# BUSINESS

*Second Edition*

*Houghton Mifflin Company    Boston*

*Dallas    Geneva, Illinois    Palo Alto    Princeton, New Jersey*

# BUSINESS

## Second Edition

## Robert Kreitner
*Arizona State University*

## Barry L. Reece
*Virginia Polytechnic Institute
and State University*

## James P. O'Grady
*St. Louis Community College
at Florissant Valley*

## Credits

Opening vignettes: Chapter 5, p. 124, from Kenneth Labich, "The Seven Keys to Business Leadership," *Fortune*, October 24, 1988, p. 59. Copyright 1988 *Fortune* Magazine. Reprinted by permission of the publisher. Chapter 6, p. 156, 162, from Alex Taylor, III, "The Tasks Facing General Motors," *Fortune*, March 13, 1989, pp. 52–53. Copyright 1989 *Fortune* Magazine. Reprinted by permission of the publisher. Chapter 20, p. 604, from K.J. McIntyre, "Bringing Risk Management to the Jungle," *Business Insurance*, April 18, 1988, p. 152. Copyright 1988. Used by permission of the publisher. Chapter 23, p. 696, from F. Washington and D. Pauly, "Driving Toward a World Car?" p. 48. From NEWSWEEK, May 1, 1989. © 1989, Newsweek, Inc. All rights reserved. Reprinted by permission; p. 704, from Julie Lieblich, "If You Want a Big, New Market . . ." *Fortune*, November 21, 1986, p. 181. Copyright 1986 *Fortune* Magazine. Reprinted by permission of the publisher.

Business Issues: Chapter 2, p. 44, adapted from "Corporations with a Conscience," *Business & Society Review*, winter 1988, pp. 58–59. Reprinted by permission of the publisher. Chapter 6, p. 171, Ellen Paris, "Managers as Entrepreneurs," pp. 62–63. Excerpted by permission of *Forbes* magazine, October 31, 1988. © Forbes Inc., 1988. Chapter 8, p. 231, excerpted from Cheryl Sullivan, "Various Test Approaches: A Look at Pros and Cons," *The Christian Science Monitor*, January 25, 1989, p. 8. Reprinted by permission from *The Christian Science Monitor*. © 1989 The Christian Science Publishing Society. All rights reserved. Chapter 10, p. 285, from J. Braham, "Marrying Goods & Services." Reprinted with permission from Industry Week, November 7, 1988. Copyright, Penton Publishing, Inc., Cleveland, Ohio. Chapter 16, p. 479, from Andrew Kupfer, "Now, Live Experts on a Floppy Disk," *Fortune*, October 12, 1987, p. 70. Copyright 1987 *Fortune* Magazine. Reprinted by permission of the publisher.

Experiencing Business: Chapter 1, p. 9, excerpted from the business I.Q. quiz in *Fortune*, January 1989. Copyright 1989 *Fortune* Magazine. Reprinted by permission of the publisher. Chapter 2, p. 58, from H. Becker and D.J. Fritzche, "A Comparison of the Ethical Behavior of American, French, and German Managers," *The Columbia Journal of World Business*, winter 1987, pp. 87–95. Reprinted by permission of the publisher. Chapter 5, p. 130, "For Your Information," reprinted with permission from PERSONNEL JOURNAL, Costa Mesa, California. Copyright September, 1984. All rights reserved. Chapter 6, p. 168, Randi Blaun, "Plugging into the Power Source," November/December 1988, p. 20. From *Executive Female*, the publication of the National Association of Female Executives, New York City. Chapter 7, p. 188, data from Kenneth A. Kovach, "What Motivates Employees? Workers and Supervisors Give Different

Answers," p. 59. Reprinted from *Business Horizons*, September–October, 1987. Copyright 1987 by the Foundation for the School of Business at Indiana University. Used with permission. Chapter 12, p. 349, Data from Edward C. Baig, "Name That Brand," *Fortune*, July 4, 1988, pp. 11–12. Copyright 1988 *Fortune* Magazine. Reprinted with permission of the publisher. Chapter 15, p. 458, from the 1988 annual report of The Goodyear Tire & Rubber Company. Copyright 1989. Used by permission. Chapter 17, p. 535, from "Bank Credit Card Interest Rates," *Wall Street Journal*, April 10, 1989, p. C19. Reprinted by permission of *Wall Street Journal*, Dow Jones & Company, Inc. 1989. All Rights Reserved Worldwide.

Chapter and part opener photos: p. 3, Jean-Paul Nacivet/After Image; p. 36, TRW, Inc. p. 67, Rob Nelson/Picture Group; p. 95, Bob Kramer; p. 125, Tim Brown/Tony Stone Worldwide; p. 155, Mark Joseph Photography; p. 185, Charles Feil/Stock, Boston; p. 215, © RJ Muna; p. 249, Harold Sund/The Image Bank; p. 280, © Thomas Grosscop; p. 311, © Edward Alfano; p. 339, Jeffrey Scales; p. 367, © Chris Sorensen/The Stock Market; p. 398, © Joseph Mulligan; p. 431, Suzanne Anderson and Associates, Inc.; p. 467, Reprinted with permission from 1987 Sallie Mae Annual Report to Stockholders—Jeff Zaruba, photographer; p. 507, © Steve Weber, 1987/Stock, Boston; p. 541, Jake Rajs/The Image Bank; p. 573, © John Chiassan/Gamma-Liaison; p. 603, Chip Mitchell/Picture Group; p. 635, George Peet, Keller and Peet Associates; p. 663, Steve Starr/Picture Group; p. 691, R. Michael Stuckey/Comstock

Cover illustration © Stanislaw Fernandes/The Image Bank

Printed in the U.S.A.
Library of Congress Catalog Card Number: 89-85582
ISBN: 0-395-433606

ABCDEFGHIJ-VH-9543210/89

*To Margaret, with lots of love*
Robert Kreitner

*To Vera, Lynne, Mark, Monique, Michelle and Colleen*
Barry L. Reece

*To my parents, Jim and Nellie; my wife, Pattie; and four sons,
Pat, Mike, Dan, and Tim*
James P. O'Grady

# Brief Contents

# Contents

*Chapter* 2

## Social Responsibility and Business Ethics     36

## Part Two
## Management and Organization

### Chapter 5  Management

*Chapter* **7** Human Relations in Business     184

*Chapter* **13** Distribution Strategy 366

## Channels of Distribution

*Chapter*

# 19 Securities Markets ......... 572

## How Securities Change Hands ......... 575

## The New York Stock Exchange ......... 579

## Sources of Financial Information ......... 586

EXPERIENCING BUSINESS  Watching Your Stock ......... 589

## Regulation of Securities Trading ......... 589

BUSINESS ISSUES  A Look Back at the Market Crash of 1987 ......... 592

*Chapter*

# 20 Risk Management and Insurance ......... 602

## The Nature of Risk ......... 605

# *Preface*

Many students sign up for introductory business courses not knowing what to expect. Unsure of the path to pursue through school and into the professional world beyond, they're wondering what business has to offer them. They may come to the class with no more than the idea that business is a practical thing to study or perhaps someone they know is "in business." An introductory business text serves the critical purpose of revealing to these students the choices and possibilities the business world makes available to them. *Business* 2/e by Robert Kreitner, Barry Reece, and James O'Grady teaches the fundamental concepts of business in a way that brings this world to life for students, a world that is exciting, rewarding, and powerful, the inner workings of which have a broad effect on our lives.

*Opportunity and Challenge*    *Business* 2/e teaches students about business by allowing them the opportunity to participate in it and the challenge to think critically about it. After reading about consumer behavior and the process of gathering market research in Chapter 11, the student is presented with a number of forecasted demographic trends and asked to apply them to a marketing plan for the Carnival Cruise Lines company. Chapter 8, "Managing Human Resources," asks, "How well informed are you about human resource management trends?" Is it legal for a department store manager to have applicants for a head cashier's job take a lie detector test? What is the number-one reason why good employees quit? Chapter 22 explores the relationship between government and business, and presents the student with a different kind of task, one that is representative of the kinds of dilemmas the business community faces today: As the Chief Financial Officer for a small semi-conductor firm, how would you choose to dispose of your firm's toxic wastes? Should you have them disposed of here in the United States, where disposal is expensive and carefully regulated, or ship them to a less developed country that has no such environmental regulations and charges little for waste disposal?

*Relevant*  Kreitner, Reece, and O'Grady highlight business issues and events today that will affect students as they enter the workforce tomorrow. Both male and female students will be affected by how corporate America treats women in business who want families as well as careers. Chapter 9, "Labor-Management Relations," considers what has popularly come to be known as "the mommy track," one woman's hotly debated solution to this issue. What do today's organizations need to be successful and effective? Chapter 6 talks about the criteria upon which *Fortune* evaluates companies in its well-known annual survey, and considers the most recent crop of winners, among them Merck, Rubbermaid, and Herman Miller. Chapter 13, "Distribution Strategy," analyzes the events in the super-retailer arena where newcomer Wal-Mart has challenged the reigning giants, Sears and K mart, closing the gap in annual sales.

*Tools for Business*  *Business* 2/e and its support package are designed to provide students with the tools they'll need to get the most from this course. Each chapter begins with a color-coded model illustrating how the seven parts of the text relate to each other and providing the student with an instant map for determining which chapters and parts have been studied, and which are still to be covered. The model helps students make sense of what they have accomplished, and what lies ahead. One Experiencing Business box in every chapter provides a situation where students must think critically and actively participate, while Business Issues boxes explore current real-world examples of what the student is learning. Finally, learning objectives are an organizing thread running through each chapter: they appear listed at the beginning of every chapter, are highlighted in the margins as each is discussed, and are then reprinted at the end of the chapter for review, accompanied by brief discussions. Key terms, which provide students with their business vocabulary and are so important in making concepts understandable, also appear in the margins as they are discussed, and again at the end of each chapter in a list.

The *Business* 2/e support package includes the following items:

- *Study Guide.* Each chapter of the study guide includes a thorough chapter summary, a list of learning objectives, a matching exercise using key terms, 25 completion questions, 10 multiple choice questions, and 10 true-false questions. Answers to all exercises appear at the end, including explanations for both correct and incorrect answers in the multiple choice. A computerized version of the study guide is also available.
- *Instructor's Manual.* A new, more accessible instructor's manual has been developed for the Kreitner/Reece/O'Grady package, including a number of valuable instructional aids new to this edition. Suggested answers to the end of chapter discussion questions and the case questions in the text are provided, as well as a comprehensive lecture outline, a controversial issue related to chapter material designed to generate class discussion, and a supplemental lecture using examples beyond those covered in the text chapter. Comprehensive lecture outlines from the instructor's manual are available on a microcomputer program called *Lecture Bank*.
- *Business Careers.* Robert Luke's book compiles information about salary, career ladders, and getting ahead in careers in marketing, management,

accounting, entrepreneurship, and finance in an informal style that students will find enjoyable.

- *Test Bank.* The test bank accompanying the *Business* 2/e text has over 150 test items per chapter, including multiple choice, true-false, completion, matching, and essays. Items are coded according to difficulty, text page number, and corresponding learning objective. The test bank is also available as a microcomputer program.

- *Transparency package.* A package of 150 two, three, and four-color acetate transparencies is included in the Kreitner, Reece, and O'Grady package, for effective classroom use of the main text art program.

- *Project manuals. Investing in Business,* 2/e; *Opening a Business,* 2/e; *Careers in Business,* 2/e. Each project has its own set of objectives and is independent of the other projects. These projects offer students an opportunity to apply basic business principles discussed in the text to real-world situations, and to make decisions comparable to those made in the business world.

- *Entrepreneur: A Simulation,* 2/e. This simulation challenges student players with a real-world situation involving the takeover and continuing operation of a retail store. Ongoing decisions include areas of pricing, advertising, quality control, cash flow, market research, and inventory management.

- *Videos.* The *Business* 2/e package includes 20 videos, organized according to the seven parts of the text, which highlight real-world companies, products, and issues.

- *Business Papers.* The *Business Papers* include 75 different documents commonly encountered in the business world, such as policies, tax forms, legal documents, applications, and others.

Together these items form a complete package of everything needed to make the introductory business course a meaningful experience for both student and instructor.

Robert Kreitner<br>
Barry L. Reece<br>
James P. O'Grady

# *Acknowledgements*

Kreitner/Reece/O'Grady is the end result of a dedicated effort by a dedicated team. The following academic and professional reviewers should be acknowledged for their contribution to this effort:

James Agresta
*Prince George Community College*

David Aiken
*Hacking Technical College*

Phyllis C. Alderdice
*Jefferson Community College*

Dimitry N. Alexander
*Miami Dade Community College*

Nikki Altman
*DeVry Institute of Technology*

Dominic A. Aquila
*Rochester Institute of Technology*

Barry Ashmen
*Bucks County Community College*

Toby Atkinson
*Brevard Community College*

Gregory A. Bach
*University of North Dakota*

Ray Balcerzak
*Ferris State University*

Barbara Barrett
*St. Louis Community College at Merramec*

Alec Beaudoin
*Triton College*

John R. Beem
*College of Dupage*

Harvey R. Blessing
*Essex Community College*

William J. Boeger
*St. Louis Community College at Florissant Valley*

James H. Boeger
*Rock Valley College*

Mary Jo Boehms
*Jackson State Community College*

S. Bonem
*Cincinnati Technical College*

John S. Bowdidge
*Southwest Missouri State University*

Steve Bradley
*Austin Community College*

Sonya K. Brett
*Macomb Community College*

Tom Brinkman
*Cincinnati Technical College*

Harvey S. Bronstein
*Oakland Community College*

Howard R. Budner
*Borough of Manhattan Community College*

Judith G. Bulin
*Monroe Community College*

Robert F. Byrnes
*Suffolk County Community College*

J.M. Callan
*Raymond Walters College at University of Cincinnati*

Joseph A.M. Camardo
*Cayuga Community College*

J.E. Cantrell
*Deanza College*

Robert Carrel
*Vincennes University*

Lawrence Chase
*Tompkins Cortland Community College*

Jill Chown
*Mankato State University*

J. Michael Cicero
*Highline Community College*

Robert Coiro
*Laguardia Community College*

Ronald L. Cooley
*South Suburban College*

Helen A. Corley
*Oxnard College*

Robert J. Cox
*Salt Lake Community College*

Lewis K. Cushing
*Illinois Valley Community College*

Rex R. Cutshall
*Vincennes University*
Dexter Dalton
*St. Louis Community College at Merramec*
Kathy Daroy
*Pierce College*
Kathy Daruty
*Los Angeles Pierce College*
Helen M. Davis
*Jefferson Community College*
Dale Dickson
*Mesa State College*
Sam Dunbar
*Delgado Community College*
John Egan
*Jersey City State College*
Tony Enferua
*Lakeland Community College*
Ruben C. Estrada
*Pima College, Downtown Campus*
Frank Falcetta
*Middlesex Community College*
Roy Farris
*Southeast Missouri State University*
Carol Ferguson
*Rock Valley College*
Gilbert Fleming
*Guilford Technical Community College*
Thomas Forsythe
*Mott Community College*

Donald M. Freeman
*Pikes Peak Community College*
William Friedman
*Fontbonne College*
Michael Fritz
*Portland Community College*
G. Gelderloos
*Grand Rapids Junior College*
David Gennrich
*Waukesha County Technical Institute*
Martin Gerber
*Kalamazoo Valley Community College*
Roger D. Gillingham
*Vincennes University*
Chaim Ginsberg
*Borough of Manhattan Community College*
Donald S. Gordon
*Illinois Central College*
W. Michael Gough
*Deanza College*
David K. Graf
*Northern Illinois University*
Joseph Gray
*Nassau Community College*
Janet M. Green
*San Bernadino Valley College*
Glennon Grothaus
*St. Louis Community College at Merramec*

Roy R. Grundy
*College of Dupage*
John Gubbay
*Morraine Valley Community College*
E.C. Hamm
*Tidewater Community College*
Carnella Hardin
*Glendale Community College*
Sanford B. Helman
*Middlesex Community College*
Paul Hegele
*Elgin Community College, Fountain Square Campus*
Douglas G. Hereter
*Ferris State University*
Nathan Himelslin
*Essex County College*
Louis Hoekstra
*Grand Rapids Jr. College*
Raymond L. Howerton
*Portland Community College*
Paul F. Jenner
*Southwest Missouri State University*
Owens Jensen
*North Dakota State School of Science*
Jenna Johannpeter
*Belleville Area College*
Gene Johnson
*Clark College*
Ike Kaim
*Delta College*

Ann Kane
  *Rose State College*
Bob Kegel
  *Cypress College*
David Kelmar
  *Santa Monica College*
Bernie Kestler, C.F.P.
  *President, Kestler
  Associates, Inc.*
Edward J. Kirk
  *Vincennes University*
Steve Kirman
  *Dyke College*
Rod Krug
  *State University of New
  York*
Marvin Levine
  *Orange County
  Community College*
Mona Levine
  *Montgomery College*
Thomas W. Lloyd
  *Westmoreland County
  Community College*
Patricia A. Long
  *Tarrant County Jr. College*
Paul James Lonndrigan
  *Mott Community College*
Anthony L. Lucas
  *Community College of
  Allegheny*
Gary Lyons
  *East Texas State University*
Sheldon A. Mador
  *Los Angeles Trade
  Technical College*
Donald D. Manning
  *University of Northern
  Colorado*

Allen D. Mason
  *Stephens College*
Robert Masters
  *Fort Hays State University*
Bob Matthews
  *Oakton Community
  College*
Robert McDuffy
  *Delta College*
Catherine C. McElroy
  *Bucks County Community
  College*
James M. McHugh
  *Forest Park Community
  College*
Robert C. McNally
  *Washtenaw Community
  College*
Randall D. Mertz
  *Mesa Community College*
Nancy Meyer
  *Northwestern Business
  College*
James Mezsaros
  *County College of Morris*
Ina Midkiff-Kennedy
  *Austin Community College*
Jan A. Miller
  *Thomas Nelson
  Community College*
Edwin F. Miner
  *Phoenix College*
William F. Motz, Jr.
  *Lansing Community
  College*
M. James Nead
  *Vincennes University*
Mary K. Nelson
  *University of Minnesota*

Lee H. Neumann
  *Bucks County Community
  College*
C.E. Nieuwejaar
  *New Hampshire College*
David Oliver
  *Edison Community College*
George Palz
  *Erie Community College*
Kenneth Papenfuss
  *Ricks College*
Dennis D. Pappas
  *Columbus State
  Community College*
Richard W. Perry
  *Santa Rosa Jr. College*
Constantine G. Petrides
  *Borough of Manhattan
  Community College*
Joseph Platts
  *Miami Dade Community
  College*
Raymond E. Polchow
  *Muskingum Area Technical
  College*
Richard Randall
  *Nassau Community
  College*
Richard Randolph
  *Johnson County
  Community College*
Bob Redick
  *Lincoln Land Community
  College*
Monique Reece
  *King Soopers*
James A. Reinemann
  *College of Lake County*
David Reiter
  *Richard J. Daley College*

John H. Rich
*Illinois State University*
Deborah Roebuck
*Kennesaw State College*
Christopher W. Rogers
*Miami Dade Community College*
Rich Rowray
*Ball State University*
Gabe Sanders
*Jersey City State College*
Paul D. Sanders
*West Valley College*
Richard E. Schallert
*Black Hawk College*
Dennis E. Schmitt
*Emporia State University*
Daniel J. Schneck
*San Joaquin Delta College*
J. Martin Sipos
*Paine Webber, Inc.*
Robert W. Sexton
*Cuyahoga Community College*
Dennis D. Shannon
*Belleville Area College*
Alan P. Shields
*Suffolk County Community College*
Lynette Klooster Shishido
*Santo Monica College*
Eleanor Simon
*Santa Monica College*
Curtis J. Smith
*Community College of the Finger Lakes*
Carl J. Sonntag
*Pikes Peak Community College*

Martin S. St. John
*Westmoreland County Community College*
Jeffrey D. Stauffer
*Ventura College*
William A. Steiden
*Jefferson Community College*
E. George Stook
*Anne Arundel Community College*
David Streifford
*St. Louis Community College at Forest Park*
William S. Sugg, Sr.
*Lakeland Community College*
Lynn H. Suksdorf
*Salt Lake Community College*
Jim Van Tassel
*Mission College*
Jack L. Taylor
*Charles County Community College*
Ray Tewell
*American River College*
James B. Thurman
*George Washington University*
Jay Todes
*North Lake College*
Cynthia Tomes
*Des Moines Area Community College*
Charles E. Tychsen
*Northern Virginia Community College*

Ted Valvoda
*Lakeland Community College*
Robert Wagley
*Wright State University*
George Wang
*St. Louis Community College Merramec*
P.A. Weatherford
*Enbry-Riddle Aeronautical*
Bernard W. Weinrich
*St. Louis Community College at Forest Park*
Stephen L. West
*El Palo Community College*
Harold Weyser
*Rockland Community College*
Charles White
*Edison Community College*
Roberta Whitney
*University of Nevada at Las Vegas*
Mildred M. Whitted
*St. Louis Community College at Forest Park*
F. Christian Widmer
*Tidewater Community College*
Gregory J. Worosz
*Schoolcraft College*
William F. Wright
*Mt. Hood Community College*
Marilyn J. Young
*Tulsa Jr. College*

We would also like to extend our thanks and appreciation to our colleagues and friends for their continuing wise counsel and support. Finally, we give our deep thanks to our families, without whom our work on this project would not have been possible. We lovingly dedicate this book to them.

# BUSINESS

*Second Edition*

# The Business System

*W. L. Gore and Associates is, without a doubt, one of America's most interesting companies. It was started by Bill Gore, an innovative person with a strong entrepreneurial spirit. The company's most famous product is Gore-Tex, a high-tech fabric used in the construction of boots and other outdoor apparel. Today, millions of people stay dry in the rain because of Gore-Tex clothing. W. L. Gore and Associates has not only achieved economic success, it has been recognized as a company with a strong social conscience. In Part I we will discuss how America's free market system fosters the development of new businesses. We will also discuss the evolution of social responsibility in an economic climate that emphasizes freedom and individualism. This section also reviews the various forms of business ownership and introduces entrepreneurship, the nature of small business, and franchising.*

PART ONE

# 1 The Challenge of American Business

After you have completed this chapter, you will be able to do the following:

**1.** Define the term business and explain how it involves the "value-added" concept.

**2.** Explain, from the standpoint of different roles people play, why it is important to study business.

**3.** Discuss how business managers learn to manage.

**4.** Contrast socialism, communism, and capitalism.

**5.** Explain the ideology of American free enterprise.

**6.** Discuss the interrelationship of demand, supply, and equilibrium.

**7.** Contrast the four forms of economic competition.

**8.** Trace our economic system's historical development.

**9.** List and explain at least four major challenges facing American business.

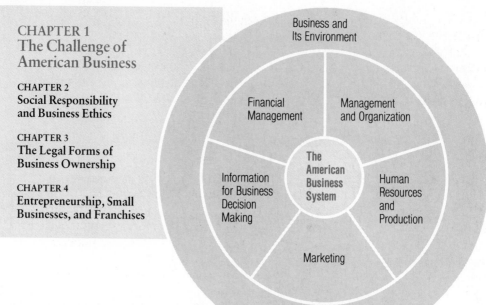

Business and
Its Environment

Financial
Management

Management
and Organization

The
American
Business
System

Information
for Business
Decision
Making

Human
Resources
and
Production

Marketing

T he son of a Texas cotton broker at whose knee he says he learned his first business principle (treat the customer right), [Ross] Perot started to work at the age of 7, making an honest buck breaking horses at $1 each. He acquired the habit of square dealing from his father and an appreciation of charity's blessings from his mother. President of his senior class at the U.S. Naval Academy, Perot disliked the Navy's seniority system, and left to work for IBM in 1957. Five years later he quit to found EDS [Electronic Data Systems] with $1,000 in savings. He was unable to sell stock in the shaky-looking venture, but that early blow to a salesman's pride had its salve: Perot had to keep all the stock himself, which goes a long way toward explaining his present worth of around $2.5 billion.[1]

**profit**  the excess of revenues over expenses

By any standard, Ross Perot's achievements have been extraordinary. Even more extraordinary is the American business system that enabled Perot to turn $1,000 into $2.5 billion. It is a system that challenges *anyone* and *everyone* to turn their good ideas and hard work into **profit**—the excess of revenues over expenses. Like any other economic system, the American business system has its own unique set of strengths and limitations. This chapter introduces you to the American business system by exploring the study of business, basic economic concepts, and modern business challenges.

**business**  the profit-motivated buying, producing, and selling of goods and/or services

Business is typically taken for granted because it is an ever-present feature of modern life. But what is business? In general terms, **business** is the profit-motivated buying, producing, and selling of goods and/or services. Some critics question the pursuit of profit, treating it as a dirty word. The real question, however, is: "How was the profit earned?" There is a world of difference between, for example, the profits derived from processing and selling illegal drugs on one hand and developing, marketing, and responsibly pricing a new life-saving medicine on the other. The former is outside the law, whereas the latter is socially and legally acceptable. This distinction helps make the point that business is a "value-added" economic process subject to social, political/legal, and technological constraints. Because those constraints are constantly changing, business is an endlessly challenging and exciting endeavor. One way to accept the challenge is by taking time to study business systematically.

*1.* *Define the term business and explain how it involves the "value-added" concept.*

# Why Study Business?

Businesspeople speak their own specialized language. One basic reason for studying business is simply to learn that language. For instance, do you know the difference between a partnership and a corporation, between a line position and a staff position, between an asset and a liability, and between a stock and a bond? Successful businesspeople do, and so will you after reading Chapters 3, 6, 15, and 18. You will encounter dozens of other important business terms along the way.

A second basic reason for studying business is that each of us, during any given day, plays a number of different roles (see Figure 1.1). A working knowledge of business can help us do a better job of playing the following

*2.* *Explain, from the standpoint of different roles people play, why it is important to study business.*

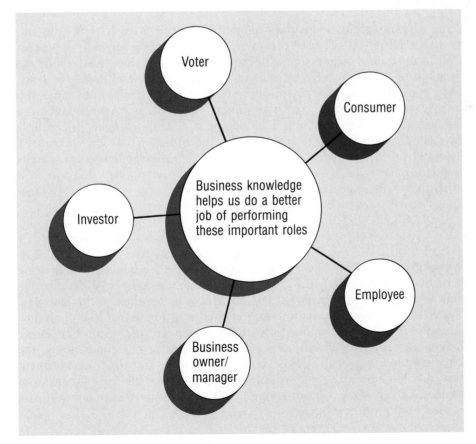

FIGURE 1.1 Business Knowledge Helps in Many Ways

important roles: consumer, employee, business owner/manager, investor, voter. Let us briefly review each of these roles from a business perspective.

## Be a Smarter Consumer

Studying business helps you to think like a businessperson. Consider, for example, how the purchasing manager for a bicycle manufacturer goes about buying key parts such as tires, pedals, and drive chains. Each purchased part must satisfy design specifications and be reasonably priced. Suppliers of the various parts must be reliable and capable of consistent product quality. Shipping costs and delivery dates must also be considered. Likewise, consumers who make important buying decisions in a businesslike manner do their homework first. When you buy a car, for instance, it is a good idea to consult market research journals such as *Consumer Reports* or watch *Motorweek* on the PBS network to see what sort of track record the vehicle has. Smart consumers who use good business sense also have a clear goal in mind when they make major buys. That way the family of four that really needs an economical minivan won't end up with a turbo-charged sports coupe that was "just the right color."

## Be a Better Employee

Being a good employee involves more than getting to work on time and satisfying basic job requirements. For example, nonmanagerial employees who have studied business tend to have a better idea than most about the dynamic relationship between sales revenue, expenses, and profit (or loss). They appreciate the importance of controlling all expenses, both large and small. Consider the job of concert promoter. Many concertgoers are convinced that promoters must be getting rich, judging from the high ticket prices these days. But as the figures in Table 1.1 demonstrate, a concert promoter's potential profit is rapidly eaten up by a wide variety of expenses. Profits could turn into losses if the concert promoter's employees don't keep a watchful eye on expenses.

## Be a Successful Business Owner/Manager

If you have the entrepreneurial spirit, you probably have thought of starting your own business. But this route is not for the faint-hearted because the mortality rate for new businesses in America is astounding. Although exact figures are not available, venture capital experts estimate that half of all new businesses do not survive the first year and 80 percent fail within five years.[2] A survey of 1,002 small business owners from across the country found the leading cause of small business failures to be "lack of management expertise."[3] Good ideas, enthusiasm, and hard work—all key ingredients of business success—are still not enough. Solid business management skills are needed to make a new business succeed.

6

TABLE 1.1    The Economics of a Concert

| | |
|---|---:|
| **Gross [From Ticket Sales]** | **$189,392** |
| **Tax 6%** | **10,720** |
| **Net** | **178,662** |

| | | |
|---|---:|---:|
| **Expenses** | | **$163,829** |
| Artist's advance | | $50,000 |
| 15% of after-concert receipts paid additional fee to artist | | $34,111 |
| Total for Artist | | $84,111 |
| ***Additional Expenses:*** | | |
| Rent for building | | $25,000 |
| Liability insurance ($10,000,000 worth) | | 1,347 |
| Production cost | | 10,000 |
| Licensing fee | | 26 |
| ASCAP/BMI (publishing fee) | | 410 |
| Private security | | 800 |
| T-shirt security | | 295 |
| Stage hands | | 4,344 |
| Potted plants | | 55 |
| Furniture | | 579 |
| Messenger | | 100 |
| Piano tuner | | 140 |
| Catering | | 2,109 |
| Backstage phone bill | | 350 |
| Advertising & promotion | | 17,488 |
| Limousine service | | 660 |
| Postage | | 12.50 |
| Misc. | | 2.50 |
| Reserve claim (for building) | | 1,000 |
| Support act | | 15,000 |
| Total Expenses | | $163,829 |

| | |
|---|---:|
| **Profit** | **$14,843** |
| **Personal profit** | **$7,421.50** |
| **Co-promoter** | **$7,421.50** |

Source: "So You Want to Be a Concert Promoter," *Black Enterprise,* December 1984, p. 57. These are figures from a concert by a top-name recording artist, provided by Birmingham promoter John Ray. Copyright December 1984, The Earl G. Graves Publishing Co., Inc., 130 Fifth Avenue, New York, NY 10011. All rights reserved.

## Be a Wiser Investor

Investing is not solely for the well-to-do. Employees who contribute to a personally funded or company-sponsored retirement fund also are investors. Regardless of whether you invest directly or indirectly in stocks, bonds, or a variety of other ventures, a working knowledge of good business practice and economic cycles can provide a winning edge.

Success in business requires management expertise   *Entrepreneurs Richard Williams and Jim Scott had the kind of managerial expertise necessary to succeed. As college juniors the two began a business producing strapless sun visors to help pay for tuition. Anticipating problems with distribution and delivery dates, Williams and Scott bought a van and started Bull Dog Movers, Inc. Today both businesses are thriving, having both been named in the* 1988 Inc. 500 *list of companies by* Inc. *magazine.*

## Be an Informed Voter

Important economic matters unavoidably end up in the political arena. During the 1988 presidential election, for instance, voters were presented with a number of economic issues. Among these were: raising the minimum wage, providing day care for employees' children, balancing the budget, correcting the foreign trade deficit, improving productivity, and preventing higher inflation. Because successful businesspeople are necessarily well informed, they are in a position to weigh economic issues intelligently when voting.

## TEST YOUR BUSINESS I.Q.

How well informed are you about general business affairs? Try the following questions and check your answers with the ones at the back of the book.

1. Airline fares have bounced up and down since 1978, when a major policy affecting competition in this and other industries went into effect. What policy was it?
2. After co-founder Steve Jobs left Apple Computer, he started a new computer company. What is it called?
3. The late Ray Kroc is an example of a visionary entrepreneur who started a wildly successful business that changed the nature of franchising in America. Name the company he founded.
4. *True or false:* A manager who feels his employees must be closely supervised probably believes in Theory X.
5. It took six years getting from the idea to reality, but the little yellow squares of paper with a strip of non-binding adhe-

sive on the back quickly became a popular and much-copied innovation. Name the original product and the company.
6. Which of the following products is not made by Procter & Gamble?
   a. Citrus Hill orange juice   c. Fab detergent
   b. Crest toothpaste          d. Ivory soap
7. After the 1987 stock market crash, in which he lost $500 million, the "richest man in America" commented, "It doesn't matter. It's only paper." Who is he?
8. What is the total value of all goods and services produced in one year in a country called?
9. In 1988, two countries finalized a free-trade agreement that is expected to have wide repercussions on their $150 billion-year-trade. Name the two countries.
10. What American car manufacturer popularized the "aero" design?

Source: Excerpted from *Fortune* Business I.Q. Quiz, January 1989.

# How to Learn More About Business

Some say learning about business is like learning how to ride a bike (see Experiencing Business). Get on, fall off many times, learn from your mistakes, and eventually be on your way. Though this is a rather harsh comparison, research evidence suggests that it is largely true. A study at Honeywell, maker of the familiar thermostats and other control devices, provided an answer to the question: "How do successful business managers learn to manage?"[4]

After surveying 3,600 Honeywell managers over a five-year period, the researchers came up with a 50 percent, 30 percent, 20 percent formula (see Figure 1.2). Half of what the managers knew about managing came from their job assignments; in other words, from the "school of hard knocks." Thirty percent came from personal relationships—observing and imitating role models. The remaining 20 percent was acquired through training. As

*3. Discuss how business managers learn to manage.*

Practicing for the future  *Formal study of business theory and practice and economic cycles is valuable for anyone who wants to make wise investments, regardless of the size or type of venture. These students are acting as brokers and taking calls from student "investors." The contestant whose simulated portfolio earns the most wins $25,000 and a trip to the Bahamas.*

the term is used here, training includes formal academic business studies, on-the-job training, and informal self-study. Business students need to prepare themselves to learn from all three major sources of business knowledge: job assignments, role models, and training.

## Getting a Running Start

Although college courses in business cannot fully prepare you to run a business successfully, they can and do provide a running start. Once again, learning by actually doing is the primary source of business knowledge. Formal academic training—complete with definitions, concepts, and techniques—makes learning from experience and role models that much easier.

## A Program of Self-Study Is Important

In addition to your formal college coursework, you can learn a great deal about business through a program of informal self-study. Regularly keeping up with a few of the publications and television programs listed in Table 1.2 can provide valuable self-education for present and future business managers. If you want to be a businessperson, you need to think, talk, and act like one.

Let us now turn to some basic concepts that shape the world of business.

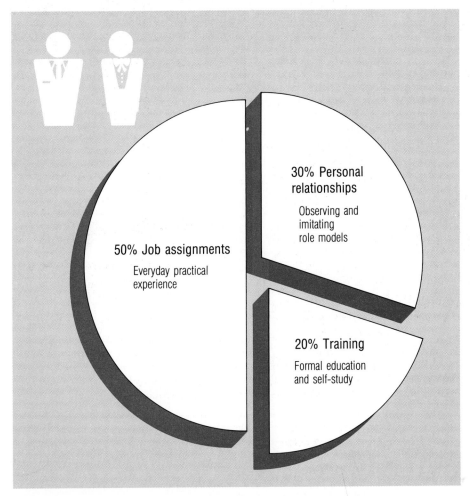

FIGURE 1.2   The Honeywell Study: How Businesspeople Learn to Manage

Source: From Ron Zemke, "The Honeywell Studies: How Managers Learn to Manage," pp. 46–51. Reprinted with permission from the August 1985 issue of TRAINING, the Magazine of Human Resources Development. Copyright 1985, Lakewood Publications Inc., Minneapolis, MN (612) 333-0471. All rights reserved.

# Economic Foundations of American Business

As mentioned earlier, business is a value-added economic process. A sporting goods company adds economic value to plastic by molding it into tennis rackets. Later, wholesalers add economic value to cartons of tennis rackets by shipping them to sporting goods stores around the country. Finally, sporting goods stores add economic value by advertising, displaying, and selling the tennis rackets to tennis players. Each step in this process is an

TABLE 1.2    Where to Find Up-to-Date Business Information

| Periodical Literature |
| --- |

**General Purpose**
   *Business Week* (weekly)
   *The Wall Street Journal* (weekdays)
   *Fortune* (biweekly)
   *Forbes* (monthly)
   *Time* Business section
   *Newsweek* Business section
   *USA Today* Business section
   Local newspapers Business section

**Special Audience**
   *Inc.* (small business focus)
   *Black Enterprise*
   *Executive Female*
   *Hispanic Business*
   Numerous trade magazines and newspapers that focus on specific industries,
   e.g., *Restaurant Business*

**General Academic Publications**
   *Harvard Business Review*
   *Business Horizons* (Indiana University)
   *Columbia Journal of World Business*

**Bibliographic Reference available in most libraries**
   *Business Periodicals Index* lists recent business articles

| Television | |
| --- | --- |
| **Network** | **Program** |
| PBS | *Nightly Business Report* |
| | *Wall Street Week with Louis Rukeyser* |
| | *Adam Smith's Money World* |
| ABC | *This Morning's Business* |
| CNN | *Moneyline* |
| | *Moneyweek* |

important part of the American economic system. We need to understand the basic dimensions of that system.

## *Economics: A Definition*

economics   the study of
how individuals and society
choose to employ limited resources and distribute the resulting goods and services

**Economics** is the study of how individuals and society choose to employ limited resources and distribute the resulting goods and services. The key word in this definition is *choose*. A company with a ton of steel can choose to turn it into either an army tank or a farm tractor. It must choose to *employ,* or put to work, that metal and the labor required to change it into another form. Similarly, a company that makes cookware must decide whether it will manufacture and distribute pans for sale in gourmet shops or

**Role model and mom** *Janine Craane of Merrill Lynch, shown here with her mother Valery Craane, her role model and colleague, learned that academic training in business can provide a running start for on-the-job training. After completing Merrill Lynch's training program, she joined her mother in Merrill's retail brokerage department where the two have become famous for the high volume of new business they bring in every year.*

in supermarkets, for a specialty market or the mass market. Under normal circumstances, no one tells an American company to make tanks or tractors or to sell its pots to supermarkets rather than gourmet shops, but a company does not make such decisions simply on instinct.

In large part, society guides those decisions. Every society—without exception—must answer these three fundamental questions:

1. What goods and services will be produced?
2. How will they be produced?
3. For *whom* will they be produced?

A society's answers to these questions, combined with the method it uses to reach them, describe its **economic system**: how a society produces and distributes goods and services. In the United States, these questions are usually answered in the **marketplace**, the forum where individuals and businesses exchange money for goods and services. Other types of economic systems approach the task of producing and distributing goods and services differently.

**economic system** the way in which a society produces and distributes goods and services

**marketplace** the forum where individuals and businesses exchange money for goods and services

# Alternative Economic Systems

*4. Contrast socialism, communism, and capitalism.*

In theory, at least, there are three basic economic systems: socialism, communism, and capitalism (see Figure 1.3). In modern reality, however, the distinctions between these alternative systems have become blurred. It is safe to say that no pure system exists today. The U.S. capitalist economy exhibits certain socialist characteristics and the Soviet Union's and China's communist economies are being restructured to include a number of capitalist practices. To prepare for what lies ahead, each basic type of economic system requires a closer look.

**socialism** an economic system in which the state owns the principal means of production, though private property of some sort still exists

*Socialism* Described by Karl Marx (1818–1883) as a forerunner of communism, **socialism** is an economic system in which the state owns the principal means of production but private property of some sort still exists. What distinguishes communism from socialism is the disappearance of private property in the later stage, communism.

Marx's view of the process from socialism to communism by means of the class struggle was neither universally accepted in his own time nor today. In

FIGURE 1.3 Three Basic Economic Systems

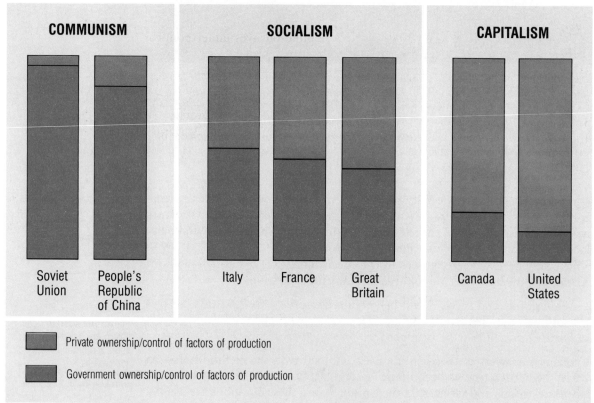

Private ownership/control of factors of production

Government ownership/control of factors of production

fact, many saw nonrevolutionary socialism as an end in itself. These so-called utopian socialists dreamed of ideal societies in which all worked according to their abilities and received what they needed. Today, in countries like Sweden, France, and Britain, Marxist and utopian socialists coexist. Their coexistence with parties advocating free enterprise has produced mixed economic systems. Between World War II and the late 1970s, these countries and others nationalized such major industries as airlines, steel, coal mining, and banking. Heavy taxation of profits usually accompanied the more serious efforts at socialist economies. These taxes were used to pay for government services, such as health care, that free-enterprise systems leave largely to the private sector.

Beginning in 1980, however, the pendulum began to swing the other way as a wave of **privatization**, the selling of government-controlled companies and industries to private investors, swept the mixed economies. In this decade private shareholders have purchased, in part or completely, almost sixty state-owned businesses around the world, valued at more than $90 billion. By the 1990s, some 2,000 more—including companies owned by countries such as Britain, France, Mexico, and Bangladesh—will share the same fate.[5]

**privatization** the selling of government-controlled companies and industries to private investors

A term often used to describe the mixed economies of Western Europe is *democratic socialism*. These countries have governments selected in free, open elections. Though their legal systems are often quite different from ours, they are designed to protect individual rights.

*Communism*   More than half the world's population lives under political systems that claim to be organized according to principles developed by Karl Marx. A great scholar and fierce political writer, Marx viewed history as a series of struggles between social classes. He foresaw conflict between the working class and the capitalist class for control over the *means of production*, the factories in which the workers toiled and the capital needed to organize and build the plants. Marx also advocated a *labor theory of value*, which holds that labor is what gives value to goods and services and labor therefore deserves to be rewarded for this production.

According to Marx, the working class would ultimately triumph. From that victory would emerge **communism**, a classless, propertyless society whose banners would read "From each according to his ability, to each according to his need!"[6] Although many *planned economies* have been based on Marxist doctrine with all property owned by the state, pure communism has never been a reality. Indeed, Mikhail Gorbachev's attempt to revitalize the stagnant Soviet economy is reversing cherished Marxist principles.

**communism** an economic system in which there are no social classes, and no privately owned property

Within Russia's still state-owned industrial sector, managers are being encouraged to pay more attention to customers and less to central planners. By the early 1990s, all but a thousand or so of the more than 500,000 prices currently fixed by Moscow are meant to be set by negotiations among individual enterprises. . . . As he vigorously peddles his *perestroika* (restructuring), Gorbachev doesn't want to hear the old Marxist dictum, "from each according to his ability, to each according to his need(s)." He lambastes past tendencies to "level off" incomes and hails reliance on performance-based pay, insisting that "no limit be set."[7]

**Profits made in Moscow** *Mikhail Gorbachev's reforms are making capitalistic practices more common in his communist country. Marina Osadshuk runs a boutique in Moscow that caters to the new class of Soviet consumer who is willing to spend 200 to 700 rubles ($320 to $1,120) on handmade suits and dresses.*

**capitalism** an economic system based on the belief that private citizens should be free to produce and sell goods and services for profit, without government interference

**modified capitalism** the American brand of capitalism, in which a relatively free marketplace is constrained by governmental rules and regulations

*Capitalism* **Capitalism** is an economic ideal based on the belief that private citizens should be free to produce and sell goods and services for profit, without government interference. This model traces back to a book written in 1776 by an obscure Scottish professor and bureaucrat. The book was titled *The Wealth of Nations* and its author was Adam Smith (1723–1790). Smith envisioned the free marketplace as the appropriate mechanism for determining wages, prices, and profits. The key to societal well-being, according to Smith, was guaranteeing the individual maximum freedom of economic action. In Smith's words, the pursuit of economic self-interest improves society as a whole as if by "an invisible hand."[8]

If Adam Smith were alive today, he would certainly be shocked at what we call capitalism. He would see minimum wage laws, price supports for farm goods, and antitrust laws that restrict profits. He would see markets that are somewhat free but subject to considerable government intervention. In fact, an estimated 50 percent of the decisions made by American businesses are in response to government decisions and actions.[9] Consequently, a more appropriate label for American capitalism is **modified capitalism**, reflecting a relatively free marketplace constrained by governmental rules and regulations. Those rules and regulations cover a mind-boggling array of public concerns such as consumer safety, environmental protection, child labor, and equal employment opportunity.

Modified capitalism is the heart of the American free-enterprise system.

## The American Free-Enterprise System

America's economic structure is a free-market or **free-enterprise system**, an economy based on the principle of voluntary association and exchange. Free enterprise is really a political/economic ideology representing a blend of democracy and capitalism.

*Free Markets*   In a free-market system, supply and demand define the price of goods and services. Competition is the ideal, and certainly it is the rule among stereo stores, camera shops, fast-food outlets, and most other types of businesses. The result is competitive prices. Wendy's hamburger prices cannot vary too much from Burger King's. If Wendy's prices are too low, they will lose potential profits. If they are too high, Wendy's will lose sales.

A voluntary exchange follows when a price is agreed upon. That exchange should result in satisfaction to the buyer and profit to the seller. Figure 1.4 illustrates a completed transaction.

**free-enterprise system**
an economy based on the principle of voluntary association and exchange

*5. Explain the ideology of American free enterprise.*

FIGURE 1.4   How the Free Marketplace Works
Source: Adapted from K. Davis and W. C. Frederick, *Business and Society,* 5th ed. (New York: McGraw-Hill, 1984), p. 102. Copyright 1984. Used by permission of the publisher.

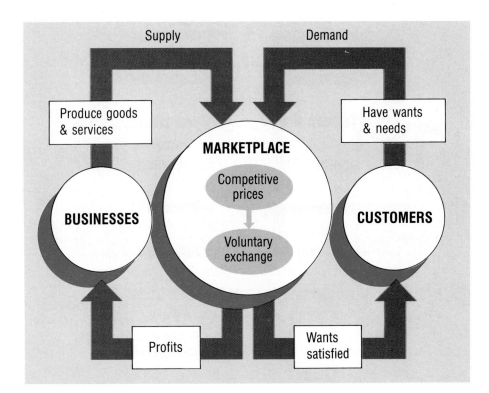

*Freedom and Individualism*   The voluntary nature of the associations and exchanges in the marketplace depends on individuals having the power and freedom to make these choices for themselves without compulsion from the state. Freedom and individualism are closely linked. It is difficult, for instance, to imagine groups rather than individuals deciding whether to buy a certain type of car. Individuals make these decisions; they are not made collectively. Both the Declaration of Independence and the Constitution emphasize that our political institutions exist to protect individuals, not vice versa.

*Private Property and Profit*   Private property and the profits to be made from it are the foundations of our economic system. If private property did not exist, free markets could not exist. Since the time of Adam Smith, economists have described the ways in which people make money from their property in terms of three **factors of production:**

**factors of production** land, labor, and capital: the three ways in which people make money from their property

1. Land: real estate and all natural resources, including minerals, timber, and agricultural products.
2. Labor: the work supplied by humans.
3. Capital: the money, plant, and equipment required to produce goods.

**product**   any good or service that may be the subject of an exchange for money

One can earn rents or interest by leasing land or capital to others and wages by selling one's labor to others. Profits, though, come only from assembling the factors of production to create a **product,** any good or service that may be the subject of an exchange for money (see Figure 1.5).

FIGURE 1.5   Factors of Production and Their Rewards

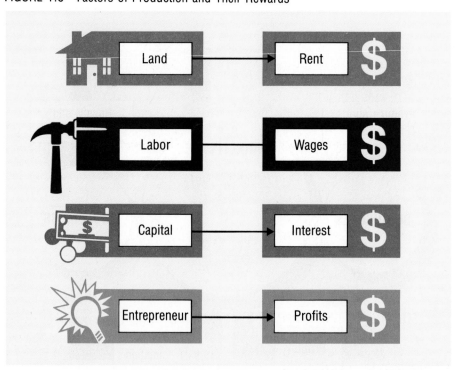

Supply and demand   *In our free-market system of voluntary exchange, the supply of and demand for a product, or a service, such as renting home videos, determines its price.*

The person who assembles the necessary factors and applies enough creativity to generate a product or service is called an **entrepreneur** or capitalist. The compensation awarded a capitalist for the efforts and risk assumed in establishing or operating a venture is *profits*. Risk is the key element here, because simply assembling the factors of production is not enough. An entrepreneur is someone like Tom Monaghan, the man who after brushes with bankruptcy turned Domino's Pizza into the nation's fastest-growing franchise chain. The willingness to bet on one's own abilities to control the various factors of production to turn out products or services for a profit is what free enterprise is all about.

**entrepreneur** a person who assembles the necessary factors and applies enough creativity to generate a product or service

## Demand, Supply, and Equilibrium

When economists study the three fundamental economic questions listed earlier, they deal with the concepts of demand and supply.

*How Much Customers Will Buy*   The willingness of purchasers to buy specific quantities of a good or service at a particular price and particular time is called **demand**. In other words, how much of something people will buy depends on its price when they want it.

**6.** *Discuss the interrelationship of demand, supply, and equilibrium.*

**demand** the willingness of purchasers to buy specific quantities of a good or service at a particular price and particular time

Figure 1.6A graphs the demand for mid-quality running shoes on July 1. The vertical scale on the left lists prices at which a pair might sell. The horizontal scale on the bottom indicates what quantities the public might be expected to buy at each specific price in a range of prices. The line reflecting the relationship between each price and the quantities demanded is the **demand curve**. Not surprisingly, more people will buy shoes at $10 than at $60. Thus, the demand curve also shows the buyers for whom the manufacturer will produce the running shoes at each price.

**demand curve** the line reflecting the relationship between each price and the quantities demanded

### *What Sellers Will Provide*

The willingness of sellers or producers to provide goods or services at a particular price and particular time is termed **supply**. In other words, how much of something people will sell or supply depends on its price when they can sell it.

**supply** the willingness of sellers or producers to provide goods or services at a particular price and particular time

Figure 1.6B graphs the supply of the running shoes that is available on July 1. The vertical scale lists specific prices within a range of prices at which the seller might sell the shoes. The horizontal scale indicates the number of pairs the seller might put on the market at each of those prices. The line reflecting the relationship between the price and the quantity is the **supply curve**. The higher the price, the more shoes the seller will be willing to sell. Thus, the supply curve also shows how many pairs of running shoes the manufacturer will produce at each price.

**supply curve** the line reflecting the relationship between the price and the quantity supplied

### *When Demand and Supply Meet*

From your experience as a consumer, you know that demand and supply directly affect each other. A manufacturer will want to sell more shoes at $50 than at $25, but the demand curve clearly

FIGURE 1.6A   Demand Curve

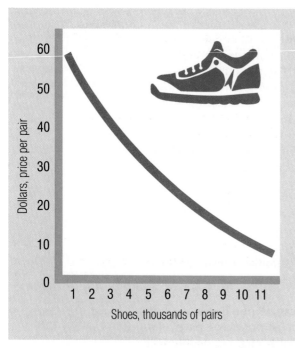

FIGURE 1.6B   Supply Curve

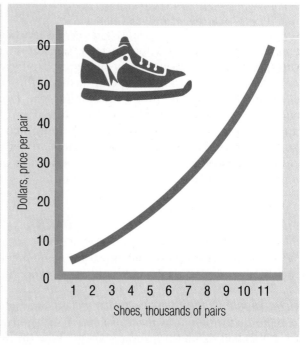

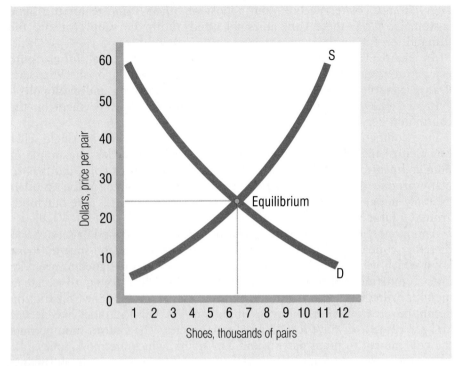

FIGURE 1.7   Equilibrium

indicates that fewer people will buy them at the higher price. By plotting the two curves on the same graph, we see that they meet at $25, the point marked E on Figure 1.7.

The E on the graph marks the point of **equilibrium**, the location at which supply and demand are in balance. At that point the intentions of the seller and the buyers coincide. Figure 1.7 shows that at $50 per pair the manufacturer would supply 10,000 pairs, but the public would buy only 1,000. At $20 per pair, the maker would supply 4,500 pairs and the public would buy 7,500. Only at $25 per pair would supply equal demand. Thus, the point of equilibrium between supply and demand identifies the **market price** of goods or services, at least theoretically. There is another factor, however—competition—which affects the two curves and therefore the market price of the goods in question.

**equilibrium** the location at which supply and demand are in balance

**market price** the point of equilibrium between supply and demand

## Competition and Markets

When two or more businesses offering similar goods or services go after the same customers, **competition** occurs. In our free-enterprise system, competition largely regulates the marketplace. Business must respond to customers' demands or else watch a competitor do so. On the other hand, businesses often survive and expand if they can meet customers' needs at a price that customers are willing to pay. In our example of demand and supply, the manufacturer is not the only seller of mid-quality running shoes. Adidas,

**competition** when two or more businesses offering similar goods or services go after the same customers

New Balance, Nike, Reebok, and a host of others compete for the same customers. What these companies do affects both the supply of and the demand for our manufacturer's shoes.

As Figure 1.8 illustrates, competition takes four general forms: pure competition, monopoly, monopolistic competition, and oligopoly. Very few, if any, examples of the polar extremes—pure competition and monopoly—exist. To one degree or another, all competition falls somewhere on the continuum between them.

**Pure competition,** or "perfect competition," occurs when no single seller can control the price of a specific good or service. The classic example of pure competition occurs with a commodity, like wheat or corn, that has so many producers that no one of them can control its selling price. Another example might be hamburgers or pizzas in restaurants and take-out foods around a large university.

A **monopoly** occurs when one company alone offers a good or service and therefore controls the market and price for it. The federal and state antitrust laws, which we will look at in detail in Chapter 22, are designed to promote pure competition. These laws prohibit activities like trying to create a monopoly that restrict competition. Nonetheless, the law and the Constitution permit the creation of certain types of monopolies. Public utilities like electric and gas companies have legal limited monopolies. The Constitution permits the government to grant patents and copyrights, which are monopolies.

Despite such exceptions, the bias in our economic system is clearly against monopolies and in favor of pure competition. Between the competitive extremes are two other types, though, which we will now examine.

**Monopolistic competition** occurs when a relatively large number of sellers market similar but not identical products. These products are usually interchangeable. For example, blank audio or video cassettes are almost indistinguishable within the same grade, except to the expert. Yet Sony, Maxell, Scotch (3M), TDK, Realistic (Radio Shack), and others spend millions each year to convince you that they are better than their competitors.

*7. Contrast the four forms of economic competition.*

**pure competition**  occurs when no single seller can control the price of a good or service

**monopoly**  occurs when one company alone offers a good or service and therefore controls the market and price for it

**monopolistic competition**  occurs when a relatively large number of sellers market similar but not identical products

FIGURE 1.8   Competition Continuum

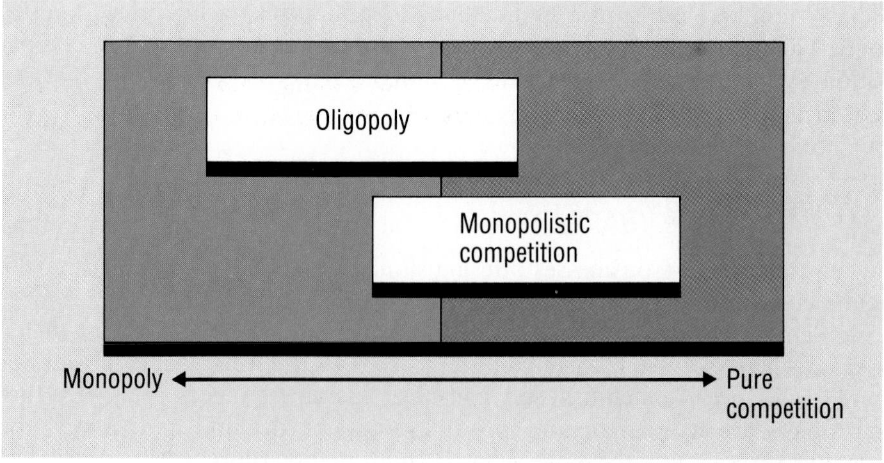

Oligopoly

Monopolistic competition

Monopoly ←————————————————→ Pure competition

Monopolistic competitors generally have some limited control over price. Although they can do little to discourage other companies from entering the market, they can exert influence over the retail outlets that sell their goods to consumers. For example, the producers of high-quality, prestige-priced stereo equipment might choose not to sell to the so-called deep discounters like Crazy Eddie, 47th Street Photo, Circuit City, or Silo.

The final type of competition is an **oligopoly**, a market dominated by a few large sellers, usually in industries that require huge initial investments in plant and equipment. An oligopoly can take one of two forms. In the first, a few sellers market products that are identical. The aluminum industry is an example of this form of oligopoly. In the second, a few sellers sell products that differ somewhat from each other. The domestic and foreign auto makers compete in this fashion.

**oligopoly** a market dominated by a few large sellers, usually in industries that require huge initial investments in plant and equipment

# The Development of Our Economic System

Since the Revolution, the face of American business has completely changed. We have passed from a primarily agricultural and natural-resource–based economy through industrialization to a service-oriented, information-based economy.

*8. Trace our economic system's historical development.*

## The Earliest Years

As early as the 1630s, American colonists residing in the richer, more established colonies lived as well as their European counterparts. Unlike their European cousins, however, the colonists achieved their standard of living largely by **barter**, trading goods for goods or services rather than for money. Throughout the colonial period, money in the form of gold or silver was in critically short supply. This shortage made accumulating the capital required for large-scale enterprises very difficult.

**barter** trading goods for goods or services rather than for money

Before the start of the nineteenth century, most American businesses were small, owned either by individuals or partners who ran them. Between 1700 and 1776, only seven business corporations came into existence in the American colonies. By 1800 there were 335 corporations, over half of which had been created since 1796.[10]

## The Industrial Revolution

The Industrial Revolution began in about 1750 in Great Britain and about 1800 in the United States. It had three distinct characteristics:

- Newly invented machines came to replace human labor.
- Work became centered in the factory, not the home.
- A division of labor in producing goods replaced the single artisan who had made a product from start to finish.

The Industrial Revolution began as a textile revolution. Cloth, when it could be bought, was extremely expensive. The process of making clothes—from converting raw cotton or wool into a dress, a shirt, or a pair of pants—was highly labor intensive. Factory production of cloth began in the late eighteenth century, and ready-to-wear apparel eventually appeared in the mid-nineteenth century. One of the earliest ready-to-wear producers was Levi Strauss. In the early 1850s, he invented blue jeans to sell to miners in the California gold rush.[11]

*The Growth of Industry*   Factories organized around the new machinery sprang up in New England. A surplus of cheap labor, abundant water power, and a growing concentration of capital made Massachusetts in particular an ideal location. Working conditions, hours, and pay in the mills were grim by today's standards but were often better than those on the farms the workers had left.

The principles that worked so well in producing textiles plainly applied to manufacturing many other goods. In Connecticut, Eli Whitney, who had made almost nothing on his cotton gin, did make money on mass-produced firearms. In Illinois, Cyrus McCormick invented a reaper for harvesting grain in 1834 and opened his first factory in 1847. A well-developed system of water travel and a rapidly growing rail system opened up most of the United States east of the Mississippi to the new manufacturing during this period.

The Civil War (1861–1865) marked a major turning point in America's business history. The North put over 2.2 million men in uniform, an unheard-of number for that time, and mobilized its resources, developed transportation systems to move men and war supplies, and created new lines of communications. This genius for organization, production, and transportation characterized American business over the next several generations.

Within ten years after the war ended, the shape of industrial America had emerged. New immigrants, largely from Europe, kept wages low. The nation's expansion led to new products and transportation lines. Except for two major recessions, the times were generally prosperous. With the exceptions of the nine-month war with Spain in 1898 and World War I, the nation was mainly at peace until 1941.

*The Production Era*   The period from the Civil War until just after World War I might be characterized as a production era. During this period, the demand for products exceeded many manufacturers' production abilities. Manufacturers thus focused on improving production capacity and efficiency and on lowering costs.

Production, regarded as the key to success, dominated all other business functions. In many industries competition was limited because only a few firms were capable of consistent, efficient production. Marketing's main jobs in these industries were simply the taking and filling of orders. Other marketing activities were not required when firms with ample production capacity and robust product demand could sell all they could make.

The production era nurtured Thomas Edison, Alexander Graham Bell, and dozens of other innovative entrepreneurs who reshaped communications and transportation. Others built gigantic industrial empires. The names of many of their founders are still familiar: Philip Armour (meats); Frederick Wey-

24                                                          *PART I / THE BUSINESS SYSTEM*

**Women in the factory** *During World War II every sector of the U.S. economy had to be carefully planned and regulated. While the male labor force was drained by the war effort, women were recruited to work on the assembly lines.*

erhaeuser (lumber); Eli Remington (arms); John D. Rockefeller (oil); Andrew Carnegie (steel); Gail Borden (dairy products); and Marshall Field (general merchandise).[12]

The ready availability of capital and the irresistible urge to generate ever-greater profits led men like Collis P. Huntington (1821–1900) to attempt to control entire business sectors. His career began when he helped found the Central Pacific Railroad, the western half of the first transcontinental rail line, completed in 1869. The construction of that government-subsidized line made his fortune. By the time of his death, he and his associates controlled most western rail transportation.

*Reform and Regulation*  The great transportation, industrial, and natural resource combinations of the late nineteenth and early twentieth centuries were known as trusts, a term that describes the unique business form adopted to avoid state corporation laws. Between 1890 and 1914, the states and the federal government enacted antitrust laws to free markets from the monopolists. (We will discuss these in more detail in Chapter 22.) These laws were the first serious attempt to impose any restriction on the practice of *laissez faire* (French for "hands off"). Other attempts, such as the creation in 1887 of the Interstate Commerce Commission to regulate transportation, failed, largely because of weak laws and ineffective or unsympathetic administrators.

The Great Depression of 1929–1939 began in the midst of several major business scandals, hundreds of bank failures, crashing prices on the major U.S. stock exchanges, and the onset of a global economic crisis. Those events also brought on an era of intense government activity in economic affairs.

In 1932, American voters elected Franklin D. Roosevelt president, but they did not give him a mandate to regulate the marketplace. The economic situation when he took office was so desperate, however, that he and the country were willing to try anything. Banks and corporations selling stocks or bonds became closely regulated by new agencies like the Securities and Exchange Commission (discussed in Chapters 18 and 19). With 25 percent unemployment, labor harmony became a major goal. As we will see in Chapter 9, Congress enacted several major labor laws, one of which created the National Labor Relations Board to oversee labor-management relations.

When World War II began in 1939, the country was just beginning to emerge from its decade-long economic depression. As the Civil War had proved, a modern war requires planning, organization, and control in all sectors. During the United States' participation in World War II (1941–1945), the government tightly controlled what was produced, bought, sold, earned, and developed. Every single sector of the economy experienced rationing of labor and resources and had to follow government plans.

After the war, many controls were abolished or modified, but some remained in place. For twenty years after World War II ended, no nation experienced the level of prosperity that ours did. There were recurring complaints about overregulation of business. It was hard, however, to argue seriously with a low inflation rate, high employment, and an ever-increasing gross national product (GNP).

## The Sales and Marketing Era

From the end of World War I to the beginning of the Korean War in 1950, production capacity was no longer a major problem. Now, instead, firms could not be sure of selling all they could produce. Many companies' marketing strategies consisted of producing all they could, then figuring out how to sell what they had. The result was close attention to advertising and

**The service sector** *Today the production and distribution of services and information account for the largest segment of the American economy. With a highly trained work force and sophisticated technology AT&T is able to offer long distance telephone service to points around the world in a matter of seconds.*

A bedtime story in Aomori.

Told across an ocean.

"Is she still awake?"
"Barely."
"Let me kiss her good-night."
"Hi, Grandpa."
"Hiroko, what are you going to dream tonight?"
"That it's 4 o'clock in the morning and I'm dancing around the house because Mommy and Daddy forgot to put me to bed."
"Good-night, Hiroko."

Dreaming of a visit with your granddaughter in Japan? With AT&T, it costs a lot less than you'd think. So go ahead. Reach out and touch someone.

**AT&T**
The right choice.

to the hiring, training, and deploying of an effective sales force. Marketing's role thus began when there was product to sell. Sales personnel were expected to sell it, regardless of its quality or whether it met consumer needs.

The great post–World War II boom brought a new consumer attitude and forced firms to evolve new marketing approaches. For the first time, most American families had **discretionary income**, or more income than is required to obtain the necessities of life. They used their discretionary income to satisfy needs with different kinds of products and to acquire wants. For example, consumers who before could afford flour only for baking could now buy ready-made bread, cake mixes, Bisquick biscuit flour, or other flour-based products.

**discretionary income** more income than is required to obtain the necessities of life

The implications of this change were immense. No longer could companies count on their sales forces alone to sell what was produced. Instead, they had to produce what customers wanted. Firms responded by introducing marketing at the beginning rather than the end of the production cycle and by integrating marketing into each phase of the business. Marketing assumed a more prominent role in product planning, pricing, product scheduling, and inventory control, as well as in distribution and servicing of the product.

Research became increasingly important. Marketers developed and improved their models to describe customer behavior. New-product planning grew increasingly sophisticated. Television advertising, branding strategy, and self-service dominated business thinking well into the 1970s.

## The Rise of the Service and Information Sectors

Five harsh realities led to a fundamental restructuring of American business, starting in the mid-1970s:

- The demise of the smokestack industries—steel, shipbuilding, coal, and the like—that had been our economy's backbone since the Civil War
- The shock of oil crises that demonstrated how vulnerable we were to foreign energy suppliers
- A loss of confidence that came with major recessions and staggering inflation
- The astonishment at how easily foreign products could displace American goods in electronics and autos
- A heightened consciousness of the problems of unemployment and underemployment as a new generation with great expectations joined the work force

**The New Industries** Fortunately, one major effect of the shocks of the 1970s was to accelerate the growth of two sectors of our economy in which we were becoming world leaders: the service sector and the information sector. These sectors have close connections.

The **service sector** consists of businesses that perform work for others that does not involve producing goods. Education, for example, lies in the service sector, as do all the other professions. It is important to note, incidentally, that a person may provide a service that involves selling or creating a good.

**service sector** consists of businesses that perform work for others that does not involve producing goods

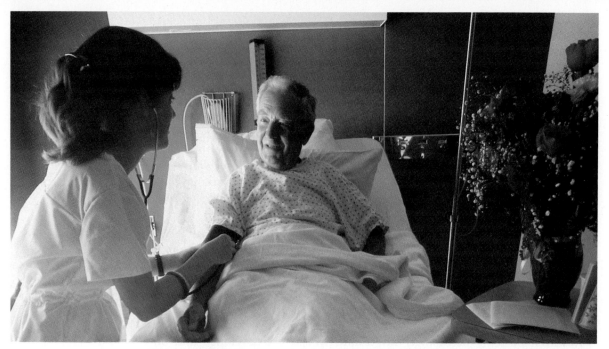

The new industries  *Since the mid-1970s American business has undergone major change, marked by the accelerated growth of the information and service industries.*

For example, a dentist may sell a patient a gold tooth, but the character of the transaction is predominantly a service involving the fitting of the tooth.

A major element in the service sector consists of those who operate the new computer and information-processing technologies. The businesses that produce computers and related equipment and instructions are providing support for the information sector of our economy. Computers are essentially devices for the manipulation of information, like account information for banks and credit cards.

*Deregulation*  In 1977, for the first time since Franklin D. Roosevelt, a president, Jimmy Carter, took seriously business's complaint about over-regulation. He began intensive deregulation of the transportation and financial industries. The idea was to let a freer marketplace encourage competition. His successor Ronald Reagan accelerated the deregulation process, particularly in those two areas. Deregulation had some unintended consequences, however. For example, a total of thirty U.S. airlines in 1978 grew to 125 by 1988. But despite the apparent increase in competition, the U.S. airline industry actually became more concentrated. The five major airlines that now account for some 70 percent of passenger traffic (a hefty 10 percent increase from a decade before) were in business well before deregulation became a reality.[13] Meanwhile, the declining condition of the U.S. savings and loan industry, reshaped by the forces of financial services deregulation, had become a national crisis.[14] Needless to say, the concept of industrial deregulation remains the subject of great controversy. Some call for more government control of the marketplace; some call for less. America's economic experiment goes on.

28

# Looking Ahead: Some Major Challenges for American Business

It has been said that the future is important because we are going to spend the rest of our lives there. What lies ahead for American business? No perfect crystal ball is available, but forward-thinking people have sketched the rough outlines of some major challenges. For example, an instructive agenda has been offered by the Hudson Institute, a private nonprofit research organization in Indianapolis. The Hudson researchers have challenged American business to respond creatively and boldly to the following six problems between now and the year 2000:

- *Stimulating balanced world growth:* The U.S. must pay less attention to its share of world trade and more to the growth of the economies of the other nations of the world, including those nations in Europe, Latin America, and Asia with whom the U.S. competes.
- *Accelerating productivity increases in service industries:* Prosperity will depend much more on how fast output per worker increases in health care, education, retailing, government, and other services, than on gains in manufacturing. [By the year 2000, an estimated 88 percent of the U.S. work force will be employed in the service sector of the economy.] [15]
- *Maintaining the dynamism of an aging work force:* As the average age of American workers climbs toward 40, the nation must insure that its work force does not lose its adaptability and willingness to learn.
- *Reconciling the conflicting needs of women, work, and families:* Despite the huge increases in the numbers of women in the work force, many of the policies and institutions that cover pay, fringe benefits, time away from work, pensions, welfare, and other issues have not yet been adjusted to the new realities.
- *Integrating black and Hispanic workers fully into the economy:* The shrinking numbers of young people, the rapid pace of industrial change, and the rising skill requirements of the emerging economy make the task of fully utilizing minority workers particularly urgent between now and 2000.
- *Improving the education and skills of all workers:* Human capital—knowledge, skills, organization, and leadership—is the key to economic growth and competitiveness. [16]

*9. List and explain at least four major challenges facing American business.*

To this list we would add a seventh challenge for American business: *Preventing continued destruction and pollution of the natural environment.* The traditional debate over jobs versus the environment has become obsolete in a world choking on its own garbage. Creative solutions are needed to produce jobs *and* environmental protection (see Business Issues).

These challenges are subject to debate because they strive to improve the overall economy and quality of life rather than cater to selected special interests. The first challenge, for instance, would probably get a cold reception from those sectors of the U.S. auto industry presently experiencing great pressure from foreign imports. But the Hudson researchers believe that a rising worldwide economic tide will "lift all boats." Please note that these seven challenges are not presented as final answers. They are intended to stimulate public discussion, debate, and creative problem solving.

## A FACE-OFF: INDUSTRY VERSUS THE ENVIRONMENT

Acid rain, air and water pollution, toxic waste, global warming, and the depleted ozone layer are all threats to our environment. Their effects are already being felt, and those effects are not good. What's at stake is not just a change in the quality of our lives but the survival of this planet.

Take global warming, or the greenhouse effect. The problem is caused in large part by carbon dioxide in the atmosphere. Carbon dioxide acts like a greenhouse, letting the rays of the sun in but keeping excess heat from radiating out. What happens? The earth's temperature rises, weather patterns change, storms intensify, fertile lands become deserts.

Much of the carbon dioxide in the atmosphere is a by-product of the fossil fuels burned to generate power. And much of that power is being generated for industry. Industry can reduce the amount of carbon dioxide in the atmosphere by cutting back its consumption of fossil fuels, by conserving energy and using alternate sources of energy (the sun, atomic power). But conservation affects productivity, and expensive new technology affects profits. And this is why industry has been slow to face up to its responsibilities to the environment.

In the 1960s and 1970s, public outcries about pollution forced the federal government to step in. Environmental protection laws were drawn up and passed, and regulatory agencies were formed. But regulation has been costly and has met with limited success. Moreover, the political climate in Washington has changed. Conservatives don't like regulation; they don't want government interfering in business.

Clearly, regulation is not working. So what do we do now? One suggestion is an incentive system, a system of credits, refunds, and permits that would encourage—not force—industry to deal with environmental problems. Actually, the idea isn't new. Since 1979, the Environmental Protection Agency has allowed companies to earn and trade pollution credits. (A company that does more than the environmental protection laws require in one area earns credits that allow it to do less than regulations require in another.) But for the first time the pollution credit notion is receiving the support of environmentalists as well as economists.

Industry versus the environment. The struggle has been going on since the turn of the century, when Teddy Roosevelt set out to protect the nation's wilderness. But today the issue isn't saving trees; it's saving our future and our children's future. And when the stakes are this high, we all have a responsibility to see the struggle end.

Sources: Michael D. Lemonick, "The Heat Is On," *Time,* October 19, 1987, pp. 58–63, 67; Jeremy Main, "Here Comes the Big New Cleanup," *Fortune,* November 21, 1988, pp. 102–103, 112; Daniel B. Wood, "*National Geographic* Begins Its Second Century with a Warning," *Christian Science Monitor,* December 1, 1988, pp. 1, 32.

## *A Topical Model for the Study of Business*

Because business is a complex subject with many important topics, we need a road map for our trip through the subject. Figure 1.9 displays just such a map. The major topics correspond to the seven parts of this textbook.

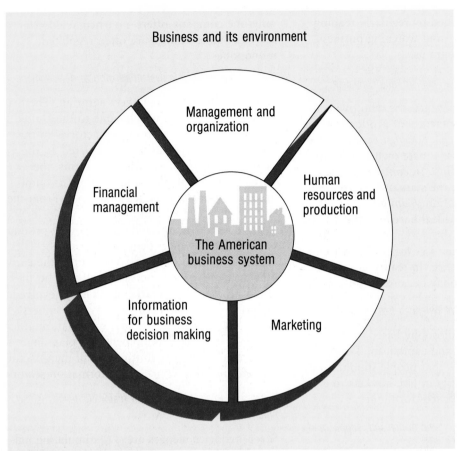

Business and its environment

Management and organization

Human resources and production

Financial management

The American business system

Information for business decision making

Marketing

FIGURE 1.9   A Topical Model for the Study of Business

# CHAPTER HIGHLIGHTS

*1. Define the term* business *and explain how it involves the "value-added" concept.*

*Business* is the profit-motivated buying, producing, and selling of goods and/or services. Businesspeople add economic value to goods and services by producing, storing, transporting, and selling them.

*2. Explain, from the standpoint of different roles people play, why it is important to study business.*

A working knowledge of business terminology and practices helps one be a smarter consumer,

better employee, successful business owner/manager, wiser investor, and informed voter. This is true because business touches every aspect of modern life.

*3. Discuss how business managers learn to manage.*

According to the Honeywell study, managers learned half of what they knew about business management from job assignments (firsthand experience). Thirty percent of their management knowledge reportedly came from personal relationships (role models). The remaining 20 percent came from training (formal education and self-study). A good deal about current business practices can be learned by regularly reading business publications and watching business-related television programs.

### 4. Contrast socialism, communism, and capitalism.

The key distinguishing factor is who owns and controls the primary factors of production, the state or private citizens. *Socialist* economies are characterized by mostly state ownership with some private ownership. In *communist* (or planned) economies, the state owns virtually all the factors of production. *Capitalism*, by definition, is an economic ideal based on the belief that private citizens should be free to produce and sell goods and services for profit, without government interference. In reality, no pure type of economy exists today because of intermixing.

### 5. Explain the ideology of American free enterprise.

It is an economic philosophy based on the principles of democracy and capitalism. The free-enterprise ideal holds that people should be able to associate voluntarily in free markets to exchange goods and services for money.

### 6. Discuss the interrelationship of demand, supply, and equilibrium.

*Demand* is the willingness of purchasers to buy specific quantities of a good or a service at a particular price at a particular time. *Supply* is the willingness of sellers or producers to provide goods or services at a particular price at a particular time. *Equilibrium* is the point at which demand and supply are in balance.

### 7. Contrast the four forms of economic competition.

The four primary types of economic competition range along a continuum from pure competition at one end to monopoly at the other. *Pure competition* occurs when no single seller can control the price of a single good or service. *Monopolistic competition* occurs when a relatively large number of sellers market similar but not identical products that are easily substituted for one another. An *oligopoly* is a market dominated by a few large sellers, who exert significant control over price and entry into the mar-

ket. A *monopoly* refers to a market in which only one company offers a particular good or service. Public utilities are often regulated monopolies.

### 8. Trace our economic system's historical development.

Colonial America was largely agrarian. The Industrial Revolution, which came to the United States in about 1800, brought factories to this country. Industrialization was spurred by the development of transportation systems, the needs of the Civil War, and the flow of immigrants to work in America's factories. From the time of the Civil War until just after World War I, businesses concentrated on improving production capacity to meet demand. During the sales era from the end of World War I until the early 1950s, the focus was on selling all that business could produce. The marketing concept evolved as business saw the need to assess consumers' wants and needs and use that information at all stages of product development and planning. American business is shifting out of manufacturing and into the service and information sectors.

### 9. List and explain at least four major challenges facing American business.

Seven major challenges are: (1) stimulating balanced world growth so that a healthy global economy will benefit all nations; (2) accelerating productivity increases in service industries—the service sector is the largest and least productive sector of the U.S. economy; (3) maintaining the dynamism of an aging work force—as the work force grows older, it is important to promote adaptability and willingness to learn; (4) reconciling the conflicting needs of women, work, and families because workplace practices have not kept pace with the greater number of women in the work force; (5) integrating black and Hispanic workers fully into the economy because there is a danger of creating a permanent underclass of minority citizens; (6) improving the education and skills of all workers because well-trained *people* are the key to economic growth and competitiveness; and (7) preventing continued destruction and pollution of the natural environment because jobs are of little use in a world we cannot live in.

# KEY TERMS

| | | | |
|---|---|---|---|
| Profit | Communism | Demand | Pure competition |
| Business | Capitalism | Demand curve | Monopoly |
| Economics | Modified capitalism | Supply | Monopolistic competition |
| Economic system | Free-enterprise system | Supply curve | Oligopoly |
| Marketplace | Factors of production | Equilibrium | Barter |
| Socialism | Product | Market price | Discretionary income |
| Privatization | Entrepreneur | Competition | Service sector |

# REVIEW QUESTIONS

1. What does the term *business* mean?
2. Why is it worthwhile to study business?
3. What three fundamental questions must every economic system answer?
4. How can one distinguish between socialism, communism, and capitalism?
5. What are the three factors of production?
6. What do the concepts of supply, demand, and equilibrium involve?
7. What is the difference between a monopoly and an oligopoly?
8. What were the three distinct characteristics of the Industrial Revolution?
9. Why did the production era prompt a wave of reform and regulation between 1890 and 1914?
10. What are at least three major challenges facing American business between now and the year 2000?

# APPLICATION EXERCISES

1. In the early 1980s, American Telephone and Telegraph (AT&T) was the nation's largest regulated monopoly. This giant company owned the Bell Telephone system and other subsidiaries. In 1982, after many years of legal battles, AT&T's management signed a consent decree which required the firm to sever its relationship with each subsidiary that provides local phone service to consumers in specific geographic areas. The Justice Department took legal action because it believed AT&T was monopolizing the entire phone industry and stifling competition. In your opinion, was this action justified? Should AT&T have been allowed to continue in the role of a regulated monopoly? What has been the effect of the breakup of AT&T in your community?

2. Make a list of five business firms in your community that have been in operation for at least two years. The list should include several types of businesses. For each business, answer the following questions. Do the forces of supply and demand appear to have a strong influence on the prices charged for the firm's products and services? Would more competition result in lowering the prices of products and services offered by the firm?

# CASES

## 1.1 Wal-Mart: Retailing Good Guy or Bully?

It officially begins like most every other event at Fayetteville's Barnhill Arena—with a prayer and the National Anthem. However, this invocation at the home of the University of Arkansas' basketball Razorbacks doesn't carry any of the usual athletic allusions. And instead of the Hog Wild Pep Band, a prerecorded orchestra plays accompaniment to "The Star-Spangled Banner" as patriotic images flash on overhead video screens. It is touted as the world's largest shareholders' meeting, and no one has challenged the claim.

The sport that brought more than 6,000 people here today is capitalism, and the home team is Wal-Mart Stores Inc., based just up the road in Bentonville . . . [1988 sales: nearly $20 billion]. This fast-growing retail chain, whose sales have reportedly increased by 240 percent over the last five years, plays the game differently than the competition.

So different in fact that some industry analysts say this once little-known outfit could become the nation's largest retailer as early as 1991. They also believe the company could achieve this feat without expanding beyond its current territory of 25 states spread primarily across the Sun Belt. For the time being, Wal-Mart is No. 3 in terms of yearly sales behind Sears, Roebuck & Co. at $28.1 billion and K Mart Corp. with $25.6 billion.

"Sears and K Mart are losing market shares," says Cathleen Mackey, retail analyst with New York–based Smith Barney, Harris Upham & Company. "Wal-Mart's pricing strategy allows it to capture market share quickly. Its productivity feeds upon itself. . . . No one else has the financial wherewithal, the management and technology. Frankly, I wouldn't want to be in Wal-Mart's way."

"We're writing a chapter in retailing that's never been written before," says Sam Walton, chairman of the board who co-founded the company, along with his brother James, 26 years ago.

Wal-Mart built its foundation and reputation in rural middle America, placing stores mainly in cities of 25,000 or less—a market most retailers viewed as marginal. "There was a lot more business in those towns than people ever thought," Sam Walton has quipped in the past.

True enough. But Wal-Mart's entry into rural American markets, a phenomenon that in the words of some critics "tears at the civic fabric of small-town life," has drawn mixed reviews from local citizens.

Some say that Wal-Mart's success is coming at the expense of small, family-owned stores whose roots run deep in communities like Pawhuska, Oklahoma. Cries of unfair competition have come from critics who point to vacant downtown shops that were forced to close, they say, because of Sam Walton's predatory pricing that gobbles up customers. A group of Oklahoma drug stores has reportedly sued the company over a little-known state law that requires retailers to sell their goods above cost.

Others praise the chain for bringing big-city retailing—with its wide selection at discount prices—to their small town. They also point to the increased traffic of rural consumers who now come to their town to shop instead of trekking to the big cities.

### Questions

1. What is the relationship between Wal-Mart's pricing strategy—"the lowest prices in town"—and the company's incredible success and growth?
2. What would Sam Walton and the owner of a small-town store driven out of business by Wal-Mart each have to say about American free enterprise?

Source: Excerpted from George Waldron, "Bargains and Billionaires," Southwest *Spirit*, November 1988, pp. 34, 36–37, 48. Reprinted courtesy of Southwest SPIRIT, carried aboard Southwest Airlines, © 1988; East/West Network, publisher.

## 1.2 Should the U.S. Postal Service Go Private?

To most Americans, postal problems mean delayed deliveries and rising stamp prices.

It also means questions like this one from a Massachusetts woman: "If a post card can get from Tibet to Boston in two days, why does a pair of overshoes take six weeks to go first class from New York to Boston?"

These are important issues, but do not deal with underlying difficulties.

When postal experts consider what to do to improve the oft-criticized performance of the United States Postal Service, they quickly get to a fundamental issue. They call it privatizing. Would mail service be better if private profit-making companies did more of the job?

Taken to the ultimate, the question becomes: Should private, competitive industry replace the Postal Service, with its 800,000 workers and its monopoly on delivery of first-class mail?

Experts sit on all sides of these questions. The Postal Service itself is "all for" more contracting with private companies for postal services, says Deputy Postmaster General Michael S. Coughlin. It seeks to improve its efficiency. But, not surprisingly, it vehemently objects to replacing the Postal Service with profitmaking firms, or even opening up first-class mail delivery to competition.

That's entirely the "wrong approach," says Daniel Oliver, commissioner of the Federal Trade Commission. The real problem, he told a conference on postal privatization last year, is that "the Postal Service is a monopoly, and monopolies behave like monopolies no matter who's in charge of them." Mr. Oliver says the ultimate solution is "to manage the politics" of the situation, and get Congress to approve an end to the monopoly status. . . .

"There is a role for the private sector," Warren Cikens, an expert on privatization, insists, "in setting a challenge or standard in areas that traditionally have been public sector," such as the Postal Service. He especially mentions standards of individual productivity (long a Postal Service problem) and administration. He calls for establishing "a middle ground," between continuation of status quo and the Oliver concept of ending such postal monopolies as first-class letter delivery.

### Questions

1. What are the major arguments *in favor of* ending the government's monopoly on the delivery of first-class mail?
2. What are the major arguments *against*?
3. Which side of the debate do you find most convincing? Why?

Source: Excerpted from Robert P. Hey, "Putting the Mails in Private Hands," *The Christian Science Monitor,* January 6, 1989, p. 8. Reprinted by permission from *The Christian Science Monitor.* © 1989 The Christian Science Publishing Society. All rights reserved.

# 2 Social Responsibility and Business Ethics

**LEARNING**

**OBJECTIVES**

*After you have completed this chapter, you will be able to do the following:*

*1. Define the term* corporate social responsibility.

*2. Discuss the arguments for and against social responsibility.*

*3. Distinguish between altruism and enlightened self-interest.*

*4. Outline the evolution of the concept of social responsibility.*

*5. Describe the four different social responsibility strategies.*

*6. Describe the development and application of the social audit.*

*7. Explain three reasons why today's managers need to be concerned with business ethics.*

*8. Discuss specific steps managers can take to encourage ethical conduct.*

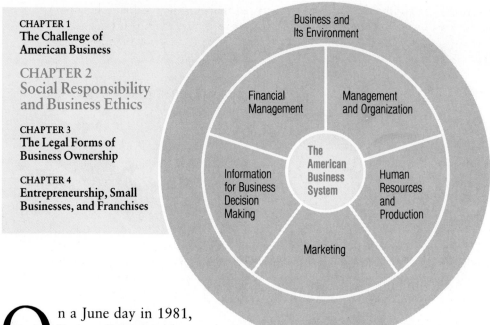

O n a June day in 1981,
Eugene Lang stood on a
podium in East Harlem in New York
City. A self-made multimillionaire and president of REFAC Technology Development Corporation, Lang was giving the commencement address at P.S. 121,
which he had attended fifty years earlier. In the midst of his speech, he realized
that he wanted to leave his audience with something more than the usual words
of inspiration. He proceeded to tell the sixty-one graduating sixth-graders that
if they completed high school he would pay for their college educations.

This gesture turned out to be more than a hollow promise because Lang backed
it up with money and his own personal time. He funded remedial education and
counseling programs for the East Harlem youngsters. Lang developed lasting
personal relationships with them as well. The results were amazing. Although
the average dropout rate in ghetto schools continued to hover around 75 percent,
Lang's P.S. 121 class achieved a 93 percent graduation rate in 1987. By the Fall
semester of 1988, thirty-four were still in college.

Lang, who has donated more than $23 million to educational institutions,
provided more than hope for a few fortunate kids. He has become an inspiring
role model for corporate social responsibility. Many executives and companies
across the country are imitating his grass-roots support of education.[1]

The story of Eugene Lang and those who have followed his example is a
wonderful one, but it is not exceptional. People in business and businesses
themselves make enormous contributions to the betterment of their communities. Just consider a few examples of the sort that could fill a book:
sponsoring Little League teams, buying books for libraries, funding AIDS
research, providing labor for drug-abuse centers, and paying for alcohol-

awareness programs. It is generally accepted that businesses, from the largest to the smallest, and the people who own them have obligations to society. The great debate is over the nature and extent of those obligations. This discussion is the focus of this chapter.

# Corporate Social Responsibility: Definition and Background

**Corporate social responsibility** encompasses obligations to society above and beyond making a profit for stockholders, obeying laws, or honoring contracts.[2] It is important to keep in mind that companies still need to make profits. Otherwise they would be socially irresponsible by going out of business. The key theme here is taking action "above and beyond" making a profit. Social responsibility as a concept does not require that a business adopt a particular point of view or that it promote certain specified ends. For this reason, most definitions of social responsibility emphasize the means that a business chooses to employ rather than the ends it may seek to achieve (see Table 2.1).

Whether one believes that businesses have obligations to society beyond the minimal requirements imposed by law and contracts depends largely on whether one sees a business as just an economic organization created solely to increase the value of its owners' investments. If its only purpose is conceived of as that of making money for its owners, then its only obligation to society is to act within the law. As the influential economist Milton Friedman has written,

> [There] is one and only one social responsibility of business—to use its resources and engage in activities designed to increase its profits so long as it stays within the rules of the game, which is to say, engages in open and free competition without deception and fraud.[3]

**corporate social responsibility** encompasses obligations to society above and beyond making a profit for stockholders, obeying laws, or honoring contracts

*1.* Define the term corporate social responsibility.

*2.* Discuss the arguments for and against social responsibility.

TABLE 2.1    Ten Commandments of Corporate Social Responsibility

I. Thou Shall Take Corrective Action Before It Is Required.
II. Thou Shall Work with Affected Constituents to Resolve Mutual Problems.
III. Thou Shall Work to Establish Industrywide Standards and Self-Regulation.
IV. Thou Shall Publicly Admit Your Mistakes.
V. Thou Shall Get Involved in Appropriate Social Programs.
VI. Thou Shall Help Correct Environmental Problems.
VII. Thou Shall Monitor the Changing Social Environment.
VIII. Thou Shall Establish and Enforce a Corporate Code of Conduct.
IX. Thou Shall Take Needed Public Stands on Social Issues.
X. Thou Shall Strive to Make Profits on an Ongoing Basis.

Source: Excerpted from L. D. Alexander and W. F. Matthews, "The Ten Commandments of Corporate Social Responsibility," *Business and Society Review*, number 50, Summer 1984, 62–66. Used by permission.

Shopping for a better world   *The Council on Economic Priorities, a public interest research group, works to improve corporate social responsibility by educating consumers on the products they're buying and the companies that manufacture them. The Council publishes a booklet called* Shopping for a Better World: A Quick & Easy Guide to Socially Responsible Supermarket Shopping," *a report card of sorts, which grades over 130 companies in areas like charitable donations, women's and minority advancement, animal testing, and the environment. The Council wants to show business that consumers care.*

According to Friedman and his followers, business's sole responsibility is to ensure its survival by making a legal profit. Arguments for and against corporate social responsibility are summarized in Table 2.2.

## Voluntary Actions

Milton Friedman's views do not represent the mainstream of current thinking on social responsibility. For example, consider the lesson that Japanese executives learned when they opened a truck plant in Tennessee:

> Marvin T. Runyon, the new president of Nissan Motor Manufacturing Corp. USA in Tennessee, didn't think much about it when he earmarked $100,000 of his first-year budget for charity. To Runyon, who had spent 37 years at Ford Motor Co., donating money was standard business procedure. But Nissan's president at the time, Takashi Ishihara, was stunned when he noticed the item in Runyon's 1981 plan. "You don't make money yet," Ishihara said. "How are you going to give it away?" Replied Runyon: "It's the American way." Eventually, Ishihara relented, and Nissan became a prominent donor.[4]

Although corporate charity to outsiders is still not common in Japan, Japanese companies have learned that this custom is all part of doing business in the United States.

**TABLE 2.2   The Arguments For and Against Social Responsibility**

| For | Against |
| --- | --- |
| 1. Business is involved in social issues whether it wants to be or not. | 1. Business's focus on profits already brings about the most efficient allocation of societal resources. |
| 2. Business has the resources to deal with some of the most difficult problems that society confronts. | 2. Business lacks the ability to pursue economic and social goals at the same time. |
| 3. Business is a major beneficiary of every improvement in society. | 3. Business has more than enough power over economic matters as it is. |
| 4. Business invites government intervention, rather than avoiding it, when it fails to act on its own. | 4. The public does not elect business managers, unlike its public officials. Managers are not directly accountable to the public, so they should not be asked to determine what society ought to do. |

Today the debate centers on the nature of business's responsibility to society, not on whether that responsibility exists. It is generally agreed that social responsibility has three dimensions:

- How a firm behaves as it pursues its goal of making profits
- What charitable efforts a firm undertakes that are not related to its normal business activities
- What positions a firm takes on issues of public policy that affect both business and society

The field within which a firm can act in fulfilling its social responsibility is defined by two boundaries: the minimum requirements for responsible social conduct expressed by laws, and the maximum boundaries permitted by its competitive economic position (see Figure 2.1).[5]

Within this range, a business is free to define social responsibility in its own way. In other words, a business's actions in this arena are *voluntary*. For example, after a psychopath poisoned Extra-Strength Tylenol capsules, causing eight deaths, Johnson & Johnson, the maker of this aspirin substitute, immediately recalled 30 million bottles of it, at a cost of $100 million. Johnson & Johnson did not wait for an order from the Food & Drug Administration or a state agency. Rather, it did what it believed would best protect the public. The company received much praise—and customer loyalty—for its action. Most commentators failed to note, incidentally, that the company is also one of the largest corporate philanthropists.

By contrast, over a period of years the A. H. Robins Manufacturing Company disregarded mounting evidence that its Dalkon Shield birth-control device was causing serious health problems in users. When it was sued, it lied to the courts, hid documents, and defamed the individuals who had been its product's victims. The company finally recalled the defective product from the market, but it ended up in bankruptcy nevertheless.

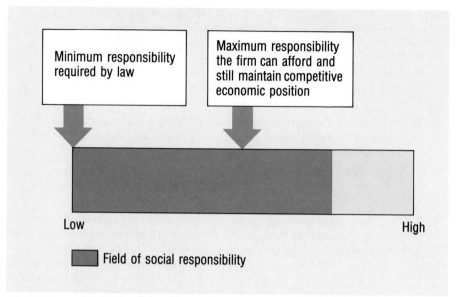

FIGURE 2.1   The Field within which a Firm Can Act in Fulfilling Its Social
Responsibility

*Source:* David Vogel, "Foreword" to Thornton Bradshaw & David Vogel, *Corporations and Their Critics* (New York: McGraw-Hill, 1982), pp. viii–ix.

## *Toward Greater Social Responsibility*

Business has assumed ever-greater social responsibility in recent years. Some observers go so far as to claim that business can survive only by taking an aggressive role in social issues, especially since public attitudes toward business are not as good as they could be. In a nationwide poll of 1,250 Americans taken in 1987, only 18 percent described their attitude toward business as "very favorable" (see Figure 2.2). The largest percentage of respondents described their attitude only as "somewhat favorable."[6] The survey results reveal *broad but shallow* public support for business. Such an attitude is not surprising in view of highly publicized insider trading scandals, defense industry fraud, and other corporate misdeeds. Moreover, popular movies like *Wall Street* and television shows such as *Dallas* and *Dynasty* consistently paint a negative picture of the corporate world. J. R. Ewing's antics do little to build public confidence in business.[7] Consequently, many businesspeople feel strongly about getting their firms more deeply involved in the social issues confronting Americans today.

As shown in the Business Issues box, American businesses are answering the call for greater social responsibility in a wide variety of ways. Each of the actions taken by the companies profiled was *voluntary* and *above and beyond* legal requirements.

42

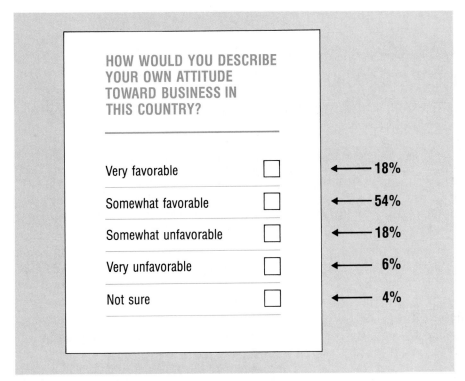

HOW WOULD YOU DESCRIBE YOUR OWN ATTITUDE TOWARD BUSINESS IN THIS COUNTRY?

| | |
|---|---|
| Very favorable ☐ | ← 18% |
| Somewhat favorable ☐ | ← 54% |
| Somewhat unfavorable ☐ | ← 18% |
| Very unfavorable ☐ | ← 6% |
| Not sure ☐ | ← 4% |

FIGURE 2.2   Public Attitudes Toward Business Are Not as Good as They Could Be

*Source:* Data from Stuart Jackson and Harris Collingwood, *"Business Week*/Harris Poll: Is an Antibusiness Backlash Building?"* Reprinted from July 20, 1987, issue of *Business Week* by special permission, copyright © 1987 by McGraw-Hill, Inc.

## *Enlightened Self-Interest*

What motivates a company's management to engage in social responsibility programs? The answer is one or a combination of three different motives: (1) **altruism**—an unselfish concern for others' well-being; (2) avoidance of government regulation; and (3) enlightened self-interest. Altruism and avoidance of regulation are self-explanatory. The third motive, however, requires a closer look.

**Enlightened self-interest** involves the belief that a business ultimately helps itself when it helps to solve society's problems. In other words, a cleaner, safer, more fair-minded world is a better place in which to do business. A prime example is 3M Corporation's waste reduction program mentioned in the Business Issues box. Copper sheeting was formerly cleaned at the company's Columbia, Missouri, electronics plant with a toxic chemical mixture spray. A group of employees was able to reduce the health hazards involved in this process by devising a machine that scrubs the copper with an abrasive, leaving behind a nonhazardous sludge. This relatively inexpensive piece of equipment did away with an extra 40,000 pounds of liquid hazardous waste every year. The 3M Corporation states further that its worldwide

**altruism**   an unselfish concern for others' well-being

*3. Distinguish between altruism and enlightened self-interest.*

**enlightened self-interest** involves the belief that a business ultimately helps itself when it helps to solve society's problems

## CORPORATE SOCIAL RESPONSIBILITY IN ACTION

At a ceremony in New York in 1988, the following companies received America's Corporate Conscience Awards from the Council on Economic Priorities:

| Company | Nature of Social Contribution | Explanation |
| --- | --- | --- |
| Gannett Company | Fair employment for women | Four women are on Gannett's board of directors, the publisher of *USA Today* is a woman, and women head twenty-three of Gannett's subsidiaries. |
| IBM | Family concerns | Notable programs include: AIDS education and support program and an extra $50,000 in company-paid health coverage for employees with handicapped children. |
| Procter & Gamble | Animal rights | P&G has been a leader in reducing the number of animals used in consumer product safety testing and developing alternatives to animal testing. |
| 3M Corporation | Environmental protection | 3M's waste recovery, van pooling, and energy-saving programs have become models for U.S. businesses. |

Source: Adapted from "Corporations with a Conscience,"
*Business and Society Review*, Winter 1988, pp. 58–59.

program, known as Pollution Prevention Pays, saved the company $400 million through 1988.[8]

3M's waste reduction program is a win-win situation. Employees at 3M facilities and the communities in which they operate win because of reduced exposure to hazardous waste. The company itself wins by saving vast sums of money because preventing pollution is cheaper than cleaning it up later and settling related lawsuits.

From a broader perspective, companies can derive three benefits from enlightened self-interest: enhanced reputation, favorable publicity, and improved recruiting (see Figure 2.3).

*Reputation Value*   Enlightened self-interest operates on several levels. At the highest level, it represents an understanding that nothing is more important to the long-term success of any business than its reputation. Unless a company is prepared to sacrifice its own immediate financial advantage to protect the

44

*"Still–in a way–nobody sees a flower–really–
it is so small–we haven't time–
and to see takes time, like to have a friend takes time."*
—*Georgia O'Keeffe*

Red Poppy, 1927  Oil on canvas 7" × 9", Private collection, Geneva          Photography by Malcolm Varon

## GEORGIA O'KEEFFE 1887-1986

*National Gallery of Art, Washington · November 1, 1987-February 21, 1988
The Art Institute of Chicago · March 12-June 26, 1988
Dallas Museum of Art · July 31-October 16, 1988
The Metropolitan Museum of Art, New York · November 19, 1988-February 5, 1989*

**Southwestern Bell Corporation**

*An exhibition organized by the National Gallery of Art and made possible by a grant from Southwestern Bell Foundation.*

**Social responsibility and the arts**  *Southwestern Bell Corporation expresses its commitment to social responsibility and community service by funding cultural events such as a Georgia O'Keeffe exhibit which traveled around the country in 1988. Corporations which make financial sacrifices in the community's interest believe that they are investing in long-term business success by earning the loyalty and respect of the public.*

public interest, it cannot expect the public to care about the company's long-term well-being.

Many companies encourage employees to take on community projects, such as United Way campaigns, that cut into work time. Some businesses even allow employees to work full time on a community project while on a paid leave of absence. The most noted program of this type is the Xerox Social Service Leave Program, which started in 1972. Qualified Xerox employees may apply for a six-month to one-year paid leave to work on a community-service program. Afterward, they are guaranteed their old job back or a similar one.

REPUTATION VALUE    PUBLICITY VALUE    RECRUITING & KEEPING PERSONNEL

FIGURE 2.3    Potential Corporate Benefits of Enlightened Self-Interest

*Publicity Value*    On another level, enlightened self-interest requires accurate calculation of the long-term benefits expected to be derived from the short-term costs of social responsibility. The corporate charitable contribution is the classic example of this. Its real benefit comes from the publicity and recognition that gifts attract. Research bears out this finding. A study of corporate charitable donations in thirty-six different industries led the researchers to call such generosity "profit-motivated advertising."[9]

Along the same lines, American Express has introduced "cause-related marketing," which is designed at once to create social benefits and to generate greater profits. During the campaign for funds to restore the Statue of Liberty, the firm pledged a penny for every American Express card transaction and a dollar for every new member. The three-month campaign raised $1.7 million for the Statue while boosting card use by 28 percent and applications for cards by 45 percent.

*Recruiting and Keeping Personnel*    Companies with strong reputations for their social commitments have a significantly easier time in recruiting and keeping personnel with similar interests. Firms with good records on hiring and promoting women and minorities tend to attract increasing numbers of qualified job applicants from these groups.

Businesses with a highly visible commitment to the communities in which they operate also tend to have better records in attracting and keeping personnel. Wang Laboratories has made its area of eastern Massachusetts a much better place to live through its generous donations to cultural affairs and its funding of Boston's Wang Center. Despite recent reversals in Wang's business fortunes, it retains a high reputation.

Many businesses have programs that pay part or all of an employee's tuition for courses taken outside of work hours. Such programs improve employee morale by demonstrating a firm's commitment to helping its personnel improve their chances of getting ahead. And tuition aid helps fill local college classrooms with committed students. Some businesses have taken these programs a step further by giving employees paid leaves of absence to complete their degrees or to obtain advanced training.

As an instructive backdrop for the rest of this chapter, let us take a brief historical look at how the concept of corporate social responsibility evolved in the American free-enterprise system.

# The Evolution of the Concept of Social Responsibility

The idea that business has social responsibility has undergone change since the nation's founding.[10] In Chapter 1, we saw that Adam Smith introduced the principle of laissez faire. To have a marketplace free of government interference was a radical break from the close regulation of trade and prices that had existed since medieval times. The concept of laissez faire dominated social and political thinking of the next century and a half (see Figure 2.4).

*4. Outline the evolution of the concept of social responsibility.*

FIGURE 2.4   The Evolution of the Concept of Social Responsibility

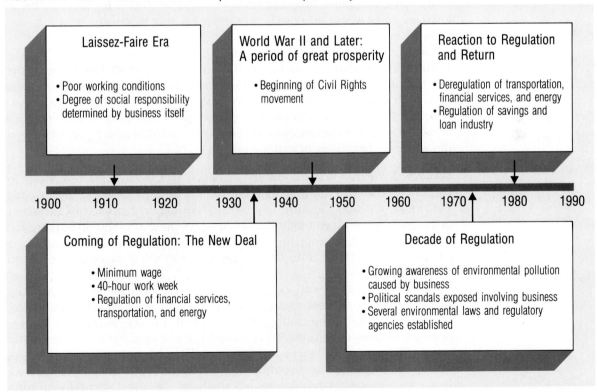

# Caveat Emptor and the Nature of Contracts

**caveat emptor** a Latin term meaning "let the buyer beware"

Laissez faire found expression in the prevailing philosophy of the marketplace, **caveat emptor,** a Latin term meaning "let the buyer beware."

*Responsibility for Products*   Laissez faire suggested that the invisible hand that Adam Smith described as working through the marketplace would reward those who produced goods that the public wanted. Those who sold inferior or dangerous goods would fail. For the concept to work, however, some buyers had to receive shoddy goods or be maimed by dangerous products.

**contract** an agreement between two or more parties that the law will enforce

The concepts of laissez faire and caveat emptor also affected the courts' view of the nature of a **contract,** an agreement between two or more parties that the law will enforce. The courts of the time regarded contracts as being the product of bargaining in which each side protected its own interests. Thus, a contract between a retailer and a buyer for the sale of a product did not give the buyer the right to hold the manufacturer responsible for injuries from a defective product, because the manufacturer did not deal directly with the thousands of people, perhaps, who might have a claim against it. For example, someone named MacPhearson once bought a Buick.[11] A defective wheel came off and MacPhearson was injured. The dealer was not at fault, because the manufacturer made the wheel. But the manufacturer was not responsible either, for it had not dealt with the buyer itself. MacPhearson could have protected himself only by carefully inspecting the car before buying it or by negotiating with the dealer for protection—or by not buying the car at all. Until 1916, this was the law in the United States, and the notion did not entirely disappear until 1966.[12]

The effect of this narrow interpretation of the right to sue was to assign the defining of business's social responsibility to business. Anyone who insisted that society should have a say in the process was told that business's self-interest was the best protection the public could have. What ended the argument was not the question of responsibility for products but the one of the working conditions of employees.

*Responsibility for Worker Safety*   Implicit in the laissez-faire concept of contracts is another notion, that the parties to a contract are in an equal bargaining position. Because any two parties are free either to contract or not to contract, it was thought that legislatures and courts should not interfere with the parties' agreement. This view dominated the interpretation of employment contracts until the 1930s, and important aspects of it remain the law today.

Nineteenth-century working conditions were almost uniformly appalling. The standard work week exceeded 60 hours even until the 1930s, and paid vacations and health insurance were unknown. Efforts on the state level to improve working conditions largely failed. For instance, New York attempted to limit bakers' work weeks to 60 hours. The U.S. Supreme Court voided the statute, though, as unconstitutional interference with the right to contract. In effect, the courts refused to acknowledge the fundamentally unequal bargaining positions of employer and employee.

Again, the task of defining business's responsibility to society was assigned solely to business. Employers who wished to improve working conditions faced a hard choice. Any investment in better working conditions would put them at a competitive disadvantage, because their own costs would go up but their competitors' would not. Some employers nevertheless tried to improve their workers' lots, but most did not.

## The Coming of Regulation

Starting in the 1880s, public opinion began to favor the imposition of minimum standards of conduct on business by government. Under their **police powers,** the state and local governments' powers to protect the health, safety, and welfare of their citizens, governments started the long process of assuring safe and sanitary workplaces and residences.

For many the event that marked the end of the laissez-faire era in working conditions occurred in 1911. A 20-minute fire on the ninth floor of the Triangle Shirtwaist Company building in New York City left 147 workers dead. The image of more than fifty young women leaping from windows to escape the flames came to haunt the public. Later revelations about blocked exits and generally unsafe conditions gave impetus to the gathering movement toward regulation of the workplace.[13]

**police powers** state and local governments' powers to protect the health, safety, and welfare of their citizens

The consumer advocate *In 1965 Ralph Nader first drew attention with the publication of a book detailing serious structural problems in the Corvair. The movement he began eventually forced General Motors to stop production of the car. Since then Nader has gone on to fight the consumer's battle on many fronts.*

*The Depression and the New Deal*  The depression of 1929–1939 shook Americans' confidence in the laissez-faire concept. By the time Franklin Roosevelt took office in 1933, one-quarter of the work force had no jobs and America's industrial output had fallen by 50 percent. Revolutions and dictatorships such as those afflicting Russia, Germany, and Italy seemed a real possibility in the United States.

Through programs like unemployment insurance, Social Security and federal bank deposit insurance, and various government regulations, Roosevelt hoped to protect Americans from capitalism's rough edges. The intense regulation of financial services, transportation, and energy dates to this period.

After Roosevelt replaced several of its members, the U.S. Supreme Court became much more favorably inclined toward laws regulating such working conditions as wages and hours. Roosevelt signed legislation enacting a national minimum wage and establishing the 40-hour work week as standard. Suddenly business found itself with a set of governmental minimum standards of performance and even higher public expectations of performance.

*World War II and a Period of Great Prosperity*  Where the New Deal might eventually have taken the relationship between government and business and how a prolonged depression would have altered people's relationships with business remain unknown. World War II arrived, requiring the United States to pull itself together. It emerged from the war as the strongest and most prosperous nation the world had yet seen. The New Deal reforms had become generally accepted as business's social ground rules. The public and business agreed that these reforms represented in effect floors and that business's principal responsibility was to create jobs and prosperity. The prosperity was enormous enough to hide the inefficiencies and waste that regulation was forcing on all the transportation systems other than the automobile and on the financial-services industry.

Perhaps the most important development in the period after World War II was the Civil Rights movement. It began in the South among blacks who demanded equal treatment under the laws. Their successes profoundly changed the nature of the workplace. For example, in the 1960s Levi Strauss opened a plant in Virginia, for which it wanted to hire both blacks and whites. The white workers demanded separate restrooms and drinking fountains, with preferably a wall between white and black workers. Strauss refused these demands, which were not unreasonable by local standards, insisting upon an integrated facility because the company felt it was the right thing to do.[14]

The gains made by blacks led directly to the opening of the workplace to other minorities, women, and the handicapped. By the late 1960s, equal opportunity had become a societal goal.

## The Decade of Regulation: The 1970s

By the early 1970s, the U.S. public's postwar confidence in business had eroded. A growing awareness of environmental pollution focused attention on businesses that could not or would not clean up their operations without being compelled to do so by the government. The Vietnam War, which began in earnest in 1965, put a spotlight on firms supplying war materials. One such company, Dow Chemical, attracted considerable attention because its defoliants had serious environmental as well as military consequences. The prevalence of such occupational diseases as black lung among coal miners and brown lung among cotton-mill workers led to demands for more effective regulation of the work place. The great political scandals of the early 1970s centered largely on the role of corporations in both the national and international political processes. Finally, the consumer movement, led initially by Ralph Nader, drew public attention to the shoddy and sometimes dangerous quality of many products.

At all levels of government, the response to these unsettling events was a burst of regulation. Environmental laws and regulations came in a flood. Agencies such as the Federal Election Commission, the Occupational Safety & Health Administration (OSHA), and the Consumer Product Safety Commission appeared seemingly overnight.

## The Reaction to Regulation

A reaction against regulation began in the late-1970s. President Jimmy Carter initiated a series of deregulation programs that were aimed particularly at the energy, financial-services, and transportation industries. These efforts were well underway by the end of his term in 1981.

**5.** *Describe the four different social responsibility strategies.*

The election of President Ronald Reagan was expected to bring an era of deregulation and what we describe as nonregulation in Chapter 22. Things did not work out quite as imagined, however. In fact, there was a general consensus in favor of regulation. One desirable effect of regulation is that it denies a cost advantage to those who do not act in a socially responsible manner. Also, it is hard to argue that pollution or unsafe products benefit society. Although the pace of business regulation slowed as the 1980s progressed, only small parts of the regulatory structure disappeared entirely. George Bush's first major decision as President, rescuing the ailing savings and loan industry, involved a huge dose of government regulation of business.

# Social Responsibility Strategies

With today's complex web of governmental regulations, business managers may choose from among four classes of social responsibility strategies reaction, defense, accommodation, or proaction (see Figure 2.5).

## RECOGNITION OF CORPORATE SOCIAL RESPONSIBILITIES

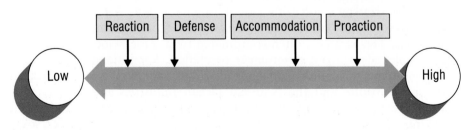

FIGURE 2.5 Social Responsibility Strategies Visualized

Giving back to the community   *Leslie Schilling is a real estate developer who has earned millions of dollars buying, selling, and managing properties in San Francisco. Although her real estate projects keep her busy, the Hong Kong–born developer has made the time to help San Francisco's Asian community. As the first woman to head the city's Asian Business League, her primary goal is to see that the league's members overcome a cultural shyness and learn to say what they think.*

## The Reaction Strategy

**reaction strategy**   when business denies responsibility for something while at the same time developing an argument for continuing the status quo

A business follows a **reaction strategy** when it denies responsibility for something while at the same time it is developing an argument for continuing the status quo. For example, despite mounting medical evidence of the link between cigarette smoking and lung cancer, tobacco companies vigorously deny the connection as a basis for justifying the sale of cigarettes. A. H. Robins, mentioned earlier, followed a reaction strategy.

## The Defense Strategy

**defense strategy**   the use of public relations, legal maneuvering, and whatever other means are necessary to avoid assuming additional obligations

The **defense strategy** involves the use of public relations, legal maneuvering, and whatever other means are necessary to avoid assuming additional obligations. This strategy, often coordinated by a trade association, is most often employed to avoid government regulation. For instance, the leading opponents of the regulation of offshore oil drilling operations are the American Petroleum Institute and the National Ocean Industries Association. The National Coal Association resists surface-mining regulation. A few individual companies, like Mobil Oil Company, have adopted this strategy. For some years, Mobil has bought advertising space in newspapers to present its views (a practice called *advocacy advertising*).

## The Accommodation and Proaction Strategies

The accommodation and proaction strategies have in common a willingness to assume responsibility for their actions rather than to deny it. The difference between the two strategies lies in the motivation underlying the assumption of responsibility.

When a company assumes more social responsibility because of pressure from an interest group or the government, it adopts an **accommodation strategy**. If, for example, a company sets up stringent promotion goals for women and minorities under the threat of a lawsuit by its employees, it is using an accommodation strategy.

In contrast, Genentech, a biotechnology firm, recently exhibited a **proaction strategy** of voluntary, constructive social action by offering to make available its anticlotting drug Activase free of charge to hospitals treating low-income patients suffering from heart attacks. (Activase, created through genetic engineering, normally sells for $2,200 a dose.)[15] Those corporate programs listed in Business Issues are further examples of proactive social responsibility.

**accommodation strategy**   when a company assumes more social responsibility because of pressure from an interest group or the government

**proaction strategy**   voluntary, constructive social action

A proaction strategy at work   *Many companies are taking corporate social responsibility into the public schools, volunteering money, equipment, and people. Some, like Los Angeles–based Arco Oil & Gas Co., are sending employees—from secretaries to officers—into the classroom to tutor minority students.*

# The Social Audit

social audit  an annual
assessment of a company's
effects on society and
the environment

By law, every corporation that has more than 500 shareholders and a value
exceeding a certain minimal level must have its books audited. Shareholders
and the investing public are thus provided with an accurate picture of the
business's financial condition. Some people have applied this same concept
to a business's interaction with society and encourage a **social audit**, an
annual assessment of a company's effects on society and the environment.

## *Developing a Social Audit*

*6. Describe the development
and application of the social
audit.*

A business would normally expect to perform a social audit annually, just
as it issues an annual report. An accumulation of audits over the years would
provide a good means of evaluating a company's long-term social contribution.

A social audit requires a five-step process (see Figure 2.6). First, the
company must develop a list of all its programs that affect the public. The
list might include such programs as pollution-control efforts, minority
employment outreach programs, energy-conservation campaigns, workplace
safety awards, and charitable contributions. Second, the company must
identify the objectives and purposes of each activity—what the company
hopes to achieve and what society stands to gain. Third, the company should

FIGURE 2.6  Five Steps in Conducting a Social Audit

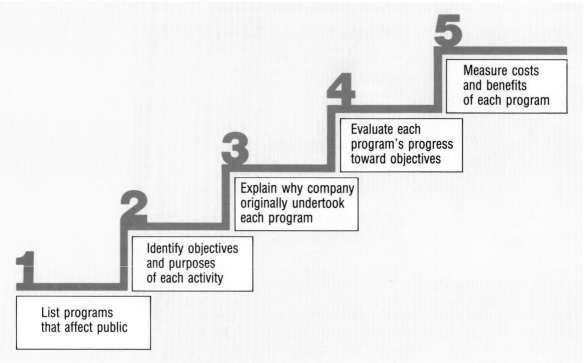

**Making money with compassion** *As an insurance company John Hancock offers all kinds of insurance programs, including AIDS Case Management—what the company bills as a "cost containment program with compassion." Case managers are registered nurses who coordinate the medical care of AIDS patients. They also see to the other needs of these patients and their families, referring them to community educational resources and coordinating in-home health care programs.*

explain why it originally undertook each program. Fourth, it should evaluate each program's progress during the audit period in question. Finally, when it is possible to do so, the company should measure the costs and benefits of each program.

## Objections to the Social-Audit Concept

A well-accepted body of accounting and legal standards governs financial audits. The standards for fiscal audits are objective and uniform across the whole range of American businesses. The basic problem with the social-audit concept is that no such body of standards exists for social criteria. Political, philosophical, and religious beliefs would all affect a social audit. Recall, for example, Milton Friedman's view of the entire concept of social responsibility. And consider, for example, whether, say, ServiceMaster Industries' express commitment to operate in accordance with Christian values[16] would be regarded in the same way by all who reviewed its social audit. In short, the objectivity required for a uniformly accepted social audit would be hard to come by.

## The Future of the Social Audit

Few corporations have greeted the social-audit concept with enough enthusiasm actually to undertake one. If the social audit proves useful to the companies that are pioneering it, others will follow. It is worth noting that more than 90 percent of the nation's top 500 corporations now include some disclosure of the social consequences of their activities in their annual reports. It thus seems likely that in the future a disclosure of the social consequences of corporate policy will in one form or another become a permanent part of businesses' reports to their owners and investors.

# Business Ethics

What the law does not prohibit, a business can do, without fear of legal penalty. It does not follow, however, that doing anything not forbidden by law is acceptable. For instance, in most cases a person can ignore another's cry for help without threat of any legal penalty, but ignoring that cry is not morally right. William S. Kanaga, head of the U.S. Chamber of Commerce, recently put it this way for businesspeople: "Mere obedience to rules and

*"This month we're featuring our Entrepreneur Starter Set—desk, chair, file, and a beautifully framed ethics pledge."*

Ethics training at Apple   *Apple Computer was faced with an ethics problem recently when it was discovered that workers were leaking information about the company's product plans. John Sculley, chairman of Apple, opted to deal with the problem in a six-minute video used for employee training. Sculley appears in the video wearing pajamas and dreaming of the loss of major company secrets. As the nightmare unfolds, Apple is destroyed, and, with it, the employees' profit-sharing program. Of course it's only a dream, but Apple hopes to get the point across.*

laws is not enough. Legality must be a floor, not a ceiling."[17] Just how far a person or a business should go in this regard is the subject matter of business ethics. Let us explore this important and interesting area.

## *What Does Business Ethics Involve?*

The study of moral, as contrasted with legal, obligations is called **ethics.** **Business ethics** is the study of the moral problems that confront members of business organizations and others who engage in business transactions. Business's role is to provide the goods and services that society requires, in the most efficient manner possible. In some cases this role conflicts with other important values. A common problem involves technological change. What should a company do with an excellent employee who cannot adapt to a new technology or who is made redundant by it? Sheer efficiency dictates termination, but loyalty to employees who have merited it may require another solution or a termination that is both gradual and generous.

**ethics**   the study of moral, as contrasted with legal, obligations

**business ethics**   the study of the moral problems that confront members of business organizations and others who engage in business transactions

## PUT YOUR ETHICAL JUDGMENTS TO AN INTERNATIONAL TEST

*Instructions:* Please read the following situations and circle your response choices on the scales provided. Comparative responses for samples of American, French, and German managers are provided at the back of the book.

### Situation 1

Rollfast Bicycle Company has been barred from entering the market in a large Asian country by collusive efforts of the local bicycle manufacturers. Rollfast could expect to net 5 million dollars per year from sales if it could penetrate the market. Last week a businessman from the country contacted the management of Rollfast and stated that he could smooth the way for the company to sell in his country for a price of $500,000.

If you were responsible, what are the chances that you would pay the price?

Definitely
would not

Definitely
would

1—2—3—4—5—6—7—8—9—10

### Situation 2

Master Millers has developed a special milling process which yields a wheat flour which when used for bread provides a lighter more uniform texture than conventionally milled wheat flour. Unfortunately, the process gives off more dust than the emission control equipment presently installed can handle and still maintain emissions within legal limits.

Due to lack of availability, the company is unable to install new emissions control equipment for at least two years; if it waited that long to introduce the new process, however, competitors would very likely beat it to the market.

The general manager wants to use the new process during the third shift which runs from 10 p.m. to 6 a.m. By using the process at that time, the new flour could be introduced and the excess pollution would not be detected due to its release in the dark. By the time demand becomes great enough to utilize a second shift, new emission control equipment should be available.

If you were responsible, what are the chances you would approve the general manager's request?

Definitely
would not

Definitely
would

1—2—3—4—5—6—7—8—9—10

Source: Vignettes excerpted from Helmut Becker and David J. Fritzsche, "A Comparison of the Ethical Behavior of American, French, and German Managers," *Columbia Journal of World Business,* Winter 1987, pp. 87–95.

The ethical dimension of management is not limited to a knowledge of the differences between right and wrong. It extends to choosing among different principles of moral obligations. In other words, ethical decisions may require choices between different alternatives that are each right in their own way. Ethical conduct is not learned by memorizing a handbook. A manager can fall back only on the knowledge that every action has ethical implications that require careful consideration.

How well developed is your ethical judgment? Take a few minutes to complete the questionnaire in Experiencing Business and see how your answers compare with those given by American, French, and German managers.

## Why Be Concerned with Business Ethics?

The subject of business ethics has received renewed attention in the business press and popular media in recent years. This wave of concern is driven by at least three different influences. First, there has been a public outcry about corporate and managerial misdeeds. Second, the courts are showing an increasing tendency to hold managers personally accountable for their companies' misconduct. Stiff fines and even jail terms await convicted executives. Third, influential members of the business community are calling for more ethical conduct in the workplace. Each of these three influences deserves brief discussion.

*7. Explain three reasons why today's managers need to be concerned with business ethics.*

*Public Concern about Business Ethics*  Daily news stories of insider trading scandals on Wall Street and other corporate misconduct have taken their toll on the public's opinion of business's ethics. For example, the same nationwide *Business Week*/Harris poll referred to earlier uncovered a rather gloomy mood. Of those surveyed, only 2 percent rated the ethical standards of corporate executives as "excellent." The majority rated them as "only fair." Worse yet, 49 percent of those surveyed believed white-collar crime was "very common" (see Figure 2.7).[18] Thus, public opinion is pushing state and federal legislators and prosecutors for tough new regulations and enforcement.

*Increased Personal Legal Accountability for Managers*  For many years, managers were largely shielded from personal legal prosecution by the so-called corporate veil. But no more. Courts in the United States are increasingly holding individual managers *personally* accountable for illegal corporate activities. After all, the logic goes, individuals (not corporations) make decisions.

For example, in June of 1988, two former top executives of the Beech-Nut Nutrition Corp. were fined and sentenced to prison for selling fake apple juice for children. The supposedly "100% Pure" apple juice was actually a concoction of sugar, flavoring, and water, without a trace of real apple juice. It was the largest consumer fraud case on record. Each former Beech-Nut official was fined $100,000 and sentenced to a year and a day in jail. Moreover, the company had to pay a $2.2 million fine to the government and $7.5 million to settle a class-action suit.[19] In this and other similar cases, the message to business managers is clear: if you break the law, you go to jail. Consequently, managers are paying keener attention to calls for improved business ethics.

*Calls for Action from the Business Community*  Although many business leaders have called for a strengthening of business ethics, one message is particularly memorable. It comes from Thomas R. Horton, president and chief executive officer of the American Management Association:

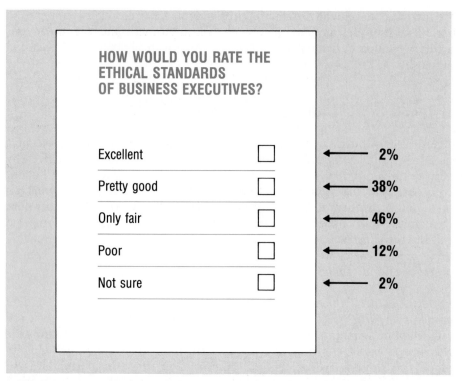

FIGURE 2.7   Business Executives Do Not Receive High Marks from Most Americans for Their Ethical Standards

*Source:* Data from Stuart Jackson and Harris Collingwood, *"Business Week*/Harris Poll: Is an Antibusiness Backlash Building?"* p. 71. Reprinted from July 20, 1987, issue of *Business Week* by special permission, copyright © 1987 by McGraw-Hill, Inc.

In my view, this tide can be turned only by deliberate and conscious actions of management at all levels. Each manager needs to understand his or her own *personal* code of ethics: what is fair; what is *right*; what is *wrong*? Where is the ethical line that *I* draw, the line beyond which *I shall not go*? And where is the line beyond which I shall not allow my *organization* to go?[20]

Horton's message is forceful because it is *personal.* Who is primarily responsible for improving business ethics? A look in the nearest mirror provides the answer.

## *Encouraging Ethical Conduct*

*8. Discuss specific steps managers can take to encourage ethical conduct.*

It is not enough for a company simply to encourage its employees to act ethically. Appropriate actions must accompany such statements. Top management can demonstrate its commitment to doing business ethically by starting companywide ethics-training programs. Many firms already have such programs. Some such corporations include the Cummins Engine Company, BankAmerica Corp., the Avco Corporation, and the Prudential Insurance Company. The defense industry particularly has emphasized these programs. The General Dynamics Corporation, a major defense contractor, has even established an "ethics hot line" that employees can call if confronted with ethical problems they can't resolve.[21]

Another technique is to develop a corporate code of ethics, such as Xerox Corporation's fifteen-page ethical code that says among other things: "We're honest with our customers. No deals, no bribes, no secrets, no fooling around with prices. A kickback in any form kicks anybody out. Anybody."[22] Experts agree on the three things needed to make a company code of ethics work: (1) a widely distributed code that mentions *specific practices;* (2) *top management support* and ethical behavior; and (3) *strict and evenly enforced penalties* for noncompliance.

Some corporations, the federal government, and some state governments have developed elaborate plans for protecting whistle blowers. **Whistle blowers** are employees who report unethical or illegal conduct to their superiors or a government agency.[23]

**whistle blowers** employees who report unethical or illegal conduct to their superiors or a government agency

# One Company's Approach to Improving Business Ethics

After a series of scandals involving its defense businesses, General Dynamics instituted an aggressive ethics program at the request of the Secretary of the Navy. The company asked Stanford University business professor Kirk O. Hanson, an expert on ethics, to help draw up suggestions for creating an ethical work environment. The company then circulated these guidelines, part of which are in Table 2.3, to its managers.

One of the toughest dilemmas facing managers today may be how to communicate ethical values to their employees. General Dynamics gave its managers the suggestions in Table 2.4. Most companies do not try to teach their employees right from wrong, assuming that most people know the distinctions. Instead, they try to encourage employees to do the right thing. General Dynamics went so far as appointing a full-time corporate ethics director, who in turn appointed ethics directors for the corporation's divisions. Over a period of several months, more than 100,000 General Dynamics

TABLE 2.3    General Dynamics Guidelines for Creating an Ethical Work Environment

- Which action maximizes benefits to all parties, reduces harm, respects rights, and treats people fairly?
- Would I be comfortable explaining my decision to my family or on the *Today* show?
- Am I willing to make my decision become a general rule for the company?
- Will this decision look as good a month and a year from now as it does today?

Source: Adapted from "Developing Ethics Code Mom Would Be Proud Of," *St. Louis Post-Dispatch,* March 30, 1986, p. 8A. Used by permission.

**TABLE 2.4    General Dynamics Guidelines for Communicating Ethical Values**

- Create an open environment in the workplace that makes employees feel comfortable in bringing problems or ethical dilemmas to superiors.

- Be consistent and reward ethical behavior. For example, don't tell employees that you want an ethical environment at work and then issue an ultimatum—"The quarterly profit goals had better be reached, or else."

- Ask questions on value-related issues when visiting offices or factories.

- Include criteria in performance-evaluation systems that incorporate performance according to key ethical values.

- Prepare a statement of the values or "way" certain kinds of business problems should be handled.

- Use employee publications and other media to demonstrate and reinforce key values.

- Establish special ethics training or integrate such discussions into existing programs.

- Instruct by a good personal example.

Source: Adapted from "Developing Ethics Code Mom Would Be Proud of," *St. Louis Post-Dispatch*, March 30, 1986, p. 8A. Used by permission.

employees were given copies of a twenty-page pamphlet titled *General Dynamics Standards of Business Ethics and Conduct*. Additionally, all managerial and nonmanagerial employees attended ethics seminars. Effectiveness of the General Dynamics program was demonstrated by 3,646 calls to the ethics hot line in 1986 alone.[24]

The question that sticks in many people's minds is this: How proactive are programs like the one at General Dynamics? Would the company have invested the necessary resources in these programs without the threat of losing government contracts for further violations? In short, is the program purely an accommodation strategy? Only the company's long-term ethical *behavior* will tell.

# CHAPTER HIGHLIGHTS

*1. Define the term* corporate social responsibility.

Corporate social responsibility encompasses obligations to society above and beyond making a profit for stockholders, obeying laws, or honoring contracts. *Voluntary* behavior *above and beyond* the letter of the law is central to this concept.

*2. Discuss the arguments for and against social responsibility.*

Those who favor corporate social responsibility put forth four arguments: (1) Business is already

socially involved; (2) business has the resources to deal with social problems; (3) business benefits from societal improvements; and (4) social responsibility helps avoid government regulation of business. Four counterarguments offered by opponents of social responsibility are: (1) Profit-seeking efficiently allocates societal resources; (2) businesses are meant to pursue economic goals, not social goals; (3) businesses already have enough power in society; and (4) business managers are not accountable to the public at large because they are not elected; so they should not be asked what society ought to do.

*3.* Distinguish between altruism and enlightened self-interest.

*Altruism* involves unselfishly serving the needs of others. *Enlightened self-interest* holds that a business ultimately helps itself by trying to solve societal problems (a win-win situation).

*4.* Outline the evolution of the concept of social responsibility.

The traditional principles of laissez faire (hands off) and *caveat emptor* (let the buyer beware) led to abuses in the marketplace. Abuses in the workplace also occurred. These conditions prompted the age of business regulation. The Reagan era slowed the regulatory process, but a complex system of regulations still requires businesses to perform many acts above and beyond making a profit.

*5.* Describe the four different social responsibility strategies.

Businesses may choose from among four classes of social responsibility strategies: reaction, defense, accommodation, and proaction. A business follows a *reaction strategy* when it denies responsibility for something while developing an argument for a continuation of the status quo. The *defense strategy* involves the use of public relations, legal maneuvering, and all other means necessary to avoid assuming additional obligations. *Accommodation* and *proaction strategies* have in common a willingness to assume responsibility rather than to deny it. The difference between the two lies in the motivation underlying the assumption of responsibility. A company that assumes greater social responsibility because of pressure from an interest group or a government agency is adopting an *accommodation* strategy. When a company displays

greater social responsibility without any pressure, it has adopted a *proactive* strategy.

*6.* Describe the development and application of the social audit.

The *social audit* is an annual assessment of a company's effects on society and the environment. The audit involves a five-step process. Step 1 involves preparation of a list of all its programs that affect the public. The list might include such things as pollution control efforts or energy conservation campaigns. During step 2 the company identifies the objectives and purposes of each activity. Step 3 involves an explanation of why the company originally undertook each program. An ongoing evaluation of each program's progress during the audit period makes up step 4. Step 5 involves the assessment of costs and benefits of each program.

*7.* Explain three reasons why today's managers need to be concerned with business ethics.

Three driving forces behind the heightened concern for business ethics are: (1) growing public concern about corporate misdeeds; (2) more and more managers are being held personally accountable for corporate misdeeds; and (3) business leaders are issuing strong calls for better business ethics.

*8.* Discuss specific steps managers can take to encourage ethical conduct.

Proven techniques include: ethics and values training; ethics hot lines for employees of large corporations; corporate codes of ethics (that mention specific practices, are supported by top management, and strictly enforced); and whistle blowing.

# *KEY TERMS*

| | | | |
|---|---|---|---|
| Corporate social responsibility | Caveat emptor | Defense strategy | Social audit |
| | Contract | Accommodation strategy | Ethics |
| Altruism | Police powers | | Business ethics |
| Enlightened self-interest | Reaction strategy | Proaction strategy | Whistle blowers |

# REVIEW QUESTIONS

1. What is the key to determining whether or not a corporate action is socially responsible?
2. Which arguments do you find most persuasive, those for or against social responsibility?
3. Why would businesspeople probably find enlightened self-interest more appealing than altruism?
4. Why did the 1970s become the decade of regulation?
5. How does a defense strategy to social responsibility differ from a reaction strategy?
6. How does a proaction strategy to social responsibility go beyond an accommodation strategy?
7. Why is it safe to say that the measurement of costs and benefits is the most difficult part of social auditing?
8. Why might many managers think twice before engaging in illegal corporate activities?
9. Why must the improvement of business ethics ultimately be a personal responsibility?
10. What does it take to make a corporate code of ethics work?

# APPLICATION EXERCISES

1. Assume the role of vice president of marketing for a large bank. In the weeks ahead the bank will establish a telemarketing department that will be used to market two new services. One service will be a second mortgage loan plan for people who want to borrow money, using their home as collateral. The second service will be a special checking account that offers a higher interest rate. The staff of this new department will include a department manager, assistant department manager, and eight persons who will be involved in telephone sales. Prepare a series of guidelines that can be incorporated into a code of ethics for the department.
2. Review recent issues of *The Wall Street Journal, Business Week, or Fortune,* and identify a company that is currently involved in some type of legal action. Explain how the problem(s) could have been avoided with social auditing and an ethics program.

# CASES

## 2.1 Steve Wolf's Class Act: Straight Talk in the Classroom

It's a gray January afternoon on Chicago's South Side—35 miles and a world away from UAL Corp.'s suburban headquarters—as Stephen M. Wolf speaks. The audience is captive, and decidedly noncorporate. "I'm from east Oakland, which is 75% black and 25% tough," the towering chief executive tells several hundred black elementary school students at the John W. Cook School. "I didn't get to be chairman because I had wealthy parents. No one gave the job to me, and no one is going to give it to you. But with education, you can do it."

Wolf, 47, has made the improvement of education his private crusade. Last September at New York's Wings Club, he chided a surprised audience of airline executives for not doing enough to raise the quality of local schools. Recently he challenged other businessmen to get personally involved.

**Road Show** With little fanfare, Wolf and a black pilot and flight attendant have been visiting several schools in poor areas of Chicago to proclaim hope through education. Last summer, Wolf put a 15-year-old he met at one of the schools on his own payroll to do odd jobs around headquarters. (The teenager was too young for United to hire.)

When Wolf speaks at the Cook School, the kids in the aging auditorium listen intently. "United Airlines is a terrific place to work," he tells them as they read cards listing the airline's job requirements. "But there are two things you must do: Graduate from high school and don't fool around with drugs—and I mean no fooling around, because we test."

The delivery is not as stirring as Jesse Jackson's, but Wolf's message also comes from the heart. The subsequent applause shows he may have hit the mark. Asks one particularly ambitious student: "Mr. Wolf, how long are you going to be chairman?"

## Questions

1. What sort of social responsibility strategy is Mr. Wolf following? Explain.
2. How would someone who supports the concept of corporate social responsibility respond to the following comment: "Wolf's job is to run UAL and make sure it keeps making a profit, not run around trying to impress school kids."

Source: James E. Ellis, "Steve Wolf's Class Act: Straight Talk in the Classroom," *Business Week,* February 6, 1989, p. 57. Reprinted from February 6, 1989 issue of *Business Week* by special permission, copyright © 1989 by McGraw-Hill, Inc.

## 2.2  Kicking a Deadly Habit

The latest evidence is that smoking kills 390,000 Americans annually (nearly three jumbo jetloads every day), that it causes strokes in addition to heart and lung disease, and that it may cause uterine cancer in women. . . . the proportion of Americans who smoke has fallen from 40 percent to 29 percent since 1965—a decline that could save 3 million lives by the end of the century.

. . . While the smoking rate has declined substantially among certain classes of American men, it has fallen only slightly among women. And women are now paying the price for taking up the habit in such great numbers in the middle of the century: their lung-cancer rates have quadrupled since the 1960s. By the same token, blacks, blue-collar workers and people without high-school educations are all doing more than their share of the smoking and dying.

The tobacco industry's critics say that these trends are no accident. They charge that the cigarette makers, long aware that affluent white males are fleeing the weed, have simply taken aim at other segments of the market. By designing special cigarettes for women, directing ads and promotions at minority groups and increasing exports to developing countries, they say, the industry has simply shifted the burden of illness. Matthew Myers, head of the Coalition for Smoking or Health, argues that without "dramatic" measures—perhaps a ban on cigarette advertising—American life expectancy will become more and more a function of class and race.

**"Clear Message"**  The cigarette companies take strong exception to such talk. Industry officials have long held that advertising serves only to promote particular brands among confirmed smokers. They accuse critics like Myers of implying that women and blacks can't think for themselves, and they maintain that ad restrictions would violate the First Amendment [freedom of speech].

## Questions

1. Do you believe the tobacco industry's claim that its advertising is aimed at confirmed smokers (rather than at converting nonsmokers)? What are the social responsibility implications of your answer?
2. What is your business ethics perspective on producing and selling cigarettes? A tobacco company stockholder's perspective? A public health official's perspective?

Source: From G. Cowley, "Kicking a Deadly Habit," p. 60. From NEWSWEEK, January 23, 1989. © 1989, Newsweek, Inc. All rights reserved. Reprinted by permission.

# 3

# The Legal Forms of Business Ownership

After you have completed this chapter, you will be able to do the following:

*1.* Identify and describe three basic legal forms of business ownership.

*2.* Outline the advantages and disadvantages of the three legal forms of business organization.

*3.* Distinguish between general partnerships and limited partnerships.

*4.* Describe how a corporation is organized and managed.

*5.* List and describe three other legal forms of business organization that exist for specialized purposes.

J ohn B. Connally at various points in his career was Secretary of the Treasury, Secretary of the Navy, governor of Texas, senior partner in an enormously prestigious Houston law firm, and a plausible presidential candidate. His partner Ben Barnes, a former political protege who became lieutenant governor in the 1960s, was commonly called the boy wonder of Texas politics. Together they set up a private real-estate development firm, Barnes-Connally Partnership. As businessmen, the pair apparently never heard the word "no" from bankers.

Tough times hit the state of Texas. The oil economy was in shambles, the farm economy was almost as sick, and you could not give away office space. The Barnes-Connally partnership emerged as one of the more spectacular plunges in Texas real estate. The pair personally guaranteed much of several hundred million dollars in debt. Bank of New England, which helped finance a $13 million complex of office condominiums, declared the partnership in default on $4.1 million of loans and threatened to auction the property to the highest bidder.

As you read about the legal forms of business organization in this chapter, consider whether John B. Connally and Ben Barnes were well advised in their choice of legal relationship.[1]

Partnerships are one of the three principal legal forms of business. The other two are sole proprietorships and corporations. Which form of business is best? The best business form is simply the one that fits. One form will not fit all businesses. What is good for General Motors is probably not good for Ma & Pa's Superette. The most that can be said about the best form is that as businesses grow, they tend to become corporations, if they are not already structured that way.

This chapter has two purposes. First, it describes the principal legal forms for business used in the United States. Second, it illustrates how those forms affect the people who work for or deal with businesses.

# Sole Proprietorships

The form of business in which one individual (the *sole proprietor*) owns all the assets of the business and is alone responsible for its debts is a **sole proprietorship**. A sole proprietor may run almost any kind of business, from a dry cleaner to a movie theater to a computer store to an accounting practice. About the only industries that sole proprietors cannot enter are banking and, in most states, public utilities.

Sole proprietorships make up 70 percent of American businesses. As Figure 3.1 shows, however, they account for only a small share of business revenues or income. Many small businesses are not designed to grow beyond the size of business that their owners can manage by themselves. Others may have such a small market or such inadequate financing or limited management talent that they simply are not destined to grow. Table 3.1 shows some

*1. Identify and describe three basic legal forms of business ownership.*

**sole proprietorship** form of business in which one individual (sole proprietor) owns all the assets of the business and is alone responsible for its debts

FIGURE 3.1   A Breakdown of the Three Forms of Business
Source: *Statistical Abstract of the United States* (Washington, D.C.: U.S. Gov't., 1988), p. 495, Table 823

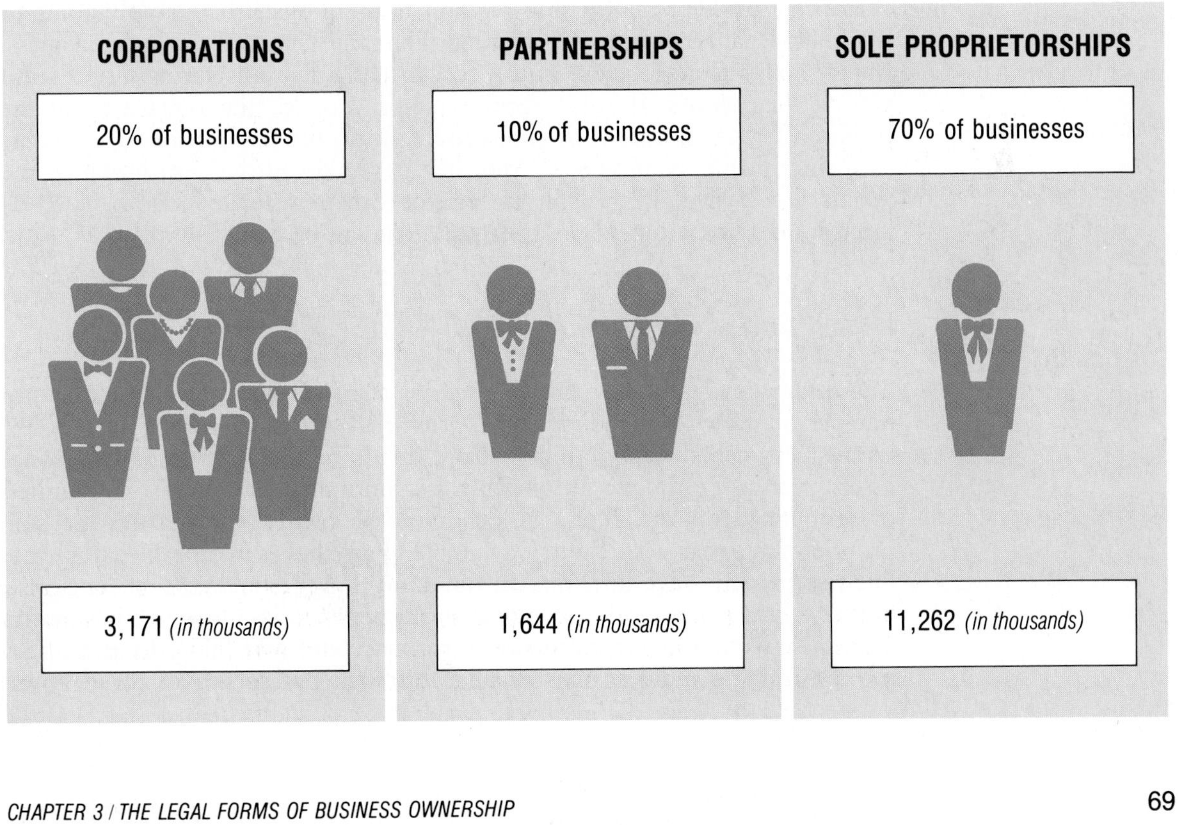

| CORPORATIONS | PARTNERSHIPS | SOLE PROPRIETORSHIPS |
|---|---|---|
| 20% of businesses | 10% of businesses | 70% of businesses |
| 3,171 *(in thousands)* | 1,644 *(in thousands)* | 11,262 *(in thousands)* |

**TABLE 3.1  Advantages and Disadvantages of Sole Proprietorships**

| Advantages | Disadvantages |
|---|---|
| Control and independence | Unlimited financial liability |
| Secrecy | Lack of continuity |
| Ease of formation and dissolution | Limited financing |
| Ownership of all profits | Management limitations |

advantages and disadvantages of sole proprietorships. Still others may just be in their infancy. As a business grows, it comes to demand additional capital and more diverse managerial skills. At that point, many sole proprietorships change form, becoming partnerships or, more likely, corporations.

## Advantages of a Sole Proprietorship

*2. Outline the advantages and disadvantages of the three legal forms of business organization.*

Ask sole proprietors what they like most about their businesses and they will say, "Independence!" Sole proprietors have only themselves to answer to. Their judgments, good or bad, are their own responsibility. They can add a new product, hire a new employee, or relocate. Taking a vacation is easy, at least theoretically. Sole proprietors also have the advantage of secrecy. With no partners, shareholders, or government agencies requiring periodic reports, sole proprietors have only themselves to blame if a competitor learns of their product strategy, for example.

Starting a sole proprietorship requires nothing more than simply going to work. No legal formalities are required. The same is true of closing a business. Many small businesses close simply by canceling their answering services and closing their doors. If sole proprietorships succeed, the reward is all the profits, after taxes, from their enterprise. Sole proprietors pay taxes on profits as if their profits were wages. And they pay taxes in the year in which the profits are earned. If the sole proprietor can itemize deductions, such as interest on a home mortgage, this treatment can be beneficial.

## Disadvantages of Sole Proprietorships

The disadvantages of sole proprietorships stem from the fact that they are one-person shows. The individual proprietor is responsible for the full amount of business debts. This liability also extends to the proprietor's personal assets, such as house and automobile. Its continuity may be severely limited or terminated on the illness or death of the owner. Ordinarily, the sole proprietorship has less capital available than the two other legal forms; likewise, it may have difficulty in obtaining long-term financing. It is also limited by the proprietor's viewpoint and experience. A proprietor who starts a business using the proprietorship form may later find these disadvantages too constraining and thus may consider forming a partnership or corporation.

Doing it her way  *Jackie likes doing business her way and as the owner and chef of Jackie's Nouvelle Cuisine Restaurant, she can. Though sole proprietorship is the answer for Jackie right now, if she wants to open a second restaurant or finds she's working too many hours, she may choose another form of business in the future— a partnership or even a corporation.*

# Partnerships

Federal law defines a **partnership** as "an association of two or more persons to carry on as co-owners of a business for profit."[2]

## An Association of Co-owners

*Voluntary Nature*  A partnership is an **association**, a voluntary organization of people with a common interest. Partnerships are characterized by **mutual agency**, the authority of each partner to act on behalf of the other partners and the partnership as a whole. An agency relationship is always voluntary, so there is no such thing as an involuntary partner.

It is not necessary, however, for a person to agree formally to be a partner. Not even a handshake is necessary. When two or more people act like partners by transacting business together and sharing the profits, the law will treat them as partners. Suppose that Alice and Barbara are independent real

**partnership**  an association of two or more persons to carry on as co-owners of a business for profit

**association**  a voluntary organization of people with a common interest

**mutual agency**  the authority of each partner to act on behalf of the other partners and the partnership as a whole

estate brokers who decide to share an office. Over time, they help each other on sales, cover calls for each other, and divide commissions on sales. The law will treat them as partners even though they may have no formal written or oral **partnership agreement**, a contract between two persons stating the terms on which they agree to be partners (see Figure 3.2).

*Partnership Shares* A partner is a co-owner of a partnership. **Co-owner** means joint owner, not equal owner. A partnership must have two or more co-owners. These co-owners may be either individuals or other businesses. If Alice and Barbara are partners, they are by definition co-owners of the partnership. They may agree that Alice owns 40 percent of the business and Barbara 60 percent, for instance. If, however, there is not clear evidence of such an agreement, such as a division of profits according to this formula, a court will presume their shares to be equal. This presumption is one reason a written partnership agreement is so important. In almost all states the law does not require one, though.

FIGURE 3.2   A Sample Partnership Agreement

Source: Arnold J. Goldman and William D. Sigismond, *Business Law: Principles and Practices,* 2d Ed. (Boston, MA: Houghton Mifflin Co., 1988), p. 528. Used by permission of the publisher.

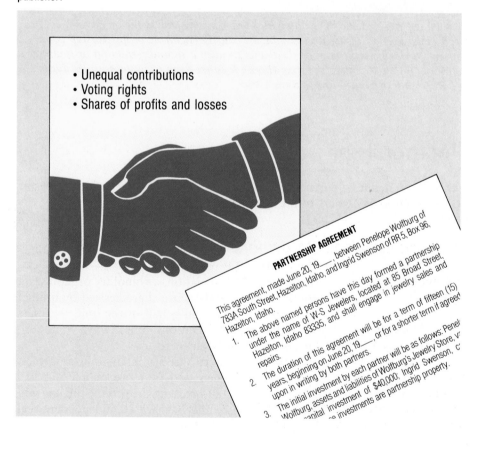

- Unequal contributions
- Voting rights
- Shares of profits and losses

**PARTNERSHIP AGREEMENT**

This agreement, made June 20, 19___, between Penelope Wolfburg of 783A South Street, Hazelton, Idaho, and Ingrid Swenson of RR 5, Box 96, Hazelton, Idaho.

1.  The above named persons have this day formed a partnership under the name of W-S Jewelers, located at 85 Broad Street, Hazelton, Idaho 83335, and shall engage in jewelry sales and repairs.

2.  The duration of this agreement will be for a term of fifteen (15) years, beginning on June 20, 19___, or for a shorter term if agreed upon in writing by both partners.

3.  The initial investment by each partner will be as follows: Penel Wolfburg, assets and liabilities of Wolfburg's Jewelry Store, v          initial  investment of $40,000; Ingrid Swenson, c                ae investments are partnership property.

Celebrity partnership   *Olivia Newton-John, best known for her bubbly pop hits and roles in movies such as "Grease," and "Xanadu," is also a partner in a successful business venture. In 1983 she teamed up with former singing partner and fellow Australian Pat Farrar to open "Koala Blue," a boutique specializing in Australian-flavored fashions.*

Another important presumption flows from the co-ownership concept: partners share both profits and losses. Courts treat people who share profits and losses as partners unless they can prove otherwise. Again, the partners may alter the profit and loss percentages by mutual agreement. For example, Alice and Barbara may choose to divide their profits equally but absorb their losses on a 40:60 basis.

*Partnership Contributions*   The ownership percentages in a partnership often depend on a partner's **capital contribution**, a partner's investment—whether in cash or property—in the business. For instance, one partner may contribute $10,000, another contribute inventory and a store, and a third his or her twenty years of experience in the trade. The law will presume the three to be equal partners and their contributions to the partnership to be of equal value. Their partnership agreement, however, might assign them 25, 50, and 25 percent interests, respectively, and value their contributions at $10,000, $20,000, and $0. Placing a value on partnership contributions can thus be seen to be extremely important. When a partnership terminates, after all its debts are paid the partners' contributions are repaid before the remaining assets are divided among the partners.

**capital contribution**   a partner's investment—whether in cash or property—in the business

## FORMING A PARTNERSHIP

You and two friends are thinking about going into business. You intend to open a sandwich and salad shop, at 1012 Main Street, just across the street from a large office building in the center of the business district. Your preliminary estimates indicate that the noon hour walk-in business will allow you to break even. However, deliveries will also be available.

Your group's plan calls for each person to contribute $2500 to get started. Profits and losses will be shared equally. The work arrangement calls for you to manage the store and to handle telephone orders. Your first friend will be in charge of making the sandwiches. Your other friend will not be involved in the day-to-day affairs of the business. Other workers will be hired depending on the amount of business.

Although it is not legally required, your group agrees that it would be good for the partnership agreement to be in writing. Using the items listed, prepare a partnership agreement for your business.

1. Date
2. Names of partners
3. Nature of business
4. Name and location of business
5. Duration of partnership
6. Investments of partnership
7. How partners will share
8. Accounting system for the business
9. Rules for partners' drawing money from the firm
10. Duties of partners
11. Restraints on partners
12. Termination of partnership

*Partners' Liability*    A partner, like a sole proprietor, generally has unlimited liability, which is a major disadvantage of the partnership form. A partner is legally responsible—**liable**—for any and all debts of the partnership. A creditor can force a single partner to pay an obligation of the partnership even though there might be other partners (see Experiencing Business).

**liable** being legally responsible for any and all debts of the partnership

## *To Carry on a Business for Profit*

In the definition given earlier of partnership, the phrases "to carry on" and "a business for profit" have highly specific meanings with a number of variations.

**general partnership** the usual form of partnership

A **general partnership**, the usual form of partnership and the one we have been describing, is an ongoing business involved in a series of transactions. Suppose that Anne, Bill, and Cheryl begin buying and subdividing land and reselling it for home lots. After they have sold some lots, they reinvest part of their profits in more land. They would be operating a partnership. On the other hand, if they had bought a farm together and were holding it as an investment, they would not be partners. They would have formed instead a **joint venture**, an association of individuals for a limited, specific, for-profit

**joint venture** an association of individuals for a limited, specific, for-profit business purpose business purpose. The participants in a joint venture do not normally have mutual agency authority.

A nonprofit partnership is a legal impossibility. If two nonprofit organizations like the American Red Cross and the American Cancer Society, say, jointly founded a clinic, their relationship could not be a partnership.

There are many terms used to describe a partner's relationship to the other partners in a general partnership. Table 3.2 lists some of them. The key point to remember, however, is what makes a partner a partner: either mutual agency or sharing profits and losses—or both.

## Advantages and Disadvantages of Partnerships

Like the proprietorship, a partnership can be set up with relative ease. Legal formalities and expenses are few compared with the requirements for the creation of a corporation. Another advantage to partnerships is the flexibility they offer for partners to specialize in the firm's management. For example, one partner in a car dealership might take charge of sales and car purchasing while the other supervises repairs and parts. In large accounting and law partnerships, specialties tend to be quite narrowly defined. The general rule is: the larger the partnership, the higher degree of specialization. In a partnership, it is often possible to increase financial capacity through the combined assets and borrowing power of the partners.

Partnerships share two major disadvantages with proprietorships. These are unlimited financial liability and lack of continuity. The partners may

TABLE 3.2   The Types of Partners

**Silent Partner**
A partner whose active involvement in the firm is not acknowledged publicly.

**Dormant Partner**
A partner who does not take an active role in the firm's management and whose participation is not known to the public.

**Nominal Partner**
A person who is not actually a partner but who with a partner's knowledge represents him- or herself as such. If a third party had reason to rely on such a representation, a nominal partner could obligate the partnership just like a real partner.

**Junior Partner**
A partner recently admitted to an existing partnership who usually makes a relatively small capital contribution, receives a minor share of the profits, and plays a small role in management.

**Senior Partner**
A partner of some tenure with a substantial investment in the firm, a significant share of the profits, and major responsibility for managerial decisions.

come to disagree on the direction the firm should take, or they may begin to take different career paths. One partner may feel that he or she is carrying more of the load than the other partners. The range of potential causes for disagreement is almost limitless. Because a written agreement is not a legal requirement for a partnership, the dissolution or buying out of a partner may be difficult in terms of partner interests, additions, and dispute settlements. Table 3.3 summarizes the advantages and disadvantages of partnerships.

## Limited Partnerships

*3. Distinguish between general partnerships and limited partnerships.*

**limited partnership** form of business in which the general partners have the same rights and liabilities as partners in a general partnership while the limited partners have virtually no management rights

**limited partner** investor in a partnership whose liability is restricted to the amount invested

In the business form called the **limited partnership**, the general partners have essentially the same rights and liabilities as partners in a general partnership while the limited partners have virtually no management rights. In essence, **limited partners** are investors in a partnership whose liability is restricted to the amount they invest. The number of limited partners in a partnership can range from one to thousands. General partners, who often are corporations, manage the investments and normally receive both a fee and a percentage of the profits. A sample certificate of limited partnership in Figure 3.3 illustrates items that partners might include in specifying limitations of the partnership.

The main appeal of limited partnerships today is that limited partners can participate in a venture, such as real estate development or producing a movie, without risking anything beyond their initial investment. However, recent tax reform legislation has severely restricted writing off any losses a partnership generates to offset the partners' taxable income.

## Ending a Partnership

**dissolution** an act that indicates that a partner has ended the business relationship

**winding up** liquidation of the partnership's assets, payment of its debts, repayment of the partners' capital contributions, and division of the remaining funds

Compared with closing a sole proprietorship, ending a partnership is a complicated matter. It involves a three-stage operation: dissolution, winding up, and termination. At the point of closing a partnership, partners may regret the lack of a written partnership agreement.

A **dissolution** is an act, like dying or saying "I quit," which indicates that a partner has ended the business relationship. The significance of a dissolution is that it forces the **winding up**—the liquidation of the partnership's assets, payment of its debts, repayment of the partners' capital contributions, and division of the remaining funds. A partnership agreement may establish a

TABLE 3.3    Advantages and Disadvantages of Partnerships

| Advantages | Disadvantages |
|---|---|
| Ease of formation | Unlimited financial liability |
| Management flexibility | Lack of continuity |
| Increased financial capacity | Partner conflicts |
| | Dissolution problems |

## CERTIFICATE OF LIMITED PARTNERSHIP

The undersigned, desiring to form a Limited Partnership under the Uniform Limited Partnership Act of the State of _____ , make this certificate for that purpose.

**§ 1. Name.** The name of the Partnership shall be "_____".

**§ 2. Purpose.** The purpose of the Partnership shall be to [describe].

**§ 3. Location.** The location of the Partnership's principal place of business is _____ ____ County, _____ .

**§ 4. Members and Designation.** The names and places of residence of the members, and their designation as General or Limited Partners are:

| | | |
|---|---|---|
| _____ | [Address] | General Partner |
| _____ | [Address] | General Partner |
| _____ | [Address] | Limited Partner |
| _____ | [Address] | Limited Partner |

**§ 5. Term.** The term for which the Partnership is to exist is indefinite.

**§ 6. Initial Contributions of Limited Partners.** The amount of cash and a description of the agreed value of the other property contributed by each Limited Partner are:

| | |
|---|---|
| [Name] | [Describe] |
| [Name] | [Decribe] |

**§ 7. Subsequent Contributions of Limited Partners.** Each Limited Partner may (but shall not be obliged to) make such additional contributions to the capital of the Partnership as may from time to time be agreed upon by the General Partners.

**§ 8. Profit Shares of Limited Partners.** The share of the profits which each Limited Partner shall receive by reason of his contribution is:

| | |
|---|---|
| [Name] | _____ % |
| [Name] | _____ % |

Signed _____ , 19 ____

_____
_____
_____
_____

Signed and sworn before me, the undersigned authority, this _____ , 19 ____

Notary Public
_____ County, _____

FIGURE 3.3   Sample Certificate of Limited Partnership

formula for dividing the firm's assets. If it does not, the law requires an equal division of them. During the winding up, the partnership must not engage in any new business. The partnership agreement, however, may contain a provision allowing the remaining partners to buy out the departing one and continue the business without interruption.

**Termination** is simply recognition of the fact that the winding up stage is complete and the partnership has therefore ended. Until termination, the partners continue to owe fiduciary duties to one another and to the partnership.

**termination** recognition of the fact that the winding up is complete and the partnership has therefore ended

# Corporations

Corporations are the most complex of the three business forms. As defined by Chief Justice John Marshall in the Dartmouth College decision in 1819, a corporation "is an artificial being, invisible, intangible, and existing only in contemplation of the law." In other words, a **corporation** is that form of business organization authorized by state law which comes into existence when the state's secretary of state issues a *certificate of incorporation*. The certificate of incorporation, sometimes called a *corporate charter*, is a document that certifies that the corporation has come into existence and is authorized to do business. A corporation is a distinct legal entity separate from the individuals who own it. It also has the right to sue and be sued and to hold property.

**corporation** the form of business organization authorized by state law that comes into existence when that state's secretary of state issues a *certificate of incorporation*

## The Key Characteristics of Corporations

*4. Describe how a corporation is organized and managed.*

Corporations have four fundamental characteristics that distinguish them from partnerships and sole proprietorships. These are:

1. The necessity to meet certain formal requirements before the corporation can come into existence
2. Unlimited life, independent of the lives of the corporation's owners and managers
3. Separation of ownership and management
4. Limitation on the financial liability of the firm's owners under certain circumstances

*Requirements for Creation*   A corporation cannot come into existence on a handshake the way a partnership can. In order to receive a certificate of incorporation, an **incorporator** must sign and file two copies of the proposed articles of incorporation with the secretary of state of that state. (Some states require two incorporators.) An incorporator can be anyone but is often the lawyer who represents those setting up the corporation. The incorporator's only functions are to sign and file the articles.

**incorporator** person who signs and files two copies of the proposed articles of incorporation with the secretary of state of that state

This section will discuss what the articles of incorporation should contain. Here, though, is a list of items that the law requires the articles to contain that we will *not* be discussing:

- The corporation's name and address
- The corporation's purposes, which may simply be described as "the transaction of any or all lawful business for which corporations may be incorporated"
- The number, names, and addresses of the corporation's initial board of directors
- The name and address of each incorporator
- The number of shares of stock the corporation may issue as well as the classes of shares, if any, and their respective rights[3]

The secretary of state's office reviews the articles of incorporation to make sure that they are in the proper form. If they are and all filing fees have been paid, the secretary of state issues a certificate of incorporation.[4]

*Unlimited Life*  Unlike both a partnership and a sole proprietorship, a corporation has a life apart from the human beings who create it. It can remain alive as long as it pays the state an annual **franchise tax**, a fee for the privilege of doing business as a corporation. It is important to note, however, that just because a corporation can live forever does not mean that it will. Most corporations are small and, like partnerships, tend to die with their founders.

**franchise tax**  a fee for the privilege of doing business as a corporation

*Separation of Ownership from Management*  A corporation's owners may work for it, but most do not, and certainly they are under no obligation to

**The new leaner corporation**  *More and more U.S. companies are trying to save money and increase efficiency by reducing the size of their corporate staffs. Steelmaker Nucor is a model of this new leaner style: pictured here are all but two of its corporate staff.*

do so. The owners of a corporation are called **shareholders**, persons who own shares in a corporation. **Shares** are the units into which ownership of a corporation is divided. The articles of incorporation will specify whether there are to be five shares or 137 million (the number that Coca-Cola presently has)[5] or some other number. In theory, the ownership of a corporation is completely separate from the management of it. And in practice, in large corporations like General Electric with its 462 million shares,[6] the two are indeed separate. In **closely held corporations**, however, firms with fifty or fewer shareholders like the Pulitzer Publishing Company in St. Louis with its 5,470.5 shares held by about 20 shareholders,[7] the owners or a faction of them manage the company.

Shares in most large corporations are **publicly traded**, meaning that they are bought and sold on stock exchanges. Shareholders can usually sell their ownership interests if and when they want to. This *liquidity* is one of the great advantages of owning the shares of publicly traded corporations. The shares of only 10,000 U.S. corporations are publicly traded, however. The interests that shareholders have in the remaining 3 million or so corporations are not nearly so liquid. In general, minority shareholders in corporations that are not publicly traded must be prepared to stick with the management that is in place whether they like it or not. Even so, unless the articles of incorporation or another agreement restrict the sale of shares, it is easier to transfer ownership in a corporation than in a partnership.

The corporation's separate existence means that it pays taxes as an entity in its own right. This separate taxation holds another enormous advantage for its shareholders. With a partnership, every dollar of net income is divided among the partners, and they must pay taxes on it. Even if the income is retained in the partnership for, say, new office equipment, the partners pay taxes on it in the year they earn it. This problem does not exist with corporations. Historically, corporations have paid taxes at a significantly lower rate than have their shareholders. More important, they can retain aftertax earnings and their shareholders do not pay taxes on them. Corporations are therefore superior to partnerships and sole proprietorships as a form for accumulating investment capital. It is worth noting, though, that when corporations do distribute their earnings to shareholders, those earnings are taxed again, as income to the shareholders.

*Limited Shareholder Liability*  The *Ltd.* at the end of the name of a corporation stands for "limited liability," which means to the British what *Inc.* means to us. It is not surprising that *Ltd.* came to mean "corporation." One of the corporation's key characteristics is the limitation of a shareholder's liability for a firm's obligations to the amount of his or her investment.

Limited liability is extremely important to the shareholders of a corporation faced with, say, responsibility for a large personal injury award. Shareholders in the Manville Corporation found themselves in that situation in recent litigation over asbestosis. Limited liability also protects shareholders when a company's debts have their source in contracts. John B. Connally and Ben Barnes might have considered incorporation in the situation that was described at the beginning of this chapter. The smaller the corporation, however, the

**TABLE 3.4   Advantages and Disadvantages of Corporations**

| Advantages | Disadvantages |
|---|---|
| Limited financial liability | Expense of formation |
| Permanence | Legal restrictions |
| Increased financial capacity | Taxation |

less protection that limited liability offers on contractual debts. Because of the risk involved, financial institutions will often not make loans to small corporations unless one or more shareholders agree to cosign as individuals. By cosigning, the shareholders waive their limited liability in respect to that loan. Suppose that Al, Barbara, Charlie, and Darlene are the four shareholders in the ABCD Corporation, which needs a $100,000 loan. Last Resort National Bank agrees to make the loan—if the four shareholders cosign the note. If ABCD defaults, the bank may force any or all of the cosigning shareholders to pay the debt.

## Advantages and Disadvantages of Corporations

The corporate form of business offers several advantages over the other two legal forms (see Table 3.4). A stockholder's liability is limited to the amount of his or her investment. Because the corporation enjoys a separate and continuing legal existence, ownership of the corporation can be readily transferred. When owners delegate authority to hired managers, the corporation can draw on the expertise and skills of more than one individual. Capital can be acquired by issuing stock. It is also relatively easy to secure long-term financing from lending institutions by utilizing corporate and personal assets of stockholders and principals or guarantors.

Disadvantages of corporations include the considerable expense involved in formation when compared to the proprietorship and partnership. These expenses include legal fees; filing fees; taxes; and burdensome local, state, and federal reports. Additionally, the corporation's activities are limited by its corporate charter and by laws that specifically cover the corporate legal form. Last are the numerous and sometimes excessive taxes. Corporate income is taxed initially when it is earned by the corporation and a second time when it is distributed to individual stockholders as personal income.

## Types of Corporations

As Figure 3.4 shows, there are ten basic types of corporations.

*Public, Quasi-Public, and Private*   A **public corporation** is one set up by Congress or a state legislature for a specific public purpose. The Tennessee Valley Authority, the Student Loan Marketing Association, and many local

**public corporation** corporation set up by Congress or a state legislature for a specific public purpose

Private corporations  *Private corporations are able to raise capital by selling ownership shares. Coca-Cola has used its resources both to expand its markets in the soft drink industry and to create new markets in the entertainment industry. Its entertainment operation—Columbia Pictures Entertainment—produces movies and television programs and owns a chain of three hundred theaters.*

**quasi-public corporation (public utility)** a corporation that is granted a monopoly by a government unit to provide certain kinds of services to the public

**private corporation** corporation organized by private individuals or companies for some purpose other than for providing utility service

**nonprofit corporation (not-for-profit corporation)** an organization set up for charitable, educational, or fraternal purposes

**for-profit corporation** organization created to make profits for its owners

school districts are examples of public corporations. A **quasi-public corporation** or **public utility** is one granted a monopoly by a government unit to provide certain kinds of services to the public. These companies usually provide electric, local telephone, water, or natural gas services in specifically defined areas. The vast majority of corporations are **private corporations**, however, meaning that private individuals or companies have organized them for some purpose other than for providing utility service.

*Nonprofit and For Profit*  A **nonprofit corporation** or **not-for-profit corporation** is an organization set up for charitable, educational, or fraternal purposes. The American Heart Association, most private colleges, and the Elks and Rotary clubs are nonprofit corporations. Our focus throughout this book is on **for-profit corporations**. Their name describes them perfectly: they are created to make profits for their owners.

*Publicly and Not Publicly Traded*  For-profit corporations themselves fall into two general categories. The first, publicly traded corporations, was discussed earlier. (It should be noted that many quasi-public corporations are publicly traded, like Commonwealth Edison, which supplies electricity to the Chicago area.) Another category includes the vast majority of corporations, those that are *not publicly traded.* This designation simply means that a corporation's stock is not traded on a stock exchange. The term does not necessarily reflect a company's size. For instance, Hanson Industries and Revlon, numbers 167 and 172 on the 1989 Fortune 500 list, are not publicly traded.[8]

*Professional and Closely Held Corporations*  Two types of corporations that are not publicly traded bear special mention. **Professional corporations,** the newest form of corporation, are firms whose shareholders offer such professional services as medical, legal, and engineering work. In some parts of the country professional corporations are rapidly replacing partnerships, because until recently the federal tax laws permitted corporations—but not partnerships—to set up highly advantageous pension and insurance plans.

We have already mentioned closely held corporations. Because of the small number of shareholders involved in them and because their shareholders tend to operate the corporation, some states' laws allow closely held corporations to operate like a partnership. The principal advantage of this treatment is that it allows them to dispense with having a **board of directors,** a group of individuals elected by the shareholders to oversee business operations.

**professional corporation**  newest form of corporation, in which shareholders offer such professional services as medical, legal, and engineering work

**board of directors**  group of individuals elected by the shareholders to oversee business operations

FIGURE 3.4  Types of Corporations

Source: Lawrence S. Clark and Peter D. Kinder, *Law and Business* (New York: McGraw-Hill, 1986), p. 399. Copyright 1986. Used by permission of the publisher.

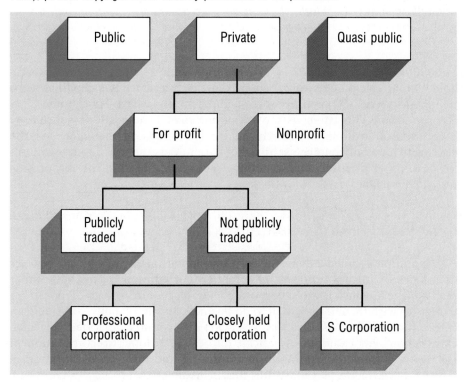

Closely held corporations  *Rupert Murdoch's News Corp. has acquired substantial interests in newspapers, magazines, books, television, and movies all over the world. It's an enormous organization, but it's very much under Murdoch's control; he and his family own half the shares of the corporation. This kind of control gives Murdoch the freedom to make a decision and act on it quickly.*

**Subchapter S (S corporation)**  corporation with thirty-five or fewer shareholders that elects under Subchapter S of the Internal Revenue Code to be treated for federal tax purposes essentially as a partnership

*Subchapter S Corporations*  A corporation with thirty-five or fewer shareholders that elects under Subchapter S of the Internal Revenue Code to be treated for federal tax purposes as a partnership is a **Subchapter S** or **S corporation**. This choice is the only thing that distinguishes a subchapter S corporation from other closely held corporations of the same size. By electing to have Subchapter S status, the shareholders can use the corporation's losses to offset their income, something they could not do if the corporation was the taxpayer.

## Classification of Corporations

**domestic corporation**  what a corporation is called in the state in which it receives articles of incorporation

**foreign corporation**  what a corporation is called in any state other than the one in which it was incorporated

**alien corporation**  American corporation that does business in a foreign country

A corporation is called a **domestic corporation** in the state in which it receives its articles of incorporation. It is a **foreign corporation** in any state other than the one in which it was incorporated. (States require foreign corporations to register with them if they wish to do business locally.) Finally, an American corporation that does business in a foreign country is called an **alien corporation**. For example, American Express is a domestic corporation of Delaware, a foreign corporation in California and an alien corporation in Great Britain. Figure 3.5 illustrates these classifications.

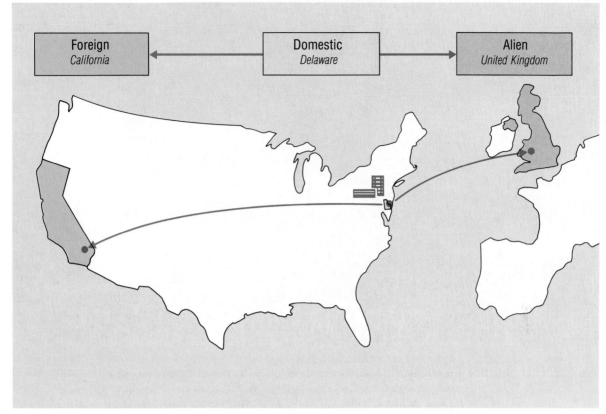

| Foreign<br>*California* | Domestic<br>*Delaware* | Alien<br>*United Kingdom* |
|---|---|---|

FIGURE 3.5    Domestic, Foreign, and Alien Corporations

## *Managing the Corporation*

Logic suggests that because shareholders own the corporation, they should run it. That is not how a corporation works, though. Officers, who are elected by a board of directors, who in turn are elected by the shareholders, run the company.

*The Shareholders' Role*    Shareholders have only one function that relates to the management of their company: electing the board of directors. Apart from having a right to vote on certain extraordinary transactions, such as selling the company or most of its assets, voting annually for directors is all they do. Shareholders are not corporate agents and therefore do not have fiduciary duties to the corporation.

*The Board's Role*    The board of directors represents the interests of the shareholders. It sets general policy for the corporation and elects the company's top management. Although board members are not corporate agents, their duties to the corporation are fiduciary.

A board has to meet only once a year, but it is more likely to meet quarterly. The law requires that a board act by resolution after a formal

# THE JOYS OF KINDER-CARE.

**The corporation**   *Most of the nation's largest businesses are publicly-owned corporations whose shares are publicly traded on recognized stock exchanges.*

---

**minutes**   secretary of the board's record of the votes in a board meeting

vote. The secretary of the board records the votes in the meeting's **minutes** or records. These formalities emphasize the corporation's existence separate from its shareholders and board members. If the board fails to observe the formalities, it jeopardizes the shareholders' limited liability. States that permit closely held corporations to do away with their boards have reasoned that such boards serve no purpose when the shareholders are serving essentially as the management.

**bylaws**   rules adopted for the corporation's internal operations

The relationship between the board and the officers it elects is defined by the articles of incorporation and the corporation's **bylaws**, the rules adopted for the corporation's internal operations. In essence, the relationship is one of accountability.

**corporate officers**   a president, one or more vice presidents as specified in the bylaws, a secretary, and a treasurer, elected by the board

*Management's Role*   The board must elect **corporate officers:** a president, one or more vice presidents as specified in the bylaws, a secretary, and a treasurer.[9] A corporation must have officers, because they are its agents. A corporation is not a living person and could not transact business without agents. The board may appoint any other officers or agents that the bylaws permit. If the board wanted to appoint a board member to be a corporate agent for some purpose, it would have to adopt a resolution to that effect. No board member is automatically an agent of the corporation. Similarly, no shareholder is an agent of the corporation unless appointed by the board.

# Other Business Forms

A number of other legal business forms exist for relatively specialized purposes. Let us examine them briefly here.

**5.** List and describe three other legal forms of business organization that exist for specialized purposes.

## Joint Ventures

We have already mentioned one specialized business form, the joint venture. In essence, it is a partnership without mutual agency and without a continuing general business purpose. A joint venture has a single defined objective, though it may take years to achieve. The most common joint ventures are oil and gas development projects in which oil companies join to share the costs and risks of an exploratory well. But they are becoming increasingly common in areas marked by high entry costs. For example, Kodak and Cetus have joined forces to develop biotech diagnostic systems, while AT&T and Olivetti are working together to introduce AT&T's computers to Olivetti's European markets.[10]

## Syndicates

A temporary association formed to carry out a specific, usually short-term investment is a **syndicate**. A syndicate resembles a joint venture but rarely develops an administrative structure, as some joint ventures do. Syndicates are often formed to underwrite and distribute large issues of stocks and bonds, to purchase expensive real estate for resale, and to spread the risk of owning expensive resources such as stallions and bulls used for breeding.

**syndicate** temporary association that forms to carry out a specific, usually short-term investment

## Cooperatives

A corporation or association formed to perform services so its owners or members can make a profit—but without making any profit itself—is a **cooperative**. Some examples of major cooperatives are Ocean Spray, a cooperative formed by cranberry growers, and Land o' Lakes, a cooperative formed by Minnesota dairies to market their products. Cooperative members may be individuals or have any business form (see Business Issues).

**cooperative** corporation or association formed to perform services so its owners or members can make a profit but without making any profit itself

# Business Forms: A Perspective

To discuss a category that includes 17 million or so entities, we must focus on common threads and characteristics and avoid exceptions. And yet it is a safe bet that anyone who pays attention to the news has heard a lot more about conglomerates than about subchapter S corporations, although there are a lot more of the latter than the former. A **conglomerate** is a corporation that owns several other corporations that are in different industries. A conglomerate makes **acquisitions**, purchases of other companies.

**conglomerate** a corporation that owns several other corporations that are in different industries

**acquisition** the purchase of other companies

# AGRICULTURAL COOPS GO BIG TIME

"If we don't have an equal return on assets with other people in the business, they're going to outrun us sooner or later, and we'll cease to exist," says William Gaston, chief executive of Gold Kist Inc. These are predictable words from the head of a business with $1.2 billion in sales in fiscal 1986. But are they what you would expect to hear from the head of a poultry, grain, and farm-supplies cooperative? Agricultural coops, founded as the farmers' answer to big business, are behaving more like big businesses every day.

Considering the size of some coops, this development is not so surprising. Many smaller coops have either failed or merged in recent years, and the sales figures for the larger survivors compare to those of the larger shareholder corporations. Land O'Lakes Inc., a Minnesota-based dairy cooperative, had $2.2 billion in sales in 1987. Sunkist Growers Inc., a western citrus-farmers' cooperative, had $855 million. Ocean Spray Cranberries Inc. had $736 million.

This increase in size has been accompanied by an increase in the capitalization of the cooperatives, whose function it is to sell the products of the member farmers and pass the profits back to them. In turn, the increase in capitalization has, many feel, increased the distance between the coops and the farmers.

Traditionally, the coops have been thinly capitalized by farmers who were not interested in high administrative costs or fancy marketing techniques. To an extent, this mentality persists. "A farmer is very happy to invest in a plant," says Richard L. Fogg, group vice president of Land O'Lakes. "That's tangible. For the same $10 million, he doesn't feel too good about a guy from New York with suede shoes running an ad campaign."

Like it or not, however, the suede shoes may well be in the barnyard to stay. Extensive marketing is especially important given the emergence of a world agribusiness market. Citrus fruit from Chile, Spain, and Israel has cut Sunkist's domestic share almost in half in the last 10 years. A few years ago, Blue Diamond, a California almond growers cooperative, had no overseas sales. Today over two-thirds of its nuts are shipped abroad.

The marketing efforts behind these successes cost money—money the farmers may not be willing to put up. In consequence, some coops have considered raising funds through public offerings. Land O'Lakes was ready to offer 37 percent of Country Lake Foods Inc., one of its subsidiaries, when the stock market tumbled in 1987. The coop is now waiting for the right moment to make the offering. Gold Kist made the move in 1986, going public with a quarter of one of its subsidiaries.

G. Howard Morse Jr., a cranberry grower and former chairman of Ocean Spray, dislikes this approach. He feels that the independent source of income drives a wedge between the company and the growers.

Not every coop farmer can make this claim. Even before the public offering, the chicken farmers of Gold Kist had no more say in chicken production than farmers working for Frank Perdue. When Gold Kist makes a profit, the farmers receive only a small fraction of their share in cash. The average member farmer, who produces only about .06 percent of Gold Kist's chickens, has little to say about this. So, it seems, does Chief Executive Gaston, to whom selling chickens is selling chickens, no matter what the basis or form of the business.

Sources: "Giving Thanks for Cranberries," *The Economist,* January 10, 1987, p. 57; David Henry, "Capitalist in the Henhouse," *Forbes,* January 26, 1987, p. 37; Ellen Paris, "Sunset in the Groves?" *Forbes,* March 23, 1987, pp. 35–36; Corie Brown, "Why Farm Co-ops Need Extra Seed Money," *Business Week,* March 21, 1988, p. 96; "Nuts!" *Forbes,* October 17, 1988, p. 8.

**Cooperatives**  *Cooperatives can be big business as the farmers who own Blue Diamond, Land O'Lakes, Sunkist, and Ocean Spray are finding out. Right now, many of these multimillion dollar cooperatives are facing a major decision. As they continue to grow they will need capital beyond what their owners' profits can supply. The farmer-owners may eventually have to consider selling shares to the public to raise capital.*

Many critics argue that conglomerates are dinosaurs that have grown so large that they will topple from their own weight. They reason that most conglomerates' acquisitions are made to build an empire rather than for sound business reasons. Certainly that appears to be happening with four of the conglomerate kings in the period from the 1960s through the 1980s: Dart & Kraft, Gulf + Western, Beatrice Foods, and ITT. All four have sold individual companies—and sometimes whole divisions—that did not relate to a newly defined core of businesses.

Growth by acquisition today centers largely on **mergers**, the acquisition of companies in related businesses. As we will discuss in Chapter 22, mergers are either *horizontal* (the acquired company is a direct competitor) or *vertical* (the acquired company is in the same chain of supply). When Coca-Cola acquires one of its bottlers, the merger is vertical. If it had acquired Dr. Pepper, the merger would have been horizontal.

**merger**  the acquisition of companies in related businesses

Whatever happens with the big acquisitions, opportunities abound in small businesses, as the next chapter reveals. It is fun to watch the dinosaurs battle each other and the government, but for many it is more fun to make big money with ventures of their own.

# CHAPTER HIGHLIGHTS

*1.* Identify and describe three basic legal forms of business ownership.

A *sole proprietorship* is a form of business in which one individual (the *sole proprietor*) owns all the assets of the business and is alone responsible for its debts. This form of business ownership makes up 70 percent of American businesses. A *partnership* is defined as an association of two or more persons who serve as co-owners of the business. A *corporation* is a form of business organization authorized by state law which comes into existence when a secretary of state issues a certificate of incorporation. To receive a certificate of incorporation, an *incorporator* must sign and file the proposed articles of incorporation with the secretary of state.

*2.* Outline the advantages and disadvantages of the three legal forms of business organization.

The major advantages of a sole proprietorship include control and independence, secrecy, ease of formation and dissolution, and ownership of all profits. Disadvantages include unlimited financial liability, lack of continuity, limited financing, and management limitations. Partnerships are also easy to form, provide management flexibility and increased financial capacity. Disadvantages of partnerships include unlimited financial liability, lack of continuity, partner conflicts, and dissolution problems. The major advantages of corporations are limited financial liability, permanence, and increased financial capacity. The disadvantages include expense of formation, legal restrictions, and taxation.

*3.* Distinguish between general partnerships and limited partnerships.

A *general partnership* is an association of two or more persons who carry on as co-owners and all partners are liable for the debts of the business. A *limited partnership* is a form of business in which the general partners have essentially the same rights and liabilities as partners in a general partnership while the limited partners have few management rights and limited liability.

*4.* Describe how a corporation is organized and managed.

The first step in organizing a corporation is to obtain a certificate of incorporation from the secretary of state where the corporation will be incorporated. In most cases the legal papers are prepared and filed by an attorney who represents those setting up the corporation. Officers, elected by the board of directors who in turn are elected by the shareholders, manage the company.

*5.* List and describe three other legal forms of business organization that exist for specialized purposes.

A *joint venture* is essentially a partnership without mutual agency and without a continuing general business purpose. A joint venture has a single defined objective. A *syndicate* is a temporary association formed to carry out a specific, usually short-term investment. For example, a syndicate might be formed to purchase expensive real estate for resale. A *cooperative* is a corporation or an association formed to perform services so its owners or members can make a profit.

# KEY TERMS

Sole proprietorship
Partnership
Association
Mutual agency
Partnership agreement
Co-owner
Capital contribution
Liable
General partnership
Joint venture
Limited partnership
Limited partner
Dissolution
Winding up
Termination

Corporation
Incorporator
Franchise tax
Shareholder
Share
Closely held corporation
Publicly traded
Public corporation
Quasi-public corporation
    (public utility)
Private corporation
Nonprofit corporation
    (not-for-profit corporation)
For-profit corporation

Professional corporation
Board of directors
Subchapter S (S corporation)
Domestic corporation
Foreign corporation
Alien corporation
Minutes
Bylaws
Corporate officers
Syndicate
Cooperative
Conglomerate
Acquisition
Merger

# REVIEW QUESTIONS

1. What is a sole proprietorship? Why is it the most commonly used form of business ownership?
2. What are the major advantages and disadvantages of sole proprietorships?
3. Define a partnership. What are the advantages and disadvantages of this form of business ownership?
4. What is the difference between a general partnership and a limited partnership? Why are limited partnerships established?
5. What are the four characteristics that distinguish the corporation from other types of businesses?
6. Describe the day-to-day management of a typical corporation. What roles are assumed by shareholders, the board, and management?
7. What is a joint venture? Why are joint ventures formed?
8. What is a cooperative? What are its advantages? Can you identify a cooperative in your immediate area?
9. Describe a conglomerate. List at least three conglomerates that currently operate in the United States.

# APPLICATION EXERCISES

1. You are currently interested in establishing the following types of businesses. What forms of business ownership would you consider?
   a. A frame shop that will offer professional picture framing.
   b. A real estate firm that will maintain residential and commercial divisions. In addition, a property management division will be established.
   c. A furniture manufacturing plant that will specialize in casual wood furniture.
2. For the past five years you have been the advertising director for a small chain

of appliance stores. You plan and coordinate the advertising for all of the company's retail stores. Recently a friend who operates a successful graphic design agency contacted you and discussed the possibility of forming an advertising agency. He suggested the creation of a general partnership. Would this be the best form of business ownership? What are the major advantages of forming a general partnership? Disadvantages?

# CASES

## 3.1  Steve Jobs and NeXT

You are 30 years old. You are worth over $90 million. You have just been forced out of the dream company you largely inspired, by the person you brought in to run it. What do you do?

If you are Steve Jobs, a founder and to many still the image of Apple Computer, Inc., you start over. This time you go first class. You set up shop not in a garage, where the Apple legend began, but in a carefully patrolled, landscaped setting in Palo Alto. You stock the company's designer kitchen with designer fruit juices. You order cellular phones for all the company's European cars. Money comes in. You value your company at $128 million.

Jobs's new company is called NeXT, and his new computer is determinedly innovative, both outside and in. Housed within a striking black cube is an 8-megabyte storage capacity (ten times that of its competitors), a sound quality equivalent to a compact-disk player (whole symphonies can be passed from computer to computer), a 17-inch diagonal monitor, sharp displays, and stunning graphics. The NeXT computer is not only easy to use, it is easy to program. Steve Jobs believes he has five great products in him, and he is convinced this is one of them.

Not everyone agrees. Referring to NeXT's lack of a color display, William H. Gates, chairman of Microsoft Corp., declares the machine uncompetitive. It will not accept Apple or IBM software. It was designed not for the $15 billion corporate market, but for the $2 billion educa-

tional market. And its $6,500 price tag is far above the $3,500 student resistance level.

And then there is the question of Jobs's management skills and philosophy. Jobs was pressured to leave Apple because of his quirky, nonstop, never-take-no-for-an-answer style. He campaigned for sales and other divisions to operate almost as separate companies. As far as he was concerned, R&D should not be subject to top-management constraints. (This was how he developed the Macintosh. At the time Apple was proceeding along more restrained lines with its main project—the now-forgotten Lisa.) Jobs was chairman of Apple, but he never really had control. At NeXT he is not only chairman, he owns 63 percent.

Critics read trouble into NeXT's eighteen-month delay in getting its product on the market. The delay has given NeXT's competitors time to catch up. H. Ross Perot, who has invested $20 million in NeXT, has a different view. "They spent an inordinate amount of time striving for perfection. He's done it again."

### Questions

1. Might Steve Jobs be pressured out of NeXT, as he was from Apple? Why?
2. For a spirited entrepreneur like Jobs, what are the advantages of a closely held corporation? What are the disadvantages?

For more information, see *Business Week*, October 24, 1988, pp. 74–80; *Fortune*, May 23, 1988, pp. 10, 84–88; and *Inc.*, October, 1987, pp. 49–60.

## 3.2 The Corporate Raid

One of the key characteristics of a large corporation is the separation of shareholders and management. Shareholders own the corporation; very few of them have anything to do with day-to-day management. Shareholders do, however, have a say in how management is working. Some exercise their ownership rights by attending and voting at annual stockholders' meetings. But most let management act for them by giving management their proxy.

Then there's Carl Icahn. Icahn is a corporate raider. He looks for a company whose stock he feels is undervalued, buys up as much of that stock as he can, then stages a fight for control of the organization. Icahn believes companies whose stock is selling below true value are badly managed, and bad management makes Carl Icahn mad.

In one successful takeover bid, Icahn acquired control of TWA in 1986. He used that control to make himself chief executive officer and to initiate widespread changes in the management of the airline. Those changes, he insists, generated earnings of $106.2 million in 1987, the first profits for the carrier since 1984.

In 1988, Icahn took on the management of Texaco in one of the most publicized takeover attempts ever. First he bought up 15 percent of the company's stock. Then he took out full-page ads offering shareholders $60 for each share of stock, $10 over the trading price. When Texaco's board rejected his bid, Icahn geared up for a proxy fight. He hired a firm to solicit proxies

from Texaco shareholders. These proxies would give him the number of votes he needed to win five seats on the company's fourteen-member board, the first step in taking control of the company. In the meantime, Texaco's management mounted its own campaign, running anti-Icahn ads and filling shareholders' mailboxes with letters defending its record.

In the end, Icahn lost and management won. The majority of shareholders voted (or allowed management to vote for them) to keep top management in place. But the battle may be far from over. Icahn still holds a large block of Texaco stock. He could decide to dump it, opening the door for some other corporate raider, or he might decide to try again himself. In the meantime, Texaco's management has been put on notice. Now, more than ever, it has to produce.

### Questions

1. How can shareholders control the actual operation of a corporation? What determines each shareholder's influence?
2. What effect did Icahn's takeover of TWA have on the airline's shareholders? How does this compare with the effect of the proxy fight on Texaco's shareholders?

For more information see *Fortune*, February 29, 1988, pp. 54–55, 58; *Newsweek*, June 13, 1988, p. 50; *Newsweek*, June 27, 1988, p. 44; and *Business Week*, August 1, 1988, p. 88.

# 4 Entrepreneurship, Small Businesses, and Franchises

LEARNING
OBJECTIVES

After you have completed this chapter, you will be able to do the following:

**1.** Describe the characteristics of an entrepreneur.

**2.** State the various definitions of small business and explain why there is more than one definition.

**3.** Discuss why certain fields attract small businesses.

**4.** Analyze why small businesses succeed and fail.

**5.** Describe the services of the Small Business Administration.

**6.** List the advantages and disadvantages of franchising.

**7.** Describe the protections offered by law to franchisees.

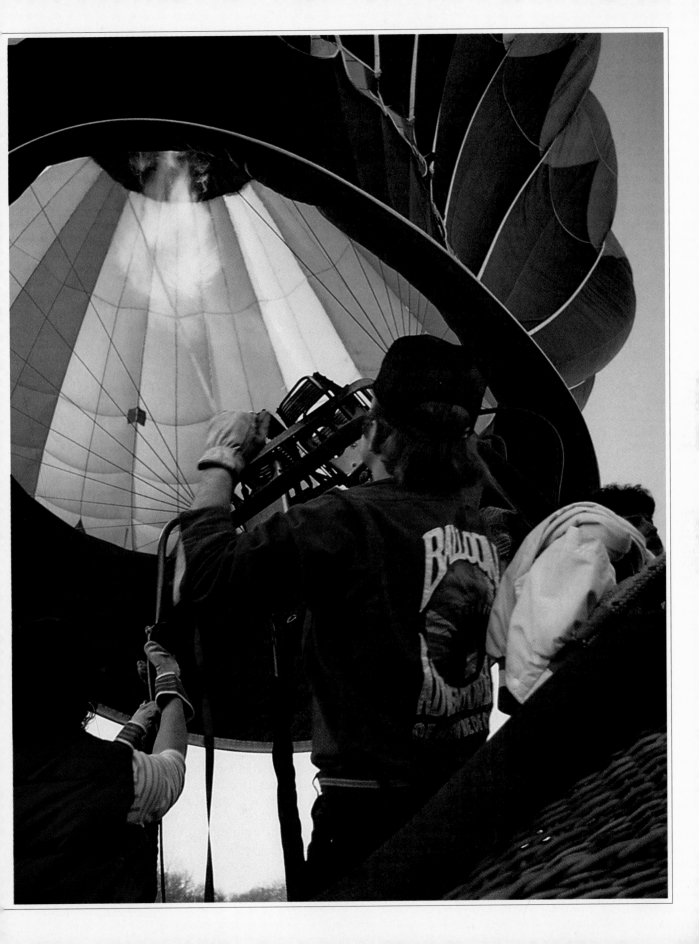

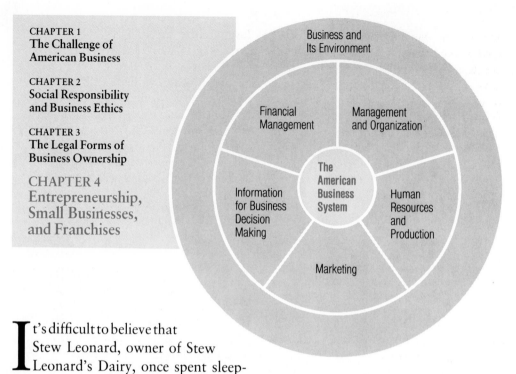

It's difficult to believe that Stew Leonard, owner of Stew Leonard's Dairy, once spent sleepless nights worrying about the success of his new business. As it turned out, he didn't need to worry. Stew Leonard's Dairy, located in Norwalk, Connecticut, boasts the largest sales per square foot of any retail store in the world.[1] With help from his local bank, Leonard obtained a small business loan for $485,000 that was used to build his new store. From the beginning his philosophy has been to sell the freshest items at low prices and make shopping fun for the customer. Excellent service is also part of his business philosophy. Etched in stone at the store's entrance are his two commandments: Rule 1: The customer is always right; Rule 2: If the customer is ever wrong, reread Rule 1.[2]

# Entrepreneurs and Entrepreneurship

**entrepreneur** a person who organizes, operates, and assumes the risk of a business venture in the hope of making a profit

**entrepreneurship** the capacity for innovations, investment, and expansion in new markets, products, and techniques

Stew Leonard is an **entrepreneur**, a person who organizes, operates, and assumes the risk of a business venture in the hope of making a profit. In the past, the word *entrepreneur* described only those who created their own businesses. Today, the word applies to anyone who runs a business and who builds and innovates.[3] As Professor Nathaniel H. Leff describes it, "**Entrepreneurship** is the capacity for innovations, investment, and expansion in new markets, products, and techniques."[4] Normally, entrepreneurs are associated with small businesses, and that will be our context.

Thousands of people decide each year to set out on their own. Figure 4.1 illustrates the steady growth of new incorporations during the past decade.

Some want independence, some look for large profits, and others hope to have some effect on society's ills. The same skills that enable one person to create a thriving business allow someone else to erect a community center, develop a civic orchestra, or establish a museum. Successful entrepreneurs possess the vision to identify needs and to develop ways to satisfy them. William L. Gore, the inventor of Gore-Tex fabrics and one of America's most innovative businesspeople, expressed the entrepreneurial drive in his own way: "The creative, emotional urge that leads to the risk-taking and tremendous energies of entrepreneurs is a real factor in their accomplishments. Creative urges are widely present in humans and need only freedom and opportunity to be released."[5]

## The Characteristics of an Entrepreneur

Entrepreneurs are a varied lot. It is extremely difficult to pigeonhole them or their goals for their businesses. Some want to become giants in their fields, whereas others want just a small, secure niche. Maryles Casto, for instance, parlayed a $3,000 investment in a tiny travel agency into a $30-million business—Casto Travel, headquartered in Santa Clara, California—which she is aggressively expanding.[6] Vince Hansen started his fresh juice business—Hansen Juices, Inc., in Los Angeles—on a shoestring, too. Hansen was a product of the Depression, however, and he did not want to grow at the price of going into debt. He has deliberately kept his business small and

*1. Describe the characteristics of an entrepreneur.*

FIGURE 4.1   The Number of New Business Incorporations Continues to Rise

Source: Statistical Abstract of the United States (Washington, D.C.: U.S. Govt., 1988)

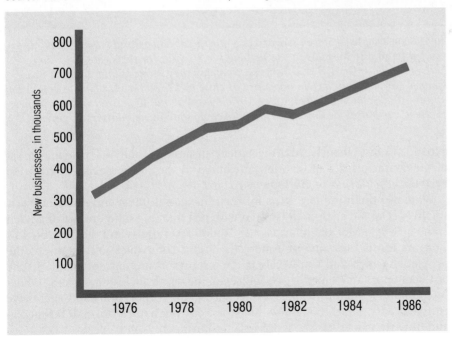

**Doing something fun** *Steven Udvar-Hazy (pictured) and Louise Gonda knew they wanted to go into business in "something fun," which for them, both aviation buffs, meant airplanes. These days the company they formed, International Lease Finance Corporation, has an inventory of close to $2 billion. Airplane leasing is big business today: in the United States carriers lease about 40 percent of their planes; overseas, an enormous market has developed as state-owned airlines go private.*

expanded only when he had the money in hand.[7] Table 4.1 provides a list of the characteristics most often attributed to the entrepreneur, as reported by the *Encyclopedia of Entrepreneurship.*[8]

Whatever their ultimate goals for their businesses, most entrepreneurs start small. McDonald's, after all, started with just one store and one set of golden arches. Today, McDonald's has over 10,000 restaurants and the McDonald's Corporation is now one of America's largest companies. Yet many of the people who own and run McDonald's restaurants are entrepreneurs. In the last section of this chapter we will examine the franchising system, which often makes for happy marriages between giant corporations and aggressive entrepreneurs. First, though, we must look at the nature of small businesses and how they operate (see Experiencing Business).

## DETERMINING YOUR ENTREPRENEURSHIP POTENTIAL

Are you a good candidate for an entrepreneur? Take a moment to consider the following questions:

1. Has someone in your family started his or her own business?
2. Are you confident in your ability to achieve the goals you set for yourself?
3. Do you enjoy making your own decisions?
4. Do you find yourself frequently thinking up new ideas?
5. Would you be willing to work long hours to achieve a goal?
6. Are you willing to take chances?
7. Do you tend to be tireless and have a high energy level?
8. Do you find it difficult to focus your attention on "small" details?

Note: Persons with the potential to become a successful entrepreneur usually answer "yes" to these questions.

# The Nature of Small Business

*Small* is a relative term. It implies the question: Compared to what? Peter Norton Computing Inc., with annual sales of approximately $11 million and a work force of 38 people,[9] is small compared to IBM, with sales of about $50 billion and 400,000 employees.[10] But Peter Norton Computing Inc. is hardly small when compared with a neighborhood beauty salon or a mom-pop grocery store.

TABLE 4.1    Ten Characteristics of the Entrepreneur

1. Good physical health
2. Superior conceptual abilities
3. The broad thinking of a generalist
4. High self-confidence
5. Strong drive
6. Basic need to control and direct
7. Moderate risk taking
8. Great realism
9. Moderate interpersonal skills
10. Sufficient emotional stability

Source: C. Kent, D. Sexton, and K. Vesper, *Encyclopedia of Entrepreneurship*, © 1982, p. 29. Reprinted by permission of Prentice-Hall, Inc., Englewood Cliffs, NJ.

## A Working Definition of Small Business

Let's define **small business** as any business that is independently owned and operated, is not dominant in its field, and does not employ more than 500 persons. There is, in fact, no generally accepted definition of a small business. We can see why by looking at the elements of this definition.

Some commentators argue that franchised operations, like the National Video Stores outlets, are not true small businesses.[11] The franchiser, in this case National Video Stores, sets management standards that the store owner must observe. By this reasoning, the store owner—the franchisee—is not truly independent. We will see in the last section of this chapter why many franchisees argue that this assistance only reduces, but does not eliminate, the risk of entrepreneurship.

Depending on how *field* is defined, a small business fitting our definition could dominate its field. For example, Peter Norton Computing Inc. was the first company to develop software that allows users to retrieve deleted files. Peter Norton, founder of the company, discovered a **market niche**, the area in which a firm specializes or holds a unique position. Like many good ideas, Norton's was easy to copy, and soon many competing products appeared on the market. Peter Norton Computing Inc. is still a major competitor in this field but no longer dominates it.[12]

For many people, describing as "small" a business that employs up to 499 employees flies in the face of common sense. Just to pay 500 employees only $100 per week for a year would mean that the company would have to earn $2.6 million just to meet the payroll. There is a good reason behind this element in our definition, though. The **Small Business Administration (SBA)**, an agency of the federal government that offers both managerial and financial assistance to small businesses, has adopted a basic definition of small business that parallels ours. The SBA also uses additional standards to determine which businesses can receive its help. The SBA's services are described later in this chapter.

Studies have shown that the public in general uses a very restrictive definition of the term *small business*. The average person uses it to refer to an owner-managed business that employs only a handful of people, not more than, say, twenty or twenty-five.

## The Economic Importance of Small Business

However small business is defined, one fact is not disputable: small businesses are critical to the soundness of our economy. In terms of numbers, small businesses dominate the U.S. economy. As Table 4.2 indicates, most of the businesses in America, more than 80 percent, employ fewer than twenty workers. And the great majority of American workers are employed by a business that meets the 500-employee criterion of our small business definition.

Small businesses account for most of the new jobs in America. David Birch, a leading expert on small business and author of *Job Creation in America* notes that the formation and expansion of firms that employ fewer than twenty people have generated almost all (98 percent) of America's employment gains during the past decade. By contrast, the nation's 500

**Focusing on a market niche** *Today more parents are having their children later, and have more money to spend on dressing them. Whit's End is a retail operation that has targeted a specific market niche by catering to such parents.*

largest companies have dropped over 2 million employees during this same period.[13]

Birch and others also note that small firms are also the source of most innovations. Many of the successful new businesses are built on innovation. For example, Lane Nemeth started her company, Discovery Toys, because she could not find an educational toy suitable to give a friend's 1-year-old

TABLE 4.2    Distribution of Establishments and Employees in the U.S., by Enterprise Size

| Enterprise Size (Number of Employees) | Percent of Establishments | Percent of Employees |
|---|---|---|
| 0–19 | 83.4 | 25.2 |
| 20–99 | 9.9 | 19.8 |
| 100–499 | 3.2 | 16.7 |
| 500–4,999 | 1.9 | 18.3 |
| 5,000 or more | 1.5 | 19.8 |
| | 100.0 | 100.0 |

Source: Redrawn with permission of The Free Press, A Division of MacMillan, Inc. from *JOB CREATION IN AMERICA: How Our Smallest Companies Put the Most People to Work*, by David L. Birch. Copyright © 1987 by The Free Press.

child as a present. Her idea was to sell quality toys through home demonstrations, just as Amway, Avon, and Tupperware sell their goods. In 1977, she started with a borrowed $25,000. Today, she has a sales force of 12,000 and gross sales of more than $40 million.[14] Ray Kroc, the driving force behind the development of McDonald's, didn't invent the hamburger, but he did develop a new way to serve this popular item.

## Fields That Attract Small Business

3. Discuss why certain fields attract small businesses.

Certain fields, such as retailing, services, and high technology, are more attractive to entrepreneurs than others. These fields tend to be easier to enter and require low initial financing. Also, it is easier to pick a market niche in these fields. (Chapter 11 discusses in more detail how to select a niche.) New firms thus suffer less from heavy competition, at least in the early stages, than do more established firms.

*Retailing*   A businessperson who acquires goods from manufacturers, producers, or wholesalers, then sells them to consumers is a **retailer**. Retailing has always attracted entrepreneurs. Any main street or shopping strip is lined with independent record stores, sporting goods shops, dress boutiques, drugstores, groceries, and hardware stores. Retailing particularly attracts entrepreneurs because it is so easy to gain experience and exposure in this field. Retailers always need sales help, and all but the smallest need many other types of employees, such as buyers or window dressers.

**retailer** a businessperson who acquires goods from manufacturers, producers, or wholesalers, and then sells them to consumers

It is also relatively easy financially to open a store. The retail entrepreneur does not have to make the heavy investment in equipment and distribution systems that a manufacturing business would require. All that the new retailer needs is a lease on store space, a minimal amount of merchandise, and enough capital to sustain the business through the always difficult start-up period. For example, in 1977 Julee Rosso and Sheila Lukins opened The Silver Palate, a 165-square-foot gourmet food shop featuring freshly cooked foods. This store serving New York's upper West Side attracted a large clientele of hard-working people who wanted to eat well at home but lacked time to cook. The partners were soon able to branch out into such high-profit ventures as catering and writing cookbooks.[15]

**service** work that is done for others that does not involve the production of goods

*Services*   The term **service** describes work done for others that does not involve the production of goods. Think about all the examples of service firms to be found on a main street, shopping strip, or in an office district: real estate and insurance and personnel agencies, barber shops, banks, computer repair shops, accounting firms, and many others.

Service industries attract entrepreneurs for much the same reasons that retailing does. And services also attract individuals whose skills are not always needed by larger businesses, such as beauticians, morticians, and jewelers (see Business Issues).

**high technology** new and innovative types of businesses that depend heavily on advanced scientific and engineering knowledge

*High Technology*   With its emphasis on emerging scientific advances, high technology seems an unlikely area to attract entrepreneurs. **High technology** is a broad term for the new and innovative types of businesses that depend

## FREE ENTERPRISE AND THE MAIL

They're springing up in busy neighborhoods all across the country. They could be barber shops or dry cleaners, but you don't come here to have your hair cut or your clothes pressed; they're storefront post offices. They do just about everything that U.S. post offices do, and make money doing it.

In large part, storefront post offices are a response to problems within the U.S. Postal Service. The Postal Service is overstaffed and undermechanized. And when it needs money, it raises the price of stamps without improving the quality of service.

Most economists blame these problems on the legal monopoly the Postal Service enjoys over the delivery of letter mail. This monopoly dates back to 1845, when Congress enacted the private express statutes, laws that prevent private carriers from delivering first- and third-class mail.

Supporters of the statutes argued that private carriers would take over the most profitable routes, in heavily populated areas, leaving less profitable routes to a U.S. mail service "crippled and broken down for the want of means." Opponents insisted that competition would improve service and lower costs. These same arguments are still being heard today.

The statutes may limit competition in the mail "industry," but they haven't done away with it completely. There's fierce competition in the overnight-delivery arena. (Package deliveries are not protected by the private express statutes.) Here, Federal Express, Purolator Courier, United Parcel Service, and other private companies hold 90 percent of the market. And in the last few years, chains of private post offices have begun to compete in other service areas.

Mail Boxes Etc. is the largest of these chains, with some six hundred franchises in forty states. Each outlet sells stamps (usually at a penny more than what the Postal Service charges), wraps packages for mailing or delivery, and rents post office boxes. There's a charge for these services, but people are willing to pay it to avoid long lines and for the convenience of local service. In 1988, Mail Boxes Etc. made over $1 million on over $5 million in sales. Storefront post offices are a small business that's getting bigger every day.

Sources: "Storefront Post Offices," *Time,* 12 January 1987, p. 57; "Reinventing the Post Office," *Fortune,* 19 January 1987, p. 8; Janice Castro, "Charging More and Delivering Less," *Time,* 28 March 1988, p. 50; James C. Miller III, "It's Time to Free the Mails," *Consumers' Research,* March 1988, pp. 11–14.

---

heavily on advanced scientific and engineering knowledge. Yet it is precisely the people who have been able to identify innovations or new niches in the field of computers, biotechnology, genetic engineering, robotics, and a dozen other markets who have become today's high-tech giants. Many of them started out working in garages, basements, or kitchens. Recent research indicates that high-tech businesses start small but tend to get bigger faster than most other companies. They are also less likely to go out of business than other types of businesses.[16]

Bill Gates began writing computer software in his teens and later founded Microsoft, a successful high-tech company. By the time he was 30, he had become one of America's 100 richest persons.[17] And although it requires

**Technology on the farm**  *Farmer James Webb has a phone in his tractor and it's helping him make money. It allows him to keep working in the fields and still be there when a grocer wants to place an order or when he needs to check the weather or touch base with an employee.*

more capital to develop hardware than software, there are many success stories relating to hardware. Apple Computer, for instance, began in a garage.

# Owning a Small Business

An entrepreneur does not need an engineering degree to use new technology. Applying high-tech solutions in a stodgy business can lead to great success. Former Wall Street money manager Robert Waggoner bought Burrelle's Information Services, Inc., a 100-year-old clipping service whose employees were still relying on razor blades and newspapers. Today, Burrelle's depends on computers and databases and is a high-growth company. Waggoner is probably not typical of people who own small businesses—but only because there is no typical entrepreneur. Waggoner, however, does share one characteristic with many small businesspeople: he bought into Burrelle's because he wanted to call his own shots. Independence is one of the great rewards of entrepreneurship.

## The Rewards of Small-Business Ownership

The desire to be your own boss certainly is a major reason for going into business for yourself (see Table 4.3). During the last five years, entrepreneurs have created new corporations at a rate exceeding 700,000 per year. That number does not, of course, include any of the other business forms (sole proprietorships and partnerships) discussed in Chapter 3.

Many people strike out on their own because they believe that they can do better for themselves than they could by remaining with their current employers. They often feel stuck on the corporate ladder, which is what happened to Janice Jones. She left a Wall Street house to found her own firm, Chartwell & Company, a $2 million venture that specializes in investing and financial consulting.[18]

Entrepreneurs are sometimes persons who simply cannot work for someone else. More often, they just want the freedom to choose who they work with, the flexibility to pick where and when to work, and the option of working in a family setting. Many new entrepreneurs start their new business in their own home. Home-based businesses are growing at a rapid pace throughout America. Some estimates indicate that as many as 20 percent of the new small business enterprises are operated from the owner's home.[19] These business owners are involved in catering, custom sewing, computer research, photography, the planning of weddings, and a host of other enterprises.

Historically, immigrants to the United States found that starting their own businesses was the best way to enter the American mainstream. This pattern continues today among Hispanics, blacks, Asians, and women.

## The Rise in Women Entrepreneurs

The rapid growth of women-owned businesses is one of the most important economic developments of recent times (see Figure 4.2). Women now own approximately 30 percent of American businesses compared to 5 percent prior to the 1970s. They are starting businesses at more than twice the rate of men and could well own and operate 50 percent of the nation's businesses by the year 2000.[20] A majority of women-owned businesses are small retail or service firms and tend to be owned by one person.

TABLE 4.3    The Rewards and Risks of Small-Business Ownership

| Rewards | Risks |
|---|---|
| 1. To gain control over your own destiny. | 1. Uncertainty of income. |
| 2. To reach your full potential. | 2. Losing your entire invested capital. |
| 3. To reap unlimited profits. | 3. Quality of life until the business gets established. |
| 4. To make a contribution to society. | 4. Complete responsibility. |

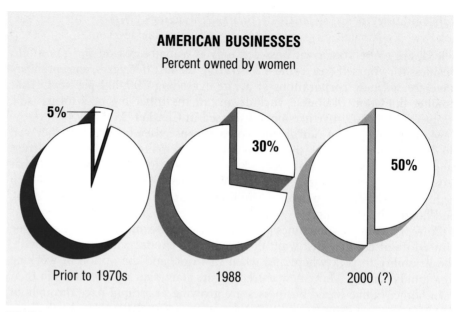

**AMERICAN BUSINESSES**

Percent owned by women

5%

30%

50%

Prior to 1970s          1988          2000 (?)

FIGURE 4.2   The Growing Number of Businesses Owned by Women

Source: "New Economic Realities: The Rise of the Women Entrepreneurs," *A Report of the Committee on Small Business,* House of Representatives, June 28, 1988 (Washington, D.C.: U.S. Government Printing Office, 1988).

Many women entrepreneurs acquired valuable business experience while working for a large corporation. Mary Ann Jackson, owner of My Own Meals Inc., learned about financial and strategic planning at Beatrice Companies. She has developed and marketed a line of children's meals that will be sold by supermarkets. Jackson spent eighteen months studying her market and developing her product before starting the business.[21]

## The Risks of Small-Business Ownership

Running a small business certainly is alluring, which is why so many people dream of it. Sad to say, though, of every ten small businesses formed, eight go out of business within the first ten years after they open their doors.[22] The financial risks of running a small business are very high, although some businesses are considerably less risky than others.

Even if the business keeps going, the odds are not in the entrepreneur's favor that he or she will have the next Ben & Jerry's Ice Cream Company, New England's leading premium ice cream vendor. It is more likely that the business will produce a living for its owner, but not much more. And there are always worries about new equipment, expanding inventory, rent increases, or competition. Ben & Jerry's, for instance, found itself shut out of supermarkets as a result of competition from Häagen-Dazs, the original premium ice cream maker whose owners sold it to Pillsbury. It took a lawsuit to open the supermarket doors to Ben & Jerry's again.[23]

In addition to facing financial and psychological stresses, entrepreneurs tend to be victims of physical stress. The small businessperson often must be the owner, manager, sales force, shipping and receiving clerk, bookkeeper, and custodian. Sixteen-hour days quickly become standard, and vacations are rarely possible. And women business owners often face major challenges as they attempt to manage a home and a business at the same time.

A key element in the definition of an entrepreneur is that he or she takes risks. If the potential rewards—whether financial or psychological—were not enormous, no one would go into a small business. A million or so people each year balance the risks and rewards of entrepreneurship and decide to become entrepreneurs. Our society rewards innovation and risk taking, if the entrepreneur can persist. Many creative persons succeed or fail not in their business concepts but rather in how they manage their businesses once they start.

## The Keys to Success

Despite their failure rate, small businesses have some advantages over their larger competitors.

*4. Analyze why small businesses succeed and fail.*

*Flexibility*   Small size can give a business's owners the flexibility to adapt to changing market demands. Small businesses usually have only one layer of management, the owners. Decisions therefore can—and should—be made and carried out quickly. By contrast, in larger firms decisions on even routine matters can take weeks, because they must pass through two or more management levels before an action is authorized. Some large companies have recognized this lesson and have eliminated certain layers of management. For instance, an aggressive young steel manufacturer, the Nucor Corporation, has only two levels of management between its mill workers and its chief executive officer.

*Focus*   Small firms can focus their efforts on a few key customers or on a precisely defined market niche. Large corporations, on the contrary, often must compete in the mass market or for large market segments. Firms like L. L. Bean, Inc., the outdoor wear cataloger, begin by identifying a niche, capturing a market, then gradually expanding their lines and customer base. Bean's originally specialized in hunting and fishing gear; today it is a major force in outdoor and casual clothing.

*Reputation*   Because of their capacity to focus on narrow niches, small firms can develop enviable reputations for quality and service. A good example is the Brookstone Company, with its unqualified returns policy that demonstrates a commitment to customer satisfaction.

## The Paths to Failure

Small businesses fail for many reasons. A poor business concept, like a snow removal service in a Southern state, will produce disaster nearly every time.

Trying to expand a hobby into a business can work if a market niche genuinely exists, but all too often people start such a business without identifying a real need for the goods or services. Overoptimism is a great trap. Other notable causes of small business failures include disproportionate burdens imposed by government regulation, insufficient reserves to withstand slow sales, and vulnerability to competition from larger companies.

Two major paths to failure deserve a closer look. These are an inability to develop a business plan (including profit projections) and a lack of capital to continue the business.

*Failure to Develop a Business Plan*  When a prospective entrepreneur fails to put together a business plan and make profit projections, the stage is set for business failure. The plan provides a path to follow during the critical

FIGURE 4.3  Developing a Business Plan

Source: Reprinted from *Going into Business*, (U.S. Small Business Administration: Washington, D.C.).

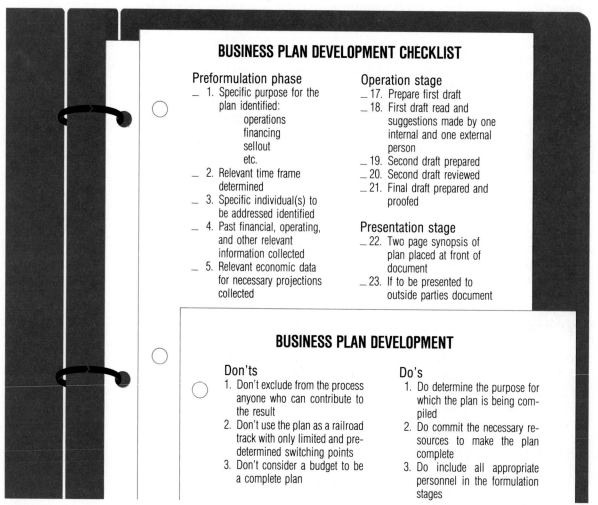

**BUSINESS PLAN DEVELOPMENT CHECKLIST**

Preformulation phase
\_ 1. Specific purpose for the plan identified:
    operations
    financing
    sellout
    etc.
\_ 2. Relevant time frame determined
\_ 3. Specific individual(s) to be addressed identified
\_ 4. Past financial, operating, and other relevant information collected
\_ 5. Relevant economic data for necessary projections collected

Operation stage
\_ 17. Prepare first draft
\_ 18. First draft read and suggestions made by one internal and one external person
\_ 19. Second draft prepared
\_ 20. Second draft reviewed
\_ 21. Final draft prepared and proofed

Presentation stage
\_ 22. Two page synopsis of plan placed at front of document
\_ 23. If to be presented to outside parties document

**BUSINESS PLAN DEVELOPMENT**

Don'ts
1. Don't exclude from the process anyone who can contribute to the result
2. Don't use the plan as a railroad track with only limited and predetermined switching points
3. Don't consider a budget to be a complete plan

Do's
1. Do determine the purpose for which the plan is being compiled
2. Do commit the necessary resources to make the plan complete
3. Do include all appropriate personnel in the formulation stages

early stages of business development and operation. A sound plan tells you what to do and when to do it. It should include a definition of your business, an assessment of your competition, estimates of income and expenses, and other information. A sound business plan is often the key to acquiring financial support from bankers and suppliers (see Figure 4.3).

*Undercapitalization*   The quickest and most common way to fail in business is **undercapitalization,** the lack of sufficient funds to operate a business normally. More than 50 percent of small businesses fail within a year after they open, most often because they are undercapitalized. All too many entrepreneurs have thought that all they needed was enough money to get their doors open. They thought that the business could live on its cash flow after that. Almost all businesses, however, suffer from seasonal variations in sales when cash is tight, and very few businesses make money from the start.

**undercapitalization** the lack of sufficient funds to operate a business normally

Figure 4.4 charts the monthly sales figures for jewelry stores. A moment's thought reveals why jewelry sales peak in June and December. In May and June, jewelers sell class rings to students and engagement and weddings rings to the soon-to-be-married. December, of course, brings the holiday gift rush.

To avoid the problem of undercapitalization, the prospective small business owner should prepare an estimated income statement. The statement will usually include an estimate of sales, controllable expenses, and fixed expenses (such as rent) for the first year of operation.

**FIGURE 4.4**   Jewelry Stores' Percentages of a Year's Total Sales, Month by Month. What types of retailers might have the opposite peaks or no peaks at all?

Source: Roanoke Times and World News, *Advertising Planbook* (Roanoke, VA: 1989). Reprinted with permission from the Newspaper Advertising Bureau.

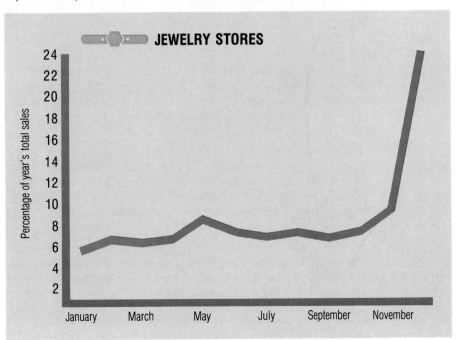

# Financing the Small Business

In the popular view, the entrepreneur is the person who invents the better widget or the way to sell it. A more accurate view might be that the successful entrepreneur is the one who obtains adequate financing to produce or market the better widget. We will discuss financing fully in Chapters 17 through 19.

Even a small retailer will probably need fifty thousand dollars to rent space, add necessary equipment and furnishings, and buy an initial inventory. In addition, the retailer needs **working capital**, the money necessary to fund the business's regular operations. Ideally, the entrepreneur should put up a significant percentage of the necessary capital. Few new entrepreneurs have

**working capital** the money necessary to fund the business's regular operations

**Creative financing** *In July 1988, Carolyn Gorsuch and Barbara Allen couldn't have picked a better time to start a business. Savvy and MasterCard BusinessCard were giving away a $25,000 entrepreneurial grant in a contest for women entrepreneurs. Gorsuch and Allen won the contest grant, and with $55,000 in personal loans, they had the start-up capital they needed to create Shop Talk, a small business that produces greeting cards for everyday happenings.*

the entire amount, however. They must therefore look to other sources for additional financing. These sources include:

- The owner's resources
- Family and friends
- Financial institutions
- Vendors

## The Owner's Resources

The most important source of funds for any new business is its owner. Most people have more wealth than they realize. One form it often takes is **equity**, ownership interest, either in a home or accumulated value in a life-insurance policy or in a savings account.

Alternatively, the owner may have assets that could be used in the business and thereby become part of his or her equity in the firm. A computer, a typewriter, desks, and the like are common examples. The owner can also provide working capital for the business by reinvesting any profit back into the business or simply by not drawing a full salary.

**equity** ownership interest, either in a home or accumulated value in a life-insurance policy or in a savings account

## Family and Friends

Entrepreneurs often look to family and friends as sources for loans or **capital**, assets that are exchanged for an ownership interest in a business. Family and friends are often hard put to turn down an entrepreneur in need of cash, but if the business goes bad the emotional losses for all concerned may greatly exceed the money involved. As with any other serious transaction, anyone loaning a friend or family member money for a venture should state the agreement clearly in writing.

Despite their potential disadvantages, loans from family members are appealing to the entrepreneur. Usually he or she can structure a favorable repayment schedule and even sometimes negotiate an interest rate below the current rate offered by banks.

**capital** assets that are exchanged for an ownership interest in a business

## Financial Institutions

Inevitably, businesses must at some time borrow from a financial institution. As we will see in Chapter 17, savings and loans institutions, banks, trust companies, and investment companies are the major types of financial institutions.

Typically, entrepreneurs start shopping for financing in their local institutions. These sources know the environment in which the entrepreneur is operating. When Tidewater, Inc., of New Orleans decided to go into the business of servicing offshore oil-drilling platforms, it sought start-up financing from the Whitney National Bank in New Orleans. The bank not only made the loan but also granted the new company an extension when it could not make its first payment.[24] That is the kind of service entrepreneurs look for from local institutions.

Start-up ventures sometimes borrow up to 75 percent of their needs, depending on a bank's evaluation of the venture's likelihood of success and of the entrepreneur's ability to repay the loan. The institution will often require the entrepreneur to give it a **security interest**, a financial interest in personal property or fixtures that secures the payment of a debt or obligation. The property securing the debt is called **collateral**. Collateral may consist of some of the new firm's assets, such as its office equipment. Especially in the case of start-ups, the entrepreneur may have to offer some personal property as collateral, such as the entrepreneur's home. In this case the security is called a **mortgage**, a security interest in real property. If the entrepreneur or firm fails to repay the loan, the lending institution may eventually claim the collateral and sell it to recoup its loss.

Financial institutions can also grant a small business a **line of credit**, an agreement by which a financial institution promises to lend a business a predetermined sum on demand. A line of credit permits an entrepreneur to take quick advantage of opportunities that require a bank loan.

## Trade Credit

Many vendors will grant buyers financing in the form of **trade credit**, an agreement whereby the supplier sells goods or services to the buyer but does not require immediate payment. Sometimes payment is not due for a specific period, such as thirty days. In other cases payment is due in periodic installments.

## Other Sources of Funding

Financial institutions are not the only sources for loans. Some community groups sponsor revolving loan funds to encourage the development of particular types of businesses. State and local agencies may guarantee loans, especially to minority businesspeople or for development in certain areas. The Small Business Administration offers several financial assistance programs. Four of these programs are described here:

- Direct loans   Usually made only to businesses that do not qualify for loans from financial institutions.
- Guaranteed loans   Guaranteeing that a loan made by an institution to a qualified small business will be repaid.
- Participation loans   A mix of a guaranteed loan and a direct loan in which the SBA guarantees an institution's loan for part of the firm's needs and makes up the balance in a direct loan.
- Minority Enterprise Small Business Investment Companies (MESBICs) Financing companies partially funded by the SBA that make loans to minority-run businesses.

Matchmaking, small business style   *The Chicago-based Inventors' Council is Don Moyer's brainchild. The Council matches inventors with manufacturers, ideas with production capabilities. Companies describe the kinds of products they want to produce, and inventors submit their proposals. According to Moyer, the process works whether a match is made or not. It gets both inventors and manufacturers thinking about new ideas, and to Moyer, this is what success in business is all about.*

# Where to Go for Help

The key role that small business plays in our economy and social fabric has resulted in many efforts to improve the entrepreneur's ability to compete.

## *Entrepreneurial Training Programs*

Creativity and innovation, two keys to the entrepreneur's success, cannot be taught. What *is* being taught, in seminars and college classrooms from Harvard to the University of Washington, is management and financing techniques. As previously noted, these skills are crucial to a venture's success.

Jack Thorne, a professor at Pittsburgh's Carnegie Mellon University, recalls that when he started teaching entrepreneurship fifteen years ago, such courses were offered at only four or five other schools in the country.[25] Today, hundreds of courses in entrepreneurship are taught at two- and four-year colleges.

Workshops for prospective small business owners have become very popular in recent years. These programs focus on the risks and rewards that accompany business start-ups.

Many new ventures are nursed through those trying early days by **business incubator programs**. Like the laboratory units for which they are named, business incubators nurse fragile new enterprises in an artificially supportive environment until they are strong enough to make it on their own.[26] The first business incubator was established at University City Science Center in Philadelphia over twenty-five years ago. Today there are over 300 incubator programs nationwide. The fledgling enterprise is usually offered a variety of support services such as expert advice from faculty members, assistance with research, and access to university libraries and laboratories.

## Small Business Administration

When most people think of government help for small businesses, they think of the Small Business Administration. The SBA offers many types of management assistance to small businesses, including

- Counseling for firms in difficulty
- Consulting on improving operations
- Training for owner/managers and their employees

### Small Business Development Centers (SBDCs)

The SBA funds a number of **small business development centers**, business clinics usually located on college campuses that are set up to provide counseling at no charge and training at only a nominal charge. These centers are often the SBA's principal means of providing direct management assistance where they exist.

### Small Business Institute (SBI)

The **Small Business Institute** program draws on the talents of faculty members and students at colleges and universities. The program is usually housed in the school of business and involves students who are working toward degrees. Under the supervision of a professor, the students assist small business owners with their problems. Today over 500 colleges and universities support SBI programs.

### Service Corps of Retired Executives (SCORE) and Active Corps of Executives (ACE)

SCORE and ACE are volunteer agencies funded by the SBA to provide advice for small firms. Both are comprised of experienced managers whose talents and experience the small firms could not ordinarily afford.

In addition to these programs, the SBA sponsors or cosponsors many of the workshops for prospective business owners previously described. The SBA also makes available a wide range of publications that focus on such topics as employee training, advertising, and bookkeeping.

**business incubator programs** programs that nurse fragile new enterprises in an artificially supportive environment until they are strong enough to make it on their own

5. Describe the services of the Small Business Administration.

**small business development center (SBDC)** a business clinic usually located on a college campus that is set up to provide counseling at no charge and training at only a nominal charge

**Small Business Institute (SBI)** program in which business students assist small business owners with their problems, under the supervision of faculty members

**Service Corps of Retired Executives (SCORE) and Active Corps of Executives (ACE)** volunteer agencies funded by the SBA to provide advice for small firms

114

# Franchising

Many entrepreneurs choose to start a franchised operation in the hopes that they can avoid the pitfalls of starting a completely new business. For instance, many expect to receive management assistance from the **franchiser,** the company that sells the franchise. Franchises have their own unique types of risks, however, of which the **franchisee,** the person who buys a franchise, must beware.

**franchiser**  company that sells a franchise

**franchisee**  person who buys a franchise

## The Franchising Relationship

A license to sell another's products or to use another's name in business, or both, is a **franchise.** In such a business relationship, the franchisee acquires the rights to a name, logo, certain methods of operation, national advertising, products, and other elements associated with the franchiser's business. Rent-

**franchise**  a license to sell another's products or to use another's name in business, or both

A franchise for Charlotte   *Despite heavy opposition George Shinn was determined to get a National Basketball Association (NBA) franchise for Charlotte, North Carolina. Shinn, a wealthy businessman, went to the city government and worked a deal on the playing space, the city's new coliseum. Then he got the fans involved, with contests to name the team and mascot. When he faced NBA officials, he made them an offer they couldn't refuse. In 1988, the Charlotte Hornets suited up and played ball. Their principal owner: George Shinn.*

a-Wreck and Kwik-Kopy, for example, are franchisers with well-known logos and national visibility.

Generally, the franchisee pays a flat fee to the franchiser for the franchise. Depending on the quality of the franchise, the initial fee can range from $5,000 to more than $500,000. As Table 4.4 shows, the amount invested by the franchisee varies greatly. In addition, the franchisee pays the franchiser a monthly or annual fee based on a percentage of sales or profits.

## Advantages and Disadvantages of Franchises

**6.** List the advantages and disadvantages of franchising.

Franchises have unique characteristics that can either increase or decrease the entrepreneur's risks.

*Advertising and Promotion* Most franchisers provide advertising and promotion for their entire system. The promotion might include nationally recognized logos like Wendy's freckle-faced girl or Midas Muffler's crowned logo. Many franchisers are not national, though, and their marketing help may be quite limited. For instance, Smokey Mountain Log Cabins, Inc., is a franchise of outlets for its prefabricated log cabins in Virginia, North and South Carolina, Mississippi, and Texas.[27]

*Management Assistance and Training* Some franchisers offer their franchisees extensive management assistance and training. The older and more successful the franchiser, the better this help is likely to be. Some firms, like McDonald's, even have training centers for their franchisees.

As noted earlier, some people question whether a franchisee is really an entrepreneur. They argue that the franchisee has a tendency to become too dependent on the franchiser for guidance on management decisions. The franchisee's success or failure also depends to a large extent on that of the

TABLE 4.4    Approximate Amount of Investment by Franchisee*

| Franchiser | Type of Business | Minimum Investment |
|---|---|---|
| Comprehensive Accounting Services | Accounting service for small businesses | $42,000 |
| Fantastic Sam's | Beauty salon | $20,000 |
| Kwik-Kopy | Printing | $30,000 |
| Maid Brigade | Cleaning service | $25,000 |
| Gingiss Formalwear | Formalwear rental | $75,000–$90,000 |
| Subway Sandwiches and Salads | Restaurant | $29,000 |
| Check Express | Check cashing | $19,000 |
| Physicians Weight Loss Centers | Weight loss | $17,500 |

*In addition to these franchise fees, the franchisee may be required to invest in equipment, supplies, and other items.

franchiser. This dependence can be a distinct disadvantage if the franchiser runs into problems.

*Central Purchasing and Product Consistency*   Many franchisers provide the supplies that franchisees need to do business. The hamburger chains usually sell the beef patties to their franchise stores. The advantages to the individual franchisee are assured supplies and uniform quality throughout the system, a major factor in customer decisions. A major disadvantage to centralized purchasing may be prices that are higher than in the open market.

Some franchisers do not offer central purchasing or do not carefully monitor the quality of what franchisees buy. Product inconsistency in such systems can hurt franchisees badly.

*Financial Requirements*   The sometimes stiff fees and capital requirements associated with franchises can be both an advantage and a disadvantage to the franchisee. If properly administered, the fees and capital requirements of franchising assure the financial integrity of the franchiser and the system (see Figure 4.5). Some franchisers, like Tubby's Sub Shops, also look for franchisees who will finance no more than 50 percent of their total investment, which in this case would be half of approximately $375,000.[28]

If a system is not well run or its promotion is not effective, the franchise fees can become an insupportable burden. Computerland franchisees forced the franchiser to reduce its fees and to increase and improve its promotion when its national advertising campaigns proved unsuccessful.

*Franchisee Protections*   The earliest major franchisers were the automobile manufacturers and oil companies. Their retail dealers were, and still are, franchisees. In both industries, the franchisees are protected by federal laws from arbitrary terminations of their franchises.[29] Other types of franchisees may not be protected.

*7. Describe the protections offered by law to franchisees.*

The principal legal protections for franchisees are contained in the Federal Trade Commission's regulations. These stipulations require the franchiser to supply a prospective franchisee with a disclosure statement at least ten days before the franchisee signs a franchise agreement. The best protection, however, is an aggressive investigation of the franchiser and its competitors, the opportunities and risks in the franchise area, the terms of the franchise agreement, and all the other factors that go into a business plan.

# Small Business: A Parting Look

Small businesses are the heart of our economic and social system because of the great opportunities they offer and because they express the freedom that Americans have to make their own destinies. The risks are indeed great— but the opportunities for success, both financial and psychological, are greater.

The characteristics of the successful entrepreneur are rewarded in other business areas, too. Creativity, innovation, and willingness to take risks also characterize the most successful managers in large businesses and government.

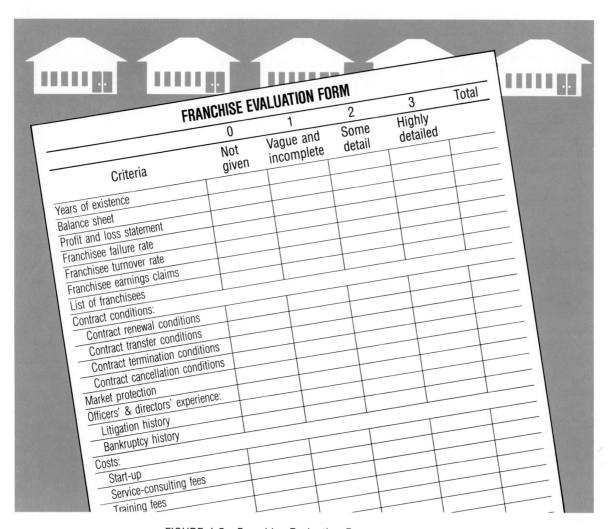

| FRANCHISE EVALUATION FORM | 0 | 1 | 2 | 3 | Total |
|---|---|---|---|---|---|
| Criteria | Not given | Vague and incomplete | Some detail | Highly detailed | |
| Years of existence | | | | | |
| Balance sheet | | | | | |
| Profit and loss statement | | | | | |
| Franchisee failure rate | | | | | |
| Franchisee turnover rate | | | | | |
| Franchisee earnings claims | | | | | |
| List of franchisees | | | | | |
| Contract conditions: | | | | | |
| Contract renewal conditions | | | | | |
| Contract transfer conditions | | | | | |
| Contract termination conditions | | | | | |
| Contract cancellation conditions | | | | | |
| Market protection | | | | | |
| Officers' & directors' experience: | | | | | |
| Litigation history | | | | | |
| Bankruptcy history | | | | | |
| Costs: | | | | | |
| Start-up | | | | | |
| Service-consulting fees | | | | | |
| Training fees | | | | | |

FIGURE 4.5    Franchise Evaluation Form

Source: Adapted from *Journal of Accountancy*, March, 1986 issue. Copyright © 1986 by the American Institute of Certified Public Accountants, Inc.

# CHAPTER HIGHLIGHTS

*1. Describe the characteristics of an entrepreneur.*

Entrepreneurs are a varied lot, but most successful entrepreneurs flourish in an atmosphere of moderate risk taking and are optimistic and energetic. Most entrepreneurs are very goal and achievement oriented.

*2. State the various definitions of small business and explain why there is more than one definition.*

As this text uses the term, a small business is independently owned and operated, is not dominant in its field, and does not employ more than 500 persons. The Small Business Administration's definition, which is similar, classifies businesses by industry and sets different limits for each for the number of employees and amount of sales. A White House conference on small business limited small businesses to those that employ fewer than 400 employees. The Committee for Economic Development included several other criteria: a small number of individuals responsible for capital contributions, a local orientation to the business, and a small market share when compared to its industry as a whole.

Because *small* is a relative term and because different industries make different demands in terms of initial investment costs to start up and also require an appropriate number of employees, no single definition has satisfied all groups.

### 3. *Discuss why certain fields attract small businesses.*

Retailing, services, and high technology are among the fields that are most attractive to small businesses. These fields tend to be fairly easy to enter, require less initial financing than other types of businesses, and allow firms to serve a smaller part of the market. In these fields it is relatively easy for the entrepreneur to parlay his or her own knowledge or skill into a successful business.

### 4. *Analyze why small businesses succeed and fail.*

Small businesses have some advantages over their larger competitors. Flexibility, the ability to focus their efforts on a few key customers or on a precisely defined market niche, and the chance to develop a reputation for quality and service are some advantages small businesses have over their larger competitors.

Small businesses can fail for dozens of reasons. Undercapitalization and the inability to cope with growth are major problems for small businesses. A poor business concept or failure to identify a real need for their goods or services, disproportionate burdens imposed by government regulation, insufficient reserves to withstand slow sales, and vulnerability to competition from larger companies also contribute to the failure of a small business.

### 5. *Describe the services of the Small Business Administration.*

The Small Business Administration offers counseling, consulting, and training services. Small Business Development Centers (SBDCs), often located on college campuses, provide low-cost or free counseling and training and are one of the SBA's principal means of providing direct management assistance. The Service Core of Retired Executives (SCORE) and Active Core of Executives (ACE) provide assistance to individual businesses through the efforts of experienced volunteers. The SBA also offers some financial assistance to businesses that cannot obtain funding from other sources.

### 6. *List the advantages and disadvantages of franchising.*

Four of the most important advantages of franchising are the availability of a proven product and marketing plan, having the benefit of the franchiser's advertising and promotion program, management assistance and training, and the economies of central purchasing and control. Stiff financial requirements may prevent some potential franchisees from entering the business. Although this restriction may be viewed as a disadvantage, it does help entrepreneurs avoid some of the problems of undercapitalization. Lack of independence and control is often seen as a significant disadvantage of the franchise arrangement. The most important drawback, though, is that an individual franchisee's success or failure often hinges on the reputation of other franchisees and the performance of the franchiser.

### 7. *Describe the protections offered by law to franchisees.*

Investors have a right to receive a disclosure statement prepared by the franchiser and delivered at least ten business days before the individual may make a commitment to purchasing a franchise. Franchisers must provide a written explanation of all earnings claims. Franchisees have a right to obtain any promised refund as long as they meet all the conditions for obtaining it.

# KEY TERMS

Entrepreneur
Entrepreneurship
Small business
Market niche
Small Business
  Administration (SBA)
Retailer
Service

High technology
Undercapitalization
Working capital
Equity
Capital
Security interest
Collateral
Mortgage

Line of credit
Trade credit
Business incubator
  programs
Small Business Devel-
  opment Center
  (SBDC)
Small Business Institute
  (SBI)

Service Corps of
  Retired Execu-
  tives (SCORE)
Active Corps of
  Executives (ACE)
Franchiser
Franchisee
Franchise

# REVIEW QUESTIONS

1. Define *entrepreneur* and describe the characteristics associated with entrepreneurs.
2. Compare and contrast the various definitions of *small business*.
3. Which fields tend to attract small businesses most? Why? Explain.
4. What are the principal reasons for the high failure rate among small businesses?
5. Describe the potential advantages small businesses have over their large competitors.
6. What are the potential advantages and disadvantages of owning a small firm?
7. What types of financing do small entrepreneurs typically use? What are the pros and cons of each?
8. What types of financial assistance does the Small Business Administration (SBA) provide?
9. List the types of management assistance that the SBA offers.
10. Describe the franchising relationship.
11. What are the risks and benefits of buying a franchise?

# APPLICATION EXERCISES

1. Make a list of 20 small business firms that opened approximately two years ago in your community. Then place a check mark beside the name of each business that is no longer open. In your opinion, what are some of the reasons why these firms closed? What about the others has helped them endure?

2. Assume you are planning to open a small convenience food store in your community. One option is to seek a franchise. A second option is to open your own store and purchase the merchandise from a wholesale food distributor. What are the advantages and disadvantages of each option?

# CASES

## 4.1 The Entrepreneurial Women

Charlotte Taylor, author of *Women and the Business Game*, notes that the spirit of Horatio Alger is alive and well in America. And that

spirit has been reincarnated with the name Horatia: approximately 30 percent of all business enterprises in America are owned by women, and women are starting new businesses at more than twice the rate of men. One of the best-known women entrepreneurs is Debbie Fields, who founded Mrs. Fields, Inc., a chain of more than 400 stores that sell those chewy chocolate chip cookies. Fields opened her first store at age 21.

Some successful women entrepreneurs started their business a little later in life. Carmen Jones, bored with retirement, opened a pizza shop in Wausau, Wisconsin when she was 61. Two years after starting her first store, she established Kids Korner Fresh Pizza, Inc. Today Carmen's business has grown to over thirty stores, most of which are franchises.

Achieving success in small business is often more challenging for women than men. When the House of Representatives' Committee on Small Business held hearings on problems faced by women entrepreneurs, many witnesses said women business owners face discrimination. When seeking financing, for example, they are often not judged by the same criteria as men. At the close of these hearings, which were the result of lobbying by the 3,000-member National Association of Women Business Owners, the committee concluded that more needs to be done to expedite or facilitate the entrepreneurial process for women.

## Questions

1. What do you think might be some of the major reasons that so many women are starting their own businesses?
2. Do you agree or disagree that women face special problems when they attempt to start a new business?
3. The National Association of Women Business Owners says that women often find it difficult to balance the demands of entrepreneurship with a marriage. Do you agree?

Sources: For more information see "She Calls All the Shots," *Time*, July 4, 1988, pp. 54–57; Nancy L. Croft, "It's Never Too Late," *Nation's Business*, September 1986, pp. 18–24; "Debbie Fields," *Inc.*, August 1988, p. 46; Charlotte Taylor, *Women and the Business Game*, Washington, D.C.: CTA Management Group, 1986.

## 4.2   America's Youngest Billionaire

Bill Gates is thirty-three years old and he's a billionaire. In fact, according to *Fortune* magazine, he's America's youngest billionaire.

Gates made his money in computer programming. He started writing programs when he was in high school, and he has never stopped. His company, Microsoft, developed the operating systems software that drives all IBM and IBM-compatible computers, a product line that helps generate over $500 million a year in revenues for the firm.

Others have started high-tech companies that have since become enormously profitable, but few are still working in those companies. Gates is. He combines technical wizardry with marketing savvy and the ability to lead an organization with over 2,000 employees. And he's been smart enough to get help when he needs it. In 1983, he hired Jon Shirley to manage day-to-day operations at Microsoft. Shirley and a team of professionals work on finances and planning, freeing Gates to concentrate on programming and long-term strategies.

Microsoft went public in 1986. Gates's 45 percent share of the company today is worth billions of dollars. Yet he still works 60 hours a week. He has no intention of leaving Microsoft, or even slowing down much, at least not until he's helped place a computer on every desk and in every home in the United States.

## Questions

1. It's obvious that Microsoft has an excellent product. What other factors have contributed to the success of this high-tech company?
2. Are there reasons why an entrepreneur would want to keep a firm like Microsoft small? What means does an entrepreneur have for restricting the growth of a company? Is the process risky?

For more information see *Inc.*, May 1985, pp. 57–67; *Parade Magazine*, January 26, 1986, pp. 4–5; *Money*, July 1986, pp. 49–70; *Business Month*, April 1988, pp. 59–60; *Maclean's* 101 (May 30, 1988), p. 42; and *Business Week*, September 12, 1988, pp. 104, 108.

# Management and Organization

*Several years ago, United Technologies Corporation put an advertisement in the* Wall Street Journal *that featured a bold headline: LET'S GET RID OF MANAGEMENT. The main theme of the copy was that business leaders should stop managing and start leading. There is, of course, a difference between management and leadership. Good managers are able to do both. In Part II we will describe the process of management and distinguish between management and leadership. We will also discuss the organization process, or how managers group employees and distribute work for maximum efficiency. This section also focuses on the human side of enterprise. We then review the factors that influence worker performance and attitudes.*

## PART TWO

# 5 Management

*After you have completed this chapter, you will be able to do the following:*

*1. Describe the management process and who and what it involves.*

*2. Explain what a management hierarchy represents and relate it to the three types of management skills.*

*3. Show how Henry Mintzberg's ten managerial roles can be divided into three main categories.*

*4. Describe the five steps in the managerial decision-making process.*

*5. Identify and define the five management functions.*

*6. Identify and describe four leadership styles and explain why there is no one best style.*

*7. Define the term* corporate culture *and list the characteristics of one.*

*8. Identify the key concepts of the management excellence movement.*

124

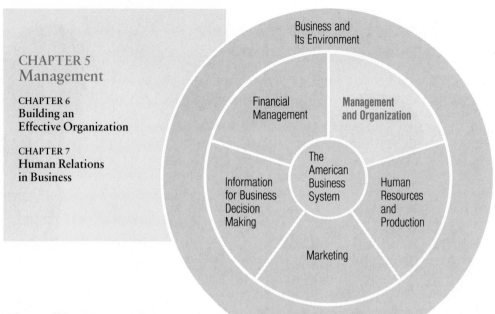

Business and
Its Environment

Financial
Management

Management
and Organization

The
American
Business
System

Information
for Business
Decision
Making

Human
Resources
and
Production

Marketing

M anagement experts say the key to making a high-commitment organization work is mutual trust between top executives and employees. The ability to engender that trusting relationship has become the number one leadership test. . . .

Beth Pritchard tried it, and it worked. She heads S. C. Johnson Wax's insect control division, which markets products such as Raid ant and roach spray and Off mosquito repellent. The division was already the leader in the field when Pritchard, 40, took over two years ago. But she has set it on an even more successful course, radically changing formulas for key products, revamping packaging, and redeploying her top staff to zero in on the needs of customers in each region of the U.S. (the rationale being that Northeastern bugs are quite different from Southwestern ones). She accomplished all that by recognizing the potential of the people working for her and delegating as much authority as possible. Says she: "My philosophy is that you can't do anything yourself. Your people have to do it."[1]

Beth Pritchard is a good manager because she does three important things particularly well. First, she knows the technical details of her job and is in touch with her customers' needs. Second, she has the vision to see how things *could be* rather than simply accepting things as they are. Finally, Beth Pritchard realizes that she can accomplish most through her people by making them powerful and independent. This chapter explores these and other related management activities needed to make business ideas come to life.

# The Nature of Management

The process of coordinating human, informational, physical, and financial resources to accomplish organizational goals is called **management** (see Figure 5.1). A **manager**, therefore, is a person who coordinates an organization's resources. Human resources are those people who actually make the organization's products or provide its services, other employees, and outside vendors and suppliers. Information resources include the knowledge and data necessary to the business, such as market research, legal advice, scientific or technical materials, and economic reports. Physical resources include the business's tangible property, such as its raw materials, manufacturing machinery and facilities, office equipment, and real estate. Finally, a company's

**management** the process of coordinating human, informational, physical, and financial resources to accomplish organizational goals

**manager** a person who coordinates an organization's resources

*1. Describe the management process and who and what it involves.*

FIGURE 5.1   The Management of Resources for a College Basketball Coach

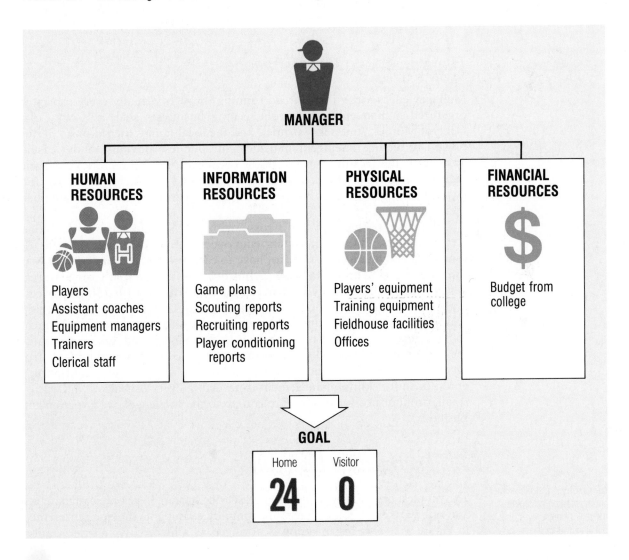

TABLE 5.1    Where to Read about Management Resources in This Textbook

| Resources | Chapter | Example of Topics Covered |
|---|---|---|
| Human | 5, 6, 7, 8, 9 | Planning, organizing, motivation, employee selection, negotiation |
| Informational | 11, 16, 19 | Market research, cost of goods sold, computers, sales reports |
| Physical | 10, 16 | Production, computers |
| Financial | 18, 19, 20, 21 | Balance sheet, investment opportunities, insurance vehicles |

financial resources are its intangible property that may with more or less difficulty be converted into cash. Some examples include bank accounts, accounts receivable, loans, stocks, and bonds. Table 5.1 shows where each of these resources is discussed in detail in your textbook.

## The Universality of Management

Management is a common thread running through virtually every aspect of organized human endeavor. Profit-seeking businesses such as Coca-Cola, General Motors, American Airlines, and the local family-owned pizza parlor obviously require intelligent management. But less obvious to the casual observer is the fact that not-for-profit organizations also require systematic management. How else could the American Red Cross, for example, and government agencies such as the U.S. Department of Education accomplish their objectives?

Although the American Red Cross—with its 250 field stations, 57 blood service centers, 700 headquarters employees, 3,000 chapters, and tens of thousands of volunteers—does not have to earn a profit, it cannot be allowed to run at a loss. The 1980s were turbulent years for the Red Cross. Annual deficits approaching $8 million forced management to lay off 250 employees, improve efficiency, do a better job of identifying clients' needs, and develop additional sources of funding.[2] These management challenges were identical to those faced by business managers during the same period. Like their profit-seeking counterparts, Red Cross managers had to identify and take control of resources, set goals, and allocate resources to achieve the organization's goals. In short, skillful management is needed in every organization, large or small, profit or not-for-profit. (Are you up to the challenge? See Experiencing Business.)

## The Management Hierarchy

**hierarchy** classification of an organization according to the rank or authority of the positions within it

The simplest organizations, like a small service station, have only one manager and one worker. A somewhat more complex example is the one represented in Figure 5.2. This organization is arranged as a **hierarchy**, an organization

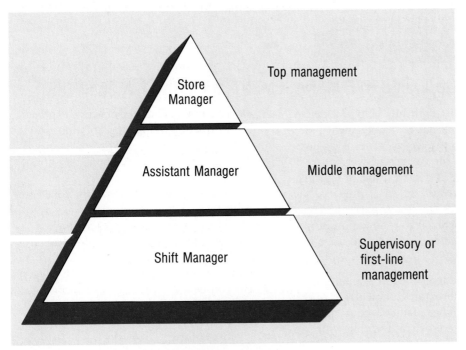

FIGURE 5.2   A Management Hierarchy

classified according to the rank or authority of the positions within it. At the top of the pyramid sits top management, the person or persons responsible for the entire operation. Beneath the top managers is middle management, and below that are the first line or supervisory managers. We will discuss their functions in concrete terms later.

*2.* Explain what a management hierarchy represents and relate it to the three types of management skills.

Normally, a person's position in the hierarchy indicates his or her status and responsibility in the organization: the higher in the hierarchy, the greater the status and the responsibility. But this rule has notable exceptions. If a storeowner's mother works behind the counter, her status is likely to be considerably higher than anyone else's in that category.

## Management Skills

A good manager needs three types of skills. First, he or she must have **human skills,** the ability to work with and for people, to communicate with others, and to understand others' needs. Second, a manager needs **technical skills,** the ability to use the tools, equipment, procedures, and techniques of a specialized field. Finally, a manager requires **conceptual skills,** the ability to understand all the organization's activities, how its various parts fit together, and how the organization relates to others. For example, as a successful division head at S. C. Johnson Wax, Beth Pritchard has to have a good understanding of the dynamic relationship among product formulas, manufacturing, customer needs, packaging, and personnel management.

**human skills**   the ability to work with and for people, to communicate with others, and to understand others' needs

**technical skills**   the ability to use the tools, equipment, procedures, and techniques of a specialized field

**conceptual skills**   the ability to understand all the organization's activities, how its various parts fit together, and how the organization relates to others

# EXPERIENCING BUSINESS

## ARE YOU EXECUTIVE MANAGEMENT MATERIAL? A SELF-TEST

The following short quiz may help you determine if you have executive management potential. Answer the questions as honestly as possible; don't assume the correct answer.

Lauer, Sbarbaro Associates, Inc., a Chicago-based executive [recruiting] firm, prepared the quiz. Although they say it is slightly subjective, the test can give you a good indication of whether or not you are, indeed, executive management material.

1. Are you more interested in planning new programs than maintaining current ones?
2. Would you rather maintain your cultural and social interest than devoting your entire effort to the job?
3. Do you believe that good communication is more important than attention to detail?
4. Do you believe that a good sense of humor is just as important as a working knowledge of the balance sheet?
5. Do you enjoy a variety of work experiences rather than concentrating on your specialty?
6. Are you somewhat impetuous and not always analytical?
7. Are you extremely interested in your compensation package, and not always that concerned with the long-term benefits?
8. Are you concerned with the political realities of your company as they relate to current assignments and your overall progress?
9. Do you believe in giving your subordinates enough rope to hang themselves rather than staying close to a project to protect them against failure?
10. Would you rather beat a customer in golf than let him win to protect the business relationship?

Source: "For Your Information," *Personal Journal*, Sept. 1984, p. 10. Answers are provided at the back of the book.

All managers must have these three types of skills, but the mix of skills a manager requires varies with his or her rank in a hierarchy, as shown in Figure 5.3. Technical and human skills are most important in lower-level managers, for instance. The superintendent of a construction project needs good personal skills to deal with laborers as well as good technical skills to make certain that the construction is done right.

FIGURE 5.3 The Mix of Managerial Skills

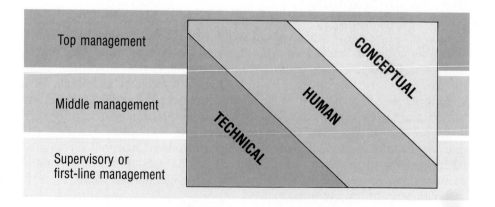

Equality at Herman Miller, Inc. *While Chairman Max Depree uses different skills than the managers below him, at his company such hierarchical distinctions are not emphasized: Herman Miller is well known for its participative style of management.*

By contrast, a top manager must have excellent conceptual skills to manage an entire organization. Human skills are still important, but having strong technical skills becomes less and less critical as one moves up in the hierarchy. The middle manager needs a balanced mix of all three types of skills: human skills to work with people above and below in the hierarchy, technical skills to deal with day-to-day operational problems, and conceptual skills to manage the relationships among departments.[3]

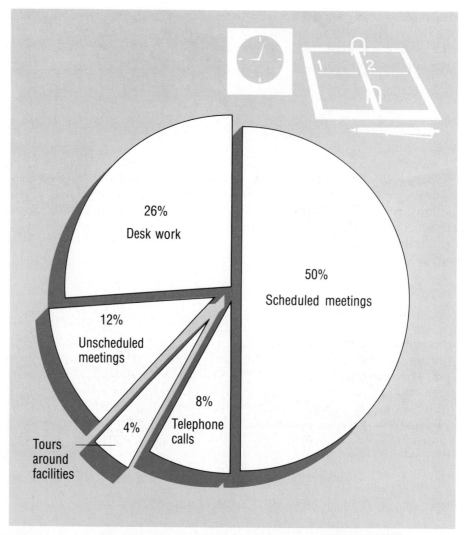

FIGURE 5.4   How Managers Spend Their Time During a Typical Day

Source: Reprinted by permission of L.B. Kurke and H.E. Aldrich, "Mintzberg Was Right!" *Management Science,* Volume 29, Number 8, August, 1983. Copyright 1983, The Institute of Management Science. Adapted from Table 2, p. 979.

## *A Day in the Life of a Typical Manager*

Direct observation of managers at work has enabled researchers to give us a fairly clear picture of the typical manager's day (see Figure 5.4). Of course, we could expect variations depending upon a manager's level and area of specialization. Overall, however, managers tend to be very busy people whose days are filled with a variety of short episodes and lots of interruptions. The pace tends to be hurried and hectic. For example, the 26 percent portion of Figure 5.4 devoted to desk work is typically not achieved in one nonstop session. Rather, the manager has to piece together the 26 percent at his or her desk with 15 minutes here and 5 to 10 minutes there. Also significant is the fact that managers spend most of their time communicating (predominantly face-to-face communication). Improvement of communication skills should be a high priority for all managers.

# Managerial Roles

A manager, like an actor, must play many different roles. Unlike an actor, who plays one role and then moves on to another, however, a manager may play several roles in the same day and sometimes two or more at once. These roles often require different mixes of management skills. In a classic observational study, Henry Mintzberg identified ten managerial roles. These fall into three broad categories: interpersonal, informational, and decisional roles.[4]

*3. Show how Henry Mintzberg's ten managerial roles can be divided into three main categories.*

## Interpersonal Roles

The roles that primarily require a manager to deal with people are the **interpersonal roles**. In the *figurehead* role, in which the manager engages in symbolic activities, he or she may have to appear at an awards ceremony or make a public presentation. As a *leader*, a manager directs the activities of certain employees, coordinates the work of others, sometimes hires and fires subordinates, does performance evaluations, and recommends employees for promotion. Finally, in the role of *liaison*, the manager serves as a communications link between people and groups.

**interpersonal roles**
roles that primarily require a manager to deal with people

## Informational Roles

**Informational roles** are those roles that require a manager to gather and communicate information within the hierarchy and to the outside world. As a *disseminator*, a person who spreads information, a manager delivers information to subordinates. As a *monitor*, a manager who gathers information, he or she reports important changes, problems, and opportunities to higher levels in the hierarchy. The disseminator and monitor roles taken together reveal why managers are an organization's vital communication links.

A manager's third informational role is that of *spokesperson*, a person who transmits information to outsiders for an organization. The spokesperson role may seem to overlap with the figurehead role, but there is a distinction. When the main purpose of a public appearance is to communicate information, a manager acts as a spokesperson. When the primary purpose is symbolic, he or she acts as a figurehead. A manager can, of course, fulfill the two roles at once. Lee Iacocca, the well-known head of Chrysler Corporation, is a classic case in point. While personally advertising Chrysler cars on television, Iacocca not only promoted his company's products, he symbolically represented the rejuvenation of American manufacturing.

**informational roles**
roles that require a manager to gather and communicate information within the hierarchy and to the outside world

**The Muppets' front man**   *Appearing briefly with co-host Kermit at the beginning of each segment of his new T.V. show "The Henson Hour," Jim Henson has come to occupy the managerial role of figurehead. Though he is the creator of the original Muppets Henson has several people working for him today and describes himself as "the front man for the organization."*

## Decisional Roles

**decisional roles** roles
that center on solving problems and making choices

Roles that flow from and are based on a manager's interpersonal and in-formational roles are known as **decisional roles**. These roles center on solving problems and making choices. In an *entrepreneurial role,* a manager looks for and implements new ideas to make his or her group more effective. A marketing manager might, for instance, adopt a new promotional idea, or a production manager might accept a subordinate's suggestion for streamlining a manufacturing process.

As a *disturbance handler,* a manager makes decisions to keep his or her group operating in the face of circumstances that are out of the ordinary. In this role, a manager might have to devise a way to keep parts coming into an assembly line despite a strike that has closed down a primary supplier.

A manager acting as a *resource allocator* decides how a group will use all the available resources. Managers rarely have all the resources they feel they need, so they must decide who gets additional clerical help, who must give up a computer terminal, what types of machines to buy, and dozens of similar issues. Of course, a manager does not make these decisions in a vacuum.

Subordinates will provide input, whether wanted or not. The intensity of such discussions may be matched by those encountered in the manager's final role. As a *negotiator*, the manager acts as a company representative either in dealings externally with outside vendors or government agencies or internally in resolving disputes between subordinates. And, depending on the company, a manager may also have to perform this role in convincing another department to provide the support that his or her group needs for a project.

# The Managerial Decision-Making Process

As the preceding discussion of a manager's decisional role implies, a **decision** is a choice of actions by means of which a manager seeks to achieve the organization's goals. Managers rarely make decisions based on mere inspiration. Most decisions come instead out of the process portrayed in Figure 5.5. This process has five important steps.

decision   a choice of actions by means of which a manager seeks to achieve the organization's goals

**4.** Describe the five steps in the managerial decision-making process.

## Step 1: Define the Problem

The first and most important step in decision making is to define the problem. A **problem** is defined as the difference between actual and desired. "Actual" refers to how things presently are and "desired" reflects one's objective or goal. For example, the problem for someone who is in St. Louis but wishes to be with a loved one in Seattle is how to deal with the 2,135 miles between the two cities. Is air travel an affordable option? If not, perhaps a less costly train ride or even an inexpensive letter will have to suffice.

problem   the difference between actual and desired

Similarly, business managers face the challenge of how to get from here to there. When James R. Houghton, the founder's great-great grandson, took over the top spot at Corning Glass Works in 1983, the firm had unproductive divisions and was barely earning a profit. The first thing Houghton did was to set tough financial objectives and make quality improvement the company's top priority. By late 1988, according to *Fortune* magazine, Corning's gap

FIGURE 5.5   The Decision-Making Process

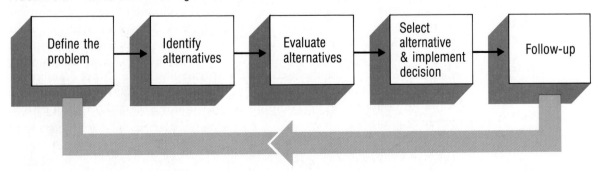

between actual and desired had closed a bit: "The targets: a return on equity of over 17% (he isn't there yet), annual inflation-adjusted revenue growth above 5% (not there yet either), a debt-to-capital ratio below 25% (he's there), and an average dividend payout of 33% of earnings (he's met that goal over the past five years)."[5]

## Step 2: Identify Alternatives

The second step in the managerial decision-making process is to identify alternatives for closing the gap between actual and desired. Clearly, these alternatives must be reasonable—there is no sense wasting time on useless solutions. Time and money always restrict the range of alternatives, but what is an impractical alternative at one time may become a practical one later. Managers should also decide how they will measure success. If they select measurement criteria at an early stage, managers will more likely be objective in determining at the end whether they have achieved their original goals.

## Step 3: Evaluate Alternatives

Once a manager has identified the reasonable alternatives, he or she must evaluate them. An intelligent appraisal requires detailed information on each alternative. Then the manager evaluates them in turn, asking these questions about each alternative: Will this alternative solve the problem as defined? Could a potential solution to the problem jeopardize another organizational goal? Are the time and money available to implement this alternative?

A manager's evaluation will often require projections and predictions. No method for forecasting the future is perfect, and the further into the future the predictions go, the greater will be the probability of error. The key to minimizing the possibility of error lies in having reliable data.

## Step 4: Select an Alternative and Implement the Decision

After evaluating the various alternatives, a manager decides on one to put into action. Successful implementation demands a manager's full commitment: the willingness to devote his or her managerial skills and the group's resources to making the chosen course of action succeed. Managers may find their interpersonal skills tested by the need to motivate subordinates to support the decision. If subordinates believe that a manager may change the decision, they may not commit themselves fully to carrying it out, thus dooming it. James Houghton's actions to revitalize Corning Glass Works have left little room for doubt about his commitment to trimming costs through improved product quality.

Like a proper visionary, he preaches the gospel on 40 to 50 trips to far-flung divisions each year, and all new Corning employees take courses that emphasize

**Evaluating alternatives**  *Faced with a number of reasonable alternatives, a manager must gather detailed information about each one, evaluate its potential effectiveness, its feasibility, and what, if any, risks are involved.*

the company's commitment to quality. By 1991 every worker will spend more than two weeks a year on additional training. Says Houghton: "Quality applies to everything we do. This is a lifelong journey, not a destination."[6]

## Step 5: Follow Up on Implementation

The final step in the decision-making process is to follow up on implementation. A manager must make certain that his or her group carries out the decision after the initial enthusiasm and thrust have ended. In other words, the manager must maintain the momentum. A manager must also monitor the results to determine whether the decision is having the planned effect. Monitoring measures the results against the goal.

This last stage in decision making is thus very much like the first. If the gap between actual and desired remains, the manager must reformulate the problem and begin the process anew.

# Management Functions

**5.** *Identify and define the five management functions.*

As we have seen, management is the coordinating of resources to accomplish a goal or objective. Reaching the goal requires the manager to make decisions in order to plan, organize, staff, lead and motivate, and control. A manager often carries out aspects of several functions at the same time. Still, for discussion purposes, we will separate these functions into the sequence pictured in Figure 5.6. As you look at the various management functions, keep in mind that a manager must be adept at all of them. Unlike, say, a basketball coach, who can always substitute a player, organizations rarely have the luxury of being able to shift managers to deal with particular situations. A manager must therefore be versatile.

## *Planning*

**planning** the process of formulating objectives and determining how to achieve those objectives with available resources

**Planning** is the process of formulating objectives and determining how to achieve those objectives with available resources. Because it sets the stage for everything managers do, planning has been called the *primary management function*. A well-written plan is made up of two key components: (1) an

FIGURE 5.6  Managerial Functions

**Planning at Monsanto** *A plan consists of an objective, describing what is to be accomplished, and when, and an action statement that explains how the objective is to be accomplished. Managers at Monsanto follow this formula when developing plans for research and development.*

objective (or goal) specifying "what" is to be accomplished and "when," and (2) an *action statement* telling "how" the objective is to be accomplished.

Ideally, the precision of plans is enhanced by stating objectives in concrete, measurable terms such as dollars, units, or percentage of increase or decrease. All too often, however, poorly written objectives get the planning process off to a bad start. People cannot be held accountable when objectives and plans are written in vague terms. For instance, how much improvement does the following plan actually involve: "I intend to improve my grade point average by studying harder." A student could satisfy this plan by taking one easy course and raising his or her grade point average a mere .001 of a point. Moreover, people generally are not motivated by vague plans. For example, the statement, "I want to lose some weight," would probably fail to prompt any significant loss. On the other hand, the statement, "I plan to lose 10 pounds in sixty days by eliminating desserts and exercising three days a week," would be more likely to produce results. This statement qualifies as a good plan because it specifies (in measurable terms) what, when, and how. The power of this plan would be enhanced if it were announced publicly, thus taking advantage of peer pressure.

**objective** what is to be accomplished; the goal

*Three Types of Planning* Organizational planning takes on at least three different faces as it moves down the managerial hierarchy. *Strategic* plans formulated by top management tend to be general in scope and long term.

strategic planning
involves determining what
business a company is in and
generally how it intends to
remain in business

In contrast, middle and lower management's *tactical* and *operational* plans tend to be more specific in scope and shorter term. **Strategic planning** involves determining what business the company is in and generally how it intends to remain in business. Strategic planners take a long-range perspective. Consider, for example, the long-range thinking of Michael D. Eisner, the respected chief executive of Walt Disney Company.

"I think in terms of decades," he says. "The Nineties are Euro-Disneyland. I've already figured out what we can do for 1997, and I've got a thing set for 2005." (He won't say what.) Eisner's most ambitious goal may be for the theme parks. Before he leaves Disney—whenever that might be—Eisner hopes to lure 100 million visitors a year to Disney's fantasylands (including those in Japan and Europe), about double the current number. Getting there will require major investments and perhaps additional parks outside the U.S. Eisner admits doing "a lot of thinking about China."[7]

At the middle manager level, we find strategic plans translated into more specific tactical plans. **Tactical planning** involves allocating available resources to specific projects. For example, the managers of Disney's various theme parks annually determine how many new employees will have to be hired and trained, based on park attendance forecasts. **Operational planning,** carried out by first-level supervisors, deals with day-to-day scheduling and operations. A Disneyland wardrobe supervisor, for example, would make sure the right number of properly cleaned and mended Disney character costumes are available each morning.

*The Planning Process*   As Figure 5.7 reveals, planning is a multistep process. These stages, like the management functions, are rarely visible in isolation since most managers have several projects going at any given time. Some organizations do have a formal planning period, for budgeting, for example, in which managers develop plans for the following year.

*Step 1: Analyze the Environment*   The first phase of planning is an **environmental analysis,** a study of conditions that might affect an organization. The political, legal, regulatory, technological, economic, and societal environments directly affect business. All firms, of whatever nature, should engage in environmental analysis on an ongoing basis. A large corporation might analyze foreign competition not only for threats to its existing product lines but also for opportunities to expand, either by beating the foreign firms to the punch or by providing more highly customized products or services to the domestic market.

environmental analysis
a study of conditions that
might affect an organization

Small businesses need to monitor the environment even more closely than large ones because they generally lack the large business's resources to survive a mistake. Small businesses should be on the lookout for new businesses moving into their locales, either as competitors or as new customers. If apartments for the elderly or new college facilities are built in a town, the mix of potential customers may change. If zoning regulations are up for review, businesses will want to make their views known to voters and politicians. If the state government is offering tax breaks to businesses that move into areas with high unemployment, a firm should know about the program in order to take advantage of it.

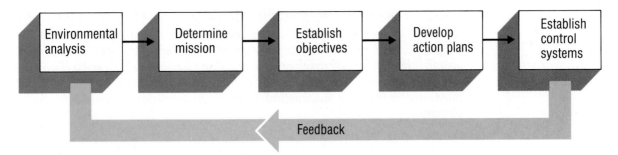

FIGURE 5.7   The Planning Process

*Step 2: Prepare a Mission Statement*   In the second phase of planning, managers define the organization's mission in a statement of the reason the organization exists. Many organizations have mission statements dating back to their founding. Over time, however, their missions probably change. For example, a small city's general hospital founded in the 1920s may have as its mission the providing of comprehensive health care to those in its community. Eventually, though, with greater levels of state regulation, increasing specialization, and the soaring costs of medical technology and malpractice insurance, that mission may no longer be possible.

*Step 3: Set Objectives*   After determining the organization's mission, managers next set its objectives or goals. Establishing objectives, once again, is the most important phase of the planning process. Objectives serve as reference points for every decision maker and guide the organization's routine activities.

Rubbermaid, maker of familiar plastic products including kitchen sink dish drains and trash containers, is a highly successful and respected company driven by carefully conceived objectives. Strategic objectives for 15 percent-a-year increases in sales revenues, profits, and earnings per share were exceeded for the five years from 1984 to 1988. To encourage innovation, a strategic objective at Rubbermaid calls for introducing no less than 200 new products every year.[8]

*Step 4: Develop Action Plans*   The fourth step in planning is to develop action plans to accomplish the objectives. Plan development begins with the ranking of projects according to how they contribute to accomplishing one or more of the objectives. Those that rank highest should receive a greater portion of the resources to be allocated than those ranking lower. Action plans also should reflect the impact of unexpected environmental changes. For example, in response to a 50 percent jump (more than $100 million) in raw materials costs in 1988, Rubbermaid improved productivity, cut costs, and raised prices. Action plans can result in shedding or altering the character of resources. An action plan could call for a significant reduction in a company's work force or for the sale of an entire operating division. In developing plans, managers will use basically the same decision-making process previously outlined.

*Step 5: Establish Control Systems* The final step in planning is to establish control systems that enable managers to measure and adjust for what actually happened, as opposed to what they planned. Establishing control systems is actually the fifth major management function (see Figure 5.6), to be discussed in detail later in the chapter. For now, note that one of the main managerial functions, control, is an integral step in accomplishing another function, planning.

## Organizing

**organizing** assigning to the appropriate position the tasks required to achieve the organization's objectives, along with the authority and responsibility for accomplishing those tasks

Assigning to the appropriate position the tasks required to achieve the organization's objectives, along with the authority and responsibility for accomplishing those tasks, is the process of **organizing**. The broad tasks might be to staff the organization, manufacture the product, sell it, account for the money paid for the product, and invest the proceeds. Clearly, management will have to divide each of these broad tasks into many smaller jobs. The assigning of authority and responsibility for tasks often follows an organizational chart, such as the much-simplified example in Figure 5.2. We will take a close look at organizing in the next chapter.

## Staffing

**staffing** the process of locating, selecting, and assigning people to the tasks designed to achieve an organization's objectives

The process of locating, selecting, and assigning people to the tasks designed to achieve an organization's objectives is called **staffing**. Staffing is closely related to organizing. Managers must match the tasks that are assigned to certain positions with the right persons for the slots. Organizations often create new positions in order to accomplish new objectives. If no one already in the organization can do the task assigned to the position, management must hire and train a new employee. (Organizing and staffing are discussed in Chapters 6 and 8.)

## Leading/Motivating

**leading/motivating** involves influencing, persuading, and directing people to accomplish an organization's objectives

The managerial function of **leading/motivating** involves influencing, persuading, and directing people to accomplish an organization's objectives. Organizations exist because they enable people to accomplish together what they could not accomplish working separately. By leading and motivating, managers *energize* organized effort. Because motivation is discussed in detail in Chapter 7, we will focus here on leadership.

*6. Identify and describe four leadership styles and explain why there is no best style.*

*Leadership Styles* As we know from personal experience with parents, teachers, and managers, not all leaders handle people in the same way. Some are strict, some are not. Some are caring, some are not. Accordingly, researchers have identified different leadership styles. Four distinct styles, as shown in Figure 5.8, are directive, supportive, participative, and achievement-

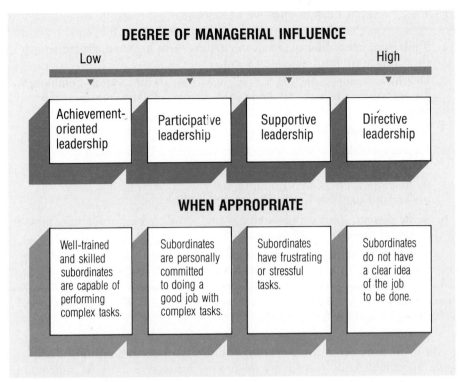

**DEGREE OF MANAGERIAL INFLUENCE**

Low                                High

| Achievement-oriented leadership | Participative leadership | Supportive leadership | Directive leadership |

**WHEN APPROPRIATE**

| Well-trained and skilled subordinates are capable of performing complex tasks. | Subordinates are personally committed to doing a good job with complex tasks. | Subordinates have frustrating or stressful tasks. | Subordinates do not have a clear idea of the job to be done. |

FIGURE 5.8    Leadership Styles for Different Situations

oriented leadership. Each style involves a different relationship between leader and subordinates.

- *Directive leadership:* Subordinates are told what to do and are given specific rules, schedules, standards, and guidance. = autocratic
- *Supportive leadership:* Subordinates are treated as equals by a friendly leader who strives to keep them satisfied. Leader still makes all key decisions, however.
- *Participative leadership:* Leader actively seeks suggestions from = democratic subordinates and seriously considers their ideas when making decisions.
- *Achievement-oriented leadership:* Leader sets challenging goals, emphasizes excellence, and seeks continual improvement because subordinates are viewed as dedicated and responsible. Subordinates exercise a good deal of self-control.[9] = free-rein style

Which of these alternative leadership styles is the best? There is no single best leadership style, according to the currently popular *situational theory* of leadership. In other words, different situations and different follower personalities require managers to vary their styles. Imagine the difficulties a hospital administrator would encounter by using a directive leadership style with a team of highly skilled heart surgeons. An achievement-oriented leadership style would be more appropriate because the surgeons would resent being told by someone outside their specialty exactly what to do and how

TABLE 5.2    Seven Keys to Effective Leadership

1. **Trust your subordinates.** You can't expect them to go all out for you if they think you don't believe in them.

2. **Develop a vision.** Some executives' suspicions to the contrary, planning for the long term pays off. And people want to follow someone who knows where he or she is going.

3. **Keep your cool.** The best leaders show their mettle under fire.

4. **Encourage risk.** Nothing demoralizes the troops like knowing that the slightest failure could jeopardize their entire career.

5. **Be an expert.** From boardroom to mailroom, everyone had better understand that you know what you're talking about.

6. **Invite dissent.** Your people aren't giving you their best or learning how to lead if they are afraid to speak up.

7. **Simplify.** You need to see the big picture in order to set a course, communicate it, and maintain it. Keep the details at bay.

Source: Kenneth Labich, "The Seven Keys to Business Leadership," *Fortune*, October 24, 1988, p. 58. Copyright 1988 *Fortune* Magazine. Reprinted by permission of the publisher.

to do it. In contrast, a drill sergeant could obtain desired military discipline from untrained Army recruits by relying on a directive style. As indicated in Figure 5.8, each style has its appropriate place.

*Keys to Effective Leadership*    After interviewing top executives, management consultants, and business professors, *Fortune* magazine developed seven instructive guidelines for today's leaders. The seven keys to effective leadership listed in Table 5.2 call for leaders who are technically competent, visionary, open and trusting, and adaptive.

## Controlling

**controlling** the process of measuring an organization's performance against its plans

The final management function is **controlling**, the process of measuring an organization's performance against its plans and taking corrective action. Control is a four-step process:

1. Establish measurable performance standards.
2. Measure actual performance.
3. Compare actual performance to performance standards.
4. Take corrective action, if necessary.

It is important to note that control includes not only the measures that managers may take to *prevent* breakdowns but also those they take to *remedy* breakdowns.

*Step 1: Establish Measurable Performance Standards*    The first step toward management control is to establish measurable performance standards to help an organization achieve the objectives set in the planning process.

For example, a restaurant manager today may use a computer to track what sells and what does not. Over time, he or she can then set standards for waiters as to what they ought to sell in one shift. Standards do not always deal only with the bottom line, however. Quite often, for instance, restaurants establish employee dress codes, rules on cleanliness, and how servers and cashiers should deal with the public.

*Step 2: Measure Actual Performance*   Measuring actual performance may or may not be easy. In the case of the computerized restaurant, the manager can follow the night's orders almost as they are entered, a technique pioneered by McDonald's. Measuring performance can also be expensive and time consuming, though. A specialty metals company manufacturing parts for space vehicles will find the government's specifications to be highly precise. Determining whether a given part meets the specifications for it requires complex laboratory analysis and expensive, objective testing. In contrast, a manager's assessment of a restaurant's employees' dress, cleanliness, and courtesy can be extremely subjective.

*Step 3: Compare Actual Performance to Performance Standards*   Once the actual performance has been measured, a manager should have little difficulty comparing it to the established standards. Of course, this is the critical step, because it determines whether corrective action is required. Suppose that a restaurant manager's figures indicate that one waiter sells significantly fewer desserts than the restaurant's standard. The manager may then decide whether

- The waiter needs instruction on how to sell more desserts.
- The dessert cart needs a more prominent location to attract customer attention.
- The waiter is incompetent and should be replaced.

*Step 4: Take Corrective Action, if Necessary*   Taking corrective action is the final control step. The comparison tools may tell the manager what needs corrective action, but he or she must have the will, resources, skills, and knowledge to do what is required. Corrective action often requires bold leadership to overcome resistance to change. For example, during the late 1980s General Motors' chairman, Roger B. Smith, significantly reshaped the giant auto maker in response to a shrinking market share. Smith encountered a great deal of internal and external resistance as he streamlined GM's five car divisions, closed some factories and modernized others, and revitalized product styling and design.[10]

# Contemporary Trends in Management

In recent years, the books topping the business best-seller lists have dealt with successful management techniques. One reason is that no two groups of people are alike, and therefore no one set of management principles works all the time everywhere. A company's management techniques should respond

**Warm culture at Sun** *Under the leadership of CEO Scott McNealy employees enjoy a liberal corporate culture at Sun Microsystems. McNealy's style of management relies on strong individual initiative from employees and grants them large shares of responsibility with little managerial supervision. However, as the company continues to expand at a rapid pace, industry observers fear that the loose style may be too unstructured to maintain control.*

to its changing environment. The penalty for failing to adjust to, say, changes in the nature of the work force may mean disaster in the workplace. Many managers therefore constantly study techniques that have worked elsewhere, looking for effective ways of managing their human, informational, physical, and financial resources. Two concepts, both framed within recent years, dominate management theory today: corporate cultures and excellence.

## Corporate Cultures

**corporate culture** a system of informal rules that spells out how people are to behave most of the time

*7. Define the term* corporate culture *and list the characteristics of one.*

"A system of informal rules that spells out how people are to behave most of the time" describes a **corporate culture**.[11] The two management consultants who developed this concept, Terrence E. Deal and Allan A. Kennedy, believe that the quality and strength of a corporation's culture determines its success or failure.

A corporate culture has four essential elements: values, heroes, rites and rituals, and a cultural network. Values are the organization's basic beliefs that define the elements of success for it and its people. Heroes are the

## MANAGEMENT WITH RESPECT

Herman Miller, Inc., has been manufacturing office furniture since the turn of the century. Today the company's commitment to improving the work environment extends beyond its product to its own human resources policies.

This concern actually began in the 1930s, when a machine operator died at work. Visiting the worker's widow, company founder D. J. De Pree learned that the man had written beautiful poetry. He wasn't surprised at the man's talent. But he was angry with himself for failing to really know the man, for not seeing him as more than a machine operator.

Over the next two decades, De Pree translated his feelings into action. In 1950, he adopted profit-sharing and employee-incentive programs long before these kinds of services were the thing to do. His son Max, now the chairman of the firm, has carried on the tradition. He's talked about a covenant between employer and employee "based on a shared commitment to ideas, to issues, to values, to goals, and to management processes."

A lot of what's happening at Herman Miller has to do with respect for workers and their opinions. There's a willingness here to listen. People work in teams and meet regularly with team leaders to exchange ideas. And all have access to top management and are encouraged to speak their minds when something is bothering them.

This commitment to its workers keeps turnover rates at Herman Miller low. It also brings in a large number of college graduates who are willing to start out on the shop floor.

According to Mike Busch, the company's president, "Management is not a class. . . . It's a function." This is an important distinction. At Herman Miller, the job of management is to bring out people's special gifts, making them more productive, and the work more than work, in the process.

Sources: Robert Levering, Milton Moskowitz, and Michael Katz, *The 100 Best Companies to Work for in America* (Reading, Mass.: Addison-Wesley, 1984), pp. 217–220; Beverly Geber, "Herman Miller: Where Profits and Participation Meet," *Training*, vol. 24, no. 11 (November 1987), pp. 62–66; Kenneth Labich, "Hot Company, Warm Culture," *Fortune*, February 27, 1989, pp. 74–76, 78.

corporation's high achievers who personify its values and thereby set an example for others in the organization. Rites and rituals are the routine behavior patterns in the organization's daily life that are necessary for its success. For example, companies like Genentech and Advanced Micro Devices regularly schedule parties to develop a sense of community among employees who often operate alone or in small groups during the week.[12] Corporations often make ceremonies out of their rites and rituals. Finally, the cultural network consists of informal communication channels within the organization that carry its values to everyone who works for the organization.

Deal and Kennedy suggest that a strong corporate culture is the key to humanizing the workplace (see Business Issues). By describing what is expected of employees, strong cultures make people feel better about their work and give them a sense of belonging. As Deal and Kennedy point out, at the Xerox Corporation the culture dictates hard work at a very fast pace. Managers there make decisions and take action quickly. In contrast, at General Electric people work hard, too, but decisions and action come at a more thoughtful pace. Quite probably, a successful GE employee would find Xerox's culture stressful and frustrating. Speed and excitement are critical elements of Xerox's culture, however, as they are at many high-tech and biotech companies. The lesson is that a firm must develop its own unique culture—it cannot buy one off the shelf.

For three reasons, as Deal and Kennedy see it, having a strong corporate culture will become increasingly important. First, the environment in which businesses operate is becoming increasingly complex. Second, the rate of technological, social, and environmental change is accelerating. Third, competition, which corporations must now define in global terms, is intensifying. Deal and Kennedy argue that these forces are leading to what they call atomized corporations: companies that consist of smaller, task-oriented organizations subject to more local control but connected to the parent organization by computerized links and by culture. They contend that success in this new world depends on the cultural ties that will come to bind small units together. Those ties require the evolution of values, heroes, rites and rituals, and a cultural network within the corporation.

## Excellence

In a best seller of the early 1980s, *In Search of Excellence,* Thomas J. Peters and Robert H. Waterman, Jr., tried to identify the characteristics of the best-run corporations. Their eight principles of management excellence are listed in Table 5.3.

*8. Identify the key concepts of the management excellence movement.*

The importance of the excellence concept lies in its identification of fundamental truths about management that fancier theories usually overlook. Although Peters and Waterman have not introduced anything particularly new, they have refocused management's attention on the basics. Take their

TABLE 5.3    The Eight Basics of Management Excellence

1. A bias for action
2. Closeness to the customer
3. Autonomy and entrepreneurship
4. Productivity through people
5. A hands-on, value-driven approach
6. A "stick to the knitting" view of the business
7. A simple organizational form and a lean staff
8. Simultaneous loose-tight management properties

Source: Condensed from T.J. Peters and R.H. Waterman, *In Search of Excellence: Lessons from America's Best Run Companies* Harper & Row, Publishers, Inc., 1982, pp. 13-15. Used with permission.

first point, "a bias for action," for example. Peters and Waterman say that excellent managers tend to do *something* rather than to analyze a problem forever. Such managers often engage in "management by walking around" (MBWA). They keep themselves informed about what is happening and stay in touch with their people by getting out of their offices and making direct contact.

Like Kennedy and Deal, Peters and Waterman emphasize the human dimensions of management. Technological innovation has hidden the continued (and perhaps increased) importance of the human element in contemporary corporations. Peters and Waterman point out that giants like IBM, 3M, and Procter & Gamble have met this challenge. Despite their complexity, these large corporations still demand a simple organizational form and a lean staff. They focus on their people and customers and "stick to their knitting," the lines and products they know best. The bottom line seems clear: managers striving for excellence should make sure that they do the simple things well.

# CHAPTER HIGHLIGHTS

*1.* Describe the management process and who and what it involves.

*Management* is the process of coordinating human, informational, physical, and financial resources to accomplish organizational goals. *Managers* are the people who coordinate the organization's employees and outside vendors and suppliers; the knowledge and data necessary to carry on the business; the organization's tangible plant, property, and equipment; and its financial resources so that the organization can achieve its objectives.

*2.* Explain what a management hierarchy represents and relate it to the three types of management skills.

The *management hierarchy* is a classification of the positions within an organization in terms of their rank or authority. Often depicted as a pyramid, the management hierarchy shows the position with the greatest authority at the top and the various levels of positions ranked below it. A good manager must have human skills, technical skills, and conceptual skills. Top management must have excellent conceptual and human skills, with less need for strong technical

skills. Middle managers need a good balance of all three types of skills. First-line managers need strong technical and human skills, with less need for conceptual skills.

*3.* Show how Henry Mintzberg's ten managerial roles can be divided into three main categories.

Mintzberg identified ten managerial roles, which can be categorized as interpersonal, informational, and decisional roles. Interpersonal roles include serving as figurehead, leader, and liaison. Informational roles consist of disseminator, monitor, and spokesperson. Decisional roles are entrepreneur, disturbance handler, resource allocator, and negotiator.

*4.* Describe the five steps in the managerial decision-making process.

The five managerial decision-making steps are: define the problem; identify alternatives; evaluate alternatives; select an alternative and implement the decision; and follow up on the decision to see if performance meets expectations. If the problem has not been solved, it must be redefined and the process begun again.

**5.** *Identify and define the five management functions.*

The five management functions are: planning, organizing, staffing, leading/motivating, and controlling. *Planning* is the process of determining an organization's objectives. *Organizing* is the process of assigning to the appropriate position the tasks required to achieve an organization's objectives, along with the authority and responsibility for accomplishing those tasks. *Staffing* is the process of locating, selecting, and assigning people to the tasks designed to achieve the organization's objectives. *Leading/motivating* is the process of influencing, persuading, and directing people to accomplish the organization's objectives. *Controlling* is the process of measuring an organization's performance against its plans to make certain that actual operations conform to plans.

**6.** *Identify and describe four leadership styles and explain why there is no one best style.*

Four leadership styles are: directive, supportive, participative, and achievement-oriented leadership. A directive leader tells subordinates exactly what to do and how to do it. Supportive leaders make all key decisions while showing special concern for subordinates' feelings and satisfaction. A participative leader actively seeks input from subordinates before making key decisions. An achievement-oriented leader lets skilled and self-motivated subordinates pursue performance goals in their own way. Because people and situations vary, so too must leadership styles vary. One style is not appropriate for all situations.

**7.** *Define the term* corporate culture *and list the characteristics of one.*

A corporate culture is a system of informal rules that spells out how people are to behave most of the time. It has four essential elements: values, heroes, rites and rituals, and a cultural network. *Values* are the organization's basic beliefs that define the elements of success for it and its people. *Heroes* are the corporation's high achievers who personify its values and thereby set an example for others in the organization. *Rites and rituals* are the routine behavior patterns in the organization's daily life that are necessary for its success. The *cultural network* consists of informal communication channels within the organization that carry its values to everyone who works for it.

**8.** *Identify the key concepts of the management excellence movement.*

The eight key concepts of the management excellence movement are:

1. A bias for action
2. Closeness to the customer
3. Autonomy and entrepreneurship
4. Productivity through people
5. A hands-on, value-driven approach
6. A "stick to the knitting" view of the business
7. A simple organizational form and a lean staff
8. Simultaneous loose-tight management properties

# KEY TERMS

| | | | |
|---|---|---|---|
| Management | Interpersonal roles | Objective | Organizing |
| Manager | Informational roles | Strategic planning | Staffing |
| Hierarchy | Decisional roles | Tactical planning | Leading/motivating |
| Human skills | Decision | Operational planning | Controlling |
| Technical skills | Problem | Environmental analysis | Corporate culture |
| Conceptual skills | Planning | | |

# REVIEW QUESTIONS

1. What is management? Do managers of small organizations have anything in common with managers of large ones?
2. What are the three types of skills needed by a good manager? Which of these skills are most important at the top of the management hierarchy?
3. How do management's informational roles and decisional roles differ?
4. Which of the five steps in the typical managerial decision-making process do you think is the most and least important? Why?
5. What is the nature of each of the five management functions? Why is it necessary for a manager to be adept at all of them?
6. What does organizational planning involve?
7. How can you tell if a plan is well written?
8. Participative leadership is a popular concept today, but why is it not appropriate for all managers and all situations?
9. What is meant by the term *corporate culture* and what are the four essential elements of culture in an organizational setting?
10. What are the eight major goals of management excellence?

# APPLICATION EXERCISES

1. Several weeks ago you applied for the position of pool manager at a local community center. After two interviews, you were given the position. This three-month summer appointment will involve hiring and training of all personnel, updating pool regulations, contacting vendors who will supply food and soft drinks for the snack bar, developing work schedules, ordering pool supplies, and making other preparations for opening day. Throughout the summer you will manage day-to-day pool operations with the help of an assistant manager. You will maintain all payroll records.

   Review the five functions of management, then rate your potential for success in each area. In which of these areas will you be most effective? Least effective?
2. Using the summer job situation described in exercise 1 and any reasonable assumptions about it, write at least five job-related plans. How can you be sure if they are well-written plans?

# CASES

## 5.1   Taking Chances at J&J

Jim Burke's first stay at Johnson & Johnson didn't last long. He had come to the company in 1953, but he left after just one year. "The company was centralized and stifling," Burke recalls, "and I was bored." In addition, he says, "we did not have a new-products division, and when I left I suggested we should have one."

It wasn't three weeks before Burke was back at J&J. His former bosses took him up on his suggestion and created a new-products division—and asked him to head it. Burke began developing a number of new ideas, but one morning he was summoned to the office of the chairman, General Robert Wood Johnson. The problem: One of Burke's first stabs at innovation, a children's chest rub, had failed dismally. Burke worried that his second stint at J&J might be as short as his first.

When Burke walked in, General Johnson asked, "Are you the one who just cost us all that money?" Burke nodded. The General said, "Well, I just want to congratulate you. If you are making mistakes, that means you are making decisions and taking risks. And we won't grow unless you take risks."

Some 30 years later [as the head of Johnson & Johnson], Burke, 63, is still spreading that word. "Any successful growth company is riddled with failures, and there's just not any other way to do it," he says. "We love to win, but we also have to lose in order to grow."

Burke believes that innovation can be nurtured through creative conflict. "I have tried to encourage that sort of conflict without fear of retribution," he says. "You end up with a lot more ideas." . . .

Long ago he forsook a conventional desk for a more expansive conference table, made of wood from the floor of a room at the Palace of Versailles. Says Burke: "I do most of my work with people, so I needed something they could all sit around."

Burke is careful not to dominate. To do so would contradict his fervent belief in decentralization. "Those of us in top management often say to each other that we had more fun running a J&J company than anything since," he says. "If you are having as much fun running a big corporation as you did running a piece of it, then you are probably interfering too much with the people who really make it happen."

### Questions

1. Which managerial roles are evident in this case? Explain your evidence.
2. Why was General Robert Wood Johnson a great manager?
3. How would you characterize Jim Burke's leadership style? Explain.

Source: From H. J. Steinbreder, "Taking Chances at J&J," *Fortune*, June 6, 1988, p. 60. Copyright 1988 *Fortune* Magazine. Reprinted by permission of the publisher.

## 5.2 McGuffey's Self-Managed Restaurants

It started with Employee Days. Keith Dunn, president of McGuffey's Restaurants Inc., had been reading books by Tom Peters and others encouraging companies to adopt an organizational structure in which workers are on top, with middle managers acting as facilitators. Last year Dunn decided to experiment by letting employees run the restaurants—planning the menu and drink specials, handling scheduling, choosing uniforms—for two days every six months.

Employee Days have boosted morale and have "been a wash, financially," says Dunn. Labor costs usually soar during the two days, but sales increase because employees tell friends and customers to stop by.

Last fall Dunn couldn't find anyone to manage the kitchen at his Asheville, N.C., restaurant. He decided to make *every day* Employee Day; he turned Asheville into a "self-managing store" for a three-month trial. It works just the same as Employee Days, except that employees are handed certain monthly financial goals. If they beat those goals, they receive half the difference in cash. "You don't dry your hands with a napkin anymore because you know how much these things are costing you," says Lori Emory, a bartender.

In October 1988 management handed dining-room employees two goals: keep labor costs below 6.5% (they came in at 6.48%), and hit sales of at least $221,000 (they reached nearly $222,000). As a result, employees earned a bonus of $184.70, which amounted to only about $8 per person. "They still wanted to stick with it," Dunn says. Bar employees earned about $30 apiece, based on meeting goals for labor costs and pouring costs. The kitchen crew earned $45 per person.

Aside from flying a Jolly Roger flag out front, employees have responded tamely. Servers voted to wear black T-shirts and pants instead of the McGuffey's uniform of white oxford shirt, tie, and green apron. The dining-room staff gave the lunch crew a raise from $2.01 an hour to $3.35 per hour to make that shift—when tips are lower—more attractive. The dining-room staff now has a say in hiring decisions. And they may get to help write an entirely new menu.

Instead of leaving right after their shifts, some employees are staying around to serve on committees, such as the one that is revamping the complicated Service Excellence recognition program.

Dunn has already eliminated two assistant kitchen manager positions, saving at least $3,000 a month. Soon, he hopes to eliminate at least two more, and he may try self-management at one of the other McGuffey's. The new system has changed employees "in motivational terms, in feeling like they are more involved," says Dunn. "It's not earth-shattering. But it's the next step so that someday—three to five years out—McGuffey's will be a truly employee-involved company."

## Questions

1. What leadership style did Keith Dunn rely on in this case? Explain.

2. How would you respond to a restaurant manager who made the following statement: "The typical restaurant employee just doesn't give a darn about the business. They have to be told every move to make."

Source: From J. Hyatt, "A Self-Managing Restaurant," p. 66. Reprinted with permission, *Inc.* Magazine, February 1989. Copyright © 1989 by Goldhirsh Group, Inc., 38 Commercial Wharf, Boston, MA 02110.

6

# Building an Effective Organization

After you have completed this chapter, you will be able to do the following:

*1.* Describe the elements of an organization.

*2.* Define organizational structure *and explain how that concept relates to an organization chart.*

*3.* Explain why division of labor is the key concept in modern organizations.

*4.* Define departmentalization and describe the four basic departmentalization models.

*5.* Draw a distinction between authority and power and identify the five bases of power.

*6.* Identify the different qualities of centralized and decentralized structures.

*7.* Contrast line-and-staff organizations with matrix organizations.

*8.* Define the terms informal organization *and* effective organization.

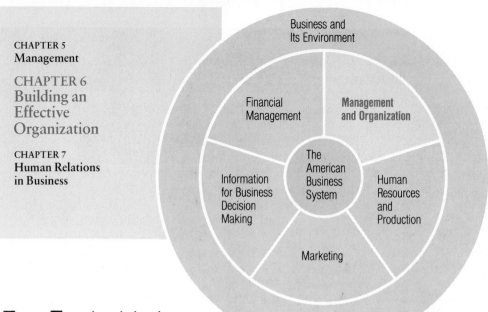

Metaphors help when contemplating something as enormous as General Motors, with its $123.6 billion a year in sales, a payroll (766,000) larger than the population of Washington, D.C., and operations in 122 U.S. cities and 34 foreign countries. So compare it to an archipelago with islands of excellence—a hot-selling line of trucks, a triumphant European car business. But there are lesser atolls, some mere outcroppings of coral. And then there is the placid lagoon: GM's worldwide bureaucracy of 110,000 white-collar workers.

A standout performance in the islands of excellence helped power an earnings surge in 1988 after a string of sorry years.

But it's too early to proclaim a renaissance. Chairman Roger Smith, 63, concedes that GM's North American car operations, the traditional heart of the business, were only marginally profitable last year; security analysts believe this part of GM lost money in 1987. Market share, which thudded from 44% to 36% in four years, was still eroding slowly in the early weeks of 1989. Smith's epochal reorganization of 1984 has left the leaders of the world's largest industrial corporation still wrestling with a fundamental question of organization. An enterprise of GM's heft can reap enormous economies of scale from centralized operations, but only decentralization can foster a fleet, flexible response to the market and a diversity of models for the full spectrum of consumer tastes. How GM resolves the dilemma will play a large role in determining its success.[1]

Organizational questions have been a giant headache for General Motors in recent years. Its huge, slow-moving bureaucracy with many layers has had to become more lean and flexible to keep pace with shifting consumer tastes and stiff foreign competition. Between 1985 and 1989, GM let go 43,000 white-collar employees, enough to populate a small city. GM's struggle to become a more adaptable organization is not unique. In fact, it is the norm because a virtual revolution in organizational structure is underway today.

Using such terms as *downsizing, turnaround,* and *retrenchment,* many American industrial mainstays went on strict diets during the 1980s. For instance, Eastman-Kodak cut 10 percent of its work force, AT&T eliminated 35,251 jobs, and Xerox cut its employment rolls by 20 percent.[2] Each of these organizations has reshaped itself into what one management consultant calls the organization of the 1990s: flat, lean, and flexible.[3] Looking farther down the road, tomorrow's organizations are likely to contain half the present levels of management. Some organizations will not even resemble the familiar pyramid shape. Instead, experts predict that "tomorrow's corporate structure will look like an hourglass—with the fewest managers in the middle."[4]

In this chapter, we explore the structure and effectiveness of modern organizations. This is an important area of study because organizations are the primary social tool for turning individual effort into collective achievements. Organizations allow people to do things otherwise impossible, such as conquering polio, putting a man on the moon, or mass-producing affordable personal computers.

# What Is an Organization?

An **organization** exists when two or more people coordinate their efforts, on an ongoing basis, to strive for a common purpose. Thus, two fishing buddies who buy a boat and try to make a living with a charter business qualify as an organization. Two occasional fishing companions, on the other hand, do not. Let us examine the important elements of this definition (see Table 6.1).

**organization** exists when two or more people coordinate their efforts, on an ongoing basis, to strive for a common purpose

## The Elements of an Organization

An organization is founded on people; it cannot exist without them. It has a purpose that directs the efforts of the people within it toward a goal, though the goals of individuals in the organization may be quite different.

*1. Describe the elements of an organization.*

TABLE 6.1    The Elements of an Organization

■ People

■ A purpose

■ Division of tasks

■ A system to coordinate tasks

■ A definable boundary separating those inside from those outside the organization

# Our approach to structuring an organization is a little bit different.

*Organizational structure  Traditionally organizations have followed a pyramid structure, with top management at the peak, radiating out to a broad base of supervisors and lower level managers. Today's organizations are following a flattening trend, however, cutting out excess layers of management in the middle. AIG insurance companies pride themselves on their organizations' own version of the traditional structure, in which they claim to offer decision-making responsibility at every level.*

An organization deliberately structures its members' activities by dividing tasks among them and developing a system to coordinate these tasks. Finally, an organization has a definable boundary that makes clear who is included and who is excluded from it.

## Organizational Structure

*2. Define organizational structure and explain how that concept relates to an organization chart.*

**organizational structure**  a pattern of task groupings, reporting relationships, and authority within an organization

Since the dawn of recorded history, humans have broken tasks down into subtasks to be performed in a structured fashion to accomplish an ultimate goal. Today's entrepreneur may be a sole proprietor employing no one, but he or she has to structure activities in order to succeed. When an entrepreneur considers taking on another person, the time has arrived for creating an **organizational structure**, a pattern of task groupings, reporting relationships, and authority within an organization.

Suppose that Jayne, a student, schedules a part-time job mowing lawns and doing garden work around her classes and social life. By doing large projects on weekends and small ones on weekdays, before or after classes,

**The organization** *The Australian band INXS demonstrates the essential elements of an organization in its coordination of individual efforts toward a common purpose. The band has been very successful in achieving its purpose: INXS has had a number of hits and its 1988 album* Kick *has gone triple platinum.*

Jayne has thus divided her work into parts to manage her time better. Let's assume that after she graduates, Jayne's Lawn & Garden Service has more work than she can handle. If she wants the business to grow, she will need a helper. Before deciding on what type of person to hire, Jayne begins to organize. She divides her work into four groups of tasks: mowing, edging and weeding, equipment maintenance, and clerical. While outlining these tasks, she considers whether and how to divide them with another person and how to relate to a new employee.

## The Organization Chart

Usually, people describe a business in terms of an **organization chart**, a diagram of the positions and reporting relationships within an organization. As Figure 6.1 reveals, an organization chart consists of boxes linked by lines. Each box represents a specific job or function. In a simple organization chart like Part B of Figure 6.1, the two boxes represent very broadly defined positions. A general assistant essentially does whatever the owner-operator assigns.

**organization chart** a diagram of the positions and reporting relationships within an organization

As an organization matures, the boxes in the chart come to represent increasingly specific tasks. Part C of Figure 6.1 pictures a mature organization, in this case a corporation. The top box normally represents the president, the firm's top manager. Below the president comes a second level, made up of vice presidents, each of whom has specific responsibilities. Note that each vice president has responsibility for an operational area that the owner-operator held in parts A and B. Again, note how much more specific the vice presidents' tasks are, even on this hypothetical chart, than those of the general assistant in Part B. We will have more to say about the definition of tasks when we discuss the division of labor.

The lines that connect the boxes in an organization chart represent reporting relationships, the responsibility of a person to report information to his or her superior and vice versa. Lines connect the boxes representing all the positions that report to a manager to the box representing the manager. The **chain of command** the vertical reporting and authority relationships in an organization chart.

An organization chart reveals an organization's skeletal structure much as an X-ray reveals human bone structure. A structure supports the organization's activities and identifies the connections among its parts. It is not the structure

**chain of command** the vertical reporting and authority relationships in an organization chart

FIGURE 6.1   Organization Charts for Three Organizations at Varying Levels of Maturity

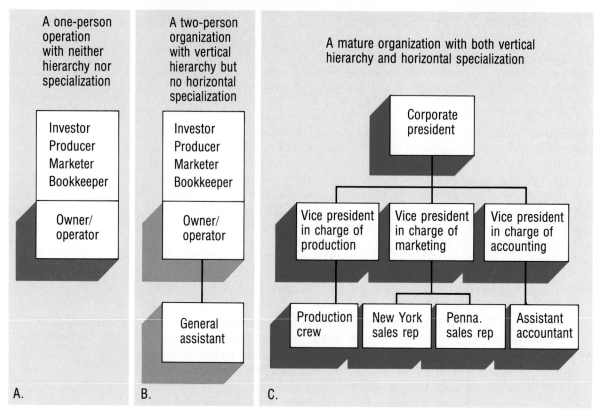

that does the work, however. Rather, the people represented by the positions on the chart give life to the organization through their work and enable it to meet its goals.

# The Principles of Organizational Design

The essence of structuring an organization lies in dividing labor into tasks to be performed and in regrouping these tasks to achieve coordinated action. The goal of balancing these competing needs underlies the design of all organizations.

## The Division of Labor

The concept of the division of labor is so much a part of our culture that it is difficult to realize that there is an alternative: everyone could try to do everything. Suppose that Jayne hires someone to do jobs on the east side of town for her Lawn & Garden Service while she works on the west. This arrangement would require two trucks, two complete sets of equipment, and two people with a full range of gardening skills. It is quite possible, though, that Jayne and her employee will have very different yet complementary skills. So an arrangement where everyone does everything would not seem to make the best use of Jayne's resources.

*3. Explain why division of labor is the key concept in modern organizations.*

In fact, one of the major contributions of the Industrial Revolution was the realization that dividing work into smaller and smaller tasks increased productivity and profits dramatically. As early as 1776, Adam Smith noted how much more efficiently pins could be manufactured if managers assigned workers to individual parts of the process instead of having one worker produce a pin from start to finish.[5] The division of labor into particular tasks and specialization by workers were keys to the development of modern management. Part C of Figure 6.1 illustrates specialization as it functions in a modern corporation.

In manufacturing operations or the construction industry, where tools and equipment are a major expense, the division or specialization of labor minimizes the outlay needed for equipment by limiting the number of people working with it (see Table 6.2). Also, specialization makes those who work with tools and machinery more competent because of constant practice. An assembly line is the ultimate application of the division of labor.

One disadvantage to the division of labor is that finding temporary substitutes for ill or vacationing employees can sometimes be difficult. Far more important, workers can become bored with what they are doing. This tendency has led companies to stimulate employee involvement through participative management programs. General Motors, for example, has saved huge sums of money by fighting boredom among hourly employees.

TABLE 6.2    Division of Labor: The Pluses and Minuses

| Advantages | Disadvantages |
|---|---|
| Efficient use of labor | Routine, repetitive jobs |
| Reduced training costs | Reduced job satisfaction |
| Increased standardization and output uniformity | Lower worker involvement and commitment |
| Increased expertise due to task repetition | Increased worker alienation |

Source: From Gregory Moorhead and Ricky W. Griffin, *Organizational Behavior,* 2nd ed., p. 226. Copyright 1989 Houghton Mifflin. Used by permission of the publisher.

Workers who were once expected to shut up and follow orders are now encouraged to use their brains. A team of hourly and salaried employees figured out how to reduce from 52 to 30 the number of parts in the rear floor of Cadillacs and big Oldsmobiles. That squashed the number of stamping dies from 93 to 38 and the number of presses used from 93 to 10, while trimming the weight from 117 pounds to 105. Annual savings: a dazzling $52 million.[6]

## Departmentalization

**departmentalization** the arranging of divided tasks into meaningful groups

*4. Define* departmentalization *and describe the four basic departmentalization models.*

**Departmentalization** is the arranging of divided tasks into meaningful groups. As Figure 6.2 shows, there are four basic departmentalization methods:

- Departmentalization by function
- Departmentalization by product or service
- Departmentalization by customer
- Departmentalization by location

*Functional Departments*    Departmentalization by function groups tasks according to the basic business functions with which they are associated. For example, a company might divide itself into marketing, finance, engineering, and production divisions. This arrangement allows people dealing with the same types of activities and issues to pool their skills and solve complex problems. Such was the case recently at Honeywell Bull, Inc., the French-American-Japanese computer manufacturing partnership. Jerome J. Meyer, the new corporation's president, inherited a loose and uncoordinated computer operation in the United States. Small computers were produced in Boston and large systems were manufactured in Phoenix, with virtually no cooperation between the two units. Separate hardware and software facilities also multiplied costs. Meyer tightened the company by reorganizing it along functional lines. Honeywell Bull now has more coordinated operations, with departments focusing on strategic planning, product development, manufacturing, and marketing.[7]

*Product/Service Departments*    Departmentalization by product or service groups tasks according to the product or service with which they are involved.

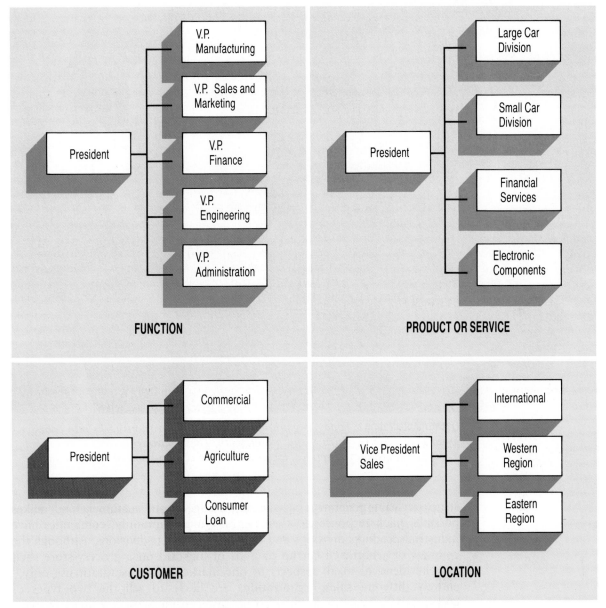

FIGURE 6.2  Four Departmentalization Models

General Motors, for example, traditionally organized its auto-manufacturing divisions according to brand prestige, with Chevrolet in one division, Cadillac in another. In 1984, GM regrouped its divisions into a large-car division and one for small cars. Those working on a particular product or service coordinate their efforts. Their focus on output often leads to greater efficiency through a sense of teamwork.

*Customer Departments*  Departmentalization by customer arranges employees according to the particular groups of customers they serve. This

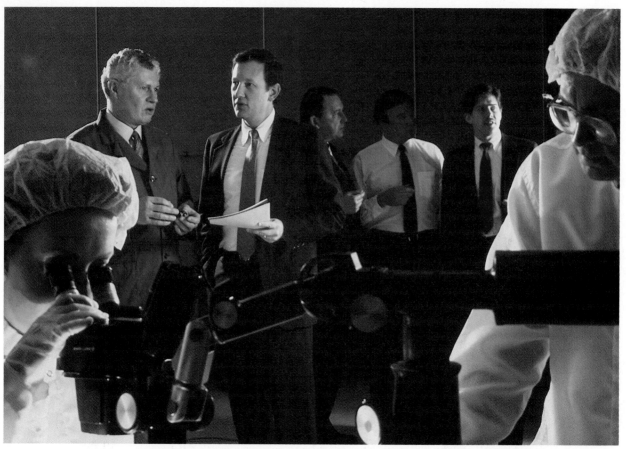

**Departmentalization**  *Today, organizations arrange their various tasks into cohesive groups for greater efficiency and productivity. The departments can be structured by function, product or service, location, or by a combination of these methods.*

structure helps generate extensive knowledge about customers and makes possible quick responses to their needs. Quite commonly, companies have industrial-products divisions and consumer-products divisions. Although the contents of a bottle of catsup or a jar of mustard on a grocery-store shelf may be identical in all respects to one marked "for restaurant use only," entirely different sales organizations are likely to sell the two types of containers. Full-service banks also organize, in part, by customer. A single bank might have a commercial division to work with businesses, a consumer division to handle personal loans, and an agricultural section to deal with farm loans.

*Location Departments*  Departmentalization by location arranges groups according to the physical location of people doing the tasks. A company will often divide its sales force into regional units to cover each potential market. In hospitals, the nursing staff is often divided into teams responsible for patient care on a single floor or ward. Grouping by location enhances communications considerably because the lines are short and direct. When a company tries to cover large segments of the country with local offices, though, administrative costs and the logistical efforts needed may rise.

*Multiple Departmentalization*   Multiple bases of departmentalization, as the term implies, is a mixture in one firm of two or more forms of departmentalization. Most large organizations, like the one shown in Figure 6.3, use at least two forms. Apple Computer, Inc., for example, is presently organized into four main units, representing a combination of functional and location departmentalization. The Apple Products unit is a functional department responsible for new product development. Apple USA, Apple Europe, and Apple Pacific are responsible for all operations in their respective geographic domains.[8] This form of multiple departmentalization gives Apple balanced

FIGURE 6.3   Multiple Bases of Departmentalization

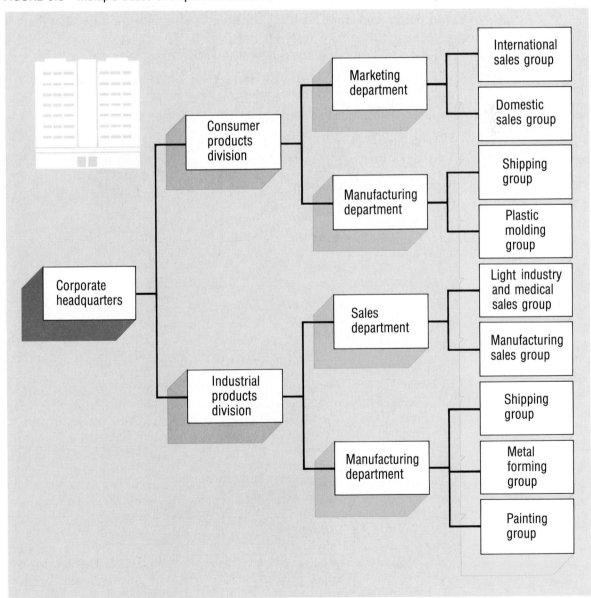

geographic marketing coverage even as it retains a specialized focus on new product development.

## Authority and Power

5. *Draw a distinction between authority and power and identify the five bases of power.*

**authority** the designated right to control the use of specified organizational resources

**power** the ability to control the actions of others

Once the basic structure of an organization is in place, as evidenced by an organization chart, things need to be set in motion. This is where authority and power come into play. **Authority** is the designated *right* to control the use of specified organizational resources. Authority may involve directing the actions of others, acting on the organization's behalf, or both.

**Power**, in contrast, is the *ability* to control the actions of others. As illustrated in Figure 6.4, effective managers operate in the area where authority and power overlap. This ideal situation is often not the case, however. A

FIGURE 6.4 Effective Managers Have Both Authority and Power

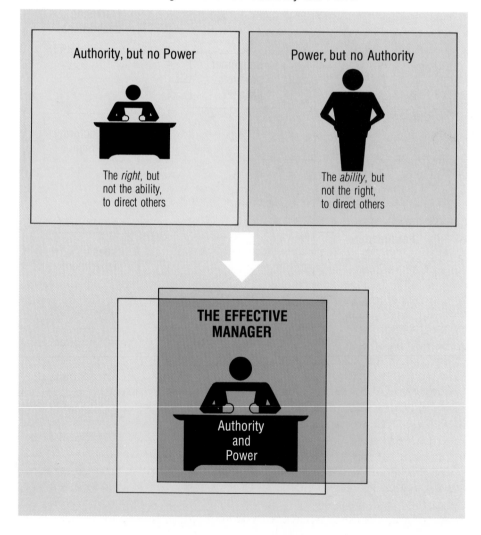

166

teacher with a misbehaving class is ineffective because he or she has authority but no power. In other words, the teacher has the *right* to quiet the students but not the *ability*. At the other extreme, an hourly employee who leads a sitdown strike to protest working conditions in a lumber mill has power but no authority. Because power is essential to getting things done in organizations, let us briefly examine different bases of power.

*Bases of Power*   Experts on the subject have identified five bases of power.[9] Each base involves a different approach to getting others to do what you want them to do.

- **Reward power:** People do things for you because you promise or grant them rewards.
- **Coercive power:** People do things for you because you threaten to punish them or actually punish them.
- **Legitimate power:** People do things for you because of your formal authority.
- **Expert power:** People do things for you because you share your knowledge or expertise with them.
- **Referent power:** People do things for you because they like you or in response to your *charisma*.

Not surprisingly, researchers have found that people respond negatively to coercive power but positively to the other four types of power.[10]

*Putting Power into Perspective*   Does the term *power* have a negative connotation for you? If so, you're not alone. Many people equate power with abuse of authority. This opinion is partly justified because power too often is abused by those in positions of authority. Nonetheless, from a managerial standpoint power can be a positive and constructive social force in organizations. Indeed, today's managers cannot hope to get anything accomplished with and through others if they have no power. Those who carry power have an obligation to understand it fully and use it in a socially responsible manner (see Experiencing Business).

## Policies and Procedures

An important means of achieving coordinated action is through *policies and procedures*. They are necessary features of almost any organization in which one person's or group's actions must mesh with another's. Policies and procedures may be as simple as deciding when a shop will be open or as complex as determining how an engineering and design unit will account for the time its employees spend on projects. Policies and procedures should make interaction easier, define the scope of an organization's activities, clarify responsibilities, and simplify and make routine procedures uniform.

For example, we will see in Chapter 8 that most companies have an employee performance-appraisal system on which the company bases raises, promotions, and other personnel decisions. Virtually all companies with such systems have detailed procedures covering how the appraisals are to be

**reward power**   power achieved by promising or granting rewards

**coercive power**   power achieved by threatening people with punishment or actually punishing them

**legitimate power**   power achieved because of formal authority

**expert power**   power achieved by sharing knowledge or expertise with others

**referent power**   power achieved through being liked or in response to your charisma

## EXPERIENCING BUSINESS

### SOME PRACTICAL TIPS ON MANAGING POWER

1. *Power is mercurial and fleeting.* It lasts only as long as the person who exercises it lasts in the job. Use it or lose it.
2. *Power must be earned.* It isn't conferred. You have to pursue it, ardently, by being innovative and productive, and by helping colleagues be the same.
3. *Power must advertise.* If you have a strong record of accomplishments, toot your own horn (politely, of course).
4. *Don't resent power plays by peers.* They're just trying to get ahead, too.
5. *Power isn't portable.* You can't transplant power from one job or one company to another. It's always a new ball game.
6. *Power is a tranquilizer.* Even if you don't care to scale the corporate heights, making yourself more powerful via relationships,

etc., can make your work flow more smoothly. And that will help you sleep better at night.

7. *Powerful people are discreet.* Tell people just enough about your personal life so that they know you're human.
8. *Powerful people are very good listeners.* That's how they got so powerful: They learned what they needed to know.
9. *The more power you have, the less work you have to do.* Because you've got all those allies, and know where to go instantly for the right facts and favors, your workload will get magically lighter. And you're bound to have more fun on the job.

Source: Randi Blaun, "Plugging into the Power Source," *Executive Female,* November/December 1988, p. 20.

performed and ultimately used. A key element of a performance-appraisal system is usually a standardized form used to evaluate all employees so that their work can be equitably compared.

## The Span of Management

**span of management**
determined by the number of people who report directly to a manager

The number of people who report directly to a manager is that manager's **span of management,** or span of control, as it is sometimes called. Spans of management vary in size. Narrow spans consist of from two to four subordinates; moderate, from five to nine; and wide, ten or more.

The real question, however, is not how many people report to a manager but how many people he or she can manage *effectively.* The rule of thumb is that the more defined and limited the subordinates' tasks are, the wider the span may be. Conversely, the more complex and dispersed the subordinates' work is, the narrower the span should be. Of course, unquantifiable factors such as the personalities of the individuals involved also play a role in determining an appropriate span of control.

# Centralization and Decentralization

Perhaps the most common means of coordinating action is **centralization**, an organizational arrangement in which all decisions are passed along to top management before being implemented. Harold Geneen, former head of ITT, probably put the argument for centralization best when he said:

> I don't believe in just ordering people to do things. You have to sort of grab an oar and row with them. My philosophy is to stay as close as possible to what's happening. If *I* can't solve something, how the hell can I expect my managers to?[11]

By contrast, **decentralization** is an arrangement in which decisions are pushed down the organization to the level where the functional expertise lies. At W. L. Gore & Associates, maker of waterproof Gore-Tex clothing, decisions are always made on the lowest possible level. In a centralized organization, the spans of management tend to be narrower than in decentralized organizations. Thus, centralized organizations with many layers and narrow spans of management are said to be *tall*; decentralized organizations with few layers and wide spans of management are termed *flat*. Figure 6.5 compares tall and flat organizations.

Because the same group makes all decisions in centralized organizations, they produce well-coordinated decisions, but the group may take a long time to reach a conclusion. It takes time to read and write reports, discuss issues, evaluate alternatives, and develop implementation strategies. The virtues of decentralization lie in its flexibility. Decisions that centralized organizations might agonize over tend to be made quickly at the level of the decentralized

**centralization** an organizational arrangement in which all decisions are passed along to top management before being implemented

*6. Identify the different qualities of centralized and decentralized structures.*

**decentralization** an arrangement in which decisions are pushed down the organization to the level where the functional expertise lies

FIGURE 6.5   Tall and Flat Organizations

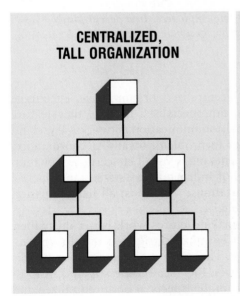

**CENTRALIZED, TALL ORGANIZATION**

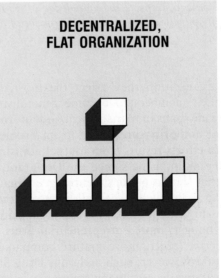

**DECENTRALIZED, FLAT ORGANIZATION**

**Decentralization**   *Avis CEO Joe Vittoria, talking here with bus driver Marcos Santiago, respects the knowledge of front-line employees. In a decentralized organization there is a flexible chain of authority where decisions are delegated to the level they most affect.*

organization they affect the most. Decentralized organizations encourage their members to become generalists, not specialists, because they feature wide spans of management and informal communication networks. The chain of authority often shifts from problem to problem. Ideally, a coordination of efforts results from mutual adjustments made by all concerned. Benjamin Franklin, as he signed the Declaration of Independence, stated the principle that should guide decentralized organizations: "We must all hang together, or assuredly we shall all hang separately."

In general, decentralized organizational structures work better in smaller, younger, more entrepreneurial firms. Centralized structures usually characterize larger, more mature companies. There are many exceptions to this rule, however, such as Longs Drug Stores, Inc. (see Business Issues). And to varying degrees many companies incorporate aspects of both centralized and decentralized organizations.

# DECENTRALIZATION IS A HEALTHY PRESCRIPTION FOR LONGS DRUG STORES

The links in a chain of stores are, by definition, supposed to be pretty much alike. They stock and sell the same items at more or less the same prices. Store managers, rarely well paid, take orders from headquarters and run their stores by the company handbook.

But centralized control and cookie-cutter merchandising aren't for everyone. Take $1.8 billion (fiscal 1988 revenues) Longs Drug Stores, Inc. With 234 stores in six western states, Walnut Creek, Calif.–based Longs consistently outperforms the retail drugstore industry by discarding the usual chain-store formula. . . .

"Our store managers can think and reason for themselves," says Chief Executive Officer Robert Long, 50. His father, Joseph (now 76 and chairman), cofounded the company with his brother Thomas 50 years ago. "They literally customize their stores to the customers they serve. We don't believe in cookie-cutter stores." . . .

Such decentralized decision making, of course, depends on good managers. To get them, Robert Long does more promoting from within than raiding competitors. Says William Combs, vice president–administration and treasurer: "You're turning the keys over to an individual to operate an $8 million store, and if they don't know what the heck they're doing, you're in big trouble."

Longs deals with its managers almost as if they were independent entrepreneurs and pays them accordingly. Including salary and bonus (a percentage of net profits), a Longs manager, by one outside estimate, can make up to $80,000 a year. "I like to think of myself as the chairman of an $8 million company," says Walnut Creek manager [Larry] Gherlone, 45, a manager for 12 years.

Clearly, Longs managers really do call the shots. The majority of their merchandise is purchased at the store level, either direct from manufacturers or from local wholesalers and jobbers. Advertising, too, is done locally. Managers choose which departments to have and how large to make them. One Longs manager noticed there wasn't a good greeting card shop in his area, for instance, so he expanded his and does nicely with cards and wrapping paper.

So what does headquarters do? Only 400 of the chain's 12,000 employees work at the head office. Headquarters offers legal support and helps the stores with invoicing, accounting, and purchasing fixtures and equipment. "The stores," says Combs, "should be concentrating on merchandising and their customers." There is a book of operational guidelines, but it contains general information on benefits, personnel, check cashing and the like.

Source: Excerpted from Ellen Paris, "Managers as Entrepreneurs," *Forbes*, October 31, 1988, pp. 62–63.

## Delegation

Overload is a typical problem for business managers today. They simply have too much to do and too little time in which to do it. Delegation can help ease their situation. **Delegation** involves the assignment of varying

**delegation** involves the assignment of varying degrees of decision-making authority to subordinates

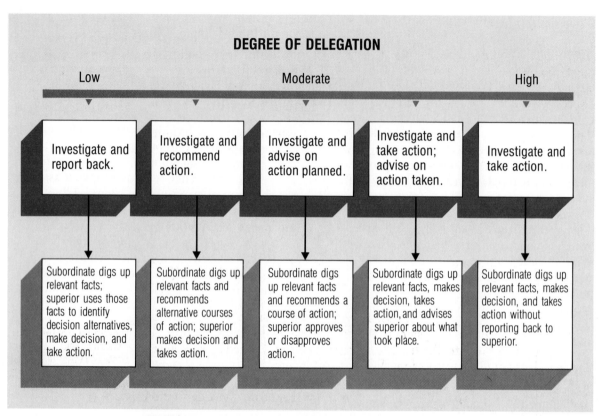

**DEGREE OF DELEGATION**

| Low | | Moderate | | High |
|---|---|---|---|---|

| Investigate and report back. | Investigate and recommend action. | Investigate and advise on action planned. | Investigate and take action; advise on action taken. | Investigate and take action. |
|---|---|---|---|---|
| Subordinate digs up relevant facts; superior uses those facts to identify decision alternatives, make decision, and take action. | Subordinate digs up relevant facts and recommends alternative courses of action; superior makes decision and takes action. | Subordinate digs up relevant facts and recommends a course of action; superior approves or disapproves action. | Subordinate digs up relevant facts, makes decision, takes action, and advises superior about what took place. | Subordinate digs up relevant facts, makes decision, and takes action without reporting back to superior. |

FIGURE 6.6   Degrees of Delegation

Source: From Marion E. Haynes, ''Delegation: There's More to It Than Letting Someone Else Do It!'' *Supervisory Management,* January 1980, pp. 9–15, as adapted in Robert Kreitner, *Management,* 4th ed. (Boston: Houghton Mifflin, 1989), p. 333. Used by permission of Marion E. Haynes and Houghton Mifflin Company.

degrees of decision-making authority to subordinates (see Figure 6.6). Delegation plays a key role in decentralization. There is a major catch, however. Namely, ultimate responsibility for accomplishing the job in question still rests in the hands of the superior. In effect, a manager who delegates is sharing (not permanently giving) a portion of his or her job with a subordinate.

Many managers are afraid to delegate because they are untrusting or afraid their subordinates will fail and make them look bad. But delegation to properly trained subordinates can improve job satisfaction and motivation as well as provide an excellent training ground for career advancement.

# Forms of Organizations

Organizations assume many structural forms, as evidenced by the variation in organizational charts. This section examines the four main ones. Table 6.3 shows the advantages and disadvantages of these organizational forms.

## Line Organization

The oldest and simplest organizational structure is the **line organization,** in which top management has total, direct control and each subordinate reports to a single supervisor.[12] The concept of the *line* evolved over time to refer to everyone involved in actually producing or distributing what a firm sells. The workers involved are called line employees, their managers line managers. Line managers have line authority, the right to make decisions that directly affect the firm's output. In a steel mill, for instance, the people who pour the molten steel are line employees, as are those who work on the shipping platform. The plant manager is a line manager.

**line organization** organizational structure in which top management has total, direct control and each subordinate reports to a single supervisor

## Functional Organization

Early in this century, Frederick Taylor introduced the concept of scientific management at Bethlehem Steel. Taylor believed that the division of labor concept applied not just to the work of laborers and steel handlers but also to the responsibilities of managers. Based on that insight, he devised the **functional organization,** a system in which the various functions involved in supervising a worker are divided into separate tasks performed by specialists. A salesperson might report to a marketing boss who concentrates on planning sales strategies, a training boss concerned with training and development, a compensation boss who handles salaries, and any other bosses the organization might see fit to include.

**functional organization** a system in which the various functions involved in supervising a worker are divided into separate tasks performed by specialists

The functional form of organization overcame some of the major deficiencies of the line form, namely, too many responsibilities for each supervisor and too many areas in which a supervisor was expected to demonstrate expertise. In short, Taylor introduced managerial specialization. Although the functional organization showed early promise, today's corporation is more likely to use the line-and-staff form described next. Nonetheless, Taylor's concept of management specialization has not just survived, it has flourished.

## Line-and-Staff Organization

In a modern organization, many employees and managers, called **staff,** are not directly involved in producing or distributing the goods and services it sells. Yet they are crucial to the firm's success because they supply support, information, and advice to line personnel. Typical staff positions include those relating to personnel, marketing, food services, and accounting. A staff position in one organization may of course be a line position in another. An accountant employed by Borden's would be a staff employee, but the same accountant working for a giant public accounting firm like Touche Ross would be a line employee. Determining whether a member of an organization is a line or a staff employee depends on the contribution of his or her job to the goods or services the organization sells.

**staff** employees and managers not directly involved in producing or distributing the goods and services an organization sells

*7. Contrast line-and-staff organizations with matrix organizations.*

TABLE 6.3　Advantages and Disadvantages of Organizational Forms

| Form | Advantages | Disadvantages |
|---|---|---|
| Line | Simple and easy to understand<br>Authority and responsibility clearly delegated<br>Speedy decision making<br>Direct communication | Top management bogged down in operational decisions<br>No specialization |
| Functional | Specialization<br>Line managers have time to manage<br>Limited area of authority and responsibility | Responsible to more than one manager<br>Possible overlapping authority and responsibility<br>Possible breakdown in discipline |
| Line and Staff | Responsible to only one manager<br>Availability of technical specialists | Possible conflict between line and staff<br>Staff advice may be seen as giving orders<br>Increases firm's overhead costs |
| Matrix | Flexibility<br>Specialization | Responsible to more than one manager<br>Possible conflicts between project and function managers<br>Difficulty in developing team spirit |

## *Matrix-Structured Organization*

**matrix organizational structure** one that combines horizontal and vertical lines of authority and also functional and product departments

An arrangement of information into a grid made up of rectangular boxes that can be read both horizontally and vertically is a matrix. A **matrix organizational structure** is one that combines horizontal and vertical lines of authority and also functional and product departments. This structure is sometimes referred to as *project management* because it brings together personnel drawn from different departments to focus on a given project. The matrix form probably first appeared in 1959 at the aerospace giant TRW.[13] It has since been used throughout high-tech industries.

The matrix form combines the common pool of technical specialists working together in the functional form with the special attention that only people assigned to one project can give to a specific product or problem. Project groups can be created by drawing on individuals permanently assigned to functional departments.

Companies often adopt a matrix structure when they come under extreme competitive pressures on significant projects and there is a limit to the resources they can devote to the project. Such situations require quick responses, something a matrix structure can provide. Project coordination in a matrix structure is better because instead of several functional managers there is only one project leader, who reports to the projects manager. Also, communication tends to be better because those assigned to a project can discuss problems across functional lines as well as with others assigned to their home department. Members of a project team can be reassigned when it ends or as the need arises. Giants like General Motors, Monsanto, and the Chase Manhattan Bank are using this form of organization in selected areas of their companies.

Matrix structures have their faults, however. The most serious is the dual reporting problem. Each employee has two supervisors: the supervisor in the functional department—say, accounting or engineering—and the project leader. Cooperation and communication between the two supervisors are the keys to keeping employees happy in matrix structures. Project managers in this structure sometimes find that the dual reporting problem limits their control over their teams. They must negotiate, persuade, and exchange favors with functional managers to get what they need because they lack line authority. Firms like Texas Instruments and Citibank have adopted matrix organization forms but then abandoned them, often because of their complexity.

# The Informal Organization

Boxes and lines on a formal organization chart do not tell the whole story. Beneath the surface, so to speak, is an entirely different organization. This second organization can seriously hamper a manager who tries to pretend it does not exist, and it is responsible for much of the resistance to change that managers encounter when implementing new programs or techniques. This behind-the-scenes network is called the **informal organization** because it is based on voluntary personal relationships rather than on formal authority.

**informal organization**
a behind-the-scenes network based on voluntary personal relationships rather than on formal authority

## Friendship Groups

The informal organization is made up of friendship groups that cut across hierarchical distinctions and technical specialties. For example, a research engineer may have lunch every day with her best friend, the head of the accounting department, and a couple of other friends who are recruiters for the firm. Suppose the engineer mentions one day at lunch that she has a cousin who is getting his business degree and needs a job. Between the accounting executive and the two recruiters at the lunch table, something positive is likely to happen for the young job hunter. Belonging to this sort of informal network within the organization greatly enhances an individual employee's reward, expert, and referent power. Accordingly, managers need to build support in the informal organization when trying to introduce changes such as a new computer system.

*8. Define the terms informal organization and effective organization.*

**Grapevine communication** *The grapevine is the informal, unofficial communication network within an organization. Information traveling along the company grapevine is often accurate, though managers are urged to monior it in order to prevent seriously inaccurate rumors from getting passed along.*

## The Grapevine

**grapevine** the informal, unofficial communication network within an organization

Nothing moves information faster than the **grapevine**, the informal, unofficial communication network within an organization. Contrary to popular belief, the grapevine tends to be quite accurate. In fact, experts say the grapevine is accurate about 75 percent of the time.[14] The most important thing for managers to keep in mind when dealing with the grapevine is that they cannot kill it. The grapevine may be an invisible part of organizational life, but it is nonetheless permanent. Managers are advised to monitor grapevine communication quietly through trusted grapevine participants and take steps to correct any seriously misleading information that occasionally comes along. A health-care executive has been quoted as saying, "Sure, I use the grapevine. Why not? The employees sure use it. It's fast, reaches everyone, and employees believe it—no matter how preposterous. I limit its use, though."[15] Some companies use rumor-control hot lines to correct misleading grapevine communication.

# Organizational Effectiveness:
# A Perspective

As both foreign and domestic competitive pressures intensify for American businesses, increased attention has been focused on organizational effectiveness. There is a growing reluctance to equate short-term profitability with effectiveness. It is possible for a company to show a quarterly profit through creative accounting techniques while at the same time being socially irresponsible and short-sighted by cutting new product research. From a broad perspective, a company that engages in these practices does not deserve to

**Effective organizations**   *CEO Stanley Gault has brought Rubbermaid, Inc. to second place on* Fortune's *annual list of "America's most admired corporations" for 1989.* Fortune *evaluated companies on eight effectiveness criteria including quality of product, innovativeness, and quality of management.*

**effective organization**
an organization that satisfies multiple effectiveness criteria ranging from profitability to social responsibility

be called effective. **Effective organizations** are those that satisfy *multiple criteria,* ranging from profitability to social responsibility. An instructive list of effectiveness criteria can be found in *Fortune*'s annual "Most Admired Corporations" survey.

## Eight Effectiveness Criteria

According to the editors of *Fortune,* there are eight attributes of corporate reputation:

1. Innovativeness
2. Value as long-term investment
3. Community and environmental responsibility
4. Ability to attract, develop, and keep talented people
5. Financial soundness
6. Use of corporate assets
7. Quality of management
8. Quality of products or services[16]

TABLE 6.4   America's Most Effective Companies: 1989

| Rank | Company | Score |
|------|---------|-------|
| 1 | Merck<br>Pharmaceuticals | 8.87 |
| 2 | Rubbermaid<br>Rubber products | 8.41 |
| 3 | 3M<br>Scientific/photographic equip. | 8.18 |
| 4 | Philip Morris<br>Tobacco | 8.15 |
| 5 | Wal-Mart Stores<br>Retailing | 8.12 |
| 6 | Exxon<br>Petroleum refining | 8.05 |
| 7 | PepsiCo<br>Beverages | 8.04 |
| 8 | Boeing<br>Aerospace | 8.03 |
| 9 | Herman Miller<br>Furniture | 7.99 |
| 10 | Shell Oil<br>Petroleum refining | 7.96 |

Source: From Carol Davenport, "America's Most Admired Corporations," *Fortune,* January 30, 1989, p. 69. Copyright 1989 *Fortune* Magazine. Reprinted by permission of the publisher.

Taken together, these attributes provide an excellent framework for assessing an organization's effectiveness. Thus, a truly effective business is not a one-dimensional quarterly profit machine. In addition to being profitable it also is a developer of ideas and people and a good corporate citizen.

## America's Most Admired and Effective Corporations

For its 1989 rankings, *Fortune* surveyed nearly 8,000 corporate directors, top executives, and financial analysts. A total of 305 American corporations representing 32 different industries were ranked from 0 (poor) to 10 (excellent) on each of the eight effectiveness criteria. For the third year in a row, Merck, the giant pharmaceutical company, took top honors (see Table 6.4). In fact, Merck (rhymes with "perk") ranked number one in six of the categories (1, 2, 4, 6, 7, and 8). Johnson & Johnson topped the list in community and environmental responsibility. Exxon was viewed as having the greatest financial soundness.

# CHAPTER HIGHLIGHTS

*1.* Describe the elements of an organization.

The elements that characterize an organization are its people, its purpose, division of tasks, a coordinating system, and a definable boundary that divides members from nonmembers.

*2.* Define organizational structure *and explain how that concept relates to an organization chart.*

An *organizational structure* is a pattern of task groupings, reporting relationships, and authority in an organization. An organization chart provides a graphic representation of how an organization is structured. Positions at the top of the chart have more formal authority than those lower on the chart. The lines joining boxes on an organization chart indicate reporting relationships and the chain of command.

*3.* Explain why division of labor is the key concept in modern organizations.

Division of labor allows complex organizations to function by breaking tasks down into smaller segments that can be handled by one person or by members of a single department. It allows

individuals to become expert in particular areas and also cuts down on the amount of equipment necessary to do a job. Once tasks grow beyond what one person can handle, applying the concepts of specialization and division of labor usually improves productivity more than it raises costs.

*4.* Define departmentalization *and describe the four basic departmentalization models.*

*Departmentalization* is the arranging of divided tasks into meaningful groups. Departments are generally organized by function, by product or service, by customer, or by location. In addition, many organizations use more than one basis for departmentalization.

*5.* Draw a distinction between authority and power and identify the five bases of power.

Authority is the *right* to control organizational resources, whereas power is the demonstrated *ability* to get others to do things. Authority and power may or may not overlap. Five bases of power are reward, coercive, legitimate, expert, and referent.

**6.** *Identify the different qualities of centralized and decentralized structures.*

In a *centralized organization,* important decisions are passed along to the top of the management hierarchy. Top executives maintain strict control of subordinates as well as of any divisions or other businesses owned or managed by the organization. There are generally many layers of organization and narrow spans of management. *Decentralized organizations* are characterized by just the opposite traits. Decisions are generally made as far down the organization as possible, there tend to be few layers of organization, managers have broad spans of management, and there tends to be a high degree of delegation.

**7.** *Contrast line-and-staff organizations with matrix organizations.*

In a *line-and-staff organization,* line managers have line authority, the right to make decisions that directly affect the firm's output. Staff managers, on the other hand, have specialized expertise. They advise and support the functions of many line managers and employees, but they do not have direct authority over or control of the organization's output. For example, members of the training staff may put together company manuals and instruction brochures that explain how certain jobs are to be performed. Members of the marketing department may develop an organization advertising campaign. But none of the staff in these departments would have the authority to decide how a product should be manufactured or what production equipment should be installed. They might advise line managers, but they could not ordinarily insist that their advice be followed.

In a *matrix organization,* tasks or projects are assigned to members of different departments who work together as a team or committee. In that way, expertise in many different areas—engineering, financial management, and marketing, for example—is available to the group as a whole. A major difference between the two forms of organization is that, in a line-and-staff organization, an employee reports to a single boss. In a matrix organization an employee normally reports to both a functional boss and a project or team leader.

**8.** *Define the terms* informal organization *and* effective organization.

The *informal organization* is a behind-the-scenes collection of friendship groups based on voluntary personal relationships rather than on formal authority. An *effective organization* satisfies multiple criteria, ranging from profitability to social responsibility.

## KEY TERMS

| | | | |
|---|---|---|---|
| Organization | Power | Span of management | Staff |
| Organizational structure | Reward power | Centralization | Matrix organizational |
| Organization chart | Coercive power | Decentralization | structure |
| Chain of command | Legitimate power | Delegation | Informal organization |
| Departmentalization | Expert power | Line organization | Grapevine |
| Authority | Referent power | Functional organization | Effective organization |

## REVIEW QUESTIONS

1. What is the difference between a large group of people in a movie theater and an organization?

2. What is the practical value of an organization chart? How do charts vary from organization to organization?

3. Which type of departmentalization is the best? Explain your reasoning.
4. What sort of power do you presently have? How can you tell?
5. What difference would it make if the span of management were too large or too small?
6. Would you rather work in a centralized or decentralized organization? Explain.
7. If a manager can delegate authority, why can't he or she delegate responsibility to others?
8. Would you rather have a line or staff job? Explain.
9. Why is it useless for a manager to try to kill the grapevine?
10. What makes a business effective?

# APPLICATION EXERCISES

1. Draw an organization chart for the college or university you are currently attending. Include all major administrative positions and departments. As you prepare the chart, be sure to distinguish between line and staff positions.
2. Assume that you are the chief administrator of a medium-sized hospital. In recent months you have noticed that the informal organization has become very active. You have heard rumors that have greatly exaggerated the issues and problems in the hospital. What steps could you take to make the informal organization less active?

# CASES

## 6.1 A Study in Contrasts at General Motors

GM controlled more than half the U.S. auto market . . . [during the 1960s], and the talk around Detroit was that the government might try to dismantle it under the antitrust laws. To make the corporation more efficient—and, some say, harder to break up—the company stripped the five car divisions of their factories and handed them over to a new, centralized manufacturing organization called the General Motors Assembly Division (GMAD). . . .

By the early 1980s, the car divisions had shriveled into little more than marketing organizations. Instead of developing unique cars for Buick customers, Buick engineers spent their time devising minor alterations in trim and handling qualities on a platform also used by Chevrolet. GMAD, meanwhile, had grown into a monster answerable at times only to GM's president. Along with Fisher Body, a corporatewide organization that produced body parts, it squabbled with the divisions over how the cars would be built. Since responsibility was divided, vehicle quality suffered. If a rattle developed in a new Citation, Chevy would blame GMAD for building the car badly while GMAD would berate the platform team for an incompetent design.

[Chairman Roger] Smith's grand reorganization was an effort to end the infighting and restore discipline. He scrapped GMAD and Fisher Body and divided the car business into two supergroups. One included Chevrolet, Pontiac, and the Canadian factories; the other comprised Buick, Oldsmobile, and Cadillac. The idea was to make each group accountable for the quality, performance, and profitability of its products. Few doubt that a change in this direction was necessary, but the reorganization caused wholesale confusion, and GM is still trying to get things right. . . .

The two supergroups set out on strikingly different paths. Buick-Oldsmobile-Cadillac, as it is known, has headed partway back to the decentralized pre-1960s era. It set up three subgroups that roughly correspond to the old Buick, Olds, and Cadillac organizations. Instead of sitting in a central office, Buick engineers work close to the assembly line in Flint, Michigan, striving to make Buicks ride and handle like Buicks.

Chevrolet-Pontiac-Canada, by contrast, emerged as a highly centralized organization—"a perfect image of the corporation," as [one observer] puts it—and on balance it seems to work less well. With engineers headquartered in a Detroit suburb supervising plants that stretch from Quebec to California, the group has further eroded divisional distinctiveness and complicated decision-making.

## Questions

1. What steps could Chairman Roger Smith have taken to ensure a smoother reorganization?
2. Why do you suppose the more decentralized Buick-Oldsmobile-Cadillac group apparently is outperforming the Chevrolet-Pontiac-Canada group?

Source: From Alex Taylor III, "The Tasks Facing General Motors," *Fortune*, March 13, 1989, pp. 56, 58. Copyright 1989 *Fortune* Magazine. Reprinted by permission of the publisher.

## 6.2 The Importance of Organization

On January 28, 1986, the space shuttle Challenger exploded soon after takeoff from Kennedy Space Center, killing its crew of seven. An investigation of the disaster determined that the immediate cause was the cold-weather failure of synthetic rubber O-rings, used to seal the sections of Challenger's solid-fuel booster rocket. It seems likely that a contributing cause was management failure within the National Aeronautics and Space Administration (NASA). The investigating committee recommended that astronauts become more involved in managing the shuttle program, especially where safety was involved.

NASA, the organization that administers the U.S. space flight program, has, in recent years, been beset by budget cuts and personnel reductions; by the problem of trying to reach overly ambitious space-flight goals; by occasional lack of cooperation and even jealousy among its several components (such as the Marshall, Kennedy, and Johnson Space Flight Centers); by the increasing isolation of NASA's leaders in Washington, D.C.; and by the temporary loss of its top executive, who was on a leave of absence. Probably no one of these managerial problems could have caused a breakdown of NASA's carefully structured system for handling last-minute flight decisions. But together they did.

Of late, NASA's top executives have had to spend much of their time lobbying Congress for funds. This has allowed them less time to keep tabs on and control their organization. NASA's component organizations, each concerned with its own part of the shuttle operation and its own budget and independence, seem to have found that situation agreeable. Staff cuts have helped to reduce the upward flow of information, weakening communication beween lower and higher levels of management.

Six months before the Challenger launch, NASA executives were warned that the O-rings posed a safety threat. They were also told that the rings posed a budget threat; it would cost perhaps $350 million to eliminate the problem. Lack of funding and personnel seems to have led officials to consider the O-rings as a long-term problem that could not be solved immediately. They may have felt reasonably safe in doing so, since the rings had already been given a special safety waiver. Waivers are required for all parts that do not meet NASA's fail-safe specification. However, the O-ring waiver was actually issued before the safety problem was discovered.

The Challenger flight had already been delayed twice due to cold weather. Just before the January 28 launch, Morton Thiokol's senior engineer at the launch site argued strongly for another delay. (Morton Thiokol is the firm that manufactured the booster rocket.) The engineer, Alan McDonald, refused to certify that the rocket was ready and safe for flight.

Some insiders believe that McDonald's argument and refusal should have been communicated to top NASA executives. Traditionally, the top administrator or his deputy is at every launch; however, for this launch the top executive was on leave and his deputy was in Washington. Instead, personnel from Marshall Space Center (which is responsible for NASA rocketry) communicated with executives at Morton Thiokol. They overrode McDonald, and the launch went ahead. Managers from Marshall maintain that a routine technical matter was involved, and that it was their responsibility.

Ironically, two of NASA's top executives were at the launch site. Both were plugged into a communications network that allows all personnel to hear what takes place during the countdown, and both had the authority to delay the launch. But the argument never came through on the network, and no one brought it to their attention.

## Questions

1. How did each of NASA's problems contribute to the "organizational breakdown" that permitted the Challenger launch? How would you characterize that breakdown?
2. What type of organizational structure would minimize or eliminate the chance of such a breakdown? Why?

For more information see *Newsweek*, June 23, 1986, pp. 66–68; *Fortune*, May 12, 1986, pp. 26–32; and *The Wall Street Journal*, March 18, 1986, p. 5.

# 7 Human Relations in Business

## LEARNING OBJECTIVES

*After you have completed this chapter, you will be able to do the following:*

*1. Define human relations.*

*2. Explain what motivation is and describe the origins of the modern approach to it.*

*3. Describe Abraham Maslow's hierarchy of needs.*

*4. Describe Frederick Herzberg's Motivation-Maintenance Model.*

*5. Explain the differences between Douglas McGregor's Theory X and Theory Y assumptions about what motivates people.*

*6. Describe some important internal and external motivators in the workplace.*

*7. Describe strategies for involving employees in decision making.*

*8. Identify four types of alternative work patterns in use today and describe their prospects.*

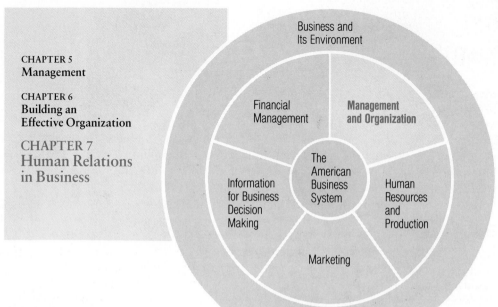

Business and
Its Environment

Financial
Management

Management
and Organization

Information
for Business
Decision
Making

The
American
Business
System

Human
Resources
and
Production

Marketing

One of the traditions at Publix Super Markets, Inc., a Florida-based company with over 300 stores, is the opening-night banquet. The banquet is held before the opening of each new supermarket and gives new employees the opportunity to meet executives of the company. The cover of the banquet program is adorned with a slogan that seems like an accurate description of this unique company: "Where working is a pleasure."

For the banquet guests, this event serves as an exciting orientation to one of America's most successful employee-owned companies. Throughout the evening corporate executives and managers from various stores describe the career opportunities offered by the company. They describe people who started as grocery baggers and now manage a Publix Supermarket.[1]

Daniel Yankelovich, author and noted analyst of social trends, said after interviewing scores of Publix employees: "The people who work there are the most highly motivated people I have ever seen in a large organization." He reported that the most common single comment he heard from Publix employees was that they felt treated "like a person, not like a number."[2]

Publix is not the only American business to build a family atmosphere among its employees. Some, like Publix, have had the same philosophy since their founding. Others, from steel companies to hotels, have concluded that attention to the human side of their enterprises may lead to solutions to the contemporary challenges discussed in Chapters 1 and 2.

# The Nature of Human Relations in Business

Most business organizations that survive for a long period maintain a balance between a concern for success (growth or profit) and regard for their people. Modern businesses require the interaction of large numbers of individuals. Often, what appear to be policy, procedural, and organizational problems are really disguised conflicts between individuals. Better work relationships in contemporary businesses thus begin with an understanding of how people interact.

In its broadest sense, **human relations** covers all the types of interactions among people: conflicts, cooperative efforts, and group relationships.[3] A human is a complex being. Each person is a unique mixture of emotional stability, physical fitness, mental alertness, self-image, morals, and values orientation (see Experiencing Business). Some employers may wish that they could hire just the brain or the brawn of their workers, but they have no choice except to hire the entire person.[4] If the whole person can be improved, the firm will benefit. Thus, an increased understanding of human relations will help identify ways to improve employee and organizational effectiveness.

**human relations** refers to all the types of interaction among people: conflicts, cooperative efforts, and group relationships

*1. Define human relations.*

## Morale

Human relations does not begin and end at the company's door. What goes on outside the workplace affects what happens inside it. Good human relations in an organization usually means high **morale,** a state of psychological well-being based on such factors as a sense of organizational purpose and confidence in the future. Morale is the enthusiasm that workers display toward their jobs, their fellow employees, and their employers.

**morale** a state of psychological well-being based on such factors as a sense of organizational purpose and confidence in the future

Many of America's most successful companies have discovered that high morale is good for the "bottom line." One such company is Federal Express Corporation, the nation's leading provider of overnight, door-to-door delivery of packages and letters. This is a company that adheres to a no-layoff policy, pays good wages, offers profit sharing, and maintains excellent communication with employees. One way Federal Express keeps the lines of communication open is to schedule brown bag lunches at which top company officials meet with employees during lunch breaks. Fred Smith, founder and chairman of Federal Express, says, "We are interested in making this a good place to work, where people are dealt with as human beings rather than as some number."[5] We can see that top executives at Federal Express and Publix share a common view of how employees should be treated.

The emotional and physical health of individuals are closely linked. Quality of work, whether at a desk or on a plant floor, often relates directly to an individual's diet and physical fitness. The menus in the cafeterias of the Northwestern Mutual Life Insurance Company report how many calories each item contains.[6] The Adolph Coors Company invested $600,000 in a "wellness center," a health education and group exercise center in a former

## WHAT DO YOU WANT FROM A JOB?

What do employees want most from their jobs? Is it good pay? Job security? Interesting work? Although most people want a job that offers a combination of several morale-building factors, they rank some factors higher than others. What do you want most from a job? Consider the following list of factors and rank them from highest to lowest priority. Studies have been done to see how managers think their employees would rate these factors, and how employees themselves actually do rate these factors. When you have finished your own ranking, check it against the rank-ings of the managers and employees in the study at the back of the book. How do the three differ? How are they similar?

- Help with personal problems
- Promotion and growth
- Interesting work
- Good pay
- Full appreciation of work done
- Involvement
- Job security
- Good working conditions
- Loyalty to employees

supermarket near its headquarters.[7] The Stride-Rite Corporation sought to improve the working environment by restricting smoking in its headquarters and four manufacturing plants.[8]

# Motivating Workers

**motivation** the factors that cause people to behave in a certain way

*2. Explain what motivation is and describe the origins of the modern approach to it.*

One of the most important dimensions of effective human relations within an organization is **motivation**, the factors that cause people to behave in a certain way.[9] Put another way, motivation is what drives a person to accomplish a certain goal. In a work setting, motivation makes people want to work, but precisely what is it that motivates people? No question about human behavior is asked more often and is more difficult—or more important—to answer. For generations, managers have believed people to be primarily motivated by money. However, as the playwright Neil Simon has pointed out, "Money brings some happiness. But, after a certain point, it just brings more money."[10] Today, following sixty years of research, a growing number of organizations have come to assume that employee motivation centers on factors besides money.

## The Hawthorne Studies

Researchers became more aware of the complex nature of motivation as a result of studies conducted in the 1920s. A Harvard University research team headed by Elton Mayo initiated a series of experiments to determine

Meridian goes Caribbean *Harvey Kinzelberg, chairman of Meridian Group, a computer-leasing firm, boosts executive employees' morale by sponsoring a bi-annual Caribbean scuba and brainstorming excursion. Attention to the emotional and physical well-being of employees means high morale, and high morale improves employee and organizational effectiveness.*

relationships between changes in physical working conditions and employee productivity, which may be considered "the level of output of goods and services achieved by the resources of an organization"[11] Their research took place at Western Electric's Hawthorne plant outside Chicago, so these landmark reports are now known simply as the **Hawthorne studies.**

In one experiment, Mayo and his colleagues selected two groups of employees who did similar work under like conditions. The team increased the lighting for one group but kept it constant for the other. Productivity increased with the increase in lighting. To verify their results, the researchers began to dim the lights for the group being studied. To their surprise, productivity actually increased. Indeed, the workers reached one of their highest output levels when the light was quite dim. Some factor besides lighting was plainly influencing productivity.

When Mayo and his team began interviewing the employees, they quickly made two important discoveries. First, the attention focused on the test group made them feel important and appreciated. For the first time, they had gotten

**Hawthorne studies**
experiments conducted in the 1920s to determine relationships between changes in physical working conditions and employee productivity

feedback on their job performance. Second, the way the experiments had been conducted had allowed the employees greater freedom from supervisory control. These circumstances had boosted their morale and motivation, so their productivity rose.

The Hawthorne studies did not immediately convince managers that they should change their approach to motivating employees. Inevitably, the discovery that human factors, such as the need to be involved and the desire for feedback, affect productivity had a major impact. Managers began to consider motivation tools other than money and job security. Even more important, the Hawthorne studies led to an awareness of the average worker as a complex combination of needs, values, and attitudes. This recognition brought about the birth of the human-relations movement, whose principal assumption is that employees who are satisfied with their work are motivated to perform better than employees whose needs are unsatisfied.[12]

Today, responses to the Hawthorne studies range from highly critical to supportive. Critics often cite flawed methodology and statistical inaccuracies as weaknesses of this research.[13] Nevertheless, the Hawthorne studies can be credited with turning our attention to a wider range of employee motivation strategies.

# The Nature of Needs

**need** something that disturbs our satisfied physical or psychological state

Motivation is, of course, a concept not limited to understanding the productivity of the workplace. Rather, it is a term used to describe the force that prompts us to move toward the satisfaction of a **need**, something that disturbs our satisfied physical or psychological state.

After studying the relationship between needs and motivation, the psychologist Abraham H. Maslow concluded that

- People have a number of different needs that each require some measure of satisfaction.
- Only those needs that have not been substantially satisfied influence behavior. A satisfied need does not motivate.
- People tend to satisfy their basic human needs in a specific order, which Maslow called their **hierarchy of needs**.

**hierarchy of needs** the order in which people tend to satisfy their basic human needs

As Figure 7.1 reveals, Maslow's hierarchy of needs looks like a pyramid. The following sections examine the blocks from which this pyramid is built.[14]

*3. Describe Abraham Maslow's hierarchy of needs.*

## *Physiological Needs*

**physiological needs** food, clothing, sleep, and shelter; the "survival" needs

Abraham Maslow termed food, clothing, sleep, and shelter—the basic **physiological needs**—the "survival" or "lower order" needs. The satisfaction of these physiological needs, what a human requires biologically to survive and function, comes first. In most work environments, basic needs rarely dominate. During periods of economic stress, however, such as the prolonged

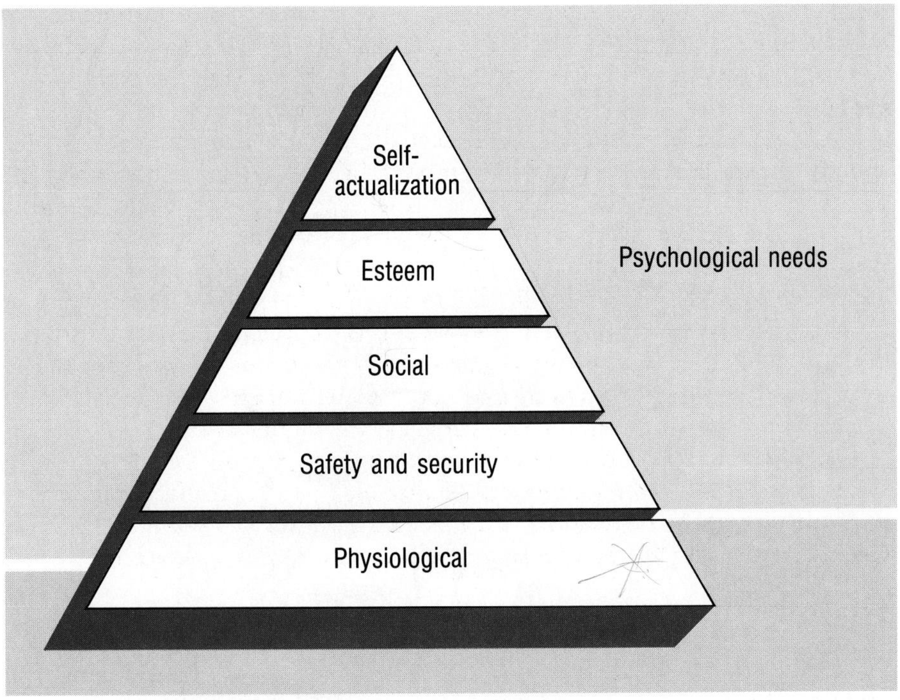

FIGURE 7.1 Abraham Maslow's Hierarchy of Needs

recession of 1977–1985 in the western Pennsylvania steel industry, people take and keep any jobs they can find simply to put food on their tables.

## Psychological Needs

Sometimes called **secondary needs**, the needs of the mind—**psychological needs**—are distinct from the needs of the body. Maslow believed that psychological needs, the pyramid's top layers, were of a higher order than physiological ones.

**pyschological (secondary) needs**
the needs of the mind

*Safety and Security*   The need for safety and security reflects a desire for order and predictability. Employees feel more secure when they know that they will not lose their jobs, they will be able to provide for their families, and they will have sufficient resources after retirement to be able to enjoy their lives. Organizations satisfy these needs, at least partly, by offering employees pension, profit sharing, and insurance programs. A few companies, like Johnson & Johnson Products, Inc., maintain a "no layoff" policy similar to that of Federal Express.

A company can satisfy its employees' need for security by emphasizing fairness. Federal Express has what may be the nation's most fully developed system for handling employee grievances. Its Guaranteed Fair Treatment (GFT) procedure gives employees a series of steps to follow when they have conflicts with their supervisor.[15]

**Safety and security**  *Chairman Max DePree of Herman Miller, Inc. is directly accessible to employees with serious grievances. By investigating complaints and correcting injustices, a company helps satisfy its employees' needs for a sense of security.*

*Social*  Social needs center on our desire for affection and approval from others. They include our wish for a sense of belonging to and identification with a group. To some extent, we satisfy our social needs by joining professional associations, religious groups, sports teams, or social clubs. The other members presumably share our interests, values, and goals.

For many, jobs satisfy their social needs, and wise employers address that need. Mary Kay Cosmetics, Inc., in Dallas, takes several steps to be sure that its home office and manufacturing employees feel themselves part of the family. Within a month after being hired, employees meet with company chairperson Mary Kay Ash. On their birthdays, they receive a voucher for dinner for two. Everyone at Mary Kay eats in the same cafeteria. No titles appear on office doors, helping foster the attitude that there are no lower echelons at Mary Kay.[16]

**esteem**  how a person is regarded by others and by himself or herself

*Esteem*  The next-to-the-top level of Maslow's hierarchy of needs is **esteem**, how a person is regarded by others and by himself or herself. Each of us needs to feel worthy in the eyes of others. From the satisfaction of this need, we gain a sense of competence, personal worth, and adequacy.

As Maslow uses the word, esteem includes self-esteem, how a person feels about himself or herself. The need for self-esteem cannot be overstated. The psychologist Arthur Witkin has written, "Perhaps the single most important thing is to be aware of a worker's need for self-esteem."[17] For many workers, even a passing word of praise or appreciation can be a strong motivator. Some companies have gone much further than that. At each Marriott Hotel, the staff picks an "employee of the month" whose picture is then prominently displayed. The employee also receives a gift.

*Self-actualization*   At the top of Maslow's hierarchy is **self-actualization,** which means self-fulfillment or the tapping of one's potential to one's own satisfaction. Few people do not wish to be better at what they do. The desire to be a better gardener, musician, carpenter, teacher, engineer, or salesperson is often triggered by the need for self-actualization. For nearly thirty years, Jack Lemmon made a name for himself as a light comedic actor. *The Odd Couple* and *Some Like It Hot* were two of his biggest hits. He then decided to test himself in dramas, including *The China Syndrome* and *Missing*, for which he won the Academy Award for Best Actor. To much acclaim, Lemmon returned to the stage as the lead in what is commonly regarded as American drama's most difficult play, Eugene O'Neill's *Long Day's Journey into Night*. At a time when many people might be expected to retire, Jack Lemmon made the critics reappraise him as a multidimensional actor.

**self-actualization** self-fulfillment or the tapping of one's potential to one's own satisfaction

## The Hierarchy of Needs Today

Maslow based his theory about a hierarchy of needs on two observations. First, people satisfy their needs systematically, starting with the survival or physiological needs, then moving up the pyramid. Second, survival needs take priority over higher needs. We may say, however, that situations in life are not quite as precisely defined as Maslow made them appear. At any one time, a complex array of needs motivates an individual, and one activity may satisfy a number of them. Consider a business lunch, for example. You not only conduct business with your client but also satisfy the need for food and drink, and may well satisfy your social needs and fulfill your need for esteem as well.

To a great degree, American business has been able to satisfy its workers' survival needs—but it has not been so successful with their higher-order needs. This historic problem may become acute in the future because the generation now entering the work force has greater expectations than those that preceded it. These workers are better educated and want more from a job than just a paycheck and good fringe benefits. They are more apt to be motivated by the opportunity for participation in problem solving and decision making. Thus, the compensation they seek also includes meaningful work and recognition for what they do. These higher expectations place a considerable burden on management to develop a sophisticated understanding of human behavior.

# Frederick Herzberg's Motivation-Maintenance Model

*4.* Describe Frederick Herzberg's Motivation-Maintenance Model.

**Motivation-Maintenance Model**
Herzberg's model for human behavior at work, in which people require certain motivational and maintenance factors

**motivational factors**
work experiences that tend to motivate employees to achieve higher production levels and feel more committed to their jobs

**maintenance (hygiene) factors**  the elements that form the work environment

Frederick Herzberg, another psychologist, studied human behavior at work. He called his theory the **Motivation-Maintenance Model.**

**Motivational factors** are work-related experiences such as the following:

- Achievement
- Recognition
- Responsibility
- Advancement and growth
- The work itself

When these experiences are present, they tend to motivate employees to achieve higher production levels and to feel more committed to their jobs.

**Maintenance** (or **hygiene**) **factors** consist of the elements that form the work environment. They take their name from Herzberg's view that keeping these factors in good order is necessary to avoid the discontent that would reduce everyday levels of performance.[18] This notion parallels the idea of preventing illness through good personal *hygiene*. These factors include:

- Salaries and benefits
- Working conditions
- Relationships with superiors, coworkers, and subordinates
- Job security

In short, maintenance factors are the basic benefits, rights, and conditions considered essential to any job. They are workplace rewards that do not function as strong motivators. A reduction in their quality, however, can create a level of dissatisfaction that may result in low productivity. At best, all that maintenance factors can do is combat dissatisfaction. It remains for motivational factors to boost job satisfaction and performance.

Motivational factors are those benefits above and beyond a job's maintenance factors. A regular paycheck is certainly a maintenance factor. Although wages are important and their reduction will lead to dissatisfaction, they are of low motivational value when they are present in adequate amounts. Both Herzberg and Maslow agree that the higher-order needs are more likely to motivate workers over the long run (see Figure 7.2). A worker's sense of personal satisfaction in his or her work, an opportunity to grow on the job, and a feeling of being important seem to be lifelong motivating factors.

# Douglas McGregor's Theory X and Theory Y

Supervisors and managers play key roles in motivating employees. The supervisors' overall management philosophies and attitudes toward their subordinates often determine the success of efforts to motivate employees

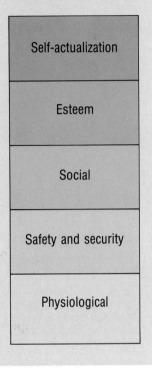

FIGURE 7.2 Maslow's and Herzberg's Models Compared

**HERZBERG'S MOTIVATION/ MAINTENANCE FACTORS**

| Motivators | Achievement Work itself Responsibility Growth |
| | Advancement Recognition |
| Maintenance (hygiene) factors | Status |
| | Interpersonal relationships with supervisors, peers, and subordinates |
| | Company policy and administration |
| | Job security |
| | Working conditions |
| | Salary and some benefits Personal life |

**MASLOW'S HIERARCHY OF NEEDS**

Self-actualization

Esteem

Social

Safety and security

Physiological

and the quality of employee relations. To illustrate how supervisors affect their relationships with subordinates, Douglas McGregor, in his classic book *The Human Side of Enterprise*, described two opposing models of management. He called them Theory X and Theory Y (see Figure 7.3).[19]

McGregor's **Theory X** holds that people really do not want to work and will avoid it if possible. To make people productive, it is necessary to push them, supervise them closely, and threaten them with some type of punishment. Because workers have little or no ambition, they prefer to avoid responsibility and will seek security above all.

Some have called this pessimistic theory a "carrot and stick" approach that combines rewards and punishments to motivate workers. In most cases, the reward is pay. Theory X managers and supervisors view employees as lazy, incompetent, and reluctant to accept responsibility, and they often treat employees with suspicion and little respect.

By contrast, McGregor's **Theory Y** holds that work is as natural to people as recreation and rest. Workers do not dislike work and, under the right conditions, will accept—in fact, seek out—responsibility. This theory says that employees do not want to be rigidly controlled or threatened with punishment. Instead, they look to work to satisfy many of their social, esteem, and self-actualization needs. It is up to the supervisor and the employer to provide an atmosphere in which they can do so.

**Theory X** McGregor's theory that people really do not want to work and will avoid it if possible

*5. Explain the differences between Douglas McGregor's Theory X and Theory Y assumptions about what motivates people.*

**Theory Y** McGregor's theory that work is as natural to people as recreation and rest

| THEORY X | THEORY Y |
|---|---|
| 1. People do not like work and try to avoid it. | 1. People do not naturally dislike work; work is a natural part of their lives. |
| 2. People do not like work, so managers have to control, direct, coerce, and threaten employees to get them to work towards organizational goals. | 2. People are internally motivated to reach objectives to which they are committed. |
| 3. People prefer to be directed, to avoid responsibility, to want security; they have little ambition. | 3. People are committed to goals to the degree that they receive personal rewards when they reach their objectives. |
| | 4. People will both seek and accept responsibility under favorable conditions. |
| | 5. People have the capacity to be innovative in solving organizational problems. |
| | 6. People are bright, but under most organizational conditions their potentials are underutilized. |

FIGURE 7.3   Theory X versus Theory Y

Source: Douglas McGregor, *The Human Side of Enterprise* (New York: McGraw-Hill Book Co., 1960), pp. 33–34, 47–48.

Moog, Inc., a thirty-five year old heavy manufacturing company, typifies Theory Y management. Its 3,000 employees do not punch time clocks but report their own time. Floor inspectors do not check every product; employees check their own work. After ten years with the company, and every five years from then on, each employee gets an additional seven days of paid vacation. Moog's employees have responded by making its turnover rate less than 1 percent per year, and it has never had a work stoppage. Bill Moog, the company's founder and president, believed from the start that people "would be much more effectively motivated in an environment of trust, respect, positive rewards, and reinforcement than in an environment of coercion, punishment, and threats."[20]

# The Dimensions of Motivation

Earlier in this chapter, we saw that motivation can be described as the drive to accomplish a particular goal. This definition suggests that in a work setting motivation is the result of rewards that a person receives while actually performing the job. These factors are the rewards known as internal motivators. Rewards that are quite apart from what the job itself offers, however, can provide their own motivation. These rewards are referred to as external motivators.

## Internal Motivators

An intrinsic reward that occurs when a duty or task is performed is an *internal motivator*. In other words, it is the good feeling that one gets from doing something well.

*6. Describe some important internal and external motivators in the workplace.*

*Job Enrichment* As Frederick Herzberg noted, work itself can be a motivational factor. For that reason, many companies have come to focus on the job itself as a motivator. After research found that work conditions can shape employee attitudes positively, many organizations started **job enrichment programs**, whose major goal is to make routine jobs more challenging and interesting by giving employees more independence and responsibility. Job enrichment can be as simple as giving a receptionist the responsibility for ordering supplies, or it can mean redesigning the work of an entire department. The Northwestern Mutual Life Insurance Company has reduced the drudgery associated with handling its overwhelming paperwork by redefining jobs. In the Milwaukee-based company's new-business department, sixty-four distinct job descriptions became six. Now the same number of people handle a variety of tasks, rather than just one each, so the work is less routine and more challenging. Maytag, the Corning Glass Works, IBM, and Motorola have also adopted job enrichment programs of one form or another.

**job enrichment programs** programs whose major goal is to make routine jobs more challenging and interesting by giving employees more independence and responsibility

*Job Enlargement* A concept related to job enrichment is that of **job enlargement**, adding similar duties from the same job level to a worker's basic responsibilities. A common means of job enlargement in manufacturing is to assign all the tasks involved in assembling a certain unit to one person rather than assigning one task to each of, say, five people. A simple example would be having an auto assembly line employee assemble all windows in a car, instead of just the windshield.

**job enlargement** adding similar duties from the same job level to a worker's basic responsibilities

**Variety at National Steel** *Workers at National Steel such as Jim Slifka participate in a job rotation system. Through job rotation employees learn to perform multiple tasks at their level in the company, thereby reducing stress, boredom, and fatigue. A flexible work force can also help companies increase quality, efficiency, and productivity.*

**job rotation** a system in which workers switch for a time from one job to another

## Job Rotation

In a **job rotation** system, workers switch for a time from one job to another. Many companies use job rotation to give workers a more comprehensive view of the business or of production processes. The employee remains at a job long enough to become proficient in it before moving on to another job at the same level within the organization. Other companies use job rotation to alleviate stress, fatigue, or boredom. For example, many stores arrange to have an employee handle telephone calls from customers, a high-stress task, for no more than a few hours. The employee then works at a cash register or performs clerical tasks.

## External Motivators

The most usual form in which *external motivators* appear is as rewards or other types of positive reinforcement provided to someone by another person. Reinforcement exerts a motivational force when a particular reward causes workers to respond in the same way again. In recent years, managers have tried many different types of external motivators to stimulate their subordinates' performance. Let us examine the more common ones.

*Positive Reinforcement* A major component in productivity is employee satisfaction. Both Frederick Herzberg and Abraham Maslow cited the need for recognition and esteem as motivating forces. Demonstrations of appreciation for work well done can be cost-effective external motivators. A few sincere words of praise, an attractive plaque presented with ceremony to a loyal worker, or a letter of appreciation are common forms of **positive reinforcement**, actions following particular behavior that are designed to increase the likelihood of that behavior's being repeated. Positive reinforcement is perhaps the least expensive, most effective way to improve productivity and raise employee morale. As the authors of *The One Minute Manager* suggest, good managers try to "catch people doing something right!"[21] Employees who feel unappreciated often do not perform to the best of their abilities. In settings where supervisors emphasize what is wrong with employee performance, employees often become demoralized and defensive.

**positive reinforcement** actions following particular behavior that are designed to increase the likelihood of that behavior's being repeated

*Management Expectations*   The expectations of others can greatly influence people. Studies have shown that if teachers expect their students to be high achievers, the students often live up to those expectations. Other studies on workplace motivation have shown that the same principle applies to managers and workers. A manager's failure to be clear about his or her expectations can result in decreased motivation and increased frustration in an employee. Managers can motivate employees just by clearly communicating their expectations, letting their subordinates know what they want done, and when and how to do it. Managers can create an atmosphere in which their subordinates expect positive reinforcement and behave accordingly.[22] It is then up to the manager to monitor performance and provide positive feedback when it is merited.

*Awards and Premiums*   Every year, American companies hand out about $8 billion in awards and premiums to their employees. These include color televisions, vacations, rings, pins, certificates, pens and pencils, and a host of other items. By giving these bonuses to employees, management intends to get certain results. The principal goals are to

- Reduce absenteeism
- Improve sales
- Improve quality control
- Increase application of training program content
- Improve customer relations
- Reduce on-the-job accidents

This motivational technique dates back to at least the late 1800s when John H. Patterson, the founder of the National Cash Register Company (today's NCR), used a variety of award programs to motivate his sales force. Many businesses also use awards and premiums to stimulate suggestions for cost-saving practices. During the energy crisis of the late 1970s and early 1980s, the Gillette Company offered cash bonuses for useful ways to cut its electric and oil bills. In one remarkable case, a General Motors employee earned $30,000 in one year for his suggestions and had earned more than $70,000 for suggestions made over the years before that.[23] Some companies also offer merchandise awards, in addition to or in place of cash.

Award and premium programs are not without their critics. One concern is that they tend merely to "paper over" problems. For instance, a company that decides to offer trading stamps or other incentives to reduce absenteeism

*"Don't you ever worry about your lack of long-range goals?"*

may overlook the bad working conditions or poor supervisors that are causing the problem. Such programs may also reinforce the wrong behavior. A salesperson set on winning a bonus trip to Hawaii or Bermuda may push a customer into buying a product that is not right for that person's needs. Despite these and other criticisms, however, the popularity of award and premium incentive programs continues to grow.

*Financial Incentives*　　Money is, of course, one of the most common forms of external motivation. Although Herzberg and others regard cash as a maintenance—not a motivational—factor, one cannot overlook the power of financial incentives. An employee's pay often represents more than just money to that person. Pay levels also signify recognition and esteem. Employees commonly use the company pay scale to compare their worth and achievements with others. A host of corporations use financial incentives to boost productivity, improve quality, reduce operating expenses, improve attendance, or some combination of these goals. In the future, American businesses seem likely to experiment with a variety of "pay for performance" plans. *Merit pay*, for instance, is on the upswing.

# Involving the Employee in Decision Making

**7.** *Describe strategies for involving employees in decision making.*

The idea of bringing employees into the decision-making process in the workplace is not new. The merits of increased worker involvement have been discussed for many years. In 1960, Walter Reuther, then president of the

United Auto Workers, said, "I think in addition to earning your bread and butter that work ought to give you a sense of participation in the creative process." [24] Some companies have involved employees in decision making for years, but for the vast majority it is a new experience.

## The Quality of Work Life Movement

The drive to achieve a better workplace environment for employees while increasing profitability for the employer is known as the **Quality of Work Life (QWL) movement.** Achieving its goals requires a process through which people become involved in creating an organization that achieves a satisfactory balance of business, human, and social needs.[25]

The key word in the QWL process is **involvement,** which brings employees, unions, and management closer together for their mutual benefit. QWL also involves people in the day-to-day decision-making process on the job.[26] More than 3,000 companies have QWL programs today, including IBM, General Motors, Sprague Electric, and Friendly Ice Cream. But even small firms can benefit from QWL. In the 1970s, John Simmons headed the World Bank's program to implement decentralized decision making. He became convinced that in QWL lay the key to revolutionizing American business. He left the World Bank to take over the firm his family had owned for generations, Simmons Construction Company. He immediately decided to practice what he preached by selling the firm to its employees. Simmons, who remained as chairman, proudly noted recently that under employee control the company had "made more money in the last four years than it did in the previous fifteen." [27]

**Quality of Work Life movement (QWL)** the drive to achieve a better workplace environment for employees while increasing profitability for the employer

**involvement** the element of the QWL process that brings employees, unions, and management closer together for their mutual benefit

## Theory Z

The QWL movement received a boost in 1981 from William G. Ouchi's best seller, *Theory Z*.[28] At that time, Japanese productivity was the highest in the world and productivity in the Western world had been declining for years. In **Theory Z,** Professor Ouchi outlined how American business could meet the challenges Japan poses. He provided new insights into the relationships between Japanese workers and their employers. He also made it clear that technological innovation was not the only reason for Japan's extraordinary success—employee involvement in a wide range of problem-solving and decision-making activities played a central role in their productivity record (see Figure 7.4).

Since *Theory Z*'s publication, we have learned a great deal more about Japanese organizations. Many Japanese companies emphasize lifetime employment, shared responsibility for making and implementing decisions, and a close working relationship between management and labor. Perhaps most important, Japanese organizations foster a climate of *trust*. Without trust, as many companies of the Theory X type have discovered, human relationships degenerate into conflict.

The bottom line, as QWL advocate John Simmons puts it, is quite clear: "High performance firms today are idea factories. They have learned how

**Theory Z** William Ouchi's 1981 book, which outlined how American business could meet the challenges Japan poses

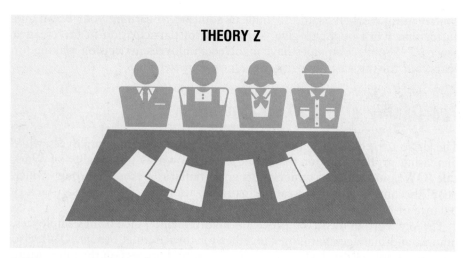

**THEORY Z**

FIGURE 7.4   Theory Z

to generate, nurture and implement ideas and do it quickly. At Toyota, the average Japanese worker produces 44 ideas per year. Employee participation is the only way to do that, and the most cost effective way to do that."[29]

## Quality Circles

**quality circles** groups of workers that volunteer to meet regularly to discuss ways to improve work procedures, eliminate defects, and perform their work more efficiently

One of the ways the Japanese have improved the quality of their products and increased their productivity is by organizing groups of workers into **quality circles.** These groups volunteer to meet regularly, often on a weekly basis, on company time to discuss ways to improve work procedures, eliminate defects, and perform their work more efficiently. The groups are usually small, commonly from six to eight people. Members receive special training that enables them to participate effectively. They share with management the results of their discussions.

The International Association of Quality Circles lists about 2,000 American companies among its members. Program objectives vary from one company to another but generally include one of the following:

- Improve quality
- Reduce waste
- Improve communications
- Develop group problem solving
- Increase work satisfaction

Quality circles as well as other aspects of Japanese management do not always translate directly into American successes. Many Americans have different views on competitiveness and cooperation. For example, American workers tend to concentrate on short-term individual goals. Many do not see anything wrong with competition among workers. In the future we should look more closely at the culture and contexts in which Japanese methods of management have evolved and function. Although we can learn a great deal by studying Japanese management practices, cultural differences make blind

**Quality circles** *Many American companies have adopted the Japanese management practice of using quality circles: small organized groups of workers discuss ideas for improving aspects of the organization, from increasing work satisfaction to improving quality of the product or service.*

imitation of them both impractical and unwise. *Adaptation,* not imitation, of Japanese management practices is the best course.

# Alternative Work Patterns

With better communications between workers and management has come clearer understanding of their respective needs. Particularly in the area of work scheduling, management now reacts more favorably to innovative proposals (see Figure 7.5).

## *Flexitime*

Some companies have adopted a policy of replacing traditional fixed work hours with a more flexible time (**flexitime**) schedule set by employees within the company's guidelines. Typically, companies using this policy divide the

**flexitime** a plan in which traditionally fixed work hours are replaced with a more flexible time schedule within a company's guidelines

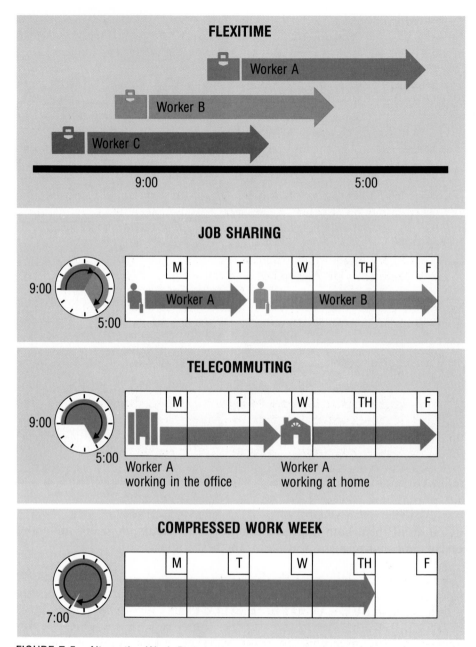

FLEXITIME

Worker A

Worker B

Worker C

9:00                    5:00

JOB SHARING

9:00

5:00

| | M | | T | | W | | TH | | F |
Worker A                    Worker B

TELECOMMUTING

9:00

5:00

| | M | | T | | W | | TH | | F |

Worker A
working in the office

Worker A
working at home

COMPRESSED WORK WEEK

7:00

| | M | | T | | W | | TH | | F |

FIGURE 7.5    Alternative Work Patterns

*8. Identify four types of alternative work patterns in use today and describe their prospects.*

work day into two categories: core time and flexible time. During core time, all employees must be at work. Core time at most companies is from 9:30 A.M. to 3:00 P.M. Flexible time is usually the 3 to 3½ hours on either side of the core time. Employees are free to choose when to arrive and leave during those periods, as long as they work for the required number of hours.

Control Data Corporation introduced flexitime in the United States in 1972. Since then the Nestlé Food Corporation and the Occidental Life Insurance Company along with many others have adopted it. In Europe, about 40 percent of the Swiss work force, 30 percent of the West German, and 20 percent of the French take advantage of flexitime.[30] As flexitime evolves in America, we are seeing many variations of this alternative work pattern. Perkins Geddis Eastman, an architecture firm in New York City, is liberal in its use of flexible work schedules. Parents who wish to spend more time with their children are permitted to work one or two days a week at home.[31]

Most studies of flexitime report benefits to both the organization and its workers. Employees can set their own work hours to avoid traffic tie-ups and other commuter problems. They adjust their work hours to match their own energy rhythms, which can help avoid stress and ultimate burnout. In addition, flexitime permits people to take care of personal business, such as banking or dealing with public agencies, during regular work hours without taking a day off. From the companies' point of view, supervisors can make better use of their employees' time. Many companies report that flexitime has raised employee morale, reduced tardiness and absenteeism, and cut turnover rates.

## The Compressed Work Week

Some companies have adopted a variant of flexitime, the **compressed work week**, a scheduling system that permits workers to vary the number of days they work from the traditional five—without changing the total number of hours worked. A compressed work week often permits workers to put in four 10-hour days instead of five 8-hour days. Workers at Electro Scientific Industries, Inc., in Portland, Oregon, not only have these options but may also work four 8.8-hour days and a half day on Friday.[32]

**compressed work week** a scheduling system that permits workers to vary the number of days they work from the traditional five without changing the total number of hours worked

## Job Sharing

A program in which two people share one job is known as **job sharing**. It is particularly popular among working mothers. One such mother took maternity leave to have her baby and faced a difficult decision when her leave ended. She did not want to give up her career as a lawyer, but she also wanted to spend time with her child. Job sharing in a program sponsored by the New York State Department of Law where she worked allowed her to do both. She now works half time and receives half her normal pay.

**job sharing** a program in which two people share one job

Job sharing is likely to increase in the future. It will continue to appeal to mothers who work, but it will also benefit the increasing numbers of middle-aged persons who must take care of elderly family members. A recent study of employees at the Travelers Insurance Company in Hartford, Connecticut, revealed that 28 percent of the employees surveyed, all of whom were over 30, spent an average of 10.2 hours per week caring for aged relatives and friends.[33]

## *Telecommuting*

telecommuters persons who work at home or in a satellite office and electronically transfer the information needed to do their job between home/satellite and headquarters

A growing number of Americans are **telecommuters**. According to Jack Nilles, the University of Southern California professor who coined the term,[34] these are persons "who work at home or in a satellite office and electronically transfer the information needed to do their job between home/satellite and headquarters."

Of course, some jobs, like sales, often center on activities outside the office, but telecommuting is substantially different from such traditional work. Within the next few years, about 5 million people will come to work at home two or three days each week. What is more, an even higher number could do so if they and their employers were willing. The technology is ready and waiting.

To date a number of companies have successfully experimented with telecommuting. The J. C. Penney Co., Inc., the American Express Company, and the Blue Cross and Blue Shield Association are among them. For the last several years, the New York Telephone Company has had a group of employees who work at home. The company has noted significant gains in productivity among its telecommuters. Their jobs center primarily on writing training materials, screening employment applications, and financial forecasting (see Business Issues).

# Human Relations: A Perspective

In the 1990s, managers are very likely to give even greater attention to human relations in business. The service industry is growing rapidly in America and this trend will require a different work ethic. Karl Albrecht and Ron Zemke have pointed out in their best seller, *Service America*, that relationships in a service economy are more important than physical products. Restaurants, banks, hospitals, public utilities, colleges, airlines, and retail stores all have the problem of gaining—and retaining—their clients' and customers' patronage. Every service firm has, perhaps, thousands of "moments of truth," those critical incidents when customers come into direct contact with the organization. It is those moments when customers form their impressions of the organization's quality and service.[35]

Beyond this interaction between members of an organization and the public, managers have had to look carefully at the relationship between employees and their tasks and among the employees themselves. Managers have come to realize that productivity and job satisfaction increase when employees work as teams and can make decisions about how to perform their tasks. This emphasis exists in the service sector, where it is quite common to hear phrases like "the health care team."[36] The approach is becoming equally common on the manufacturing floor. The most important change in orientation, however, is among managers themselves. As Crawford H. Greenewalt of Du Pont has noted: "Teams of laborers built the pyramids and teams of craftsmen the medieval cathedrals. Now, for the first time, however, management itself has become a team effort."[37]

# WORKING NINE TO FIVE

■ Some workers at Merck and Company, a large pharmaceutical firm, have a choice about the time they go to work and the time they leave. They must be at their desks between 10:00 A.M. and 3:30 P.M., but their day can start at 7:30 A.M. or end at 6:00 P.M.

■ At Perkins Geddis Eastman, a small architectural firm in New York City, workers (both men and women) with young children have the option of working one or two days a week at home.

■ The head of Radcliffe's career services department works a 32-hour week, and she's organized the department to allow employees to set their own schedules. Her assistant's position is shared by two people.

■ Touche Ross, a major accounting firm, allows women with young children to work four days a week without sacrificing opportunities for advancement.

Flexitime. Part time. Job sharing. The shortened work week. These alternative work patterns are becoming more and more common in the workplace. The steady erosion of the nine-to-five workday, five days a week, is a response to societal and economic trends.

Probably the most important of these trends is the growing number of women in the workplace. Almost 70 percent of American women are working or actively looking for work. As more of them occupy professional and managerial positions, companies are finding it harder to ignore the conflict many women face between career and family.

Other trends are economic. In the recession of the early 1980s, companies with overloaded payrolls were forced to lay off workers. Now these same companies are looking for "contingent" workers whose hours accommodate the fluctuating needs of their companies.

Finally, we're witnessing enormous growth in the service sector of the economy. It is here, particularly in retail operations, that we find the greatest number of flexible work patterns.

There is no question that a shift to flexible scheduling means an investment in time and effort on the part of both company and employee. Probably the most important challenge comes in redefining the traditional work ethic—in acknowledging that good and valuable work can be done even if an employee shares a job or regularly goes home at 3:00 P.M. And there are the simple logistics of handling a full-time business with a variety of work schedules.

But it seems the effort is worthwhile. There's more to it than the worker's morale or level of stress. By meeting the needs of valued experienced workers, employers save the time and expense of training new workers. And there are other benefits. A 1983 study by Goodmeasure, Inc. and Rosabeth Kanter, a consultant, compared the financial performance over twenty years of two groups of companies. The "progressive" companies were highly responsive to the needs of their workers for flexible scheduling; the "nonprogressive" companies offered few if any alternative work schedules. The study found that in measures of sales, assets, return on equity, and return on total capital, the progressive companies were doing far better than the more traditional firms.

Sources: Alex Taylor III, "Why Women Managers Are Bailing Out," *Fortune,* August 18, 1986, pp. 16–23; Beverly Geber, "Pushing for Part Time," *Training,* December 1987, pp. 59–61, 64–66; "A Look at Alternative Work Schedules," *Training,* March 1988, p. 74; Ellen Wojahn, "Bringing Up Baby," *Inc.,* November 1988, pp. 64–66, 70, 74–75.

# CHAPTER HIGHLIGHTS

**1.** *Define human relations.*

*Human relations* includes all the types of interactions among people: conflicts, cooperative efforts, and group relationships.

**2.** *Explain what motivation is and describe the origins of the modern approach to it.*

*Motivation* can be defined as the factors that cause a person to behave in a certain way or to accomplish a certain goal. The modern approach to the study of motivation began in the 1920s with the Hawthorne studies by Elton Mayo and his colleagues at Western Electric.

**3.** *Describe Abraham Maslow's hierarchy of needs.*

Maslow proposed a theory of motivation based on a *hierarchy of needs:* physiological, safety and security, social, esteem, and self-actualization. Needs are generally satisfied systematically (that is, from the lowest to the highest), and only needs that have not been satisfied are motivators.

**4.** *Describe Frederick Herzberg's Motivation-Maintenance Model.*

According to Herzberg, needs can be divided into two primary categories: motivational factors and maintenance factors. *Motivational factors,* which cause workers to be more productive and to feel more committed to their jobs, include experiences of achievement, recognition, responsibility, advancement and growth, and inherent satisfaction in the work itself. *Maintenance factors* do not serve as motivators in themselves but lead to dissatisfaction when they are lacking. They include salaries and benefits, working conditions, interpersonal relationships, and job security.

**5.** *Explain the differences between Douglas McGregor's Theory X and Theory Y assumptions about what motivates people.*

*Theory X* states that people do not want to work and will avoid it if they can. They must be pushed, closely supervised, and threatened with punishment if they are to be productive. They have little ambition and seek security above all. *Theory Y* argues that work is as natural as rest and recreation and that workers will seek out responsibility on their own. Managers must provide an environment in which workers can satisfy their social, esteem, and self-actualization needs.

**6.** *Describe some important internal and external motivators in the workplace.*

*Internal motivators* are the rewards one gets from feelings inside oneself. Many companies today use the job itself as a motivator. People's feelings of reward and self-worth are enhanced through job enrichment (making routine jobs more challenging and interesting by giving employees more independence and responsibility), job enlargement (combining similar tasks at the same skill and job level), and job rotation (providing an opportunity for workers to perform a number of jobs at the same level). *External motivators* are rewards given to someone by another person. They include positive reinforcement that may come in the form of positive feedback about an employee's abilities and performance, awards and premiums, and financial incentives.

**7.** *Describe strategies for involving employees in decision making.*

The *Quality of Work Life (QWL) movement* focuses on bringing employees, unions, and management closer together for their mutual benefit and attempts to decentralize decision making, thus fostering a sense of involvement throughout the organization. William G. Ouchi expanded upon this idea in *Theory Z,* which attempted to explain the reasons for Japan's extraordinary business success. Ouchi pointed out that Japanese organizations are based on trust, an expectation of lifetime employment, shared responsibility, and a close relationship between management and labor. Theory Z organizations such as IBM try to promote such attitudes in the United States. *Quality circles* are another idea adopted from the Japanese. Small groups of workers meet to discuss ways to improve work procedures, promote quality, and increase efficiency. Members generally receive special training. Quality circles can improve communications throughout an organization and may lead to significant cost savings. American managers need to study and adapt, rather than blindly imitate, Japanese management practices.

*8. Identify four types of alternative work patterns in use today and describe their prospects.*

Four common alternative work patterns are flexitime, the compressed work week, job sharing, and telecommuting. *Flexitime* has been adopted by many organizations and has been found to benefit both the organization and its workers. The *compressed work week*, in which employees work the same number of total hours per week but vary the number of work days, has not been as widely adopted. *Job sharing*, in which two people share a single job, is likely to increase in the future. As the number of working women with young children or middle-aged people with elderly family members increases, the attractiveness of job sharing will doubtless rise. *Telecommuting* (working at home or in a satellite location and transferring information to the main office electronically) will become even easier and more affordable.

## KEY TERMS

Human relations
Morale
Motivation
Hawthorne studies
Need
Hierarchy of needs
Physiological needs
Psychological needs
   (secondary needs)

Esteem
Self-actualization
Motivation-Maintenance
   Model
Motivational factors
Maintenance (hygiene)
   factors
Theory X
Theory Y

Job enrichment
   program
Job enlargement
Job rotation
Positive
   reinforcement
Quality of Work Life
   movement (QWL)

Involvement
Theory Z
Quality circles
Flexitime
Compressed work week
Job sharing
Telecommuters

## REVIEW QUESTIONS

1. Define human relations.
2. What is the relationship between high morale and human relations in an organization?
3. What was the most important finding by researchers involved in the Hawthorne studies? If the study were to be duplicated today, would the findings be different?
4. Briefly describe Abraham Maslow's hierarchy of needs. How are a person's needs related to his or her motivation?
5. Is it possible to achieve self-actualization in the modern workplace? Explain.
6. Briefly describe Frederick Herzberg's Motivation-Maintenance Model. Explain the difference between maintenance (hygiene) factors and motivation factors.
7. Compare Douglas McGregor's Theory X and Theory Y. Why is it important for modern managers to study these two motivational theories?
8. What is the difference between internal and external motivation? Give examples of each.
9. Describe the terms *job enrichment* and *job enlargement*. Give examples of each.
10. What are some of the principal goals of incentive programs?
11. Describe the Quality of Work Life (QWL) movement. In what ways has Theory Z contributed to the QWL movement?

# APPLICATION EXERCISES

1. Within the next week, talk to three persons who hold supervisory or management positions. Ask them which is the bigger challenge in their business careers: people problems or technical problems. If time permits, discuss the problems with them in detail, and record their responses in writing.

2. Many organizations experience high employee turnover. In many retail businesses the turnover rate is 60 percent annually. In some service industries, such as fast foods, the turnover rate is 90 percent annually. What rewards might be used to reduce turnover and increase worker productivity?

# CASES

## 7.1 UPS: Model of Efficiency

When *Fortune* magazine conducted a national survey to identify America's most admired corporations, United Parcel Service was ranked number one in the transportation category. With a combination of good management, a well-trained work force, and a carefully developed package delivery system, the company has been able to deliver quality service year after year.

UPS believes that its employees should give the firm a fair day's work for a fair day's pay. The package delivery firm seems willing to give more than a fair day's pay. Its drivers earn about $1 more per hour than drivers at any other trucking company. But in return, UPS expects maximum output from its employees.

Since the 1920s, the firm's industrial engineers have been studying every detail of every task performed by most UPS employees. From their studies have come time and motion standards that govern how those tasks are performed and how long they should take. Drivers, for example, are expected to walk to a customer's door at a speed of exactly three feet per second. They are told to knock as soon as they get there rather than waste time looking for a doorbell.

Work engineers are continually riding with drivers, timing everything from stops at traffic lights, to waits at customers' doorways, to stairway climbs, to coffee breaks. And they are not averse to pointing out the occasional inefficiency—as when a driver handles a package more than once. In addition, supervisors ride with the "least best" drivers, noting how they work and constantly correcting them until their work is up to standard.

The work standards extend to package sorters at UPS depots as well. Each sorter is expected to handle 1,124 packages every hour, reading the Zip code on each one and then placing it on a conveyor belt. One mistake is allowed every 2,500 packages.

The object of all this work engineering is efficiency—and UPS has been called one of the most efficient companies anywhere. It is also a highly profitable company. Most drivers take the regimentation in stride; many show pride in meeting the UPS standards each day. Others, however, feel that they are constantly being pushed, that it is impossible for them to relax at work. UPS officials claim that the standards provide accountability. And, they say, employees who work according to UPS standards should feel less tired at the end of the day.

UPS's approach to employee development and motivation seem to be quite effective. The company, however, will continue to face major competition from Purolator Courier, Federal Express, Emery Worldwide, and many other carriers.

### Questions

1. Discuss UPS's relations with its drivers in terms of the Maslow, Herzberg, and McGregor motivation models.
2. What might UPS gain, and what might it lose, by involving its drivers in workplace decision making?

Source: *Fortune*, January 30, 1989, pp. 68–94. For more information, see *The Wall Street Journal*, April 22, 1986, pp. 1, 23; *New England Business*, April 21, 1986, pp. 57–64; and *Newsweek*, February 7, 1983, pp. 55–56.

## 7.2 Work Life at Steelcase

Eighty-eight percent of the people working at Steelcase Inc., a Grand Rapids, Michigan, manufacturer of office furniture, were working there ten years ago. Seventy-two percent of its employees were there fifteen years ago. Many are second- and third-generation employees. The firm receives about 30,000 unsolicited job requests each year but hires according to a somewhat unique policy. Twenty percent of new employees are recruited from minorities, families in hardship, and some former employees. The remaining 80 percent must be sponsored by current employees. And because so many friends and relatives are sponsored whenever the company requests applications, applicants are considered according to the seniority of the sponsor.

Why the clamor for jobs at Steelcase? Average factory workers' earnings at the firm are about 20 percent higher than the regional average, the company contributes 15 percent to a profit-sharing plan, and has both bonus and incentive programs, along with a wide range of employee benefits.

And there's a lot more besides:

- The firm is developing robots to perform the most tedious manufacturing operations. The final assembly line has been replaced with assembly benches where pairs of workers do complete assembly. The newer system requires more employee training but involves much less drudgery.
- Steelcase designs and builds all new machinery in-house. The firm continually solicits input from the person who will be operating each machine, and when it is delivered to the work area it bears a plate with that employee's name on it.
- The firm's incentive plan, by which employees have added as much as 80 percent to their paychecks, is run on the honor system. Employees keep track of their own incentive bonuses.

In return, Steelcase demands the best from its employees. The firm has a reputation for quality and for meeting promised delivery dates, and employees must work toward both goals. Quality is checked first by the workers themselves, then by supervisors. Work that is not up to standard must be redone.

Steelcase also has a formal system for taking disciplinary action. Various infractions result in the assessing of points; for example, an employee who is late without an excuse gets 10 points, and infractions such as careless workmanship, theft, drinking during working hours, and insubordination are worth up to 120 points. A worker who accumulates 160 points is summarily dismissed—but along the way, he or she will have been counseled at least once concerning the problem. If an employee is unhappy with treatment from a supervisor, he or she can go to top management where an open door policy exists. Many of those who lose their jobs are eventually rehired—and most of them remain.

One thing Steelcase does not have to demand from its employees is loyalty; that develops naturally. Since it was founded in 1912, the firm has never had a work stoppage, and 96 percent of its shipments (valued at over $1 billion per year, from twenty-one plants) arrive on time. Steelcase seems to practice what *Inc.* magazine has called *workstyle*, and which might best be characterized as a concern for the quality of work life. Obviously, most people are quick to respond to that concern.

### Questions

1. Would you describe Steelcase as a Theory X- or Theory Y-oriented company?
2. Is Steelcase too demanding of employees in some ways? Explain.
3. Does Steelcase's approach to employee relations increase or decrease the work and responsibility of management? Why?

Source: For more information see *Inc.*, January 1986, pp. 45–54; *Management Review*, November 1985, pp. 46–51; *Forbes*, October 7, 1985, pp. 90–99; and *The 100 Best Companies to Work for in America*, 1985, pp. 347–352.

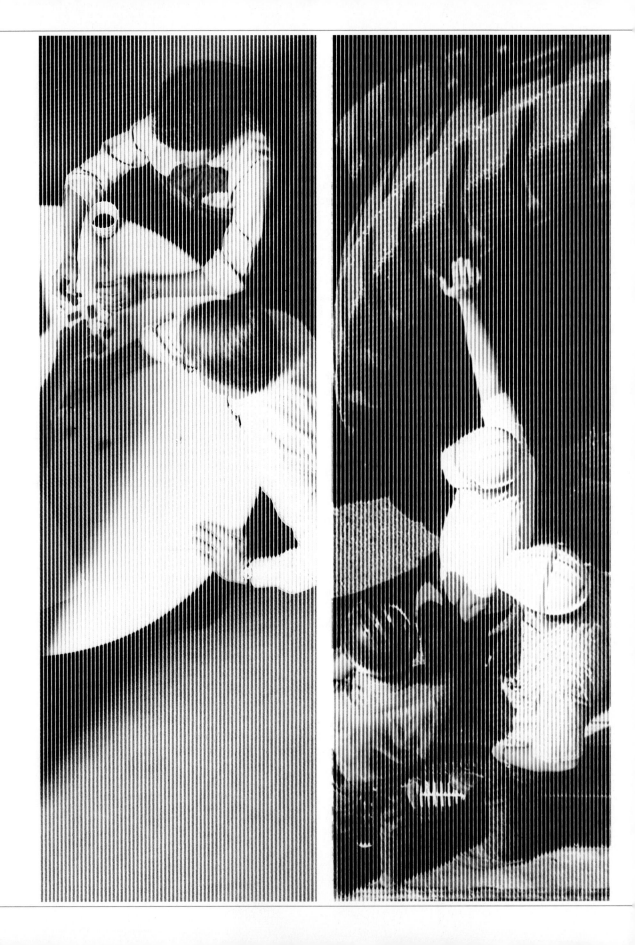

# Human Resources and Production

| | |
|---|---|
| CHAPTER 8 | MANAGING HUMAN RESOURCES |
| CHAPTER 9 | LABOR-MANAGEMENT RELATIONS |
| CHAPTER 10 | OPERATIONS MANAGEMENT |

*John Naisbitt and others who have carefully studied the American business scene say that human capital has replaced dollar capital as the strategic resource. To develop this resource, American companies are spending $30 billion each year on training and education programs. And a growing number of union bargaining agreements contain components for the education and training of workers who need retraining. In Part III we examine the broad field of human resource management, including labor-management relations. Operations management, the process of coordinating the production of goods and services with all the activities associated with production, is also discussed in this section.*

PART THREE

# 8 Managing Human Resources

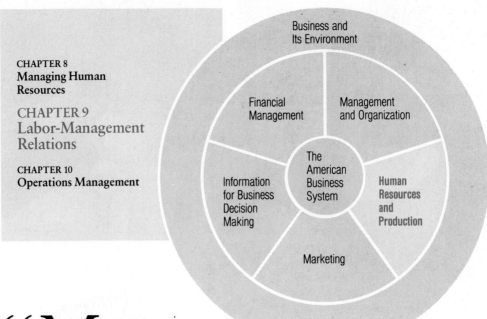

"My mommy is coming to take me to lunch," Monica Hogge, a wide-eyed 4-year-old, tells a visitor at a child-care center in an office park in Tysons Corner, Va. "We're going to Pizza Hut."

Taking her daughter out for lunch is a weekly ritual for Cindy Hogge, whose office is just a short walk from her daughter's child-care center.

A single mother, Hogge used to take Monica to a neighbor's house, then drive 45 minutes to the office. But now "we get an extra 1½ hours a day in the car together," Hogge says.

Cindy Hogge is a purchasing agent for Engineering Research Associates, Inc., a designer of computer systems. She is one of three employees at her company taking advantage of its support of the Tysons Corner Play and Learn Children's Center (PAL). Launched by a consortium of 22 companies, the genesis of PAL shows how local businesses can pool resources to minimize the costs of setting up a child-care center for their employees.[1]

Taken at face value, this mother-daughter situation seems rather unremarkable. Symbolically, however, it represents today's changing work force and business's response to those changes. In Cindy Hogge's case, she belongs to the rapidly growing army of female employees (many of whom are single parents). Her employer, for its part, has accommodated her special day-care needs to keep her as a valued and satisfied employee. Rather than being an isolated event, a single mother's use of a day-care center cooperatively formed by twenty-two companies is an encouraging sign of the times.

# The Evolution of Human Resource Management

The last two decades have seen a marked change in **human resource management,** the process of acquiring, deploying, and developing people for organizational success. Each of the three words in this key term reflects a separate change in the field. Until the mid-1960s, the people involved in human resource work were usually called *personnel managers.* Their duties normally centered on staffing activities such as hiring, keeping employment records, attending to minor medical benefits problems, and organizing company teams and outings. Since then, dramatic changes have occurred in our society and in the make-up of the American work force. No longer can companies afford to look at people as a commodity to be exploited to exhaustion and then discarded. In today's organizations employees are viewed as human *resources* that need to be carefully nurtured, accommodated, and developed.

**human resource management**   the process of acquiring, deploying, and developing people for organizational success

*1.* Explain what human resource management is and describe the factors that have contributed to its importance.

## America's Changing Work Force

Important among the work force trends prompting the evolution of human resource management practices are:

- A more diverse work force. Women, minorities, and recent immigrants will make up 80 percent of the new job seekers by the year 2000.
- A decline in entry-level workers, reflecting a low birth rate in the 1970s and early 1980s.
- An older work force. By the year 2000, 39 percent of the work force will be below the age of 35, down from 49 percent now.
- More women in the work force. Women now represent about 50 percent of the American work force.
- More working mothers. By 1987, 55 percent of married mothers with children under 6 years old were working, up from 12 percent in 1950.[2]
- Growing educational mismatches. According to one executive: "The top third of America's young people is the best educated in the world, but the middle third is slipping into mediocrity, and the bottom third is at Third World standards."[3] In our increasingly service-oriented economy, we thus face the dilemma of a polarized work force with both over-educated and undereducated job seekers.

Human resource management is a rapidly changing field because of these work force trends; by the year 2000 new economic and social conditions will transform the employee/employer contract in every area from hiring to retirement.[4] It is thus more important now than ever before for today's and tomorrow's business managers to be well informed about human resource management trends and issues (see Experiencing Business).

## HOW WELL INFORMED ARE YOU ABOUT HUMAN RESOURCE MANAGEMENT TRENDS AND ISSUES?

Select one answer for each of the following items and then consult the scoring key at the back of the book.

1. Is it legal for a department store manager to have applicants for a head cashier's job take a polygraph (lie detector) test?
   a. Yes
   b. No
2. What is the number-one reason why good employees quit?
   a. Poor advancement opportunity
   b. Dissatisfaction with supervision
   c. Personal problems
   d. Dissatisfaction with pay
3. The pay gap between men and women working fulltime in the United States has been growing
   a. narrower.
   b. wider.
4. The purpose of performance appraisal is
   a. evaluation.
   b. to strengthen the corporate culture.
   c. evaluation and development.
   d. to measure productivity.
5. Which of the following is the most widely used training technique in business and industry today?
   a. Games/simulations
   b. Lectures
   c. One-on-one instruction
   d. Videotapes

6. Is it legal for a company to ask on its job application if you have ever been arrested?
   a. Yes
   b. No
7. Employees tend to get less productive as they get older.
   a. True
   b. False
8. Between now and 1995, which occupation will produce the greatest number of new jobs in the U.S.?
   a. Medical assistants
   b. Cashiers
   c. Computer programmers
   d. Computer operators
9. What percent of American high school students drop out before graduation?
   a. 10%
   b. 15%
   c. 19%
   d. 29%
10. What term applies to the recent practice of letting employees pick their own combination of benefits?
    a. Portable pensions
    b. Sliding scale benefits
    c. Cafeteria-style benefits
    d. Gainsharing

## The Legal Environment

**antidiscrimination laws**
laws that forbid treating people differently on the basis of their religion, color, sex, race, age, or national origin

Beginning in the 1960s, government action began to reflect society's changing attitudes about how people should be treated at work. Collectively, these federal, state, and local regulations are known as the **antidiscrimination laws**, since they forbid treating people differently—particularly in employment and housing—on the basis of their religion, color, sex, race, age, or national origin. Table 8.1 lists the major federal antidiscrimination laws, regulations, and executive orders.

*The Civil Rights Act of 1964*   The law foremost in the minds of those responsible for human resources management is the **Civil Rights Act of 1964**,

**Civil Rights Act of 1964 (Title VII)**   law that declares it illegal to discriminate in employment against any individual in respect to his or her compensation as well as the terms of employment because of that individual's race, color, religion, sex, or national origin

TABLE 8.1   Key Laws, Regulations, and Executive Orders Affecting Human Resource Management

| | |
|---|---|
| Fair Labor Standards Act (1938) | Regulates child labor; establishes minimum wage; regulates overtime pay for nonmanagerial workers. |
| Equal Pay Act (1963) | Prohibits wage discrimination on the basis of sex for jobs with "substantially equal" duties. |
| Civil Rights Act, Title VII (1964); Equal Employment Opportunity Act (1972); Affirmative Action Programs | As discussed in text. |
| Executive Orders 11246 and 11375 (1965–1967) | Prohibit discrimination by contractors and subcontractors for the federal government; require preparation of affirmative action plans for achieving equal employment opportunity. |
| Age Discrimination in Employment Act (1967) | Forbids discrimination in compensation, terms and conditions of employment, or privileges on account of age; applies to employees between the ages of forty and seventy; forbids forced retirement under seventy. |
| Occupational Safety and Health Act (1970) | Requires federal government to establish health and safety standards and to conduct inspections. |
| Vocational Rehabilitation Act (1973–1974) | Requires federal contractors and subcontractors to take affirmative steps to hire the handicapped. |
| Employee Retirement Income Security Act (1974) | Regulates pension plans so covered employees receive their pensions. |
| Pregnancy Discrimination Act (1978) | Requires pregnant employees to be treated as all other employees for the determination of benefits. |
| Uniform Guidelines on Employee Selection Procedures (1978) | Establish criteria for federal agencies to use in judging the compliance of federal contractors and subcontractors with antidiscrimination laws. |
| EEOC Sexual Harassment Guidelines (1980) | Prohibit sexual harassment that affects decisions about employment conditions, promotions, and raises. |

which is commonly referred to as **Title VII**, after its key section. That part declares it illegal to discriminate in employment against any individual in respect to his or her compensation as well as the terms and conditions or privileges of employment because of that individual's race, color, religion, sex, or national origin.

In 1972, Congress amended *Title VII* of the Civil Rights Act by means of the **Equal Employment Opportunity Act**. This act created the **Equal Employment Opportunity Commission (EEOC)**, which enforces the employment-related aspects of the antidiscrimination laws. This independent board consists of five members appointed by the president. The EEOC's staff of attorneys and investigators evaluates complaints of discrimination. If a complaint appears to be valid, the staff first attempts to work out a settlement with the employer. If this effort fails, the staff seeks the commission's permission to file a lawsuit against the employer.

Enforcement of the antidiscrimination laws is not limited to the EEOC. All the states, many localities, and individual lawsuits can enforce these laws.

*Affirmative Action Programs*   Beginning with the Civil Rights Act of 1964, selected employers were ordered to develop **affirmative action programs**. Unlike equal employment opportunity that strives to avoid *future* discrimination, affirmative action attempts to correct imbalances caused by *past* discrimination. These programs consist of written plans to hire, train, and promote minority workers and women. A plan typically states a program's goals, the steps to achieve them, and timetables that the employer has committed itself to follow.

Not all employers must develop affirmative action programs. Certain federal contractors and subcontractors do have to develop them in order to obtain government contracts. And courts will sometimes order employers to develop affirmative action programs to correct an employer's past pattern of discrimination.

Despite efforts by the Reagan administration to weaken affirmative action and recent court decisions eliminating its most aggressive forms, business support for these programs remains strong. In a recent poll of 202 chief executive officers of large U.S. companies, 59 percent said they did not plan to change their present affirmative action programs.[5] Still, equal employment opportunity protection is not perfect. Individual courage, persistence, and initiative are often needed to overcome deep-seated prejudice. Jerry O. Williams, president and chief operating officer of Chicago's AM International since 1985, is an example of this persistence. He is next in line to become the chief executive officer of AM International, making him the first black chief executive of a *Fortune* 500 company.[6]

## Responsibility for Human Resource Management

The responsibility for who handles human resource management in a firm depends on the business's size. In smaller firms, the owner and the other managers perform these functions. Then, as firms grow, they develop a need for human resource professionals.

**Equal Employment Opportunity Act**   act that created the Equal Employment Opportunity Commission (EEOC)

**Equal Employment Opportunity Commission (EEOC)**   agency that enforces the employment-related aspects of the antidiscrimination laws

**affirmative action programs**   programs that consist of written plans to hire, train, and promote minority workers and women

Protecting equal opportunity *Despite weakening government support for affirmative action programs, business support from companies like The Equitable Company, an insurance company, remains strong.*

In large businesses, a human resource department and other managers in the organization generally share the responsibilities. In some companies, operating management plays an active role in all hiring decisions. In others, it simply takes a final look at the human resource department's candidate. All companies need to treat their human resources as carefully as they do their other resources—by planning strategically for their acquisition and use.

# Human Resource Planning

Imagine you had the task of finding 3,000 employees for a brand-new automobile assembly plant. That is precisely the challenge Toyota Motor Company faced in 1987 while its new factory was being built in Georgetown, Kentucky.[7] This situation dramatizes the need for **human resource planning**, the systematic process of forecasting the future demand for employees and estimating the supply available to meet that demand. Employees represent a substantial investment, and their deployment and redeployment require as much planning as for other assets.

**human resource planning** the systematic process of forecasting the future demand for employees and estimating the supply available to meet that demand

*2. Explain the human resource planning process.*

## *Forecasting Demand*

Human resource planners consider both internal and external factors when forecasting a firm's demand for workers. Internal factors include possible shifts in goods or services, planned expansions or contractions in operations, purchases of new equipment, and likely personnel changes such as retirements and leaves of absence. Suppose that the K mart Corporation plans to open twenty-five new stores during the next two years. Twenty-five store managers and assistant managers alone must be hired, just for the new stores. K mart will also have to find replacements for the managers it expects to lose by **attrition**, the normal loss of employees from retirement, job changes (see Figure 8.1), death, and the like.

**attrition** the normal loss of employees from retirement, job changes, death, and the like

Perhaps the most important external factor to consider in planning for workers is the state of the nation's economy. Rising or falling interest rates, for example, can affect a firm's sales and hence its demand for human resources. Other important external factors include government regulations, technological changes, and the level of competition a firm faces.

## Estimating the Supply of Workers

Among the most important external factors affecting the supply of workers are the number of high school or college graduates available, existing patterns of worker mobility and migration, general economic conditions (especially the unemployment level), and the overall characteristics of the labor force a

FIGURE 8.1   Why Do Good Employees Quit?

According to a poll of 1,099 human resource managers, five reasons why good employees quit their jobs were ranked as shown here.

Source: Data from Phil Farish, "HRM Update," *Personnel Administrator,* July 1988, p. 18. Used by permission of the publisher.

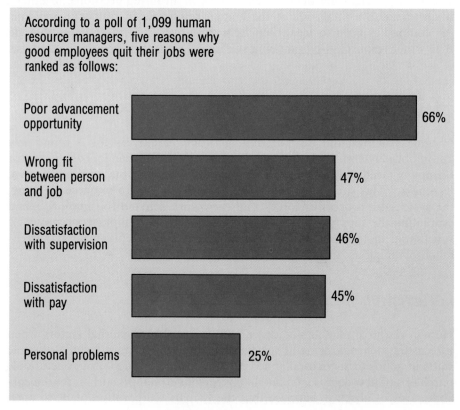

According to a poll of 1,099 human resource managers, five reasons why good employees quit their jobs were ranked as follows:

| Reason | Percentage |
|---|---|
| Poor advancement opportunity | 66% |
| Wrong fit between person and job | 47% |
| Dissatisfaction with supervision | 46% |
| Dissatisfaction with pay | 45% |
| Personal problems | 25% |

given business can tap. For example, over the next two decades the work force will age considerably as the baby boom generation grows older. Also, as mentioned earlier, a shortage of adequately educated entry-level employees is being experienced. McDonald's and other heavy users of entry-level talent are feeling the pinch.

Forecasting the supply of workers available from within a company requires estimating how many current workers are qualified to move into anticipated vacancies. The human resources department also needs to assess production schedules and budgets, Equal Employment Opportunity goals, and possible relocations, plant closings, turnover and absenteeism rates, and transfers within the firm. One method of making this evaluation is to use a **skills inventory**, a data bank containing each employee's employment history, skills, interests, and performance record that can be used to match personnel with new jobs or to select candidates for promotion, transfer, or added responsibilities. If this data is stored in a computer, finding the right employee for a job can often be relatively simple.

**skills inventory** a data bank containing each employee's history, skills, interests, and performance record

## Planning to Meet Needs

After the human resources specialists have forecast the demand and supply of personnel, they develop a plan to assure a work force appropriate for the company. If they anticipate a greater demand than the supply available, their plan will focus on attracting new employees. If, on the other hand, they see supply exceeding demand, they will plan for a reduction of the work force. Many firms hope to deal with work force reductions through attrition, but attrition takes time—layoffs are much quicker. Of course, layoffs have a negative impact on employee motivation, trust, and loyalty. Some companies, such as IBM, rely on transfers and retraining while trying to maintain a no-layoff policy.

## Job Analysis

Hiring, training, and evaluating employees is a lot easier when both the employer and the prospective employee know precisely what a job entails. This information should come from a **job analysis**, a systematic study of each employee's duties, tasks, and work environment. Among the questions a job analysis addresses are

**job analysis** a systematic study of each employee's duties, tasks, and work environment

- What are the actual job activities?
- What equipment is used on the job?
- What specific job behaviors are required?
- What are the working conditions under which the job is performed?
- What interaction with other employees and superiors is required?
- Does the job require the employee to supervise others?

A job analyst may gather this information by observing the worker on the job site, interviewing the employee, having the person fill out a questionnaire, or using a combination of these methods.

Planning for the organization's demand for workers  *When forecasting the supply of workers available managers consider several external factors, such as level of unemployment and the number of high school or college graduates available.*

After determining what a job involves, the job analyst identifies the knowledge, skills, and abilities required to perform it successfully. Then the analyst prepares two documents, a job description and a job specification.

A **job description** is a written summary of the duties, tasks, and responsibilities associated with a job. The first part of a job description, the identification section, states the job title, the department in which the job is located, and the supervisor to whom the applicant would report. The second part, the general summary, briefly describes the job. The specific duties section, the third area, describes what those functions are.

A **job specification** lists the key qualifications a person needs to perform a job successfully. Human resource professionals classify qualifications into three categories: knowledge, skills, and abilities. Some of the factors considered are education or training, experience, specific work skills, mental or physical abilities, and personal abilities. Suppose that the Levi Strauss Company wanted to hire an individual to supervise its physical fitness program for pregnant workers. The qualifications for this position might include a master's degree in health and physical education, two years' work experience in a physical fitness facility, certain teaching skills, and the ability to interact well with people.

**job description**  a written summary of the duties, tasks, and responsibilities associated with a job

**job specification**  a listing of the key qualifications a person needs to perform a job successfully

# The Employment Process

The procedure by which a firm matches its hiring needs with the available human resources is the employment process. It includes **recruitment**, the process of attracting qualified people to apply for jobs; **selection**, the identification of appropriate candidates; and **orientation**, the systematic introduction of new employees to their new organization, job, and coworkers. Figure 8.2 illustrates the sequence of the employment process. At any point in this procedure, the employer may determine that its needs and the job applicant's do not match and reject the application. Applicants may also withdraw at any point.

**recruitment**  the process of attracting qualified people to apply for jobs

**selection**  the identification of appropriate candidates

**orientation**  the systematic introduction of new employees to their new organization, job, and coworkers

## *Recruiting*

The objective of recruiting is to attract a pool of qualified applicants from which to choose the most appropriate person for a particular job. If recruiting produces only as many candidates as there are jobs, the employer cannot be selective. If, on the other hand, the efforts to recruit result in a flood of applicants, the firm needs to have a systematic screening apparatus in place. For example, Toyota received an incredible 90,000 applications for jobs at its new assembly plant in Kentucky. Part of Toyota's rigorous screening procedure involved 14 hours of technical, manual dexterity, reading, and math tests. Workplace simulations and panel interviews followed.[8] Recruiting

*3. List the steps in the employment process.*

FIGURE 8.2  The Employment Process

To prospective applicants, the job process is a string of steps that must be completed before an applicant can be chosen for a job.

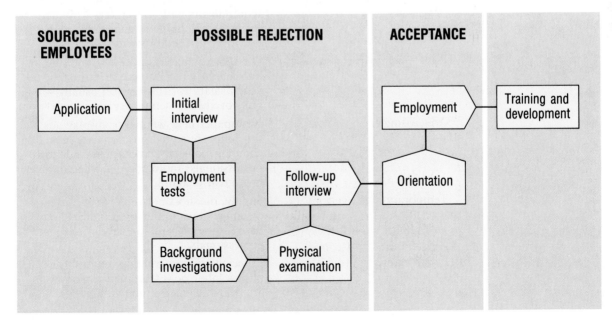

a robust and talented pool of job applicants is a never-ending challenge for managers.

When companies have openings above the entry level, many prefer to hire from within, but all occasionally have to hire from outside. To solicit applications, firms rely on job postings, advertising, personnel agencies, or management recruiters. Other good sources include local schools and colleges, unions, government agencies, and current or former workers (see Table 8.2).

## TABLE 8.2  Sources of Employees

*The human resources department's greatest challenge is to provide a qualified pool of candidates for every job opening. It must draw on many sources for these applicants. This table charts the most significant sources.*

Source: From Alex Taylor, III, "Tomorrow's Chief Executives," *Fortune,* May 9, 1989, p. 33. Copyright © 1988, *Fortune* Magazine. Reprinted by permission of the publisher.

| Internal Sources | |
| --- | --- |
| Job posting and bidding | Promotion or transfer from within. Vacancy notices posted throughout the facility, giving employees a set time to apply; union rules often require this procedure before a job can be offered to outsiders. |
| Current employees | Pass the word to family members, friends, etc. |
| Past employees | Also refer candidates; sometimes willing to return themselves. |
| **External Sources** | |
| School recruiting | Type of school approached varies with candidates required; e.g., high schools for minimal-skill jobs; technical schools for technicians or computer programmers; colleges for professional and managerial candidates. |
| Public (state) employment agencies | Try to match employer's stated requirements with job seekers who are referred; no charge to either the employer or the job seeker. |
| Private employment agencies | Use same matching process as the state but charge 10 to 20 percent of first-year's salary for this service; usually—but not always—employer pays fee. |
| Advertising | Newspaper help wanted or display ads for nonprofessional positions are most common; journal and magazine ads for professionals; radio and TV where labor is in great demand. |
| Temporary-help agencies | Supply, on short notice, a broad range of nonprofessional help on a day-to-day basis; some provide low-level professionals. |
| Labor unions | Especially in construction, unions establish a labor pool from which workers are drawn to meet employers' needs. |

## Selection

Employee selection may be described as a screening or sifting process that identifies applicants who should be extended a job offer. It is constrained by Equal Employment Opportunity regulations and historically has been plagued by haphazard practices and outright abuses. Various types of testing, interviews, physical examinations, and reference checks are all part of this sometimes lengthy sorting-out process. Employee selection is also a costly process. Not only is it expensive in terms of the time and effort put into screening procedures, but in terms of bad hiring decisions as well. By one estimate, losing a new employee after a few months costs, in terms of training and lost productivity, from $5,000 for an hourly worker to as much as $75,000 for a manager. A bad choice who *doesn't* quit can cost a company a great deal more in the long run, in real losses and lowered morale.[9] Each major part of the selection process deserves a closer look.

*Employment Application*    As the first step in the hiring process, candidates must usually complete an employment application. Figure 8.3 is a typical job

Steps in the hiring process    *Candidates complete an employment application as the first step in the hiring process. Some job seekers try to give themselves a competitive edge by supplementing their applications, such as this woman, who hopes to impress prospective employers with a video resume.*

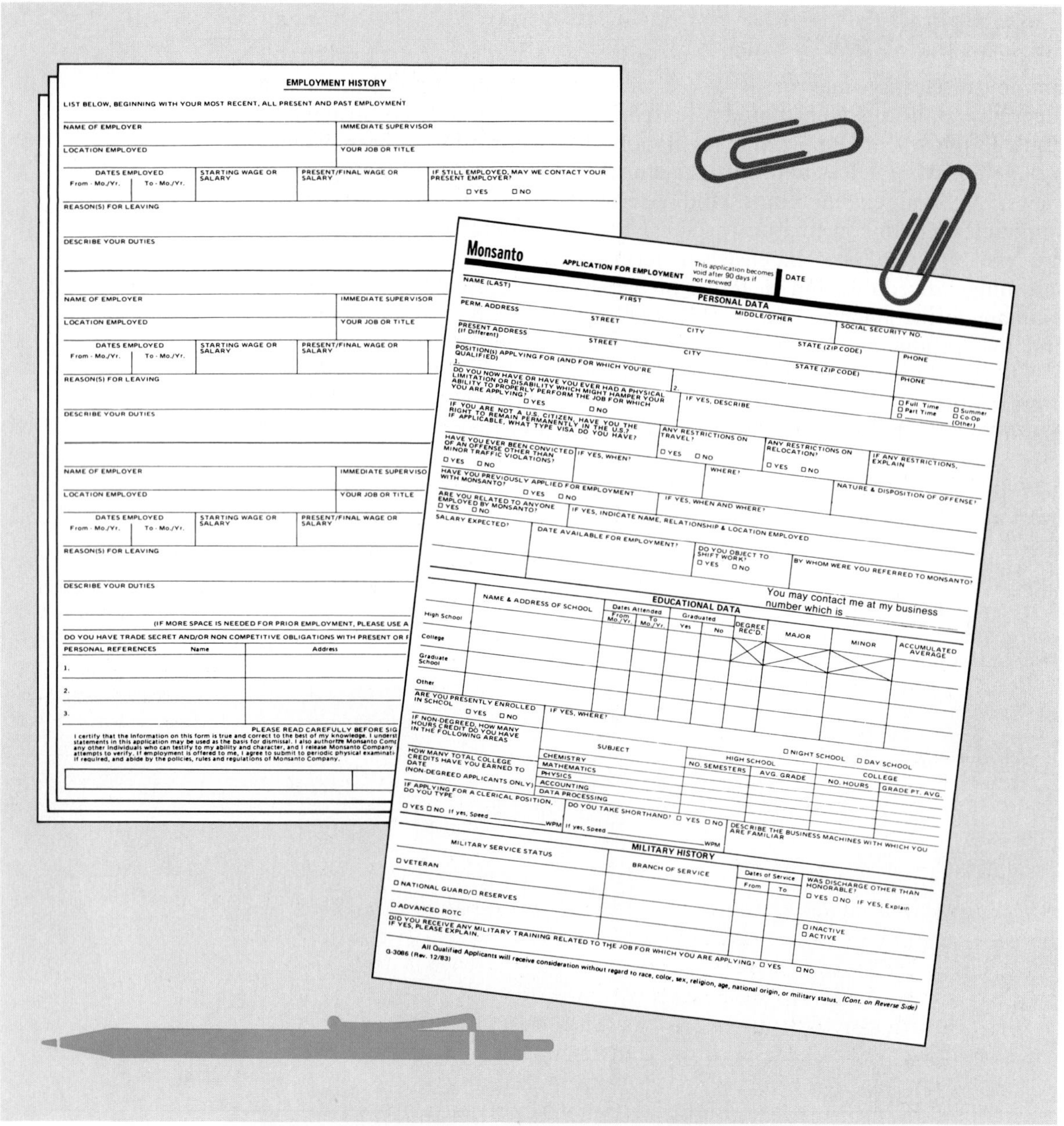

FIGURE 8.3 Sample Employment Application Form
Source: Used by permission of Monsanto Company.

application. An employment application serves three purposes. First, it records the candidate's interest in the firm. Second, it provides a profile of the candidate, which the human resources department can use to determine whether the applicant is qualified for the job and merits interviewing. Third, it becomes the basis of the successful applicant's employment records.

An employer must draft the employment application so that it avoids questions that might lead to charges of illegal discrimination. Some questions that on the surface seem proper could still result in discrimination. For example, "Have you ever been arrested?" seems neutral. Many people, however, are arrested for crimes yet are not prosecuted, much less convicted. Of course, an employer may ask whether a person has been convicted. Note that if an employer cannot include a question on an application form, it cannot ask the question at any point in the employment process.

*Employment Tests*   Many companies require job applicants to take **employment tests**, standardized screening devices intended to predict the applicant's potential for successful job performance. Employment tests can serve one or both of the following purposes: (1) identify "high-potential" applicants; and (2) screen out "high-risk" applicants. Four important considerations in choosing one of the testing techniques listed in Table 8.3 are "cost, relevance, legality, and ethics."[10] Clearly, there is no one best testing device.

Equal Employment Opportunity Commission guidelines specify that all employment tests must be valid, reliable, and nondiscriminatory predictors of job performance. A **valid employment test** measures what it is supposed to measure (such as typing speed). A **reliable employment test** consistently measures what it is supposed to measure. Above all, an employment test should not discriminate against protected minorities. If challenged by the EEOC, employers must be able to support with statistics the validity, reliability, and fairness of their employment testing techniques. Let's try these concepts out with the following real-life example:

> Russell Reynolds Jr., who heads a New York executive search firm that bears his name, likes to take a serious job candidate out for a sail, with an eye to seeing what kind of crew member he makes. Does he pitch in without being asked, or does he do little or nothing for fear of making a mistake? Says Reynolds: "I have found this an ideal way to spot life's 'givers' and 'takers.'"[11]

If Reynolds were actually hiring or not hiring corporate executives on the basis of his sailing "test," would it hold up in court? Almost certainly not, because this little adventure would systematically screen out people subject to chronic sea sickness, those deathly afraid of water, and those whose experience with sailboats was limited to seeing them on television. In short, the sailing test probably would be an undefendable employment test for any job other than that of sailboat crew member.

A good deal of controversy surrounds employment testing, and rightly so. Abuses through the years have led to government regulation. The most recent example of a federal curb on employment testing abuses is the Employee Polygraph Protection Act of 1988. As of December 27, 1988, it is illegal to require applicants for nongovernmental jobs to take a lie detector test unless the job involves security services or access to drugs. Current employees cannot be forced to take a polygraph test unless it is part of an ongoing investigation.[12] Drug testing is also a likely candidate for regulation because of its growing use. In fact, 37 percent of the companies polled in a recent nationwide survey reportedly used employee drug testing.[13] The pros and cons of various approaches to workplace drug testing are outlined in Business Issues.

**employment test** a standardized screening device intended to predict the applicant's potential for successful job performance

*4. Explain what the Equal Employment Opportunity Commission wants to see in an employment test.*

**valid employment test** test that measures what it is supposed to measure

**reliable employment test** test that consistently measures what it is supposed to measure

*Background Investigations*   To protect themselves against falsified resumes and lies on employment applications, employers often perform background checks on applicants who reach the final stages of the selection process. These investigations can be as simple as checking references or as detailed as verifying all of the applicant's claims.

TABLE 8.3   Employment Testing Techniques: An Overview

| Type of Test | Comments |
| --- | --- |
| ■ **Pencil-and-Paper Psychological and Personality Tests:** Measure attitudes and personality characteristics such as emotional stability, intelligence, and ability to deal with stress. | Renewed interest based on claims of improved validity; can be expensive when scoring and interpretations are done by professionals; validity varies widely from test to test. |
| ■ **Pencil-and-Paper Honesty Tests:** Assess candidate's degree of risk for engaging in dishonest behavior | Inexpensive to administer; questionable validity; growing in popularity since recent curtailment of polygraph testing. |
| ■ **Job Skills Tests (clerical and manual dexterity tests, math and language tests, assessment centers, and simulations):** Competence is assessed in actual "hands-on" situations. | Generally good validity if carefully designed and administered; assessment centers and simulations can be very expensive. |
| ■ **Polygraph (Lie Detector) Tests:** Measure physical signs of stress such as rapid pulse and perspiration. | Growing use in recent years severely restricted by federal (Employee Polygraph Protection Act of 1988), state, and local laws. Questionable validity. |
| ■ **Drug Tests:** Urine, blood, or hair samples submitted to chemical analysis for controlled substances. | Rapidly growing in use despite strong employee resistance and potentially inaccurate procedures. |
| ■ **Handwriting Analysis (graphoanalysis):** Personality characteristics and styles inferred from samples of handwriting. | Popular in Europe and growing in popularity in U.S.; sweeping claims by proponents leave validity in doubt. |
| ■ **AIDS/HIV Antibody Tests:** Blood samples tested for evidence of AIDS virus. | An emerging area with undetermined legal and ethical boundaries; major confidentiality issue. |

Sources: Adapted from discussion in Paul L. Blocklyn, "Preemployment Testing," *Personnel*, February 1988, pp. 66–68; Eric Rolfe Greenberg, "Workplace Testing: Results of a New AMA Survey," *Personnel*, April 1988, pp. 36–44; Karen M. Evans and Randall Brown, "Reducing Recruitment Risk Through Preemployment Testing," *Personnel*, September 1988, pp. 55–64; and James G. Frierson, "New Polygraph Test Limits," *Personnel Journal*, December 1988, pp. 84–92.

# THE PROS AND CONS OF WORKPLACE DRUG TESTING

Interest in on-the-job drug testing—both in the public and private sectors—has skyrocketed since the White House began pushing the concept in 1986. Below are the pros and cons of some types of drug testing used in the workplace.

- *Random testing.* In this most controversial form of testing, when your number comes up, you are tested.

  Private-sector employers are generally wary of random testing, which is currently under legal challenge.

  Advocates say that it deters drug use and that it prevents supervisors from singling out certain workers to punish or embarrass them.

  Opponents say that it could be unconstitutional. Police cannot search a person's house without obtaining a warrant; neither should employers be allowed to conduct a personal "search" of an employee without reasonable cause, they argue.

- *Periodic testing.* All workers take drug tests, usually at the time of their annual physical exams. The arguments pro and con are similar to those for random testing.

- *Preemployment testing.* In one of the most popular tests used in the private sector, job applicants submit to testing as part of the hiring process.

  Advocates say employers should have a right to know if a prospective employee is a drug user, particularly in jobs involving national security or public safety. Opponents say applicants have even fewer rights than employees.

  An initial positive test will probably disqualify an applicant, even though more-thorough (and expensive) testing could prove the result of the initial test to be false.

- *Postaccident testing.* Drugs tests are required any time a worker is involved in a job-related accident.

  The US Supreme Court will soon rule on the constitutionality of post-accident testing, in a case involving train crews in the federally regulated railroad industry.

- *Reasonable-cause testing.* You are tested if your employer suspects you of drug use.

  Advocates say this is the least pernicious type of testing, because the government (or the employer) must show reasonable suspicion before conducting a bodily search.

  Opponents say it could stigmatize workers and lead to unfair practices by employers. Supervisors, they add, do not have the training to identify the symptoms of drug use.

Source: Cheryl Sullivan, "Various Test Approaches: A Look at Pros and Cons," *The Christian Science Monitor,* January 25, 1989, p. 8.

References are usually the starting point in any background investigation. They are not, however, always valuable to an employer. Financial references have little relevance to job performance, and personal references are usually not worth much, since no one would deliberately refer a potential employer to someone who would give negative information. Information from previous employers is more valuable. Immediate supervisors especially have had the opportunity to observe the applicant's behavior and performance. Employers seldom want academic references for applicants who have been working for some years. These are quite helpful, though, when an applicant is about to graduate and has only part-time or summer work experience.

*Physical Examinations*   Some firms require applicants to take physical examinations. Either the company doctor or a doctor approved by the employer performs the examinations, which the firm pays for. Where jobs require heavy lifting or other major forms of exertion, physicals are a must. Firms hiring for food service positions must have prospective employees tested for communicable diseases like tuberculosis.

Some firms use preemployment physicals to protect themselves against insurance or worker's compensation claims for conditions employees had before taking the job. Not long ago, an insurer ran an ad featuring a picture of a high-school football player being carried off the field on a stretcher. The caption urged employers to insure with that company because its record-keeping would eliminate claims for injuries that had occurred earlier.

*Interviews*   Two common types of interviews during the selection process are initial and selection interviews. An *initial interview* should determine whether an applicant meets the firm's minimum qualifications for the jobs it has open. The interview should cover the type of work the applicant wants, his or her pay expectations, and possible starting dates.

*Selection interviews* are conducted in much more depth than initial interviews. They typically come after the employer has all the information it wants on the applicant. The interviewer can probe an applicant's personality and give him or her an opportunity to elaborate on information in the application. At this time, the interviewer should also tell the applicant more about the company and the position available. The success of the employment process may depend on how clearly the interviewer and the applicant understand each other on the terms and conditions of the job. The applicant should ask questions in the same penetrating vein as the interviewer.

The number of selection interviews an applicant will have depends on the nature of the position. An applicant for, say, a retail sales position is likely to have only one interview, probably with the sales manager. By contrast, an applicant for an entry-level auditing position with a major accounting firm can expect several selection interviews. One may be with a human resources professional, the others with potential coworkers and supervisors.

Selection interviews are of three types. The first and most common is the **structured interview**, in which the interviewer asks a series of prepared questions based on the job specifications. This type is also known as a guided, directed, or patterned interview. Its structured nature protects against untrained interviewers by ensuring that the same questions are put to all interviewees. The second type is the **unstructured interview**, in which the interviewer does not have a firmly set structure for the interview and the interviewee does most of the talking. This format is more common in grievance, counseling, and exit interviews.

The third type of selection interview is the **stress interview**, in which the interviewer deliberately annoys, embarrasses, or frustrates the applicant to determine his or her reaction. Businesses use stress interviews for positions

**structured interview**
interview in which the interviewer asks a series of prepared questions based on the job specifications

**unstructured interview**
interview in which the interviewer does not have a firmly set structure for the interview and the interviewee does most of the talking

**stress interview**   interview in which the interviewer deliberately annoys, embarrasses, or frustrates the applicant to determine his or her reaction

that are primarily managerial, particularly in customer and employee relations, where it is important to remain calm and in control under pressure.

*Selection Decision*   Usually, the human resources department and the manager filling the position make the selection decision cooperatively. A joint decision improves their chances for making a good choice. Such a decision brings to bear the expertise both of employment professionals and of the person for whom the new employee will work.

## Orientation

Soon after a new employee joins a firm, he or she should receive an orientation, the process of introducing new employees to their new organization and job. During the orientation the human resources representative commonly covers background like the company's history, organizational structure, product or service lines, and key managers. Other topics may include the company's employee policies and procedures like sick leave and vacations, the availability of health and life insurance, and safety regulations. For example, a new hire at either Disneyland or Walt Disney World can expect to spend at least three days at "Disney University" being oriented and trained:

> The orientation consists of two day-long "traditions" courses followed by one to fourteen days of on-the-job training. The first day of traditions courses, often referred to as "Traditions I," gives the cast member an overview of the history, achievements, and philosophy of Disney World, a rundown on an individual cast member's "role" in the show, and a tour of the Disney property. The second day of classes includes an introduction to Disney policies and procedures, a summary of the social and recreational benefits available to the cast, and an introduction and orientation to the cast member's new work area.[14]

Because the new employee's major source of information about the new work environment will come from the orientation session, it is critically important that the company's expectations and demands be fully explained. The new employee's supervisor should describe the requirements of the position in detail and how it relates in a larger way to what the company does. Other topics the supervisor should cover include the policies on coffee breaks and lunch hours, the physical layout of the work area, and the nature of the new employee's on-the-job relationships with other employees.

# Evaluating and Developing Job Performance

Once people have been hired, constructive steps must be taken to keep them productive, relatively content, and up to date. This is where performance appraisal, employee assistance programs, and training and development come into play. We examine each of these important human resource management activities in this section along with a look at promotion, transfer, and discharge.

## Performance Appraisal

performance appraisal
a formal assessment of how
well employees are doing their
jobs

Most public and private organizations big enough to have a formalized management system conduct some type of performance appraisal. A **performance appraisal** is a formal assessment of how well employees are doing their jobs. One study of 589 personnel administrators found that 87 percent had some sort of performance appraisal system in place. Significantly, only 54 percent of those with a formal performance appraisal system were satisfied with it.[15] Although many managers are uncomfortable with the notion of evaluating others, effective performance appraisal is a cornerstone of good management.

5. Identify the primary purposes of performance appraisals and describe three appraisal techniques.

*Purposes of Appraisal*   Performance appraisals serve two kinds of purposes. First, they help evaluate employees, including determining eligibility for pay raises and promotion and deciding which employees to retain. Second, they help develop employees because they are future oriented and aimed at improving the employee's career potential.

Because an employee's immediate supervisor is in the best position to observe the employee, he or she usually conducts the performance appraisal. In some companies, however, the employees do self-appraisals, which the supervisor then reviews with them. In a few companies, coworkers review each other's performance.

management by
objectives (MBO)
employee performance-
appraisal technique based on
objectives established jointly
by the employee and his or
her supervisor

*Appraisal of Techniques*   A widely used employee performance-appraisal technique based on objectives established jointly by the employee and his or her supervisor is called **management by objectives (MBO)**. The employee's progress is reviewed periodically during the course of the period for which the goals were set. Some organizations use MBO primarily as a planning technique.

Other appraisal techniques include graphic rating scales in which specific aspects of job performance are rated on graphic scales of 1–7 or 1–10, performance checklists (see Figure 8.4), and rank-order appraisals. A rank-order appraisal requires the supervisor to rank all employees under his or her supervision from best to worst on a global performance scale. This simple technique becomes quite difficult to use with large numbers of employees.

Performance appraisals are an empty exercise if the employer does not communicate the results to the employee. In most cases, the immediate supervisor conducts the postappraisal interview. This supervisor should tell the employee the results of the appraisal, encourage the employee to continue his or her positive behavior, and plan for future improvement as well as explain salary or promotion decisions.

## Employee Assistance Programs

People do not leave their personal problems on the doorstep when they go to work. Drug and alcohol, domestic, financial, and emotional problems accompany employees into the workplace. An estimated 18 percent of the U.S. work force is plagued by personal problems that can have a negative and costly impact on job performance.[16] Employee drug and alcohol abuse

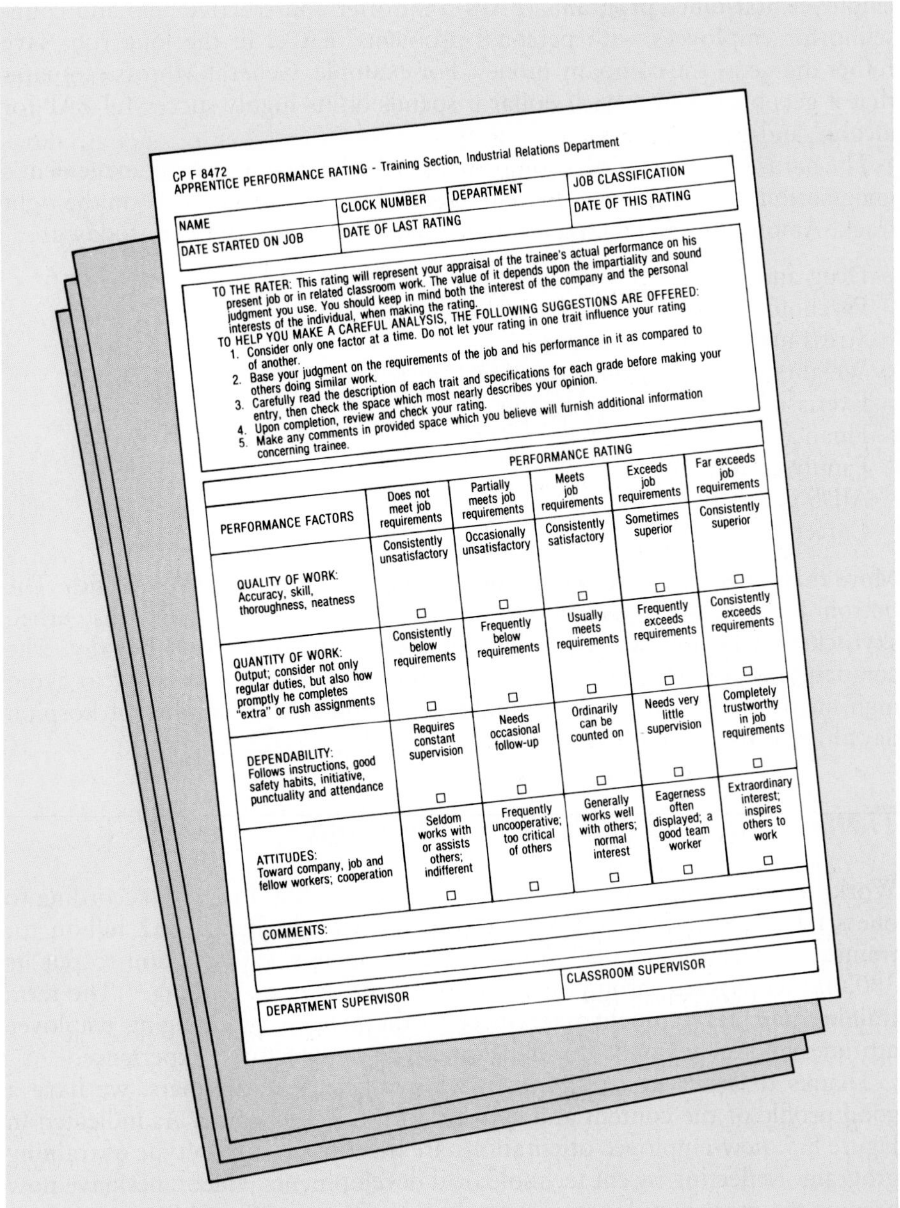

CP F 8472
APPRENTICE PERFORMANCE RATING - Training Section, Industrial Relations Department

| NAME | CLOCK NUMBER | DEPARTMENT | JOB CLASSIFICATION |
|---|---|---|---|
| DATE STARTED ON JOB | DATE OF LAST RATING | | DATE OF THIS RATING |

TO THE RATER: This rating will represent your appraisal of the trainee's actual performance on his present job or in related classroom work. The value of it depends upon the impartiality and sound judgment you use. You should keep in mind both the interest of the company and the personal interests of the individual, when making the rating.
TO HELP YOU MAKE A CAREFUL ANALYSIS, THE FOLLOWING SUGGESTIONS ARE OFFERED:
1. Consider only one factor at a time. Do not let your rating in one trait influence your rating of another.
2. Base your judgment on the requirements of the job and his performance in it as compared to others doing similar work.
3. Carefully read the description of each trait and specifications for each grade before making your entry, then check the space which most nearly describes your opinion.
4. Upon completion, review and check your rating.
5. Make any comments in provided space which you believe will furnish additional information concerning trainee.

| | PERFORMANCE RATING | | | | |
|---|---|---|---|---|---|
| PERFORMANCE FACTORS | Does not meet job requirements | Partially meets job requirements | Meets job requirements | Exceeds job requirements | Far exceeds job requirements |
| QUALITY OF WORK: Accuracy, skill, thoroughness, neatness | Consistently unsatisfactory ☐ | Occasionally unsatisfactory ☐ | Consistently satisfactory ☐ | Sometimes superior ☐ | Consistently superior ☐ |
| QUANTITY OF WORK: Output; consider not only regular duties, but also how promptly he completes "extra" or rush assignments | Consistently below requirements ☐ | Frequently below requirements ☐ | Usually meets requirements ☐ | Frequently exceeds requirements ☐ | Consistently exceeds requirements ☐ |
| DEPENDABILITY: Follows instructions, good safety habits, initiative, punctuality and attendance | Requires constant supervision ☐ | Needs occasional follow-up ☐ | Ordinarily can be counted on ☐ | Needs very little supervision ☐ | Completely trustworthy in job requirements ☐ |
| ATTITUDES: Toward company, job and fellow workers; cooperation | Seldom works with or assists others; indifferent ☐ | Frequently uncooperative; too critical of others ☐ | Generally works well with others; normal interest ☐ | Eagerness often displayed; a good team worker ☐ | Extraordinary interest; inspires others to work ☐ |

COMMENTS:

| | |
|---|---|
| DEPARTMENT SUPERVISOR | CLASSROOM SUPERVISOR |

FIGURE 8.4 Sample Performance Checklist Appraisal
Source: Champion International Corporation. Used with permission.

alone costs the U.S. economy an estimated $60 to $100 billion a year. This huge drag on the economy is worsened by impaired employees who do more shoddy work, have more accidents, and accrue more absenteeism and sick leave than their sober coworkers.[17] Progressive employers no longer fire or simply ignore troubled employees. Instead, many companies have developed

**employee assistance
program (EAP)** program
that offers constructive help
and counseling for employees
with personal problems

**6.** Explain what an
employee assistance program
(EAP) is.

employee assistance programs (**EAPs**) that offer constructive help and counseling for employees with personal problems. EAPs, in the long run, save rather than cost the company money. For example, General Motors estimates that it gets back $3 for each dollar it spends on its highly successful EAP for alcohol and drug abusers.[18]

The nature and extent of a company's EAP is limited only by management's imagination and willingness to help troubled employees get back on the right track. Among the EAP activities found in business and industry today are:

- Drug and alcohol abuse counseling and treatment
- Psychological counseling for emotional problems
- Stress management training
- Weight control and quit smoking clinics
- Exercise and wellness programs
- Financial counseling
- Family counseling
- AIDS counseling
- Career counseling

More than altruism drives companies into these types of EAP activities. The bottom line is also a powerful incentive. Quaker Oats Company has curbed skyrocketing health care costs by helping its employees stay healthy. The company installed a fitness center and conducts programs on how to avoid high medical bills. As a result Quaker has reduced the number of hospital days logged by its employees by 58 percent.[19]

## Training and Development Programs

Workplace training today is an immense undertaking. In 1987, according to one study, U.S. public and private organizations budgeted $32 billion for training and development.[20] Annually, IBM spends $900 million to put its 390,000 employees through 5 million student days of training.[21] The term **training and development** refers here to the process of changing employee attitudes and/or behavior through some type of structured experience.

**training and
development** the process
of changing employee attitudes
and/or behavior through some
type of structured experience

**7.** Identify the most
common type of training and
the most widely used training
technique.

Thanks to a survey of 2,830 *Training* magazine subscribers, we have a good profile of the content and delivery of modern training. As indicated in Figure 8.5, new-employee orientations are the most common type of training program. Reflecting recent technological developments, videotapes have now become the most popular training technique. The traditional lecture method is still a strong second.

A recent training trend of great importance is an emphasis on remedial education. In view of the fact that 29 percent of American high school

FIGURE 8.5   Research Reveals the Content and Delivery of Today's Training

Source: Data from Chris Lee, "Where the Training Dollars Go," *Training*, October 1987, pp. 60, 64, as adapted by Robert Kreitner, *Management*, 4th ed. (Boston: Houghton Mifflin, 1989), p. 368. Reprinted with permission from the October, 1987, issue of TRAINING, The Magazine of Human Resources Development. Copyright 1987, Lakewood Publications, Inc., Minneapolis, MN (612) 333-0471. All rights reserved.

## TYPES OF TRAINING
### Percent providing

New-employee orientation
75.8

Performance appraisals
63.5

Time management
61.4

Leadership
58.8

Word processing
56.6

Stress management
53.1

Team building
51.5

Hiring/selection
51.0

New-equipment operation
50.6

Goal setting
49.2

Problem solving
46.0

Safety
46.0

Product knowledge
45.9

Interpersonal skills
44.2

Motivation
44.2

Managing change
42.8

Train-the-trainer
42.7

Listening skills
41.4

Planning
41.0

Personal computer applications
39.4

## INSTRUCTIONAL METHODS
### Percent using these methods for employee training

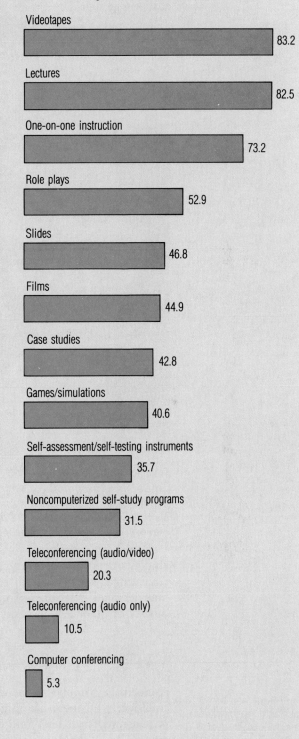

Videotapes
83.2

Lectures
82.5

One-on-one instruction
73.2

Role plays
52.9

Slides
46.8

Films
44.9

Case studies
42.8

Games/simulations
40.6

Self-assessment/self-testing instruments
35.7

Noncomputerized self-study programs
31.5

Teleconferencing (audio/video)
20.3

Teleconferencing (audio only)
10.5

Computer conferencing
5.3

**Training for the job** *Today's organizations are spending heavily on training and development programs for their employees. American Express and Shearson Lehman Hutton are investing in a different kind of training. In cooperation with New York public schools, the two companies established the Academy of Finance, a two-year program that offers classroom instruction as well as practical work experience.*

students drop out before graduation, companies are having to take up the educational slack through remedial courses in reading, writing, math, and interpersonal relations. America's competitiveness is tied directly to the quality of its new workers.

## Promotion, Transfer, and Discharge

**promotion** an advancement granted to an employee to a higher position, greater responsibility, or more prestige

Aside from compensation (discussed in the next section), the reality of an employee's business life might be summed up in terms of three activities: promotions, transfers, and separations. A **promotion** is an advancement granted to an employee to a higher position, greater responsibility, or more

238

prestige. An increase in salary often accompanies a promotion. Organizations promote on the basis of performance, seniority, or both. Union contracts usually require promotion on the basis of **seniority**, the length of employment with a given employer in relation to the time that all the other employees in the unit have worked for the employer. For example, in a unionized steel mill all union members have the right to bid on a job, but the job will usually go to the bidder who has worked there the longest.

Sometimes a promotion includes a *transfer,* a shift from one job to another in an organization that may or may not require a change in the employee's place of work. Transfers can also be horizontal changes that do not involve a promotion.

**Separation** is the ending of the employment relationship. One form of separation is *quitting,* an employee's voluntary departure from a job. *Retirement* is a form of separation. So, too, are **layoffs**, separations caused by the employer's lack of work, which may become permanent. There is a growing trend toward the use of outplacement to ease the trauma of layoff for an employee. **Outplacement programs** teach laid-off employees job-hunting skills and help them find suitable employment. A **discharge** or *termination* is a permanent separation initiated by the employer, usually for cause, such as absenteeism or poor job performance.[22]

seniority the length of employment with a given employer in relation to the time that all the other employees in the unit have worked for the employer

separation the ending of the employment relationship

layoff a separation caused by the employer's lack of work

outplacement program a program that teaches laid-off employees job-hunting skills and helps them find suitable employment

discharge a permanent separation initiated by the employer, usually for cause, such as absenteeism or poor job performance

# Compensation and Benefits

Employees work for **compensation**, the money or benefits or both for which an employee exchanges work.

compensation the money or benefits or both for which an employee exchanges work

## The Purposes of a Compensation System

A business's compensation system has three main purposes: attracting qualified employees, retaining those employees, and motivating higher levels of performance from them. A firm achieves each of these goals through the various aspects of the compensation system.

*8. Explain how compensation systems achieve their three primary purposes.*

*Attracting Qualified Employees* A company's ability to attract qualified employees depends in part on how its general level of pay compares with that of other firms competing for the same type of employee. The average pay for a particular position among comparable firms is called the *going rate.* Businesses do not want their pay scale to vary much from the going rate. A company that sets, say, entry-level credit supervisors' salaries at $20,000 when the going rate is $23,500 will not attract as many qualified applicants as its competitors. To determine what the going rate is, companies consult a **wage/salary survey**, a review of pay rates within comparable industries in a particular region. Thus, a retail clothing chain centered in the New York metropolitan area might look at credit supervisors' wages at consumer electronics outlets in and around New York. Data from Dallas would be of little use. A business, a consulting firm, a human resources trade association, or a government group might take or commission the survey.

wage/salary survey a review of pay rates at companies within comparable industries in a particular region

*"Although the portions were large, overall I found the health care a bit weak, the vacation plan too lightly seasoned, and the retirement plan past its prime."*

*Retaining Employees*   Hiring an employee is expensive, so retaining productive employees is a key goal of compensation systems. Keeping workers is primarily a function of maintaining a fair **pay structure**, the relationship among the rates of pay for various jobs within the company. Employees dissatisfied with a pay structure often look for new jobs.

The relative importance of jobs to the company determines their rates of pay. For instance, a defense contractor would pay a research engineer more than a bookkeeper, but an engineer would make less than the vice president of the division in which he or she works.

## Types of Compensation

A compensation system includes base pay, incentives, and benefits. A good system motivates effective performance by establishing fair individual rates of compensation and by effectively linking performance to compensation.

**Base pay** refers to the basic wages or salaries that workers receive. For example, a job description stating a wage of $7.50 per hour, $300 per week, or $1,200 per month states the position's base pay. **Incentives** refers to bonuses and other plans designed to encourage employees to produce work beyond the minimum acceptable levels. Incentives take many forms, including cash bonuses, options to buy stock, and gifts. **Benefits** are services that employees receive that are paid for by the employer, like health insurance, pensions, and vacations. Benefits are a major cost consideration for businesses because they had grown to 40 percent of the American payroll by 1987.[22] Because health-care costs (insurance premiums and direct payments to doctors

**pay structure**   the relationship among the rates of pay for various jobs within the company

**base pay**   the basic wages or salaries that workers receive

**incentives**   bonuses and other plans designed to encourage employees to produce work beyond the minimum acceptable levels

**benefits**   services that employees receive that are paid for by the employer, like health insurance, pensions, and vacations and hospitals) are the primary contributor to higher benefits costs, businesses have pushed some of the burden onto employees in the form of higher deductibles.

Because individuals have different benefits needs, some employers have established *flexible-benefit programs* (also known as **cafeteria-style benefit programs**), which permit employees to choose from an array of benefit programs, up to a preset limit (see Figure 8.6). The employee's choices are like those of a person entering a cafeteria with just a $5 bill. The person may select whatever he or she wants, as long as the total cost does not exceed $5. The American Can Company, for example, allows its employees to design their own benefits, drawing from five benefit areas: medical insurance, life

**cafeteria-style benefit programs** programs that permit employees to choose from an array of benefit programs, up to a preset limit

FIGURE 8.6   Flexible Benefits

Because individuals have different benefit needs, some employers have established flexible benefit programs that permit employees to choose from an array of benefit programs.

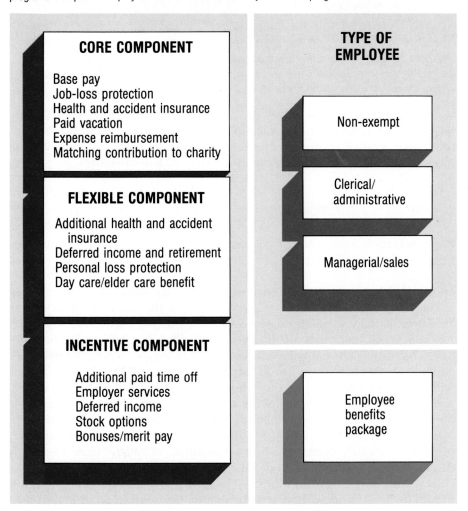

**Employee benefits** *By meeting the personal needs of its employees, through affordable day-care within the office complex, a company can receive a higher rate of employee recruitment, retainment, and productivity.*

insurance, disability insurance, vacations, and retirement programs. A healthy, unmarried woman in her twenties can thus create a very different mix of benefits from that of a chronically ill married man in his sixties.

## Bases of Compensation

Employers can choose among three bases of compensation: time, productivity, or a combination of the two.

**wages** compensation usually calculated according to the number of hours an employee actually worked

*Time*   Employees paid on the basis of the time they work may receive **wages**, compensation usually calculated according to the number of hours an employee actually worked. Employees covered by the Fair Labor Standards Act who work more than 40 hours in a given week must receive overtime pay. That rate is normally one and a half times the usual hourly rate. Thus, an employee whose wages are $6 per hour who works 44 hours in a week will receive $9 per hour for the 4 hours of overtime. In contrast, **salary** is compensation calculated usually on a weekly, monthly, or yearly basis and not normally related to the number of hours actually worked. The Fair Labor Standards Act exempts many salaried employees from its overtime pay provisions. Hence, human resource specialists normally refer to hourly employees as *nonexempts* and to salaried employees as *exempts*.

**salary** compensation calculated usually on a weekly, monthly, or yearly basis and not normally related to the number of hours actually worked

*Productivity*   Compensation systems that pay employees according to their productivity are called *incentive systems*. We are able to discuss only the two

242                                                                 *PART III / HUMAN RESOURCES AND PRODUCTION*

most important of the many incentive systems. A **piece-rate system** is an incentive system that compensates a worker according to the number of units of a product he or she produces. The employer determines wages by multiplying the number of units produced times the piece rate for one unit. The other main incentive system is the **commission basis,** in which sales employees receive either a fixed amount or a percentage of the value of the sales they make. The commission system in effect gives employees a double incentive. On the one hand, if they do not sell anything, they get no pay. On the other, there usually is no upper limit on what they can earn.

*Time and Productivity*   Perhaps the most common compensation systems combine the time and productivity criteria. The weight given each element depends on both the company and the job.

Many firms pay their employees a **bonus,** a payment beyond the employees' base pay or commissions. Often, only upper management receives bonuses, but some firms distribute them to all employees after a successful year. Companies calculate bonuses usually on either a lump sum or a percentage of salary basis. Anaheim Custom Extruders, a plastic tubing manufacturer, assigns 28 percent of its profits to a bonus pool, which it then distributes in proportion to the employees' base salaries. This company is built on incentives. At the end of each shift, supervisors hand out $15 and $25 cash bonuses and six-packs of beer or soda to workers who make their productivity goals.

A **profit-sharing program** distributes a set portion of a company's profits to its employees, according to a standard formula. For example, a firm might set aside 15 percent of its profits for distribution to its employees, based on

**piece-rate system**   an incentive system that compensates a worker according to the number of units of a product he or she produces

**commission basis**   an incentive system in which sales employees receive either a fixed amount or a percentage of the value of the sales they make

**bonus**   a payment beyond the employees' base pay or commissions

**profit-sharing program**   program that distributes a set portion of a company's profits to its employees, according to a standard formula

Working out at work   *With the rising cost of providing health care benefits, more companies are recognizing the value of investing in their employees' "wellness" by providing sports facilities for their workers.*

a formula related to their salaries. Ryan Transfer in Green Bay, Wisconsin, offers a variant on profit sharing. Employees who choose to participate divide 40 percent of the company's gross sales with management, up to and including the president, instead of receiving wages.

# Today's Human Resources Challenges

At no other time in history has business faced so many and such complex human resources challenges as it does today. It is worth summarizing them:

- How to establish and maintain equal employment opportunities for women and minority group members.
- How to cope with the increasingly complex legal requirements relating to employee compensation and benefit plans.
- What to do about the skyrocketing costs of health care, which directly affect the cost of medical insurance.
- How to set up equitable rates of pay to reflect female and male employees' comparable worth to the firm.
- What businesses can use to motivate employees when labor market conditions dictate that entry-level salaries must nearly match those being paid to senior employees in the same job classification (a problem called *wage compression*).
- How to motivate new hires in a two-tier system who will never achieve the base pay of senior employees in the same job classification.
- Seek out solutions to curb on-the-job use of alcohol and drugs.
- How to make up for the educational deficiencies plaguing entry-level employees.
- How to balance the employee's right to privacy with the employer's right to know in the areas of drug and AIDS testing.
- How to deal with AIDS and fear of AIDS in the workplace.

# CHAPTER HIGHLIGHTS

*1. Explain what human resource management is and describe the factors that have contributed to its importance.*

*Human resource management* encompasses the activities involved in acquiring, deploying, and developing people in a business. The work force has changed dramatically over the last two decades. Four changes in particular have raised the importance of human resource managers in a firm: the entry of minorities into skilled jobs and the professions, an enormous increase in the number of women in the workplace, an aging work force, and educational mismatches.

*2. Explain the human resource planning process.*

The *human resource planning process* consists of several stages: forecasting demand, estimating the supply, and planning to meet the needs. To plan effectively, businesses must engage in job analysis, the systematic study of an employee's duties, tasks, and work environment. After studying a job, analysts prepare a *job description*—a written summary of the duties, tasks, and responsibilities associated with a job—and a *job specification*—a list of qualifications a person needs to perform a job successfully.

**3.** *List the steps in the employment process.*

The three steps in the employment process are *recruitment*, the process of attracting qualified people to apply for jobs; *selection*, the process of identifying appropriate candidates; and *orientation*, the process of introducing new employees to the organization and the job.

**4.** *Explain what the Equal Employment Opportunity Commission wants to see in an employment test.*

The EEOC wants all employment tests to be *valid* (measure what they are supposed to measure), *reliable* (consistently measure what they are supposed to measure), and *nondiscriminatory* (fair to minorities).

**5.** *Identify the primary purposes of performance appraisals and describe three appraisal techniques.*

*Performance appraisals*, the formal assessment of how well employees are doing their jobs, serve two kinds of purposes: evaluation purposes and development purposes. Their evaluation purposes include determining eligibility for pay raises and promotion and deciding which employees to retain. Their development purposes are future-oriented and are aimed at improving the employee's career potential.

**6.** *Explain what an employee assistance program (EAP) is.*

An employee assistance program is a company-sponsored program offering constructive help and counseling to employees with personal problems including drug and alcohol abuse, stress management, financial counseling, and family problems.

**7.** *Identify the most common type of training and the most widely used training technique.*

According to recent research, new-employee orientation is the most common type of training today and videotapes are the most widely used training technique.

**8.** *Explain how compensation systems achieve their three primary purposes.*

A business's compensation system has three main purposes: attracting qualified employees, retaining those employees, and motivating higher levels of performance from them. When a firm pays the going rate or better, it is likely to attract employees. Retaining employees is primarily a function of maintaining a fair pay structure. Incentive systems that involve bonuses, pay that is tied to productivity, and/or profit-sharing plans serve to motivate employees to perform better.

# *KEY TERMS*

| | | | |
|---|---|---|---|
| Human resource management | Skills inventory | Performance appraisal | Pay structure |
| Antidiscrimination laws | Job analysis | Management by objectives (MBO) | Base pay |
| Civil Rights Act of 1964 (Title VII) | Job description | Employee assistance program (EAP) | Incentives |
| Equal Employment Opportunity Act | Job specification | Training and development | Benefits |
| Equal Employment Opportunity Commission (EEOC) | Recruitment | Promotion | Cafeteria-style benefit programs |
| Affirmative action programs | Selection | Seniority | Wages |
| Human resource planning | Orientation | Separation | Salary |
| Attrition | Employment test | Layoff | Piece-rate system |
| | Valid employment test | Outplacement program | Commission basis |
| | Reliable employment test | Discharge | Bonus |
| | Structured interview | Compensation | Profit-sharing program |
| | Unstructured interview | Wage/salary survey | |
| | Stress interview | | |

# REVIEW QUESTIONS

1. Why is human resource management especially important today?
2. In what ways is America's work force changing?
3. What do the following terms mean: job analysis, job description, job specification?
4. What are four major sources of potential employees?
5. What are the steps in the employment process? Explain each step.
6. Which employment test in Table 8.3 is the best? Explain your reasoning.
7. Why are employee orientations important?
8. Why do you suppose nearly half of the users of formal performance appraisals are dissatisfied with them?
9. What should a good compensation system accomplish?
10. What are the two ways of paying employees on the basis of time? Distinguish between them.

# APPLICATION EXERCISES

1. Recently you assumed the management duties at a shoe store in a large metropolitan area. This store has a history of high employee turnover and low morale. These problems have had a negative impact on profits of the business. To correct these problems, you have decided to improve the employee selection and screening process. Briefly describe the steps that might be taken to identify capable employees. How would you screen applicants?

2. In recent weeks you have applied for several part-time positions. One position is with a small manufacturing plant. The starting hourly wage is $8.00 and you will be able to work from 20 to 25 hours each week. The other position is with a large manufacturing company that uses a piece-rate compensation system. The hours will be the same, but the potential for higher hourly earnings exists. At the present time, the average hourly pay earned by employees is $8.60. Which position would be most appealing to you? What are some of the major advantages and disadvantages of each compensation plan from your standpoint? From the employer's standpoint?

# CASES

## 8.1 "Pixie Dust" Is Disney's Secret to Managing People

The Walt Disney Company, which operates the original Disneyland in California and Walt Disney World in Florida, has long been one of the best-known names in family entertainment. One of the main reasons for that name recognition is the Disney organization's unique approach to inspiring commitment and motivation in its employees—an approach that has earned it a reputation as one of the best-managed companies in America.

Now the Disney company has developed a seminar designed to share its management philosophy and strategies with human resources managers and other business professionals. Inspired by Thomas J. Peters and Robert H. Waterman's *In Search of Excellence* (Warner Books, 1984) and initiated in January 1985 at Walt Disney World, "The Disney Approach to People Management" offers an intensive three-day look at "how Disney does it."

Managing the Disney operation is indeed an imposing task. Located on 28,000 sprawling acres, Walt Disney World—which consists of the Vacation Kingdom complex and the EPCOT (Experimental Prototype Community of Tomorrow) Center—requires 1,100 types of jobs filled by more than 25,000 full-time and part-time employees to entertain the 25 million guests who visit the resort each year.

How does Disney successfully direct the energies of so many employees toward achieving its goals? The secret, according to seminar manager Rick Johnson, is "pixie dust," a magic ingredient that inspires Disney employees to provide the best in service for their guests.

The formula for pixie dust is simple: Training + Communication + Care = Pride. By carefully training and developing cast members, by making all cast communications timely and effective, and by encouraging a friendly and caring work environment, Disney creates a strong sense of pride in each cast member, which in turn inspires him or her to give first-rate service to all Disney guests. The participants in the people management seminar learn first-hand how the pixie-dust formula is applied to all aspects of the Disney World operation.

## Questions

1. Why do you think the "pixie dust" formula has worked so well for Disney?
2. Which part of the "pixie dust" formula do you think is most crucial? Explain your reasoning.

Source: Excerpted from Paul L. Blocklyn, "Making Magic: The Disney Approach to People Management," *Personnel,* December 1988, pp. 28–29.

## 8.2 A Human Resources Nightmare at U.S. Air

*Hi, Ray. I think it's sort of ironical that we end up like this. I asked for leniency for my family, remember. Well, I got none and you'll get none.*

—A note purportedly written by U.S. Air employee David Burke to his former supervisor, Raymond Thomson.

The above note, which was reprinted in the December 12, 1987 edition of *The San Diego Union,* was found at the crash site of Pacific Southwest Airlines Flight #1771. Forty-three people died in the crash—including David Burke and Raymond Thomson.

This tragic scenario, while extreme in the sense of desperation that it conveys, highlights the chaos that can follow an employee's termination. In this case, Burke was fired for allegedly stealing $69.00 in beverage receipts from U.S. Air, Inc. (which owns Pacific Southwest Airlines) and for drinking on the job. According to newspaper accounts, however, the feud between Burke and Thomson had apparently started at least five months before the tragedy when Burke stated in an informal complaint to the California Department of Fair Employment and Housing that he had twice been passed over for promotion because of his race and had accused Thomson of discrimination. While we may never know all the details of the meetings between these two men, one thing is clear. An employee was fired, and in the aftermath of that firing he carried out a vengeful act against his former boss that left 43 people dead and their families devastated.

## Questions

1. Should managers who read this account be afraid to fire anyone for fear they will be creating a mass murderer? Explain.
2. What role could an employee assistance program (EAP) have played in this situation?

Source: From Miriam Rothman, "Employee Termination, 1: A Four-Step Procedure," pp. 31–32. Reprinted, by permission of the publisher, from PERSONNEL, February/1989 © 1989. American Management Association, New York. All rights reserved.

# 9 Labor-Management Relations

After you have completed this chapter, you will be able to do the following:

**1.** Describe the role of Samuel Gompers in the development of the American labor movement.

**2.** Identify the antitrust acts that affected the labor movement's effort to organize American industry.

**3.** List the key features of the National Labor Relations Act, the Taft-Hartley Act, and the Landrum-Griffin Act.

**4.** List the steps in the unionization process and summarize each.

**5.** Identify the subjects that may and may not be discussed in collective bargaining.

**6.** Describe the stages of a grievance proceeding.

**7.** Define givebacks and discuss the effects of this concept on bargaining today.

**8.** Analyze the phases of collective bargaining.

**9.** Identify the weapons each side in collective bargaining has to force an agreement.

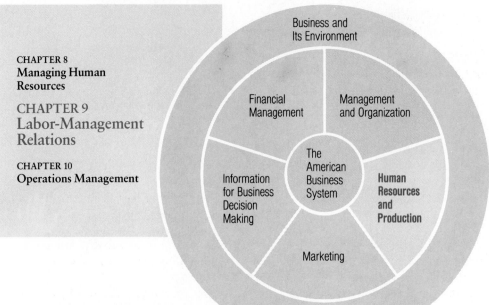

Business and
Its Environment

Financial
Management

Management
and Organization

The
American
Business
System

Information
for Business
Decision
Making

Human
Resources
and
Production

Marketing

Frederick W. Smith, founder of Federal Express Corporation, has an overwhelming desire to be number one. Yet in one area victory has eluded Smith: Federal Express continues to struggle to be a major player in international deliveries. Smith, who was awarded the now infamous "C" on an economics paper that outlined his idea for an overnight delivery service, plans to improve his company's chances by paying $880 million for a resurgent Tiger International, Inc., the world's biggest heavy cargo airline, best known for its Flying Tiger Line.

The merger represents a step toward Smith's goal of making Federal Express the best and largest transportation company in the world. Among the hurdles Smith faces is the task of combining Tiger's unionized work force of 6,500 with Federal's nonunion employees. Any consolidation could compromise Smith's paternal "no-layoff" credo and dilute Federal's entrepreneurial culture. An industry consultant warns that "this merger will have to be handled like two porcupines making love—very carefully." Smith disagrees. "It's a big challenge, no question," he says. "I don't know that it's a bet-the-company move. We get a lot of hard assets with this acquisition."[1]

**union** an organization through which employees combine their strength to advance their common interests

**organized labor** workers represented by unions

This chapter's focus is on **unions**, organizations through which employees combine their strength to advance their common interests. Relations are not always harmonious between management and **organized labor**, workers represented by unions. In fact, when most people think of labor-management relations, what come to mind are often harsh words and bitter strikes. But as GM and the UAW are proving, traditional foes can work together to meet challenges not dreamed of when unions first succeeded in organizing American industry.

# The Early Union Movement

In 1787, representatives of the thirteen original states met in Philadelphia and drafted our Constitution. Five years later, a small group of Philadelphia shoemakers formed the first union. When they went on strike, their employers quickly crushed the union—with the help of local authorities. This pattern persisted for the next 140 years.

## The First Organizing Efforts: 1830–1865

Conditions in the mid-nineteenth century workplace were so awful as to be simply unimaginable to people today. The noise, dirt, lack of sanitary facilities, poor ventilation, and absence of fire exits would not be tolerated in any modern workplace. As the Industrial Revolution progressed, workers increasingly looked to unions as a way to bring pressure to bear on unresponsive management and government.

Although the union movement gradually gained strength from the 1830s through the 1850s, it could claim few successes. Tailors in New York City and women cotton-mill workers in Lowell, Massachusetts, made up two of the unions defeated in this period. To gauge how far unions have come, one need only consider their principal demands in the late 1830s: free public education and a 10-hour work day, six days a week.[2]

## The Emergence of Strong Unions: 1865–1914

The Civil War marked the beginning both of modern warfare and of the modern industrial economy. It marked as well a turning point for the labor movement. The victorious North had organized its population, industrial production, and financial resources during the war years to a degree unequaled in history. This momentum did not slow after the war ended. The railroads, for example, carried the U.S. economy forward. By 1869, when the first transcontinental rail line was completed, the railroads employed tens of thousands of skilled and unskilled workers alike.

### The Knights of Labor
The year 1869 also saw the founding of the **Knights of Labor**. The Knights' goal was to organize all workers, regardless of their skills or industry, into one organization. In 1885, the Knights won organized labor's first two great successes through strikes against the Missouri Pacific Railroad. The issues were pay cuts and the railroad's discrimination against members of the Knights in hiring and promotion. In the next year, membership in the Knights soared from 100,000 to 700,000. The Knights' successes were short-lived, however. On May 6, 1886, someone threw a bomb during an anarchist rally in Chicago, leaving seven policemen dead. The Knights were blamed and could not recover their original momentum, even though the charges were never proved.

Labor unions have always been vulnerable to charges of being the tools of radicals. Today, in France and England, Marxists and Socialists dominate

**Knights of Labor** an organization formed in 1869 whose goal it was to organize all workers, regardless of their skills or industry, into one organization

several large labor unions. For the most part, American unions bear little resemblance to their European counterparts. The work of one man, Samuel Gompers, is the main reason that American unions focus on their members' material needs rather than on political philosophies.

*1.* *Describe the role of Samuel Gompers in the development of the American labor movement.*

**American Federation of Labor (AFL)** an umbrella organization for craft unions

**trade (craft) union** a union made up of skilled workers of the same or related vocations

*Samuel Gompers* Gompers understood the inherent weakness of organizations that tried to represent all types of workers in all industries, the way the Knights of Labor and its radical offshoot, the International Workers of the World (the "Wobblies"), had attempted to do. American workers and industry were much too diversified to be capable of being organized in one all-encompassing union.

In 1881, Gompers founded the **American Federation of Labor (AFL)**, an umbrella organization for craft unions. A **trade** or **craft union** is a union made up of skilled workers of the same or related vocations. Over the next

Pioneer labor union organizers  *Samuel Gompers (right) founded the AFL in 1881, a national organization of craft or trade unions for skilled workers. John L. Lewis organized all the industrial unions of unskilled workers, forming the CIO in 1935. In 1955 the two merged to form the world's largest union organization.*

four decades Gompers built the AFL into the nation's most important labor organization. More important, he established the political and social philosophy that guides unions even today. That philosophy, **business unionism**, emphasizes that American unions exist primarily for the economic improvement of their workers, not to engage in a class struggle to alter the American form of government or to promote socialism.[3] Indeed, Gompers once declared, "I want to tell you Socialists that I have studied your philosophy; read your works on economics. . . . Economically, you are unsound; socially, you are wrong; industrially, you are an impossibility."[4]

What Gompers wanted was **collective bargaining**—negotiation of the terms and conditions of employment between management and an organization representing employees. He believed collective bargaining to be the only way that workers could gain enough strength to negotiate effectively with management for labor's proper share of the capitalist pie.

*The Sherman Act*   Ironically, the legislation originally designed to curb large companies' abuses of the market system, the **Sherman Antitrust Act** (1890), became business's main tool against unions. Typically, when a union began to organize a company, the firm would seek an **injunction**, a court order forbidding certain actions. The companies claimed, often successfully, that organizing employees to bargain collectively with employers had the effect of restraining trade and therefore violated the Sherman Act.

For forty-two years, Gompers and organized labor fought to neutralize this unintended result of the Sherman Act. What Gompers wanted from the federal government was impartiality. He felt that labor should be free to negotiate with management without government's interference.

**business unionism** the philosophy which emphasizes that American unions exist primarily for the economic improvement of their workers

**collective bargaining** negotiation of the terms and conditions of employment between management and an organization representing employees

*2. Identify the antitrust acts that affected the labor movement's effort to organize American industry.*

**Sherman Antitrust Act** legislation originally designed to curb large companies' abuses of the market system

**injunction** a court order forbidding certain actions

# The Modern Era: Regulation of Labor Relations

Ten years before his death in 1924, Gompers got part of what he wanted. Within ten years after his death, however, it had become clear that government neutrality could not alone create an atmosphere in which labor and management could coexist.

## The Era of Government Neutrality: 1914–1932

In 1914, Congress adopted the Clayton Act, which amended the Sherman Act. In it Congress declared that

> [the] labor of a human being is not a commodity or article of commerce. Nothing in the antitrust laws shall be construed to forbid the existence and operation of labor . . . organizations.[5]

Despite this language, the Supreme Court regularly interpreted the new law to let employers continue using injunctions to block organizing. It was eighteen years later that Congress, in the Norris-LaGuardia Act of 1932, effectively removed that obstacle to unionization.

*The Rise of Industrial Unions*  The removal of antitrust restrictions did not swell the AFL's rolls. Most major crafts were already unionized, so union organizers shifted their focus to the mass of unskilled workers being recruited for America's major industries: steel, mining, and autos. The Utility Workers, the United Rubber Workers, the Amalgamated Clothing and Textile Workers, the Oil, Chemical and Atomic Workers International, and other unions like them are **industrial unions**, unions whose membership includes all the workers in an industry, regardless of the tasks they perform.

industrial union  a union whose membership includes all the workers in an industry, regardless of the tasks they perform

The distinction between craft and trade unions on the one hand and industrial unions on the other is an important one. When the New York Knicks play the Los Angeles Lakers in Madison Square Garden, members of the electricians' craft or trade union work on the lighting, members of the plumbers' union fix clogged sinks, members of the carpenters' union make any last-minute adjustments to the movable seating, and members of the NBA Players Association actually play the game. They are all members of craft or trade unions. When a new Corvette rolls off a General Motors assembly line, however, every one of the thousands of parts in that car was installed, assembled, adjusted, and inspected by members of just one industrial union: the United Auto Workers.

**Congress of Industrial Organizations (CIO)** an umbrella organization for industrial unions

The leading figure in the industrial union movement was the United Mine Workers' president John L. Lewis. In 1935, Lewis founded the **Congress of Industrial Organizations (CIO)**, an umbrella organization for industrial unions. Several years earlier, it had become clear that the government neutrality established by the Clayton Act would never make a reality of Gompers's ideal of having labor and management negotiate their differences. Bloody organizing strikes, especially in coal and steel, and the onset of the Great Depression in 1929 convinced the public that Congress would have to act.

## The Era of Legislation: 1932–1959

3. List the key features of the National Labor Relations Act, the Taft-Hartley Act, and the Landrum-Griffin act.

Between 1932 and 1959, the peak period in union membership and strength, Congress enacted several major labor laws. Table 9.1 identifies their key provisions as well as those of some other related statutes.

**National Labor Relations Act (NLRA)** also known as the Wagner Act; act that made labor-management relations a federal matter and established the National Labor Relations Board to regulate them

*The National Labor Relations Act (NLRA)*  The **National Labor Relations Act** of 1935, popularly called the **Wagner Act**, made labor-management relations a federal matter and established the National Labor Relations Board (NLRB) to regulate them. Called "labor's Magna Carta," the act makes it unlawful for an employer to interfere with its employees' rights to form, join, and participate in a union or for management to try to subvert the union itself. The NLRA forbids employers to discriminate against workers who join a union or to retaliate against those who file charges of **unfair labor practices**, violations of the laws that the NLRB enforces. In addition, it

**Unfair labor practice** a violation of the laws that the NLRB enforces

TABLE 9.1  Federal Laws Governing Labor-Management Relations

| Statutes | Major Provisions |
| --- | --- |
| Clayton Act (1914) | Declared union activity not subject to the antitrust laws. |
| Railway Labor Act (1926) | Designed to keep interstate commerce flowing despite labor difficulties. (1) Governs railroad and airline collective bargaining; (2) Created National Mediation Board to conduct union elections and resolve disputes between labor and management. |
| Norris-LaGuardia Act (1932) | (1) Outlawed contracts under which management could fire a worker if he or she joined a union; (2) Prohibited federal courts from issuing injunctions against lawful union activities, including picketing and strikes. |
| National Labor Relations Act (Wagner Act) (1934) | (1) Created National Labor Relations Board (NLRB); (2) Prohibited unfair labor practices; (3) Guaranteed employees the right to join and participate in unions. |
| Taft-Hartley Act (1947) | (1) Outlawed unfair labor practices by unions; (2) Abolished the closed shop; (3) Permitted states to enact right-to-work laws; (4) Allowed president to order 80-day "cooling off" period in disputes of national importance; (5) Created the Federal Mediation and Conciliation Service, to assist parties in resolving disputes. |
| Landrum-Griffin Act (1959) | (1) Gave the Secretary of Labor powers to monitor and control union corruption; (2) Serves as bill of rights for union members. |

Source: Adapted from R. N. Corley et al., *The Legal Environment of Business*, 6th ed. (New York: McGraw-Hill, 1984), p. 246. Copyright 1984. Used by permission of the publisher.

compels an employer whose employees select a specific union as their exclusive bargaining agent to bargain with that union.

The **National Labor Relations Board (NLRB)**, a five-member board appointed by the president to carry out the federal labor laws, has two major responsibilities. First, it supervises elections in which employees decide whether to be represented by a union. Second, it determines the validity of charges that an employer or a union has committed some unfair labor practice.

Not surprisingly, the Wagner Act boosted union membership dramatically, from 3 million in 1933 to 9 million in 1940. By 1945, unions claimed almost 15 million members.[6]

**National Labor Relations Board (NLRB)** a five-member board appointed by the president to carry out the federal labor laws

### The Taft-Hartley Labor Act

While World War II raged abroad, labor and management agreed on peace at home. When peace came, however, workers tried to make up for the minimal raises granted during the war.

The **Taft-Hartley Act** reflected the public's wish to blunt union drives for more wages, benefits, and—most important—power. The Taft-Hartley provisions that labor most bitterly resented abolished the closed shop and authorized the states to enact **right-to-work laws**, which outlaw union shops. A *shop* is simply a workplace. There are five types of shop. A **closed shop** is one that requires workers to belong to the union before they can be hired. A **union shop** is one in which workers do not have to be union members when hired but must later join, usually within thirty days. An **agency shop** is one in which employees may choose not to join the union. Since they receive the benefits of the union's bargaining on their behalf, however, the employer deducts from their pay a sum equal to the union's dues and pays that to the union. In a **maintenance shop**, an employee who joins a union must remain in it only so long as he or she works in that bargaining unit.

Finally, an **open shop** is one in which union membership is not a condition of employment. It is this type of shop that most right-to-work laws require. The union shop is the principal means by which unions protect their status in the workplace. For this reason, unions have rightly regarded right-to-work laws as direct threats to their existence. Today, twenty-four states have right-to-work laws.

The Taft-Hartley Act also imposed on labor the requirements that the Wagner Act had imposed on management. For example, it requires unions to bargain in good faith, as discussed later.

Union membership continued to grow until the early 1950s, when it peaked both in numbers and in percentage of the work force. Total union membership has declined almost continuously since then (see Figure 9.1). Nonetheless, the AFL and CIO, which merged in 1955, still form the largest union organization in the world. Only the Teamsters and the National Education Association are not affiliated with it.

### The Landrum-Griffin Act

In many organizations, corruption accompanies growth and power. Labor unions have been no exception to this trend. For instance, various congressional hearings and trials have exposed racketeering in the Teamsters Union. The 1954 Academy Award–winning movie *On the Waterfront* accurately portrayed intimidation, bribery, theft, and even murder in the dockworkers' unions. As a result of revelations like these, in 1959 Congress enacted the **Landrum-Griffin Act**. This act's bill of rights for union members guarantees them the right to vote in union elections, speak at union meetings, receive union financial reports, and be treated like other members.

Only a few unions suffered the same ills as the Teamsters and dockworkers. Unions and their leaders accomplished much good during the mid-century period. John L. Lewis of the United Mine Workers redefined the benefits, such as health care and pensions, that workers should receive. Walter Reuther of the United Auto Workers played a key role in the social movements of the 1950s and 1960s. And George Meany, head of the AFL-CIO, played a critical role in the effort to keep European unions noncommunist.

**Taft-Hartley Act** act that reflected the public's wish to blunt union drives for more wages, benefits, and—most important—power

**right-to-work law** a law that outlaws union shops

**closed shop** one that requires workers to belong to the union before they can be hired

**union shop** one in which workers do not have to be union members when hired but must later join

**agency shop** one in which employees may choose not to join the union

**maintenance shop** one in which employee who has joined a union must remain in it only so long as he or she works in that bargaining unit

**open shop** one in which union membership is not a condition of employment

**Landrum-Griffin Act** provides a bill of rights for members, guaranteeing them the right to vote in union elections, speak at union meetings, receive union financial reports, and be treated like other members

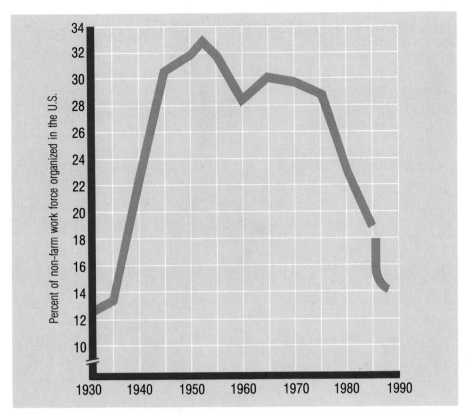

FIGURE 9.1    Union Share of the Work Force

Source: Data from 1930–1985 from L. Troy and N. Shevlin, *Union Sourcebook* (West Orange, NJ: Industrial Relations Data Information Services, 1985). Used by permission of the publisher. Data from 1985–1988 from *Employment and Earnings* (U.S. Bureau of Labor Statistics); January, 1987; January, 1988; January, 1989.

# Unions Today and Tomorrow

Unions continue to play an important—but changed—role in American life. Nonunion operations have reduced the number of workers in the trades on which Samuel Gompers built the AFL. Membership in industrial unions, the foundation of the CIO, has dropped as jobs have gone overseas. Membership dropped 27 percent in the United Auto Workers and 42 percent in the Steelworkers during the 1970s. Unions, as a whole, lost over 4 million members between 1979 and 1987. Membership increased slightly in 1988.[7]

## *The Emerging Service Sector*

The shape of the American work force has changed. As Figure 9.2 indicates, workers are shifting into the service sector of the economy. Office workers, hotel and restaurant employees, and civil servants—teachers, police, and

FIGURE 9.2 The Shape of the American Work Force Has Changed

Workers are moving away from production-oriented industries to service industries. The percentage of total employment employed by service industries continues to grow.

Source: *Statistical Abstract of the United States, 1988.* Table no. 631.

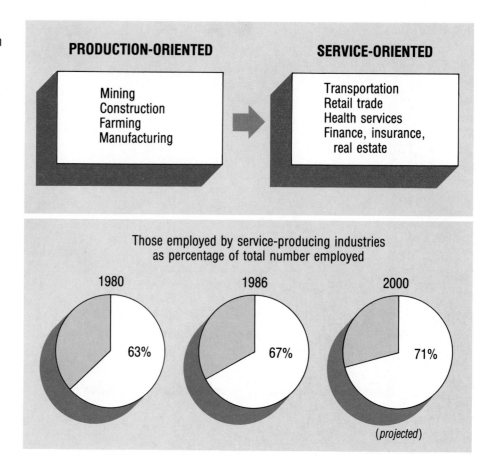

**PRODUCTION-ORIENTED**

Mining
Construction
Farming
Manufacturing

**SERVICE-ORIENTED**

Transportation
Retail trade
Health services
Finance, insurance,
  real estate

Those employed by service-producing industries as percentage of total number employed

1980 — 63%

1986 — 67%

2000 — 71% (*projected*)

government workers—are service workers. Today, for example, more people work at McDonald's restaurants than for General Motors. The unions that are growing are those that represent service workers.

Women and minorities tend to dominate service unions. Service jobs often require fewer skills and are less well paid than those in the trades or heavy industry. As more jobs are lost in traditionally male-dominated fields, more white men are likely to join service unions.

## Growing Numbers of Women and Minorities

Overall, the number of women in the workplace has increased dramatically, as seen in Figure 9.3. A major reason for this increase is the Civil Rights Act of 1964, discussed in Chapter 8 (see Business Issues).

That law has also led to a greater number of minority group members entering the unionized work force. Today, blacks make up 15 percent of the 17.4 million unionized workers. Not surprisingly, some of the most bitter organizing battles in recent years have centered on groups of workers dominated by minorities.

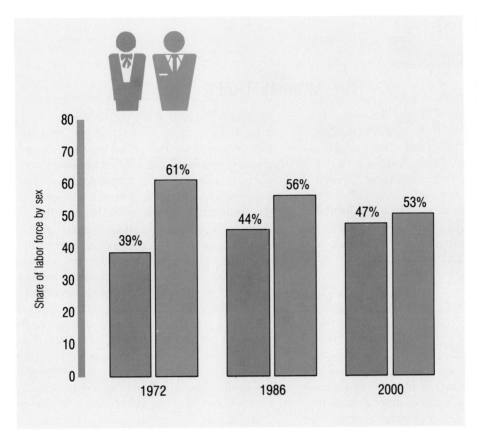

# The Unionization Process

Unions thrive when workers believe that employers are not treating them fairly. Workers join and support unions because unions increase their power in bargaining for wages and benefits, because they encourage greater job stability and predictability, and because they protect workers from arbitrary firings or demotions. This section describes the unionizing process.

*4. List the steps in the unionization process and summarize each.*

## The Organizing Drive

Either the workers themselves or a union may take the necessary steps toward unionization, which are collectively called the **organizing drive**. Sometimes a union may already represent some workers at the same firm. At other times the union may represent workers at similar firms.

**organizing drive** taking the steps toward unionization

Normally, the union makes its initial moves very quietly to avoid tipping its hand to management. Then the union gradually becomes more public about its efforts. In some cases, unions are creative in their attempts to win workers. For instance, the Amalgamated Clothing & Textile Workers offered

# THE MOMMY TRACK

What do Congresswoman Pat Schroeder, Du Pont executive Faith Wohl, and research director Fran Rodgers have in common? All three are upset with Felice N. Schwartz. Schwartz, founder and president of Catalyst, a research and advisory organization dedicated to the advancement of women in the workplace, is not the sort of person you would expect to earn the ire of three prominent female leaders. The cause of the friction is an article Schwartz wrote for the *Harvard Business Review*.

That article, "Management Women and the New Facts of Life," states that many of the arguments corporate male executives have made against the advancement of women in the business world are essentially correct. Yes, says Schwartz, the rate of turnover in large corporations is much higher among women than it is among men. Yes, many women who take maternity leave return to work later than agreed or not at all. Yes, a lower percentage of women than men are anxious to advance straight to the top of the corporate ladder. Yes, for all these reasons women are more expensive than men to employ.

All this is not to suggest that Schwartz has soured on her cause. Past professional problems, she feels, are not attributable to the nature of women, but to the attitudes of men—attitudes that should now change.

Demographics, argues Schwartz, are on women's side. A high percentage of new entrants into all levels of the work force will be women. In terms of qualifications, women will number among the top applicants for corporate-suite-track jobs. Corporations will have to hire women and should want to make the best use of them.

The prejudice against career-and-family women, says Schwartz, is rooted in the feeling that because their interests are divided, these women will not give the corporation all that it needs from them. Schwartz argues that the move-up-or-move-out philosophy leads to a clustering of frustrated and incompetent people in middle-level jobs. Employers should be happy to have career-and-family women in these mid-range positions. In this way the company is more likely to have qualified and satisfied people in these jobs. Meanwhile, the women are assured of responsible positions that leave them time and energy for their families. When the women are ready, they should be given the option of reentering the fast track.

Women leaders have reacted strongly to the Schwartz article. "It's tragic," says Congresswoman Schroeder, referring to what some disparagingly call the "mommy track." "It reinforces the idea, which is so strong in our country, that you can either have a family or a career, but not both if you're a woman."

"What's so disturbing about Felice Schwartz's article," says Fran Rodgers, president of Work-Family Directions, a research and referral group, "is that it is devoted to fitting women into the existing culture, instead of finding ways to change that culture."

Responds Schwartz: "At this point in time women do take a larger part of the responsibility for childrearing. Unless we acknowledge those differences and costs, we won't address the problems women face." She adds that what she really wants to do is give women the flexibility they need. "I tell business leaders that if they're requiring women to come back to work six weeks after they have a baby, they're getting a disabled person."

Sources: Felice N. Schwartz, "Management Women and the New Facts of Life," *Harvard Business Review,* January/February 1989, pp. 65–76; "Study Sees Two Tracks for Women," *St. Louis Post-Dispatch,* March 12, 1989, pp. 1, 8; Elizabeth Ehrlich, "The Mommy Track," *Business Week,* March 20, 1989, pp. 126–134.

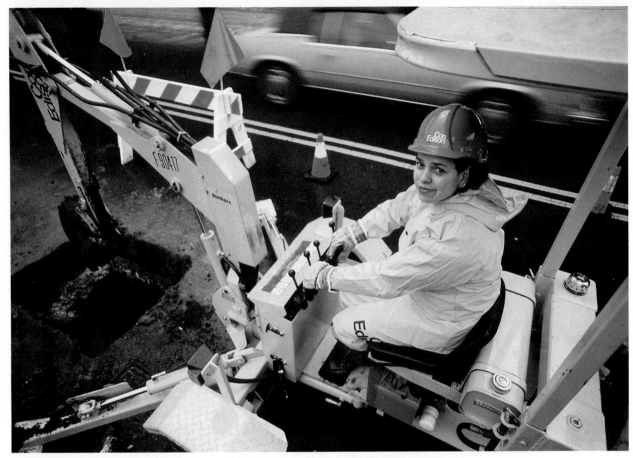

The changing shape of the unionized work force *The passage of the Civil Rights Act of 1964 led to a steady increase in the number of women and minorities in the workplace and in unions.*

employees at the Hanes Corporation a simple cardboard slide rule so that they could calculate their earnings under Hanes's extremely complicated compensation system.[8]

Once the organizing drive has gained what the union feels to be sufficient strength, the union requests that management recognize it as the workers' representative. The request is almost never granted. Typically, when the union requests recognition, it tells management that more than 30 percent of the workers have signed **authorization cards**, forms signed by employees that either authorize the union to represent them or to request a representation election (discussed next), or both.

**authorization card** form signed by employees that either authorizes the union to represent them or to request representation election or both

## The Representation Election

If the employer refuses to recognize the union, the union uses the cards to support a petition filed with the National Labor Relations Board to hold a **representation election**, an election to determine whether a union will represent a particular group of workers. After receiving the petition, the NLRB meets with the union and the employer. It tries to gain the parties' agreement on

**representation election** an election to determine whether a union will represent a particular group of workers

The unionization process  *Workers join and support unions because unions increase their power in bargaining for wages and benefits, because they encourage greater job stability and predictability, and because they protect workers from arbitrary firings or demotions.*

**consent election**  a representation election agreed on by union and management

**bargaining unit**  a group of employees who share common interests in wages and working conditions and have common skills

the date, time, and place of the election; the form of the ballot; and a definition of the bargaining unit. If the parties can be led to agree on all these issues, the NLRB holds a **consent election**, a representation election agreed on by union and management. If the parties disagree on even one of these points, it is up to the NLRB to decide whether to hold an election.

First, the NLRB judges whether the workers seeking the election make up an appropriate **bargaining unit**, a group of employees who share common interests in wages and working conditions and have common skills. The parties may hotly contest this issue. The union will want the bargaining unit defined broadly enough to contain the greatest number of employees favoring unionization. The company will, of course, want the opposite. Once the NLRB has defined the bargaining unit, it must determine whether at least 30 percent of the unit's employees are interested in union representation. Normally, the authorization cards provide a ready answer.

Before a representation election can take place, each side presents its case to the workers. There are some restrictions on what can be said and done. For example, management cannot either directly or indirectly threaten workers with the loss of their jobs if they vote for the union. The workers vote by secret ballot during working hours at the job site.

Representation elections can involve more than one issue on the ballot. The workers may have two or more unions to choose from, as well as "no union." If no one choice receives a majority, the NLRB stages a run-off election between the top two choices in the first one. If the majority of voters chooses to be represented by a union, the NLRB certifies that union as representing all workers in the bargaining unit for the purposes of collective bargaining.

# The Subjects of Collective Bargaining

Parties may negotiate on any subject that a federal or state law does not forbid them to. In other words, they can agree on discussing any topic that does not involve breaking the law. For instance, the Sheet Metal Workers could negotiate a wage agreement with a construction company—but the agreement could not waive time and a half for overtime work. The **Fair Labor Standards Act** discussed in Chapter 8, also known as the *minimum wage law* or the *wages and hours law*, requires it.

5. Identify the subjects that may and may not be discussed in collective bargaining.

**Fair Labor Standards Act** law that requires time and a half for overtime work

The Taft-Hartley Act requires that labor and management negotiate about wages, benefits, hours, and working conditions. Each of these mandatory subjects for collective bargaining is discussed in turn. There are also voluntary subjects for collective bargaining, such as any subjects that the parties might bargain about that are neither illegal nor mandatory. These topics usually fall under the heading of management rights or union rights.

## The Respective Rights of Management and Union

In a collective bargaining agreement, management will want to retain as much control as it can over the conduct of employees on the job. It will also want to reserve the right to control the type and pace of production. For example, management will want to control the scheduling of overtime so that it can respond quickly to fluctuations in demand for its products. Paying overtime is always cheaper than hiring new workers, so management will want a small permanent work force. The union will want employees to be able to refuse overtime so that they can choose between leisure time and overtime. Unions have historically argued also that every person has a right to a job, and unions are committed to creating permanent jobs.

The rights that concern the union most include control over the definition of the bargaining unit, the scope of the employer's recognition of its right to negotiate on behalf of the bargaining unit, the duration and renewal schedule of the collective bargaining agreement, and the way in which jobs are to be assigned. For example, one of the hottest issues in recent years between New York's transit management and the Amalgamated Transit Union involved the contracting out of repair work on subway cars and buses to companies whose workers were not ATU members. Other unions have made the issue of part-time nonunion workers a major collective bargaining point.

Management protects its rights by inserting a clause in collective bargaining agreements saying that it retains any rights that it has not expressly given up.

## Wages and Benefits

Under normal circumstances, wages and benefits are the most important subjects of collective bargaining.

**base wage rate** the minimum paid per hour to any worker in the bargaining unit

**cost-of-living adjustments (COLAs)** changes to the base wage rate to reflect increases in the inflation rate for the preceding quarter or year

**Consumer Price Index** index of the inflation rate provided by the government

*Base Wages and COLAs* The **base wage rate**, the minimum paid per hour to any worker in the bargaining unit, is the basis upon which everything else is calculated. Until quite recently, contracts routinely called for **cost-of-living adjustments (COLAs)**, changes to the base wage rate (up to an established maximum) to reflect increases in the inflation rate for the preceding quarter or year. COLAs were designed to ensure that inflation did not reduce real wages. A contract might call for an annual COLA of up to 3 percent, assuming that the inflation rate, usually measured by the government's **Consumer Price Index**, equaled or exceeded 3 percent. As inflation increased and productivity declined in the decade from 1975 to 1985, however, the reduction of COLAs became a key management objective in collective bargaining.

**seniority differential** an incremental pay increase determined by the length of the worker's service with the employer

**shift differential** an incremental pay increase for working nonstandard time periods

*Wage Differentials and Incentives* Some contracts call for a **seniority differential**, an incremental pay increase determined by the length of the worker's service with the employer. This differential is usually defined in terms of years worked. Contracts involving employers who operate on other than a strictly nine-to-five, Monday-through-Friday basis often call for a **shift differential**, an incremental pay increase for working nonstandard time periods. This differential is for working at times that other workers do not want to work. The graveyard shift, from 11 P.M. to 7 A.M., almost always carries the highest shift differential.

**incentive rate formulas** pay increments awarded for increased productivity

**piece-work rates** rates that pay employees according to what they produce, not by the time they work

As we discussed in the last two chapters, employers often pay premiums for above-average productivity. **Incentive rate formulas** are pay increments awarded for increased productivity. These formulas are not always tied to the base wage rate. Unions traditionally oppose incentive rates because they resemble **piece-work rates** that pay employees according to what they produce, not by the time they work. In the past, when employers used this pay method they often adjusted upward the output requirements and reduced the piece rate. For that reason, machine quotas and speeds are hot issues when labor and management are negotiating incentive rates.

*Benefits and Health Insurance* Of course, direct wages paid to workers are not the employer's only costs. Benefits make up a significant component of those costs, as seen in Chapter 8. Two of the most expensive benefits are pensions and health insurance. In both cases, the employer makes payments to specific funds, not directly to the employee.

In the case of pension funds negotiated by unions, the company pays in a sum equal to a percentage of each worker's wages. Upon retirement, the employee receives a monthly check for the rest of his or her life, if the system works as it is supposed to, though it does not always work that way.

As the cost of health care has soared, so have employers' contributions to their employees' health-care plans. Today, for instance, General Motors spends $3 billion for employee health benefits.[9] When a new GM car rolls off the assembly line, the largest single cost component in it is for employee and dependent health care, not for steel, rubber, or glass as one might guess.

## Hours

As already noted, the hours that employees work are the subject of federal and state laws and also of collective bargaining agreements. The issues related to hours go well beyond questions of shift differentials and the length of the work week. They also include paid vacation time, unpaid leave, maternity/paternity leave, paid holidays, breaks, and rest periods.

## Working Conditions

Virtually all collective bargaining agreements deal with the question of working conditions. **Working conditions** is a catch-all term to describe all aspects of the relationship between employer and employee that are not related to the area of compensation. Coal miners, for example, engage in some of the most routinely dangerous work in American industry. Like anyone else, a coal miner wants to take home the maximum pay. From their earliest collective bargaining agreements, however, the United Mine Workers have emphasized safety.

**working conditions** a catch-all term to describe all aspects of the relationship between employer and employee that are not related to the area of compensation

**Risky business** *Job safety is one of the most important issues for negotiation on the collective bargaining table, especially for workers in industries that regularly require dangerous work conditions, like drilling and mining.*

There are other working conditions typically covered in collective bargaining agreements. Some of them are:

- Shift assignments: Will management, or employees (using seniority), determine who works which shifts?
- Work schedules: What periods of the day will shifts fall into?
- Work rules: What will be the rules of the workplace, and how much say will the union have in them?

## Job Security

Job security has two components: the right to employment and the right to receive unemployment compensation when work is not available.

One's **right to employment** refers to the methods by which promotions, transfers, and layoffs are determined within a bargaining unit. For the most part, unions have insisted that all three factors be determined on the basis of **seniority**, a system in which the order of hiring determines the order of promotions, layoffs, rehirings, and the exercise of all other employment rights. For the employer, seniority means that the most experienced—and most highly paid—workers are the last to be laid off. For the worker, seniority gives more security. It is usually easier for younger workers to find a new job or trade than for older ones. Still, in the face of widespread plant shutdowns, as in the steel industry, seniority is of little value.

Workers who are laid off are entitled to **unemployment compensation,** payments from a pool created by employer contributions and required by state law to be made for a certain period to laid-off workers. Some collective bargaining agreements also require the employer to make supplemental payments to laid-off workers. For instance, under the United Auto Workers program, when big layoffs hit the auto industry in the early 1980s, some workers received for a time almost 95 percent of their normal wages, paid from a combination of government benefits and employer contributions.

## The Grievance Process

A **grievance** is an employee complaint about wages, hours, working conditions, or disciplinary action for which the collective bargaining agreement provides a procedure for resolution. The procedure both assures the just resolution of employee complaints and identifies recurrent problems in a workplace. It is the primary means for seeing that management lives up to the collective bargaining agreement (see Figure 9.4).

*Discussions Between Management and Union* Normally, an employee starts the grievance process by taking a complaint to the **shop steward**, a union member elected to represent the other members employed in a particular work unit in their day-to-day dealings with the employer. An employee might complain to the shop steward if, for example, he or she thought the supervisor had filed inaccurate performance reports or if he or she had been fired for fighting in the lunchroom. The shop steward would then take the matter up with the employee's supervisor.

---

**right to employment** the methods by which promotions, transfers, and layoffs are determined within a bargaining unit

**seniority** a system in which the order of hiring determines the order of promotions, layoffs, rehirings, and the exercise of all other employment rights

**unemployment compensation** payments from a pool created by employer contributions and required by state law to be made for a certain period to laid-off workers

**grievance** an employee complaint about wages, hours, working conditions, or disciplinary action

**6.** *Describe the stages of a grievance proceeding.*

**shop steward** a union member elected to represent the other members employed in a particular work unit in their day-to-day dealings with the employer

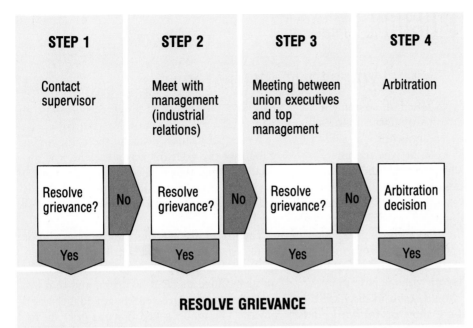

FIGURE 9.4  A Typical Grievance Procedure

| STEP 1 | STEP 2 | STEP 3 | STEP 4 |
|---|---|---|---|
| Contact supervisor | Meet with management (industrial relations) | Meeting between union executives and top management | Arbitration |

Resolve grievance? — No — Resolve grievance? — No — Resolve grievance? — No — Arbitration decision

Yes — Yes — Yes — Yes

**RESOLVE GRIEVANCE**

If the supervisor decided not to reconsider the action or reduce the punishment, the grievance might go to the union's **chief steward**, an elected union official for the employee's department or plant who represents the members in grievances and oversees the execution of the collective bargaining agreement. The chief steward meets with the employee's department head.

A grievance that goes beyond the chief steward becomes the subject of negotiations between the company's human resources director and the union's **grievance committee**, a union committee that meets with management to resolve matters relating to the contract that the stewards are unable to resolve. It may include officers of the local union, the union's **business representative** or **business agent** (a person employed by a union to represent it in matters with management), and the chief steward.

*Arbitration*   The final stage in most grievance procedures is **arbitration**, the submission of a dispute to a neutral third party, an **arbitrator**, who makes a decision binding on the parties who submitted the matter. There are two principal sources for arbitrators: the American Arbitration Association, a private group; and the Federal Mediation and Conciliation Service, an agency created by the Taft-Hartley Act that maintains a list of arbitrators. Arbitration works somewhat like a court trial, but it is less formal. The arbitrator's decision is usually final (see Experiencing Business).

## Givebacks

Someone once asked Samuel Gompers what labor wanted. His reply could not have been clearer: "More, more, and more!"[10] After World War II, unionized workers grew used to wage increases, benefit expansions, and more advantageous working conditions in every new contract. In recent years,

**chief steward**  an elected union official for the employee's department or plant who represents the members in grievances and oversees the execution of the collective bargaining agreement

**grievance committee**  a union committee that meets with management to resolve matters relating to the contract that the stewards are unable to resolve

**business representative (business agent)**  person employed by a union to represent it in matters with management

**arbitration**  the submission of a dispute to a neutral third party

**arbitrator**  the neutral third party who makes a decision binding on the parties who submit a dispute

## YOU BE THE ARBITRATOR

Apex Motors had negotiated an agreement with the union that stated that it could discipline for just cause. The grievant was a fifteen-year employee when he was terminated. Before January of the past year, the company did not have an attendance policy. When a shop foreperson was appointed, she began to record employee absences.

On March 11, the grievant was given a written warning in which he was informed that the next time he was absent, he would be given a three-day layoff without pay; the next absence thereafter would result in discharge. On April 6, he did not show up for work, did not call in, and was given the three-day layoff. On September 30, the grievant called the company at 6:55 A.M., stating that he had overslept because his girlfriend's alarm clock failed to go off. He arrived at work at 8:15 A.M. At 10:00 A.M. he was terminated for excessive tardiness and absenteeism. The company based its decision on his record.

At the arbitration hearing, the company argued that the grievant was aware he was on final warning, that it needed a regular employee, that no animosity existed, and that it did not volunteer a day of vacation on September 30.

The union argued that the company did not state a time limit for the warnings, that the grievant was a long-term employee and had an unspecified medical problem, and that he had previously corrected his attendance behavior. The union asked that the grievant be reinstated and compensated for the lost wages, benefits, and seniority.

If you were the labor arbitrator, how would you decide the case? For Apex Motors or for the union? Why?

---

though, several trades and industries have slumped in the face of foreign competition and advancing technology, and others have virtually disappeared. In 1917, for example, 180,000 coal miners worked in anthracite pits. In 1985, they numbered only 3,000.[11]

**givebacks** a union's forgoing of wages or benefits or working conditions won in earlier collective bargaining

Today, almost every collective bargaining agenda lists **givebacks**, a union's forgoing of wages or benefits or working conditions won in earlier collective bargaining. Up to 40 percent of the contracts negotiated in recent years have contained givebacks. Many of them have been negotiated in an atmosphere of joint management and labor concern for the future of their industries and jobs. Some have come after long strikes.

7. Define givebacks and discuss the effects of this concept on bargaining today.

Workers in steel, coal, meatpacking, airlines, and nonferrous metals, to list just a sampling of industries, have agreed to wage and benefit cuts. Perhaps more important, unions have agreed to changes in work rules. Such givebacks enabled Firestone Tire & Rubber to boost productivity 10 percent and Jones & Laughlin Steel to reduce the man-hours required to produce a ton of steel from 6 to 3.5.[12] When the United Auto Workers became convinced that sacrifices by its members might ultimately save their jobs, it agreed to contracts with the "Big Three" American automakers (GM, Ford, and Chrysler) in which

- Wages were frozen.
- Nine paid holidays were given up.
- Wage increases created by COLAs were deferred for eighteen months.
- Management obtained new power to discipline workers for excessive absenteeism.
- Management gained greater discretion in organizing production.

Givebacks often have a significant price to the employer. General Motors, for instance, agreed not to close several plants it had planned to, created a profit-sharing plan for union workers, guaranteed income to any employee with ten years' seniority who was laid off, and promised to lay off supervisors in proportion to unionized workers. Chrysler had to agree to put the president of the United Auto Workers on its board of directors.

# The Collective Bargaining Process

In the last section, we examined some topics that a collective bargaining agreement usually addresses. Now let's go back a step and look at how the parties actually reach an agreement (see Figure 9.5).

The Taft-Hartley Act requires that labor and management "meet at reasonable times and confer in good faith with respect to wages, hours and other conditions of employment." This description is a good definition of the collective bargaining process itself.

*8. Analyze the phases of collective bargaining.*

## Preparations for Bargaining

Before negotiations start, both sides spend substantial energy preparing.

Union officials begin their preparation by determining what the members want and then drawing up a set of demands. Next they assemble information to support these demands, such as data on wage rates at the company's competitors. Issues relating to working conditions, such as production quotas, also require documentation. At the same time that union officials are preparing their demands, they publicize and explain what they are doing. Not only must the union's negotiating team reach an agreement with management, it must also convince its own members of the rightness of its strategy and of the justice of the final contract package.

Management generally prefers to respond to proposals from labor rather than to offer proposals itself, to avoid tipping its hand. Management tries to anticipate the union's demands and to have ready an appropriate response to every union demand.

Management's principal concern is cost. It will therefore develop detailed statistical summaries and formulas to take into the negotiating sessions that will permit its negotiating team to estimate costs quickly. These summaries typically categorize employees by age, sex, seniority, and job classification. If the union asks for changes in, say, paid vacation time or health insurance coverage, management can plug these demands into formulas and quickly calculate their costs.

## Negotiating Teams

**national negotiation** form of negotiation in which national union negotiates wages and benefits on an industry- or companywide basis and the local unions negotiate working conditions

**pattern bargaining** form of negotiation in which local unions in a single company or industry negotiate on their own under the supervision of the national union

**council bargaining** form of negotiation in which several local unions join to negotiate together

**independent bargaining** form of negotiation in which a local negotiates for itself, without any help from the national or any other local unions

Each side in the collective bargaining process is represented by a negotiating team. On the union side, the relationship between the local and its national union determines who is on its negotiating team and what it negotiates. This relationship can take one of four forms.

1. **National negotiation:** The national union negotiates wages and benefits on an industry- or companywide basis and the local unions negotiate working conditions. The United Auto Workers uses this type of negotiation system.
2. **Pattern bargaining:** The local unions in a single company or industry negotiate on their own under the supervision of the national union.
3. **Council bargaining:** Several locals join to negotiate together.
4. **Independent bargaining:** The local negotiates for itself, without any help from the national or any other local unions.

FIGURE 9.5  The Nature of Collective Bargaining

Collective bargaining involves negotiations between labor and management from their initial positions to within the bargaining zone.

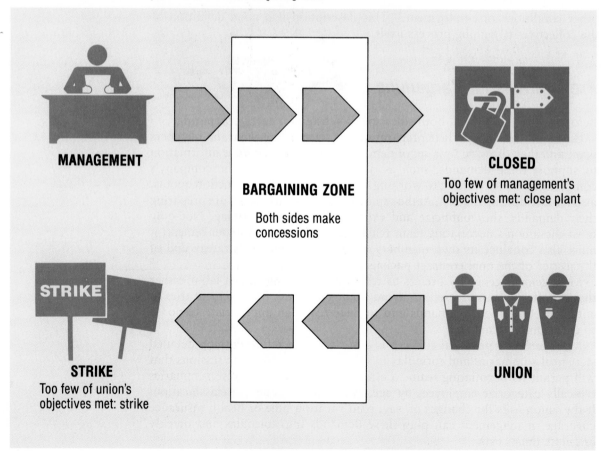

**MANAGEMENT**

**CLOSED**
Too few of management's objectives met: close plant

**BARGAINING ZONE**

Both sides make concessions

**STRIKE**
Too few of union's objectives met: strike

**UNION**

Sitting down to the bargaining table. *Union representatives come to negotiations with a list of demands and supporting statistics to help defend their case, and management arrives with a strategy that tries to anticipate these demands, and oppose them.*

Regardless of which relationship is used, the local union selects its own negotiating team, usually at a meeting of the local's membership. The team is often made up of a combination of the local's officers and regular members.

On the other side of the bargaining table, management's team consists usually of the human resources director or labor relations director and the plant managers and superintendents whose departments are involved in the negotiations.

## The Bargaining

Since the 1930s, collective bargaining negotiations have followed a well-defined pattern. Some significant variations in the pattern have appeared since the late 1970s, however.

As noted earlier, management traditionally has preferred to respond to union demands rather than to propose its own initiatives. Recently, though, companies in such fiercely competitive industries as airlines, copper, and rubber have begun to make demands themselves. And unions have had to give back benefits won in past collective bargaining to keep their companies afloat.

The early bargaining sessions often proceed slowly, sometimes bogging down in disputes over procedural issues. The serious bargaining begins with the noneconomic issues, such as management rights or the form that union recognition is to take. The parties usually agree, however, that nothing is to be considered settled until both parties have agreed on the whole contract. Each side agrees to accept some of the other's points and drop some of its own demands.

When they have resolved all the noneconomic issues, the negotiating teams turn to wages and benefits. Now bargaining becomes intense. Both sides make concessions, labor perhaps trimming its wage demands in exchange for concessions on benefits. The negotiators exchange proposals and counter-proposals until each knows how far the other will go.

At that point, if the sides are not too far apart they often split the differences and agree on a contract. If the gap is too large, the union may strike. Under normal circumstances, however, both sides have options for bridging an impasse, which they will examine carefully before giving up on the negotiating process.

*Selling the Contract*    The collective bargaining process does not end when the teams reach agreement. The contract must have the strong support of both negotiating teams, because both teams' constituents must ratify it.

Management's team must convince senior management that it should sign the contract. Normally, this amounts to a formality. And though it rarely happens, the union's membership can vote to reject the contract. Union leaders must therefore conduct an intensive education campaign to sell the contract to their fellow members. If a majority of the members voting agree to support the contract, the collective bargaining process is at an end—until it is time to negotiate a new contract.

## Mediation, Arbitration, and Factfinding

**mediation**  the process in which an impartial third party helps the parties settle their unresolved issues

**mediator**  the impartial third party who helps negotiating teams settle their unresolved issues

When the negotiating teams cannot resolve their differences, they sometimes resort to **mediation**, the process in which an impartial third party, a **mediator**, helps the parties settle their unresolved issues. The mediator suggests non-binding alternatives for their consideration. The Federal Mediation and Conciliation Service will supply mediators, as will some states. In some cases, the parties draw up lists of acceptable mediators themselves. Regardless of how a mediator becomes involved, the goal is the same: to avoid work stoppages.

Mediation should not be confused with arbitration. An arbitrator makes decisions that bind the parties. Some state laws require binding arbitration when a public-sector employer like a city, county, or state government unit cannot reach agreement with certain types of workers. These laws most often affect teachers, police, and firefighters. Binding arbitration laws are often

Linemen on the picket line  *NFL players picketed outside the Los Angeles Memorial Coliseum when they were on strike during the 1987–88 season. A union will sometimes call on its members to strike in an attempt to force management's compliance with the union's economic demands.*

highly controversial, because arbitrators have tended over the years to make decisions without regard for their overall impact on an employer's budget.

Another device commonly used in public-sector (but not private-sector) bargaining is **factfinding**, the process by which an outside factfinder narrows the issues that are before the negotiating parties.

**factfinding**  the process by which an outside factfinder narrows the issues that are before the negotiating parties

## When the Parties Cannot Agree

Unions and management both have weapons to force the other side to meet their terms. If they did not, collective bargaining could not take place.

For their part, unions can threaten either strikes or picketing. And management has the options of lockouts, injunctions, or bringing in strikebreakers.

*9. Identify the weapons each side in collective bargaining has to force an agreement.*

## Strikes

When a union, in an effort to put economic pressure on management, calls on its members not to work, a **strike** occurs. Strikes are usually characterized by **picketing**, the patrolling of the entrances to an employer's facilities by members of a labor union often carrying signs to inform other employees and the public that a strike is in progress and to persuade them not to enter.

The law imposes significant restraints on how unions are allowed to conduct strikes. For instance, unions may not throw up mass picket lines, nor may pickets block entrances to an employer's facility. Employers can get injunctions in state courts limiting both the number and the placement of pickets.

## Lockouts

One of the techniques management has to put economic pressure on a union is to close its doors to the unionized workers, a procedure known as a **lockout**. As a weapon, the lockout is a two-edged sword. The workers lose wages, but management also loses production—and therefore profits. Lockouts were more common earlier, when an industry or groups of companies typically negotiated contracts with unions together. Until the 1970s, for instance, all the New York City newspapers bargained together so that a strike against one triggered lockouts at all the papers. Lockouts are now rare.

## Legal Restraints

A party that wants to modify or end a contract must give the other at least sixty days' notice before the effective date of the proposed modification or termination. If a strike or lockout takes place before the end of that period, the party taking the action commits an unfair labor practice. Before a strike or a lockout can occur, the side taking the action must give the other advance notice.

A union has unique legal restraints on it during a strike or lockout. It cannot stage a **secondary boycott**, a refusal to work for, purchase from, or handle the products of another company with which the union has no dispute in order to force that company to stop doing business with the company with which the union does have a dispute. Suppose that the printers strike a certain newspaper. The union may not organize a boycott of the paper's newsprint supplier, for example, in order to pressure the paper to settle. In contrast, a union is allowed to organize a **primary boycott**, an action by a union to try to persuade others not to deal with an employer against whom it has a dispute. Boycotts organized by the United Farm Workers against produce grown on nonunion farms had some successes in the 1970s and 1980s.

## Strikebreakers

Persons hired to replace striking employees, either in an effort to force the union to come to terms or to destroy its effectiveness by minimizing the strike's effect on the employer's operations, are referred to as **strikebreakers** or **scabs**. In 1981, the Professional Air Traffic Controllers Organization (PATCO) went on strike, severely disrupting air travel. The government immediately moved to replace the strikers with new employees and never settled with the union. A major argument against hiring strikebreakers is that it forever poisons relations between union and management. Strikebreakers are thus a last-resort weapon.

---

**strike** practice in which a union, in an effort to put economic pressure on management, calls on its members not to work

**picketing** the patrolling of entrances to an employer's facilities by members of a labor union often carrying signs to inform other employees and the public that a strike is in progress

**lockout** management technique in which doors are closed to unionized workers

**secondary boycott** a refusal to work for, purchase from, or handle the products of another company with which the union has no dispute in order to force that company to stop doing business with the company with which the union does have a dispute

**primary boycott** an action by a union to try to persuade others not to deal with an employer against whom it has a dispute

**strikebreaker (scab)** a person hired to replace striking employees

The PATCO strike involved special circumstances. The government exercised its rights as an employer confronted by an **economic strike**, a strike called because of failure to reach agreement on wages and benefits. In such a case, the employer can hire strikebreakers and need not rehire the strikers even if the strike ends. If a strike is over something other than economic issues, however, the employer commits an unfair labor practice by bringing in strikebreakers.

**economic strike** a strike called because of failure to reach agreement on wages and benefits

# Labor-Management Relations: A Perspective

America's labor movement had fallen on hard days by the 1980s. Unions like the United Auto Workers, used to organizing successes, found themselves rejected by workers in new plants like Honda's Marysville, Ohio facility. Other unions, like the flight attendants', found themselves in the position of having to admit defeat after long strikes when their employers kept operations going with strikebreakers. Still other unions found themselves forced to accept givebacks and layoffs.

Some commentators have predicted a continued decline for labor unions, based on current trends. Whether that in fact happens will depend not only on the unions themselves but in large part on how management treats its workers. Unions have traditionally based their appeal on an "us versus them" perception, saying workers were overworked, undercompensated, and generally unappreciated. Should management allow such perceptions to flourish, unions will no doubt grow stronger. Much depends on management's learning and implementing the lessons that U.S. automakers have learned the hard way. Cooperation is a two-way street, and if any need appears certain, it is the need for continued cooperation of management and labor.

# CHAPTER HIGHLIGHTS

*1. Describe the role of Samuel Gompers in the development of the American labor movement.*

In 1881, Samuel Gompers founded the American Federation of Labor, an umbrella organization for craft unions. Over the next four decades he built the AFL into the nation's most important labor organization and established the philosophy of business unionism. This philosophy holds that American unions exist primarily for the economic improvement of workers, not to engage in a class struggle to alter the American form of government or to promote socialism.

*2. Identify the antitrust acts that affected the labor movement's effort to organize American industry.*

Two antitrust acts significantly hampered labor's effort to organize American industry. They were the Sherman Antitrust Act and the Clayton Act.

*3. List the key features of the National Labor Relations Act, the Taft-Hartley Act, and the Landrum-Griffin Act.*

The National Labor Relations Act, also known as the Wagner Act, made labor-management relations a federal matter and established the National Labor Relations Board to regulate them. The act made it unlawful for an employer to interfere with its employees' rights to form, join, and participate in a union or to try to subvert the union itself. The Taft-Hartley Act abolished the closed shop and authorized states to enact right-to-work laws, which outlaw union shops. The Landrum-Griffin Act guarantees union members the right to vote in union elections, speak at union meetings, receive union financial reports, and be treated like other members.

*4. Summarize the steps in the unionization process.*

The unionization process begins with the organizing drive, the union's first attempt to gain worker support. If enough workers have signed authorization cards and if management refuses to recognize the union, then the union files a petition with the NLRB to hold a representation election. If the union and the employer agree on the date, time, and place of the election, the form of the ballot, and the definition of the bargaining unit, a consent election is held. If they do not agree, the NLRB decides whether the workers seeking an election make up an appropriate bargaining unit and whether 30 percent of the workers want an election. Each side presents its case to the workers before a representation election is held.

*5. Identify the subjects that may and may not be discussed in collective bargaining.*

Unions and management may negotiate on any subject a federal or state law does not expressly forbid. They must negotiate about wages, benefits, hours, and working conditions.

*6. Describe the stages of a grievance proceeding.*

A *grievance* is an employee complaint about wages, hours, working conditions, or disciplinary action for which the collective bargaining agreement provides a procedure for resolution.

An employee starts the grievance process by taking a complaint to the shop steward. If the shop steward and the employee's supervisor cannot resolve the matter, it goes to the chief steward, then to the company's human resources director and the union's grievance committee. The final stage in most grievance procedures is arbitration. An arbitrator's decision is usually final.

*7. Define* givebacks *and discuss the effects of this concept on bargaining in the 1980s.*

*Givebacks* are a union's forgoing of wages or benefits or working conditions won in earlier collective bargaining agreements. As America's basic industries slumped or disappeared, unions were willing to give up benefits they had won in previous negotiations in order to prevent their employer from going bankrupt or closing down facilities. It is likely that unions will continue to show flexibility on work rules and other changes as long as it seems their jobs might otherwise disappear. In return for union givebacks, companies have had to make concession's relating to job security.

*8. Analyze the phases of collective bargaining.*

Collective bargaining has three primary phases: preparations, negotiations, and selling the contract. If agreement cannot be reached, the process moves on to mediation, arbitration, or factfinding. During the first phase, unions assemble information and draw up their demands. Management tries to anticipate the union's demands and makes ready its response. During negotiations each side hammers out areas of agreement. Each side agrees to accept some of the other side's points and to drop some of its own demands. Once the teams have agreed, the union must convince its members to vote to support the contract. When the sides cannot agree, they can seek help from impartial outsiders—either mediators, arbitrators, or factfinders.

*9. Identify the weapons each side in collective bargaining has to force an agreement.*

Management and unions each have weapons they can use to force an agreement. Unions rely on strikes and picketing. These tactics not only do economic damage to the employer, they also publicize the union's position. Management can turn to lockouts and to strikebreakers.

# KEY TERMS

Union
Organized labor
Knights of Labor
American Federation
  of Labor (AFL)
Trade (craft) union
Business unionism
Collective bargaining
Sherman Antitrust Act
Injunction
Industrial union
Congress of Industrial
  Organizations (CIO)
National Labor Rela-
  tions Act (NLRA);
  the Wagner Act
Unfair labor practice
National Labor Rela-
  tions Board (NLRB)
Taft-Hartley Act

Right-to-work law
Closed shop
Union shop
Agency shop
Maintenance shop
Open shop
Landrum-Griffin
  Act
Organizing drive
Authorization card
Representation
  election
Consent election
Bargaining unit
Fair Labor
  Standards Act
Base wage rate
Cost-of-living
  adjustments
  (COLAs)

Consumer Price
  Index
Seniority differential
Shift differential
Incentive rate formulas
Piece-work rates
Working conditions
Right to employment
Seniority
Unemployment
  compensation
Grievance
Shop steward
Chief steward
Grievance committee
Business representative
  (business agent)
Arbitration
Arbitrator
Givebacks

National negotiation
Pattern bargaining
Council bargaining
Independent bargaining
Mediation
Mediator
Factfinding
Strike
Picketing
Lockout
Secondary boycott
Primary boycott
Strikebreaker (scab)
Economic strike

# REVIEW QUESTIONS

1. Briefly describe the labor movement from 1865 to 1914. What were some of the most significant events?
2. What influence did the National Labor Relations Act (the Wagner Act) have on the American labor movement? What effect did the Taft-Hartley Act have on the labor movement?
3. What are some of the major factors that motivate workers to join and support unions?
4. When a labor union decides to initiate an organization drive, what steps does it follow?
5. What are some of the most common subjects of collective bargaining? What are the mandatory subjects? Voluntary subjects?

6. From the employees' standpoint, what are the advantages of a seniority system? Disadvantages?
7. Describe the major steps in the collective bargaining process.
8. What are the major contributions of the mediator?
9. Discuss the bargaining issues that have surfaced in the past decade. Why are strikes and lockouts less common today?
10. In what ways does mediation differ from arbitration?

# APPLICATION EXERCISES

1. Contact a person who is a member of a union representing service workers. Conduct an interview and obtain answers to the following questions:
   a. What are the major subjects of collective bargaining upon which labor and management are negotiating?
   b. What issues are most difficult for negotiators to agree on?
2. Review selected issues of *Fortune, Business Week,* and *Nation's Business* published during the past six months. Identify the contemporary issues and problems facing organized labor.

# CASES

## 9.1  Frank Lorenzo vs. the Eastern Airline Unions

"America's Toughest Bosses," screamed the headline of an article in a February, 1989, issue of *Fortune.* At the top of the list was Frank Lorenzo, empire-building, union-busting leader of Texas Air.

In less than a decade, Lorenzo had built his airline from a small regional carrier to the second largest in the United States. His first big step had been the take-over of Continental in the early 1980s. Initially, Lorenzo reduced the size and payroll of his new acquisition by selling assets, laying off workers, and demanding union concessions. When machinists and flight attendants balked, he filed for bankruptcy. The unions caved in. With wages only half of what they had been, he rebuilt the airline. In the end Continental was larger than ever.

Three days after filing for bankruptcy at Continental, Lorenzo had the carrier flying again. At Eastern, which he took over in 1986 and where he tried to implement exactly the same strategy, he was not so lucky. The main reason? There was no one to fly the planes. At Continental, pilots had made an early, separate peace. At Eastern, pilots had joined the machinists and flight attendants when they walked out. Insofar as he contributed to the creation of a united front between the elite Air Line Pilots Association and the militant International Federation of Machinists, two unions not known for their harmonious relations, Lorenzo unwittingly accomplished something the labor movement might never have accomplished by itself.

Many analysts maintain that Lorenzo, for all his reputation as a troublemaker for unions, had no choice but to seek to cut wages. In spite of high revenues and the lucrative East Coast routes it dominated, Eastern had lost a billion dollars over the preceding decade. At the time of the strike, losses were estimated at $1.5 million a day. There were indications that the unions, which felt that Lorenzo was spinning off assets to make the carrier appear in worse shape than it really was, knew they would have to grant concessions and were primarily engaged in a personal strike against Frank Lorenzo. At one point Lorenzo went so far as to file racketeering charges against the unions for conspiring to find a buyer for the troubled airline.

### Questions

1. At the time of the Continental negotiations, the airline business was in a slump. At the time of the Eastern negotiations, business was booming, and pilots and mechanics were in great demand. How might an improved economy have worsened Lorenzo's negotiating position? Should he have tried a different strategy at Eastern? If so, what?
2. Pilots earn four to five times more than mechanics. How might this have affected the

pilots' less militant approach in the Continental negotiations?

Source: For more information, see *Business Week*, December 19, 1988, pp. 71–80; *Fortune*, February 27, 1989, pp. 40–41; *The Wall Street Journal*, March 10, 1989, pp. A1, A10–11; *New York Newsday*, April 7, 1989, p. 42.

## 9.2 Health Care Costs

Corporate health care is a big business. In 1987, General Motors alone paid out close to $3 billion for medical plans covering about one percent of all Americans.

Corporate health care is also a booming business, at least in terms of costs. GM's bill for 1987 had risen roughly 50 percent in just two years.

The company's attempt to bring these expenses under control had been flexible, imaginative, and, for a while at least, successful. Working in cooperation with the United Auto Workers, GM had encouraged union members to—for example—get second opinions and use less expensive health-care options. The second opinions were no prescription for lower costs. With certain kinds of minor surgery being handled in outpatient clinics, those costs did decline—temporarily. But soon outpatient-clinic charges began to go up dramatically. Other attempts to use less expensive services were also met by rising prices.

The General Motors example is not unique. Companies everywhere are seeking relief from rising health-care costs. Many are including health maintenance organizations (HMOs) among their employee options and offering incentives for employees to join them. For example, the use of private doctors or more expensive health services may require a substantial—even prohibitive—copayment by the employee.

HMOs are the cheapest option because most of their physicians are on staff or under contract. But, as with other health-care alternatives companies have explored, HMOs, too, are becoming increasingly expensive. The quality of health care in HMOs is not always first rate. Physician salaries tend to be low. Turnover is high. Darkening this picture are the gloomy financial figures for HMOs, which have been losing billions of dollars a year.

### Questions

1. How might a union react to a company's attempt to impose or radically increase copayments?
2. Should companies finance union-administered health-care programs, rather than pay for such programs directly? Why?

Source: For more information, see *Fortune*, August 29, 1988, pp. 44–46; *Business Week*, October 31, 1988, p. 120; and *Fortune*, December 19, 1988, pp. 133–140.

# 10 Operations Management

After you have completed this chapter, you will be able to do the following:

1. Define operations management *and describe the elements that go into it.*

2. *Classify the types of production processes.*

3. *Describe the steps that go into the strategic planning of an operation.*

4. *List the steps in the PERT process for scheduling production control.*

5. *Identify the criteria that go into a facilities location decision.*

6. *Describe the principal considerations in designing the layout of production facilities.*

7. *Describe the advancements being made in operations management with robots and computers.*

8. *Identify the key elements involved in implementing an operational plan.*

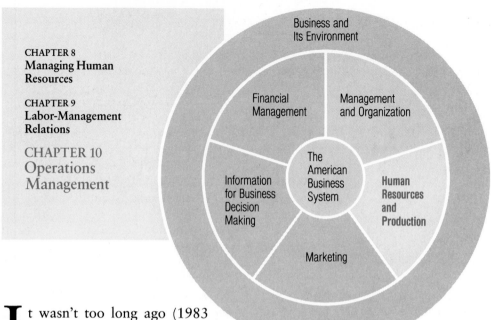

I t wasn't too long ago (1983
to be exact) that Harley-Davidson,
the premier maker of heavyweight
motorcycles in the U.S., came close to being run off the road and out of the
market by the competition. That was the year Honda nearly left Harley in the
dust by grabbing 44.3% of the market to Harley's 23%.

Today, though, Harley is back in the lead with nearly 40% of the market, and
Honda is trailing by more than 10 percentage points. And a lot of other U.S.
companies making a lot of other products under intense competition from abroad
are looking closely at the Harley turnaround and what it has to teach them.
Harley's winning strategy: Use short-term government import controls to buy
enough time to turn around it's own operations, improve quality and cut costs.[1]

You don't have to be a motorcycle enthusiast to recognize Harley-Davidson's
comeback as an inspiring example for American business and industry. In
the face of devastating foreign competition, Harley-Davidson did not hide
behind permanent trade barriers. Instead, the eighty-seven-year-old company
increased its competitiveness by doing a better job of transforming raw
materials and ending with a higher-quality product. In short, Harley-Davidson
became more productive. It did so not by any magic formula, but by cost
cutting, employee training, inventory discipline, and quality improvement.
This chapter focuses on the production function of business, the area where
Harley-Davidson was able to make substantial changes. As we will see,
production involves making goods and services for sale in the marketplace,
as well as the decisions surrounding making these goods and services, such
as quantities to be produced, the various methods available, and the design
of the production facility.

# Products and Operations Management

From Chapter 5 you may recall that management is the process of coordinating human, informational, physical, and financial resources to accomplish an organization's goal. The goal this chapter discusses is creating a marketable product. A **product** is a good, a service, or a combination of goods and services that an organization sells. People normally associate the term *product* with a tangible good like a typewriter, but the sense of this word also includes the concept of an intangible service like a checking account, or a combination of the two, like a restaurant meal, which is both prepared and served. In the case of PPG Industries, for example, the *product* it sells General Motors includes a unique combination of a tangible good, paint, and an intangible service, expertise and management (see Business Issues).

One way that production occurs is through **manufacturing**, the management of the resources necessary to convert raw materials into finished goods. A furniture maker, for example, might buy cherry wood, a raw material. The company's workers then apply tools and their skills to the raw material in order to turn it into, say, rocking chairs. This process of transforming wood into rockers is manufacturing.

Manufacturing, however, is only a part of the larger concept called *operations*. When you see a doctor in a clinic during a checkup, this examination is a service. The bill the clinic sends you is associated with the production of its service. Billing is a part of the clinic's operation. The process of planning and coordinating the production of goods and services is called **operations management**.

**product** a good, service, or a combination of goods and services that an organization sells

**manufacturing** the management of the resources necessary to convert raw material into finished goods

**operations management** the process of planning and coordinating the production of goods and services

# The Transformation Process

The key concept in operations management is **transformation**, the conversion of input (resources) into output (goods or services). For example, AT&T takes plastic and electromechanical parts and transforms them through design, manufacturing, and assembly into telephones. Figure 10.1 illustrates some transformation systems.

The term *transformation* implies physical changes, but today it also includes the conversion of resources into services. For instance, an educational institution takes its primary inputs—enrolled students, curriculum, faculty, and facilities—and produces employable graduates.

**transformation** the conversion of input (resources) into output (goods or services)

*1.* Define operations management *and describe the elements that go into it.*

## Division of Labor and Specialization

We saw in Chapter 6 that modern organizations are based on the related concepts of division of labor and specialization. It is hard to conceive of a productive system today that does not rely on these concepts. From fast-food restaurants to automobile assembly lines, tasks are divided and workers specialized.

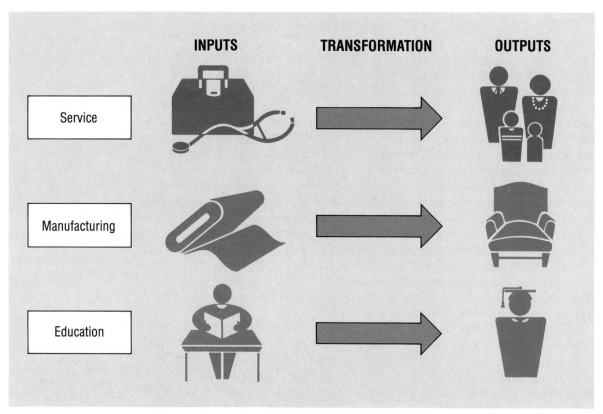

| INPUTS | TRANSFORMATION | OUTPUTS |
|---|---|---|
| Service | | |
| Manufacturing | | |
| Education | | |

FIGURE 10.1   Transformation Systems

## A Classification of Production Processes

*2. Classify the types of pro-duction processes.*

Production processes are classified according to the variety and quantity of goods produced under them. In general, the greater the quantity and the less the variety of goods produced, the more structured the process is (see Figure 10.2).[2]

*Production to Order and Production to Stock*   All production organizations are either production-to-order systems or production-to-stock systems. A **production-to-order system** produces only what customers or clients demand, as the order comes in. Catering services or custom upholstery shops are examples of production-to-order systems. A **production-to-stock system** produces goods to be held in inventory. The automobile industry is a classic example of production to stock. One of the most closely watched barometers of economic health is the national inventory of new cars.

*Continuous-Flow System*   The production-to-stock process that produces large quantities of a single standardized product is called the **continuous-flow system** or **continuous-process system**. Industries using continuous-flow systems, such as petroleum refining, are capital intensive and are often highly automated.

**production-to-order system**   system that produces only what customers or clients demand

**production-to-stock system**   system that produces goods to be held in inventory

**continuous-flow system (continuous-process system)**   the production-to-stock process that produces large quantities of a single standardized product

## PPG SELLS GENERAL MOTORS A LOT MORE THAN PAINT

At General Motors' Buick Reatta plant in Lansing, Mich., painting of the new $25,000 luxury sports car is being performed in a unique manner. Both the paint preparation and application as well as the administrative management of the paint shop at this low-volume "craft center" are being supervised not by GM, but by the supplier, PPG Industries Inc.

At the Reatta center the goal was to achieve the highest possible quality. GM realized it could not provide the painting expertise expected for such a luxury car, so it turned to PPG. After a year of production, with PPG's twelve supervisors in complete charge of the paint operation, including GM's fifty-six United Auto Workers employees, both supplier and customer agree that that target has been reached. J. Robert Thompson, the GM manager of the center, calls the high-gloss paint job "one of the best in the world."

PPG is achieving this while containing costs within the per-vehicle amount it had agreed upon with GM. The two companies also are profiting from their warranty-sharing agreement, in which they split equally any savings or expense.

"Our experience has been phenomenal," Mr. Thompson exclaims. "We are 75 percent below the [warranty-savings] goal. When you have warranty costs down where we have ours, where the customer says the paint job is great and doesn't need repair, that's big dollars." This success has erased early GM worries about not developing its own painting skills.

Source: Excerpted from James Braham, "Marrying Goods & Services," *Industry Week*, November 7, 1988, pp. 69–70.

---

*Mass Production or Assembly-Line Production*   The production-to-stock process that produces large quantities of identical or nearly identical products is **mass production** or assembly-line production. The auto industry was the one that brought these terms into our everyday vocabulary. Originally, the variation in products was tiny. Today, in contrast, some claim that part of Detroit's disadvantage in competing with Japan lies in the hundreds of different equipment configurations that can be provided on an American car. General Motors is in the process of remedying this situation by producing 132 models by 1992, down from 175 in 1987.[3]

**mass production**   the production-to-stock process that produces large quantities of identical or nearly identical products

*Batch Processing or Intermittent Processing*   The system of production called *batch processing* or *intermittent processing* is a production-to-stock system that generates lower quantities of goods than a mass-production system. This system, however, is likely to use processes similar or identical to those in mass-production systems. A restaurant uses this method when the cook prepares salads, then biscuits, and then soup.

*Job-Shop Processing or Job-Order Processing*   The production-to-order process in which the producer makes a quantity of goods to the customer's

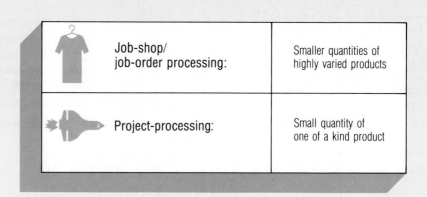

**PRODUCTION TO STOCK SYSTEM**

Produces goods to be held in inventory

| | | |
|---|---|---|
| gas | Continuous-flow/ continuous-process: | Large quantities of single standardized product |
| | Mass production/ assembly-line production: | Large quantities of identical or nearly identical products |
| | Batch processing: | Smaller quantities of identical or nearly identical products |

**PRODUCTION TO ORDER SYSTEM**

Produces only as much as consumers demand

| | | |
|---|---|---|
| | Job-shop/ job-order processing: | Smaller quantities of highly varied products |
| | Project-processing: | Small quantity of one of a kind product |

FIGURE 10.2   A Classification of Production Processes

satisfaction is the *job-shop processing* or *job-order processing* system. Such shops produce a far greater variety of types of goods than the three production systems we have just discussed, but the quantities they produce are quite small by comparison. Individually tailored clothes and custom-built houses are produced this way. Hair styling salons and barber shops rely on job-shop processing to accommodate individual customers.

*Project Processing*   The production-to-order system in which the manu-facturer produces a one-of-a-kind item is *project processing*. Production of such relatively unique products as telecommunications satellites or nuclear power plants is usually on a project basis.

Production to order   *There are no shirts on the shelves at Manhattan custom-shirt maker Seewaldt & Bauman—just fabrics and the paper-patterns kept for each customer. Shirtmaker Stan Seewaldt cuts and stitches each shirt to order. The minimum order he accepts is six shirts. Says Seewaldt, "If a guy has a paunch, I can do a lot to hide it."*

# Strategic Operations Planning

A firm's vision of itself and of its future dictates the kind of operation it should develop. Operations planning begins with strategic planning. Once a firm's senior management has adopted a strategy, its middle management can develop the tactics to carry out this strategy while its first-line managers develop operational plans to execute the tactics.

*3. Describe the steps that go into the strategic planning of an operation.*

## The Strategic Decision

In the last decade, no strategic decision has been more analyzed than IBM's to enter the highly competitive personal computer (PC) market. During the late 1970s the PC field belonged to upstarts Apple and Commodore. IBM

Strategic planning   *Sandra Kurtzig began creating software for business microcomputers at a desk in her bedroom to supplement the family income. She has since moved her thriving firm, ASK, to Silicon Valley. The expansion of Kurtzig's firm required careful timing and planning.*

made a strategic decision to build a personal computer because that rapidly growing market sector was virtually the only one in which IBM did not have an entry. Although IBM's development of a popular PC often is characterized as a happy accident, it was instead a key feature of IBM's strategy for achieving greater connectivity among its wide range of computers.[4]

Until its PC model, IBM took great pride in developing and manufacturing its own unique machines. All IBM product development was structured to occur in a centralized, integrated environment under the direct supervision of top management. IBM did many things differently in producing its personal computer, not the least of which was to set up what amounted to an independent subsidiary to develop this product.

## The Make-or-Buy Decision

Once a firm decides to develop a certain new product, it must decide whether it is to be a manufacturer or a packager of that product. In other words, should the firm make the product or merely buy it from other companies and put its own label on the package?

288

Such a decision has an impact not just on the one company but on the entire national economy. Over the last twenty years, increasing numbers of American corporations have abandoned domestic manufacturing operations in favor either of buying products from other vendors—usually foreign ones— or manufacturing goods abroad themselves. The practice of buying parts from outside vendors is called **outsourcing** and is perceived by unions to be a serious threat to job security.[5] By 1989, Chrysler was outsourcing 70 percent of its parts; the figures for Ford and General Motors were 50 percent and 30 percent, respectively.

**outsourcing** the practice of buying parts from outside vendors

The flight from domestic manufacturing led *Business Week* to call American firms that "import components or products from low-wage countries, slap their own names on them, and sell them in America" **hollow corporations.**[6] IBM's PC initially went a similar route. About 73 percent of its parts, including the keyboard, video monitor, and disk drives, for instance, were manufactured abroad, but the "brains," like the microprocessors made by Intel Corporation, were American, as was the final assembly. IBM has since come to rely more on in-house components.

**hollow corporations** American firms that "import components or products from low-wage countries, slap their own names on them, and sell them in America"

## The Nature of the Business

The make-or-buy decision relates to the fundamental question: What is the nature of a given business? Many writers have hailed IBM's development of the PC as exhibiting marketing genius, and so it did. IBM must have carefully weighed the cost of manufacturing the entire PC against the cost of buying its components. It seems likely, however, that IBM's principal tactical consideration was ultimately its understanding of its basic business: selling and servicing, as opposed to manufacturing, business equipment. Its choice proved to be a brilliant one. Here is an example of what the authors of *In Search of Excellence* would call "sticking to your knitting."

## High-Tech versus Low-Tech Decisions

In some business sectors, companies may have a choice between high-tech and low-tech manufacturing methods. For example, a company manufacturing pianos can choose between applying modern production techniques to the pianos' parts and final assembly or constructing its pianos the way they were made a century ago. Steinway has chosen the older method, which is why it takes thirteen months to produce a Steinway piano.

The 1960s marked the beginning of a renewed interest in crafts. Despite a continuation of that trend, it has proven difficult for artisans to provide sufficient quality and uniqueness to overcome the price differential favoring machine-made goods, which are often imported.

Despite space-age technologies that have become commonplace, successful products still spring from surprisingly low-tech decisions. For example, New Pig Corp. makes a sausage-shaped product called a "pig" that can soak up four times its weight in oil and other greasy fluids in half a minute. What is the secret ingredient that has machine shop owners and other customers breaking down New Pig's doors to place orders? "Pigs" are little more than nylon stockings stuffed with ground-up corn cobs![7] The object lesson here is not to overlook simple solutions to difficult problems.

## Production Planning and Control

The management function called **production planning and control** involves the scheduling and monitoring of operations relating to the production of goods or services. Its goals include:

- High-quality production
- High productivity of human and physical resources
- Low operating costs
- Customer satisfaction

For example, a job shop can achieve high productivity and minimize operating costs by reducing the number of **setups**, modifications of a process or a machine to meet the specifications for a new order, that it must do. Scheduling jobs together that have similar requirements can reduce costs and delays.[8]

### Product Planning

Production and marketing departments need to work together to develop products that meet the market's requirements. These decisions are generally tactical ones made in the context of a strategy outlined by top management. In a new company the production and marketing departments may of course consist of one person, the entrepreneur.

Planning a service operation has much in common with planning a manufacturing operation. The emphasis on quality may be higher in service, and certainly the planning of a service operation must center on the personnel who will perform the services. In making high-quality chocolates, for instance, a confectioner like Mother Myrick's, in Manchester, Vermont, must control the quality of its product from the creation of the recipe through the sale to the consumer.[9] Likewise, a financial planner must train his or her employees to produce clean, precise work for presentation to clients.

### Scheduling Techniques

The function of production control that sets the time for and duration of tasks is called **scheduling**. Its goal is to bring people and materials together at the right moment in the right place so that resources will be used efficiently. Scheduling is never simple. Ensuring that workers have the thousands of parts required to build a Boeing 757 Jetliner—when they need them—requires great organization. Making appointments requires both organization and tact for a busy hair stylist, since such a business is built on customer relations.

One of the most popular scheduling techniques for production control is known as **Program Evaluation and Review Technique (PERT)** (see Figure 10.3). The PERT process's first step is to identify all the major activities required to complete a project. Completion of each activity is called an *event*. For example, in building an apartment house, laying the foundation and putting on the roof are activities that become events when completed.

The second step in the PERT process is to arrange the events into a sequence to separate the events that can happen simultaneously from those

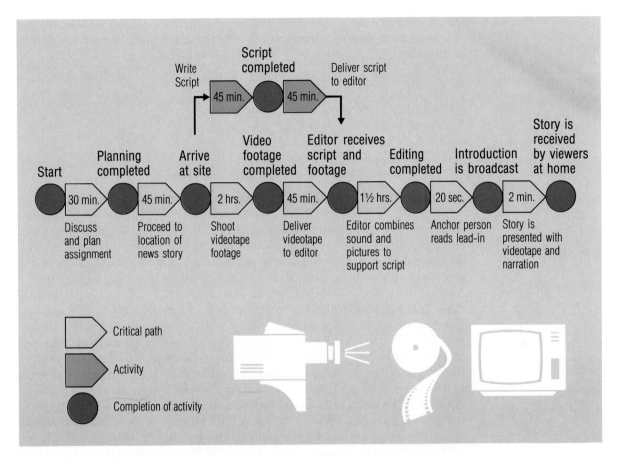

FIGURE 10.3  PERT in Action

that must occur sequentially. For instance, a roof can be shingled at the same time the windows are being installed, but the wiring cannot go in before the walls are up.

Step three in the PERT process requires estimating the time it will take to complete each activity. The planners then total the time required for each path, a series of sequential events in the production process. The path with the longest total time from start to finish is called the **critical path**. If any of the activities on the critical path lag, the project almost certainly cannot be completed on time.

*4. List the steps in the PERT process for scheduling production control.*

**critical path**  the path with the longest total time for completion of a series of sequential events in the production process

## Facilities Location

A large corporation that needs to develop a new facility faces three basic decisions in locating it:

1. In what part of what nation should it locate?
2. In what community should it locate?
3. On what site within the community should it locate?

The smaller the firm, the more likely it is to begin with the second or third question. Even so, every business faces the same decision criteria in choosing a location:

- Proximity to raw materials and/or markets
- Availability of qualified personnel
- Availability of appropriate transportation
- Affordability and availability of energy
- Attractive government inducements
- Favorable local regulations and taxes
- Congenial general living conditions in the area

These factors will have different weights in each firm's decision. For instance, when Borden's moved its headquarters from New York City to Columbus, Ohio, an important consideration was Columbus's reputation as a good place to raise a family. When Honda located its first U.S. plant 50 miles northwest of Columbus in Marysville, the key factors were favorable state taxes and the ready availability of all three major types of ground transportation.

### Proximity to Raw Materials and/or Markets

Virtually every type of business must locate its facilities close to either a source of raw materials or a key market or both. The ideal is of course to be located close to both, but that is often impossible. Adolf Coors Company decided to locate its first Eastern brewery in Virginia, because the water quality there matched that in Coors's home state of Colorado and because the plant would be near its new markets. Although Coors has put off construction of its Eastern brewery for the time being, it is using its Virginia site as a packaging and distribution center to serve its Eastern customers more efficiently than before.[10]

When raw materials are large, bulky, or heavy, a manufacturer usually locates its operation near the source of such materials, to avoid high transportation costs. If, however, the cost of transporting raw materials is only a minimal part of the cost of production, firms tend to locate near markets.

A more exotic approach to locating facilities near raw materials or markets is a computerized mapping technique called *geosystems*. This approach marries maps with geological, demographic, or market research information. A color-coded geosystem map can tell a petroleum company where to drill for oil or a bank where to locate a branch nearest the greatest concentration of high-income households.[11]

### Availability of Qualified Personnel

All firms obviously require qualified personnel to operate them. The nature of the jobs determines whether the availability of qualified personnel will be a determining factor in the decision about where to locate a facility.

### Appropriate Transportation

A firm must have appropriate transportation facilities, including parking, for receiving its raw materials or for receiving customers and clients. These facilities must be able to handle both the firm's finished products and departing customers or clients. Finally, the firm's employees must have appropriate transportation facilities available to them to reach work comfortably and conveniently.

Appropriate transportation  *Traveling to and from Union Pacific Resources'
production platforms off the Louisiana coast created a special problem. The
company solved it with the aid of helicopters.*

*Affordability and Availability of Energy*  The price and availability of the
energy needed for production often plays a key role in site selection. For
instance, the process of manufacturing aluminum requires enormous quantities
of electricity. It is thus not surprising that the aluminum industry has
concentrated in areas like that served by the Bonneville Power Authority in
the Pacific Northwest. The federal government originally established these
public corporations to supply low-cost hydroelectric power in their service
regions to attract jobs.

*Government Inducements*  Other government inducements to locate in
specific regions include a possible tax forgiveness for a certain period,
industrial revenue bonds to finance a project at very low cost to the business,
and the construction of necessary water and sewer hookups and facilities.
Governments often use these inducements to lure businesses into blighted
areas or to train minorities.

Government also has a broad range of powers that it can use to either
hinder or promote a business in choosing a particular site. For instance,
within localities, zoning regulations specify the uses to which land and the
buildings on it can be put. The local zoning authority may at its discretion
grant variances from the regulations in order to permit a business to use land
for its own purposes.

Not surprisingly, government inducements to attract business can cause problems and breed resentment if they are excessive. For example, according to *Fortune:*

> Kentucky's package of goodies to cash-rich Toyota, including interest on funds the state had to borrow, will cost its citizens more than $280 million over 20 years. The cost of the come-ons per job created, which worked out to $11,000 when Tennessee bagged Nissan in 1980, ballooned to $50,000 in Kentucky. Wallace Wilkinson, who won the governorship after sharply criticizing this largess, has discovered that most of Kentucky's federal funds for job training are committed to Toyota.[12]

# The Layout of Production Facilities

**layout** the physical arrangement of a production facility

Very early in the stage of planning for a new facility, management must decide on the new plant's **layout,** the physical arrangement of a production facility.

## Design Considerations

*6. Describe the principal considerations in designing the layout of production facilities.*

The design of a facility's layout should maximize the efficient use of a firm's human and physical resources. No operation, however, can be designed with just these considerations in mind. For instance, management must also take into account such limitations as state and federal safety requirements.

*Manufacturing Operations* Manufacturers want a layout that will promote the smooth flow of materials within a plant. Raw material must enter the plant at an appropriate point for easy input into the manufacturing process. The process of transforming raw materials into salable goods should move smoothly, without bottlenecks, to the moment the finished products leave the facility.

**process layout** a layout model which groups machinery or activities according to their purposes

An operations-management team has a number of layout models from which to choose (see Figure 10.4). A **process layout** groups machinery or activities according to their purposes. In a pipe factory, for instance, all the machines that put threads on household water pipes would be placed together. Normally, small operations with differentiated product mixes, such as job shops, use process layouts. In a **product layout**, though, the equipment arrangement relates to the sequence of operations performed in manufacturing a product. Product layouts are most commonly used in assembly-line operations.

**product layout** a layout model in which the equipment arrangement relates to the sequence of operations performed in manufacturing a product

**fixed-position layout** an operational arrangement in which workers and equipment come to the product, instead of the usual arrangement

In both process and product layouts, the raw material or product moves from one processing stage to the next. In contrast, a **fixed-position layout** is an operational arrangement in which workers and equipment come to the product, instead of the usual arrangement. Commercial and military aircraft are made this way, as are medium to large ships.

*Nonmanufacturing Operations* Managers of nonmanufacturing facilities also need to address the layout question. Retailers, for example, carefully

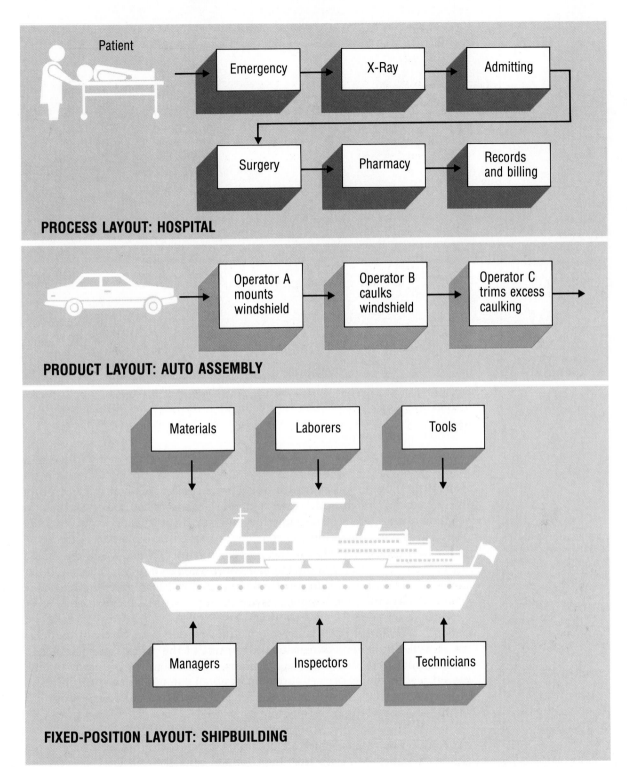

**PROCESS LAYOUT: HOSPITAL**

**PRODUCT LAYOUT: AUTO ASSEMBLY**

**FIXED-POSITION LAYOUT: SHIPBUILDING**

FIGURE 10.4   Basic Production Layouts

Source: Robert Kreitner, *Management,* 4th ed. (Boston: Houghton Mifflin, 1989), fig. 17.7, p. 697. Copyright 1989 Houghton Mifflin. Used by permission of the publisher.

**Product layout**  *Packaging orange juice is an assembly-line operation. The machines that fill the containers with juice must be set up before the machines that seal the containers. Next come the machines that pack the containers into cartons and those that seal the cartons.*

**consumer-oriented layout**  an operational layout designed to facilitate the customer's interactions with the firm's services

control the flow of customers through the display areas and into checkout lines. And the design and location of work stations can make or break a service business like a restaurant, computer-repair operation, or accounting office. In service operations, a **consumer-oriented layout** is an operational layout designed to facilitate the customer's interactions with the firm's services. Banks introduced the familiar roped waiting lines for tellers in order to end customers' frustration if they happened to pick a slow-moving line. Grocery stores instituted express-checkout lines for the same reason.

*Design Techniques*  Designing layouts that work is an art but also requires art as well. Simple one-dimensional diagrams of the process are a sufficient starting point, but two-dimensional maps are essential for proper planning. Indeed, a scale model or even three-dimensional computer drawings are often necessary to make a design come to life. Computer-assisted design programs can assist in developing the overall design.

**capacity**  the rate at which an operation can produce output over a given period

*Capacity*  The rate at which an operation can produce output over a given period is called its **capacity**. Appropriate capacity concerns the facility planners, who must forecast demand. The capacity problem is generally more acute for service companies than for manufacturing concerns. A manufacturing company can compensate for too little capacity by building up inventory during slack periods or adding extra shifts. Such service businesses as restaurants usually do not have these options, however. Overcapacity in the form of empty seats has driven bus companies, passenger train lines, and airlines into bankruptcy over the years.

Some decisions about capacity have nothing to do with the demand for a company's goods or services. Rather, the operation's manageability becomes the overriding concern. For example, at Parker Hannifin Corp., the hydraulic press manufacturer, plant size is kept down to between 300 to 400 employees. According to the firm's chief executive officer, Paul G. Schloemer, "When a division gets to a point where its general manager can't know and understand the business and be close to the customer, we split it off."[13] Consequently, Parker Hannifin has 80 divisions and 200 plants.

## Mass Production, Computers, and Robotics

One of the hottest topics in operations management is the "so-called" "factory of the future" that incorporates recent developments in computers and mechanization. Applying technological breakthroughs to operations has proven far more difficult than anyone originally imagined, however. Not only have robots been known to spray paint each other instead of the product as horrified engineers looked on, but workers also resent being displaced by robots.

*7. Describe the advancements being made in operations management with computers and robots.*

*Computerized Automation*  When the term first entered our language, **automation** referred to the substitution of machines for human labor. The word still carries that meaning, but the development of so-called *smart machines* has broadened its meaning to include the replacement of human sensory applications, too. For example, Allen-Bradley, a manufacturer of controls for electric motors, has designed an assembly line that can read bar codes so that it can produce unique controls without stopping for retooling.[14] IBM's 12-lb. laptop personal computer, though a flop in the marketplace, was a computerized automation marvel. As *Fortune* noted when IBM's laptop was still in production: "From receiving dock to exit dock, the machine is assembled, tested, packed, and shipped without a human being so much as driving a screw."[15]

**automation**  the substitution of mechanical for human labor and sensory applications

*Robots and Computer-Integrated Manufacturing (CIM)*  A **robot** is a reprogrammable machine capable of performing a variety of tasks requiring programmed manipulations of tools and materials. Some believe robots to be the key to recapturing world markets for manufactured goods because they perform routine, repetitive tasks thousands of times without a mistake.

The great benefit of robots to manufacturers lies not in having them replace human labor but in their vastly improving product quality. Robots most fully achieve this upgrading as an element of **computer-integrated manufacturing (CIM)**, a computerized operations-management system that manages data flow while at the same time directing the movement and processing of material. The resulting combination of lower labor costs and greater quality control may reduce a factory's typical breakeven point from 60 to 65 percent of capacity to as little as 25 to 30 percent.

**robot**  a reprogrammable machine capable of performing a variety of tasks requiring programmed manipulations of tools and materials

**computer-integrated manufacturing (CIM)**  a computerized operations-management system that manages data flow while at the same time directing the movement and processing of material

# Operational Implementation and Control

**8.** Identify the key elements involved in implementing an operational plan.

Many of the decisions we have been discussing, such as determining a plant's capacity, are made just once. By the time the facility is built and the necessary equipment installed, the management should have plans in place for running it. The quality of the planning will of course come to nothing if the plan is not implemented appropriately. Effective planning is a never-ending process of communication, evaluation, and reevaluation.

The key to successful implementation is **control**, the process of measuring an organization's performance against its plans to make certain that the actual operations conform with the plans. In short, "control is assuring that desired results are attained."[16]

**control** the process of measuring an organization's performance against its plans to make certain that the actual operations conform with the plans

## Operational Planning

The scheduling of an organization's day-to-day needs and anticipation of how to meet them is **operational planning**. In a sense, all operational planning supports one key decision: the amount of output the facility needs to generate over a particular planning period. For example, management must decide how many workers to hire and train to achieve the desired output. Similarly, the output target determines the quantity of raw materials that will have to be ordered.

**operational planning** the scheduling of an organization's day-to-day needs and the designing of how to meet them

## Inventory Control

**Inventory** is a general term used to describe certain classes of goods that are assets to a business. There are two classes of inventories, indirect and direct. **Indirect inventories** are the supplies a business uses that are not purchased with the intention of reselling them. The ribbons used in an office typewriter or antifreeze for a company truck fall into this class. **Direct inventory**, in manufacturing, includes raw materials, work in process (whatever stage of production it is in), and finished products. In retail and service operations, direct inventory includes all goods bought for resale. Controlling the costs and flow of direct inventory is a major concern for an operations manager.[17] There is a definite trend today toward small inventories.

Indirect inventory is not a major focus of operations management, but direct inventory is. In this chapter, when we refer to inventory we mean direct inventory.

**inventory** certain classes of goods that are assets to a business

**indirect inventories** the supplies a business uses that are not purchased with the intention of reselling them

**direct inventory** in manufacturing this includes raw materials, work in process, and finished products; in retail and service operations it includes all goods bought for resale

*The Costs of Inventory* The basic objective of inventory control is to balance two types of costs. **Carrying costs** are expenses incurred because an item is held in inventory. Among many others, carrying costs include taxes, storage charges, insurance, maintenance, and spoilage. **Ordering costs** are expenses incurred whenever a business places an order for inventory goods with a vendor. They include not only all the vendor's charges but also the

**carrying costs** expenses incurred because an item is held in inventory

**ordering costs** expenses incurred whenever a business places an order for inventory goods with a vendor

Seeing is believing   *In the final analysis, the only way to know how much inventory you have is to count it. As sophisticated as inventory-control procedures have become, there is still an important place for clipboards and gummed labels.*

costs associated with receiving and processing the order and the cost of any delays in production caused by not receiving the goods promptly.

Management's goal is to achieve a minimum total inventory cost and to balance inventory carrying and ordering costs. Achieving this goal requires two separate actions. First, management must minimize the controllable inventory costs, like spoilage. Second, it must balance the unavoidable costs against each other.

*Just-In-Time Inventory*   To accomplish these two goals, the Japanese developed the so-called **just-in-time inventory system,** an ordering system

**just-in-time inventory system**   an ordering system that aims to have inventory arrive on the premises just moments before it must enter the transformation process

that aims to have inventory arrive on the premises just moments before it must enter the transformation process. These systems have a very narrow margin of error and therefore require close cooperation between the supplier and the manufacturer. Various U.S. companies are now beginning to adopt just-in-time systems. All the auto makers and other manufacturers like Allen-Bradley are now using just-in-time inventory systems, at least in parts of their manufacturing operations.

Inventory costs are as big a problem for service operations as for manufacturing. For instance, the cost of keeping every conceivable part in stock would bankrupt a small appliance shop. Likewise, a restaurant cannot afford to throw out large quantities of unsold food regularly.

## Materials Requirements Planning (MRP)

The computerized technique used to plan and control manufacturing inventories is called **materials requirements planning** (**MRP**). MRP's purpose is to ensure that a manufacturer has available the necessary materials and components in the right quantities and at the right time so that it can complete its finished products according to the master schedule. At the operational level, management uses MRP to plan production on a short-term basis.

The enormous improvements in both computer hardware and software over the last decade have turned MRP's goals into reality for many firms. MRP has reduced inventory investment, improved work flow, reduced shortages of materials and components, and achieved more reliable delivery schedules. In addition, materials requirements planning has led to better communications and improved integration of support functions.[18]

## Purchasing

The operations function by which a business obtains the goods and services it requires is **purchasing**. Purchasing's objective is to ensure that a firm has the right materials at the right price at the right place at the right time. To do so requires good suppliers. Traditionally, purchasing managers were advised to find several suppliers for each purchased item to avoid interruptions in supply and encourage price competition. In recent years, however, the trend has been toward fewer rather than more suppliers. This is particularly true when just-in-time inventory systems are in place. "Single sourcing" has become a commonplace procedure. This apparently risky approach to purchasing is made less risky by building long-term relationships with preferred suppliers and helping them improve the quality of their output. Xerox has enjoyed better quality and lower prices by dramatically thinning the ranks of its suppliers. Between 1980 and 1987, Xerox reduced its vendors from 5,000 to 400. By 1992, Xerox wants to lower the number to 250.[19]

Small differences in pricing can turn into large sums over a long period. Quality is always a consideration, but getting the highest quality possible is

Quality as part of the product   *To make its croutons, Quality Croutons, Inc., first makes bread from flour. It then cubes the bread and toasts it. Without a thorough quality control process, however, the company would not produce a product acceptable to McDonald's, a major customer.*

not. A purchasing manager needs to be as specific as possible about the quality necessary for the product. Finally, the supplier's reliability is a critical factor in operational planning, because the probability of on-time delivery must be factored into the purchasing department's **lead time**, the period that elapses between the time of placing an order and its receipt.

**lead time**   the period that elapses between the time of placing an order and its receipt

## Quality Control

The operations management function meant to ensure that output meets product design specifications is **quality control**. A successful quality control program results in the production of goods and services of a specified uniform quality—not necessarily of the highest quality. The overriding goal is

**quality control**   the operations management function meant to ensure that output meets product design specifications

## WHAT KIND OF SERVICE HAVE YOU BEEN GETTING LATELY?

Think of the kind of treatment you have received in service establishments recently. Pick a specific restaurant, hair styling salon, bank, airline, hospital, government agency, auto repair shop, department store, bookstore, or other service organization and rate the kind of customer service you received, using the following five factors. Circle one response for each factor and total them.

1. *Tangibles:* physical facilities, equipment, appearance of personnel.

   Very                  Very
   poor              good
     1—2—3—4—5—6—7—8—9—10

2. *Reliability:* ability to perform the desired service dependably, accurately, and consistently.

   Very                  Very
   poor              good
     1—2—3—4—5—6—7—8—9—10

3. *Responsiveness:* willingness to provide prompt service and help customers.

   Very                  Very
   poor              good
     1—2—3—4—5—6—7—8—9—10

4. *Assurance:* employees' knowledge, courtesy, and ability to convey trust and confidence.

   Very                  Very
   poor              good
     1—2—3—4—5—6—7—8—9—10

5. *Empathy:* provision of caring, individualized attention to customers.

   Very                  Very
   poor              good
     1—2—3—4—5—6—7—8—9—10

Total score = _____

### Scoring Key

| | |
|---|---|
| 5–10 | Cruel and unusual punishment |
| 11–20 | You call this service? |
| 21–30 | Average, but who wants average service? |
| 31–40 | Close only counts in horseshoes |
| 41–50 | Service hall-of-fame candidate |

Source: Adapted from discussion in Leonard L. Berry, A. Parasuraman, and Valarie A. Zeithaml, "The Service-Quality Puzzle," *Business Horizons*, September–October 1988, pp. 35–43.

---

consistency. Three good reasons for improving product quality are: (1) the threat of expensive product liability lawsuits is reduced; (2) better quality means fewer product warranty claims; and (3) getting a new customer costs five times as much as keeping a current one.[20] It practically goes without saying that quality is as important in service operations as in goods-producing ones (see Experiencing Business).

**inspection** the determination of whether an input or output conforms to the organization's standards of quality

The most common quality control technique is **inspection**, "the determination, sometimes by testing, of whether . . . an input or output conforms to organizational standards of quality."[21] We should note that those with responsibility for inspection are not necessarily responsible for correcting the failings that caused the defective production. Rather, it is their job to make sure that substandard products go no further and to call attention to irregular production processes. Quite often, inspectors simply cannot check every

**TABLE 10.1   Ten Commandments of Quality**

- There is no such thing as acceptable quality. It can always get better.
- From the corner office to the shop floor, quality is everybody's business.
- Keep your ears open. Some of the best ideas will come from the most unexpected sources.
- Develop a detailed implementation plan. Talking about quality isn't enough.
- Help departments work together. The territorial imperative is your biggest obstacle.
- Analyze jobs to identify their elements and set quality standards for each step.
- Take control of your process: You must know why something goes wrong.
- Be patient. Don't expect gains to show up next quarter.
- Make extraordinary efforts in unusual situations. Customers will remember those best.
- Think beyond cutting costs. The benefits of improved quality should reach every part of the organization.

Source: From Joel Dreyfuss, "Victories in the Quality Crusade," October 10, 1988, p. 84. Copyright 1988 *Fortune* Magazine. Reprinted by permission of the publisher.

single product. Quality control therefore often involves statistical analyses of random samples (see Table 10.1).

# Operations Management: A Perspective

A few years ago, it took Motorola at least three weeks to manufacture an electronic pager after receiving an order from a customer. Now the same process takes only two hours. This fact represents much more than an interesting tidbit about the capability of American industry. It is concrete evidence of a dramatic new strategic thrust in operations management. Namely, *speed* has become an important competitive advantage. According to *Fortune*, "Quickly developing, making, and distributing products or services brings important, sometimes surprising competitive benefits."[22] When speed is accompanied by better product quality, customer satisfaction improves. Moreover, employees enjoy working for vibrant, progressive, and successful companies.

A time-based strategy, however, does not mean doing the same old things, only faster. That is a sure-fire formula for burning out employees and endangering product quality. Instead, entire operations—from product design, to production, to marketing and distribution practices—are being completely rethought to achieve greater efficiency. Waste is being hunted down and eliminated. Operations that once took months now take weeks. Those that took weeks now take hours. Needless operations are removed altogether. Why? Because companies and their employees are learning how to work "smarter, not harder." In an increasingly competitive global economy, working smarter is not just a good idea. It is an absolute necessity.

# CHAPTER HIGHLIGHTS

*1.* Define operations management *and describe the elements that go into it.*

*Operations management* is the process of planning and coordinating the production of goods or services. It requires the management of people and machinery to transform materials and resources into finished products.

*2. Classify the types of production processes.*

Production processes are classified according to the variety and quantity of goods produced. The *continuous-flow system* or *continuous-process system* is a production-to-stock process that produces large quantities of single standardized product. *Mass production* or assembly line production is a production-to-stock process that produces large quantities of a small number of products. *Batch processing* or intermittent processing is a production-to-stock system that generates lower quantities of goods than a mass production system but may use similar or identical processes. *Job-shop processing* or job-order processing is a production-to-order process in which the producer makes a quantity of goods to the customer's satisfaction. *Project processing* is a production-to-order system in which the manufacturer produces a one-of-a-kind item.

*3. Describe the steps that go into the strategic planning of an operation.*

Once a firm decides to develop a new product, it must decide whether to make the product or buy the product from other companies and just put its label on it. An increasing number of American corporations have abandoned manufacturing operations in favor of buying products from other vendors. If a company decides to produce its own product, it may be able to choose between low-tech and high-tech manufacturing methods. High-tech industries make greater use of modern production techniques such as automation and the use of robots. Planning the operation also includes decisions related to production planning and control. Production planning and control is a management function involving the scheduling of operations relating to the production of goods or services. Its goals include high-quality production and low operating costs.

*4. List the steps in the PERT process for scheduling production control.*

One of the most popular scheduling techniques for production control is the *Program Evaluation and Review Technique (PERT)*. The first step in the PERT process is the identification of all the major activities required to complete a project. The second step is to arrange the activities and events into a sequence in order to identify which of them can happen simultaneously and which must occur sequentially. The third step requires estimating the time it will take to complete each activity.

*5. Identify the criteria that go into a facilities location decision.*

The factors that must be considered in selecting a facilities location include proximity to raw materials or markets; availability of personnel; availability of appropriate transportation; cost and availability of energy; government inducements; the favorability of local regulations and taxes; and general living conditions in the area.

*6. Describe the principal considerations in designing the layout of production facilities.*

*Layout* refers to the physical arrangement of an operational facility. The design of a facility's layout should maximize the efficient use of human and physical resources. An operations management team has a number of layout models from which to choose. A process layout groups machinery or activities according to their purposes. In a product layout, the equipment arrangement relates to a sequence of operations performed in manufacturing a product such as in an assembly line. In both of these layouts, the raw material or product moves from processing stage to processing stage. In contrast, a fixed-position layout is an operational arrangement in which workers and equipment come to the product, which is usually too large to move conveniently.

**7.** *Describe the advancements being made in operations management with robots and computers.*

A *robot* is a reprogrammable machine capable of performing a variety of tasks requiring programmed manipulations of tools and materials. These machines are designed to perform routine, repetitive tasks thousands of times without a mistake. Robots are sometimes part of *computer-integrated manufacturing (CIM)*, a system that manages data flow while directing the movement and processing of material. Firms that use CIM and similar systems seek lower labor costs and greater quality control.

**8.** *Identify the key elements involved in implementing an operational plan.*

*Operational planning* is scheduling an organization's day-to-day needs and anticipating how to meet them. Inventory control is one of the key elements of the operational plan. The basic objective of inventory control is to balance two types of costs: carrying costs and ordering costs. To achieve these two goals, many companies are using the just-in-time inventory system. *Materials requirements planning (MRP)*, a computerized technique used in planning and controlling manufacturing inventories, helps ensure that the firm has available the materials and components in the right quantities and at the right time. *Purchasing*, the operational function by which a business obtains the goods and services it requires, is another element of operational planning. The final element of operational planning is quality control. Quality control ensures that output meets product design specifications.

## KEY TERMS

Product
Manufacturing
Operations management
Transformation
Production-to-order system
Production-to-stock system
Continuous-flow system (continuous-process system)
Mass production

Outsourcing
Hollow corporations
Production planning and control
Setup
Scheduling
Program evaluation and review technique (PERT)
Critical path
Layout
Process layout
Product layout

Fixed-position layout
Consumer-oriented layout
Capacity
Automation
Robot
Computer-integrated manufacturing (CIM)
Control
Operational planning
Inventory
Indirect inventories
Direct inventory

Carrying costs
Ordering costs
Just-in-time inventory system
Materials requirements planning (MRP)
Purchasing
Lead time
Quality control
Inspection

## REVIEW QUESTIONS

1. What does the term *operations management* mean? What activities does it involve?
2. How does a production-to-order system differ from a production-to-stock system?
3. What is the significance of the make-or-buy decision?
4. What are three different transformation processes? Describe them.

5. In deciding where to locate a new baseball bat factory, what criteria should management consider?
6. How does a process layout differ from a product layout?
7. How are computers and robots affecting automation?
8. What two major costs must be balanced in managing inventory?
9. How can operations managers improve product quality?
10. Why is speed becoming an important strategic competitive advantage?

## APPLICATION EXERCISES

1. Assume you have decided to begin production of a simple three-shelf bookcase to be made of fine wood. You would like to produce at least five bookcases each day. Decide whether you would use a process layout or a product layout in your production area. Prepare a sketch of the layout you select.

2. Quality control is an important operations management function. What quality control techniques would be appropriate for the following businesses:
   a. dairy
   b. hospital
   c. building contractor
   d. bank

## CASES

### 10.1  Diamond-Star Starts Fresh

Diamond-Star's production facility [a joint venture between Chrysler and Mitsubishi] in Bloomington-Normal, Ill., is staffed by auto plant novices. Fully 80 percent of the employees have never worked in an automobile manufacturing environment before. According to Glenn Gardner, Diamond-Star's chairman, "They're not normal auto worker types. They can read and write and communicate."

Gardner and company must be confident that the workers can do the job because the Eclipse/Laser is built without any shims. In other words, what comes off the robotic welding line is the final product. There is no room for adjustment.

But there is a lot of room in the plant itself, even though it is small by industry standards for its capacity. The Diamond-Star facility covers 636 acres and 2 million square feet of floor area. Most U.S. assembly plants with equivalent capacity are, on average, 1 million square feet larger. Much of the extra space is used for storage of materials—steel, glass and the like—that will be used in the production process. Diamond-Star is counting on just-in-time inventory delivery, which decreases the time between the delivery of materials and their use, to reduce the amount of space needed for inventory.

If it is possible for an automotive assembly plant to be cozy, the Diamond-Star plant is just that. Maybe it was the fact that only 20 cars a day were being built when we visited. Or perhaps it had something to do with how clean and fresh the factory was from top to bottom. Then again, it might have been the Automated Guided Vehicles (AGVs) that played "Mary Had a Little Lamb" to warn workers that they were in the area. (AGVs at American plants typically use klaxons that are as good at inducing cardiac arrest as they are of warning bystanders.) How it will look, sound and feel at full production, however, is another matter.

Sixty-three cars an hour—240,000 per year—can be built at full capacity, and a five-step manufacturing process is followed. Rolls of steel are stamped into major body panels in the press shop, and these are then stored and distributed by robot. Plastic panels, like the front and rear bumpers, are molded in the on-site plastic shop. The chassis and body panels are welded together in the body shop; approximately 90 percent of this stage is automated. The paint shop takes this skeleton, cleans it, dips it in primer, primes it again, and applies the top coat finish. Final assembly robots remove the doors, hood and hatch (to protect panel finish and ease assembly) and operating hardware is installed. When ready for the final quality check, the doors, hood and hatch are reinstalled. Then the car gets a final run on a small, unbanked oval to test for shifting ease, squeaks, rattles, and the like.

## Questions

1. What is the hidden meaning in Chairman Glenn Gardner's apparent insult directed toward American auto workers?
2. Why, from an operations management standpoint, is the new Diamond-Star facility likely to succeed (or fail)?

Source: Christopher A. Sawyer, "Diamond-Star Starts Fresh," *Autoweek,* November 21, 1988, p. 27. Reprinted with permission.

## 10.2 Why a Big Steelmaker Is Mimicking the Minimills

At the time, it seemed perfectly logical to LTV Corp. Chairman Raymond A. Hay. The union of his company with troubled Republic Steel Corp. in 1984 would sharply boost market share while creating dramatic cost efficiencies in production.

Meanwhile, James A. Todd, Jr. had an entirely different notion—one that initially provoked snickers from such big producers as LTV. As head of Alabama-based Birmingham Steel Corp., Todd began buying up small inefficient steel plants in 1985. His goal: to build a more productive "minimill" company that would convert scrap into finished steel products for niche markets.

There's little surprise in knowing who had the last laugh. Size only worsened the troubles already plaguing LTV and Republic. As Hay struggled to combine the two companies' differing cultures and bloated operations, the fast-plunging market sent LTV into Chapter 11 bankruptcy in 1986. Birmingham, by contrast, is thriving. Todd is expected to report some $40 million in net income on more than $400 million in sales for the year ending June 30.

Behind Birmingham's success are typical small-company attributes: a genuine entrepreneur-boss, flexible work rules, cost-efficient facilities, and narrow product lines. Such advantages allow Birmingham to make a ton of steel with only a third of the labor man-hours of large producers.

Instead of the traditional 8-hour work shift, Birmingham's workers put in 12-hour turns, working three days one week and four days the next. That sharply boosts productivity by cutting time-consuming shift changes to two from three.

The benefits of smallness haven't been lost on Hay. He has drastically downsized LTV, trying to make it a leaner, more market-driven company. He even has adopted many minimill labor practices by giving employees such incentives as profit-sharing, stock ownership, and a greater voice in management.

Still, small rivals are expected to win more market share from LTV and the other industry giants. Experts predict that Birmingham and other minis will capture 36 percent of the market by 2000, up from more than 20 percent today. Vows Todd: "We are going to get a bigger piece of the market."

## Questions

1. An ongoing debate in management circles pits "small is beautiful" against "bigger is better." What implications do the facts of this case have for that argument?
2. What appears to be Birmingham Steel's "secret" of success?

Source: From John A. Byrne, "Why a Big Steelmaker Is Mimicking the Minimills," p. 92. Reprinted from March 27, 1989 issue of *Business Week* by special permission, © 1989 by McGraw-Hill, Inc.

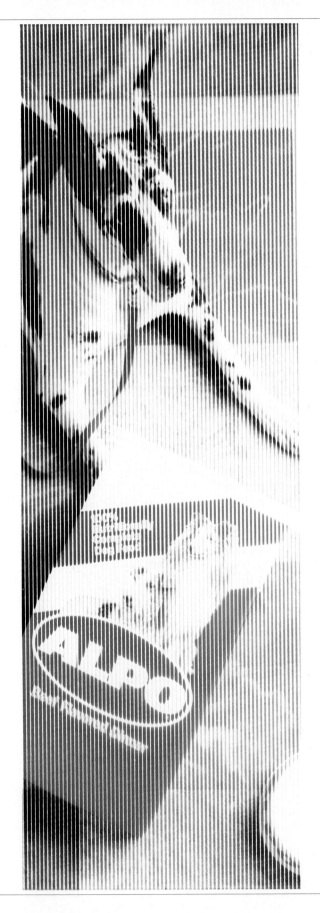

# Marketing

*Every year sees the introduction of thousands of new products to the marketplace. Some products generate millions in profits each year. The movie "Gone With the Wind" (1939) and Tide soap (1946) have produced phenomenal profits every year since their introduction. By contrast, the DeLorean automobile may have cost investors $500 million.*

*Most products are neither skyrocketing successes nor fabulous flops. What makes them profitable or causes them to disappear quickly often has less to do with the merits of the idea behind the product than with how the new product was marketed. Marketing is a broad term whose meaning includes the decisions on how a product is developed, what its packaging will look like, how it will be presented to end-users, what its price will be, how the product will be transported from its manufacturer to the next purchaser, and what types of promotion will be used to sell it. This unit explores these and other marketing issues.*

**PART FOUR**

# 11 Marketing Management

*LEARNING*

*OBJECTIVES*

*After you have completed this chapter, you will be able to do the following:*

*1.* *Define marketing and describe the functions it performs.*

*2.* *Outline the evolution of marketing.*

*3.* *Explain the marketing concept.*

*4.* *Identify and describe the elements of the marketing mix.*

*5.* *Identify and contrast the four basic types of utilities.*

*6.* *Explain the relationship between market segmentation and target markets and describe how marketers identify target markets.*

*7.* *Describe the key elements of consumer behavior.*

*8.* *Explain the importance of market information and market research.*

*9.* *Distinguish between consumer products and industrial products.*

*10.* *Evaluate the costs and benefits of marketing.*

Business and
Its Environment

Financial
Management

Management
and Organization

Information
for Business
Decision
Making

The
American
Business
System

Human
Resources
and
Production

**Marketing**

In the late 1960s H. J. Heinz decided to challenge Campbell Soup Company for a larger share of the soup market. Years later, frustrated company officials decided to give up the battle, convinced that Campbell's hold on the market was "unshakeable." It appears they gave up too soon. A growing number of competitors have eroded Campbell's U.S. market share from over 80 percent in the early 1970s to the current level of 60 percent.[1] Market share was lost to a wide range of aggressive competitors such as Progresso, Lipton, and Japanese noodle makers Maruchan and Nissin Foods. The nation's largest soup maker is fighting back with new products, bigger marketing budgets, and new marketing strategies.

Campbell no longer sees America as a mass market. The company is developing a variety of new products aimed at the growing convenience, premium, and health-conscious market segments.[2] Golden Classics, a premium-price soup, appeals to consumers who will pay extra for quality. Campbell Cup appeals to those who seek convenience. Special Request (reduced sodium) and Creamy Natural (no additives) appeal to the growing number of Americans who pay attention to their health. What happened to that large group of Americans who were satisfied with a can of condensed beef noodle soup? That mass market is gone and has been replaced by working women looking for convenience, single consumers who want smaller portions, and ethnic groups who want specialty items.

To be competitive, Campbell's has to be attuned to the markets for its products. In this chapter we will learn how companies use marketing to introduce and gain the acceptance of their products in the marketplace.

# What Is Marketing?

**Marketing** is the process of planning and executing the conception, pricing, promotion, and distribution of ideas, goods, and services to create exchanges that satisfy individual and organizational objectives.[3] In the past, marketing dealt primarily with those business activities that moved goods and services from producers to consumers or end users. Although marketing continues to fulfill that function, today it also focuses on nonbusiness, intangible services, and marketing activities for persons and organizations. For example, the National Dairy Research and Promotion Board developed a national marketing campaign to increase milk consumption. One of the major elements of this marketing campaign was a nationwide advertising program that resulted in an increase in the consumption of milk by 10 percent.[4]

> **marketing** the process of planning and executing the conception, pricing, promotion, and distribution of ideas, goods, and services to create exchanges that satisfy individual and organizational objectives
>
> *1. Define marketing and describe the functions it performs.*

## *Marketing Functions*

Approximately 33 percent of the American civilian work force have jobs in marketing. About 50 percent of every buyer's dollar goes for marketing costs.[5] With so many jobs and that much money involved, it is plain that marketing takes in an extremely broad spectrum of functions, even more perhaps than the wide-ranging definition suggests. As Figure 11.1 illustrates, at some point in the chain beginning with the producer and ending with the consumer or end user marketing performs eight basic functions. For the moment we are not concerned with who performs them; what is important to remember is that all eight are performed by someone and usually cannot be omitted.

*Collecting and Analyzing Market Information*  Market information has become a key decision-making factor in all divisions of companies. Accurate, timely market information that is intelligently analyzed greatly increases the probability that the firm will deliver products buyers want, when and where they want them, at a price they are willing to pay. Marketing activity often starts when a product is little more than a concept because firms recognize that they have a better chance to develop a successful product if they know what the end user wants. McDonald's conducts extensive research before adding a new product to its menu. Marketers generally obtain this information through surveys and other market-testing strategies.

*Selling*  Selling is marketing's most visible and identifiable function. It makes possible the **exchange process**, the transfer of money or its equivalent for goods, services, or labor. Some firms, like American Telephone & Telegraph (AT&T), make goods for their own use or consumption, but the overwhelming majority of firms sell their goods to someone else. After all, firms generate their revenue by selling.

> **exchange process** the transfer of money or its equivalent for goods

*Financing*  Someone must finance a product from the time it is completed until a customer pays for it. Sometimes even after it sells the product, the

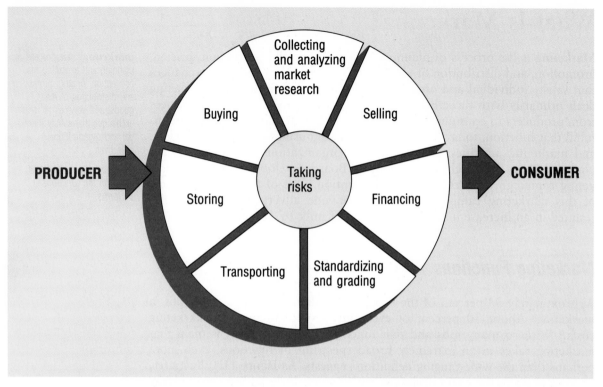

**FIGURE 11.1** Eight Basic Functions of Marketing

Marketing takes in an extremely broad range of functions beginning with the producer and ending with the consumers or end users.

**trade credit** a commercial buyer's open account arrangements with suppliers of goods or services

**marketer** a person who works in marketing

**grading** the assignment of "predetermined standards of quality classifications to individual units or lots of a commodity".

**standardization** establishing a set of uniform specifications against which particular manufactured goods are measured, or a set of classes in which agricultural and mined products are sorted or assigned

manufacturer will continue to finance the goods through the extension of **trade credit**, a commercial buyer's open account arrangements with suppliers of goods or services.[6] For example, General Motors extends credit to its dealers and auto buyers through its credit organization, General Motors Acceptance Corp. (GMAC). **Marketers**, the people who work in marketing, are often heavily involved in credit decisions because the availability of credit often influences a customer's decision to buy.

*Grading and Standardization* These marketing tasks are related but not identical. The American Marketing Association has defined both terms. **Grading** is the assignment of "predetermined standards of quality classifications to individual units or lots of a commodity."[7] When you buy meat or butter at a supermarket, it bears a United States Department of Agriculture (USDA) grade. Coal is also graded. **Standardization** is "the determination of basic limits or grade ranges in the form of uniform specifications to which particular manufactured goods may conform and uniform classes into which the products of agriculture and [mineral extraction] industries may or must be sorted or assigned."[8] The tire industry, for example, has established grading standards for various products.

*Transporting*  To facilitate the flow of products to ultimate purchasers, most businesses that produce goods have created extensive **channels of distribution**, a group of intermediaries or middlemen that direct products to customers. **Intermediaries**, or **middlemen**, are firms between the manufacturer and the ultimate user that take title or directly assist others to take title to goods. For example, Singer sells its sewing machines through its own stores, and Campbell Soups are distributed through wholesalers and retailers. When marketers are choosing a mode of transportation, they weigh such factors as speed, cost, and security.

*Storing*  Products often do not pass directly from production to a consumer. Often, products are stored first for a while at the factory where they are produced and later in wholesaler or retailer warehouses such as those owned by Kroger or Safeway.

**channel of distribution**
a group of intermediaries or middlemen that direct products to customers

**intermediary (middleman)** a firm between the manufacturer and the ultimate user in the channel that takes title or directly assists others to take title to goods

High price, high risk  *Peter L. Harris, CEO of F. A. O. Schwarz, a chain of luxury toy stores, buys his Christmas inventory months in advance. With items that go for as much as $14,000, Harris is under pressure to anticipate in summer his clientele's winter whims.*

*Buying* Many firms buy goods that they then resell with little or no processing. Good buying decisions result in products that are easily resold. When Safeway Stores buys a truckload of 1 lb. cans of Maxwell House Coffee from General Foods, it will have to do little more than put a price on the outside of the cans and place them on the shelves.

*Assuming Risks* Manufacturing goods or buying them and owning them until they are sold sometimes involves considerable risk. The risk may take many forms. Obsolescence, spoilage, or fashion changes are just a few of them. For example, Sears must buy its Christmas merchandise during the summer at the latest and take delivery well before Thanksgiving. As a result, it must carry the cost of storing these Christmas goods for several weeks. If the goods do not sell, Sears bears the loss as well.

# The Evolution of Marketing

*2. Outline the evolution of marketing.*

All eight functions of marketing must be heeded by most marketers. The amount of attention given to each function has changed over time, however. In this country we can identify three distinct eras in the history of marketing (see Figure 11.2).

FIGURE 11.2   The Evolution of Marketing
Though marketing's eight functions are constants, the emphasis marketers have given each function has changed over time.

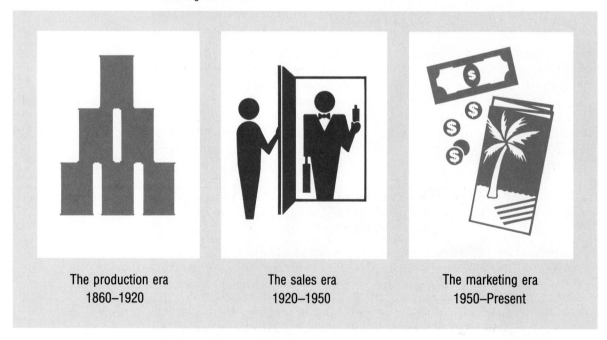

The production era
1860–1920

The sales era
1920–1950

The marketing era
1950–Present

## The Production Era: 1860 to 1920

The production era in marketing came at the same time as America's first great burst of industrial growth. From the Civil War until just after World War I, demand exceeded many manufacturers' ability to produce their goods. They therefore rightly regarded improving their production capacity and efficiency and lowering their costs as their keys to success. In many industries, the marketer's main jobs were simply the taking and filling of orders. Some of the other marketing functions were not necessary when firms with robust product demand could sell all they could make.

## The Sales Era: 1920 to 1950

In the period from the end of World War I to the beginning of the Korean War, the scope of marketing broadened greatly. Production capacity was no longer a major problem. Consistent, high-quality output had become commonplace. In the sales era, firms could no longer be sure of selling all they could produce. Successful firms recognized the need to pay attention to advertising and to the hiring, training, and deployment of an effective sales force. A common view was that "good advertising and a fast-talking sales force can sell anything." During this period marketers came to realize that they needed accurate information about the marketplace. This recognition led to the development of systematic market research, which permitted the effective planning of advertising and sales campaigns at an early point in the production process.

## The Marketing Era: 1950 to the Present

The marketing era that began with the great post–World War II economic boom has continued to the present. Economic historians have referred to America in the 1950s as the "affluent society." For the first time, most American families had **discretionary income**, more income than what is required to obtain the necessities of life. They used this extra income to satisfy their needs with different kinds of products and to acquire additional goods and services. For example, consumers started spending more on travel and recreation.

**discretionary income**
income above what is required to obtain the necessities of life

*The Marketing Concept*   Marketers now had to learn how to satisfy wants as well as needs. An excerpt from the 1952 General Electric annual report describes how this 1950s leader in marketing was meeting the challenge.

*3. Explain the marketing concept.*

> In 1952 your Company's operating managers were presented with an advanced concept of marketing. . . . This, in simple terms, would introduce the marketing man at the beginning rather than the end of the production cycle and would integrate marketing into each phase of the business. Thus marketing, through its studies and research, would establish for the engineer, the designer and the manufacturing man what the customer wants in a given product, what price he is

FIGURE 11.3
The Four Pillars
of Marketing

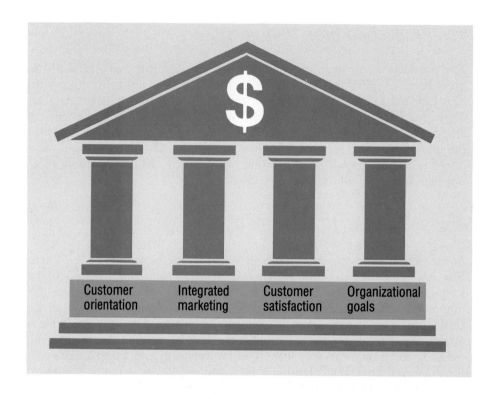

| Customer orientation | Integrated marketing | Customer satisfaction | Organizational goals |

willing to pay, and where and when it will be wanted. Marketing would have authority in product planning, product scheduling and inventory control, as well as the sales distribution and servicing of the product.[9]

**marketing concept** the "belief that the firm should dedicate all of its policies, planning, and operations to the satisfaction of the customer"

Thus, as early as 1952, firms like General Electric had begun to look toward what is now called the **marketing concept**, the "belief that the firm should dedicate all of its policies, planning, and operations to the satisfaction of the customer."[10]

*The Marketing Concept's Four Pillars*  This operating philosophy rests on four pillars (see Figure 11.3). The marketing concept is

- oriented toward the customer
- backed by integrated marketing
- aimed at generating customer satisfaction
- achievement of its organizational goals

These terms are critical to an understanding of the marketing concept.

**customer orientation** basing marketing decisions on customers' wants

Firms with a **customer orientation** base their marketing decisions on their customers' wants. For example, a consumer-oriented auto sound manufacturer like Delco would not bring out a new line of radios simply because it had the technical capacity to make this product. It would instead make its decision following an analysis of the potential demand for such a product.

**integrated marketing** viewing marketing as the job of everyone in the company, because each employee can influence the firm's ability to gain and retain customers

**Integrated marketing** plays a key role in maintaining a customer orientation. This concept views marketing as the job of everyone in the company because each employee can influence the firm's ability to gain and retain customers.

Firms like Wal-Mart Stores, Inc. and Publix Supermarkets have been built on this concept. In companies adopting an integrated marketing approach, marketers make sure that the customers' needs and the firm's response mesh. They study consumers and carefully interpret their needs to the company. The Vermont Castings wood-stove company supplies probably the ultimate example of integrated marketing. Every summer it gives an old-fashioned New England picnic for its customers, 11,000 of whom are likely to show up. The management corresponds directly with its customers, and along with every stove comes a lifetime subscription to *Vermont Castings Owners' News*.[11] Such strategies encourage the kind of two-way communication on which successful marketing depends.

Firms that can deliver **customer satisfaction** have a greater chance for long-run survival than those that do not. Customers buy products and services because of the satisfaction they receive from them. Firms must therefore remove any potential dissatisfaction that might be associated with what they sell. For instance, sports fans hate to stand in line except for the hottest contests, so minimizing the ticket line wait is every team's goal. Consequently, teams such as the Boston Celtics and Los Angeles Rams begin to promote ticket sales well in advance of the season and at a variety of locations.

> **customer satisfaction** a positive reaction in customers toward the goods and services they buy

In reality, the marketing concept's first three pillars—customer orientation, integrated marketing, and customer satisfaction—are a means of achieving the fourth—the firm's **organizational goals**, its long-range objectives. Of course, the key goal is profitability, a requirement for survival. The firm may emphasize other goals as well, among them commitments to environmental quality, affirmative action, and worker participation in decision making.

> **organizational goals** a firm's long-range goals

## Marketing Today

Throughout the past four decades the global economy has evolved from one of excess demand to one of excess supply. With few exceptions, most goods-producing industries do not operate at full capacity. Service industries, meanwhile, have mushroomed (see Business Issues). A growing number of marketers are thus attempting to expand existing markets or develop new markets, and multinational competition has increased dramatically in recent years. As noted at the beginning of this chapter, Campbell Soup Company must now compete with Anglo-Dutch–owned Thomas J. Lipton and Nissin Foods, a Japanese company. Companies operating in major industrial economies must treat the rest of the world as a source of supply and demand. A one-world market exists for products ranging from cars to computers.

IBM provides a good example of a global company. Sales from IBM's overseas operations now accounts for over half of total company revenues. Nestlé, a Swiss firm, has become the world's largest food company by learning how to transfer products and marketing methods from one country and culture to another. Some of the company's leading brands include Nestlé Crunch candy bars, Buitoni pasta, and Nescafé, the world's first instant coffee. Nestlé has even learned how to market Lean Cuisine frozen dinners in France.[12] As competition increases in America and throughout the world, marketing will assume even greater importance.

## MARKETING SERVICE BUSINESSES

America's rapidly growing service sector may have as many different marketing strategies as it has kinds of services. Walter Riley, owner of a trucking firm, took a humorous approach. Not only does Riley's Kearney, New Jersey, firm keep him laughing all the way to the bank, it tickles customers, too. When Riley learned that his company name, Guaranteed Overnight Delivery, was too close to one registered by another outfit, he toyed with the idea of using the acronym GOD. His managers said no. His ad agency did some market research and then said the same thing but Riley went ahead and used the name anyway. The result? One of the fastest-growing companies in the nation. People see one of his trucks and they remember the name. "Normally," says Riley, "it takes years to get that kind of recognition."

Debit One, a financial services franchisor, sees itself as the McDonald's of small-company bookkeeping. Representatives drive a computer-equipped recreational vehicle up to the client's door and do its books on the spot. "Privacy and speed," says Director of Franchise Relations Charles Green. "Our clients' books never leave the parking lot." Debit One believes it can offer small businesses services small accounting firms cannot. "Our franchises keep in close touch," says Green. "Clients can tap the whole body of company knowledge." The Kansas City firm has sev-enty-four franchises in twenty-seven states.

Larry A. Olsen, president of El Paso–based Tracks to Adventure, Inc., yawns at the accepted wisdom. "You just can't worry about what the other guy is going to do. You'll be distracted from doing the things necessary to make your company a success. And in a funny way, if you worry too much, you'll end up letting the competition run your business for you. You'll spend all your time reacting, or trying to anticipate their moves, and spend none figuring out where you think your company should go." Not that Olsen, whose business it is to plan tours of up to seven weeks for people who travel in their recreational vehicles, fails to pay attention. He takes to heart the anonymous written critiques he solicits from his customers. What they like, he does again. What they do not like, he stops doing. Olsen is also intensely image conscious. The mailings he sends out to ad respondents cost him between $4 and $5 each. As to his competitors, he figures if they come up with a good idea, he will hear about it. An Alaska tour, one of Olsen's biggest money-makers, was the brainchild of another tour service.

Sources: "The Miracle of the Name," *Inc.*, April 1988, p. 14; Easy Klein, "Franchised Business Services: A Boon to Small Firms," *D & B Reports,* September/October 1987, pp. 26–27; Paul B. Brown, "The Ostrich Gambit," *Inc.*," May 1988, pp. 135–138.

# The Four P's and the Concept of Utility

Marketing can be examined from the two different perspectives of buyer and seller. Students of marketing have long used the strategies known as the "Four P's" to summarize the seller's activities and the concept of utility to explain the buyer's actions.

## The Marketing Mix

The marketer's major tools that summarize the seller's activities are those called the **Four P's:**

- Product strategy
- Price strategy
- Place (distribution) strategy
- Promotion strategy

The Four P's are the variables that marketers can control, unlike the variables in the marketing environment, such as the country's economic condition or the overall demand for what their industry produces.

The recipe that marketers develop for putting these elements together becomes their marketing plan. The blend varies for each product, so the combination of the Four P's in any strategy is called the **marketing mix.** In

**Four P's** the marketer's major tools for summarizing the seller's activities, consisting of the product strategy, price strategy, place (distribution) strategy, and promotion strategy

*4. Identify and describe the elements of the marketing mix.*

**marketing mix** the combination of the Four P's in any strategy

**Marketing spectacle** *To introduce his NeXT computer, Steve Jobs rented San Francisco's Davies Symphony Hall. There, amidst a sound-and-light show, he led his computer through its tricks. Among its stunts: Giving a speech, operating four stopwatches at once, and functioning as an oscilloscope.*

the following chapters, we will examine the Four P's in detail. Here we will sketch each briefly.

*Product Strategy*   Product strategy calls for much more than just deciding to make a product. Among the crucial factors a manufacturer must determine are:

- Product quality
- Product features
- Number of models, sizes, styles, and so on
- Branding
- Packaging
- Labeling

*Price Strategy*   The major pricing decision is whether to assign a price above, below, or about even with the competitors'. Of course, a firm must consider other factors too, such as product cost, consumer demand, and the need to offer discounts.

*Place (Distribution) Strategy*   In designing a distribution strategy, a manufacturer focuses primarily on selecting the marketing intermediaries such as wholesalers and retailers. For example, a manufacturer like Black & Decker that sells to Lowe's Companies, Inc., which operates nearly 300 retail home-center stores, ships to one of Lowe's large distribution centers. There, Lowe's organizes shipments for its stores using its own trucks. Figure 11.4 shows a typical channel of distribution.

*Promotion Strategy*   A promotion strategy centers on transmitting information to potential customers. The major forms of promotion are advertising, personal selling, sales promotion, and publicity.

FIGURE 11.4   Channel of Distribution

MANUFACTURER          WHOLESALER          RETAILER          CONSUMER

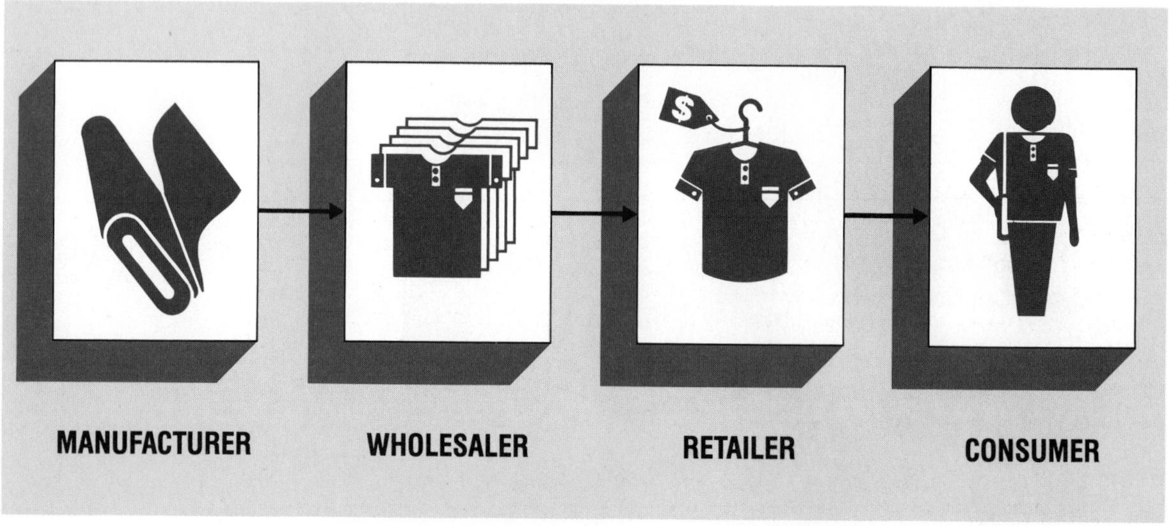

**Changing fashions** *The Limited's stores had specialized in clothes for fashion-conscious women between 18 and 40. When profits fell in 1988, however, store-division President Verna Gibson made some changes. In the future, she decided, The Limited's stores would be larger and would concentrate on clothes for successful career women in their thirties and for their children.*

## Customer Satisfaction

The purpose of marketing is to "create exchanges that satisfy individual and organizational objectives," according to one definition. The satisfaction that goods and services yield to their buyers is called their **utility**. A purchaser receives satisfaction when the product is in the right form, which is created in the production phase, is available in the right place and at the right time, and provides the satisfaction promised or anticipated from its use. If a product lacks any of these utilities, a potential purchaser probably will not buy it. Marketing bears much responsibility for creating these utilities.

*Form Utility*    Although production creates much of a product's form utility, marketing influences its form by determining what kinds of products and

**utility**   the satisfaction that goods and services yield to their buyers

*5. Identify and contrast the four basic types of utilities.*

product attributes the market demands and transmitting that information to product designers. Suppose that market researchers for a soft-drink company determine that cola drinkers want a softer, sweeter taste than their company's main cola. Their discovery might lead to a new product, as it did at Coca-Cola when it brought out New Coke.

*Place Utility*   Marketing has the primary responsibility for creating place utility by arranging for appropriate outlets for the product. Columbia Records, for example, distributes its records and tapes to a variety of outlets, ranging from discounters like Gold Circle Stores to record stores like Strawberry's to mail-order companies like the Columbia Record Club. In contrast, a specialty steel company may itself be the only outlet for its own products.

*Time Utility*   Marketing must also ensure time utility by supplying customers with the product when they want it. Marketing's job is to make certain that outlets carry sufficient inventories. Seasonal timing is important, for instance. In most parts of the country, lawn-care products have a limited selling season. Stocking stores with Scott's Turf Builder or grass seed in November makes little sense. At the other extreme, the demand for pet food products continues year round.

*Possession Utility*   Finally, marketers are responsible for possession utility. They must arrange for the transfer of ownership or title to the goods. In many cases the transfer is no more complicated than putting coins in a vending machine, pressing a button, and retrieving a can or a candy bar. In other cases, the exchange can be quite complicated, as in buying a major item like a home or a car. The real-estate developer or car dealer who simplifies the process for the customer by arranging financing and performing other such services stands a good chance of making the sale.

# Identifying Markets

**market**   a group of people or firms who currently demand or might potentially require a product or service and who have the ability, willingness, and authority to buy it

A **market** is a group of people or firms who currently demand or might potentially require a product or service and who have the ability, willingness, and authority to buy it. The identification of markets is a critical marketing function because it defines targets for the company's marketing efforts. Stated broadly, a market might consist of teenagers or retirees, working women or minorities. Most likely, it will be described in specific terms such as "single females from 17 to 25."

## *Marketing to Specific Groups*

Very few firms can afford to market their products to all consumers or all businesses in the United States. At the same time, few firms would want to, because it is a rare product that is acceptable to all consumers. Until the end of World War II, Coca-Cola was such a product. But today Coca-Cola offers

324

consumers several variations on its original cola formula as well as noncola drinks like Minute Maid Orange Juice. Most firms must choose specific groups of customers on which to focus their marketing efforts.

*Market Segmentation* The total market can be subdivided, in a process called market segmentation, into smaller groups of consumers based on identifiable common characteristics called *segmentation variables* (see Figure 11.5). **Market segmentation** is the process of dividing all potential customers into distinctive groups that might merit a specific type of marketing effort. Marriott, a leader in the hotel field, has achieved a great deal of success with a segmentation strategy. Each of Marriott's four chains, Fairfield Inns, Courtyard hotels, Residence Inns, and Marriott hotels and resorts is aimed at a specific segment of the travel market.

Segmentation variables are usually classified under four headings. **Geographic variables** include regions, counties, cities, and climate areas. The most likely purchasers of snow blowers, for instance, are suburban and rural residents in the snow belt. **Demographic variables** include age, sex, family size, income, occupation, education, religion, race, nationality, and social class. Families with children under three are likely to buy diapers; families

**6.** *Explain the relationship between market segmentation and target markets and describe how marketers identify target markets.*

**market segmentation** the process of dividing all potential customers into distinctive groups that might merit a specific type of marketing effort

**geographic variable** a segmentation variable that considers regions, counties, cities, and climate areas

**demographic variable** a segmentation variable that considers age, sex, family size, income, occupation, education, religion, race, nationality, and social class

FIGURE 11.5  Market Segmentation

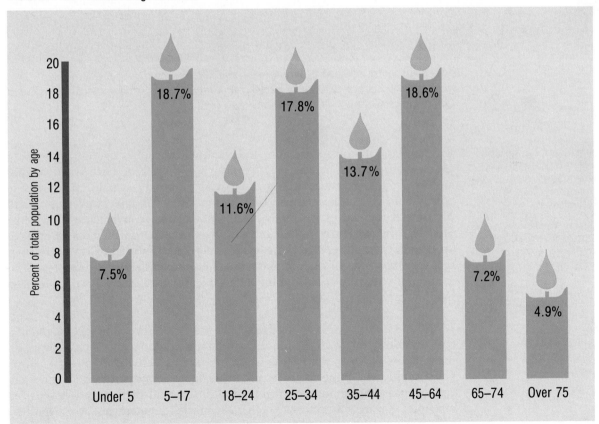

**Adventures in demography** *Pinpointing a market segment is not the same as marketing to a stereotype. Seniors are commonly thought of as quiet, stay-at-home types. This is not necessarily the case.*

**psychographic variable**
a segmentation variable that considers personality characteristics, lifestyle, and buying motives

**benefit variable**
segmentation variable that considers economy, convenience, and prestige

with children in college are not. **Psychographic variables** include personality characteristics, lifestyle, and buying motives. An average Ford Escort owner and an average Porsche 911 Carrera owner respond quite differently to the cost of auto accessories. **Benefit variables** include economy, convenience, and prestige. A two-career couple is more likely to buy convenience foods, like Stouffer's frozen entrees, than couples in which one partner does not have an outside job. As you might expect, a marketer may focus on more than one segmentation variable. Campbell has been experimenting with red bean soup in Southern areas (geographic variable) where many Hispanics (demographic variable) live.

*Target Marketing*   Once marketers have identified several market segments, they are ready to launch the process of **target marketing**, choosing the specific markets on which they will focus their marketing activities.

**target marketing** choosing specific markets on which to focus marketing activities

To qualify as a target market, a segment must be measurable. If marketers cannot measure the number of potential buyers and their income levels, for example, they may not know whether the market segment is worth pursuing.

The segments must also be accessible by the firm's marketing program. Advertising in *South Florida Home & Garden* magazine would not reach a main market for New England winter vacations. Even if the advertising reaches the right segment, however, the advertiser must have the capability of delivering its products or services. If zoning laws prohibit fast-food restaurants in a certain section of a city, it does not matter how many residents might potentially patronize a Wendy's in that area. Finally, the target segments must be large enough to be potentially profitable.

Marketers choose from two principal strategies in developing target markets. The first, a **differentiated strategy,** consists of individualized appeals aimed at particular market segments. The pain reliever market can be subdivided into customers who do or do not want aspirin. Consequently, we have Bayer Aspirin and Tylenol. A **concentrated strategy** is used when a marketer directs marketing efforts toward a single market segment. The BMW 750i, a 12-cylinder luxury sedan that sells for over $70,000, requires a concentrated marketing strategy.

**differentiated strategy**
aiming individualized appeals at particular market segments

**concentrated strategy**
directing marketing efforts at one specific market segment

**Identifying the market** *While the jeans Levi's is advertising here are designed to attract young boys, the ad is directed at their parents, who are most likely to be making the ultimate buying decision.*

WHEN HE GETS A LITTLE WEIRD AROUND THE EDGES, REMEMBER THAT HE LOVES LEVI'S JEANS.

His hair resembles nothing that occurs in nature. And his shoes look like protective packaging for radioactive materials. So how do you explain why he's so crazy about something as sturdy and sensible as Levi's jeans? Don't even try. To find out where to get Levi's jeans for boys, call **LEVI'S** 1-800-227-5600.

## Consumer Behavior

*7. Describe the key elements of consumer behavior.*

Most effective marketing decisions are based on a thorough knowledge of consumer behavior. Gaining that knowledge requires marketers to find out how and why consumers make buying decisions. Just knowing what products are selling today and to whom is not enough—marketers have to predict tomorrow.

Although sociologists and psychologists still have much to learn about consumer behavior, a wealth of knowledge does exist to guide marketers. For example, researchers have identified two categories of primary buying motives. **Rational buying motives** include the desire for dependability, durability, efficiency, financial gain, and economy. Commercial banks usually rely on rational buying motives in their promotions. **Emotional buying motives** include the wish for social approval, a desire to be different, and a need to be free of fear. Quite often, consumers make purchases based on a combination of rational and emotional motives. Marketers must determine the most relevant motives for their products, incorporate into the product the features that appeal to those motives, and focus their promotional strategies on appeals to those motives. Toothpaste ads often appeal to both rational and emotional motives. Many consumers want clean teeth so they can avoid seeing the dentist as well as wanting to look attractive.

**rational buying motive** a buying motive that includes the desire for dependability, durability, efficiency, financial gain, and economy

**emotional buying motive** a buying motive that includes the wish for social approval, a desire to be different, and a need to be free of fear

## Market Data

*8. Explain the importance of market information and market research.*

Marketers must have timely marketing information on a variety of issues such as consumer behavior, market characteristics, competitors' activities, potential substitute products, and other factors. Interpreting and, when necessary, adding to the vast array of data that marketers need requires a marketing information system and marketing research.

**marketing information system** a combination of people, equipment, and procedures organized to gather, process, and disperse information needed for making marketing decisions

*Marketing Information Systems* A **marketing information system** is a combination of people, equipment, and procedures organized to gather, process, and disperse information needed for making marketing decisions.

The sophistication of a firm's marketing information system will depend on the size of the firms range of products and its management's perception of the importance of marketing information in its overall decision making. A large firm may have a mainframe computer dedicated to its marketing information system, but smaller firms often do not even have a structured marketing information system. Their marketing information system may be in random file folders or in someone's head. With the availability of powerful, low-cost personal computers, small firms can now afford to develop marketing information systems that large firms could not have had thirty years ago. More will be discussed about computers in chapter 16.

Wrangler Womenswear, a division of Blue Bell, Inc., outfitted its entire sales force with portable computers. Sales representatives can place orders, update data files, and transmit memoranda and letters by telephone from the

# EXPERIENCING BUSINESS

## A MARKET PLAN FOR CARNIVAL CRUISE LINES

Carnival Cruise Lines is a company that offers customers a "holiday at sea" at a modest price. Each ship features the amenities you would expect to find at a fine resort. Passengers can shoot skeet, work out at a fully equipped gym, or spend time at a gambling casino. Room service is available 24 hours a day, in addition to three full meals and a midnight buffet which are served every day.

Suppose you are hired by Carnival Cruise Lines to develop a marketing plan. Which of the following demographic trends would be of greatest interest to you? Why?

- By the year 2000, the number of workers between the ages of 16 and 24 will drop by two million, while the number between 35 and 54 will be 25 million higher.[1]
- By the year 2000, about 80 percent of all entry-level employees will be women, minorities, and immigrants.[2]
- A growing number of people are starting their own businesses. Over one million new enterprises are started each year.[3]
- The average household size continues to decline, but at a slower rate than in the 1970's.[4]

- In the year 2000, today's baby-boomers will be 36 to 54 years old, right in the middle of their peak income-earning years.[5]
- The number of single (never-married) people as a percent of the total U.S. population continues to grow.[6]
- In 1995 women will occupy a 60.3 percent share of the workforce.[7]
- The number of associate degrees and bachelor's degrees awarded has increased steadily in recent years.[8]

Sources: [1] "What Managers Should Know about Work Force Changes in the Year 2000," *Personal Report*, December 1, 1988, p. 4. [2] Patricia Galogan, "Here's the Situation," *Training and Development Journal*, July 1987, pp. 20–22. [3] David L. Birch, "The Atomization of Americans," *Inc.*, March 1987, pp. 21–22. [4] *The Supermarket Industry Semi-Annual Report*, April–September 1987. Chicago: Campbell-Methuen Research Information Center. [5] Christopher Knowlton, "Consumers: A Tougher Sell," *Fortune*, September 26, 1988, p. 64. [6] *Statistical Abstracts of the United States*, 1988, Table 49. [7] "Changing Profile of the U.S. Labor Force," *U.S. News & World Report*, September 2, 1985, p. 46. [8] *Projections of Education Statistics to 1997–1998*, National Center for Education Statistics, U.S. Department of Education, 1988, p. 51.

road. Better yet, the computer gives them instant access to home-office files. Now salespeople can give customers "while you wait" information about pricing and style and quantity availability. Thus, Wrangler's 100 sales representatives can avoid the annoying situation of taking an order and then, weeks later, having to tell less-than-thrilled customers that what they wanted is unavailable.[13]

*Market Research*　When a firm's marketing information system does not contain the necessary information, its decision makers may have to initiate **market research**, the systematic gathering and analyzing of data on a particular marketing problem (see Experiencing Business). The topics of market research

**market research** the systematic gathering and analyzing of data on a particular marketing problem

might range from whether customers perceive a beer to taste great or to be less filling to sophisticated psychological evaluations of an advertising campaign's effectiveness.

A market research project involves five distinct steps:

- Defining the problem
- Planning the research
- Collecting the information
- Interpreting the information
- Reporting the findings

Data comes either from primary sources, an interview with a potential customer, or secondary sources like published reports and library materials. Researchers should start with internal secondary sources, data the firm already has. This information is usually readily available and inexpensive. Gathering new information from outside the firm is a last resort because it is time consuming, difficult, and expensive.

# Consumer and Industrial Markets

Most of what we are discussing applies to both consumer and industrial markets. The two markets, however, are different enough to consider separately.

Customers in the consumer market purchase goods and services for their own personal use or for the use of someone in their household. Anything you take off the shelf and put in your grocery cart is a consumer good. Customers in industrial markets purchase goods and services to use in the manufacture of other products. The steel that went into your grocery cart was an industrial product. Because the reasons for buying are different in each major market, marketers must adopt individual strategies to attract buyers in each.

## Consumer Products

**consumer product**
goods and services purchased in the consumer market

*9. Distinguish between consumer products and industrial products.*

**convenience goods**
products that consumers purchase frequently, generally at low prices, and for which they are willing to spend only a minimum of effort in completing the exchange

Goods and services purchased in the consumer market are **consumer products**. Consumer goods are classified into three categories, each of which requires a distinct marketing strategy based on the effort consumers are likely to be willing to exert to find the product.

*Convenience Goods*   Products that consumers purchase frequently, generally at low prices, and for which they are willing to spend only a minimum of effort in completing the exchange are **convenience goods**. Milk, bread, newspapers, soft drinks, and chewing gum are common examples. The marketers of convenience goods must, therefore, maintain competitive prices, distribute their products through many retail outlets, and center their promotional efforts on constant reminders to shoppers.

Industrial markets  *All the air in a truck is not necessarily in the tires. All the gas is not necessarily in the fuel tank. Truck manufacturers make special trucks for special industries.*

*Shopping Goods*  Typical **shopping goods** are purchased infrequently, have a relatively high unit price, and are bought only after comparison with other product alternatives. For example, homeowners needing a new lawnmower generally visit several stores to learn what features are available and to find the machine they want at an appropriate price. They may also consider the availability of service where they buy.

**shopping goods** goods that are purchased infrequently, have a relatively high unit price, and bought only after comparison with other product alternatives

**Specialty Goods**   Products for which consumers develop a strong preference and loyalty are called **specialty goods**. Generally, price is not a major consideration in the decision to buy these goods. Consumers are willing to spend a great deal of effort to locate them. For example, some consumers may buy only Curtis Mathes Corporation televisions and will search their area until they locate a dealer.

**specialty goods** products for which consumers develop a strong preference and loyalty

## Industrial Products

An **industrial product**, as noted earlier, is one that is used in the production of another good or service. Essentially, any product not for personal or household consumption is an industrial product. The electronic control in a production robot is an industrial product, as is the label on an audio cassette.

**industrial product** a product used in the production of another good or service

*Unique Market Features*   The industrial market is different from the consumer market in several ways. Perhaps the most important distinction is that the demand for industrial products is **derived demand**; that is, the demand for them is caused by the demand for other products. For example, the demand for American car radios depends largely on the number of automobiles American auto assemblers produce. As Toyota and other foreign car makers capture a larger share of car sales, American firms that make car radios sell fewer of them.

**derived demand** products for which the demand is caused by the demand for other products

Industrial markets are also more concentrated than consumer markets—there are fewer firms than people. Also, there are concentrations of similar types of manufacturing in particular localities. Two examples are the high-tech concentrations on Route 128 around Boston and the so-called Silicon Valley outside San Francisco. Of course, industrial products are also usually ordered in far larger quantities and in far larger dollar amounts than are consumer products. For that reason and because of both the buyer's and the seller's corporate bureaucracies, the purchasing process for industrial markets is considerably more complex—and more carefully planned.

*Overlap*   It is important to note that a specific product can, under different circumstances, be both a consumer and an industrial good. For instance, a video cassette recorder bought for home use is a consumer good, whereas an identical recorder bought to show training tapes to Toys "Я" Us employees is an industrial product.

# Marketing's Costs and Benefits

*10. Evaluate the costs and benefits of marketing.*

Justifying marketing costs requires an evaluation of marketing's benefits. Let's look at two major costs of marketing: distribution and promotion.

As we have seen, marketing intermediaries or middlemen operate the channels of distribution. In periods of escalating prices, people often claim that eliminating middlemen would reduce the final price of goods. Middlemen,

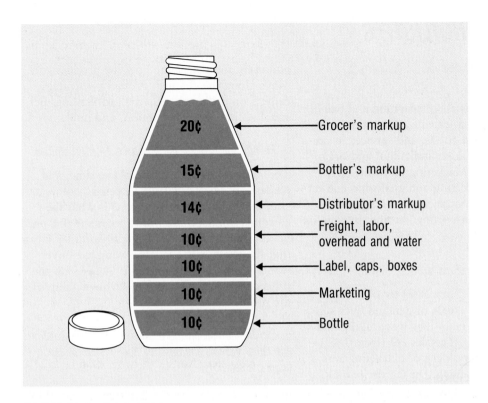

**FIGURE 11.6  Bottled Water**

Today bottled waters sell at the rate of a billion gallons per year. This figure shows where the $.89 a typical liter costs goes.

*Source:* From ''The Economics of Bottled Water,'' p. 70. Redrawn with permission, *Inc.* magazine, October, 1986. Copyright © 1986 by Goldhirsh Group, Inc., 38 Commercial Wharf, Boston, MA 02110.

however, can significantly reduce the costs and time involved in most transactions because one middleman avoids the need for each of several sellers to contact each of several buyers in the exchange of goods. As the number of transactions increases, the advantages of using a middleman increase dramatically, as we will see in Chapter 13.

Promoting the product can result in a larger number of customers learning about it. When customers use the product regularly, the product unit cost is reduced, allowing a lower price for each customer. Take, for instance, the bottled-water industry. In the mid-1970s, only ''health nuts'' bought this product, and then they bought mineral water. Today, bottled waters sell at the rate of a billion gallons per year. That is a lot of Perrier, Poland Springs, Polar seltzer water, and the like. Figure 11.6 shows where the $.89 typical cost for a liter goes. In this chapter, we have looked at many of the factors that account for the markups: product development, market analysis, and inventory carrying charges, among others. In the chapters that follow, we will look intensively at additional aspects of pricing and at the other costs listed on the bottle.

# CHAPTER HIGHLIGHTS

*1. Define marketing and describe the functions it performs.*

*Marketing* is the process of planning and executing the conception, pricing, promotion, and distribution of ideas, goods, and services to create exchanges that satisfy individual and organizational objectives. Marketing performs eight basic functions: collecting and analyzing market information, selling, financing, grading and standardization, transporting, storing, buying, and assuming risks.

*2. Outline the evolution of marketing.*

The *production era* (from 1860 to 1920) was characterized by an excess of demand over supply. The marketer's main jobs were taking and filling orders. During the sales era (from 1920 to 1950), the primary focus of marketing was on advertising and selling. During the *marketing era,* which began in the early 1950s, the focus shifted to the *marketing concept,* which has as its central premise the idea that the ultimate purpose of every business should be providing customer satisfaction.

*3. Explain the marketing concept.*

The marketing concept is characterized by an orientation toward the customer, integrated marketing practices, aimed at generating customer satisfaction, and dedicated to the achievement of organizational goals.

*4. Identify and describe the elements of the marketing mix.*

The four elements of the marketing mix are product, price, place, and promotion. *Product strategy* involves decisions about quality, features, number of styles and sizes, branding, and packaging. *Price strategy* deals with how a seller will price his or her product in relation to market demand. *Place strategy* concerns the distribution of a good or service. Producers and marketing intermediaries must develop a marketing channel, decide who will sell the product to the end user, and determine how the product will move along the channel. *Promotion strategy* centers on decisions related to advertising, personal selling, sales promotion, and publicity.

*5. Identify and contrast the four basic types of utilities.*

The four utilities are: form, place, time, and possession. *Form utility,* e.g., design, color, or size, means that what is offered is what the customer wants; *place utility* means that a product is where a buyer wants it; *time utility* means that the product is available when the buyer wants it; and *possession utility* focuses on the procedures necessary to transfer ownership of the product.

*6. Explain the relationship between market segmentation and target markets and describe how marketers identify target markets.*

*Market segmentation* is the process of dividing a large market into smaller groups at which a marketing program can be aimed. Market segments must be measurable, accessible, and substantial. They are generally classified according to their geographic, demographic, psychographic, and benefit variables.

*7. Describe the key elements of consumer behavior.*

Consumer decisions are generally based on *rational buying motives* (which include the desire for dependability, durability, efficiency, financial gain, and the like) and *emotional buying motives* (the desire for such things as social approval, the wish to be different, and freedom from fear). Many purchase decisions are based on a combination of rational and emotional buying motives.

*8. Explain the importance of market information and market research.*

*Market information* and *market research* are key elements in the marketing concept. Only by keeping abreast of consumer wants and needs can marketers hope to deliver what the consumer wants—when, where, and how the consumer wants it.

**9.** *Distinguish between consumer products and industrial products.*

*Consumer products* are goods and services purchased in the consumer market for personal use or for the use of someone in the buyer's household. An *industrial product* is a good or service used to produce another good or service. Some items can be either a consumer or an industrial product, depending on its final use.

**10.** *Evaluate the costs and benefits of marketing.*

Marketing costs claim about half the buyer's dollar, but the services that marketing provides are essential. Marketing increases the efficiency of the exchange process, raises consumer satisfaction, and leads to the development of products that satisfy consumer wants and needs.

# KEY TERMS

Marketing
Exchange process
Trade credit
Marketer
Grading
Standardization
Channel of
  distribution
Intermediary
  (middleman)
Discretionary income
Marketing concept

Customer orientation
Integrated marketing
Customer satisfaction
Organizational goals
Four P's
Marketing mix
Utility
Market
Market segmentation
Geographic variable
Demographic variable

Psychographic
  variable
Benefit variable
Target marketing
Differentiated
  strategy
Concentrated
  strategy
Rational buying
  motive

Emotional buying
  motive
Marketing information
  system (MIS)
Market research
Consumer product
Convenience goods
Shopping goods
Specialty goods
Industrial product
Derived demand

# REVIEW QUESTIONS

1. What is marketing? What major functions does marketing perform?
2. What are the elements of the marketing mix? Define each element.
3. Define *utility*. Describe the four basic types of utilities.
4. What is a market?
5. Define *market segmentation*. By what criteria do marketers segment markets?
6. How do marketers target markets? What are the two principal strategies used in developing target markets?
7. Why is a knowledge of consumer behavior important?
8. Distinguish rational from emotional buying motives.
9. List the benefits of a marketing information system.
10. What are the benefits of market research? Describe the process by which market research is conducted.
11. Distinguish consumer products from industrial products.
12. Characterize each of the classifications of consumer goods.
13. What is the key characteristic of an industrial market?

# APPLICATION EXERCISES

1. Recently you were selected to serve as chairperson of the promotion committee for a celebrity golf tournament. The tournament will match several well-known celebrities from your state against the best local golfers. Tickets will sell for $25 per person and your goal is to attract a large gallery of fans. All proceeds will be given to a local charity. As you develop a promotion plan, what segmentation variables would be most important? What buying motives would you appeal to?

2. Develop a marketing plan for a new lawn care service that will be offered to residents of a three-county area. As you prepare this plan, consider these questions:
   a. What market information will you need?
   b. How will you collect appropriate market information?

# CASES

## 11.1  Marketing for Hospitals

Natel Matschulat, the first marketing director for Mount Sinai Medical Center, says, "Marketing a hospital is a challenge because it's something that people don't really want to use." Her goal is to get people to think of this New York City hospital first when they do need medical care. To achieve this goal, she spent $2 million on television, radio, and newspaper advertising during her first year.

Traditionally, hospital administrators have considered marketing (which they equated with advertising) to be unnecessary and somehow inappropriate to their profession. But in the late 1970s they began to turn to advertising as a means of dealing with rising costs, increasing competition, and empty beds. These first efforts were decidedly unsuccessful in attracting patients. Hospitals began to advertise before they knew what they had to advertise.

Now, however, many hospitals are doing at least some basic market research. They are also attempting to expand existing services and develop new services to accommodate their markets. Their new offerings range from home health care for elderly outpatients to valet parking and room service for more affluent inpatients. One large obstetrics hospital has opened a downtown maternity clothing store, where it also holds classes for prospective parents. Hospital officials see the store as a natural extension of their patient services.

Hospitals still have the problem of deciding where to direct their marketing efforts: to physicians, who usually choose a hospital for their patients; to patients, who receive the hospital's "product"; to insurance firms, which usually pay for it; or to some combination of the three.

### Questions

1. Has the marketing concept finally penetrated the health care industry? Explain.
2. To whom should hospitals market their services? Why?

Sources: For more information see *Hospitals*, June 5, 1986, pp. 50–55 and 66–67; *Marketing & Media Decisions*, April 1986, pp. 96–101; *Healthcare Financial Management*, May 1984, p. 62; and "On the Rise," *Fortune*, December 21, 1987, p. 167.

## 11.2  A Rich Dessert

Since 1921, Reuben Mattus's family had produced hand-turned ice cream for local consumption. Theirs was one of dozens of small firms vying for distribution in New York City's neighborhoods. By the time Reuben took over the business, the competition was fierce; it got worse in the 1950s, when the large ice cream manufacturers began to use their economic power to drive small local firms out of supermarkets.

Mattus decided he'd had enough of that kind of competition, and he searched for something that would get him out of it. What he came up with, in 1960, was the first of the so-called "super-premium" ice creams—twice as rich as mass-produced ice cream, and made with only natural ingredients.

Because he believed that the Danish made superior ice cream, Mattus made up a Danish-sounding name for his product: Häagen-Dazs. He also gave it a high price, betting that plenty of people would pay more for a quality product with a foreign-sounding name.

He was right. At first he had trouble getting local supermarkets to carry Häagen-Dazs, because they didn't believe people would pay the price. Mattus refused to advertise his product, because he didn't trust advertising. But his persistence and a higher-than-usual markup convinced some supermarkets to carry it, and word-of-mouth advertising convinced the rest. Competitors soon followed Mattus's lead; the market for super-premium ice cream now is estimated at $2 billion annually, and growing by about 25 percent each year.

## Questions

1. What risks were involved in Reuben Mattus' marketing effort?
2. Describe and evaluate the Häagen-Dazs marketing mix.

Sources: For more information see *Business Week*, June 30, 1986, pp. 60–61; *Marketing & Media Decisions*, June 1986, pp. 38–46; *The New Yorker*, July 8, 1985, pp. 31–45; and *Fortune*, March 9, 1986.

# 12 Product and Pricing Strategies

## LEARNING OBJECTIVES

After you have completed this chapter, you will be able to do the following:

**1.** Describe the new-product development process.

**2.** Explain the product life cycle concept.

**3.** Explain the functions of branding, packaging, and labeling.

**4.** Describe the role of pricing in the marketing mix.

**5.** List the potential pricing objectives for a product.

**6.** Describe the principal pricing methods.

**7.** Identify the pricing strategies available for both new products and those already on the market.

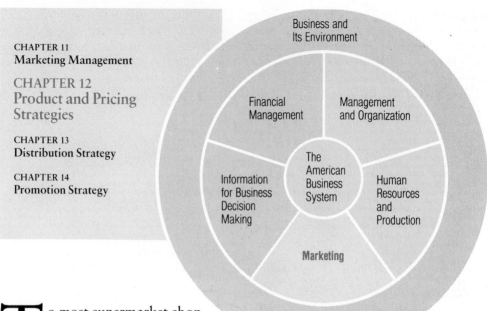

Business and
Its Environment

Financial
Management

Management
and Organization

The
American
Business
System

Information
for Business
Decision
Making

Human
Resources
and
Production

Marketing

To most supermarket shoppers Chiquita means bananas, Dole means pineapples, and Sunkist means oranges. But what brand names do you associate with tomatoes, carrots, and green peppers? Except for a few widely known brand names, most items offered by the produce department have an uncertain pedigree.[1] This situation is changing, however, as major companies such as Del Monte, Kraft, Campbell, and Pillsbury enter the market with brand-name produce items. Campbell has introduced the highly successful "Campbell's Fresh" branded mushrooms and Del Monte offers branded papaya, bananas, and pineapple.

Not everyone agrees that branded fruits and vegetables represent a good deal for the consumer. Though some say that branded produce products give the shopper additional value and convenience, others point to little or no quality difference between branded and unbranded products. Proponents maintain that a growing number of shoppers put their faith in brand names they recognize.[2] Although more branded merchandise is showing up in produce departments, it is too early to predict the future of this product category.

# Product Strategy

**product**  a good, a service, an idea, or any combination of the three that may be the subject of an exchange

As noted in Chapter 10, a **product** is a good, a service, an idea, or any combination of the three that may be the subject of an exchange. When you stop at a Texaco station, the gas you buy is a *good*, a tangible item. Signs announcing a special sale on Texaco batteries are part of a nationwide advertising campaign that an agency developed for Texaco. An advertising campaign is an idea—a concept, a philosophy, an image, or an issue promoting a product.[3] Suppose you ask the mechanic on duty to check a knock in your engine. The mechanic spends 15 minutes adjusting your spark plugs and charges you $25. That work is a service, labor or duties performed by one person at another's request. Had the mechanic installed new spark plugs, he or she would have sold you both a service—installing the plugs—and goods—the plugs.

## Developing New Products

New product introductions have increased steadily in recent years. The number of new consumer products introduced in the United States during a single year recently passed the 10,000 mark.[4] As the number of introductions increase, it is more difficult for new products to achieve success.

The challenge all firms face is to develop products that meet their customers' needs and wants. Firms must also continually improve what they sell or risk seeing their products replaced with those of their competitors. The standardized TV dinners of the 1950s lost much supermarket space to frozen entrees aimed at specific market segments: Budget Gourmet dinners for the value conscious, Lean Cuisine for the weight conscious, and Armour Dinner Classics for those seeking gourmet foods.

Markets are rarely static, and businesses cannot be either. A well-planned **new-product development process,** the six-step procedure for testing, developing, and selling a product (see Figure 12.1), reduces the risk of falling behind the competition. It also holds out the promise of achieving a competitive advantage.

**new-product development process** the six-step procedure for testing, developing, and selling a product

*Phase 1: Idea Generation* In the present context, an idea is the starting point of the new-product development process. An idea is simply a product concept that lacks a concrete form. Businesses should develop a logical

*1. Describe the new-product development process.*

FIGURE 12.1   The New-Product Development Process

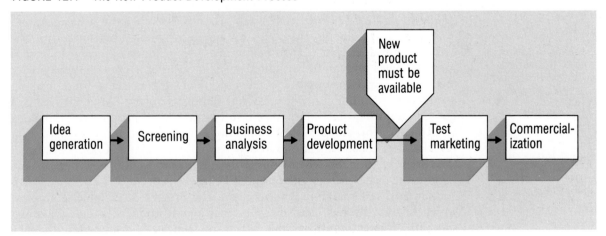

strategy for generating as many product ideas as possible. Even the most illogical-sounding idea, like contact lenses for chickens, may bring big payoffs. It is hard to believe that such a product made money for its inventor, Robert Garrison. The tinted lenses stop the birds from pecking each other. Contact lenses not only save chicken farmers the cost of debeaking their birds but also increase the egg-laying productivity of the flocks.[5]

Firms should encourage suggestions for new products. Excellent ideas can come from customers, salespeople, secretaries, janitors, competitors, and others. The more ideas a firm can generate, the better the chances are that one can be commercialized, the final stage of new-product development.

*Phase 2: Screening*   In the screening phase of the new-product development process, a firm sifts the good ideas from the bad. Companies should develop decision criteria to eliminate ideas that have little promise, do not relate to customer satisfaction, or do not fit their objectives or resources.

*Phase 3: Business Analysis*   In the business analysis phase, the firm studies the proposed product's potential costs and revenues. It also closely examines how the new product will mesh with existing products, pricing policies, distribution channels, and promotional resources. Researchers may solicit potential customers' reactions to the idea. The business analysis phase can thus be seen as a continuation of the screening phase, except that the criteria used are more precise. For example, Frito Lay's O'Grady Potato Chips required that the company buy bigger cutters and sort its potatoes to give the chip its unique texture and taste.

*Phase 4: Product Development*   A firm can take an idea through the first three phases without actually producing anything. In the product-development phase, however, the firm begins to give the idea real form. Research and development staff will prepare and test prototypes against the customer's needs and wants. Product-development time is an important key to new-product success. As discussed in Chapter 10, the company that can quickly develop, make, and distribute products or services often achieves surprising competitive benefits.[6]

*Phase 5: Test Marketing*   Once the product is ready from a business and development standpoint, the company may begin limited production (in the case of a product that is manufactured). The product is then sold in **test markets**. Sales are carefully audited to gain an insight into the behavior of the entire market. Among the most popular test markets for consumer products are Columbus, Ohio; Peoria, Illinois; Phoenix, Arizona; and San Diego, California. Test-marketing results can lead to product or packaging refinements. The Adolf Coors Company's test marketing of its light beer revealed that consumers confused light Coors with regular Coors because of their similar labels. So when Coors officially introduced its new beer, Coors Light came in distinctive "silver bullet" cans.

Prolonged test marketing is a danger. The Procter & Gamble Company, which historically has intensively test marketed products, should have cut short its eighteen-month test marketing of Duncan Hines crisp and chewy

The product development process  *Before a product like Lipton's Gentle Orange herbal tea is brought to the marketplace, it goes through several stages of testing and screening to determine how well it will perform.*

chocolate chip cookies. By the time this product went national, Nabisco Brands, Inc., and the Keebler Co., Inc., had established competing products.[7]

*Phase 6: Commercialization*  Only a very few products reach the final phase, commercialization. If the results of the test marketing are positive, the firm will then introduce the product to the entire market. A good introductory marketing program can make all the difference. When Coca-Cola introduced Diet Coke, it rented Radio City Music Hall and had well-known actors and actresses endorse the new product. Many believe that Diet Coke captured a greater market share than it would have without this spectacular introduction. Still, it is unlikely that Diet Coke would have shared the fate of seven out of ten new products: failure.[8]

If the shoe fits . . .
*Reebok wanted to find out which athletic shoes would be best received by customers. It took its designs to a Los Angeles street corner and asked people to try them on.*

## *Product Strategy—A Success Story*

Although most new products do not achieve success, some companies have had exceptional results with their new introductions. One example is Rubbermaid, a company that manufactures and sells basic products such as dish drainers, microwave utensils, and other items used in the home. The company also makes file boxes and desk organizers for use in offices. Rubbermaid launches over 100 new products each year and claims a 90 percent success rate. Why are these new products so successful? The company makes every effort to keep in touch with customers and spends millions on market research and product development efforts.[9] Rubbermaid has made *Fortune* magazine's list of Most Admired Corporations five years in a row.[10]

# The Product Life Cycle

2. *Explain the product life cycle concept.*

In many ways, products are like human beings. They are born, grow up, mature, and grow old. In marketing, this process is known as the product life cycle.

## The Basic Stages

The **product life cycle** assumes that products have lives with four identifiable stages: introduction, growth, maturity, and decline. As Figure 12.2 illustrates, a product's sales or revenues determine its life cycle. The length of each stage can vary dramatically from product to product. For example, Procter & Gamble's Ivory Soap has been in its mature phase for almost a century. By contrast, the mature phase of the Osborne computer, the first successful portable, lasted less than a year.

As you study the product life cycle, keep in mind that it is just a convenient way to classify where products are today and what happened to others in the past. Ivory Soap and the Osborne computer prove that the product life

**product life cycle** the four identifiable stages in a product's life: introduction, growth, maturity, and decline

FIGURE 12.2 The Product Life Cycle

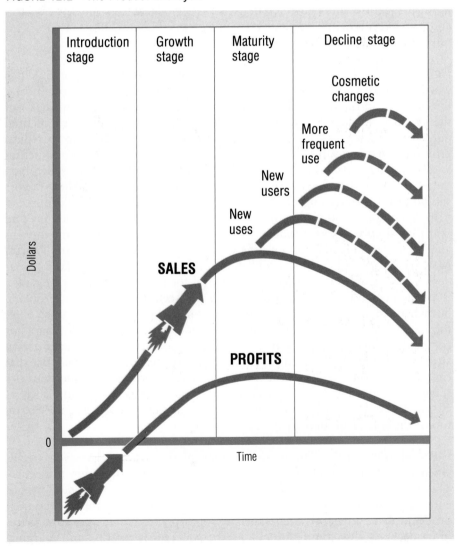

cycle is not a tool for predicting the future. In 1879, would Harley Procter, the brand's creator, have predicted Ivory would still be a top seller in the 1980s? In 1979, would anyone have predicted that Osborne Computer Corporation would be out of business by 1984?

*The Introduction Stage*    In the **introduction stage** of the product life cycle, the product is first brought to market. The introduction period varies in length from product to product. As might be expected, the major characteristic of this period is low sales and high costs per unit. High fixed costs continue until the sales volume picks up. The initial expenses associated with arranging appropriate channels of distribution can be quite high. Promotion costs are also quite high, both in terms of the number of dollars spent and as a percentage of sales.

Several years ago, the compact disc player was in the introduction stage of the product life cycle. Most potential buyers were not aware of the product's features and benefits. They were knowledgeable about tape cassettes and vinyl records but unfamiliar with compact discs. These factors kept prices high and sales low.

*The Growth Stage*    This stage begins when sales start to increase and ends when sales begin to level off. During the **growth stage**, early buyers repurchase the product and new ones enter the market. Distributors begin to seek out the product, so distribution expenses decline. As more and more potential purchasers become aware of the product, the firm may be able to reduce promotion expenditures. Because sales are increasing, promotion expenses as a percentage of sales have probably already declined significantly. In fact, the marketing costs of generating sales should generally decline. These factors should lead to decreasing fixed costs per unit and thus to greater profits.

In this stage, demand sometimes overwhelms manufacturers, who may find that they simply cannot produce what the stores can sell. For some months after they were introduced, both the Chrysler Caravan and the Ford Taurus/ Mercury Sable caused this problem for their manufacturers. To a lesser degree, 3M could not initially meet demand for its "Post-it" message pads.

Strong demand for a new product may not seem like much of a problem, but when competitors sense a profit to be made they look for ways to enter the market. A business with a successful new product should prepare for competition during the growth stage by developing a **product differentiation strategy**, a program designed to give a product distinctive characteristics that can serve as competitive advantages over similar products in the maturity stage of the product life cycle. A never-ending flow of variations, such as Classic Coke, Diet Coke, and Cherry Coke has kept the Coca-Cola Co. on top of the soft drink market in recent years.

*The Maturity Stage*    The **maturity stage** of the product life cycle begins when sales start to level off and ends when they eventually begin to decline. This stage is usually characterized by intense competition as new brands enter the market. Competition can become bitter as firms fight to keep their products alive. When this occurs, promotion expenses will increase and prices often decline. This combination puts the squeeze on profits, and marginal

**introduction stage**   the stage in the life cycle in which the product is first brought to market

**growth stage**   the stage that begins when sales start to increase and ends when sales begin to level off

**product differentiation strategy**   a program designed to give a product distinctive characteristics that can serve as competitive advantages over similar products

**maturity stage**   the stage that begins when sales start to level off and ends when sales eventually begin to decline

**Active maturity** *Smucker's jam and jelly products have been in the mature phase for years. The company keeps growing by introducing new products, like Simply Fruit. Smucker's also has a limited overseas expansion program.*

producers will begin leaving the market. This stage, however, can be very profitable for those companies that stay in the game.

To maintain a competitive advantage during the maturity stage, the marketer may change the product. A product differentiation strategy, as noted, can extend the life of the product. In an attempt to achieve a competitive advantage in the compact disc player market, Pioneer Electronics introduced the six-disc multiplay component player, which featured random programming of up to thirty-two tracks.

*The Decline Stage*  The **decline stage** of the product life cycle begins when sales begin to decrease and normally ends with the firm abandoning the product. Decreasing sales lead to decreasing profits and eventually to losses. If the firm cannot devise a way to revive sales, it drops the product. Decline and termination are not inevitable, however. Creative businesspeople can revive dying products. For instance, Miller's, a saddlery in New York City, does a good trade in buggy whips! Thus, the product life cycle cannot be used as an exact forecasting tool. Instead, it is a valuable lens through which a company can study the shift in demand for a product and the marketing strategies proposed for it.

**decline stage**  the stage that begins when sales begin to decrease and normally ends with the firm abandoning the product

## Extending a Product's Life

The real value of the product life cycle concept is as a planning tool. Managers can judge their products according to where they appear in this cycle and adjust their strategies accordingly. Most important, they can use the product life cycle as a means of identifying the proper time to look at ways to extend a product's life. A firm's survival will often depend on extending a major product's life. And even when extending a product's life is not so critical, it is often less expensive, less risky, and less time consuming to do so than to develop an entirely new product. After all, existing products usually have a base of loyal customers. Keeping them may be better than going through the whole product development process and the introduction and growth stages for a brand-new product.

*New Uses*    Most products start their lives intended for one use, but many products have more than a single potential application. Marketers can put their minds to devising new uses, but those people currently purchasing a product are a more likely source of ideas. For example, it was a consumer who came up with the idea of using baking soda as a refrigerator freshener. The need to identify new uses for products is a major reason for having a marketing information system that taps either the salespeople, who have direct contacts with purchasers, or the purchasers themselves.

*New Users*    Companies can sometimes find new customers for their products. A new promotional theme or new product features may be the key here. For example, Bounty added all-white microwave-safe towels to its line. Another source of new users may be market segments that had not previously seemed promising. Pellon made its name selling nonwoven fabrics as garment interfacing for home sewers and apparel manufacturers. Today it is successfully marketing the same type of material to computer software floppy disk manufacturers as a protective lining to go inside a diskette's cover.

*More Frequent Use*    Another way to revive a declining product is to encourage more frequent use, use in greater quantities, or the need for back-up units. Head & Shoulders shampoo, for instance, recommends two applications per washing, and Johnson & Johnson Baby Shampoo advertises that it is mild enough to use every day. Manufacturers of smoke alarms, telephones, and personal computers have used variations of these strategies. The American Express Company's "Don't leave home without it!" campaign persuaded card holders to use their cards more often.

**cosmetic change**    an alteration in a product that has little or no effect on its basic function

*Cosmetic Changes*    An alteration in a product that has little or no effect on its basic function is a **cosmetic change**. New packaging, colors, styles, sizes, and the like can boost sales without requiring fundamental changes in the product. Many of the 10,000 new consumer products introduced each year are "me-too" products fighting for shelf space. Makers of household products often stimulate sales by advertising products as "new and improved," though little may have changed save appearance and packaging. For years, auto makers have extended their vehicles' product life cycles by making minor external changes without changing what was hidden from view.

348

## THE POWER OF BRAND NAMES

Many factors contribute to the success of a brand name, from expert marketing techniques, to sizable advertising budgets, to the number of years we've been hearing the name and seeing it in the stores. Among the names listed below are ten brand names which were most often recognized in a survey of 1000 U.S. consumers. Can you select the ten most powerful brand names? Check your answers against the list at the back of the book.

| | | |
|---|---|---|
| Dairy Queen | Hershey's | Kellogg's |
| Frito-Lay | Levi's | IBM |
| Mayflower | Campbell's | Schwinn |
| Wendy's | AT&T | Ford |
| Xerox | Sears | American |
| Texaco | McDonald's | Express |
| John Deere | Pepsi-Cola | Coca-Cola |

Source: Edward C. Baig, "Name That Brand," *Fortune*, July 4, 1988, pp. 11–12.

# Branding

Lee Iacocca made his name at Ford in the mid-1960s with an idea for a car designed to appeal to the baby boomers just then reaching their twenties. His concept would have been less brilliant had it not been tied to a name and symbol that captured the spirit of the car: a Mustang at full gallop. The distinctive styling, the name, and the symbol worked together to create a product uniquely satisfying to the needs of a well-defined market segment.

*3. Identify the functions of branding, packaging, and labeling.*

## Names and Symbols

*Mustang* is a **brand**: a name, term, symbol, design, or any combination of these elements used to identify a specific product and distinguish it from its competition. Technically, *Mustang* is a **brand name**, that part of a brand that can be spoken. The running horse is a **brand symbol**, a graphic portrayal that identifies a product or firm. A brand symbol does not have to represent the words in the brand name. Coca-Cola's classic narrow-waisted bottle design is a brand symbol, as is Nike's swoosh symbol on its shoes.

When a manufacturer owns a brand, it is referred to as a **national brand** or a **manufacturer's brand**. Del Monte and Heinz are both national brands. A **private label brand** is one owned by a retailer or wholesaler. Many supermarket chains, including A&P Food Stores and Stop & Shop Companies, Inc., feature private brands (see Experiencing Business).

*Infringement* The law protects certain brand names and symbols from **infringement** or violation. When you see the symbol ® at the end of a brand name or ™ beside a symbol, it tells you that the name or symbol is a **trademark** registered with the U.S. Patent and Trademark Office.

**brand** a name, term, symbol, design, or any combination of these elements used to identify a specific product and distinguish it from its competition

**brand name** that part of a brand that can be spoken

**brand symbol** a graphic portrayal that identifies a product or firm

**national brand (manufacturer's brand)** a manufacturer-owned brand

**private label brand** one owned by a retailer

**infringement** violation of brand names or symbols

**trademark** a brand name or symbol registered with the U.S. Patent and Trademark Office

Registration gives the owner exclusive property rights to the trademark. Ralph Lauren has successfully sued clothing manufacturers who used symbols like his polo player on their clothes. And the Federal Trade Commission has forced clothes bearing imitation Izod alligators off the market.

Even when a brand name or symbol is registered, its owner must protect the trademark from becoming a **generic name**, one that has passed into common, everyday language. Examples of trademarks that became generic terms include aspirin, zipper, linoleum, and kleenex. To avoid this fate, Xerox has mounted advertising campaigns designed to keep people from using *xerox* as a synonym for *photocopy*.

**generic name** a trademark that has passed into common, everyday language

## Brand Strategies

Many consumers buy brand-name products to assure themselves of consistent quality. One package of "Campbell's Fresh" mushrooms may vary little from a non-brand package. Companies develop brands because consumers are willing to pay higher prices to satisfy brand preferences. Pepperidge Farm cookies, Skippy peanut butter, and Planters peanuts have all developed a loyal following of customers. To secure consumer loyalty, however, manufacturers must promote their brands (discussed in Chapter 14) and tightly control the quality and consistency of their products.

*Generics*    Businesses have a wide range of branding strategies to choose from. At one extreme is what might be called the no-brand strategy. Many companies do not use brands, preferring to sell generic or unbranded goods.

*Family or Blanket Brands*    For some firms in some industries, the benefits of branding outweigh the costs of creating and protecting brand names and symbols. Some adopt a **family brand** or **blanket brand strategy**, an approach based on the use of one brand name for all of a firm's products. The General Electric Company, Canon U.S.A., Inc., the Mobil Oil Company, the Eastman Kodak Company, the Campbell Soup Company, and the H. J. Heinz Co. use this strategy. The major advantage to a family-brand strategy is that promotion of one product benefits every product bearing the same brand name because it heightens name recognition. The big disadvantage is that poor quality in one product can hurt all the other products sold under the same name.

**family brand (blanket brand) strategy** an approach based on the use of one brand name for all of a firm's products

*Individual Brands*    Some firms use an **individual brand strategy**, an approach that calls for a different brand name for each product. The Lever Brothers Company and the Colgate-Palmolive Company generally use an individual-brand strategy for their products. Clearly, the major disadvantage to this strategy lies in the expense of launching each new brand. On the other hand, how many consumers can list, say, all the flops from the General Foods Corporation? When asked to think of a toothpaste associated with Colgate-Palmolive, how many would remember Cue, which was a product failure? The main advantage of the individual-brands strategy is obviously that one or even a series of failures will probably not affect the other, successful brands. Another major advantage is that the company can effectively target products to particular market segments. Each of the four hotel groups owned

**individual brand strategy** an approach that calls for a different brand name for each product

by Marriott Corporation has a different name because each is targeted at a different market segment.

Some firms use a modified version of the individual-brand strategy in which the firm name is always tied to the individual brand name. For instance, *Kellogg's* always precedes the name of one of its cereal brands, like Kellogg's Rice Krispies or Kellogg's Corn Flakes. Sears, Roebuck uses a variation of the Kellogg's model. It has multiple family names, including Kenmore, Arnie, Cheryl Tiegs, Craftsman, and several others.

# Packaging

The development of a container and a graphic design for a product are called **packaging**. The functions of packaging are to preserve, protect, promote, and provide utility (see Business Issues).

A package may serve to prevent spoilage or damage. Where the product is food, like potato chips or cookies, this function can be critical. The package

**packaging** the development of a container and a graphic design for a product

**Packaging for freshness** *Packaging not only protects a product but also insures its uniformity. In this sense, packaging does not just contain the product; it is an integral part of the product.*

## FAST PROFITS IN FAST FOODS

"Each specially bred, moisture-perfect Bachman kernel is suspended in space and bounced off pillows of hot air until it reaches the ideal popping temperature, when it explodes into a tender, fluffy super-premium morsel."

Such is the hyperbole that sparkles from the cellophane package of Smartfood, a high-priced, cheese-flavored popcorn. Premium snack foods occupy that dream space of marketers and manufacturers—a new market niche. Before 1985, there were few super-premium snack foods. Smartfood is the invention of Andrew Martin, Ann Withey, and Ken Meyers—three people in their twenties with little business, and no food business, experience. Their product is a popcorn flavored with aged white cheddar cheese.

In fact, it was not that easy. Martin and Meyer's first discussion with a distributor left him unimpressed. Having no money for the usual advertising, they had to invent techniques of their own: At Killington, Vermont, people began seeing 6-foot bags of cheese-flavored popcorn skiing down the slopes. After a year the company's financial situation was so desperate they considered closing up shop.

Then the product, which by all accounts is very tasty, began to sell itself. Said Tom Protheroe of Connecticut-based Hartford Snack Distributors Inc., "In my thirty years in the business, I have never—*never*—seen a snack-food item catch on like Smartfood has.

This stuff is completely addictive. It *flies* out of my warehouse."

Smartfood is still mainly a regional company: 75 percent of its sales are made in New England, where it controls 50 percent of an expanding market, competing against some of the major snack-food producers, who quickly developed imitations. Competitors have even adapted their own versions of Smartfood's distinctive black package.

The success of Smartfood suggests that anyone with a pot, a stove, and a creative flair with food could grow rich overnight. Protheroe suspects, however, that even a proven seller like Smartfood might have trouble expanding outside its home market. The main reason, he says, is the distributors, who, strongly influenced by the major players whose products they handle, may not be willing to push a competing product. And then there is the new supermarket charge known as the slotting allowance: only after the payment of a fee will the large chains put a new product on their shelves. For this, as well as discounts and funds for store advertising, a company might pay up to $3 million nationwide.

Sources: Trish Hall, "For New Food Products, Entry Fee Is High," *New York Times*, January 7, 1988, pp. A1, C6; Joseph P. Kahn, "The Snack Food That's Eating America," *Inc.*, August 1988, pp. 34–40; "Snack Snitching," *Women in Business*, November/December 1988, p. 6; Roberta Hershon, "These Chips Have It All," *Food & Wine*, February 1989, p. 37.

may also prevent harm to intended or unintended users. Child-resistant caps and safety seals on patent medicines belong in this category, as do pop seal tops on bottled juices. Even a manufacturer's best efforts may not deter a serious killer, however. Johnson & Johnson (J & J) promptly removed from the market all Super-Strength Tylenol capsules after someone put cyanide in random bottles. After devising a tamper-resistant package, they reintroduced the product—only to have history repeat itself. This time, however, J & J decided to abandon capsules (itself a type of packaging) for caplets. The distinctiveness of the container also serves as a basis for promotion.

Good packaging can make product use and reuse easy. A well-designed spout on a bottle of soy sauce or a comfortable handle on a container of cooking oil can make an enormous difference in consumer satisfaction. Stonyfield Farm Yogurt and other manufacturers emphasize that their containers can be reused for different purposes. Some packages are biodegradable or recyclable. As manufacturers become increasingly aware of the societal and environmental impact of their packaging, more firms are likely to adopt such containers.

# Labeling

A **label** is that part of the package or product that contains information. **Labeling** is therefore the presentation of information on a package or product. A package's basic function is, of course, to hold the product. Its total function may involve considerably more than that, however. The label may also transmit useful information to the purchaser and promote the product. Typically, a label contains the brand name and symbols, the size and contents of the package, directions for use, safety precautions, and the universal

**label** that part of the package or product that contains information

**labeling** the presentation of information on a package or product

Small but mighty   *The label on a tiny package of chewing gum must make a big statement about the product. Advances in computer technology have made more dynamic graphics possible.*

product code and symbol. A label may state the product's ingredients, warn of its hazards, and give antidote instructions in case it is used improperly. Under federal law, garment labels must state:

- The manufacturer's name
- The country in which the garment was made
- The fabric content
- Cleaning instructions

The label on processed foods must state their ingredients, in order of abundance. Any nutritional claims must also appear on the label.

A well-designed package can serve an invaluable promotion function. It gives the customer the brand name and symbol, but more importantly it creates an image for the product. Just compare any black-and-white package containing a generic dishwasher detergent with the green-and-gold Cascade package. Some packages are particularly designed to be convenient for the retailer. Items like kitchen accessories and shoelaces come in packages adapted for hanging on racks. Such packaging significantly improves their chances of winning the fight for supermarket and discount-store shelf space. Other packages are designed to prevent shoplifting. Cassette tapes come in large packages for that reason.

# The Role of Pricing

*4. Describe the role of pricing in the marketing mix.*

Pricing is a critical element in the marketing mix. It is also an important consideration in each phase of the product development process and in each stage of the product life cycle. And pricing may play a determining role in screening new product ideas and in test marketing products.

## Allocation of Resources

Pricing helps allocate markets between firms. The prices a firm assigns its products have a direct relation to the revenue the firm generates. Setting a product's price may be a firm's most complicated and important decision. Too high a price may negatively affect sales. For example, when Apple Computer, Inc., priced its Lisa at $10,000, it effectively eliminated a large part of the new model's market. The Lisa model was subsequently scrapped in favor of the highly successful Macintosh. A product may not sell at all if its price exceeds what the target market is willing or able to pay. Conversely, too low a price may prevent the firm from recapturing its development costs or may starve it into bankruptcy.

A product's price also helps consumers allocate their resources. Consumers compare the price of a product and its perceived value to them. When the value is less than the price, they are likely to drop that item from consideration. A consumer may decide to pay more for a Corvette than for a Thunderbird because of the greater satisfaction he or she anticipates.

For some consumers, low price means low quality. The first Yugo automobiles sold in America were advertised at $3,990. Consumers with the attitude "you get what you pay for" are less likely to take a close look at a car in this price range.

## Pricing Objectives

Setting prices is not a simple process. As with any critical decision, the pricing decision should be made deliberately and systematically. The first step in the pricing decision is to determine the firm's objectives. The most common ones are profit maximization, target return on investment, market share, status quo, and survival.

5. List the potential pricing objectives for a product.

*Profit Maximization*   Many firms try to set their prices to maximize their profits, but it is very hard to determine just what price will precisely do that. Profit maximizers aim for a price as high as possible without causing a disproportionate reduction in unit sales. Suppose Ford Motor Co. increases its prices by 20 percent and its unit sales decrease by only 15 percent. In that case, its profits should increase. But if unit sales decrease by 25 percent, lower profits will probably result. Unfortunately, no computer program exists that will identify the ideal balance. Experimentation is the only way to reach it.

*Target Return on Investment*   Many firms set their prices based on a target return on investment. The firm has analyzed its other investment opportunities for its money and determined that in order to justify its investment in the product, it must receive a certain return. The company may then determine—based on what it could get by putting its money in, say, a bank—that it needs a 25 percent return on every dollar it puts into a new product. In other words, if its investment were $1 million, it would need a $250,000 profit to reach its target. That figure would dictate the price per unit.

*Market Share*   In some instances, a firm will set a market-share objective. Management may decide that the strategic advantages of an increased market share outweigh the temporary reduction in profits necessary to obtain it. Suppose General Motors has a 20 percent share of the world automobile market and wants 25 percent. It may lower prices until it achieves its goal, then raise prices. This strategy has its risks, as the airlines periodically prove. When one competitor lowers prices, others follow suit so that none make money until prices go up again. A variant of this strategy, popular among banks and national auto-rental firms like Hertz and Avis, calls for giving away goods like luggage with each new account or rental.

*Status Quo*   Many firms follow what is called status-quo pricing, a strategy that might also be called "follow the leader" pricing. When a leading firm in an industry raises prices, the other firms follow suit. For generations, the U.S. Steel Corporation filled the leader's role in the steel industry and the industry maintained pricing uniformity and steady profits. However, when competition arrived in the form of European, Japanese, and Korean steel, our steel industry pricing practices were altered.

*Survival*  Survival pricing is generally a short-term objective and is often aimed at generating enough cash to pay current or past-due bills. Distress sales are an extreme type of survival tactic designed to generate enough cash to keep the business going for a few more days or weeks. One of the biggest such distress sales took place in 1989 when Eastern Airlines dropped its ticket prices shortly after a strike by the machinists' union.

# Pricing Methods

**6.** *Describe the principal pricing methods.*

A firm chooses a method that will help it meet its pricing objectives. Firms have four basic methods to choose from: economic theory–based pricing, cost-based pricing, demand-based pricing, and competition-based pricing.

## *Economic Theory–Based Pricing*

**demand**  the willingness of purchasers to buy specific quantities of a good or service at a particular price at a particular time

**supply**  the willingness of sellers or producers to provide goods or services at a particular price and particular time

Economic theory–based pricing applies the principles of supply, demand, and equilibrium as introduced in Chapter 1. **Demand** refers to the willingness of purchasers to buy specific quantities of a good or service at a particular price at a particular time (see Figure 12.3A). **Supply** refers to the willingness of

FIGURE 12.3A  A Demand Curve    FIGURE 12.3B  A Supply Curve    FIGURE 12.3C  Equilibrium

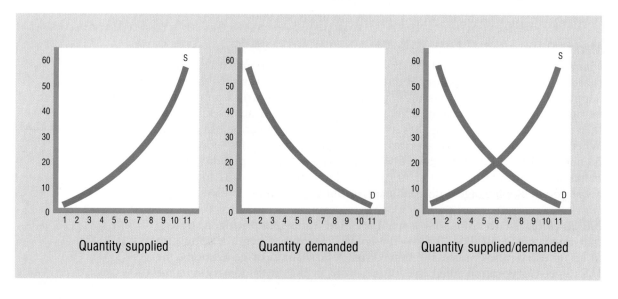

Quantity supplied          Quantity demanded          Quantity supplied/demanded

sellers or producers to provide goods or services at a particular price and particular time. In other words, how much of something people will sell depends on its price when they can sell it (see Figure 12.3B).

Demand and supply directly affect each other. By plotting their curves on the same graph, we see that they cross at the point marked *E* on Figure 12.3C. The *E* marks the point of **equilibrium**, the point at which demand and supply are in balance. It is there that the intentions of the seller and buyers coincide. The point of equilibrium between supply and demand identifies the **market price** of goods or services.

**equilibrium** the point at which demand and supply are in balance

**market price** the point of equilibrium between supply and demand

Economic theory–based pricing is critically important not only as a pricing method itself but also as the basis for the three other principal methods. It is, however, extremely hard to apply. First, constructing supply and demand curves that go beyond a narrow range of prices is very difficult. Second, supply and demand curves apply only to a particular period of time. The amount of goods demanded at a certain price can change over time, for example.

## Cost-Based Pricing

Many firms use a **cost-based pricing** approach. The cost of producing or purchasing a good serves as the starting point. The firm then adds to the product's cost a predetermined percentage of the cost called a **markup**. The formula is:

**cost-based pricing** a pricing strategy derived from the cost of producing or purchasing a good

**markup** a predetermined percentage of the cost that is then added to the cost in computing the price

$$\text{Cost} + (\text{Cost} \times \text{Markup percentage}) = \text{Price}$$

The markup must be sufficient to cover any additional costs (overhead) and provide an adequate profit. Suppose a wholesaler buys a General Electric radio for $20 and applies a markup percentage of 60 percent of cost. The calculation would be:

$$\$20 + (\$20 \times 60\%) = \text{Price}$$
$$\$20 + \$12 = \text{Price}$$
$$\$32 = \text{Price}$$

When discussing the markup percentage, it is extremely important to indicate whether the calculation is based on cost or on the selling price. Here is an example:

$$\text{Markup as a percentage of cost} = \frac{\text{Amount added to cost}}{\text{Cost}} = \frac{12}{20} = 60\%$$

$$\text{Markup as a percentage of selling price} = \frac{\text{Amount added to cost}}{\text{Selling price}} = \frac{12}{32} = 38\%$$

Simplicity is the main appeal of cost-based pricing. Otherwise this method has its problems, especially in determining the appropriate markup percentage. That percentage should produce a price appropriate for the firm's profit objectives, market demand, and competition. Some firms defeat the markup's purpose by not altering their percentage in light of current economic or business conditions.

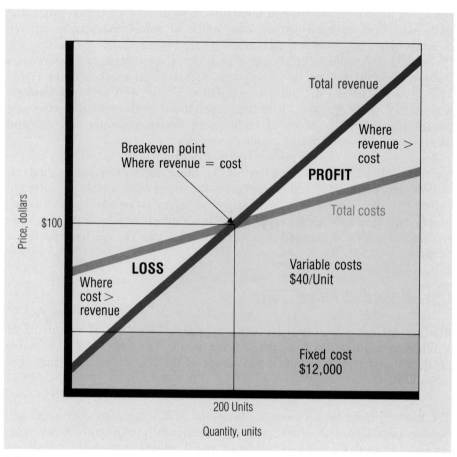

FIGURE 12.4    Breakeven Analysis

The chart labels:
- Total revenue
- Breakeven point / Where revenue = cost
- Where revenue > cost
- PROFIT
- Total costs
- $100
- Price, dollars
- LOSS
- Variable costs $40/Unit
- Where cost > revenue
- Fixed cost $12,000
- 200 Units
- Quantity, units

## Demand-Based Pricing

**demand-based pricing**
a pricing strategy that assigns price according to how much will need to be sold in order for the firm to break even

**breakeven analysis** a method used to determine the demand or sales volume required at a given price for the firm to break even

**fixed costs** costs that do not vary with the level of output or production

**variable costs** costs that depend on the number of units produced

**total costs** the sum of the fixed and variable costs

The focus of **demand-based pricing** relies on **breakeven analysis**, a method used to determine the demand or sales volume required at a given price for the firm to break even (see Figure 12.4). The formula for determining a breakeven point is:

$$\frac{\text{Fixed costs}}{(\text{Price} - \text{variable cost per unit})} = \text{Breakeven point}$$

In this formula, **fixed costs** are costs that do not vary with the level of output or production. Rent is usually considered a fixed cost. **Variable costs,** such as labor, are costs that depend on the number of units produced. **Total costs** represent the sum of the fixed and variable costs. The breakeven point is the point at which the cost of making a product equals the revenues gained from selling the product.

Suppose a business expects a product to sell for $100. The total fixed costs are $12,000 and variable costs per unit are $40. The calculation would be:

$$\frac{\text{Fixed costs}}{(\text{Price} - \text{variable cost per unit})} = \frac{\$12,000}{(\$100 - 40)} = 200 \text{ units} = \text{Breakeven point}$$

If management believes it can sell more than 200 units at $100 each, that might be the appropriate price. But if management estimates sales to be less than 200 units, it probably should recalculate the breakeven point using a lower price per unit.

## Competition-Based Pricing

Some firms, particularly in retailing and in fields where they market products similar to their competitors', use **competition-based pricing**, pricing based on competitive price levels. After determining the prices charged by the competition, management has three options: it can price higher than, lower than, or the same as its competitors. Businesses like this method because it is simple and unlikely to set off price wars. Its major flaw is that the price settled on is not necessarily related to a firm's objectives. It also assumes that the firm's marketing costs and mix are the same as its competitors'.

Food Lion, a supermarket chain serving several Southeastern states, has used a low price strategy with great success. The goal of Food Lion is to maintain price margins slightly lower than those of its competitors. To make a profit, the company operates a very efficient warehouse and distribution system and encourages store managers to keep operating expenses as low as possible. The company plans to have 800 stores in operation by the end of 1990.[11]

**competition-based pricing** pricing based on competitive price levels

# Pricing Strategies

Once a price has been set using the chosen pricing method, the firm adjusts this price in accordance with its pricing strategy. A number of pricing strategies exist, and it is not at all uncommon for a firm to use several at once, even for the same product.

*7. Identify the pricing strategies available for both new products and those already on the market.*

## New-Product Pricing Strategies

The pricing strategy for a new product must be consistent with the overall marketing strategy developed for it. Two choices here are the skimming strategy and the penetration strategy.

A **skimming price strategy** involves charging a high price when the product is first introduced. This technique takes its name from the notion of skimming the cream from the top of unhomogenized milk. This strategy works only when a sufficient number of customers are not particularly sensitive to price. Early purchasers of innovative electronic equipment fall into this category, like those who paid $1,000 for the first compact disk players. A successful skimming strategy permits a firm to recover the costs of product development

**skimming price strategy** pricing that involves charging a high price when the product is first introduced

A penetration pricing strategy   *Interac Corp. has developed The Music Sampler, which allows customers to hear excerpts from as many as 100 albums. After a one-time charge of $350, record stores may use the service for only $20 a month.*

**penetration pricing strategy**   pricing that calls for introducing a new product at a low price to attain a strong grip on a sizable market share

relatively quickly. After a time, the firm may consider lowering the price or even withdrawing from the market as new competitors, sensing a profit to be made, enter it.

A **penetration pricing strategy** calls for introducing a new product at a low price, to attain a strong grip on a sizable market share. The combination of low prices and an entrenched competitor can discourage other firms from entering the market. When a business anticipates product growth over the long term or when product development costs are extremely high, this strategy may be the best. Commodore VIC-20 was originally priced at $299, compared to $600 for the Atari 400 and $500 for the Texas Instruments 9914A. Over 1.5 million VIC-20s were sold in the first two years, and the two competitors were forced out of the market.

## Psychological Pricing Strategies

Many of the more specifically targeted pricing strategies are based on consumer behavior. These psychological strategies often influence the product's image.

**Odd/even pricing** is one of the most popular psychological pricing strategies. "Odd" prices, which end in an odd number (usually nine), are meant to give the customer the impression of low prices and convey the idea that the firm has cut prices to the last possible penny. Even prices are meant to give the opposite impression. They are usually stated in round dollar amounts, which are thought to give the consumer a sense of prestige. In theory, a bargain hunter should be attracted to an $89.99 price and the prestige buyer to a $90.00 price. Researchers have not been able either to prove or disprove the concept behind the odd/even pricing theory.

**Multiple-unit pricing** is the practice of providing discounts for purchases of two or more units. The idea here is to sell a greater total amount by convincing the customer to buy more at one time. It works best for retailers, like grocers, who can price Del Monte green beans at "two for $1."

**Prestige pricing** involves setting a very high price on an item to give an impression of high quality. Rolex watches and Porsches carry prestige prices. For years, Mercedes-Benz has maintained a prestige pricing policy for exports to America. The company knows that consumers will pay from $30,000 to $80,000 for the privilege of driving a car adorned by the three-pointed star. Prestige pricing is directly related to the familiar customer attitude that "you get what you pay for." To marketers, this saying expresses the **price-quality relationship**, which is that a high price implies high quality. If customers lack other cues on a product's quality, they will judge it by its price.

**Price lining** is a pricing strategy used primarily by retailers in which the firm selects a limited number of key prices or **price points** for certain classes of products. For example, a department store might price all its Arrow dress shirts according to a $17.50–$20–$25–$30 scheme, regardless of how much they cost at wholesale. In other words, the store would not apply a fixed markup to them.

# Product and Price: A Perspective

For three generations of consumers, General Electric was the preferred brand when it came to small appliances: irons, toasters, toaster ovens, coffee makers, and the like. One survey asked consumers to list small-appliance makers. General Electric appeared on 92 percent of the lists, Sunbeam 41 percent, and Black & Decker 12 percent. The irony was that GE had sold its small-appliance division to Black & Decker some months before.

Under the terms of the two companies' agreement, Black & Decker could use GE's name in connection with its small appliances for three years. Except in the case of irons, a fiercely competitive market, Black & Decker chose instead to relaunch the products under its own name. Black & Decker was gambling that it could take the products marketed under the best-known blanket brand in the small-appliance business and succeed with them under

**odd/even pricing** strategies in which prices ending in odd numbers are meant to suggest a low price and in which even-numbered prices suggest prestige

**multiple-unit pricing** the practice of providing discounts for purchases of two or more units

**prestige pricing** setting a very high price on an item to give an impression of high quality

**price-quality relationship** where price is directly related to quality, so that high price means high quality

**price lining** pricing strategy in which the firm selects a limited number of key prices for certain classes of products

**price points** key prices chosen for certain classes of products in the price lining process

its own name. The company spent $100 million in advertising to rename the GE brand and invested heavily in inventory to make sure that retail customers received their orders. The renaming effort worked and Black & Decker has retained leadership in the market.[12] And the company did not win customers with cost cutting. It persuaded consumers to buy Black & Decker products based on each product's features, not on its price.[13]

Black & Decker has clearly changed the product and price aspects of its marketing mix. It has also changed how it puts products in the hands of retailers and budgeted an industry record $100 million for advertising, so it has also altered the distribution and promotion strategies. In the next two chapters, we will look at these last two of the Four P's.

# CHAPTER HIGHLIGHTS

### 1. Describe the new-product development process.

The *new-product development process* consists of six phases: idea generation, screening, business analysis, product development, test marketing, and commercialization. This process depends on marketing information from the very first stage.

### 2. Explain the product life cycle concept.

The *product life cycle concept* assumes that products have lives with four identifiable stages: introduction, growth, maturity, and decline. There are no hard-and-fast rules as to how long any stage will take for a given product, and marketers can extend the life of a product by finding new uses, new users, promoting its more frequent use, or making cosmetic changes in the product. The concept is most valuable as a planning tool because it allows a company to monitor shifts in demand for its products and develop appropriate responses.

### 3. Explain the functions of branding, packaging, and labeling.

*Branding* identifies a product and distinguishes it from its competition. Brands help consumers assure themselves of consistent quality and allow companies to develop loyal customers. *Packaging* may prevent spoilage or damage,

protect against injury, promote safety, or make a product easier to use. Packaging also serves a promotion function by creating an image for a product and making the product easy to recognize. *Labeling,* the part of the package that contains information, informs the consumer what the product is and how it should be used.

### 4. Describe the role of pricing in the marketing mix.

Pricing helps firms allocate resources because a product's price is directly related to the revenue it is expected to generate. Pricing helps consumers allocate their resources by allowing them to compare the price of a product and the satisfaction anticipated from it. Price also provides some clues about quality. High prices are assumed to accompany high quality.

### 5. List the potential pricing objectives for a product.

The potential pricing objectives for a product are profit maximization, target return on investment, market share, status quo, and survival.

### 6. Describe the principal pricing methods.

There are four basic pricing methods. *Economic theory–based pricing* seeks to apply the principles of supply and demand to identify the equilibrium point and market price. *Cost-based pricing* adds a predetermined markup percentage to the cost of a product. *Demand-based pricing* relies on breakeven analysis to find out how many units of a product must be sold at a particular price to cover the cost of producing and selling the product. *Competition-based pricing* relies on the prices charged by competitors as a starting point. A business can then decide to charge more than, less than, or the same price as its competitors.

**7.** *Identify the pricing strategies available for both new products and those already on the market.*

Businesses use *skimming* or *penetration pricing* strategies for most new products. For established products, firms tend to rely on one of several psychological pricing strategies: *odd/even pricing, multiple-unit pricing,* or *prestige pricing.*

## KEY TERMS

Product
New-product
    development
    process
Test market
Product life cycle
Introduction stage
Growth stage
Product
    differentiation
    strategy
Maturity stage
Decline stage

Cosmetic change
Brand
Brand name
Brand symbol
National brand
    (manufacturer's
    brand)
Private label brand
Infringement
Trademark
Generic name
Family brand (blanket
    brand) strategy

Individual brand
    strategy
Packaging
Label
Labeling
Demand
Supply
Equilibrium
Market price
Cost-based pricing
Markup
Demand-based pricing
Breakeven analysis

Fixed costs
Variable costs
Total costs
Competition-based pricing
Skimming price strategy
Penetration pricing strategy
Odd/even pricing
Multiple-unit pricing
Prestige pricing
Price-quality relationship
Price lining
Price points

## REVIEW QUESTIONS

1. What are the basic steps in the new-product development process? Describe each briefly.
2. What is the product life cycle concept? For what purposes may it be used?
3. Identify the stages of the product life cycle and discuss each.
4. Describe the major means to extend the product life cycle.
5. The terms *brand, brand name, brand symbol,* and *trademark* describe related concepts. What are the relationships among these concepts?
6. List the major benefits of branding.

7. Describe the potential functions of packaging. How does labeling relate to packaging?
8. What is the role of pricing in marketing?
9. Define the possible pricing objectives available to a firm for a product.
10. Identify the major pricing methods. How is each different from the others?
11. What are the main new-product pricing strategies? Create examples showing how each type works.
12. Describe the main psychological pricing strategies.

# APPLICATION EXERCISES

1. For many years people living in your community have raved about your mother's chocolate brownies. A typical comment made by friends and relatives is: "If you marketed these brownies nationwide, you could make a fortune." Let's assume that the brownies are quite good and appear to have wide appeal in the marketplace. What steps in the new-product development process would be most important if a decision is made to market this product nationwide? What considerations would be part of the packaging and labeling of this product for the market?

2. Two years ago you purchased a small copy center in a college town with a population of 25,000. Most of your current customers include students and faculty members from the college. Recently the store next door was vacated and the space is available to you. You are considering expansion of your business to include a wide range of professional services such as typing resumes, legal documents, business letters, theses, and dissertations. If the expansion takes place, you will have to determine a price for each of the services. Which pricing method would you use to develop a price list?

# CASES

## 12.1  Selling Books

The late, great actor Richard Burton is reported to have expressed an interest in returning to life as an author. Famous authors, he said, make just as much money as famous actors. But the former do not have people following them around all the time.

Burton did not subscribe to the image of the poor, struggling writer. What he saw was a business where more books are published than ever before and where successful writers are multimillionaires. In 1988 Chrysler CEO Lee Iacocca earned $6.5 million, just on U.S. sales of his books. In the same year book publishing revenues reached $11.4 billion, up from $5.1 billion a decade before.

How does a publisher go about getting a good share of such a lucrative business? There is no one answer. There are no guarantees.

When it comes to subject matter, many recommend sticking to the big themes: sex, greed, and power. Movie-star confessionals and, in recent years, tales of the entrepreneur have often done well at the bookstores, but not always. The history of publishing is peppered with unlikely best sellers on unlikely themes by unlikely authors. In the 1960s, a Latin version of *Winnie the Pooh* was "must" reading. In the 1970s, *Watership Down,* a long novel populated by talking rabbits, rose high on the charts. In the 1980s, *A Brief History of Time,* by a quadraplegic physicist who could only speak with the aid of a voice synthesizer, far outsold the exposés and entrepreneurial tales.

Some books sell explosively for a while, and then die out. Other books sell steadily over the years. They may never make the best-seller list. Yet total sales may be impressive. One such volume, the philosophical novel *The Stranger,* by French author Albert Camus, first appeared in print over 40 years ago. The work has sold over three million copies in its Vintage paperback edition alone. At last count it was still selling 125,000 copies a year. According to Erroll MacDonald, Vintage's executive vice president, the success of *The Stranger* suggests a willingness on the part of American readers to "venture beyond the beaten literary path."

It also suggests smart marketing by Vintage, a unit of giant Random House. *The Stranger* is part of a line of paperback books, all on a similar level of sophistication and with uniform jacket designs. Vintage supplies stores with a

75-copy display, in which different books in the series may be shown together.

## Questions

1. How might *The Stranger* help sell an unknown book in the same line?
2. Paperbacks sell for much less than hardbacks. What advantages do paperbacks offer publishers? At what point might a publisher issue a paperback edition of a hardback book?

Sources: For more information see *Fortune*, February 13, 1989, pp. 101–103; *Publishers Weekly*, March 10, 1989, pp. 23–27; *The Wall Street Journal*, March 20, 1989, p. B4; and *The New York Times Book Review*, March 26, 1989, pp. 1, 21, 23.

## 12.2  Honda and the Big Guys

In the 1970s, inflation and the gasoline crunch created a huge demand for small, fuel-efficient cars. Many U.S. consumers purchased Japanese imports. Sales of American cars dropped sharply, and American auto manufacturers were hurting. In 1980, under the threat of formal import restrictions, the Japanese agreed to "voluntarily" limit auto exports to the United States for three years. Although the quota has been raised several times since the first agreement expired, the idea of an informal import limit has been retained.

Demand for Japanese imports has remained high, even though Detroit was able to regroup and produce its own fuel-efficient cars. To make the most of their quota, Japanese auto makers are sending their highest priced models to the United States. As a result, their profits have soared.

Japan's Honda Motor Co. began as a motorcycle producer, later added subcompact autos to its product mix, and in 1983 became the fourth largest Japanese auto maker. Honda's management felt that the firm could sell well beyond its quota of cars in the United States. For that reason, and to help reduce protectionist friction between Japan and the United States, Honda opened an auto production plant in Marysville, Ohio. Output from that plant has prompted Honda of America to assert that it is now the fourth largest auto manufacturer in the United States.

But Honda was not through importing cars. The company was so strongly associated with inexpensive subcompacts that it considered entering the $20,000-plus market as a great risk. Honda ran that risk, however. Its new cars, sold through a new system of Acura dealerships, matched the success of the tiny, air-cooled Honda Civic. Wasting no time, Honda next introduced a luxury sports coupe to sell in the $50,000 range.

## Questions

1. Why did Honda start to import higher-priced cars? Why did the company market these cars under a new brand name?
2. What does Honda gain from producing cars in the United States, given that cars cost more to produce here than in Japan?

Sources: For more information see *Barron's,* December 2, 1985, pp. 13, 48–49; *Business Week*, December 9, 1985, pp. 114, 118; *Forbes*, September 10, 1984, pp. 41–48; *Fortune*, February 20, 1984, pp. 104–108; *The Wall Street Journal*, January 11, 1989, p. B4; and *Autoweek*, February 20, 1989, p. 5.

# 13 Distribution Strategy

## LEARNING

## OBJECTIVES

*After you have completed this chapter, you will be able to do the following:*

*1. Define the term* marketing intermediaries.

*2. Describe the basic channels of distribution for consumer and industrial products.*

*3. Distinguish among intensive, selective, and exclusive distribution strategies.*

*4. List the two main types of wholesalers and identify their functions.*

*5. Specify the services wholesalers provide to producers and retailers.*

*6. List the main types of retailers and identify their functions.*

*7. Describe the organization of a physical distribution system.*

*8. Identify the principal modes of transportation for goods and discuss their advantages and disadvantages.*

*9. Explain the difference between a public warehouse and a private warehouse.*

Business and
Its Environment

Financial
Management

Management
and Organization

The
American
Business
System

Information
for Business
Decision
Making

Human
Resources
and
Production

**Marketing**

Most leaders in the retail field predict that Wal-Mart will become the nation's largest retailer within a few years. This progressive company already operates more than 1,400 stores and is adding more than 100 new stores each year. Wal-Mart is popular not only among shoppers but financial analysts as well. Margaret Gilliam, an analyst for First Boston, said, "Wal-Mart is the finest managed company we have ever followed."[1]

What is the secret of Wal-Mart's success? Observers say that one of its major strengths is a highly efficient distribution system. To obtain the lowest possible prices, Wal-Mart buys directly from the manufacturer. The products are shipped to one of the company's fourteen regional distribution centers, which are located near its stores. The company uses its own fleet of trucks to deliver products to the stores. Orders from stores are beamed via satellite to an IBM computer at corporate headquarters. In most cases, the products are delivered to the store and appear on the shelf within 36 hours of the stores' order.[2]

As a discount retailer, Wal-Mart has to be as efficient as possible because its customers are very price-conscious. The company developed its own distribution system because this approach is extemely cost-effective. Distribution costs account for less than 3 percent of sales at Wal-Mart, compared to almost 8 percent at Sears, Roebuck and Company, a major competitor.[3]

Product availability is the key concept in place utility, the third of the marketing mix's Four P's discussed in Chapter 11. For a product to deliver satisfaction, it must be where the purchasers can buy it. This chapter focuses on how products reach their ultimate user or consumer.

# Channels of Distribution

To facilitate the flow of products to their ultimate purchasers, most businesses that produce goods have created extensive **channels of distribution**, paths or routes composed of marketing intermediaries or middlemen that direct products to customers. A channel of distribution, which is sometimes called a **marketing channel** or **distribution channel**, always begins with a producer and ends with a consumer or end user. Between them, a number of different types of firms may handle the goods.

Wholesalers and retailers are the major marketing intermediaries, found in the channels of distribution for both consumer and industrial products.

## The Role of Intermediaries

Figure 13.1 shows that channels of distribution commonly contain **marketing intermediaries** or **middlemen**, firms between the manufacturer and the ultimate user or consumer that take title to the goods. These facilitating organizations directly assist others to take title to goods or assist in physically moving or storing goods while they are in the channel. For example, Pierre Cardin might ship goods by Emery Worldwide to the May Company department stores, which need them for a special promotion. As a retailer, the May Company is an intermediary between Pierre Cardin and the ultimate consumer. Emery is a facilitating organization assisting in the title exchange by physically moving the goods.

*Merchants* An intermediary—a wholesaler, distributor, or retailer—who takes title to goods and resells them is a **merchant**. Often, merchants pay for goods from the proceeds of their resale. Intermediaries of this type typically take delivery of products, hold them ready for resale, divide large shipments into lot sizes acceptable to their customers, and distribute the products to the next point in the channel of distribution.

Merchants always take **title**, the right to own property that usually (but not always) comes with physical possession of tangible personal property or real property. A better way to think of title is as the right to sell or otherwise transfer property, whether or not the seller has actual possession of the property or has paid for it.

*Agents and Brokers* In contrast to merchants, an **agent** or **broker** is an intermediary who receives a commission for bringing together buyers and sellers for the purpose of negotiating an exchange but never takes title to property.[4]

## Channels for Consumer Products

Goods and services bought by individuals for their personal or household use are *consumer products*. Figure 13.1 shows the three basic types of

**channels of distribution (marketing channels, distribution channels)** paths or routes composed of marketing intermediaries or middlemen that direct products to customers

**marketing intermediary (middleman)** a firm between the manufacturer and the ultimate user or consumer that takes title to the goods

*1. Define the term* marketing intermediaries.

**merchant** an intermediary who takes title to goods and resells them

**title** the right to own property that usually comes with physical possession of tangible personal property or real property

**agent (broker)** an intermediary who receives a commission for bringing together buyers and sellers for the purpose of negotiating an exchange but never takes title to property

*2. Describe the basic channels of distribution for consumer and industrial products.*

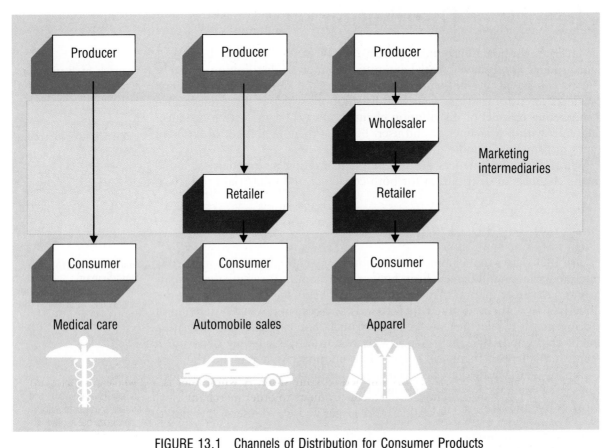

FIGURE 13.1   Channels of Distribution for Consumer Products

Most services, such as medical care, move directly from producer to consumer with no intermediary.

channels of distribution for consumer products. It is important to keep in mind that there are many variations on these types.

*Producer to Consumer*   Notice in Figure 13.1 that this channel runs directly from the producer to the consumer. Virtually all services, from haircuts to tax preparation, use this channel. Some producers sell their goods directly, and exclusively, to the public. One of the best known of these is Avon Products, Inc.'s cosmetics, which are sold door to door. Some firms use the producer-to-consumer channel as one part of their overall distribution system for goods.

Most of the major oil companies, like the Atlantic Richfield Company (Arco) and Standard Oil Company of Indiana (Amoco Oil Company), own some retail outlets—service stations, in their cases—through which they sell their products. Similarly, many of the better known franchisers, like Wendy's International, Inc., own and operate outlets, too.

The principal reason producers want direct channels of distribution is to maintain control over the distribution of their products. Marketing intermediaries often have a certain amount of control over matters such as pricing and promotion, which the producer may want to limit or eliminate. A producer-to-consumer channel also lets producers maintain close ties to consumers. Direct dealings with consumers can lead to insights about their needs and wants. Finally, this type of channel cuts out the profit that marketing intermediaries must make. Wal-Mart, as noted, decided to eliminate all intermediaries. Nevertheless, a marketing intermediary's functions often involve resources and expertise that the producer lacks. Intermediaries may be able to perform their functions more economically than the producer can.

### Producer to Retailer to Consumer

In this channel the product moves from producer to retailer to consumer. A **retailer** is a merchant who sells products or services or both to the ultimate consumer. Supermarkets, like Ralphs Grocery Company, and discount stores, like Venture Stores, Inc., are retailers. Merle Norman Cosmetics, Inc., unlike Avon, makes its own cosmetics, which it then sells to consumers through 2,500 franchised Merle Norman Studios.

**retailer** a merchant who sells products or services or both to the ultimate consumer

Many producers use producer-to-retailer-to-consumer channels because these lines are relatively short and make possible a wider range of distribution than do producer-to-consumer channels. They also facilitate the movement of bulky, perishable, and fashion-sensitive goods.

### Producer to Wholesaler to Retailer to Consumer

Most consumer goods pass through this channel. The box of Pillsbury cake mix you purchased at your nearby grocery store was very likely stored at a wholesale warehouse or distribution center before it was shipped to your store. A **wholesaler** is a business or individual who buys and resells products to other merchants such as retailers and other wholesalers and larger industrial users, but not to consumers.

**wholesaler** a business or individual who buys and resells products to other merchants, but not to consumers

Producers are likely to use wholesale intermediaries when a large number of retailers carry their products. Most electronic equipment, canned goods, office supplies, and hardware passes through such channels. The use of wholesalers may also make it easier for producers to reach different market segments. For example, a hammer manufacturer may deal with one group of wholesalers that serves hardware retailers and another that serves discount and department stores.

## Channels for Industrial Products

Producers of industrial goods can choose from many different channels of distribution. We will discuss two of the most commonly used.

### Producer to Industrial User

Producers who use this direct channel employ a sales force that sells directly to the industrial user. Producers using this channel often sell large, costly items requiring custom installation. The General Electric Company sells turbines for electricity-generating stations directly to utilities. General Electric and other producers who use this channel usually provide users with after-sale services, such as delivery, set-up, and maintenance. Quite often, the company promising the best performance on these services gets the sale.

Vertical-channel integration   *Caloric, maker of kitchen appliances, relies on large retailers such as Silo to distribute its product line. More and more retailers are absorbing the task of distribution in the appliance industry.*

*Producer to Distributor to Industrial User*   Standardized goods such as electrical supplies and janitorial supplies often pass through a distributor or wholesaler. Northland Industrial Trucks, a distributor, sells and services forklifts, trucks, and other industrial equipment to industrial users.

## Vertical-Channel Integration

**vertical-channel integration** the combination of two or more entities within the channel stretching from the producer to the consumer or end user

**corporate vertical-marketing system** a system in which the firm performs all the channel functions

**administered vertical-marketing system** a system in which one channel member dominates all the others in its channel or channels.

The combination of two or more entities within the channel stretching from the producer to the consumer or end user is called **vertical-channel integration**. Vertical-channel integration occurs when a firm either acquires another firm in its channel or sets up a division to carry out other channel functions. Some oil companies, like the Sun Refining & Marketing Company (Sunoco) or Texas Oil Company (Texaco), perform all the channel functions from the extraction of crude oil to pumping gasoline into consumers' cars. Such arrangements are called **corporate vertical-marketing systems**.

In an **administered vertical-marketing system**, one channel member dominates all the others in its channel or channels. Sears is a well-known example of a channel leader, the dominant entity in a distribution channel. It buys in such large quantities that it sets the standards for producers and other intermediaries within its channels. Wal-Mart is moving into a similar position.

Table 13.1 lists and describes the various categories of middlemen.

TABLE 13.1    Characteristics of Middlemen Serving Retailers

| Type of Middleman | Functions |
|---|---|
| Full-service merchants | Assemble, collect, and store goods; provide fast delivery, extend trade credit, and furnish market information. These services appeal especially to small- and medium-sized retailers. |
| Limited-service merchants | Charge less and provide fewer services than the full-service merchant wholesaler; generally do not grant credit or offer delivery service. Offer only fast-moving items; may do business by mail only. |
| Rack jobbers | Supply mainly nonfood items to supermarkets, set up displays, maintain merchandise assortment, and receive payment only on goods actually sold, thereby guaranteeing a markup of an agreed-upon percentage to the outlet. |
| Brokers | Receive a commission for bringing retail buyers and suppliers together; do not handle merchandise or take title to goods. Handle only a few lines, mainly grocery specialties, dry goods, fruits, vegetables, drugs, and hardware. |
| Commission agents | Similar to broker, except that they handle merchandise, but they do not take title to it. Supply mainly large retailers with dry goods, grocery specialties, and fruits and vegetables. Represent seller/producer. |
| Manufacturers' representatives | Render services similar to those of a salesperson. Restricted to a limited territory and have limited authority to negotiate price and terms of sale; sell only part of the client's output. |
| Selling agents | Similar to manufacturers' representatives except that selling agents are responsible for disposing of the entire output of the client. |
| Auctioneer | Places products on display and sells to the highest bidder. Used mainly to sell livestock and fruits and vegetables to small restaurants, large chains, or other wholesalers. |

Source: Table 8-1, adapted from *Retail Management: Satisfaction of Consumer Needs*, Second Edition, by Raymond A. Marquardt, James C. Makens, and Robert G. Roe, copyright © 1979 by The Dryden Press, a division of Holt, Rinehart & Winston, Inc., reprinted by permission of the publisher.

# Market Coverage

**market coverage** producer's choice of the number and types of outlets it wants for its products

A producer should base its choice of a channel of distribution on the **market coverage**—the number and types of outlets—it wants for its products. This choice depends, of course, on the producer's marketing objectives, marketing strategies, and resources.

## Patterns of Market Coverage

*3. Distinguish among intensive, selective, and exclusive distribution strategies.*

A producer can choose from three basic patterns of market coverage: intensive, selective, and exclusive distribution. Producers often adopt one type of market coverage for one product and another for a different one. They may also vary their coverage for one product from, say, region to region, depending on what strategy seems to work in a given area, and the nature of the product itself.

**intensive distribution strategy** strategy that takes advantage of all available retail outlets

*Intensive Distribution* The way to take advantage of virtually all the available retail outlets is with an **intensive distribution strategy**. A producer uses such a technique to saturate the market and guarantee purchasers that its brand will be available wherever they are. Cigarette companies, candy manufacturers, and soft-drink bottlers typically use this strategy because consumers will readily substitute other products for their particular ones if they are not available. It is virtually impossible to achieve saturation without relying on intermediaries, so intensive distribution gives producers very little control over retailers.

**selective distribution strategy** an approach that centers on a moderate proportion of the retailers likely to carry a particular product in a given market area

*Selective Distribution* An approach that centers on a moderate proportion of the retailers likely to carry a particular product in a given market area is called a **selective distribution strategy**. In this system, a producer carefully evaluates each potential outlet for its ability to market the product successfully. Producers of shopping goods such as clothing, furniture, and major appliances often adopt this strategy, which works well for products that consumers will seek out. A shopper who wants a Cuisinart food processor will make an effort to locate a store carrying the brand. Quite often, producers adopting a selective distribution strategy offer training for retailers as well as service facilities and promotional support.

**exclusive distribution strategy** strategy that relies on a single retail outlet or a very few outlets in a market area

*Exclusive Distribution* Another distribution arrangement, called an **exclusive distribution strategy**, relies on a single retail outlet or very few retail outlets in a market area. This strategy is most appropriate for specialty items for which consumers will gladly search, like Rolls-Royce automobiles. In return for guaranteed sales rights within a specified region, retailers often allow producers to maintain a high degree of control over the product's marketing, especially its pricing. In turn, producers generally provide a good deal of promotional and other assistance.

**Saturating the market**  *The fleet of trucks employed by the Coca-Cola Bottling Company ensures intensive distribution of its products. Coca-Cola wants its drinks to be available at all times, wherever they are normally sold.*

## Choosing a Retail Strategy

Producers select a retail strategy based on their products and their target markets. Some products, such as an ordinary candy bar or brand of cigarettes, for instance, require an intensive distribution strategy to be successful. However, for shopping goods or specialty goods, products for which a consumer will search, the most important retail strategy is to identify the target market. The manufacturer must identify the segmentation variables (discussed in Chapter 11) that characterize its market, then identify the outlets that cater to the markets the variables describe. Many considerations come into play. Does the product appeal to residents of only one region? To what age and income levels does it appeal? What types of stores does the target market frequent—shops in malls, or downtown boutiques? Is service a major consideration? If so, to what types of retailers does the target market look when it buys products like computers that have a high potential for requiring service?

Successful retailers carefully plan their stores to appeal to specific target markets. They try to create a distinct image and spark a particular emotional response among potential customers. Customers who visit a Nordstrom department store may be serenaded by a piano player and are treated like royalty by trained salespeople.[5] The variables that go into designing retail stores are called **atmospherics**. For example, what type of sales help do customers want? Do they want fashion consultants, or someone who can write up a sale? The effects of atmospherics on consumer buying are studied intently.

**atmospherics** the variables considered in designing retail stores

# Marketing Intermediaries: Wholesalers

*4. List the two main types of wholesalers and identify their functions.*

**full-service wholesaler** wholesaler who offers the widest variety of services to its customers

**limited-service wholesaler** wholesaler who offers a narrower range of services to customers

Wholesalers are those infamous middlemen whose profits so many people talk about eliminating. As we have already seen, however, wholesalers play an important role in making channels of distribution efficient. Like retailers, all wholesalers do not fit into a single mold. Each offers a different mix of services, but it is possible to divide them into two main groups. **Full-service wholesalers** offer the widest variety of services to their customers, including maintaining inventories, gathering and interpreting market information, extending credit, distributing goods, and promotional activities. **Limited-service wholesalers** offer a narrower range of services than do full-service wholesalers, and they often tend to specialize.

## Wholesalers' Services to Producers

*5. Specify the services wholesalers provide to producers and retailers.*

Wholesalers perform many functions that the producer would otherwise have to perform (see Figure 13.2).

*Sales*   The wholesaler's sales force represents the producer to retailers. Obviously, if a producer had to maintain a sales force to call on retailers, its cost of sales would be much higher.

*Inventory*   Most wholesalers maintain warehouses in which to store merchandise. If producers had to maintain and store inventories of finished products, their costs would rise dramatically. By taking care of inventory, the wholesaler bears the risk of damage, theft, and obsolescence of the goods.

*Credit*   Wholesalers reduce producers' risks by extending credit to retailers.

*Promotion*   By assisting retailers with promotions the wholesaler takes care of some of the producer's promotion and is therefore saving the company money.

*Market Information*   Obviously, in order to manufacture goods that customers want, producers must know what these wants are. Wholesalers, who deal with many retailers, can serve as conduits for this market information.

## Wholesalers' Services to Retailers

Wholesalers also provide a number of critically important services to retailers. Without them, retailers would find the cost of doing business much higher.

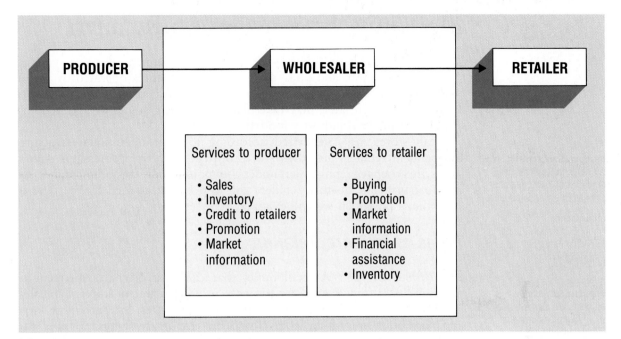

FIGURE 13.2   Services provided by wholesalers

*Buying*   The major service that wholesalers provide retailers is buying. Without wholesalers, retailers would have to deal with hosts of producers directly instead of working through a far smaller number of wholesalers.

*Promotion*   Wholesalers may provide window displays and end-of-aisle racks for specials or even designate employees to work with the retailer during special promotions. They may also offer cooperative advertising allowances, making advertising a joint venture between wholesaler and retailer.

*Market Information*   Retailers often find wholesalers to be unique, informal sources of market information because they deal both with producers and other retailers. Wholesalers know from other retailers what products are moving well and from producers what new products are being developed.

*Financial Assistance*   The extension of **trade credit** is the most common way in which wholesalers grant financial assistance to retailers. We have already noted some other ways in which wholesalers provide retailers with services they would otherwise have to pay for or forego.

**trade credit**   the most common way in which wholesalers grant financial assistance to retailers

*Inventory*   One of the most important services a wholesaler provides retailers is the inventory function. The wholesaler maintains a large inventory from which a retailer may purchase small quantities. Because the wholesaler bears the cost of maintaining the inventory, retailers can offer a larger selection of goods than they could if that burden fell on them.

# Marketing Intermediaries: Retailers

Retailers sell goods or services—or both—to consumers. Retailers vary in size from the "mom and pop" store to the giant stores operated by major chains like the R. H. Macy Company, Inc., and Albertson's, Inc. Nonstore retailing, discussed later, may take place in people's homes or at a vending machine or in the stands at a football game.

Retail stores are categorized according to their operational structure. **Independent retailers** are often sole proprietorships or partnerships. **Chain stores** are groups of retail outlets under common (usually corporate) ownership and management. In-store retailers can also be categorized by the type of store they run, which we will examine next.

## Types of In-Store Retailers

*Department Stores*   A retail outlet that carries a diverse assortment of merchandise grouped into departments is a **department store**. Typically, department stores, like the Carter Hawley Hale Stores, Inc., are quite large and may offer everything from clothes to home furnishings to tools and major appliances, luggage, and books under one roof. Department stores also usually offer services—for example, appliance repair, delivery, and gift wrapping—as part of their marketing strategy. Credit often plays a key role in marketing; most department stores offer their own charge cards. Department stores like John Wanamaker's, Macy's, and Gimbels got their start in the mid-1800s in the central business districts of major cities. Today, at least one department store anchors nearly every major suburban shopping mall, and most department stores are chain stores. Ironically, the specialty retailers and national general merchandise retailers who also choose mall locations threaten the very existence of some department stores. Figure 13.3 illustrates the wide range of competition faced by a typical department store.

Retail outlets that compete primarily on the basis of price are called **discount stores**. They offer low prices, accept lower markups or margins, and generate their profits through rapid turnover of merchandise and careful cost control. Often, cost control takes the form of fewer customer services and low-rent locations. K mart Corporation, Wal-Mart, and Target are well-known discount chains. Some discounters are now offering better services and improving the atmosphere in stores, which means, of course, higher prices to consumers. These retailers have become more like department stores (see Business Issues).

*Specialty Stores*   Stores carrying a limited line of merchandise, such as records and tapes, computers, bridal gowns, or auto parts, are known as **specialty stores**. Most specialty stores are small, focus on local markets, and are managed by their owners. Rather than competing with larger retailers on the basis of price, they compete with specialized knowledge and personal service. A few offer merchandise not sold by their larger competitors, such as the King's Collar in Philadelphia, whose owner, Nancy Gold, designs and makes custom shirts.[6]

**independent retailer**  retail stores that operate independently, and are most often proprietorships or partnerships

**chain store**  a retail outlet under common (usually corporate) ownership and management

**department store**  a retail outlet that carries a diverse assortment of merchandise grouped into departments

*6. List the main types of retailers and identify their functions.*

**discount store**  a retail outlet that competes primarily on the basis of price

**specialty store**  a store carrying a limited line of merchandise

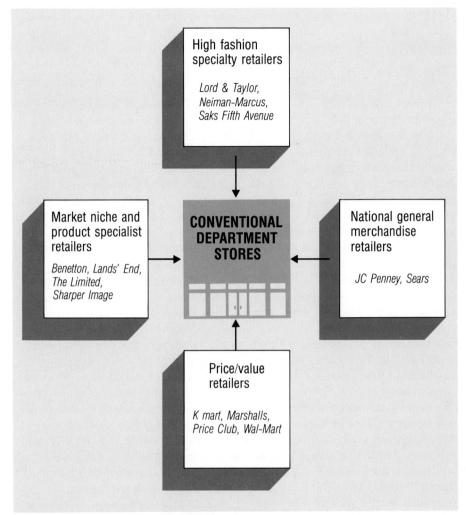

FIGURE 13.3 Conventional Department Stores and Their Competition
Source: From Leonard L. Berry, "Editor's Corner," *Retailing Issues Letter* (Center for Retailing Studies, Texas A&M University), vol. 1, no. 1, 1987, p. 4. Copyright 1987. Used by permission of Arthur Andersen & Co., Dallas, TX.

In recent years we have seen dramatic growth in specialty retail chains that feature fashion apparel and accessories. One of the fastest-growing companies is Limited, a trendy specialty retailer that operates several store divisions including Limited Stores (755 stores), Limited Express (420 stores), Victoria's Secret (326 stores), Lane Bryant (688 stores), Lerner (786 stores), and Lerner Woman (398 stores).[7]

*Catalog Showrooms* There is a special type of discount store called a **catalog showroom** in which only one unit of each product the store carries is on display. The customer selects the product he or she wants and it is brought to a pickup area from an adjacent warehouse. This arrangement

**catalog showroom** type of discount store in which only one unit of each product the store carries is on display

## NO FRILLS SHOPPING

K mart, one of the largest retailers in the United States, established its current no. 2 position by undercutting department stores. Now others are trying to undercut the undercutter. K mart faces the classic dilemma of a maturing business: If it wants to increase profits, it must consider price increases, offer lower quality products, reduce operating expenses, or use some combination of these various strategies. K mart has opted to increase prices, thereby exposing itself to competition from below.

Some of that competition comes from specialty discounters. Says President Dennis Lamm of Entertainment Marketing Inc., which supplies home electronics to discounters, "These retailers are taking the hottest item in a category, or a hot category, and running with it." And making money. Specialty discounters are among the fastest growing companies in the country. Three of the most successful: Ross Stores, Inc., which discounts clothing; Advanced Marketing Services, which discounts books; and Visit a Best Buy Co., which discounts electronics.

Also chewing away at K mart's market share are the rapidly growing warehouse clubs. Here customers explore enormous, unadorned stores, helping themselves to everything from truck tires to potato chips. The quality of the merchandise is high. The markups are very small. No sales help is provided. The largest of the warehouse clubs is Price Club, which had over $4.4 billion in sales in 1988. Costco Wholesale is next in line, with sales of $2.2 billion for the same year. The industry as a whole grew from $1 billion in 1983 to $14 billion in 1988.

The shop-by-television industry, which appears to go after the same audience as the superdiscounters, is in fact not price competitive. Expenses are too high. While such home shopping operations may not have to pay rent on a retail outlet, they must bear the cost of handling items individually instead of in bulk, and the cost of transporting purchased items to customers' homes. Still, sales growth has been impressive.

Though taking the frills out of shopping may be profitable, taking the promotional flair out of shopping may be disastrous. Perhaps this is one reason why Price Club, which enforces more exacting membership standards than the other wholesale clubs, is also more successful. Perhaps it is why Zayre's, a discount chain directly competitive with K mart but with much less splashy stores, loses to K mart in suburban communities where both have outlets.

Sources: Caroline E. Mayer, "Retailing Tackles the Last Frontier—The Living Room," *Roanoke Times & World-News*, March 1, 1987, pp. F5, F8; Gail DeGeorge, "Home Shopping Tries a Tonic for Its Sickly Stock," *Business Week*, April 25, 1988, p. 110; "Attention, K mart Shoppers," *Inc.*, May 1988, p. 104; Corie Brown with Amy Dunkin, "Zayre Zooms—Downward," *Business Week*, August 29, 1988, pp. 31–32; and Andrew Kupfer, "The Final Word in No-Frills Shopping?" *Fortune*, March 13, 1989, p. 30.

minimizes the floor space required for display and lessens the opportunities for shoplifting and accidental damage to goods. Among the better known of these increasingly popular retail outlets are the Service Merchandise Company, Inc., McDade & Company, Inc., and the Best Products Company, Inc.

**variety store** a relatively small store that offers a wide range of small, inexpensive items

*Variety Stores* A relatively small store that offers a wide range of small, inexpensive items is a **variety store**. Long known as "five and tens," the amounts the Woolworth Company charged a century ago when variety stores were a great retailing innovation, they are a dying breed. Discount stores now offer a larger selection of merchandise at competitive prices.

*Warehouse Clubs*  The **warehouse club** represents one of the fastest-growing segments of retailing. These large stores offer high-quality merchandise at very low prices. They charge membership dues that range from $15 to $25 a year. Warehouse clubs such as Costco Wholesale, Price Club, and Pace Membership Warehouse appeal to people who are willing to trade no-frill shopping for lower prices.[8]

**warehouse club**  usually a large store that charges a membership fee, and offers high-quality merchandise at very low prices

*Warehouse Stores*  A discount or off-price food store that offers approximately the same merchandise as supermarkets but has virtually no ambience or services is called a **warehouse store**. Heartland Food Warehouses in New England not only have the customer bag the groceries but charge for bags if he or she fails to bring enough. Still, many customers find the lower prices worth the effort. Among the leading warehouse chains are Edwards Food Warehouse, Warehouse Foods, and the Pic n Save Corporation.

**warehouse store**  a discount or off-price food store that offers approximately the same merchandise as supermarkets but has virtually no ambience

*Supermarkets*  The familiar large food stores known as **supermarkets** offer relatively low prices and carry many nationally recognized brands displayed in various departments, most of which are self-service. They principally sell food, but more and more supermarkets have moved into carrying nonfood items, like flowers, housewares, books, and drugs, because extremely stiff competition has led to very low profit margins on food—often 1 or 2 percent. The Kroger Company and Safeway Stores, Inc., are two of the leading supermarket chains.

**supermarket**  a large, predominantly self-serve food store that offers relatively low prices and carries nationally recognized brands

*Superstores and Hypermarkets*  **Superstores** and **hypermarkets** are large stores offering a broad selection of food, specialty food, and nonfood items. They often include a flower shop, a pharmacy, a delicatessen, a bakery, and a cafe. Some have electronic teller services connecting them to a bank. The largest hypermarket in the United States is Carrefour, located in Philadelphia. This 330,000-sq. ft. store was built on a 35-acre site.[9]

**superstore, hypermarket**  a large store carrying a broad selection of food, specialty food, and nonfood items

*Convenience Stores*  Food stores called **convenience stores** are considerably smaller than supermarkets and offer a limited range of staples and snack foods at prices considerably higher than those at supermarkets. These stores charge premium prices because they are open from 18 to 24 hours a day, seven days a week, and offer quick service. The leading convenience stores are Open Pantry Food Marts, Inc., Seven-Eleven Convenience Food Stores (Southland Stores), and Stop n Go (National Convenience Stores).

**convenience store**  a small store that offers a limited range of items at prices considerably higher than supermarket prices, but stays open from 18 to 24 hours a day

## Nonstore Retailers

Retailers who do not operate in conventional store facilities are **nonstore retailers**. They include in-home retailers, mail-order houses, and vending machines.

**nonstore retailer**  a retailer that does not operate in conventional store facilities

A giant among the retailers  *Wal-Mart Stores, a discount chain of some 1400 stores around the country, is a national retailer third in revenues behind only Sears and K mart. In addition to its regular discount stores, the company has opened several hypermarts. This five-acre Hypermart USA store is located near Dallas.*

**in-home retailer**
someone who sells directly to customers in their homes

*In-Home Retailers*  Someone who sells directly to customers in their homes is an **in-home retailer.** If the retailer books an order, the merchandise is generally delivered soon after the sale. Among the leaders in this field are World Book, Inc., for encyclopedias, Avon, and Electrolux vacuum cleaners. Decorating Den, a nationally franchised consulting service, brings designing vans to homes so consumers can choose from paint and drapery samples, carpet squares, and everything else a consumer needs to make home redecorating decisions.[10]

A relatively new form of in-home retailing is "party sales." Sales representatives recruit a cooperative customer to put on a party so that the sales person can show his or her merchandise to several customers at once. The Tupperware Division of Dart & Kraft, Mary Kay Cosmetics, Inc., and Sarah Coventry, Inc., successfully use this approach.

**mail-order retailer**  a retailer who issues a catalog from which consumers can choose items and place their orders by mail or telephone

*Mail-Order Retailers*  A retailer who issues a catalog from which consumers can choose items and place their orders by mail or telephone is a **mail-order retailer.** Such retailers generally offer competitive prices, a relatively wide

**Mail-order retailers** *Lands' End is one of the many mail-order retailers that has capitalized on the need among today's busy consumers for quick, convenient shopping by catalog.*

selection of goods, and, most importantly, convenience for busy customers. Catalogs issued by Lands' End, L. L. Bean, and Williams-Sonoma represent only three of the 7,000 mail-order catalogs sent to consumers in America. Catalog sales have been growing during a period when department store sales growth has been sluggish (see Figure 13.4). This is due in part to the increasing number of women in the work force who shop from catalogs to save time.[11] For some mail-order retailers, catalog sales are their only source of revenue. For others, like L. L. Bean, Inc., Cabela's, and Bass Pro Shops, a comparatively small portion of their receipts comes from in-store sales. For the most famous mail-order retailer, Sears, Roebuck and Company, catalog sales now make up only a small (though critical) portion of its revenues.

*Vending Machines*   When a customer inserts the appropriate amount of money, a credit card, or a code into a **vending machine**, an electromechanical device dispenses something. Vending machines offer place utility in locations

**vending machine** an electromechanical device that dispenses items when a customer inserts money, a credit card, or a code

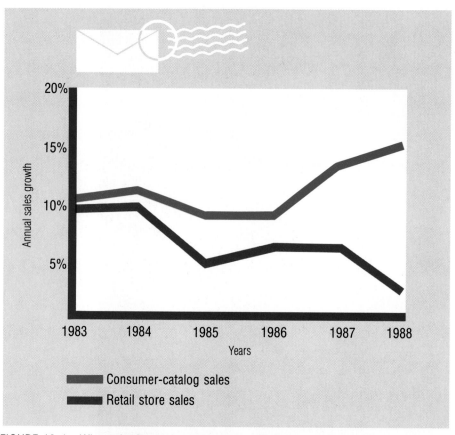

FIGURE 13.4    Where the Retail Sales Are

Source: Adapted and redrawn from Mary Rowland, "How the Busy Go Shopping," *Working Woman*, January, 1989, pp. 47–53. Reprinted with permission from WORKING WOMAN MAGAZINE. Copyright © 1989 by the Working Woman/McCall's Group. Percentages calculated using sales figures provided by Marke/Sroge Communications Chicago, and *Bernard's Retail Marketing Report*, New York.

where it is impractical to operate a retail outlet. They supply soft drinks and snacks. Recently, however, vending machines have come into use also as providers of necessities for travelers, such as toothbrushes, combs, and even airline tickets and banking services, among other things. Though vending machines are expensive to operate and maintain, the vending-machine business is growing, because their convenience makes them profitable.

## The Wheel of Retailing

**wheel of retailing**   a method of describing the evolution of retailing and retailers over time, as new competitors continue to enter the market

One method of describing the evolution of retailing and retailers over time is called the **wheel of retailing** (see Figure 13.5). This concept describes the effect of new competitors' innovations in a retail market.

A new retail entrant gets the wheel moving when it recognizes a void in the market, usually at the low end of the price spectrum. The innovator

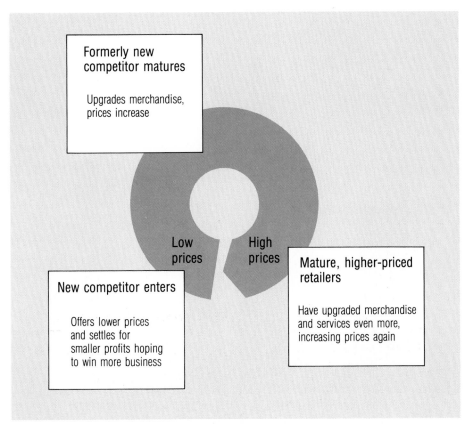

Formerly new competitor matures

Upgrades merchandise, prices increase

Low prices | High prices

New competitor enters

Offers lower prices and settles for smaller profits hoping to win more business

Mature, higher-priced retailers

Have upgraded merchandise and services even more, increasing prices again

FIGURE 13.5   The Wheel of Retailing

challenges the established retailers by offering lower prices, cutting service and ambience, minimizing expenses, and accepting a lower profit margin. As the new competitor matures, however, it upgrades merchandise, adds services, improves the store's appearance, and increases its promotional expenses— all in the quest for still-higher profits. In the end, the former innovator joins the ranks of higher margined, higher priced, mature retailers. Then it in turn becomes vulnerable to innovators filling the low-price void. K mart announced recently that it wants to upgrade the image of its stores and attract shoppers in search of more stylish merchandise. The company plans to upgrade merchandise, store appearance, and advertising.[12] It would appear that K mart is moving into the market served by Sears, Roebuck and Company, J. C. Penney Company, and others (see Figure 13.6).

Supermarkets have moved up the wheel of retailing over the years. When they first appeared, they were usually self-service operations located in buildings with limited aesthetic appeal, like old warehouses. Over time, supermarkets evolved into the typically attractive modern market that offers many services. This progress up the wheel has caused supermarket prices to increase enough to encourage a new form of food retailing, the warehouse store, which offers fewer frills and lower prices.

Another classic example of the wheel of retailing at work is Detroit's vulnerability to low-priced imports, first from Japan and Germany and now

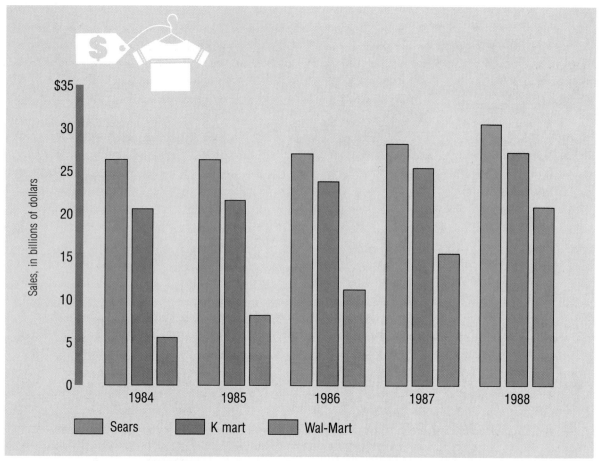

FIGURE 13.6 A Maturing K mart Moves along the Retail Wheel

Source: From Francine Schwadel, "Attention K mart Shoppers: Style Is Coming to This Aisle," *Wall Street Journal,* August 9, 1988, p. 6. Reprinted by permission of *Wall Street Journal,* © Dow Jones & Company, Inc. 1988. All Rights Reserved Worldwide. From Sears Roebuck and Co. annual report, 1988. Used by permission.

from Korea. In fact, the Japanese have largely vacated the low end of the car market in favor of higher-margined models.

# Physical Distribution

*7. Describe the organization of a physical distribution system.*

**physical distribution**
the process of transporting goods, including materials handling, order processing, and inventory control

Try to visualize all the products you bought in the last month. Did you ever ask yourself how they came to be where you bought them? One reason the American quality of life is so high is our ability to bring products from across the nation and around the world into outlets in the most remote parts of the country. This process of moving goods is called **physical distribution.** "Moving goods" brings to mind transportation, a most important part of physical distribution, but there are other critical aspects of physical distribution as well. These steps include materials handling, order processing, and inventory control.

# Transportation

The process of actually moving goods from one location to another is called **transportation**. Note, incidentally, that the transportation of goods and the passage of title to goods are entirely separate concepts. There is no necessary connection between the physical movement of goods and a change in ownership. For instance, a grain dealer may buy 100,000 bushels of wheat stored in an elevator and resell the wheat without moving it.

Before a product reaches its ultimate user or consumer, at each point in the channel of distribution someone must make a decision as to how it will reach the next point. The producer, for instance, must decide how it will reach a wholesaler. Several factors affect the transportation decision, not the least of which is cost. Other factors, however, may outweigh cost alone, such as the recipient's timely need for the goods. It is no coincidence that the U.S. Postal Service leaped into the already crowded overnight-delivery field with its Express Mail service and competed quite effectively on price. The perishability of goods may also dictate particular modes of transportation. Freshly cut tulips from Holland must be flown to Minneapolis because even the fastest boat met by the fastest train could not outrace their deterioration.

*Types of Carriers*  Firms that offer transportation services are called **carriers**. A **private carrier** is a carrier owned and operated by a shipper. For instance, some oil companies operate private carriers to distribute gasoline to service stations. A **common carrier** is a firm that offers transportation services to the public. Allied Van Lines is a common carrier. A **freight forwarder** is a common carrier that will often lease space from other carriers and combine small individual shipments into economical lot sizes. Emery Worldwide is a freight forwarder. A **contract carrier** provides service to one shipper or a limited number of shippers. Carriers provide transportation in all the categories compared and listed in Table 13.2.

*Railroads*  Railroads carry more total freight than any other transportation mode. For many large or bulky products, rail transport is the least expensive option that meets minimum speed requirements. Railroads do not reach all areas, however, nor are they generally able to move goods door to door.

**transportation** the process of actually moving goods from one location to another

*8. Identify the principal modes of transportation for goods and discuss their advantages and disadvantages.*

**carrier** a firm that offers transportation services

**private carrier** a carrier owned and operated by a shipper

**common carrier** a firm that offers transportation services to the public

**freight forwarder** a common carrier that will often lease space from other carriers and combine small individual shipments into economical lot sizes

**contract carrier** a carrier that provides service to one shipper or a limited number of shippers

TABLE 13.2  Comparing Modes of Transportation

|  | Rail | Truck | Water | Air | Pipeline |
|---|---|---|---|---|---|
| Speed | fair | good | poor | best | worst |
| Cost | moderate | high | low | highest | lowest |
| Locations served | many | most | few | moderate | fewest |
| On-time dependability | fair | good | poor | worst | best |
| Frequency | low | high | lowest | fair | highest |

Source: Adapted with permission of Macmillan Publishing Company from *Logistical Management* by Donald J. Bowersox. Copyright © 1978 by Donald J. Bowersox.

*Trucks*   Virtually no product escapes being transported by truck at some stage. Often goods are shipped by rail to a central distribution point, then by truck to retailers or smaller distribution centers. In the 1950s, innovative railroaders came up with the idea of "piggyback" service. Loaded trailers were placed on modified flat cars for shipment to central distribution facilities. There they were offloaded, hooked to tractors, and pulled to retailers or other end users. Piggybacking combined the energy efficiency and lower costs of rail transport with the convenience of truck delivery.

*Water*   Barges and cargo ships are the least expensive means of transporting goods. Their disadvantage is their relative slowness. Water transport is ideally suited for bulky nonperishable goods like iron ore, coal, grain, and motor vehicles. Barges and ships can also offer piggyback service connecting with road or rail transport.

*Air*   Air transport is the fastest and most expensive means of transporting goods. For that reason, air carriers typically transport only items of high value or goods that are highly perishable or are needed immediately. The General Motors Corporation is flying the bodies for its $50,000 Cadillac Allante from Turin, Italy, to Detroit at a cost of $2,500 to $2,800 per car. The time that would be lost and the capital tied up during the month it would take GM to transport the bodies by boat justifies this expense for them.[13] It is possible that with all the entrants into this field—from United Parcel Service to Purolator Courier Corporation to Federal Express, Inc.— air prices will decline, but not to the level of trucks.

*Pipelines*   Pipelines can carry only certain types of products, like natural gas and oil. They have very high fixed costs but low variable costs. In other words, they cost a lot to build but not a lot to maintain and operate. When they are in heavy use, their total cost per measure moved can be quite low.

## Warehousing

**warehousing**   the set of activities designed to ensure that goods are available when they are needed

*9. Explain the difference between a public warehouse and a private warehouse.*

The set of activities designed to ensure that goods are available when they are needed is known as **warehousing**. This process is not simply one of storing goods in a building called a warehouse. Among the activities of warehousing are:

- Receiving the goods
- Identifying the goods
- Sorting the goods
- Holding the goods
- Assembling shipments
- Dispatching shipments

**warehouse receipt**   the record that a public warehouseman gives a person who is storing goods

Each of these activities requires recordkeeping so that the goods are always easily retrievable. Recordkeeping is also important because goods are often sold or used as security for a loan by transferring the **warehouse receipt**, the record that a public warehouseman gives a person who is storing goods. A

Consolidation for efficiency   *Under a new, more efficient system, GC Electronics and Thorsen share a distribution center where warehousing, shipping, and distribution functions have been consolidated for the two companies. The companies, which are divisions of the Household International Corporation, formerly carried out the distribution process separately.*

public warehouse is a storage building that can be used by the general public to store goods for a fee. A **private warehouse** is one owned by a firm that has sole access to it. Maintaining a private warehouse can be expensive, especially if the firm does not use all the space.

## Materials Handling

The physical handling of items during transportation and warehousing is called **materials handling**. Efficient, effective materials handling is critically important to any business selling goods because of its potential effects on customer satisfaction and on costs from breakage or spoilage. Almost everyone has at some time bought a product that proved to be damaged when its carton was opened. Quite often, such damage results from the misuse or careless use of materials-handling devices, like forklifts. One way to reduce the likelihood of damage to goods is to minimize the number of times a product is handled. Good warehouse organization can help do this. Putting smaller units together to form a larger load—say, a pallet load or a truckload—also keeps handling to a minimum.

**public warehouse**  a storage building that can be used by the general public to store goods for a fee

**private warehouse**  a warehouse owned by a firm that has sole access to it

**materials handling**  the physical handling of items during transportation and warehousing

Fast food order processing   *New York's Second Avenue Deli relies on a fax machine for receiving orders from its customers. The Deli can process more orders more quickly this way, and customers can place orders quickly without leaving the office.*

## Order Processing

**order processing** the receiving and filling of customers' orders

The physical distribution activity known as **order processing** has as its purpose the receiving and filling of customers' orders. Fast, accurate order processing can be a major advantage for a firm. Regardless of whether they are intermediaries of some sort or end users or consumers, customers want their orders filled quickly and without errors.

## Inventory Control

**inventory control** a system that develops and maintains levels and assortments of products appropriate for a firm's target markets

The purpose of **inventory control** is to develop and maintain levels and assortments of products appropriate for a firm's target markets. If a firm holds too many items in inventory, it will have unduly high overhead costs. On the other hand, if the firm carries too low an inventory, it risks running out of certain merchandise and losing sales. Inventory control's goal is to balance these risks. Wal-Mart has developed a highly sophisticated inventory

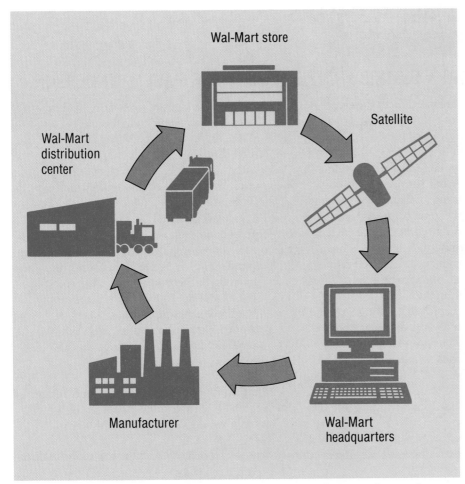

Wal-Mart store

Satellite

Wal-Mart distribution center

Manufacturer

Wal-Mart headquarters

FIGURE 13.7   Wal-Mart's Sophisticated Computer-Communications System for Broadcasting Information and Tracking Distribution

Source: John Huey, "Wal-Mart—Will It Take over the World?" *Fortune,* January 30, 1989, pp. 54–55. Based on material that originally appeared in *Fortune* magazine. Adapted with permission.

control system that minimizes out-of-stock conditions at local stores. An order from a store travels via the company's six-channel satellite system to a computer at Wal-Mart headquarters, where the order is forwarded to the manufacturer. The manufacturer ships the order to one of Wal-Mart's distribution centers and a delivery is made to the store 36 hours after the initial order was placed (see Figure 13.7).[14]

The advent of the inexpensive microcomputer has given firms almost total control over their inventories, if they choose to take advantage of the technology. The computer can tell them both how much they have in inventory and how much it is costing to carry it. Even the best computer equipment, however, cannot make up for incorrect data entry, shoplifting, and employee theft. It can help find out what happened more easily and enable the firm to act to halt the losses (see Experiencing Business).

## CHOOSING A DISTRIBUTION STRATEGY FOR PAULA HENDERSON

When Paula Henderson graduated from college she went to work for her father, owner of Henderson Woodworking Inc., a Vermont firm that was established in 1938. Henderson Woodworking manufactures fine reproductions of early American furniture. Although Paula enjoyed building and finishing furniture, she wanted to apply some of the marketing concepts she had acquired in college. A few months after returning to her father's business she developed a product that she felt had great sales potential. She designed four different wooden kitchen utensils that would appeal to people who enjoyed cooking. After experimenting with several different production methods, she determined that it cost $1.00 to produce each wooden utensil. The utensils would be sold as a four-item set for $7.00 to $8.00, depending on the costs of distribution. Paula identified five possible distribution strategies:

1. Sell her product at craft fairs held in various New England states.
2. Place an ad in selected magazines and solicit direct mail or telephone orders.
3. Attempt to have the product featured in an established mail-order catalog such as Williams-Sonoma, which has developed a catalog for cooks.
4. Approach one of the nation's large wholesale food companies such as Fleming Companies, Inc. or Super Valu Stores, Inc., and encourage them to feature the product in their catalog. These wholesalers supply hundreds of large supermarkets.
5. Approach a large retailer such as K mart or Wal-Mart and encourage them to feature this product in their stores.

What are the advantages and disadvantages of each of these distribution strategies? Which strategy would you recommend to Paula?

# Distribution: A Perspective

Talking to some people about inventory control or methods of transporting goods makes their eyes glaze over. "Dull stuff! When it gets to be a problem, then I'll think about it." In the last ten years, however, the physical distribution of goods has become a hot topic not just among penny-conscious managers but also among aggressive entrepreneurs.

**just-in-time inventory system** a program designed to ensure a continuous flow of manufacturing input from suppliers while at the same time minimizing the amount of goods held in inventory

Manufacturers, particularly in the auto industry, have noted the benefits that Japanese producers have reaped from **just-in-time inventory systems,** programs designed to ensure a continuous flow of manufacturing input from suppliers while at the same time minimizing the amount of goods held in inventory. Just-in-time systems, as discussed in Chapter 10, rely on sophisticated warehousing, materials handling, order processing, and inventory control at both ends of the industrial channels of distribution.

Just-in-time inventory systems require fast, reliable transportation systems. The everyday requirements of many businesses in our fast-paced world place demands on our transportation systems that were inconceivable fifteen years ago. Only a few insightful people like Federal Express's Fred Smith foresaw those demands. Following three years in the Marines and after developing a highly successful airplane brokerage business, Smith launched Federal Express at the age of twenty-eight.[15] Today it is hard to imagine our transportation system without Federal Express and its many competitors.

When products are in transit or in storage, time is certainly money. More than one historian has attributed our economic system's success to our willingness to innovate in transportation. With space shuttles, new generations of jet aircraft, innovative approaches to material handling, a reinvigorated rail system, and thousands of less obvious innovations, we are in the midst of another distribution revolution. Its end is not yet in sight.

# CHAPTER HIGHLIGHTS

*1.* Define the term marketing intermediaries.

*Marketing intermediaries* are firms between the producer and the ultimate user or consumer that take title or directly assist others to take title to goods or that assist in physically moving or storing goods. These are commonly wholesalers, agents or brokers, distributors, or retailers and any firms that handle the physical distribution of products.

*2.* Describe the basic channels of distribution for consumer and industrial products.

Consumer products use one of three channels (see Figure 13.1): (1) producer to consumer, (2) producer to retailer to consumer, or (3) producer to wholesaler to retailer to consumer. Industrial producers can choose from many different channels of distribution. Two of the most common are producer to industrial user and producer to distributor to industrial user.

*3.* Distinguish among intensive, selective, and exclusive distribution strategies.

*Intensive distribution* is a strategy that attempts to place a product in all available retail outlets.

With *selective distribution*, a moderate proportion of retail outlets carry a particular product in a given market. Some producers use *exclusive distribution*, in which a single retailer carries the product in a given retail area.

*4.* List the two main types of wholesalers and identify their functions.

*Full-service merchant wholesalers* take title to goods and offer the largest variety of services. *Limited-service merchant wholesalers* take title to goods but offer fewer services; they tend, however, to specialize in the services they do offer. Agents and brokers receive a commission for bringing together buyers and sellers; they do not take title to goods. These intermediaries help to move products more efficiently through the distribution channel.

*5.* Specify the services wholesalers provide to producers and retailers.

Wholesalers commonly provide the following services to retailers: buying, promoting products, gathering and interpreting market information, extending credit, and maintaining inventory.

**6.** *List the main types of retailers and identify their functions.*

*In-store retailers* include department, discount, and specialty stores; catalog showrooms; variety stores; supermarkets; superstores and hypermarkets; warehouse clubs; warehouse stores; and convenience stores. *Nonstore retailers* include in-home retailers, mail-order retailers, and vending machines.

**7.** *Describe the organization of a physical distribution system.*

Physical distribution involves transportation (the physical movement of goods), warehousing (including receiving, identifying, sorting, and holding goods, and assembling and dispatching shipments), materials handling (the physical handling of items during transportation and warehousing), order processing (the activities connected with receiving and filling customers' orders), and inventory control (the procedures necessary to develop and maintain desired levels and assortments of products for a firm's target markets).

**8.** *Identify the principal modes of transportation for goods and discuss their advantages and disadvantages.*

Of the five principal modes of transportation for goods, *railroads* are often the least expensive, but they may not be available for a given location and can only rarely provide door-to-door service. *Trucks* are moderately inexpensive, moderately fast, and offer high accessibility. They are often piggybacked on trains to combine the efficiency and low cost of rail with the convenience of trucks. *Cargo ships* or *barges* are the least expensive mode of transportation, but they are quite slow. *Air transport* is generally the fastest and most expensive way to transport goods. *Pipelines* are expensive to build and can carry only certain types of products but are inexpensive to operate.

**9.** *Explain the difference between a public warehouse and a private warehouse.*

A *public warehouse* can be used by the general public to store goods for a fee. A *private warehouse* is owned and maintained by a specific firm for its own use.

# KEY TERMS

Channels of distribution (marketing channels, distribution channels)
Marketing intermediary (middleman)
Merchant
Title
Agent (broker)
Retailer
Wholesaler
Vertical-channel integration
Corporate vertical-marketing system
Administered vertical-marketing system

Market coverage
Intensive distribution strategy
Selective distribution strategy
Exclusive distribution strategy
Atmospherics
Full-service wholesaler
Limited-service wholesaler
Trade credit
Independent retailer
Chain store
Department store
Discount store

Specialty store
Catalog showroom
Variety store
Warehouse club
Warehouse store
Supermarket
Superstore
Hypermarket
Convenience store
Nonstore retailer
In-home retailer
Mail-order retailer
Vending machine
Wheel of retailing
Physical distribution
Transportation

Carrier
Private carrier
Common carrier
Freight forwarder
Contract carrier
Warehousing
Warehouse receipt
Public warehouse
Private warehouse
Materials handling
Order processing
Inventory control
Just-in-time inventory system

# REVIEW QUESTIONS

1. Provide an overview of the channels of distribution.
2. List, then discuss, the three basic degrees of market coverage.
3. Describe the four basic consumer channels of distribution.
4. Identify two of the most common industrial channels of distribution and define their functions.
5. How do consumer channels differ from industrial channels?
6. What roles do marketing intermediaries play?
7. List the services that wholesalers provide to producers and retailers.
8. Describe the "wheel of retailing" concept.
9. What are the principal types of in-store retailers and how are they different from each other?
10. Specify the major types of nonstore retailing.
11. What factors have contributed to the increased popularity of mail-order retailers?
12. Describe the role of physical distribution in the marketing process.

# APPLICATION EXERCISES

1. During a recent vacation in Ireland you became acquainted with a line of very high-quality Irish sweaters for men and women. At the present time these products are not available to consumers in America. Describe at least three channels of distribution that might be used to direct these products to consumers. Which channel do you feel would be most effective?

2. Identify at least two wholesale firms that provide services to retailers in your community. What services to producers do these firms provide? What services to retailers do they provide? In your opinion, are these wholesalers fulfilling an important marketing function?

# CASES

## 13.1  Shopping by Mail

Not too many years ago, a direct-mail catalog was a book from which farmers ordered bib overalls. The book itself was like a huge, mid-range department store. Item after item was logically organized and methodically displayed.

Times have changed. There are still catalogs from which people living in remote areas order generic merchandise, but today's catalogs tend to appeal to affluent city-dwellers with little time to shop. The new breed of catalog is both more visually appealing and more specialized.

The catalog for Lands' End, a Wisconsin-based sports-clothing retailer, bears a strong resemblance to a magazine. Each monthly issue has a different cover and a volume and number. The catalog carries a table of contents and features about people and places connected with the operation. The Sharper Image, a San Francisco company specializing in electronic gadgets, prints customer letters in its catalog. The catalog also contains advertisements for products it does not sell.

The biggest of the big have entered the mail-order business. You may now receive a catalog from IBM or General Mills. But small firms have also gone into direct mail. Barbara Burt needed just $25,000 to establish Telltales, which sells children's books, in her garage. According to Stanley J. Fenvessy, an industry analyst, "A small mom-and-pop can make it, if it develops merchandise character, targets it properly and runs the company efficiently."

One key to success seems to lie in personalization. Call Lands' End about the fit of a particular garment and the operator can give you all the measurements for each size. Omaha Steaks' operators, who have tested everything the company sells, are trained to help customers purchase the right amount of the right meat for their parties. There are companies that feature rapid delivery and companies that offer free pick up of items you wish to return.

At a time when retail stores are suffering from declining sales, the direct-mail business is booming. During the 1980s, the number of companies producing mail-order catalogs has grown 75 percent to 7,000.

## Questions

1. What are some of the reasons that the number of mail-order companies has increased in recent years?
2. What kind of specialized catalogs might be put out by L. L. Bean, which sells outdoor wear?
3. Why do you think so many affluent city people shop by mail?

Sources: For more information see *Piedmont Airlines*, August, 1986, pp. 34–37; *Working Woman*, January, 1989, pp. 47–53; and *Fortune*, March 13, 1989, pp. 44–45.

## 13.2 Little Frookies and Giant Cookies

A researcher measures roundness and coefficient of friction on a sophisticated piece of equipment called an image analyzer. From the care with which he works you might think he is examin-ing a space-shuttle O-ring or a high-performance-car engine piston. In fact, the object of his attention is an Oreo cookie.

Such is the sophistication of the $4 billion-a-year cookie business. RJR Nabisco, which makes Oreos, controls over 30 percent of the market and spends in the neighborhood of $50 million a year on advertising. Keebler, with a 14 percent market share, spends approximately $12 million. Though Keebler's marketing symbols are elves, the players in this business are giants.

Can someone of more normal stature—a young entrepreneur, for example, armed with a good product, unbounded optimism, and a half million dollars (but no image analyzer)—succeed in such a cookie world? Judging from the case of Richard S. Worth, creator of the R. W. Frookie ("The Good For You Cookie"), the answer is yes—up to a point.

By all accounts Worth got his small, undercapitalized company off to a flying start. In his first year he had close to a million dollars in sales. By year five, R. W. Frookie had a net before-tax profit of nearly a million-and-a-half dollars. How did Worth manage to build his company up so fast? Why do experts feel he is unlikely to continue growing at the same rate? Both questions have the same answer: Distribution.

To get started, Worth sold equity in his company—at bargain-basement prices—to 20 distributors. Says Worth: " A distributor may handle 500 to 1,000 products, but if he's a share-holder you become one of the products he really devotes his time to." Says Bob Schmitt of Shur-Good Biscuit Co., a distributorship that holds nearly 2 percent of R. W. Frookies stock: "This is the most incredible product I have ever seen."

In terms of growth, however, Worth may not have hit upon the most incredible distribution strategy. "What happens if a distributor in a key marketplace falls flat on his face—yet he's a shareholder?" asks Bill Mulligan, a Cleveland-based venture capitalist. And even if Worth's distribution strategy is a good idea, adds consultant Cathy Orr, it is not one he can continue to employ. "There are too many distributors. In Los Angeles alone there are at least four or five that Worth would need."

Even with adequate financing, national distribution is a difficult proposition. Supermarkets argue that success in one region is no guarantee of success in another. They usually demand "slotting allowances" for handling new products, in order to protect themselves against those items that occupy valuable shelf space but do not sell. (See Chapter 12.) Often supermarkets require expensive promotions as a condition of accepting a new product.

## Questions

1. Worth has won over Kroger, a nationwide supermarket chain. Has this solved his problem of coast-to-coast distribution? Why or why not?
2. RJR Nabisco controls 37 percent of the supermarket shelf space and may introduce 5 new products in a month. How does this affect a small company like R. W. Frookie?

Sources: For more information see *Marketing & Media Decisions,* June, 1988, pp. 123–134; *Fortune,* July 18, 1988, pp. 32–46; *Inc.,* December, 1988, p. 24; and *Inc.,* February, 1989, pp. 55–59.

# 14 Promotion Strategy

## LEARNING OBJECTIVES

After you have completed this chapter, you will be able to do the following:

*1.* Define promotion *and* describe common promotional objectives.

*2.* Identify two major promotional strategies.

*3.* List the elements of the promotional mix.

*4.* Define advertising *and* identify the three principal types of advertising.

*5.* Weigh the advantages and disadvantages of the principal advertising media.

*6.* List the six steps in the selling process.

*7.* Describe the four major employment settings in the field of personal selling.

*8.* Define sales promotion *and* identify the principal means involved.

*9.* Distinguish between publicity and public relations.

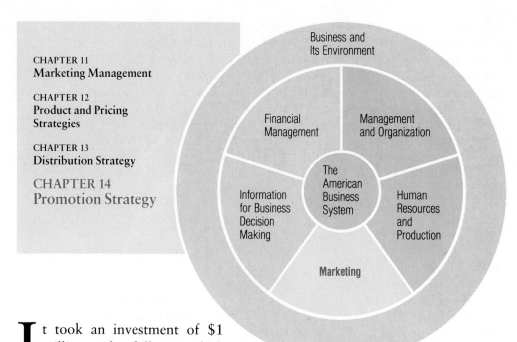

I t took an investment of $1 million and a full year of planning for Peugeot to set the stage for victory at the challenging Pikes Peak Auto Hill Climb. Why did the French auto maker invest so much time and money in a race that lasts about 10 minutes? The reason, according to company officials, was to promote the image of the new Peugeot 405 automobile in America. The French auto manufacturer has discovered that racing competition enhances the image of their cars at home and abroad. Peugeot wants to be perceived as a company on the cutting edge of advanced automobile technology.[1]

# The Nature of Promotion

**promotion** the communications that an organization uses to inform, persuade, or remind a target market about its products, its services, or itself

For most consumers, promotion is the most visible of marketing's Four P's: price, product, place, and promotion. **Promotion** describes the communications that an organization uses to inform, persuade, or remind a target market about its products, its services, or itself.

## Promotion Objectives

*1. Define* promotion *and describe common promotional objectives.*

Businesses use promotion not just to increase sales but also to manage sales. They use promotion to increase sales of specific products, increase sales at a given time, or even decrease sales or demand temporarily. Promotion can also be used to shape the image of a business. Peugeot hopes that the win at Pikes Peak will enhance the image of its automobiles.

Some firms may want to build up sales of a new product or of an established one that is generating high profits. Some companies design their promotional strategies to increase a product's market share, whereas others use promotion to differentiate their product by establishing its market niche. Another firm may hope to increase sales of its products at off-peak periods. For instance, big city hotels may advertise sharply reduced rates for weekend tourists to fill the rooms that business travelers demand during the week. And turkey breeders have successfully extended the demand for what was once only holiday fare. Today supermarkets carry turkeys all year round. Finally, when manufacturers cannot meet the demand for a new product, they should use promotion to maintain customer good will. The computer industry has frequently used this strategy when long-promised machines or software are late.

## Promotion Strategies

Effective promotion requires careful planning. In most larger corporations, the marketing manager or the advertising manager oversees and coordinates promotional activities. Promotional planning begins with the need to make a choice between two distinct promotional strategies: push or pull (see Figure 14.1).

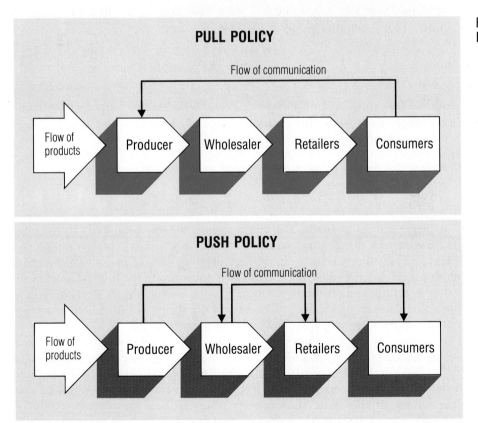

FIGURE 14.1 Push-Pull Strategies

**Push strategy** *Distributor Tom Protheroe is glad the creators of Smartfood pushed him to carry their product; its enormous popularity has changed his business. The push strategy involves directing promotional effort at the next intermediary in the channel of distribution between manufacturer and end consumer.*

**push strategy** promotion strategy that involves selling goods or services directly to the next intermediary in the channel of distribution

*2. Identify two major promotional strategies.*

A **push strategy** is directed at selling goods or services directly to the next intermediary in the channel of distribution, which we discussed in the last chapter. The success of a push strategy depends largely on the effectiveness of an organization's sales force. It is often appropriate for low-volume, high-value items like mainframe computers or construction equipment where buyers tend to rely on salespeople to answer questions and suggest appropriate options. It can also work for low-value consumer goods.

Frito-Lay, Inc., relies on a push strategy. This snack-food manufacturer's whole organization is committed to providing the best possible support to its 10,000-person sales force, who in turn make over 400,000 sales calls to retail accounts per week. To achieve this goal, Frito-Lay does things that lose money in the short run to keep stores stocked with fresh products. Sending a truck to restock a store with a few $30 cartons of potato chips can cost several hundred dollars. Braving extraordinary weather to deliver a box of potato chips or helping a store owner clean up after a hurricane, as Frito-Lay sales representatives have done, do not pay an immediate return, either. Store owners remember this dedication to service, however, which may explain how Frito-Lay has captured 70 percent of the potato chip, tortilla chip, and corn chip market in some parts of the country.[2]

The other approach, the **pull strategy**, promotes a product or service directly to the consumer, primarily through advertising or sales promotion. A pull strategy is most effective with high-volume, low-value products like laundry soap or chewing gum. When the Procter & Gamble Company developed its improved Crest toothpaste, it promoted the new product by sending sample tubes to consumers across the country. Procter & Gamble's objective was to encourage the ultimate consumers to ask their retailers for the new product. The retailer might be a Kroger supermarket or a K mart store. Both of these retailers would then turn to the next intermediary up the distribution channel, which, in both these cases, would be the company-owned distribution center. In another market, the recording industry uses videos developed for television to stimulate consumer demand from retailers. They order records and tapes from wholesalers, who in turn order them from the record companies.

**pull strategy** strategy that promotes a product or service directly to the consumer

The push and pull strategies are, of course, not mutually exclusive, and firms often use both at the same time. For example, Pella Windows & Doors, which manufactures a high-quality product, has developed a strong distribution network of home-center stores, lumberyards, and other businesses catering to builders and home owners. At the same time, it advertises in magazines like *Southern Living, Architectural Digest,* and *McCall's* to build interest among ultimate consumers.

## The Promotional Mix

Promotional activities fall into four categories:

*3.* List the elements of the promotional mix.

- Advertising
- Personal selling
- Sales promotion
- Publicity and public relations

The way a firm combines these elements in its promotion strategy is called its **promotional mix** (see Figure 14.2). We will examine each element in the following sections.

**promotional mix** the way a firm combines advertising, personal selling, sales promotion, and publicity and public relations in its promotion strategy

# Advertising

The American Marketing Association (AMA) defines **advertising** as "any paid form of nonpersonal presentation and promotion of ideas, goods, or services by an identified sponsor."[3] The AMA used *nonpersonal* in this context so that the term *advertising* would not include the face-to-face contact

**advertising** nonpersonal promotion of ideas, goods, or services paid for by an identified sponsor

FIGURE 14.2   The
Promotional Mix

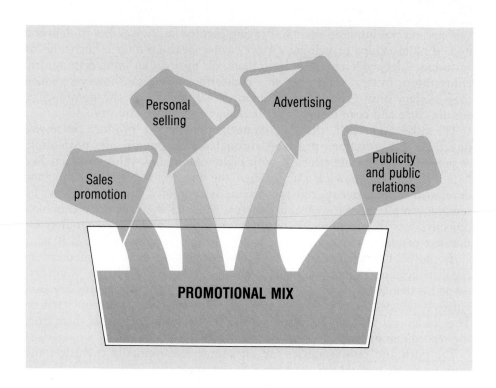

that characterizes personal selling. The word *paid* similarly excludes publicity, which is not bought.

## Advertising Objectives

In their planning processes, businesses must decide what they want their advertising campaigns to accomplish. One objective might be to provide the consumer with product information. **Informative advertising**, which performs this function, is generally used to build demand for new products or to let consumers know about improvements to mature products. When Ford launched the Taurus SHO (Super High Output), it had to promote a totally new car. Informative advertisements describe the car's ground-effect body-work, suspension, and the new 24-valve, 4-cam engine to help consumers distinguish this new product from its competitors.

Another objective in an advertising campaign may be to persuade the customer to take some action. Firms use **persuasive advertising** to influence the target market's beliefs, attitudes, or behavior. Almost all sale ads on television or in newspapers are designed to persuade. Another objective of promotion may be to remind the target market about something. **Reminder or reinforcement advertising** does just that. The "thank you for not smoking" campaigns deliberately recall past persuasive antismoking campaigns because most people, smokers and nonsmokers alike, are convinced of tobacco's dangers. Reinforcement advertising is also used to reassure consumers about choices they have already made (see Business Issues).[4]

**informative advertising**
a form of advertising that provides the consumer with product information

**persuasive advertising**
advertising that firms use to influence the target market's beliefs, attitudes, or behavior

**reminder (reinforcement) advertising** advertising that seeks to remind the target market about something

Smart.

"It's the finest pocket color TV we've tested... this set will give you a clear, sharp picture with remarkably good color."
—Video Review, March 1988

Why does the Magnavox 3" LCD Color TV deserve such rave reviews? See for yourself. Watch it anywhere, anytime. Even outdoors. The picture stays sharp. And bright. With rich, true color.

How? With the most individual picture elements in the world. Over 92,000. (But who's counting?) What's more, Magnavox added a new slant on pocket TVs, with an adjustable screen angle for better viewing.

Magnavox has always made big advances in TV technology. But putting them all into one little package, now that's pretty smart.

**MAGNAVOX**

Advertising techniques   *Magnavox is using an informational approach with this ad, by quoting a review, and with a description of the product's features. Rather than a whimsical gadget, the 3-inch TV shown here is being advertised as a "smart" sensible product to own.*

## Types of Advertising

Advertising can be classified into three broad categories:

- Selective or brand advertising
- Primary demand or generic advertising
- Institutional advertising

*4. Define advertising and identify the three principal types of advertising.*

*Selective or Brand Advertising*   The most common type of advertising is **selective** or **brand advertising**, promotion designed to encourage a consumer to buy a certain brand of product and thereby build customer patronage. The largest share of all the money spent on advertising goes to convince consumers to buy one brand—Pirelli tires or Bose speakers or Post Natural Raisin Bran, or some other brand—instead of its competitors. Some brand names have worldwide recognition. A survey to identify the best-known

**selective (brand) advertising** promotion designed to encourage a consumer to buy a certain brand of product and thereby build customer patronage

## SELLING CARS

Audi identifies its cars with heroic and free-spirited athleticism. The company has sponsored the United States Pro Ski Tour as well as rowing and sailing events. In a recent Seattle-area yacht race, the sail of a local dealers' craft sported a huge Audi logo. Will such a campaign heal a company badly wounded by past charges of cars accelerating suddenly and without warning?

Buick hired an award-winning director and a special-effects person from the movie *Star Wars* to create a commercial showing its Reatta model bursting out of a ring of fire onto a roadway. The GM division spent half a million dollars for two 30-second spots proclaiming, "The great American road belongs to Buick." Will a striking commercial help a car with a limited promotional budget compete for attention with budget-rich Chevrolet?

Jay Qualman, Buick's general director of advertising, says it will. "Each American is exposed to 1,400 commercial messages every day—that's television, print, and everything, including matchbooks, skywriting, and blimps. So we have to work hard to break through the clutter."

Marketing consultant Jay Abraham and his partner Wil Beach, however, question whether anyone knows the effect on sales of the Buick blasting out of a ring of fire or the Audi logo billowing across a sail. The issue is not academic. The automotive industry spends over a billion dollars each year.

Abraham and Beach believe companies can know exactly what they are getting for their promotional money, by using direct-response advertising. This way the company knows the number of people it's reaching because it is advertising in ways it can measure.

Abraham and Beach would not be impressed by Buick's flashy image work. "Without exception," says Abraham, "humorous, abstract, or circuitous ads or commercials are a waste." They favor "telegraphing" the benefits of the product to the potential customer.

Meanwhile, Oldsmobile promotes celebrities and their children. Chevrolet hires Aretha Franklin to sing its jingle. Hyundai gives away cars to fast-food consumers. And tiny Yugo buys the right to be official car of the U.S. men's and women's volleyball teams.

Referring to a commercial in which a red Audi 5000CS Turbo Quattro in European trim drove up a 70-meter snow-covered ski jump, that company's dealer publication bragged that the TV spot took "Audi's quest of 'pushing the limits of conformity' one better—by *defying* the limits." But did it sell cars?

Sources: Matt DeLorenzo, "Avoiding the '10 Biggest Marketing Mistakes,' " *Automotive News,* May 12, 1986, p. 26; Stephen E. Plumb, "Ad Theme: Customer Satisfaction," *Ward's Auto World,* October, 1988, pp. 61–67; "Sixty Seconds," *Automobile,* November, 1988, p. 20; "Uphill Racer," *The Spirit of Audi,* 1986, pp. 12–13; "Audi Readies Sports Activities for 1988–89" and "Seattle Dealers Hit the Big Time on Whidbey," *The Spirit,* September, 1988, p. 6.

brand names in the world found Coca-Cola and IBM at the top of the list. The next three best-known brands, in order, were Sony, Porsche, and McDonald's.[5]

For major marketers, like the McDonald's Corporation, advertising's cost effectiveness makes it an excellent way to tell people about its new products, like the McD.L.T., and to rekindle interest in Quarter Pounders and Mc-Nuggets. H & R Block, Inc., advertises its services on national television during the first four months of each year when people are focusing on their income-tax returns. Although H & R Block spends millions on advertising, its cost per person reached is actually quite low. Figure 14.3 charts the estimated annual amount of money spent on advertising in the U.S.

FIGURE 14.3 Estimated Annual U.S. Advertising Expenditures, 1977–1988

Source: Adapted from a graph prepared for *Advertising Age* by Robert J. Coen (ed.), McCann-Erickson. Reprinted with permission from Advertising Age. Copyright, Crain Communications Inc., 1988.

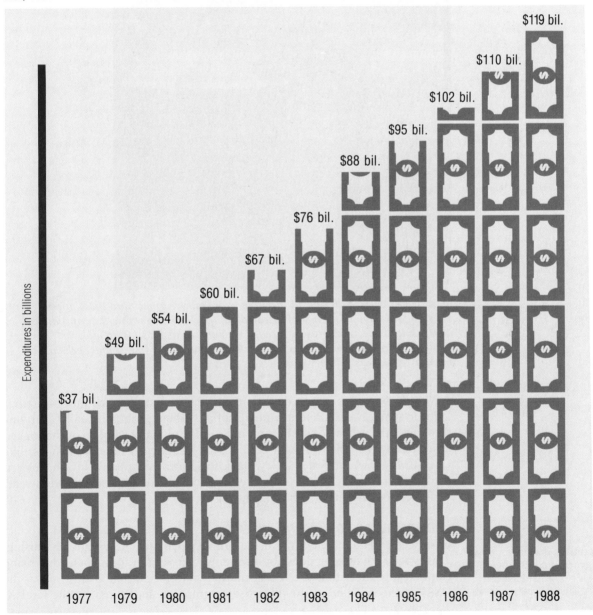

**Nouvelle calcium** *With this ad the American Dairy Farmers and the National Dairy Board have taken a sophisticated approach to promoting dairy products, advertising them as sources for needed calcium, as well as fashionable or "nouvelle" foods. The ad does not focus on a particular brand, but seeks to interest consumers in dairy products as a whole.*

Many companies have found that turning their trademark into a familiar logo or symbol can make it a powerful advertising tool. Virtually everyone recognizes the yellow-on-red Eastman Kodak Company emblem or the cocked arm holding a mallet on Arm & Hammer products. Some companies, like Coca-Cola U.S.A. and the Harley-Davidson Motor Company, Inc., have even made a lucrative sideline out of licensing their logos for use on sportswear, boots, boats, and many other products.[6]

*Primary Demand or Generic Advertising* The total demand for a product or service can be increased by using **primary-demand** or **generic advertising**. This type of advertising does not distinguish between brands. Such advertising can help products that are losing market share. "Crafted with pride in the USA" is the key line in the advertising campaign sponsored by the Crafted

**primary-demand (generic) advertising** type of advertising that does not distinguish between brands

with Pride in the U.S.A. Council, which is made up of American apparel and textile manufacturers.[7]

When consumers began to buy less beef in response to reports indicating that red meat was unhealthful, the Beef Industry Council responded with a $10-million campaign. Television and print ads emphasized that beef is now leaner and thus contains less cholesterol and fewer calories. The council supplied stores with charts to be placed next to their meat counters comparing the calories and cholesterol levels of various meat products.[8]

*Institutional Advertising*   Firms use **institutional advertising** to generate good will or enhance their image rather than to sell a specific product. Such advertising often promotes an idea or philosophy.

For more than a decade, the Mobil Oil Company has offered its political views in advertisements in leading newspapers. Mobil recognized that a great advantage of advertising is its ability to reach a large target market quickly, something that is most important to firms that market throughout the nation. The R. J. Reynolds Tobacco Company, one of the leading cigarette manufacturers, initiated a campaign to encourage everyone to "lower their voices" about smoking in public places. In the face of antismoking campaigns initiated in both the public and the private sectors, Reynolds emphasized the rights of smokers.

**institutional advertising** advertising used to generate good will or enhance a firm's image rather than for selling a specific product

## Advertising Media

Procter & Gamble, one of the nation's largest advertisers, and your local hardware store have at least one thing in common: they must decide what advertising medium to use. **Advertising media** are the means of communication used by major advertisers, including magazines, newspapers, direct mail, radio, television, and outdoor advertising. Table 14.1 compares the advantages and disadvantages involved in using these various media.

**advertising media** the means of communication used by major advertisers, including magazines, newspapers, direct mail, radio, television, and outdoor advertising

*5. Weigh the advantages and disadvantages of the principal advertising media.*

*Magazines*   Using magazines, advertisers can reach either a national audience through, say, *People* or *Time* or a specialized audience through trade magazines like *Beverage World* or *Supermarket Business*. Unlike newspapers, magazines may remain around the home or in a doctor's waiting room for months. They are thus more likely to be read and reread than are newspapers. Their high-quality reproduction of photographs and art gives them a notable advantage over newspapers. Advertisers can target markets not only by choosing the type of magazine in which they advertise but also by picking the regional or demographic editions of major publications. *Time* has 220 editions, including one that reaches 550,000 persons affiliated with educational institutions, a business edition reaching 1.6 million, and 115 test-market editions.

Magazines have some major disadvantages as an advertising medium. Because magazines often require copy several weeks in advance, they lack time flexibility. Preparing the copy also takes considerable time and is quite expensive. Small retail and service businesses usually find magazine advertising beyond their reach (see Experiencing Business).

TABLE 14.1    The Advantages and Disadvantages of the Major Media

| Medium | Advantages | Disadvantages |
|---|---|---|
| Magazines | Selectivity; long life; good reproduction of pictures and art | Lack of flexibility; long lead time; cost |
| Newspapers | Wide readership; preferred positioning; flexibility | "Lost" ads; poor reproduction of photos and color; brief ad life |
| Direct mail | Selectivity | Difficulty of maintaining lists; expensive |
| Radio | Selectivity; flexibility | Ads not available for later examination; limited only to hearing |
| Television | Vast audience; appeals to both sight and hearing; flexibility | Cost; clutter; control lost to videocassette recorders |
| Outdoor advertising | Visibility; reinforcement value | Brevity of messages; unpopularity of medium |

*Newspapers*    Newspaper advertising attracts approximately 27 percent of all advertising dollars and is the most popular advertising medium. Almost everyone buys them, so they meet the needs of both large and small advertisers. Readers can save newspapers to refer to the ads later. For example, local retail grocers know that food shoppers check the newspaper ads before going to the market. Next to the local ads, readers may find such national ads as those for the Nestlé Foods Corporation or the Campbell Soup Company's products.

**preferred position** advertising in specific sections of newspapers that are more likely to be read by the target market

Advertisers can target newspaper readers who are likely to buy their products by using a **preferred position**: a section of the paper that is more likely to be read by the target market, such as sports enthusiasts, moviegoers, or do-it-yourselfers. Some retailers negotiate **premium placement**, which means the paper will guarantee placement of the ad on a specific page.

**premium placement** a newspaper's placement of an ad on a specific page

Newspapers have some disadvantages for advertisers. An ad may be "lost" in a large metropolitan newspaper where it must compete with hundreds of other ads for reader attention. Also, newspapers do not reproduce photographs as well as magazines do, though newspaper quality has improved over the last few years. Finally, a newspaper ad has little impact the day after it is published.

**direct-mail advertising** any advertising sent through the mail directly to a target market

*Direct Mail*    Any advertising sent through the mail directly to a target market is **direct-mail advertising**. This term has become a catchall that includes everything from post cards to leaflets to sales letters to booklets to elaborate catalogs.[9]

## ADVERTISING IN MAGAZINES THAT TARGET SPECIFIC MARKETS

In recent years a number of new magazines have appeared which are aimed at specific target markets. *Quarante* (French for "40") and *Lear* are two which are designed to appeal to the growing number of women in America over 40. Both magazines are aimed at an upscale readership with high annual household incomes. Frances Lear, founder of *Lear*, notes that about 40 percent of American women are over 40 and that this number will continue to grow.

*Gentleman's Quarterly* (GQ) and *Esquire* have been leaders in the men's fashion field for many years. *MGF* (*Men's Guide to Fashion*) is a new entry into this market and is giving the established magazines strong competition. Gerald Rothberg, publisher of *MGF*,

says his magazine appeals to 18- to 29-year-olds whom he describes as "well-heeled."

*Quarante*, *Lear*, and *MGF* are supported by revenue from advertisers who believe these magazines will reach the people who will buy their products. Which advertisers would be interested in buying ads from these magazines? Think of specific brand names you might see advertised in *Quarante*, *Lear*, and *MGF*.

Sources: Cathy Trost, "Two Magazines Aimed at Women over 40 Take Different Approaches to Big Market," *Wall Street Journal*, April 6, 1987, p. 11; "A New Magazine's Mercurial Midwife," *Fortune*, January 2, 1989, p. 42; and "Magazine Aims at Younger Men," *Roanoke Times & World News*, March 27, 1988, p. E-14.

Direct mail's major advantage is its selectivity. An advertiser can target precisely the market it wishes to tap. For example, L. L. Bean, Inc., a leading direct-mail advertiser, issues different catalogs to fit its target markets. Hunters and serious outdoor enthusiasts receive one type, whereas more recreation-oriented people receive quite a different type. Direct mail's success depends on how current and of how high a quality the advertiser's mailing list is. It would do little good for Harry & David, which sells gourmet foods by mail, to mail to a Dairy Queen list. After all, each brochure or catalog may cost $1 or more to print and mail. Mailing lists must therefore contain a very high proportion of people who will at least be qualified to buy from the catalog.

An important trend in the direct-mail field is the mailing of preprinted advertising circulars to the consumer's home. Advo-Systems, Inc., is the nation's largest direct-mail advertising service. Advo's computerized files contain every residential postal address in the United States, so they can penetrate specific markets. Super X, K mart, and Sears use this direct-mail strategy to reach consumers who live near their stores.

Direct mail does have its disadvantages. Maintaining an up-to-date mailing list can be expensive. Also, many people throw away direct-mail advertising without reading it.

*Radio* Like direct mail, radio advertising offers the advertiser selectivity. Commercial radio stations develop programming targeted for particular

*"Mr. Thornton here is going to make us more visible."*

audiences: rock, easy listening, classical, all-news, and the like. The cost of radio ads tends to be lower than direct-mail ads, particularly at smaller local stations. Radio advertising is also extremely flexible. An advertiser can change messages, if need be, in just a few hours. And radio reaches large numbers of people. There are more than 470 million radios in the country—two for every person, which is an average of nearly six per household. With Walkman units and car radios, radio is the most mobile medium.

Nonetheless, radio has disadvantages. Listeners may forget radio messages because they are not available for relistening. (Repetition can sometimes compensate for this problem.) And some people can "tune out" commercials or grow adept at changing stations when ads intrude. Also, radio appeals to only one sense—hearing.

*Television*   Television advertising can have considerable impact because it appeals to two senses—sight and hearing. It is a medium that offers broad reach and image-building strengths. More than 20 percent of the nation's total advertising expenditures goes for television. Large companies like television advertising because it offers mass coverage. When Kellogg's introduced Fruitful Bran, the company's marketers chose television commercials to reach the public. Television is also a flexible medium. Advertisers can target geographic regions and, to some degree, specific types of viewers.

A great disadvantage of television is its high cost. A 30-second prime-time spot on a national network can cost $120,000—or even $675,000 for the same spot during the Super Bowl. Local rates vary widely, depending on the size of the market and type of station. The television industry and advertisers are growing increasingly concerned about **clutter**, an industry term for broadcast messages that are not part of a program: commercials, station identifications, public-service messages, and program promotional ads.[10] The industry is also concerned about the number of people who are "tuning out." The percentage of homes tuned to major TV networks has declined steadily in recent years (see Figure 14.4).[11]

**clutter** broadcast messages that are not part of a TV program

*Outdoor Advertising* Posters, billboards, signs, and the like comprise **outdoor advertising**. Despite the amount of it we see each day, outdoor advertising accounts for only 1 percent of total advertising expenditures. By necessity, a typical message is simple, easy to comprehend, and usually just six to eight words long. Outdoor advertisements are often quite effective in reaching customers who live close to the point where the products advertised are being offered for sale. Repetition is a major advantage of outdoor advertising; members of a target audience may pass by a particular sign several times a day. Also, advertisers often use the outdoor medium to reinforce other campaigns.

**outdoor advertising** advertising consisting of posters, billboards, and signs

Outdoor advertising's major disadvantages are the brevity of its messages and the controversy surrounding them. Because of billboards' unattractiveness, many areas restrict them, and some have even banned them.

FIGURE 14.4   The Decline in the Number of Homes Tuned to Major TV Networks

Source: From "This TV Season Is Prime Time for Advertisers," p. 35. Reprinted from June 13, 1988 issue of *Business Week* by special permission, copyright © 1988 by McGraw-Hill, Inc.

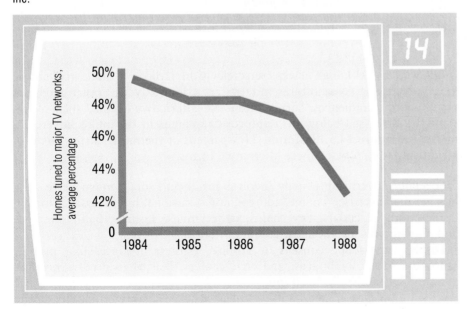

Exploring new ways to advertise   *A firm may choose to supplement its usual television, radio, and newspaper campaign advertising avenues with alternative media to promote a product.*

*Other Media*   Although newspapers, television, radio, and direct mail absorb most advertising expenditures, advertisers commonly use other media to reach specific audiences. Firms often use alternative media, such as the examples discussed below, to reinforce campaigns in the major advertising media. As Figure 14.5 illustrates, 21.3 percent of the money firms spend on advertising goes toward these alternative forms.

**specialty advertising**
producing small, inexpensive items bearing the advertiser's name, address, and occasional brief messages for free distribution

**display advertising**
product exhibits in places like airports, railroad stations, billboards, and civic centers

**Specialty advertising** usually involves producing small, inexpensive items bearing the advertiser's name, address, and occasional brief messages for free distribution. Calendars, key chains, coffee mugs, T-shirts, ball-point pens, and matchbooks are the most common items.

**Display advertising** consists of product exhibits in places like airports, railroad stations, billboards, and civic centers. It is often used to promote automobiles, hotels, or local industries.

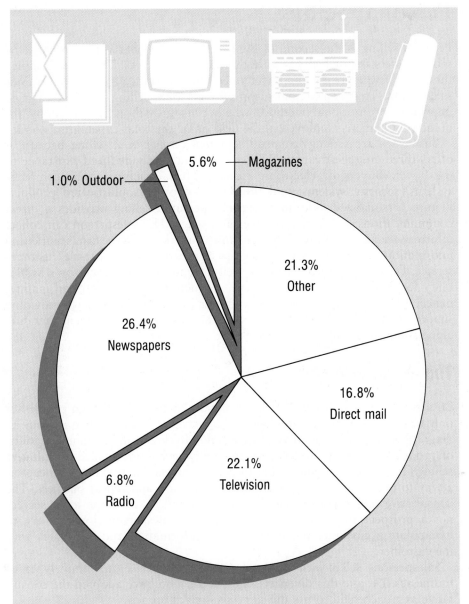

FIGURE 14.5
Advertising
Expenditures by
Medium

Source: *Statistical
Abstract of the United
States,* 1988, Table
#950, p. 552

**Targeted television advertising** aimed at specific audiences is growing in popularity with the coming of cable channels specially programmed for those who enjoy sports, country or rock music, or family entertainment.

**Shoppers' guides** are advertising circulars featuring both display and classified ads (though they sometimes contain some nonadvertising copy) that are delivered door to door or are available free at grocery stores, restaurants, or local retail shops.

**targeted television
advertising** television
advertising aimed at specific
audiences

**shoppers' guides** advertising circulars featuring both
display and classified ads that
are delivered door to door

# Personal Selling

Personal selling is the second of the four basic elements in the promotional mix. It offers major benefits to both sellers and buyers. The more complex the product, the greater the buyer's need for assistance from a well-trained salesperson. That is a major reason why personal selling is an increasingly important promotional method, whether its growth is measured by the number of persons employed in the field or by the total expenditures on it.

Businesses are willing to spend so much on personal selling because it offers three unique advantages. First, it permits individualized assistance to the buyer. Buyers of electronic cash registers, machine tools, computer systems, security systems, and thousands of other sophisticated products require personalized assistance. Second, personal selling provides a direct communications link between buyer and seller. The salesperson can collect information about the buyer's present and future needs for the firm's marketing information system. Finally, the salesperson can provide postsale customer service. Customer satisfaction may well depend on the salesperson's availability for product installation, on-site instruction in operation and maintenance, servicing warranties, following up on complaints, and providing support services. An advertising or sales promotion department standing alone could not meet these needs.[12]

## The Selling Process

*6. List the six steps in the selling process.*

**consultative selling** a sales approach used today in which salespeople serve as consultants to customers, diagnosing problems, identifying needs, and offering sound recommendations on products

Businesses spend millions of dollars annually to recruit and train people not only to sell goods and services but also to serve as consultants to customers, diagnosing problems, identifying needs, and offering sound recommendations on products. For this reason, today's sales approach is often called **consultative selling**. This approach emerged at the same time as the marketing concept as a way to provide maximum customer satisfaction and repeat business. The consultative selling concept holds that a customer is a person to be served, not a prospect to be sold. The consultative salesperson does not try to manipulate a customer but instead offers information and negotiates with the customer.

Salespersons sell a vast array of goods and services to many types of businesses. Despite this diversity, salespeople who have adopted the consultative approach tend to use the same six-step approach.

**prospecting** developing a list of potential customers

**prospects** firms or individuals who qualify as potential customers because they have the authority and financial ability to buy the product

**preapproach** planning that takes place before meeting with the customer

*Step 1: Preparing for the Sales Presentation*   The first thing a salesperson must do is called **prospecting**, developing a list of potential customers or **prospects**, firms or individuals who qualify as potential customers because they have the authority and the financial ability to buy the product. A salesperson should screen potential customers and eliminate anyone as a prospect who does not qualify in both regards.

All the planning that takes place before meeting with the customer is called the **preapproach**. During this stage, the salesperson attempts to learn as much as possible about the prospect, prepares a tentative sales presentation, and schedules an interview.

**Consultative selling**  *The consultative salesperson is there to serve, not manipulate, the potential client. The idea is to develop a negotiating relationship with the customer. By listening to and identifying needs and then offering informed recommendations, customer satisfaction is increased, meaning repeat business and a good reputation for the company.*

*Step 2: The Sales Presentation*  Unless the selling situation simply calls for taking an order because the customer knows what he or she wants, a needs assessment should be a standard part of the sales presentation. The scope of the assessment depends mainly on the sophistication and selling price of the product and on the customer's knowledge of it. For example, most insurance salespeople sell a range of policies. They use a needs-assessment strategy to determine which policy best meets a given prospect's needs. Asking questions provides one of the best ways to assess needs. Once the customer and the salesperson have identified the customer's needs, the salesperson can recommend a product or range of products to satisfy them.

*Step 3: The Sales Demonstration*  An effective sales demonstration helps verify parts of the sales story by giving customers a better understanding of the product's features. When Cuisinart, Inc., first introduced its high-quality food processors, it won many customers through its in-store demonstrations. Demonstrations must be well planned and executed if they are to be successful, however.

### Step 4: Negotiating Sales Resistance

The customer's sales resistance is a normal part of any presentation. Objections like "the price is too high" or "I don't like the color" should not trouble the salesperson, since they clarify the prospect's thinking. Customer resistance often pinpoints areas that the salesperson needs to cover in more depth.

### Step 5: Closing the Sale

Asking the prospect to buy the product comes at the point of *closing the sale*. If the salesperson has handled the presentation well, closing is normally not difficult. When some salespeople feel the prospect is ready to buy, they use a trial closing like "May I arrange for delivery?" or "How soon will you need the tapes?" The trial close becomes an attempt to determine whether the prospect is in fact ready to buy.

### Step 6: Servicing the Sale

In the broadest terms, personal selling is a two-part process: closing the sale, then servicing it. Today, servicing the sale receives more attention than it did in the past because businesses have recognized that they build profits not only by attracting new accounts but also by keeping old ones active. The services provided after a sale may include supervising the delivery and installation of the item and product orientation—making sure the customer can use and maintain the product.

General Motors established its Buick customer assistance centers to offer customers service after the sale. Buick owners receive the toll-free number of a group of specially trained advisors who can offer assistance. This service is expected to increase customer satisfaction by dealing with complaints and problems quickly and efficiently. The center can handle 1,100 calls a day.[13]


## Selling Today

The fast-talking, cigar-chewing salesman whose answer to every sales problem was more pressure on the customer is a figure of the past. Salespeople today must adopt approaches more in keeping with our market-driven economy and with a business philosophy based on customer satisfaction and repeat sales. With the modern approach to selling has come a new, well-earned status for salespeople.

*7. Describe the four major employment settings in the field of personal selling.*

The types of salespeople a firm employs depends first on where the firm is in the channel of distribution and second on its approach to sales. Also, a firm's choice of salespeople depends on its product—that is, on whether it sells primarily a good or a service.

### Selling for a Retailer

Approximately 40 percent of this country's businesses are retail firms. As everyday experience indicates, the range of retailers is vast: from "mom and pop" stores to auto dealers to computer stores to boutiques and on and on. The type of salespeople needed varies with the setting. Some businesses simply require order takers. Others demand highly trained professionals who combine hands-on product knowledge with good selling skills.

*Selling for a Wholesaler*  United States wholesalers employ over 650,000 salespeople,[14] who are normally classified as either inside or outside salespeople. **Inside salespeople** rely almost totally on telephone orders and usually follow a regular customer-contact schedule. Because of the escalating costs of personal selling, more and more wholesalers are switching to telephone sales. **Outside salespeople** or **field salespeople** typically work on the road, calling on potential buyers. Some specialize in a product niche, such as electronics or small appliances; others carry a wide range of lines. Typically, though, outside salespeople must know many products and merchandising strategies. For example, sales representatives who call on retail stores for pharmaceutical wholesalers must know dozens of different over-the-counter remedies and be able to advise their customers on advertising, display techniques, store layout, and pricing.

*Selling for a Manufacturer*  The three most common types of salespeople employed by manufacturers are field salespeople, sales engineers, and detail salespersons.

Field salespeople employed by a manufacturer usually handle well-established products that require a minimum of creative selling and technical knowledge. Persons selling standard office equipment, like desks and secretarial chairs, would be classified as field salespeople. Their major concerns are price and delivery. By contrast, **sales engineers** must have precise, detailed knowledge of their products and be able to discuss technical matters. In some instances, sales engineers may be needed to introduce products that mark technological breakthroughs. They must therefore be able to identify, analyze, and solve customer problems.

The third type of manufacturer's representative does not actually make sales. Instead, **detail salespeople** or **missionary salespeople** develop good will and stimulate demand for the manufacturer's products in target markets. Such salespersons are not paid on the basis of the sales they generate because their duties often focus on such different areas as training the customer's employees or advising on advertising campaigns. They do, however, receive indirect recognition for increased sales they may have helped generate.

*Selling a Service*  Over the last several years, the amount that consumers have spent annually on services has steadily increased. Transactions involving insurance, real estate, travel planning, finances, and business security require knowledgeable salespeople. The service sector of our economy—and with it the types of services requiring sales personnel—is likely to continue to expand.

## Telemarketing

**Telemarketing,** the art and science of marketing goods and services through telephone contact, is an integral part of many modern marketing campaigns.[15] For some marketers, the rising cost of face-to-face sales calls, now between $250 and $300 per call, makes telemarketing an attractive alternative. Telemarketing also permits a salesperson to make contact with a larger

**inside salespeople** salespeople who rely almost totally on telephone orders and usually follow a regular customer-contact schedule

**outside (field) salespeople** salespeople who work on the road, calling on potential buyers

**sales engineers** salespeople who have precise, detailed knowledge of their products and are able to discuss technical matters

**detail (missionary) salespeople** salespeople who develop good will and stimulate demand for the manufacturer's products in target markets

**telemarketing** the art and science of marketing goods and services through telephone contact

number of prospects during a given day or week. In some cases telemarketing is used as a sales support strategy. The telephone can be used to qualify sales leads and provide service after the sale. Many of the telemarketing campaigns aimed at the ultimate consumer, the person making the buying decision, are coordinated with direct mail or other media to concentrate the effectiveness.[16]

# Sales Promotion

**sales promotion** marketing activities other than personal selling, advertising, and publicity that stimulate consumer purchasing and dealer effectiveness

*8.* Define sales promotion and identify the principal means involved.

The American Marketing Association defines **sales promotion** as "those marketing activities, other than personal selling, advertising, and publicity, that stimulate consumer purchasing and dealer effectiveness."[17] Sales promotions can be as diverse as cheese sample tables in supermarkets, a $1-off coupon in a newspaper, or a frequent-flier bonus offered by airlines. In effect, each of these activities serves as a bridge to connect the other three elements of the promotional mix.[18] Sales promotion can greatly increase the effectiveness of the other activities. Here are some examples of how that happens.

*Coupons*   For many years, manufacturers have used coupons to increase the sale of products. Coupons represent the most common form of sales promotion in America.[19] During a recent one-year period, over $80 billion worth of coupons were distributed and almost $3 billion were redeemed.[20] Coupons that appear in newspapers, magazines, or direct-mail packets are often used to introduce new or improved items.

**refund**   the return of a portion of an item's purchase price

*Refunds*   The returning of a portion of an item's purchase price is a **refund**. In recent years, many small-appliance manufacturers have used rebates from three to five dollars on everything from power tools to kitchen equipment. Manufacturers use *rebates*, a form of refund like coupons, both to introduce a new product and to build sales of an existing product.

**premium**   anything of value that a customer receives in addition to the purchased item or service

*Premiums*   Anything of value that a customer receives in addition to the purchased item or service is a **premium**. Some firms concentrate on premiums to attract and hold customers. For instance, supermarkets have used towel, record, encyclopedia, dish, and silverware giveaways to attract customers into their stores. Usually, stores hand out the items with purchases above a certain size, or they are sold to the consumer at a very low price.

**sample**   a free package or container of a product

*Samples*   A free package or container of a product is a **sample**. Manufacturers often use samples to introduce new products. When Bull's-Eye Barbecue Sauce was introduced to consumers, over 8.2 million free samples and twenty-five cent coupons were mailed to homes in key markets across the United States. Full-page ads in *Supermarket News* and other grocery publications encouraged supermarkets to stock up in preparation for the promotion. This use of samples and coupons provides a good example of the *pull* promotion strategy.

Tradeshows as promotional devices  *Exhibiting a wide variety of products, usually relating to one industry, tradeshows attract many retailers and wholesalers, providing an excellent opportunity to display and effectively promote products.*

*Point-of-Purchase Displays*  Special racks, signs, and displays to increase consumer product awareness are sometimes supplied and set up by manufacturers or wholesalers in retail or service outlets. The continuing trend toward self-service buying has helped make these units, called **point-of-purchase displays**, a popular sales promotion device. They are commonly found at the end of aisles in supermarkets to make more efficient use of floor space.

**point-of-purchase display**  a special rack, sign, or display set up to increase consumer product awareness

## Trade Show

A final type of sales promotion device is in a category by itself. The **trade show** is a large exhibit of products that are, in most cases, common to one industry. Each year, for example, the National Decorating Products Show rotates from city to city, offering suppliers of paint, wallcoverings, floor coverings, and related items an opportunity to display their wares. Large numbers of retailers and wholesalers visit the show to see its varied products. Such shows also play a key role in the fashion, furniture, toy, automotive accessories and boating and recreational vehicle industries.

**trade show**  a large exhibit of products that are usually common to one industry

# Publicity and Public Relations
## *Publicity*

Quite simply, **publicity** is a communication in news-story form about a company or its products transmitted by a mass medium at no charge. Virtually any of the advertising media can serve as sources of publicity. The principal types of publicity mechanisms are the following:

■ **News releases:** Printed copy, usually in the form of brief newspaper stories, circulated generally to the news media.

**Reebok rocks** *As the sponsor of the Human Rights Now Tour, the Reebok Foundation received international publicity. The company was mentioned in the written and photographic material advertising the tour and had banners and giant displays at the concerts. By contributing to the cause Reebok achieved recognition of its name as well as a positive image, for being an organization concerned with social change.*

- **Feature articles:** Manuscripts longer than a news release (sometimes exceeding three thousand words), which the firm usually has prepared for a specific publication.
- **Captioned photographs:** Photos of a new product, a corporate officer, or something else of interest, accompanied by a brief description explaining the picture.
- **Press conferences:** Public meetings of corporate officials with the news media at which written and photographic materials are often supplied.
- **Interviews:** Private meetings of corporate officials or employees with the news media.

What is publicized is largely under the publicity seeker's control. In many cases, the goal of publicity is to shape the image of the company and its product. Publicity is not the same as advertising. A firm does not have the control over publicity that it has over advertising. Although the firm does not pay for publicity, it is not truly free. In some situations, expensive artwork or photographs may accompany a news release or be supplied to reporters. The firm must often add a full-time employee to handle publicity. Sometimes companies avoid this cost by using the services of a public relations or advertising firm.

## Public Relations

The activities designed to create and maintain favorable relations between an organization and its various publics are known as **public relations.**[21] These publics include the firm's customers, employees, and stockholders, or the government or general public. In some cases, an appropriate public relations event can reduce the negative impact of a major crisis. When Chrysler Corporation was indicted for selling as new several thousand cars and trucks that employees allegedly had driven with the odometers disconnected, chairman Lee Iacocca didn't deny wrongdoing. He held a news conference and asked: "Did we screw up? You bet we did." Experts in the field of public relations praised his candid response to the problem.[22]

# Promotion: A Perspective

When Melitta, Inc., developed its new coffeemaker system, it introduced not only a new product but also a new way to brew coffee—a double challenge. Its marketers decided to present the product directly to the top management of wholesalers and supermarket chains. Melitta customized a van in which its sales representatives traveled to various corporate headquarters. While Melitta's salespeople demonstrated their new product, their prospects sipped coffee fresh out of a Melitta system. The strategy worked.

As Melitta proved, few areas in business offer as many opportunities for creativity as personal selling and promotion. Sometimes a new idea comes merely from taking a fresh look at an everyday scene. An advertising company

**feature article**
manuscript longer than a news release, which the firm usually has prepared for a specific publication

**captioned photograph**
a photo of a new product, a corporate officer, or something else of interest, accompanied by a brief description

**press conference** a public meeting of corporate officials with the news media at which written and photographic materials are often supplied

**interview** a private meeting of corporate officials or employees with the news media

**public relations** the activities designed to create and maintain favorable relations between an organization and its various publics

*9. Distinguish between publicity and public relations.*

in Baltimore sells space on 10-inch meter-mounted signs to Minolta copiers, among others. Sometimes people who spend millions on advertising each year have to be sold on a great idea for publicity. That was the problem that Bantam Books, Inc., had when it approached Chrysler chairman Lee Iacocca about writing his autobiography. Bantam had to spend nine months convincing him to do it. In the eighteen months after its publication, *Iacocca* was on the best-seller list for 73 weeks, sold 2.6 million hardcover copies, and became the all-time best-selling nonfiction book other than the Bible.[23] The value of the publicity that Chrysler gained from the book cannot be calculated.

No small part of the reason we are in the marketing era is that people like Lee Iacocca have recognized that marketing is both critical to any business's success and personally challenging. As the millions of Americans who work in marketing can testify, it is also rewarding and fulfilling.

# CHAPTER HIGHLIGHTS

*1.* Define promotion *and describe common promotional objectives.*

*Promotion* encompasses all communication designed to inform, persuade, or remind a target market about its product, its services, or itself. Promotion can also be used to shape the image of a business.

*2.* Identify two major promotional strategies.

A push strategy is used to sell goods or services directly to the next intermediary in the channel of distribution. The pull strategy promotes the product directly to the consumer, usually through advertising or sales promotion.

*3.* List the elements of the promotional mix.

The four elements of the promotional mix are advertising, personal selling, sales promotion, and publicity.

*4.* Define advertising *and identify the three principal types of advertising.*

*Advertising* is any paid form of nonpersonal presentation and promotion of ideas, goods, or services by an identified sponsor. *Selective* or *brand* advertising encourages consumers to buy a certain brand of product and builds customer

patronage. *Primary-demand* or *generic* advertising increases the total demand for a product or service without distinguishing between brands. *Institutional* advertising generates good will, enhances an organization's image, or promotes an idea or philosophy.

*5.* Weigh the advantages and disadvantages of the principal advertising media.

*Magazines* can reach selected national or specialized audiences, they may be read and reread, and they offer quality reproduction. They require copy far in advance of publication date, however, and may be too expensive for smaller businesses. *Newspapers* attract both large and small businesses because almost everyone buys them, but ads must compete with hundreds of other ads, photographs in newspapers do not reproduce well, and their message is short lived. *Direct mail* is tremendously selective, but it is expensive, maintaining up to date mailing lists is difficult, and consumers can easily ignore it. *Radio* offers advertisers selectivity, flexibility, reasonable cost, and large audiences, but its commercials are easily forgotten. *Television* ads have high impact but are very expensive, although for large businesses the cost per person reached can be quite reasonable. *Outdoor advertising* is particularly useful for reinforcing other campaigns, but the medium is controversial and messages must be very brief.

**6.** *List the six steps in the selling process.*

The six steps are preparing for the sales presentation, the actual sales presentation, the sales demonstration, negotiating sales resistance, closing the sale, and servicing the sale.

**7.** *Describe the four major employment settings in the field of personal selling.*

The four employment settings are selling for a retailer, selling for a wholesaler, selling for a manufacturer, and selling a service.

**8.** *Define sales promotion and identify the principal means involved.*

*Sales promotion* consists of those marketing activities—other than personal selling, advertising, and publicity—that stimulate consumer purchasing and dealer effectiveness. Its principal means are coupons, refunds, premiums, sampling, and point-of-purchase displays.

**9.** *Distinguish between publicity and public relations.*

*Publicity* is communication, in news-story form, about a company or its products, which is transmitted through a mass medium at no charge. *Public relations* is a broad set of communications activities designed to create and maintain favorable relations between an organization and its various publics.

## KEY TERMS

Promotion
Push strategy
Pull strategy
Promotional mix
Advertising
Informative advertising
Persuasive advertising
Reminder
 (reinforcement)
 advertising
Selective (brand)
 advertising
Primary-demand
 (generic) advertising

Institutional
 advertising
Advertising media
Preferred position
Premium placement
Direct-mail advertising
Clutter
Outdoor advertising
Specialty advertising
Display advertising
Targeted television
 advertising
Shoppers' guides

Consultative selling
Prospecting
Prospects
Preapproach
Inside salespeople
Outside (field)
 salespeople
Sales engineers
Detail (missionary)
 salespeople
Telemarketing
Sales promotion
Refund

Premium
Sample
Point-of-purchase display
Trade show
Publicity
News release
Feature article
Captioned photograph
Press conference
Interview
Public relations

## REVIEW QUESTIONS

1. Define promotion and describe each of the basic elements a firm combines in its promotional mix.
2. What is the primary difference between a push-oriented promotional strategy and a pull-oriented strategy?

3. Most businesses seek to achieve specific promotional objectives. What are the three most common objectives?
4. What is selective or brand advertising? How is this type of advertising different from "primary demand or generic advertising"?

5. What is institutional advertising? Give at least one example not mentioned in this book.
6. What are some of the advantages of newspapers as an advertising medium?
7. Define direct-mail advertising. What are some of the factors that contribute to effective direct-mail advertising?
8. List two advantages and two disadvantages of television advertising.
9. Why do some marketers use personal selling as a promotional strategy? Give at least three reasons.
10. What are the six steps in the selling process?
11. What are the four major employment settings for salespeople?
12. Define sales promotion. List and describe the five major sales-promotion strategies.
13. What is publicity? How is publicity different from public relations?
14. What are some of the principal publicity mechanisms a business may use?

# APPLICATION EXERCISES

1. Develop a promotional plan for a new sporting goods store to be opened in a shopping center. This store will feature several lines of exclusive merchandise for golfers and tennis players. What elements of the promotional mix would be most effective in reaching potential consumers? Be specific as you describe promotional strategies that would be incorporated into your plan.

2. Consider the sporting goods store in Exercise 1 and answer the following questions:
   a. What role should personal selling play in the promotional mix?
   b. What steps can be taken to ensure that the sales staff is well prepared to perform their duties?

# CASES

## 14.1 The Cola Wars

One army is made up of Michael Jackson, Madonna, Robert Palmer, and Michael J. Fox. On the other side are Don Johnson, George Michael, Robert Plant, and Michael Jordan. Instead of guns they hold guitars. Media enthusiasts love to call this the cola wars. Coke versus Pepsi. Lavish multi-million-dollar commercials promote the competing soft-drink brands that have somehow become an integral part of the American image.

"Coke and Pepsi aren't in the product business anymore," says Clive Chajet, chairman of the New York–based corporate-identity firm of Lippincott and Marguilies. "They're in the image business, in show business." At times it is

hard to disagree. The hype for the 3D Diet Coke commercial that aired at half time of the January 1989 Super Bowl rivaled the hype for the game itself.

In fairness to Coke and Pepsi, it must be said that the companies have attempted to deal with the reality of their products. Pepsi has run blind taste tests, in which the majority of people preferred its beverage to Coke. Coke responded by adjusting its sacred formula to something sweeter and less biting—and more like Pepsi. New Coke, in spite of marketing predictions, sparked few sales but did cause a national outrage. Sophisticated business-analysis TV programs devoted their full half hours to discussion of popular hostility to the new drink, whose taste was not as well liked as the old. Coke management, it seemed, had forgotten about product loyalty.

## Questions

1. Research has established that there is no necessary correlation between the popularity of a commercial and the success of the product it promotes. Does this suggest anything about the high-priced-celebrity approach to product promotion?
2. Is the lesson to be learned here that Coke and Pepsi should stop trying to create dynamic images for their products? Why?

Sources: For more information see *Newsweek,* December 28, 1987, pp. 32–33; *Business Week,* December 12, 1988, p. 124; *Advertising Age,* January 23, 1989, pp. 1, 56; *Business Week,* March 20, 1989, pp. 162–166; and *Roanoke Times and World News,* April 2, 1989, pp. D1, D5.

# 14.2 It's a Bird, It's a Plane . . .

People have always been fascinated by airborne objects. Airplanes, hot-air balloons, blimps, and inflatables of all shapes and sizes attract our attention. This fascination has not been ignored by advertisers. Visit a parade, a festival, or a supermarket opening and you may see the giant-sized inflatable Campbell Soup Company Kid. This portable promo can be used wherever a large crowd assembles.

The Giant Texaco inflatable, in the shape of a hot-air balloon, was displayed at Miami's His-panic Heritage month celebration. It was hard to ignore this large promotion piece. Audi, the automobile manufacturer, and *Forbes,* the business magazine, used real hot-air balloons to promote their products.

Goodyear Tire & Rubber Co. has been building blimps and operating them since 1911. Its four blimps provide an unusual advertising medium and an occasional aerial platform for television cameras. Goodyear considers the blimp to be its own special symbol and contends it is a registered trademark.

Several large companies now use the blimp to promote their products and services. Fuji Photo Film Company flew its own blimp over the Summer Olympic Games in Los Angeles in 1984. A group of McDonald's franchise owners used a blimp to promote their products. People who attended the 1989 Super Bowl saw the Metropolitan Life Insurance blimp above the stadium.

## Questions

1. What are some of the major advantages and disadvantages of using hot-air balloons, blimps, and inflatables to promote products and services? What are some limitations of this advertising medium?
2. The Goodyear blimp has become a distinctive symbol. What can such a symbol do for the firm and its products?

Source: For more information, see *Business Week,* January 20, 1986, p. 30; *Newsweek,* January 6, 1986, p. 52; *Wall Street Journal,* December 27, 1985, p. 3; *Business Week,* January 26, 1987, p. 65; and *Fortune,* November 21, 1988, p. 181.

# Information for Business Decision Making

*At Ford Motor Company a very large number of employees get paid for processing information, not for making cars. Ford, like most other businesses, has moved into the information age. As we move from an industrial to an information society, computers will play a more important role in the management of information. Part V begins with an introduction to the nature of accounting, then we introduce computers and management information systems.*

PART FIVE

# 15 Accounting

After you have completed this chapter, you will be able to do the following:

*1.* Describe how managers, investors, and others use accounting information.

*2.* Distinguish between the primary types of accountants.

*3.* State the accounting equation and relate it to double-entry bookkeeping.

*4.* List the five steps in the accounting cycle and provide a one-sentence description of each stage.

*5.* Describe the functions of the three most common financial statements discussed in this chapter.

*6.* Explain briefly how analysts look at and interpret financial statements.

*7.* Analyze accounting's role in the budget process.

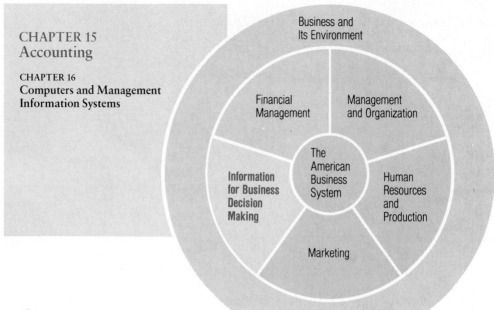

Business and
Its Environment

Financial
Management

Management
and Organization

Information
for Business
Decision
Making

The
American
Business
System

Human
Resources
and
Production

Marketing

At the end of their freshman year in college, instead of looking for a summer job, John and Kay organized a lawn service company in their city. To start their business on May 15, they each deposited $500 in a checking bank account in the name of their company, J and K Lawn Service. Their $1000 consisted of a $250 loan from each of their fathers and $250 each of their own money. Using the money in the checking account, they rented lawn equipment, purchased supplies, and hired fellow students to cut and trim lawns. On the 1st and 15th, they mailed statements to their customers.

On August 15, they were ready to dissolve their business and go back to college for the fall semester. Since they had been so busy, they had not kept any records other than the checkbook and a list of amounts owed to them by customers. When they returned the rented lawn equipment, the rental manager asked them, "How did you do?" Though they thought they did quite well, they were not sure just how successful they were. What kind of information from their record-keeping system would help make it easier to tell whether they earned a profit or loss?

# The Nature of Accounting

**accounting** the process of recording financial information, interpreting it, and then communicating it

The process of recording financial information, interpreting it, then communicating it is called **accounting**. Persons who provide accounting services, accountants, do not just compile and tabulate data. Accountants help others—managers, entrepreneurs, lenders, investors—understand what the numbers mean so that they can make informed business decisions. Accountants translate raw data into a language that businesspeople can understand and use. Thus, accounting is the "language of business." This chapter is an introduction to that language.

## Who Relies on Accounting

As Figure 15.1 reveals, owners and managers use accounting information to measure a company's performance against established standards and goals. Suppose that a corporation has set a 10 percent increase in sales as its goal for a particular quarter. The raw sales data for the quarter, translated into an understandable form by an accountant, will reveal whether the goal has

*1. Describe how managers, investors, and others use accounting information.*

FIGURE 15.1   Users of Accounting

Source: Adapted from Belverd E. Needles, Jr., *Financial Accounting,* Third Edition (Boston: Houghton Mifflin, 1989), p. 7. Copyright 1989. Used by permission of the publisher.

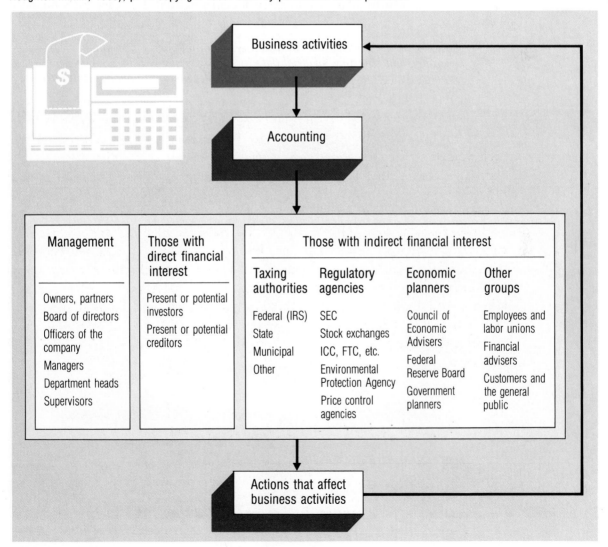

been met. Senior management can use this information to evaluate the sales manager's performance. In this way, accounting establishes accountability.

Accounting plays a critical role in controlling a corporation's present operations. For example, accounting provides a means of identifying expenses. This function is particularly important to new business, where every penny counts. The accountant's work also guides a company's planning for the future, because a business sets its goals by using as a base line what it has done in the past.

Creditors and investors also rely on accounting information to judge a firm. Bank-loan applications often require detailed information prepared by an accountant. Suppliers want similar information before extending trade credit. In deciding where to put their money, investors rely on **financial statements**, an organization's reports of its financial condition, which usually take the form of balance sheets, income statements, and statements of changes in financial position. (Each of these types of statement is described later in this chapter.) Shareholders and boards of directors judge a company's management by reference to these statements. And if a company's financial

**financial statements** an organization's reports of its financial condition

Bookkeepers and Accountants   *Bookkeepers work within the accountants' system of recording and reporting financial data for an organization. The bookkeeper supplies the accountant with raw data for the accountant to analyze and interpret for others.*

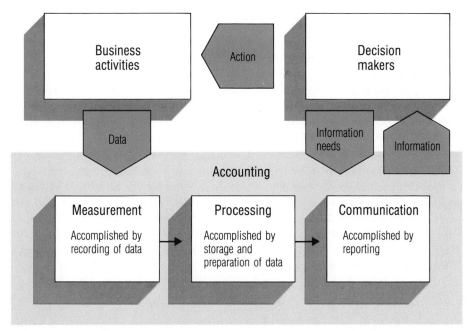

FIGURE 15.2   Accounting as an Information System

Source: Belverd E. Needles, Jr., *Financial Accounting,* Third Edition (Boston: Houghton Mifflin, 1989), p. 3. Copyright 1989. Used by permission of the publisher.

statements are available, unions analyze them before wage negotiations with management begin. Finally, a host of government agencies demand detailed financial information. The Internal Revenue Service and the various state and local taxing authorities have complex reporting requirements, with account- ants on staff to verify the reports they receive.

A business's system of reporting financial data, its accounting system, clearly must be equipped to record data accurately, be organized so that an accountant can readily translate the data, and be flexible so the data can be used for different purposes.

## Accounting's Relationship to Bookkeeping

"Accountants are just glorified bookkeepers." This common opinion could not be more wrong. A **bookkeeper** is a clerical employee who records day- to-day business transactions. A bookkeeper's thoroughness and accuracy are critically important to a good accounting system. But entry-level bookkeepers generally have only a year's in-house or comparable training. On the other hand, accountants are professionals who design and oversee an entire system of recording and reporting financial data. Bookkeepers work within that system. Accountants take the raw information that bookkeepers record, then summarize it, make adjustments to it, and interpret it for others. Figure 15.2 shows how accountants transform raw data about business activities into useful information for decision makers.

**bookkeeper**   a clerical employee who records day-to-day business transactions

## Types of Accountants

**2.** *Distinguish between the primary types of accountants.*

**public accountant** an independent professional whom individuals or companies may hire to perform specific accounting services

**audit** a formal examination of a firm's financial records

**certified public accountant (CPA)** an accountant who has passed an examination prepared by the American Institute of Certified Public Accountants (AICPA) and satisfied a state's educational and experience requirements

**private accountant (management accountant)** an accountant who is an employee of a company or government agency

**certified management accountant** management accountant who has passed the National Association of Accountants' test and has satisfied its educational and professional criteria

There are two basic classes of accountants: public and private.

*Public Accountants* An independent professional whom individuals or companies may hire to perform specific accounting services is a **public accountant**. Some public accountants practice as sole practitioners, that is, as individuals. Others form partnerships of from two to hundreds of accountants. The largest of these, listed in Table 15.1, serve primarily the nation's large corporations.

Besides the functions identified in the previous section, public accountants perform **audits**, formal examinations of a firm's financial records. An accountant then prepares financial statements based on the audit. Many lenders and government agencies require certification that the financial statements were properly prepared and fairly present the company's condition. Only a **certified public accountant (CPA)** can make that certification. A CPA is an accountant who has passed an examination prepared by the American Institute of Certified Public Accountants (AICPA) and satisfied a state's educational and experience requirements. Most states require a degree in accounting plus a period of practical training. Fewer than one-quarter of the nation's accountants are CPAs.

Those interested in a corporation's financial statements, like lenders and shareholders, rely on the independence of a CPA's certification. As have the members of other professions, accountants have found people increasingly willing to sue when they believe they have been misled. For example, some members of the Los Angeles Raiders who invested in Technical Equities Corporation sued the firm's accountants when it went bankrupt.[1]

*Private Accountants* It is important to keep in mind that the client prepares the data and financial reports that the CPA examines and tests in the course of an audit. The larger the firm, the more likely it is to have one or more accountants as employees. Accountants who are employees of companies or government agencies are called **private accountants** or **management accountants**. Management accountants can become **certified management accountants** by passing the National Association of Accountants' test and satisfying its educational and professional criteria.

### TABLE 15.1    The Nation's Largest Accounting Firms

Arthur Andersen & Co.
Ernst & Young
Coopers & Lybrand
Deloitte Haskins & Sells
Peat Marwick Mitchell & Co.
Price Waterhouse & Co.
Touche Ross & Co.

Source: Adapted from Belverd E. Needles, Jr., Henry R. Anderson, and James C. Caldwell, *Principles of Accounting*, Fourth Edition (Boston: Houghton Mifflin, 1990), p. 30. Copyright 1990. Used by permission of the publisher.

Training to become a CPA   *Only certified public accountants or CPAs have the
authority to pronounce a firm's financial records as sound and accurate to the
government's or a lending institution's satisfaction. To become a CPA most states
require that you pass the AICPA exam, and have a degree in accounting, in
addition to a period of practical training.*

# The Accounting Process

How do accountants create financial statements? What do they work from?
What is the accounting process? The easiest way to answer these questions
is to look at the operations of a hypothetical company. Suppose that two
friends, Margot and Dave, decide to open a sporting goods store specializing
in equipment for joggers and amateur runners. They lease a store, buy
inventory, and open their new business, which they decided to call Pacesetters.
They quickly find, especially when the first wave of tax forms arrives, that
they cannot keep track of their business just by using the company checkbook.
They immediately seek out an accountant who can tell them how to cope.
We will look now at what the accountant might tell Margot and Dave about
recording, classifying, and summarizing their business transactions.

# The Accounting Equation

assets   everything of value that an organization owns, its economic resources

liabilities   amounts that a firm owes to others

owners' equity   the amount the owners would have left if they used the firm's assets to pay all its liabilities

accounting equation the formula that sets liabilities and owners' equity together as claims against assets

An organization's economic resources—everything of value that it owns—are its **assets**. Cash, inventory, useful machinery and equipment, and real estate are all assets. On the other hand, the amounts that a firm owes to others are its **liabilities**. Subtracting a firm's total liabilities from its total assets produces a figure called **owners' equity**, the amount the owners would have left if they used the firm's assets to pay all its liabilities. Thus:

$$\text{Assets} - \text{Liabilities} = \text{Owners' equity}$$

Accountants regard both liabilities and owners' equity as claims against the firm's assets, so normally the formula, which is called the **accounting equation**, appears in this order:

$$\text{Assets} = \text{Liabilities} + \text{Owners' equity}$$

## Double-Entry Bookkeeping

double-entry book-keeping   a system of recording business transactions in which each transaction is recorded in at least two separate accounts

*3. State the accounting equation and relate it to double-entry bookkeeping.*

The accounting equation is the basis of **double-entry bookkeeping**, a system of recording business transactions in which each transaction is recorded in at least two separate accounts. One side of an equation must always equal the other, whether in algebra or accounting. An increase or decrease on one side of an equation requires a corresponding change on the other. This principle applies in recording business transactions, too.

Let's return to the hypothetical Pacesetters company. Suppose that it owes a jogging-suit maker $500. Margot writes a check for that sum. That transaction—paying the bill—not only reduces Pacesetters' assets by $500 in cash but also decreases its liabilities by the same amount. The equation therefore remains in balance:

$$-\$500 = -\$500$$
$$\text{Assets} = \text{Liabilities} + \text{Owners' equity}$$

Every business transaction can be thought of in this way. Figure 15.3 illustrates how several types of transactions fit into the equation.

1. Suppose that Margot and Dave invest a total of $6,000 to start Pacesetters. That amount appears on the books as both a cash asset and owner's equity.
2. When they decide to borrow $5,000, it becomes both a cash asset and a liability—they must repay the bank.
3. Pacesetters' purchase of furnishings affects only the left side of the equation. It is simply an exchange of one type of asset—cash—for another—equipment.
4. When Pacesetters needs more shoes and T-shirts, it makes a purchase on account, or a purchase on credit. The inventory becomes an asset, the obligation to pay a liability.
5. In Pacesetters' first month, it brings in $2,000 by selling $1,500 in inventory. This sales performance adds $500 to the left side of the equation. As a result, $500 must go on the right side, too—in this case under owner's equity, because it is "owed" to Margot and Dave.

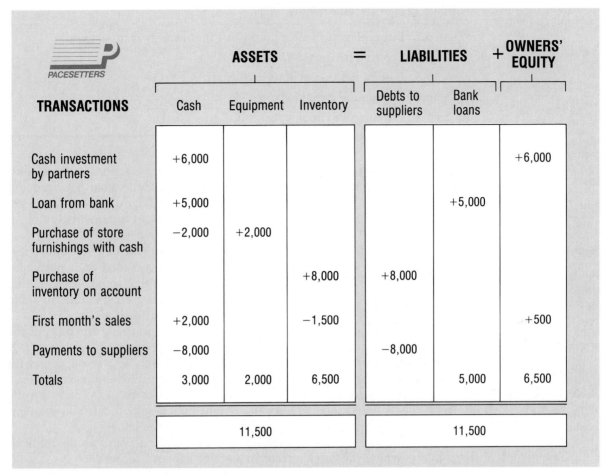

| TRANSACTIONS | ASSETS | | | = | LIABILITIES | | + | OWNERS' EQUITY |
|---|---|---|---|---|---|---|---|---|
| | Cash | Equipment | Inventory | | Debts to suppliers | Bank loans | | |
| Cash investment by partners | +6,000 | | | | | | | +6,000 |
| Loan from bank | +5,000 | | | | | +5,000 | | |
| Purchase of store furnishings with cash | −2,000 | +2,000 | | | | | | |
| Purchase of inventory on account | | | +8,000 | | +8,000 | | | |
| First month's sales | +2,000 | | −1,500 | | | | | +500 |
| Payments to suppliers | −8,000 | | | | −8,000 | | | |
| Totals | 3,000 | 2,000 | 6,500 | | | 5,000 | | 6,500 |
| | 11,500 | | | | 11,500 | | | |

FIGURE 15.3   The Accounting Equation Illustrated

6. When Pacesetters pays its suppliers for the inventory purchased on account, its liabilities decrease, but so do its cash assets.

As the last line of Figure 15.3 shows, after all these transactions the equation still remains in balance.

## The Accounting Cycle

Accounting systems typically consist of the five steps listed in Table 15.2. These steps are called the **accounting cycle** because they describe the process that takes a transaction from being mere raw data to its being summarized in the financial statements, a process repeated over and over again during a firm's life.

*Step 1: Examining Source Documents*   Accounting's source documents are the papers or computer entries which prove that a transaction actually took place. These documents include memos, checks, credit-card receipts,

*4.* List the five steps in the accounting cycle and provide a one-sentence description of each stage.

**accounting cycle**   the five-step process that takes a transaction from being mere raw data to its being summarized in the financial statements

## TABLE 15.2    The Accounting Cycle

Step 1. Examining the source documents that identify transactions.

Step 2. Entering the transactions in a journal.

Step 3. Posting the transactions in a ledger.

Step 4. Calculating a trial balance.

Step 5. Preparing financial statements.

invoices, and purchase orders. Before entering a transaction on the books, bookkeepers look at the source documents to determine what occurred and which accounts were affected. An *account* is a record of the increases, decreases, and balance of an item reported in financial statements.[2]

*Step 2: Entering Transactions in a Journal*    A **journal** or **book of original entry** is a chronological list of transactions each assigned to a particular account. A journal should include sufficient detail so that someone examining it can understand each transaction's nature. Journals are kept either by hand or on a computer, but the entry process is the same for both.

**journal (book of original entry)** a chronological list of transactions each assigned to a particular account

Figure 15.4 includes a page from the Pacesetters' journal. The titles of the two columns on the right are often confusing. In everyday usage, a credit is something positive and a debit something negative. When you deal with accounting, you must forget the terms' everyday meanings. In accounting, a **debit** is an entry on the left side of an account; a **credit** is an entry on the right side. A bookkeeper credits an account by making an entry on the right side of an account and debits it with an entry on the left.[3]

**debit** an entry on the left side of an account

**credit** an entry on the right side of the account

Every transaction has two entries: a debit to one account and a credit to another. Where the entry affects an asset or expense account:

▪ An *increase* in the account is a *debit*.
▪ A *decrease* in the account is a *credit*.

Where the entry affects a liability, owner's equity, or revenue account:

▪ An *increase* in the account is a *credit*.
▪ A *decrease* in the account is a *debit*.

These sets of rules mirror each other because they deal with the opposite halves of the accounting equation. The two sides have opposite rules of entry so that the equation will always balance.

In Figure 15.4, the entry for February 15 deals with the owners' original investment. It shows an increase in cash of $6,000. Cash is an asset, so the increase appears as a debit. The $6,000 also increases the owners' capital accounts and therefore appears as a credit to those accounts. The entry dated February 23 records a cash purchase of equipment. The increase in the equipment account appears as a debit, the decrease in cash as a credit. The February 24 entry records a purchase of supplies on account. Supplies is an asset, so the bookkeeper debited that account. **Accounts payable**—amounts due others—is a liability, so the bookkeeper credited that account. When Dave returns the defective shopping bags to the supplier, the bookkeeper will debit accounts payable and credit inventory.

**accounts payable** amounts due others

## GENERAL JOURNAL

| Date 19__ | | Account titles and explanation | Debit | | Credit | |
|---|---|---|---|---|---|---|
| Feb | 15 | Cash | 6,000 | 00 | | |
| | | Margot, capital | | | 3,000 | 00 |
| | | Dave, capital | | | 3,000 | 00 |
| | | Original investment by owners | | | | |
| Feb | 23 | Equipment | 500 | 00 | | |
| | | Cash | | | 500 | 00 |
| | | Clothing racks purchased from J. Purdy & Sons | | | | |
| Feb | 24 | Supplies | 720 | 00 | | |
| | | Accounts payable—Fischer Supply Co. | | | 720 | 00 |
| | | Purchase of imprinted bags and sales slips, | | | | |
| | | and other business forms on account | | | | |
| Feb | 27 | Accounts payable—Fischer Supply Co. | 90 | 00 | | |
| | | Supplies | | | 90 | 00 |
| | | Return of defective shopping bags to supplier | | | | |

### ACCOUNT: SUPPLIES

| Date 19__ | | Item | Debit | | Credit | | Balance Debit | | Credit | |
|---|---|---|---|---|---|---|---|---|---|---|
| Feb | 24 | Fischer Supply Co. | 720 | 00 | | | 720 | 00 | | |
| Feb | 27 | Fischer Supply Co. | | | 90 | 00 | 630 | 00 | | |

### ACCOUNT: ACCOUNTS PAYABLE

| Date 19__ | | Item | Debit | | Credit | | Balance Debit | | Credit | |
|---|---|---|---|---|---|---|---|---|---|---|
| Feb | 24 | Fischer Supply Co. | | | 720 | 00 | | | 720 | 00 |
| Feb | 27 | Fischer Supply Co. | 90 | 00 | | | | | 630 | 00 |

FIGURE 15.4   Sample Page from Pacesetters Journal

*Step 3: Posting Transactions in a Ledger*   The third step in the accounting cycle involves transferring data from the journal—a chronological listing of transactions—to an appropriate account in a **ledger**, a book or computer file in which each account appears separately. The process of transferring information from the journal to the ledger is called **posting**. Figure 15.4 indicates how the last two journal entries might appear in a ledger. Note that each transaction will still result in a debit to one account and a credit

**ledger**  a book or computer file in which each account appears separately

**posting**  the process of transferring information from the journal to the ledger

# THE ACCOUNTING PICTURE: PAINTING BY NUMBERS

As one CEO sees it, *precision* means that something is very carefully worked out, while *accuracy* means that whatever has been worked out gives a clear sense of reality. In other words, according to this executive's view, accounting figures may be precise without being accurate. Such a state of affairs may mislead the government, which regulates and taxes businesses; banks and investors, who provide businesses with financing; and even the businesses themselves, which need accurate data if they are to make informed decisions. Misimpressions may result from a misunderstanding of the rules governing the reporting of data. At times, however, financial statements may create an inaccurate and undesirable impression even when accountants have the best intentions and clearly understand the accounting rules and the company's financial picture.

Such may be the case when an American corporation is competing with a British corporation to take over a third corporation. Most likely, the price of the target company will be far more than its *book value*, which is based on the company's earnings and other figures. The amount paid that is over the book value is known as *goodwill*. By U.S. accounting rules, if the American company acquires the target it must subtract the goodwill from its earnings over a period of years. By British rules, the British company need not. The difference is far from trivial. The amount of money involved could be as much as $200 million a year for 40 years. With this much subtracted from its earnings, the U.S. company would appear to be much less profitable and could consequently have a harder time raising money.

Clearly, in the world of high finance, a dollar made is not necessarily a dollar you may say you have earned. Take the case of Company A, a franchisor of photo-developing outlets, which receives $250,000 from Company B. In return, Company A gives Company B the sole right to develop franchises in a particular city and agrees to do a certain amount of advertising in that city. In its financial reports, Company A may want to indicate the full $250,000 as earnings right away. It may not do so, however, until it has fulfilled its obligations to Company B. Magazines are in the same situation. Subscribers pay up front, but the publisher must deliver the magazines before the full amount may be declared as earnings. Such a requirement works against a franchisor seeking to raise money through a public offering. Because it could not report the high earnings it wished to report in 1986, for example, Denver-based Le Peep Restaurants, which had hoped to sell 1.7 million shares of stock at up to $10 per share, could only sell 1.3 million shares at 6½.

Sources: Charles J. Bodenstab, "Flying Blind," *Inc.*, May, 1988, pp. 141–144; Penelope Wang, "Claiming Tomorrow's Profits Today," *Forbes*, October 17, 1988, p. 78; and Penelope Wang, "The Unlevel Accounting Field," *Forbes*, November 28, 1988, p. 170.

to another, even though the corresponding entries may be pages apart. In the columns at the far right, the bookkeeper maintains a running balance on the account.

*Step 4: Calculating a Trial Balance*   If the bookkeeper has kept the books—the journal, ledger, and other accounting records—accurately, the ledger accounts should balance. The total debits across all ledger accounts should equal the total credits.

Before preparing the financial statements, an accountant will calculate a **trial balance** to make sure that a credit offsets every debit and that the arithmetic was done correctly. First, he or she brings individual accounts up to date by making adjustments to certain accounts like Supplies and Prepaid Insurance. People use papers, pencils, paperclips, typewriter ribbons, and other supplies every day. It would normally be too expensive to change the accounting records every time a secretary took out a new notepad. Therefore, at the end of the accounting period, someone counts the supplies to determine what has been used up during the period. That amount is then recorded in a journal entry. The same logic explains adjustments made to the prepaid insurance account. The firm pays the premium at the beginning of the insurance's term, which is usually a year. Each day, a portion of that benefit is used up, however. Whenever the financial statements are prepared, the prepaid insurance account is brought up to date by posting appropriate *adjusting entries*—entries made to apply accrual accounting to transactions that span more than one accounting period.[4]

After bringing the accounts up to date, the accountant sums up all accounts with debit balances and all with credit balances. Finally, the accountant checks one against the other. If the two are not equal, he or she looks for mistakes and corrects errors in accounts. Note, however, that a trial balance will not reveal all kinds of errors. If the bookkeeper reversed certain credit and debit entries or even failed to enter a transaction, the accounts would still balance (see Business Issues).

### Step 5: *Preparing Financial Statements*

An accountant prepares financial statements at the end of every accounting period. The three most common statements are:

- The balance sheet
- The income statement
- The statement of changes in financial position

The remainder of this chapter examines these three types of statement in detail.

An **accounting period** is any regular period of one year or less for which a business decides to have financial statements prepared. Many firms have them prepared quarterly or monthly as well as annually. Almost always, firms prepare statements for the same period each year, which allows users to compare the company's performance from period to period and to identify trends. In other words, a company that one year prepares financial statements for the quarter ending March 31 can be expected to prepare financials for the same quarter the next year.

After the accountant has completed the financial statements, the accounts are closed for the accounting period the statements cover. Revenue and expense accounts are returned to zero by transferring their balances to owners' equity. By the time the accountant finishes this work, a new accounting period will be under way and bookkeepers will have started entering transactions in the journal and posting them to the ledger (see Business Issues).

**trial balance** a step taken before preparing financial statements to make sure that a credit offsets every debit and that the arithmetic was done correctly

**accounting period** any regular period of one year or less for which a business decides to have financial statements prepared

FIGURE 15.5
Pacesetters Balance
Sheet

**PACESETTERS, INC.**
**BALANCE SHEET**
December 31, 19—

### Assets

| | | | |
|---|---|---|---|
| **Current assets** | | | |
| Cash | | $39,000 | |
| Marketable securities | | 8,000 | |
| Accounts receivable | $8,000 | | |
| *Less* allowance for doubtful accounts | 200 | 7,800 | |
| Notes receivable | | 2,000 | |
| Inventory | | 38,000 | |
| Prepaid expenses | | 8,200 | |
| Total current assets | | | $103,000 |
| **Fixed assets** | | | |
| Store equipment and fixtures | 76,200 | | |
| *Less* accumulated depreciation | 10,200 | 66,000 | |
| Office furniture and equipment | 27,000 | | |
| *Less* accumulated depreciation | 4,200 | 22,800 | |
| Total fixed assets | | | 88,800 |
| **Intangible assets** | | | |
| Leasehold | 6,000 | | |
| *Less* amortization | 600 | 5,400 | |
| Total intangible assets | | | 5,400 |
| **Total assets** | | | $197,200 |

### Liabilities and owners' equity

| | | | |
|---|---|---|---|
| **Current liabilities** | | | |
| Accounts payable | $41,800 | | |
| Notes payable | 10,000 | | |
| Accrued expenses | 4,200 | | |
| Total current liabilities | | $56,000 | |
| **Long-term liabilities** | | | |
| Long-term notes payable | 10,000 | | |
| Total long-term liabilities | | 10,000 | |
| **Total liabilities** | | | $66,000 |
| **Owners' equity** | | | |
| Common stock (14,000 shares at $5.00 per share) | | 70,000 | |
| Retained earnings | | 61,200 | |
| Total owners' equity | | | 131,200 |
| **Total liabilities and owners' equity** | | | $197,200 |

# The Balance Sheet

**balance sheet (statement of financial position)** summary of an organization's financial status at the end of an accounting period

The **balance sheet,** or **statement of financial position,** summarizes an organization's financial status at the end of an accounting period. Figure 15.5 shows the hypothetical Pacesetters' year-end balance sheet after the business has been operating for some years. By now, Margot and Dave have incorporated and brought in new investors. They have also diversified into other sporting goods lines.

As the headings on Figure 15.5 clearly reveal, the balance sheet is another expression of the accounting equation. Like a photograph, a balance sheet freezes a firm's financial condition at a particular moment. By law, shareholders must receive these "snapshots" at least annually.

**5.** *Describe the functions of the three most common financial statements discussed in this chapter.*

## Assets

The left side of a balance sheet lists the asset accounts in order of their decreasing **liquidity**, the ease with which the actual assets they represent can be turned into cash.

*Current Assets* Cash and any other assets that are likely to be used up or converted into cash, usually within a year, are included in **current assets**. Cash includes both money on hand, as in the cash box, and money in bank demand accounts. **Marketable securities** are securities the holder can turn into cash in only a few days. Any security traded on an exchange is marketable.

**Accounts receivable** are any amounts owed to an organization by its customers or clients. Pacesetters' customers pay primarily with credit cards or cash, so its $8,000 in accounts receivable is quite small. Some accounts receivable may become doubtful accounts, accounts receivable that appear uncollectable. For this reason, accountants make an allowance, based on the company's experience, for doubtful accounts. Notes receivable are formal, signed promises to pay a certain amount on a certain date. Generally, notes are paid over a somewhat longer period than accounts receivable, which are usually due within thirty days. In some cases, a debtor issues a note receivable to settle a past-due account.

**Inventory** is a general term used to describe certain classes of goods that are assets of a business. Inventory may represent the merchandise a company holds for sale. Pacesetters' $38,000 in inventory consists of finished products— shoes, jogging outfits, and the like. By contrast, the manufacturers who sold it these goods would include in their inventory raw materials and goods used in the process of manufacturing, too. The final type of current asset account is **prepaid expenses**, the services and supplies an organization has paid for but has not yet used. Insurance premiums are a common example. Office supplies, like paper and pens, are another.

*Fixed Assets* The tangible assets called **fixed assets**, or **plant and equipment assets**, are those that a firm expects to use for more than a year. Except for land, fixed assets tend to wear out with time. An automobile or a lathe or a computer has a limited period of usefulness before it wears out or becomes obsolete. In financial reports, companies deal with this fact through **depreciation**, the process of distributing the original value of a long-term asset over the years of its useful life. Each year, a portion of an asset's value is considered to be spent and is entered on the books as an expense. The asset's value is at the same time reduced by an equal amount. Both the accounting profession and the Internal Revenue Service have elaborate procedures for calculating depreciation. In the Pacesetters case, its office

**liquidity** the ease with which asset accounts can be turned into cash

**current assets** cash and any other assets that are likely to be used up or converted into cash, usually within a year

**marketable securities** securities the holder can turn into cash in only a few days

**accounts receivable** any amounts owed to an organization by its customers

**inventory** certain classes of goods that are assets of a business

**prepaid expenses** the services and supplies an organization has paid for but has not yet used

**fixed assets (plant and equipment assets)** those assets that a firm expects to use for more than a year

**depreciation** the process of distributing the original value of a long-term value asset over the years of its useful life

**Taking inventory**  *Inventory means different things for different organizations: for retailers it means finished goods for sale, for manufacturers it includes raw materials used for manufacturing. A farmer's balance sheet is likely to include livestock as inventory.*

furniture and equipment originally cost $27,000. Over the period that the property has been in use, the accountant has reduced its value, or depreciated it, by $4,200.

*Intangible Assets*  Long-term assets that have no physical substance but have a value based on rights or privileges that belong to the owner are **intangible assets**.[5] A trademark, like Pepsi-Cola's logo, has a real value to the company, but, unlike a bottling machine, it cannot be touched. Patents, copyrights, leaseholds (ownership of a lease), and franchises are also intangible assets. When an intangible asset has a limited life, like a patent or a leasehold, accountants show its decline in value over time by *amortization,* a process much like depreciation. Pacesetters' ten-year leasehold on its new store is carried at its original value. Each year, a portion of the original value is converted into an expense until at its expiration the leasehold disappears from the balance sheet.

An asset that appears on many balance sheets, though not on Pacesetters', is **goodwill**, a firm's extra earning power compared to other firms in the same industry. Goodwill is more than just a good reputation or a warm relationship with customers. It may come from a good location or excellent management. Goodwill does not appear on Pacesetters' balance sheet because it is not listed as long as a firm remains in the hands of its original owners. When a firm is sold, buyers will often pay a premium above the value of the company's assets. That premium is said to pay for the firm's goodwill, so the premium is assigned to that account.

**intangible assets**  long-term assets that have no physical substance but have a value based on rights or privileges that belong to the owner

**goodwill**  a firm's extra earning power compared to other firms in the same industry

## Liabilities

The balance sheet lists liabilities according to the dates when they must be paid. Like assets, liabilities are classified as either current or fixed.

*Current Liabilities*   Debts that will fall due within the next twelve months are **current liabilities**. **Accounts payable** consist primarily of debts owed to suppliers of goods and services that are due during the next accounting period. Essentially, they are the reverse of accounts receivable. Thus, a customer's debt to Pacesetters for a pair of shoes is an account receivable; Pacesetters' debt to the manufacturer for the same shoes is an account payable. **Notes payable** are notes that will fall due during the next twelve months. They are the opposite of notes receivable.

The **accrued expenses** category lumps together various kinds of obligations that were incurred during the accounting period but are not yet actually due or owing. Accrued expenses include wages that an employee has earned but are not yet due to be paid; taxes that will be due a taxing authority; interest on bank loans, and the like. If a firm takes delivery of a filing cabinet during the accounting period but has not yet been billed for it, its obligation to pay is an accrued expense. All such expenses must appear on the balance sheet in order to present a true picture of the firm's position.

*Long-Term Liabilities*   Debts that will fall due more than a year after the date of the balance sheet are **long-term liabilities**. These include mortgages, bonds, and long-term notes. Pacesetters has a $10,000 note due to the bank.

## Owner's Equity

The owner's-equity section of the balance sheet varies with the type of business it describes. A sole proprietorship's reflects simply the difference between the assets and the liabilities. Generally, its balance sheet does not distinguish the owner's original investment from later profits. The same is true of partnerships' owner's-equity sections except that the equity is divided among the partners. A corporation's balance sheet does distinguish between what the corporation has received for its stock since its founding and its **retained earnings**, profits kept in the business after any dividends are paid. Quite often, retained earnings are used to fund plant expansion and other long-term capital investments.

# The Income Statement

The balance sheet, as noted, records a company's financial position as though frozen at a particular moment. The **income statement** summarizes what an organization has earned and spent over a given period. It first totals a firm's **revenue**, the cash and accounts receivable a firm generates from its operations. Then it deducts expenses. The result is the firm's profit or loss for the period. The basic formula is as follows:

Revenues − (Cost of goods sold + Operating expenses) = Net income

Businesses can record revenues and expenses on one of two bases. On an accrual basis, the bookkeeper lists sales on the dates they take place and expenses on the dates they are incurred, regardless of whether any money

**current liabilities**   debts that will fall due within the next twelve months

**accounts payable**   debts owed to suppliers of goods and services that are due during the next accounting period

**notes payable**   notes that will fall due during the next twelve months

**accrued expenses**   various kinds of obligations that were incurred during the accounting period but are not yet actually due or owing

**long-term liabilities**   debts that will fall due more than a year after the date of the balance sheet

**retained earnings**   profits kept in the business after any dividends are paid

**income statement**   a summary of what an organization has earned and spent over a given period

**revenue**   the cash and accounts receivable a firm generates from its operations

actually changed hands. If Pacesetters sold new warm-ups to a college track team in December but the college did not pay for them until February, on an accrual basis it would treat the revenue as December's and therefore as the prior year's. Alternatively, on a cash basis, sales and expenses are listed according to the dates when money changes hands. The accounting profession and the Internal Revenue Service agree that the accrual basis more accurately reflects a company's true income. Only certain types of relatively simple businesses may use a cash basis.

## Revenues

Generally, revenues come from sales of goods and services. However, items in this category may also include income from the sale or rental of property; royalties earned on patents, copyrights, or trademarks; and interest or dividends on investments.

**gross sales** the total value of all goods or services sold during the accounting period

Let's assume that Pacesetters' annual revenues come entirely from the sale of sporting goods. The first category in the revenue category on its income statement (Figure 15.6) is **gross sales**, the total value of all goods or services sold during the accounting period. However, Pacesetters did not actually receive $294,000 for its merchandise because not all its customers paid full price and some returned the goods. The categories listed below gross sales adjust it to reality. Sales returns are the refunds allowed customers when they return something. Allowances are price reductions granted if merchandise is slightly damaged or defective. Cash discounts are given when customers are charged less than the full amount if they pay their bills promptly. Discount terms usually appear on invoices. For example, "2/10 net 30" means that the buyer may deduct 2 percent from the sale price if the invoice is paid within ten days. Otherwise, the total amount, the net, is due in thirty days.

**net sales** the amount the firm added to its assets by selling goods during the accounting period

After subtracting the adjustments from gross sales, the figure that results is **net sales**, the amount the firm added to its assets by selling goods during the accounting period. Net sales is not, however, a synonym for profit.

## The Cost of Goods Sold

**cost of goods sold** the amount that an organization spent to buy or produce the goods it sold during an accounting period

The amount that an organization spent to buy or produce the goods it sold during an accounting period is its **cost of goods sold**. Calculating the cost of goods sold varies according to which of the two basic inventory systems a firm uses. The **perpetual inventory system** records every change in inventory as soon as it happens. By contrast, the **periodic inventory method** calculates the effect of sales on inventory only at the end of an accounting period.

**perpetual inventory system** system that records every change in inventory as soon as it happens

*Perpetual Inventory* The main advantage of a perpetual inventory is that it tells managers immediately the precise value of merchandise on hand. Suppose that an automobile dealership sells a car on March 8. If it uses a perpetual inventory system, as of that date its inventory account is reduced by the cost of the car. Because managers will know exactly what inventory is on hand, they can maintain smaller inventories. Against this obvious benefit is the significantly greater cost of maintaining a perpetual inventory system.

**periodic inventory method** method that calculates the effect of sales on inventory only at the end of an accounting period

FIGURE 15.6
Pacesetters Income
Statement

**PACESETTERS, INC.**
**INCOME STATEMENT**
For the year ended December 31, 19—

| | | | |
|---|---|---|---|
| **Revenues** | | | |
| Gross sales | | $294,000 | |
| *Less* sales returns, and cash discounts | | 9,000 | |
| Net sales | | | $285,000 |
| | | | |
| **Cost of goods sold** | | | |
| Beginning inventory (January 1) | | 30,000 | |
| Purchases | $170,000 | | |
| *Less* purchase discounts | 6,000 | | |
| Net purchases | | 164,000 | |
| Cost of goods available for sale | | 194,000 | |
| *Less* ending inventory (December 31) | | 38,000 | |
| Cost of goods sold | | | 156,000 |
| Gross profit | | | $129,000 |
| | | | |
| **Operating expenses** | | | |
| Selling expenses | | | |
| Sales salaries | 46,000 | | |
| Advertising | 5,300 | | |
| Depreciation of store equipment and fixtures | 1,700 | | |
| Miscellaneous | 1,000 | | |
| Total selling expenses | | 54,000 | |
| | | | |
| Administrative expenses | | | |
| Office salaries | 20,600 | | |
| Office supplies | 1,000 | | |
| Rent | 15,500 | | |
| Utilities | 2,000 | | |
| Depreciation of office furniture and equipment | 800 | | |
| Miscellaneous | 600 | | |
| Total administrative expenses | | 40,500 | |
| Total operating expenses | | | 94,500 |
| | | | |
| **Net income before taxes** | | | $34,500 |
| *Less* income taxes | | | 6,500 |
| | | | |
| **Net income after taxes** | | | $28,000 |

Businesses that sell comparatively few but relatively high-cost units find that perpetual inventory systems work well. These systems also simplify preparation of the income statement. A perpetual inventory firm will have a continuous ledger account for the cost of goods sold and can simply enter the total for the accounting period. Today, universal product codes and electronic scanners attached to computers have made perpetual inventory systems attractive to high-volume businesses like supermarkets, which could not use them before.

*Periodic Inventory*   Firms using the periodic inventory method calculate their inventories by looking at the change in inventory during an accounting period. Pacesetters is such a firm. The first line under the cost of goods sold heading on its income statement is its *beginning inventory*—what it carried over from the prior accounting period. To that $30,000, it adds its **purchases**, the value of what it bought for inventory during the accounting period. Pacesetters received some volume discounts and some prompt-payment discounts, so their total is subtracted from the figure for purchases to produce *net purchases*. The total of beginning inventory plus net purchases equals the cost of goods available for sale during the accounting period. Of course, not all the goods available for sale were sold. To find the value of the unsold inventory, Pacesetters subtracts the inventory remaining at the end of the year from the cost of goods available for sale. The result is the cost of goods sold: $156,000.

Pacesetters' income statement calculations are typical of retailers'. A manufacturer's would be somewhat different, though. Its cost of goods sold would include raw materials or parts, labor, and factory overhead. Still, if the manufacturer used a periodic inventory system, the basic calculation would be the same.

*Gross Profit*   Subtracting the cost of goods sold from the net sales produces a company's **gross profit** or **gross margin**. Managers use this important figure to compare the company's current sales performance with it in prior accounting periods. Also, the gross profit figure offers a good standard of comparison with the performance of other companies in the industry.

*FIFO and LIFO*   The gross profit calculation seems simple, but it conceals a difficult question: How do you put a value on the ending inventory if the prices of the goods making it up change during the accounting period? Consider Pacesetters' situation when on March 1 it orders 100 pairs of running shoes at $18 apiece and then, three weeks later, orders 50 more pairs at a new price of $18.95. By the year's end, 90 of the 150 pairs are sold. In calculating income, what value should be assigned to the 90 pairs it sold?

Companies with perpetual inventory systems assign a value to each item brought into inventory and therefore do not have this problem. However, firms with relatively fast inventory turnover must choose among somewhat arbitrary methods of assigning inventory costs. The two most common are called FIFO and LIFO. The **FIFO—First In, First Out**—system assumes that the first items brought into inventory are also the first sold. Thus, it would treat the 90 pairs of shoes Pacesetters sold as coming entirely from the $18 shipment. In times of rising prices, FIFO minimizes the cost of goods sold and maximizes the gross profit, so the firm seems more successful. By inflating profits, though, it also increases the firm's taxes. More importantly, it distorts the financial picture of the firm by understating the cost of goods sold, presenting a misleading picture of what it will cost to replace inventory.

For these reasons, most accountants prefer the **LIFO—Last In, First Out—**

**purchases**   the value of what a firm bought for inventory during the accounting period

**gross profit (gross margin)**   the difference between cost of goods sold and net sales

**First In, First Out (FIFO)**   the system which assumes that the first items brought into inventory are also the first sold

**Last In, First Out (LIFO)**   the system which assumes that the last items taken into inventory are the first sold

*"When I said we'd make a profit in 1987, I misspoke."*

system, which assumes that the last items taken into inventory are the first sold. Thus, Pacesetters would treat 50 of the 90 pairs as $18.95 shoes and 40 as $18 shoes. In times of rising prices, LIFO understates profits and minimizes taxes but, far more important, it more accurately reflects the current cost of replacing the inventory. In times of falling prices, LIFO overstates profits, understates the cost of goods sold, and maximizes taxes.

## Operating Expenses

The income statement's third section, **operating expenses**, includes all costs of running the business except the cost of goods sold. Normally, an income statement divides these expenses into two general categories. **Selling expenses** are all costs directly associated with selling products or services to customers. **Administrative expenses**, also called **general expenses**, are the overall costs of operating the firm, excluding selling expenses and the cost of goods sold. Figure 15.6, Pacesetters' income statement, lists examples of both types of expenses.

## Net Income

Subtracting the total operating expenses from the gross profit produces the figure known as **net income**, the amount of profit or loss the organization

**operating expenses** all costs of running the business except the cost of goods sold

**selling expenses** all costs directly associated with selling products or services to customers

**administrative expenses (general expenses)** the overall costs of operating a firm, excluding selling expenses and cost of goods sold

**net income** the difference between the total operating expenses and the gross profit

**Monitoring costs**   *Operating expenses include all costs of running a business, except the cost of goods sold. In order to maximize net income, managers pay close attention to their organizations' expenses, continually looking for ways to reduce them and spend money more efficiently.*

has generated during the accounting period. Normally, the amount of income taxes due reduces the net income figure. The last line of the income statement is the famous "bottom line," net income after taxes.

# The Statement of Changes in Financial Position

**statement of changes in financial position** summary of changes in the firm's generation and use of cash that have taken place during the accounting period being analyzed

In addition to the balance sheet and the income statement, many firms provide a **statement of changes in financial position**, which summarizes changes in the firm's generation and use of cash that have taken place during the accounting period being analyzed. Generally, it lists the resources provided, where they came from, and how they were used. If, for example, a firm issued bonds to acquire new plant and equipment, those figures would appear on a statement of changes in financial position. This type of statement thus shows the flow of assets into and out of the organization. The Securities and Exchange Commission regards this information as critically important to investors and requires all companies subject to its regulation to provide these statements.

# Interpreting Financial Statements

Financial statements are not particularly valuable for their own sakes. They are important only for what they can tell about a business.

*6.* *Explain briefly how analysts look at and interpret financial statements.*

## Financial Ratios

Accountants, managers, owners, and investors analyze financial statements by applying **financial ratios**, certain mathematical relationships between numbers, to the components of the financial statements. In algebra, ratios always involve dividing one number by another, but there are other calculations, too, among financial ratios. Financial ratios provide important clues to the meaning of a company's reports. Table 15.3 includes the most significant financial ratios and computes them for Pacesetters, using the numbers shown in Figures 15.5 and 15.6.

**financial ratios** certain mathematical relationships between numbers used to analyze financial statements

### Percentage of Net Sales

Managers and other analysts often examine the elements of an income statement to determine the percentage of net sales that each element accounts for. Such an analysis quickly points up costs that are unusually high or low. Management then knows where problems may be developing and can concentrate on those areas. Bankers, auditors, and investors know where they should look to see if problems exist or to determine whether this firm is set for growth and expansion. Figure 15.7 illustrates the percentage of net sales breakdown for Pacesetters.

### Profitability Ratios

Although the bottom line of the income statement shows the actual amount of **profit**—the excess of revenues over expenses—it does not reveal whether the profit level is appropriate for a given firm. Larger firms usually make larger total profits, but they should. And some industries earn very high profits, whereas others have difficulty showing any profit at all. To determine whether a firm is earning a reasonable profit, most people use data from its financial statements to calculate several profitability ratios. The most commonly used are the following:

**profit** the excess of revenues over expenses

- Net profit margin, also known as return on sales
- Return on equity
- Earnings per share

The net profit margin ratio, or return on sales, measures how much profit each dollar of sales generates. The return on equity ratio shows how much the firm earns on every dollar the owners or shareholders have invested. Earnings per share states the profits realized for each share of stock the company has issued. As Chapters 18 and 19 will show, those profits can either be distributed as dividends to shareholders or kept in the firm as retained earnings.

### Short-Term Financial Ratios

These types of ratios let managers, lenders, and investors judge the liquidity of a firm. They also give the analyst important information about a company's ability to pay its debts. Even very profitable

## TABLE 15.3    Common Financial Ratios

| Name of Ratio | Ratio | Standard of Comparison |
|---|---|---|
| **Profitability Ratios** | | |
| **Net Profit Margin (Return on Sales)** | $= \dfrac{\text{Net income after taxes}}{\text{Net sales}}$ <br><br> $= \dfrac{\$\ 28{,}000}{\$285{,}000} = 0.098 = 9.8\%$ | Good; 5% for retailers |
| **Return on Equity** | $= \dfrac{\text{Net income after taxes}}{\text{Owners' equity}}$ <br><br> $= \dfrac{\$\ 28{,}000}{\$131{,}000} = 0.213 = 21.3\%$ | Very good, but young businesses often retain earnings |
| **Earnings per Share** | $= \dfrac{\text{Net income after taxes}}{\text{Common shares outstanding}}$ <br><br> $= \dfrac{\$28{,}000}{14{,}000} = \$2.00$ | Fair; IBM earns more than \$11 |
| **Short-Term Financial Ratios** | | Ability to repay short-term debts |
| **Working Capital** | $=$ Current assets $-$ Current liabilities <br> $= \$103{,}000 - \$56{,}000 = \$47{,}000$ | Not a true ratio; hard to use for comparison |
| **Current Ratio** | $= \dfrac{\text{Current assets}}{\text{Current liabilities}}$ <br><br> $= \dfrac{\$103{,}000}{\$\ 56{,}000} = 1.84$ | 2:1 the usual minimum; weak |
| **Acid-Test Ratio (Quick Ratio)** | $= \dfrac{\text{Cash + Marketable securities +}}{\text{Current liabilities}}$ <br> accounts receivable + notes receivable <br><br> $= \dfrac{\$39{,}000 + \$8{,}000 + \$\ 7{,}800 + \$2{,}000}{\$56{,}000} = 1.01$ | 1.0 is standard; quick assets should cover liabilities |
| **Activity Ratios** | | |
| **Inventory Turnover** | $= \dfrac{\text{Cost of goods sold}}{\text{Average inventory per period}}$ <br><br> $= \dfrac{\$156{,}000}{((\$30{,}000 + \$38{,}000) : 2)} = 4.6$ | Variable with industry; e.g., supermarkets in high teens |
| **Long-Term-Debt Ratios** | | |
| **Debt-to-Assets Ratio** | $= \dfrac{\text{Total liabilities}}{\text{Total assets}}$ <br><br> $= \dfrac{\$\ 66{,}000}{\$197{,}200} = 0.33$ | Normal; the lower the better for lenders |
| **Debt-to-Equity Ratio** | $= \dfrac{\text{Total liabilities}}{\text{Owners' equity}}$ <br><br> $= \dfrac{\$\ 66{,}000}{\$131{,}200} = 0.50$ | Normal; the lower the better for lenders |

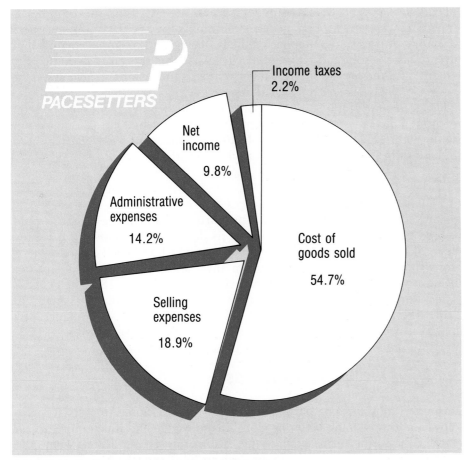

FIGURE 15.7    Pacesetters Percentage of Net Sales

firms can fail if they do not have enough money to pay their debts when they fall due. The most common short-term financial ratios are:

■ Working capital
■ Current ratio
■ Acid-test ratio (quick ratio)

*Working capital*—the difference between current assets and current liabilities—is not, strictly speaking, a ratio. It is, nevertheless, an important indicator of a company's short-term financial strength. Working capital shows how much of its assets the company would have left if it used its current assets to pay off its current debts. The *current ratio* uses the same amounts, but in this situation the current assets are divided by the current liabilities, as seen in Table 15.3. Investors generally look for a current ratio of 2:1 or better. Finally, because current assets include items like inventory as well as prepaid expenses that cannot be easily turned into cash, some analysts prefer the *acid-test ratio* to the current ratio. Because the acid-test ratio excludes all assets that are not quickly convertible into cash, the analyst using it gets a much better picture of how the company would survive a short-term crisis.

*Activity Ratios*  How efficiently an organization is using its resources is shown in its *activity ratios*. The most commonly used activity ratio measures inventory turnover, the number of times during an accounting period that inventories are sold and replaced. Analysts use this ratio to determine how long it takes the firm to convert the inventory into cash or receivables.

*Long-Term-Debt Ratios*  A company's financial health depends not only on its profitability and its power to repay short-term debts but also on how it stands with respect to long-term obligations. Bankers in particular pay heed to these ratios, the most common of which are these:

- Debt-to-assets ratio
- Debt-to-equity ratio

The *debt-to-assets ratio* shows the proportion of a firm's assets that would be used up if the firm were to eliminate its debt. This ratio also reveals how much of the firm is financed by its creditors and how much by its owners. Firms that owe a large proportion of their assets to creditors are riskier investments. (More is said about financial risk in Chapter 18.) The *debt-to-equity ratio,* which divides total liabilities by owners' equity, as shown in Table 15.3, also shows how much of the firm's activity is financed by creditors. Lenders generally look for low debt-to-equity ratios.

## Applying the Financial Ratios

Financial ratios are not particularly useful in isolation. Analysts want to know if a firm is doing better or worse than average and if it is more or less efficient than other firms of the same size in the same industry. They also want to know if a firm has enough cash to fund expansion and growth or whether lack of cash might cause the business to fail.

To get information of this sort, analysts compare financial ratios—either against the firm's own past performance or against similar firms' performance. A firm that is growing more profitable every year and using its resources more and more efficiently is likely to be a good candidate either as a creditor or as an investment. Another yardstick that financial analysts commonly use is the performance of comparable firms. A number of sources offer this information. Dun & Bradstreet publishes industry averages for operating ratios of over 150 different industries, and many trade groups and specialized publications publish similar information for particular industries (see Experiencing Business).

# Budgeting

**budget**  an organization's financial plan for the future in which it describes how it will use its resources to meet its goals

The financial statements we have analyzed describe a company's present position or its performance during a prior period. Accounting principles also play an important role in preparing a firm's **budget,** an organization's financial plan for the future in which it describes how it will use its resources to meet

Big budget  *In a large corporation most of the budgeting is done by the accounting department. Usually the other individual departments within the corporation such as this one at the Gulfstream Aerospace Corporation, which installs communication systems in jets, contribute their own budget projections to the accounting department as well.*

its goals. Normally, firms draw up budgets for a given operating period, the length of time it takes to complete a manufacturing or sales cycle. An operating period is usually a year, but it may be a quarter or any other length of time appropriate for the business.

*7. Analyze accounting's role in the budget process.*

## Types of Budgets

Budgets are based on the income statement's two basic items: revenue and expenses. A large corporation will have a **master budget**, which is an overall financial plan for the entire firm, and a number of subsidiary budgets for the units that make up the whole. A large corporation will also develop specialized budgets. For instance, an operating budget would project sales revenues, the cost of goods sold, and operating expenses. A cash budget would anticipate the flow of cash into and out of the firm. A capital budget would project expenditures on buildings and equipment over a period of years.

**master budget**  an overall financial plan for the entire firm

In addition to giving an organization a financial plan, a budget helps managers head off problems. For example, the process of developing a cash budget might reveal that in certain months the firm would not generate sufficient cash to meet operating expenses. Our hypothetical company, Pacesetters, might identify January and February as months in which cash-flow problems might arise because of a low interest in running in their area during that time of year. Margot and Dave might either set up a reserve for that period or arrange with a bank for a line of credit. July and August

# EXAMINING THE FINANCIAL STATEMENTS
# OF THE GOODYEAR TIRE & RUBBER COMPANY

The Goodyear Tire & Rubber Company is the world's largest producer of tires and rubber products. It develops, manufactures, distributes, and sells tires all over the world. It also manufactures and sells a variety of chemical and plastic products for the transportation industry, and other industrial and consumer markets.

Consult the financial statements from Goodyear's annual report below and apply the financial ratios listed in Table 15.3. How would you interpret your results? What conclusions can you draw about Goodyear's financial position? Check your answers against those in the back of the book.*

**CONSOLIDATED BALANCE SHEET**
The Goodyear Tire & Rubber Company
and Subsidiaries
December 31, 1988

(Dollars in millions)

**ASSETS**

| Current Assets: | |
|---|---|
| Cash and cash equivalents | $ 234.1 |
| Accounts and notes receivable | 1,578.4 |
| Inventories | 1,635.5 |
| Prepaid expenses and other current assets | 109.9 |
| **Total Current Assets** | 3,557.9 |
| Other Assets: | |
| Investments in affiliates, at equity | 122.3 |
| Long term accounts and notes receivable | 313.7 |
| Deferred pension plan cost | — |
| Deferred charges and other miscellaneous assets | 197.0 |
| | 633.0 |
| **Properties and Plants** | 4,427.4 |
| | **$8,618.3** |

**LIABILITIES AND SHAREHOLDERS' EQUITY**

| Current Liabilities: | |
|---|---|
| Accounts payable—trade | $ 781.3 |
| Accrued payrolls and other compensation | 412.2 |
| Other current liabilities | 347.2 |
| United States and foreign taxes | 391.0 |
| Notes payable to banks and overdrafts | 354.2 |
| Long term debt due within one year | 172.6 |
| **Total Current Liabilities** | 2,458.5 |

**LIABILITIES AND SHAREHOLDERS' EQUITY** *cont'd.*

| Long Term Debt and Capital Leases | 3,044.8 |
|---|---|
| **Other Long Term Liabilities** | 435.7 |
| **Deferred Income Taxes** | 555.4 |
| **Minority Equity in Subsidiaries** | 96.8 |
| Shareholders' Equity: | |
| Preferred stock, no par value: Authorized, 50,000,000 shares, unissued | — |
| Common stock, no par value: Authorized, 150,000,000 shares Outstanding shares, 57,430,526 (56,986,579 in 1987) | 57.4 |
| Capital surplus | 29.3 |
| Retained earnings | 2,175.4 |
| | 2,262.1 |
| Foreign currency translation adjustment | (235.0) |
| **Total Shareholders' Equity** | 2,027.1 |
| | **$8,618.3** |

---

* Hint: Remember that the figures in the statements are in *millions* of dollars, except earnings per share.
Source: The Goodyear Tire & Rubber Company, Annual Report 1988.

## CONSOLIDATED STATEMENT OF INCOME
### The Goodyear Tire & Rubber Company
### and Subsidiaries
### December 31, 1988

(Dollars in millions, except per share)

| | | | |
|---|---|---|---|
| Net Sales | $10,810.4 | Income from Continuing Operations Before Income Taxes | 537.5 |
| Other Income | 184.5 | | |
| | 10,994.9 | | |
| | | United States and Foreign Taxes on Income | 187.4 |
| **Cost and Expenses:** | | | |
| Cost of goods sold | 8,291.0 | Income from Continuing Operations | 350.1 |
| Selling, administrative and general expense | 1,745.1 | | |
| Interest expense | 238.0 | Discontinued Operations | — |
| Unusual items | 78.8 | | |
| Foreign currency exchange | 85.3 | | |
| Minority interest in net income of subsidiaries | 19.2 | Net Income | $ 350.1 |
| | 10,457.4 | | |
| | | **Per Share of Common Stock:** | |
| | | Income from continuing operations | $6.11 |
| | | Discontinued operations | — |
| | | Net Income | $6.11 |
| | | Average Shares Outstanding | 57,322,165 |

might, in contrast, be Pacesetters' biggest months, and its managers might want to arrange for some short-term investments to use up the excess cash.

## The Responsibility for Budgeting

In large corporations, the accounting department will do most of the budgeting, but every department will contribute its own projections. The overall budget lists what each department hopes to spend in the next operating period, so it tends to contain some fat, because no manager wants to be unduly restricted.

Traditionally, one year's budget is built on the prior year's. In the last fifteen years, though, another method has come into use. *Zero-based budgeting* requires managers to justify their programs—and therefore all their expenditures—each time a new budget is prepared. Instead of starting from old figures, managers start from zero to show why they need to spend what they are requesting and explain how these expenditures will produce revenues.

## Budgets as Controls

When a new operating period begins with the budget in place, managers can begin to use it as a controlling device. If a department is selling less or spending more than the budget predicted, higher levels of management will want to know why and how those in charge plan to solve their problems. This function of budgeting returns us to a concept discussed at the beginning of this chapter. Without adequate accounting procedures—starting with bookkeeping and proceeding through the development and analysis of the financial statements to end with budgeting—no manager can accurately tell where the reasons for success or failure lie. Managers will be confused about the effectiveness of their methods, and the firm's prospects will become doubtful at best.

A good accounting system makes people and programs accountable. It puts managers, owners, and investors in control of their businesses by giving them the information they need to improve their firm's present performance and to plan the company's future.

# CHAPTER HIGHLIGHTS

*1.* Describe how managers, investors, and others use accounting information.

Accounting information is useful to owners, managers, creditors, investors, and others. Owners and managers use the information to see how the business is doing and to identify its strengths and weaknesses. Bankers and creditors use financial statements and other accounting information to judge whether a business can be expected to pay its debts. Investors are interested in determining whether a firm is likely to grow. Union employees want to know what they can reasonably expect from contract negotiations.

*2.* Distinguish between the primary types of accountants.

A *public accountant* is an independent professional who is hired by individuals or companies to perform specific accounting services. *Certified Public Accountants (CPAs)* must pass an exam prepared by the American Institute of Certified Public Accountants and satisfy a state's educational and experience requirements. Only CPAs may certify an organization's financial statements. *Private accountants,* or management accountants, are employed by businesses or government agencies. *Certified management accountants* have passed the National Association of Accountants' test and satisfied its educational and professional criteria.

*3.* State the accounting equation and relate it to double-entry bookkeeping.

The *accounting equation* is:

Assets = Liabilities + Owners' equity

*Double-entry bookkeeping* is a system of recording business transactions that requires an entry in at least two separate accounts for each transaction. Accounts on the left-hand side of the equals sign (assets) record an increase as debits and a decrease as credits. Accounts on the right-hand side of the equals sign (liabilities and owners' equity) show increases as credits and decreases as debits. Any transaction that is recorded correctly leaves the accounting equation in balance.

*4.* List the five steps in the accounting cycle and provide a one-sentence description of each stage.

(1) Examine source documents to make certain that a transaction has in fact occurred. (2) Enter

the transaction in a journal, a chronological list of all the transactions that occur. (3) Transactions are then posted in a ledger. After all the accounts have been posted and brought up to date, (4) a trial balance is taken to make sure that credits equal debits and that the equation is still in balance. Mistakes and errors are corrected at this point. (5) Financial statements are prepared and accounts are closed for the period covered by the statements.

**5.** *Describe the functions of the three most common financial statements discussed in this chapter.*

The *balance sheet,* or statement of financial position, provides a snapshot of a firm's financial condition at a particular moment. Analysts use it to assess a firm's liquidity and to determine what proportion of the business is financed by creditors and what by owners. The *income statement* gives a picture of a business's performance over time. In it, expenses are subtracted from revenues to show a firm's net income for the period. The *statement of changes in financial position* summarizes changes that have taken place during the accounting period in the firm's generation and use of cash. It shows the flow of assets into and out of the

organization. The Securities and Exchange Commission requires all companies subject to its regulation to provide these statements to their shareholders and to the commission.

**6.** *Explain briefly how analysts look at and interpret financial statements.*

Analysts (including owners, managers, creditors, and investors) examine financial statements to identify trends in a firm's performance or to see how a business is doing in comparison with similar firms. An analyst usually compares financial ratios for the business with industry averages or with ratios calculated on the basis of the firm's statements for the preceding two or three years.

**7.** *Analyze accounting's role in the budget process.*

Budgets show what a business intends to achieve over the planning period and the resources it expects to use in reaching its goals. The accounting department of a large corporation usually has the major responsibility for preparing the budget as well as the responsibility to collect and interpret the raw data that allow actual performance to be compared with planned performance.

# REVIEW QUESTIONS

1. It has been said that accountants do not just compile and tabulate data. What other duties do they perform?
2. In what ways are the duties of a bookkeeper different from those of an accountant? What is the difference between a public accountant and a private accountant?
3. Define owner's equity. How would the owner of a hardware store determine his owner's equity?
4. List and briefly describe the major steps in the accounting cycle.
5. Explain the function of the balance sheet. In what ways is the balance sheet like a photograph?
6. What is the major function of the income statement? What are the major components of the income statement?
7. In what ways does a perpetual inventory differ from a periodic inventory? What are the major advantages of a perpetual inventory?
8. What is a financial ratio? List and describe at least two common financial ratios.
9. Why do business firms develop budgets? What types of specialized budgets do firms develop?
10. Owners of small business firms can utilize the services of an accountant, or compile, tabulate, and interpret their own data. What would be the advantages of employing an accountant?

# APPLICATION EXERCISES

1. Using the financial data in the income statement for Anton's Fashions Ltd. that follows, determine the net profit margin. What additional information would be needed to determine if this business is earning a reasonable profit?

2. Using the balance sheet for Anton's Fashions Ltd., review the financial data and calculate the return on equity. Also determine the debt to assets ratio.

### ANTON'S FASHIONS LTD.
Income Statement
For Year Ending December 31, 19xx

| | | | |
|---|---|---|---|
| **Revenues** | | | |
| Gross Sales | | $264,000 | |
| Less Sales Returns and Allowances | $ 4,200 | | |
| Less Sales Discounts | 2,150 | 6,350 | |
| Net Sales | | | $257,650 |
| Cost of Goods Sold | | | |
| Beginning Inventory, January 1, 19xx | | $ 38,000 | |
| Purchases | $134,000 | | |
| Less Purchase Discounts | 4,000 | | |
| Net Purchases | | 130,000 | |
| Cost of Goods Available for Sale | | $168,000 | |
| Less Ending Inventory, December 31, 19xx | | 36,000 | |
| Cost of Goods Sold | | | 132,000 |
| Gross Profit on Sales | | | $125,650 |
| **Operating Expenses** | | | |
| Selling Expenses | | | |
| Advertising | $ 3,450 | | |
| Sales Salaries | 18,200 | | |
| Sales Promotion | 3,100 | | |
| Depreciation—Store Equipment | 1,400 | | |
| Miscellaneous Selling Expenses | 720 | | |
| Total Selling Expenses | | $ 26,870 | |
| General Expenses | | | |
| Office Salaries | $ 9,200 | | |
| Rent | 18,300 | | |
| Depreciation—Office Equipment | 1,800 | | |
| Utilities | 1,350 | | |
| Insurance | 600 | | |
| Miscellaneous Expenses | 250 | | |
| Total General Expenses | | $ 31,500 | |
| Total Operating Expenses | | | $ 58,370 |
| Net Income from Operations | | | 67,280 |
| Less Interest Expenses | | | 2,100 |
| Net Income Before Taxes | | | $65,180 |
| Less Federal Income Taxes | | | 9,500 |
| Net Income After Taxes | | | $ 55,680 |

**ANTON'S FASHIONS LTD.**
Balance Sheet
July 31, 19xx

**Assets**
Current Assets
| | | |
|---|---|---|
| Cash | $ 3,700 | |
| Accounts Receivable | 4,500 | |
| Inventory | 36,000 | |
| Total Current Assets | | $ 44,200 |

Fixed Assets
| | | |
|---|---|---|
| Equipment | | 16,000 |
| Total Assets | | $60,200 |

**Liabilities**
Current Liabilities
| | | |
|---|---|---|
| Accounts Payable | $ 4,400 | |
| Notes Payable | 8,500 | |
| Payroll Taxes Payable | 2,200 | |
| Total Current Liabilities | | $15,100 |

Long-Term Liabilities
| | | |
|---|---|---|
| Long-Term Notes Payable | | 21,000 |
| Total Liabilities | | $36,100 |
| Owner's Equity | | 24,100 |
| Total Liabilities and Owner's Equity | | $60,200 |

# *KEY TERMS*

Accounting
Financial statements
Bookkeeper
Public accountant
Audits
Certified public accountant (CPA)
Private accountant (management accountant)
Certified management accountant
Assets
Liabilities
Owners' equity
Accounting equation
Double-entry bookkeeping
Accounting cycle
Journal (book of original entry)

Debit
Credit
Accounts payable
Ledger
Posting
Trial balance
Accounting period
Balance sheet (statement of financial position)
Liquidity
Current assets
Marketable securities
Accounts receivable
Inventory
Prepaid expenses
Fixed assets (plant and equipment assets)
Depreciation
Intangible assets

Goodwill
Current liabilities
Accounts payable
Notes payable
Accrued expenses
Long-term liabilities
Retained earnings
Income statement
Revenue
Gross sales
Net sales
Cost of goods sold
Perpetual inventory system
Periodic inventory method
Purchases

Gross profit (gross margin)
First In, First Out (FIFO)
Last In, First Out (LIFO)
Operating expenses
Selling expenses
Administrative expenses (general expenses)
Net income
Statement of changes in financial position
Financial ratios
Profit
Budget
Master budget

# CASES

## 15.1 Disappearing Inventory at Battery & Tire Warehouse, Inc.

Though by all appearances his company was off to a successful start, CEO Charles Bodenstab was shocked to discover an inventory shortage of $66,000 for Battery & Tire Warehouse, Inc. at the end of its first year. The unexpected loss resulted in a 25 percent decrease in the company's pretax profits. The only explanations Bodenstab could come up with for the mysterious leakage of inventory were employee theft, or a major flaw in his systems.

Bodenstab began having a physical inventory done every month and comparing the counts with the figures in the books. In the process he uncovered several errors which were causing misstatements in his company's inventory throughout the year: costs were understated in the figuring of gross margins for the truck-tire recap shop, resulting in an inflated number of inventory dollars appearing on the books; the costs of product adjustments were understated, also contributing to false figures on the books; due to paperwork foul-ups products were occasionally shipped without being invoiced; the company's suppliers had sometimes shipped the wrong quantities or charged the wrong prices, causing additional unnoticed losses; and many other problems.

According to Bodenstab it took four years of debugging and careful checking for his company to straighten out its system, so that monthly operating statements are now finally much more accurate reports of Battery & Tire Warehouse's financial position. Bodenstab notes that many other small and mid-size companies face the same year-end inventory discrepancies but do little to fix them. Some companies use year-end gains in other areas to offset inventory shortage, or build inflated costs into their systems to help explain inventory shortage later. Bodenstab is critical of such measures, since they do not provide an accurate view of a company's financial position. Though he says it's impossible to elim-

inate shrinkage completely, he suggests that companies make allowances for them each month so that they won't appear unexpectedly at the end of the year. "To my mind," says Bodenstab, "there are enough nasty surprises in running a business, without adding inventory shrinkage to the list."

### Questions

1. Why do you think it is common among other companies to ignore year-end inventory shrinkage? Can you think of other ways a company might manipulate its system to avoid acknowledging shrinkage?
2. Why is some inventory shrinkage inevitable? What kinds of problems might occur frequently and would contribute to a shrinkage?

Source: Adapted from Charles J. Bodenstab, "Surprise! Surprise!" p. 135. Reprinted with permission, *Inc.* magazine, September 1988. Copyright © 1988 by Goldhirsh Group, Inc., 38 Commercial Wharf, Boston, MA 02110.

## 15.2 Building a Profit Margin at Temps & Co.

Since opening for business, Temps & Co., a temp agency serving companies in the Baltimore-Washington, D.C. area, had seen steady growth: $21.8 million in sales for 1988, up from $20.5 million in 1987, and $12.8 million the previous year. Owner and founder Steve Ettridge had been discouraged by a continually slim profit margin, however; after salaries and expenses were taken out, not much was left.

Ettridge began to explore ways of increasing Temps & Co.'s profit margin, with 5 percent as a modest goal. He considered the traditional ways of cost-cutting, such as raising his prices for hiring temps, or cutting his temps' wages, but rejected both since the competitive market would not allow such measures. He focused on operating expenses instead, and rather than making across-the-board cuts, attacked his costs by spending *more* money in certain areas, with the hope of receiving greater returns. Some of his innovative strategies included:

■ Restructuring his system of credit analysis. With as much as 2 percent of annual sales lost to clients who skip out on the bill, he stopped running credit checks and instead began giving away $1000 to each new account as "credit," a relatively small loss in total even if some clients cheated, and also much less than the cost of running checks on all customers.

■ Cutting down on recruitment costs. Ettridge took aim at the cost of recruiting his temps, his highest cost, by paying them to report to headquarters at 9:00 every morning rather than having them wait at home for a call from Temps & Co., which usually came at 10:00 or 10:30. This eliminated the risk of losing business to another agency who might call a temp with a job earlier in the day. Ettridge calculates that it costs much less to have the temps sit idle in his office, about $10 or $20 a person, than it does to replace them, which costs him about $250.

■ Giving away service and overpaying employees. In situations where temps are not needed for the day, instead of sending them home Ettridge pays them the day's wages and sends them to companies for free. He considers giving away free service cheap advertising, since he no longer needs to pay employment agencies or advertisers. "The best possible sales call I can make," says Ettridge, "is one of our temps." When a company needs a less expensive temp than Temps & Co. has on hand,

Ettridge sends out the more expensive temp and pays the difference, rather than telling the company he can't meet their needs. Ettridge is convinced that whatever the free service and the extras cost him in the short term is more than made up in increased business later.

■ Increasing rewards to employees for bringing new-hires to the company. Ettridge rewards employees for bringing in new employees with a hefty $1000, which is still cheaper than paying employment agency fees of $2,500 to $4,000. An added advantage is that new-hires who are referred to Temps & Co. come to work already familiar with how the system works.

So far Ettridge's spend-more-to-save-more plan appears to be working. Temps & Co. has already seen positive individual responses to his strategies: bad-debt losses have dropped from 2 percent to .1 percent, and staff turnover has dropped from an annual 25 percent to 10 percent. Ettridge feels the overall prognosis is positive as well. Sales are currently growing this year, and he anticipates a gross margin of 2.8 percent, up from last year's 1 percent.

## Questions

1. Is Ettridge's impulse to spend more and spend it smarter applicable to other businesses? If so, how would you apply it to paying people more than the job is worth in a product-oriented business rather than a service-oriented one?
2. Can you see any weaknesses in Ettridge's plan, where spending more might *not* lead to as big a return as he was hoping?

Source: Adapted from Tom Richman, "How to Build a Profit Margin," p. 91. Reprinted with permission, *Inc.* magazine, February, 1989. Copyright © 1989 by Goldhirsh Group, Inc., 38 Commercial Wharf, Boston, MA 02110.

# 16 Computers and Management Information Systems

After you have completed this chapter, you will be able to do the following:

1. Explain how data differs from information.

2. Describe the various components of a computer system.

3. Classify the various types of computers used by business firms.

4. Discuss the role of management information systems in a modern business.

5. List and describe the four functions of a management information system.

6. Explain the role of statistics in a management information system.

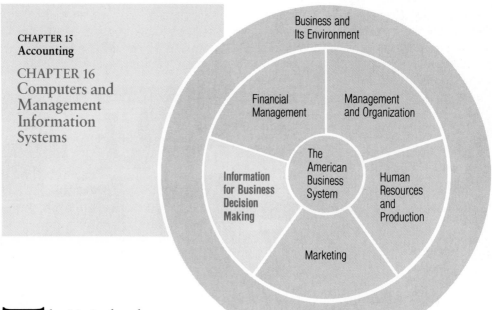

Business and
Its Environment

Financial
Management

Management
and Organization

The
American
Business
System

Information
for Business
Decision
Making

Human
Resources
and
Production

Marketing

The Limited rushes new fashions off the design board and into its 3,200 stores in less than 60 days, while most competitors still order Christmas apparel the previous May.

The [successful clothing retailer] tracks consumer preferences every day through point-of-sale computers. Orders, with facsimile illustrations, are sent by satellite to suppliers around the U.S. and in Hong Kong, South Korea, Singapore, and Sri Lanka. Within days clothing from those distant points begins to collect in Hong Kong. About four times a week a chartered 747 brings it to the company's distribution center in Ohio, where goods are priced and shipped to stores within 48 hours.[1]

As discussed in Chapter 10, speed has become an important competitive advantage for many companies. The Limited is beating its competitors to the punch in the fast-changing clothing business, thanks in large part to modern computerized information technology. Networked point-of-sale computers, facsimile (fax) machines, and satellite telecommunications effectively bring the world to the company's door. Managers who are well informed about computer technology and view information as a strategic resource tend to enjoy a significant competitive advantage.

The push toward the technology we call computers began at approximately the same time the automobile graduated from being a toy to becoming a means of transportation. The two technologies—cars and computers—that have revolutionized American life in this century matured together and are not new (see Figure 16.1). Learning to use computers is in fact much like learning to drive a car. It requires familiarity with what the machines can and cannot do and with how they respond to various commands. Just as safe driving does not require any knowledge of automotive engineering, however, the effective use of computers in the workplace does not require any conceptual understanding of computer science. This chapter is an introduction to how you go about "driving" computers. We will introduce the terms that describe computers and give you some feel for the roads they can take you down.

# Data and Information

When people talk about computers, they tend to use *data* and *information* as though these terms meant the same thing, but they do not. For example, the numbers and letters 77, DE, 75, 260, 14, YANKTON are data. When we learn that they have some relation to the Los Angeles Raiders football team, the data can take on some meaning. Number 77 was Lyle Alzado, a defensive end who is 6 feet, 2 inches (75 inches) tall and weighs 260 pounds. He was

*1. Explain how data differs from information.*

FIGURE 16.1   Time Line of Computer Development

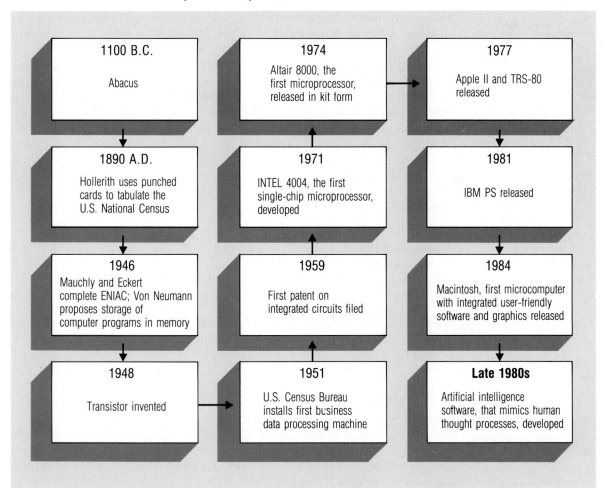

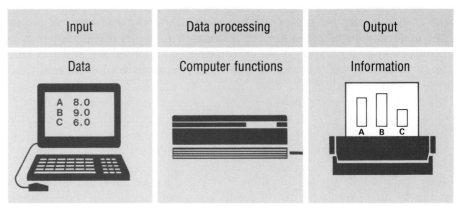

FIGURE 16.2   Information Processing System

a fourteen-year veteran who played for Yankton College. Thus, **data** are numbers, letters, facts, and figures that usually come from measurements or observations but have little or no meaning by themselves. (*Data* is the plural of *datum* but is commonly used in the singular.) The telephone book is packed with data. When you find a particular person's address and phone number, you have **information**, data that has been extracted or summarized so that it has meaning to the person who will use it.

A computer's ability to calculate, extract, and summarize turns meaningless numbers, letters, facts, and figures into meaningful information. As Figure 16.2 indicates, the data put into a computer is called **input**. The functions that a computer performs on the data are called **data processing**. The information that comes out of the computer system after processing is called its **output**. Suppose that a certain corporation sells widgets. Each month, its salespeople report their sales and a computer operator enters the data from their reports into the computer. The instructions given to the computer may be to turn the data into a sales report that presents such information as the following:

- Sales by each salesperson
- Sales by each sales office
- Sales by each region
- Sales for the current month compared to the same month last year
- Sales for the year to date as compared with original projections

These categories are common types of computer output. Later we will look at many more. First, let us examine the mechanics of computing.

# The Machinery of Computing

Strictly speaking, a **computer system** is a mechanical means of transforming data into information consisting of **hardware** (the electronic and mechanical components of a computer system) and *software* (the commands that make the machinery run). It has also been argued by many people that computer systems in addition include data, personnel, and procedures. Hardware and software are of course important, but the type of data the system will process and how much it can handle are crucial factors in any decision about buying computer equipment. Even more critical are the people who operate and rely on the system as well as the procedures a business establishes for its use.

*2. Describe the various components of a computer system.*

In short, the easiest and final element in a decision about choosing a computer system is what software and hardware to buy.[2] Evaluating the data demands, personnel usage, and procedures to be followed requires management decisions that are beyond our present scope. Our focus here is on what you can walk into a store and buy: hardware and software.

## Hardware

The machinery of a computer system is its hardware (see Figure 16.3). The three main types of hardware are

- The central processing unit (CPU)
- Input devices
- Output devices

All hardware devices other than the CPU are referred to as **peripherals,** because they are attached to but are not part of the CPU.

**peripherals** all hardware devices other than the CPU

*The Central Processing Unit* A computer system's brains, the place where the data processing actually occurs, is the **central processing unit (CPU).** A CPU has three main parts:

- The main memory
- The control unit
- The arithmetic-logic unit

**central processing unit (CPU)** the computer system's brain, where the data processing actually occurs

The **main memory** holds data and programs (discussed later) while the computer is manipulating them. The main memory consists of memory cells

**main memory** part of the CPU that holds data and programs while the computer is manipulating them

FIGURE 16.3 Computer Hardware

Input devices

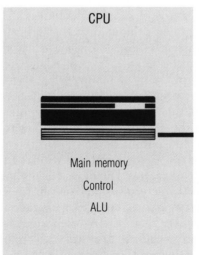

CPU

Main memory

Control

ALU

Output devices

that hold numbers expressed in a *binary* notation. Each digit in a binary number is either a 0 or a 1 and is called a binary digit, or *bit* for short. Eight bits make up a **byte**. (A single letter takes up one byte of memory because each letter of the alphabet has its own eight-bit code.)

The memory cells used to store changeable data or instructions are called the **RAM**, for **random access memory**. Depending on the power of a computer, its RAM may contain thousands, millions, or even billions of memory cells. For that reason, computer memories are usually described in terms of *kilobytes (K)*, each of which represents 1,000 bytes (actually, 1,024 bytes) of memory. Thus, a computer with 256 K of internal memory has approximately 256,000 bytes (actually, 262,144 bytes) of memory. Less common terms are *megabyte (M)*, 1,024 K, or about 1 million bytes of computer memory, and *gigabyte (G)*, 1,024 M, or about a billion bytes of memory.

The main part of the CPU, the **control unit**, tells the computer what to do and where to find or put data. The control unit interprets the computer's instructions by means of permanently stored programs. These instructions are stored in an area called the **read-only memory (ROM)**. The **arithmetic-logic unit (ALU)** handles arithmetic computations.

In addition to these three main units, the CPUs in most computers also have **auxiliary storage devices**, units in a computer system that supplement the main memory storage. The most common of these devices comes as either a floppy-disk drive or a hard-disk drive, although compact disks (CDs) are on the horizon. Auxiliary storage devices store data far more cheaply and permanently than can the internal memory.

Once a computer has processed the data in its main memory, the user can store that data in an auxiliary storage device and bring new data into the main memory. A computer's main memory is much faster to run and more costly to store data in than is auxiliary storage. It is also considered volatile, because data and programs in the main memory will disappear if there is a power failure or a major operator error. In general, auxiliary storage devices are less volatile than the main memory, though in some circumstances they, too, can lose data.

*Input Devices*    That part of a computer system which converts data from an outside source to signals which the CPU can use is an **input device**. Today, the most common input device is a keyboard. Other such devices include optical scanners, like the ones used at grocery store checkouts, magnetic tapes, magnetic disks, light pens, some appliances, readers, and a point-and-push "mouse."

*Output Devices*    That part of a computer system which transmits processed data from the computer and presents it to the user is its **output device**. The most common output devices are printers, which provide a printed record of information, and monitors, which display the data being typed in on televisionlike screens. The device in the monitor which allows the images to appear on the screen is the **cathode ray tube,** or **CRT**. Often the monitor itself is referred to as the CRT. Magnetic tape and magnetic disks are also output devices. Output devices designed to produce graphics, either on a CRT or on a printer, are especially important in computer-aided design/ computer-aided manufacturing (CAD/CAM) systems.

**byte**   eight binary digits or bits

**random access memory (RAM)**   memory cells used to store changeable data or instructions

**control unit**   the main part of the CPU that tells the computer what to do and where to find or put data

**read-only memory (ROM)**   memory cells that hold permanently stored programs

**arithmetic-logic unit (ALU)**   part of the CPU that handles arithmetic computations

**auxiliary storage devices**   units on a computer system such as the floppy or hard disk drive that supplement the main memory storage

**input device**   that part of a computer system that converts data from an outside source to signals which the CPU can use

**output device**   that part of a computer system that transmits processed data from the computer and presents it to the user

**CRT (cathode-ray tube)**   device in the monitor that allows images to appear on the screen

An exciting recent development is voice output. Some auto manufacturers have installed such devices to warn drivers that, for instance, it is time to buy gas. Some schools have used voice output for instructing special-needs students. And some telephone sales and canvassing operations have relied on it, to the great annoyance of many consumers.

## Classifying Computers

Basic criteria for classifying computers are their cost, speed, size, and the number of users who can work on them at the same time.

*3.* Classify the various types of computers used by business firms.

*Supercomputers*   As their name suggests, the largest, most powerful computers made today are the **supercomputers.** Used primarily for scientific, government, and military purposes, these giants do extensive computations with massive quantities of data. They have huge memories and often have multiple CPUs designed to operate in parallel on different parts of the same program simultaneously (see Figure 16.4). Some examples include the Cray I and the Cyber 203.

**supercomputers**   the largest, most powerful computers made today

*Mainframes*   The traditional workhorses of the computer industry are **mainframe computers,** large systems with high processing speeds and considerable storage capacity like the IBM 4381 and the Cyber 175. These large computers handle government and business data processing and extensive scientific projects. Mainframe systems are multiuser computers with enormous memories that can support hundreds of **terminals,** the input devices usually consisting of a keyboard and a CRT linked to a central computer. Walt Disney Productions runs its U.S. theme parks, hotels, cable television channel, and television and movie productions by relying primarily on five mainframe computers and 1,200 terminals.[3]

**mainframe computers** large systems with high processing speeds and considerable storage capacity

**terminals**   input devices consisting of a keyboard and a CRT linked to the central computer

*Minicomputers*   Originally, **minicomputers** were intermediate-sized computers designed to be connected directly to scientific and medical instruments to control their operation and analyze the data they produced. Later, they were connected in networks of terminals to provide computing and word-processing services for the individual departments of corporations. Large minicomputers now rival the mainframes in their size and sophistication. Also, they use operating systems, like AT&T's UNIX, that are particularly suited to research and development. Two examples include Digital Equipment Corporation's VAX series and Data General's MV series.

**minicomputers**   intermediate-sized computers originally designed to be connected directly to scientific and medical instruments to control their operation and analyze data produced

*Personal Computers*   Originally designed for the hobbyist, **personal computers** (or **microcomputers**) are becoming the backbone of corporate information systems, in settings ranging from small accounting firms to giant insurance companies. Personal computers (PCs) are smaller computers which sit on the desk top, have limited storage capacity, and usually include a monitor and a keyboard. More than 15 million PCs can be found in American businesses, a figure that is expected to reach 46 million by the year 2000.[4] The best known PCs are the IBM PC line and all of Apple's computers.

**personal computers (microcomputers)** smaller computers which sit on the desktop, have limited storage capacity, and usually include a monitor and a keyboard

FIGURE 16.4
Supercomputers: Big
Computers for Big
Jobs

Source: Based on material
that originally appeared in
Kenneth Labich, "The
Shootout in
Supercomputers,"
*Fortune,* February 29,
1988, p. 68. Copyright
1989 *Fortune* Magazine.
Used by permission of the
publisher.

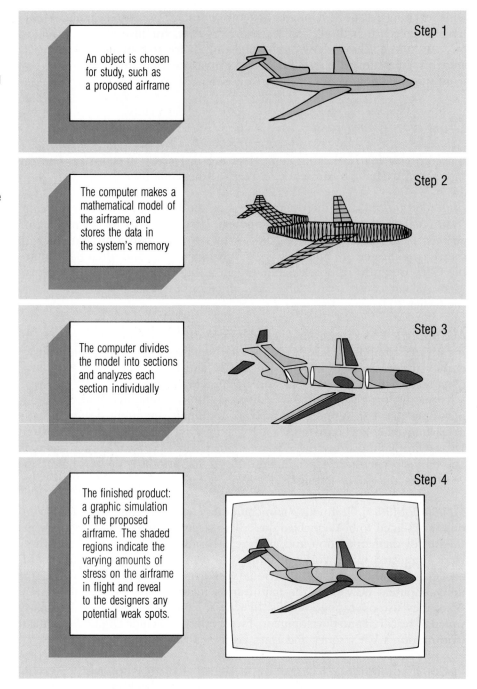

Step 1

An object is chosen for study, such as a proposed airframe

Step 2

The computer makes a mathematical model of the airframe, and stores the data in the system's memory

Step 3

The computer divides the model into sections and analyzes each section individually

Step 4

The finished product: a graphic simulation of the proposed airframe. The shaded regions indicate the varying amounts of stress on the airframe in flight and reveal to the designers any potential weak spots.

Until recently, the slower processing speeds and smaller memory capacities of PCs made them best suited for routine jobs like word processing and basic arithmetic calculations. Thanks to dramatically improved microprocessor technology, however, $5,000 PCs now have the processing and memory capabilities of mainframe computers that once cost millions of dollars.[5] A simple analogy between computers and automobiles helps demonstrate the amazing improvements in computer technology. If automobiles had developed to the degree that computers have, a Rolls-Royce would cost only $2.75 and get 30 million miles to the gallon while whisking its passengers along comfortably at 250 mph.[6]

Personal computers come in many sizes. The most familiar is the desktop model with a separate CRT, a CPU with built-in disk drives, and a keyboard. Another group, called **portable computers**, takes in a great range of machines, all the way from hand-held programmable calculators to laptop computers that can perform any function that the larger and heavier PCs can. Most portables have special or limited functions, however.

**portable computers** range of machines from handheld programmable calculators to laptop computers that can perform most functions that larger heavier PCs can

## Computer Networks

Large mainframe computers usually have a number of terminals linked to them by various means of communication, including direct wiring or telephone lines. For example, airline reservation systems consist of terminals in airports, downtown ticket offices, and travel agents' offices in many locations, all linked by telephone lines to the airline's mainframe. From any one of those terminals an agent can add, retrieve, and alter information about a passenger booked on a flight—even if the terminal is in Phoenix, the mainframe in Boston, and the flight is from Pittsburgh to Honolulu.

Mainframes have had this multiuser capacity for many years, but one of the major advances in the past decade was the development of the technology to link several minicomputers or personal computers together into networks. A *network* is a communication system that links computers so that they can either operate independently or can communicate with and share the resources of other devices linked to them. A common type of network is the **local area network (LAN)**, a network linking computers in a small geographical area or a particular building. The great advantage of a LAN is that it allows computers to send messages to other computers and to share peripherals, like printers and hard-disk drives, thus increasing the peripherals' cost efficiency. When the user is not communicating with another machine or using a peripheral device, however, the machine acts alone.

**local area network (LAN)** a network linking computers in a small geographical area or in a particular building

Other network applications of computers involve the use of a modem, a device to transmit computer signals over ordinary telephone lines. With this device an individual PC user can access (read) databanks, like the Dow Jones News Service, and use electronic bulletin boards, like the Source.

## Software

We can best describe **software** as a set of intangible commands that instruct a computer to read data into its memory from a peripheral device, perform operations on the data, store it in the main memory or in some form of auxiliary storage unit, and output the information to the user in some form. When people talk about software, they usually talk in terms of a **program**, a set of instructions for the computer to follow.[7] Without software programs to tell it how to behave, computer hardware could not function.

**software** a set of intangible commands that instruct a computer to read data into its memory from a peripheral device and perform various functions with it

**program** a set of instructions for the computer to follow

*Stored Programs*   All modern computers are *stored-program computers*, machines controlled by software stored within the hardware. A program is said to be stored because it sits in a computer's main memory while telling the computer what to do with the data that is also in the main memory.[8]

*Speaking to a Computer*   The computer's native language, its *machine language,* is built into it. Machine language is in a binary format and is very difficult for humans to read. A close relative of machine language is *assembly language,* mnemonic instructions or memory codes that are more comprehensible to humans than machine language.

*Operating Systems*   A program that does the detailed work of running hardware is called an **operating system**. In the early days of computers, the user had to specify everything a program was to do. Modern operating systems have eliminated much of this drudgery of **programming**, the designing and writing of computer programs. An operating system may perform the following tasks, among others:

1. Store and protect data in files, on peripheral devices like tape drives, hard disks, and floppy-disk drives.
2. Control the CRT, keyboard, and printer.
3. Switch the computer's resources around among multiple users.
4. Interact with other computers by means of local area network (LAN) hardware.
5. Provide informative error messages and **menus**, displays of available programs to help the computer user carry out tasks.

An operating system is usually written in a computer language that people also can read. A small program written in machine language loads the operating system's software into the computer's memory from a disk drive or magnetic tape. This program is said to "pull the operating system up by its bootstraps," or starts the computer, so the process is referred to as **booting**. On some computers, like the Apple Macintosh, the machine is preprogrammed with the operating system, which becomes available to the user as soon as the machine is turned on.

A **utility program** is a program provided by the manufacturer of the operating system that runs below the operating system. Such programs are often used to create files, edit and change files, compare them with each other, copy one file into another, and erase files.

## Software Applications Packages

The program a user employs to tell the CPU what to do with the data entered is called a **software applications package**. Such packages are generally written in a high-level language and call up utility programs to do file handling, input, and output.

*Modes*   A computer user carries out tasks in either an interactive or a batch mode. Most software applications packages are interactive.

---

**operating system**   a program that does the detailed work of running the computer's hardware

**programming**   the designing and writing of computer programs

**menu**   a display of available programs to help the computer user carry out tasks

**booting**   to "pull the operating system up by its bootstraps," or start it

**utility program**   a program provided by the manufacturer of the operating system that does routine file maintenance

**software applications package**   the program a user employs to tell the CPU what to do with the data entered

**Apollo computer in the Vatican** *These researchers are using a program on an Apollo computer terminal that will help them determine the true colors of the frescoes on the ceiling of the Sistine Chapel as part of the restoration effort.*

In the **interactive mode,** the software displays instructions called prompts to the user, which appear on either a CRT or other display device. In some programs, the user responds to prompts by typing in command lines. In others, the user directs a movable blinking symbol on the CRT, called a **cursor,** to choices on a menu. In most cases, the user can specify the input and output files wanted and instruct the interactive software to get data from them.

In the **batch mode,** the software runs directly from the operating system just like a utility program. The user creates an input file and calls up the program with this file, perhaps along with the name of an output file. A batch program will then ordinarily run without further human intervention. It will produce its results in an output file, on a CRT, or on any other specified output device. The user can print the new output file or merely look at it. Until recently, all software ran in this fashion.

*Business Applications* Software developers have written programs for almost every aspect of a business's data-processing needs. The most common types of packages are the following:

> **interactive mode** the display of prompts by the software to the user
>
> **cursor** a movable blinking symbol
>
> **batch mode** mode in which software runs directly from the operating system like a utility program

- Accounting
- Word processing
- Decision support
- Spreadsheets
- Database managers
- Computer-aided design (CAD)
- Computer-aided manufacturing (CAM)
- Computer-aided engineering (CAE)
- Computer-aided instruction (CAI)
- Desktop publishing
- Electronic mail

We will discuss a number of these packages in the next section.

*Artificial Intelligence*   Futurists have long predicted the day when computers would be able to mimic human thought processes such as perception, learning, and problem solving. In a primitive sense, that day has arrived. Artificial

Bringing an expert to the office   *Expert systems are software packages that incorporate the ability to simulate human problem solving in their programming. IBM sells an expert system package that helps with business decision making and analysis.*

## HOW ARTIFICIAL INTELLIGENCE HELPS OUT AT BOEING

Expert systems differ from conventional programs in that the driving software does not contain a precise step-by-step formula, or algorithm, for solving a well-defined problem. Instead, they use a collection of if-then rules, ranging in number from ten to several thousand, that tell a user sitting in front of a terminal what to do at each particular stage of a job. . . .

The systems are good for solving complex problems that have no "right" answer, or problems with many interacting bits of information that vary from case to case—such as the best mix of components for a big computer system. Proponents say the systems are easy to change if managers learn more about a problem after they create the program. . . .

Aerospace companies, with their big, complicated products, are natural customers for artificial intelligence, and Boeing is the exemplar of the industry. Recruits master the techniques of expert-system science during a full year of training at the company's Advanced Technology Center. The first system to go into daily service is Case, for connector assembly specification expert. Case tells skilled workers how to assemble each of the roughly 5,000 multiple electrical connectors on a typical airplane. In the old days workers had to hunt through 20,000 pages of cross-referenced specifications to find the right parts, tools, and crimping techniques for each custom-made connector (of which there are more than 500 types)—on average, a 42-minute search. Now assemblers type some basic information about a connector into a computer and get a printout of instructions in only five minutes.

Source: Excerpted from Andrew Kupfer, "Now, Live Experts on a Floppy Disk," *Fortune,* October 12, 1987, p. 70.

intelligence software, involving either *expert systems* or *neural networks,* is helping doctors and engineers use computers as technical consultants.[9] Manufacturing applications of artificial intelligence also have begun to appear (see Business Issues). Although it will be some time before computers can match the incredible data processing capabilities of the human brain, artificial intelligence is an area with exciting potential.

## *Choosing Software and Hardware*

Only when a firm knows what kind of management information system it needs, what types of demands will be made on the system, and which people will use the system and make it run is it ready to look into software and hardware. A business should look first for software that does everything it needs done, then—and only then—look for hardware to run it. Relatively speaking, hardware is the least important of the elements of a computer system.

# Management's Need for Information

Managers are paid to make decisions. Whatever their functional areas, managers require relevant, cost-efficient, and timely information on which to base these decisions (see Figure 16.5). This information may come from data collected by their companies, from their personal experience, or from external sources such as friends, news reports, television, and magazine articles. Our focus in this chapter is on the management information systems that companies develop. These systems may or may not be computerized, though today it is difficult to find any but the smallest businesses that are not at least partially computerized.

FIGURE 16.5a   Relation of Cost Value to Accuracy
FIGURE 16.5b   Value as Related to Age

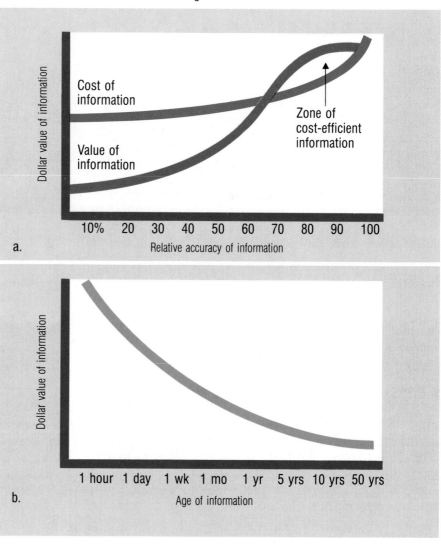

TABLE 16.1   Information Needs by Functional Area

| Functional Area | Information Needs |
|---|---|
| *Human Resources* | Compensation data; job openings; benefit packages; employee skills |
| *Operations* | Cost of materials; inventory flow; labor costs; machine use |
| *Marketing* | Customer profiles; survey research; sales; transportation availability |
| *Finance* | Cost of funds; amount needed for capital improvements; comparative investment benefits |

## Information Requirements by Functional Area

A firm's information needs depend on the nature of its business. Managers, too, have different needs, depending on their functional area. And even within a given area, managers on different levels have distinct information needs. Table 16.1 shows the four areas of managerial decision making.

*Human Resources*   The increasing complexity of hiring, training, and terminating employees makes information on recruitment, salaries, benefits, employee compensation, employee skills, absenteeism, and staffing patterns a necessity for human-resource managers. Companies affected by government employment regulations need reports showing the number of employees with various age, gender, race, salary, and job characteristics. Producing this information is the responsibility of human-resources managers. To do so, they need to maintain detailed data on the company's employees.

*Operations*   Operations managers are concerned with the materials required to manufacture their products or provide their services, the cost of production (labor and material), the cost of inventory, the efficiency of their machinery, and many other matters. Information systems can address all these needs. Materials-requirement planning (MRP) systems such as those discussed in Chapter 10 provide the information necessary to manage materials used in production. A cost-accounting system assists operations managers in determining the cost of producing their goods. Mathematical tools of various sorts help operations managers schedule the machines used in the production process.
   Many other software packages assist in operations management. For example, some packages are designed to facilitate planning, using the Program Evaluation and Review Technique (PERT) discussed in Chapter 10. Computer-aided design (CAD), computer-aided engineering (CAE), and computer-aided manufacturing (CAM) are widely used in many industries, especially automobile manufacturing. Walt Disney Productions uses computer graphics to create backgrounds for its animated features.[10]

*Marketing*   Two broad categories of information systems assist marketing managers. The first type of information system in the marketing area, the *operational system,* is the management information system designed to handle all customer orders, whether placed by mail, in person, or through a salesperson. Operational systems record what was sold and where, and by whom and to whom it was sold. Such systems can perform credit checks on customers and can help in marketing by, for example, processing lists for direct-mail operations.

The second type of information system to assist marketing managers, the *marketing information system,* is the management information system that can develop answers to questions regarding customer profiles, product penetration, and sales effectiveness. These systems give marketing managers the big picture so adjustments can be made.

*Finance*   Financial managers need information to determine, first, how much money their companies need; second, how best to obtain the money; and third—given competing alternatives—how best to spend the money. These managers often face a series of complex "what if" questions: What if sales increase by 8 percent? What if interest rates increase in the same period by 1 percent? What if new tax laws alter the depreciation allowance on the business's equipment—should that change affect the company's new equipment purchases? Financial managers can develop answers to these questions by using complicated formulas that would take considerable time to work by hand. Spreadsheet programs like Lotus 1-2-3 permit managers to change the variables in these formulas, then perform calculations far faster than any human could.

Financial managers rely on accounting data, of course. Many software makers have developed a range of off-the-shelf packages suitable for all but the largest or most complex organizations. General ledger systems, accounts payable systems, and accounts receivable and cash applications systems are among those that have taken some of the repetitiveness and drudgery out of the daily routine of accounting departments.

## Information Requirements by Management Level

The three levels of management—top management, middle management, and supervisory or first-line management—each have different information requirements. The lower the level of management, the more specialized its needs will be. And the higher the level of management, the more general will be the information required for decision making. A good top manager is a facilitator, a manager who makes other managers' jobs easier by providing the tools and information they need to do their jobs. They all, however, require information from each of the functional areas in order to make intelligent decisions.

## Sources of Data

Much of the data a firm requires comes from internal sources like the functional divisions. Other data originates outside the firm. Internal data sources provide past and present data that managers can use as a basis for

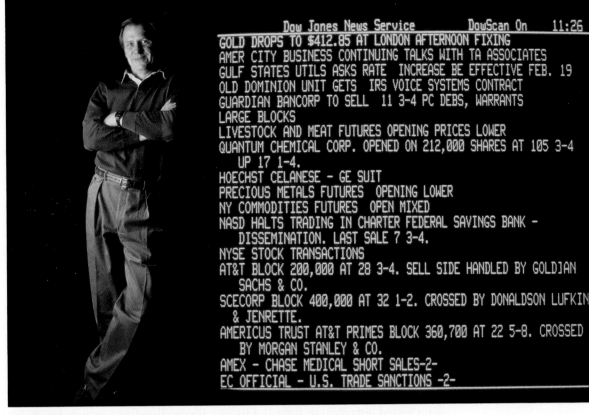

Dow Jones News Service          DowScan On     11:26
GOLD DROPS TO $412.85 AT LONDON AFTERNOON FIXING
AMER CITY BUSINESS CONTINUING TALKS WITH TA ASSOCIATES
GULF STATES UTILS ASKS RATE  INCREASE BE EFFECTIVE FEB. 19
OLD DOMINION UNIT GETS  IRS VOICE SYSTEMS CONTRACT
GUARDIAN BANCORP TO SELL  11 3-4 PC DEBS, WARRANTS
LARGE BLOCKS
LIVESTOCK AND MEAT FUTURES OPENING PRICES LOWER
QUANTUM CHEMICAL CORP. OPENED ON 212,000 SHARES AT 105 3-4
      UP 17 1-4.
HOECHST CELANESE - GE SUIT
PRECIOUS METALS FUTURES  OPENING LOWER
NY COMMODITIES FUTURES  OPEN MIXED
NASD HALTS TRADING IN CHARTER FEDERAL SAVINGS BANK -
      DISSEMINATION. LAST SALE 7 3-4.
NYSE STOCK TRANSACTIONS
AT&T BLOCK 200,000 AT 28 3-4. SELL SIDE HANDLED BY GOLDIAN
      SACHS & CO.
SCECORP BLOCK 400,000 AT 32 1-2. CROSSED BY DONALDSON LUFKIN
      & JENRETTE.
AMERICUS TRUST AT&T PRIMES BLOCK 360,700 AT 22 5-8. CROSSED
      BY MORGAN STANLEY & CO.
AMEX - CHASE MEDICAL SHORT SALES-2-
EC OFFICIAL - U.S. TRADE SANCTIONS -2-

**Electronic sources of information**  *One reason why electronic retrieval services have
not been the big money makers they were predicted to be is that calling up
information from them can be very complicated. A user must phrase a request for
information with very specific and often obtuse language, making it difficult to
know how to ask the system for what you want. William L. Dunn of Dow Jones
& Co. is hoping to change that, with a new system that provides information to
subscribers automatically, without their having to call it up, and which takes
commands in pure and simple English.*

making predictions about the future. Company records, customer records,
employment data, reports, conference minutes, memoranda, and the like
supply the bulk of the data in a firm's information system.

The external sources of data are almost limitless. Today's manager needs
to be well informed, which means keeping up with newspapers, radio,
television, journals, and the like. General business publications, such as *The
Wall Street Journal, Fortune, Business Week,* and *Forbes,* often contain
necessary information on industry and competitive conditions. Most important, industry-specific publications, often referred to as trade journals, are
must reading. For example, athletic administrators might be expected to read
*Athletic Administration, Athletic Journal,* and *Interscholastic Athletic Administration.* General media usually provide low-cost sources of data. Free sources
tend to be the informal ones, like customers, bankers, suppliers, and friends.
High-priced sources might include market research provided by outside
consultants. Managers can also access valuable information—newspaper
stories, financial data, and industry surveys—with their PCs by subscribing

to electronic news services. Subscriptions to these services can be fairly expensive, however, and some users find the very specific instructions needed to call up the information they want difficult.[11]

# Management Information Systems

*4. Discuss the role of management information systems in a modern business.*

Transformation of data into information has different meanings at different levels of an organization. J. W. Marriott, Jr., the chief executive officer of the Marriott Corporation, once recalled, "I asked for some information on a specific problem, and in response [some subordinates] brought in a computer runout several inches high. I threw them out of the office. I said, 'You're not running a business when you bring in something like that. You're not contributing.' "[12]

**management information system (MIS)** a collection of tools that provides information to a manager to facilitate that person's decision-making processes

A **management information system (MIS)** is a collection of tools that provides information to a manager to facilitate that person's decision-making processes. Specifically, an MIS should help a manager either make a better decision or make a decision more easily than he or she would have otherwise.

## Types of MIS

We have already seen that an information system may be either manual or computerized, informal or formal. Historically, well-defined reports produced on a regular basis have characterized the formal MIS. They still play an important role in it today. Such reports must be both accurate and timely if managers are to use the information properly to assist in their decision making. If the information is too old, managers either cannot or should not use it. That is why an MIS today must not only produce the regular reports it has always been expected to generate but must also respond quickly to unscheduled requests for information. A modern MIS answers "what ifs" rapidly on a CRT or else produces a printed report. The format of the MIS response is up to the manager who asks for it. For example, a sales manager might use a computer terminal to determine the projected or actual annual sales for the products sold in each of the regions under his or her direction.

## Decision Support Systems (DSS)

**decision support system (DSS)** a computer system that permits managers to call up whatever specific information they need whenever they need it

Closely related to the MIS is the **decision support system (DSS)**, a computer system that permits managers to call up whatever specific information they need whenever they need it. These systems allow managers to gain information in a less structured manner than from a traditional MIS. They assist a manager in formulating questions and gathering answers rather than in generating formal reports to answer the same questions for each period.

*Human Error*   The ever-increasing number of personal computers with decision-support software has proved a mixed blessing. In some cases, managers have made huge errors in projections because they forgot to enter

Creating a decision support system   *Union Pacific Technologies is a subdivision of the Union Pacific Corporation which develops computer and communications support systems. One system the group is marketing allows a manager to monitor every aspect of hauling goods, from origin to destination.*

some element or did not check their work. The computer cannot compensate for human error, a fact people who rely on computers are liable to learn the hard way.[13]

*Executive Information Systems*   A new type of DSS is called an **executive information system** (or executive support system). This type of computerized information system is easy to use and designed specifically for executives who might not be familiar with computers but who need to call up information quickly. The objective is to overcome *computer resistance* (see Experiencing Business) among top executives. Surprisingly, experts estimate that less than 10 percent of top executives presently use personal computers.[14] Executives generally have been reluctant to take the time for computer training and consider using a typewriterlike keyboard as an insult to their status.[15] Consequently, executive information systems are as easy to use as a touchtone telephone because the mere push of a button brings a stimulating display of neatly summarized information into view on a screen. This is possible because the systems are programmed to accommodate each executive's unique information needs. Color-coded graphics make comparisons and contrasts between divisions, products, people, and so on very easy, thus making these new systems even more attractive to computer-resistant executives.

**executive information system**   an easy-to-use computerized information system designed specifically for executives who might not be familiar with computers but who need to call up information quickly

## WHAT IS YOUR COMPUTER RESISTANCE SCORE?

*Instructions:* How well do the following statements describe you? Circle one number for each item, total your score, and check the key.

|  | Not at all like me | | | | | | Very much like me |
|---|---|---|---|---|---|---|---|

1. I have no desire to use a computer. 1—2—3—4—5—6—7

2. I don't trust computers. 1—2—3—4—5—6—7

3. I'm too old to learn how to use a computer. 1—2—3—4—5—6—7

4. I can't think of anything I would use a computer for. 1—2—3—4—5—6—7

5. Computers are too complicated for me. 1—2—3—4—5—6—7

6. The technical terms computer people use tend to intimidate me. 1—2—3—4—5—6—7

7. I'm not good enough with math to be able to program a computer. 1—2—3—4—5—6—7

8. I don't know how to type, so I can't use a computer. 1—2—3—4—5—6—7

9. I'm afraid to buy a computer because new technology will soon make it obsolete. 1—2—3—4—5—6—7

10. Computers are too expensive. 1—2—3—4—5—6—7

Total score = _____

**Key**
10–29 = Low computer resistance
30–50 = Moderate computer resistance
51–70 = High computer resistance

*Note:* See the answer key at the back of the text for interpretations.

# Functions of a Management Information System

*5. List and describe the four functions of a management information system.*

A management information system should efficiently perform four functions:

- Collect data
- Store data
- Update data
- Process data

The value of an MIS lies in its ability to accumulate data so that it can be manipulated or processed into information. Computer programs process data by summarizing, merging, selecting, and sorting it according to the needs of an MIS user. Once the computer has performed these functions, the information is ready for circulation to managers.

## Collecting Data

Before an MIS can produce information, someone must feed it data. In determining whether data belongs in an MIS, three questions have to be asked:
1. Is the data accurate?
2. Is the data timely?
3. Is the data too expensive?

Inaccurate or obsolete data is useless. And some data that is both accurate and timely may simply not be worth the cost of collection. Identifying this data requires a cost-benefit analysis.

## Storing Data

Storing data simply means saving it for later use. Once collected, MIS data is entered into the computer for later processing into information. Computer systems may store data in two places: in the main memory, or on auxiliary storage devices, such as magnetic tapes, hard disks, or floppy disks. As noted earlier, the main memory holds programs and data that the computer is currently using. For permanent storage, users can rely on auxiliary storage devices like backup disks.

The anticipated use of the data determines the type of auxiliary storage device to use in storing it. Data that will rarely be accessed, read or written, is frequently stored on magnetic tape rather like the tape in an audio or videocassette. Magnetic tape is also used when data must be retrieved by **sequential access**. In other words, if a user wants to locate a particular file, the computer must read all the entries preceding the file before it can access the file. A typical 2,400-foot reel of magnetic tape can store up to 150 million characters.

A hard disk can store hundreds of millions of characters and you can randomly access them. **Random access** means that a computer can retrieve any piece of data from the source in the same amount of time as any other piece and that the time required to access the last record will be no greater than that required for the first. Thus, random access is the opposite of sequential access. For some years, a floppy or flexible disk, with random-access capability, has been the most common type of auxiliary storage device. A floppy disk can hold up to 1.2 megabytes and is quite inexpensive.

**sequential access** the process the computer undergoes of reading all the entries preceding a user's file before it can access the file

**random access** a computer's ability to retrieve any piece of data from the source in the same amount of time as any other piece

## Updating Data

Data would be of little value if it could not be updated and refined. Updates are of three types: adds, changes, and deletes. For example, a store's MIS will include its inventory. The store will add to that inventory new classes of merchandise. It may also have to change existing entries to reflect replacements of or additions to existing data. And, finally, the store may delete items dropped from stock.

manual updating  an al-
teration of the existing data by
a person

**Manual updating** of an MIS occurs when a person does something that alters the existing data, like transferring new data to the appropriate storage device or deleting entries. Manual updating can occur on a daily, weekly, or monthly basis, as needed, depending on a firm's business. Manual-updating systems are often referred to as **batch systems,** because the data is first collected, then stored in a batch until time to process them.

batch system  manual-
updating system in which data
is first collected, then stored in
a batch until time to process
them

**Real-time updating** of an MIS occurs when computer hardware and software interact automatically to make changes to the database as new data becomes available. People do not have to intervene, because the data to be accessed, the changes, and the programs are all permanently stored on an auxiliary storage device permanently attached to the computer. For example, consider how real-time updating has helped Circuit City Stores outperform its competitors in the appliance and consumer electronics market:

real-time updating  in-
teraction of computer hardware
and software to automatically
make changes to the database
as new data becomes available

> Customers in the gigantic, 30,000-square-foot stores are served by salespeople who punch up transactions on terminals dotted around the floor. The system provides an up-to-the-moment inventory of merchandise. The company's automated distribution centers, located within a day's drive of the stores they serve, can reliably replenish stocks within 24 hours.[16]

# Perspective: Changes in the Computerized Workplace

Traditionally, managers have seen automation as a means of improving employee productivity in terms of the net profit to be derived per wage and benefit dollar. As artificial intelligence begins to realize its promise, these benefits will travel up into the professional and managerial ranks, too.

Some students of the issue believe new computer technology will cause the work force to partition itself between an elite who can work with the new machines and those who cannot. But as computers become increasingly user friendly, a greater share of the work force will have access to the new technology.

Another fear is that of possible job loss. Some jobs will, in fact, be lost as organizations are restructured around new computer technology for greater competitiveness. Computers are making organizations flatter, with fewer levels. Exxon, for example, has eliminated whole layers of middle management because computerized information systems replaced managers whose main job was checking up on the work of others. Executive information systems allow top management to do its own checking up on lower-level operations. At the same time, computers are creating jobs by the hundreds of thousands. Only time will tell if computers, on balance, will cause a net gain or loss of jobs. One thing is sure, however. Computers are causing an earthquake of restructuring in modern businesses.

Computers are having more subtle impacts on the workplace as well. Detailed computer records track the finest aspects of a person's job performance (e.g., how many key strokes per hour for a word-processing clerk as well as the timing and duration of his or her breaks). Employees and unions are expressing growing concern about computer surveillance versus employee

**The changing workplace**   *As computers become easier to use and less expensive, the share of the workforce that uses them grows. Computers are making organizations flatter, with fewer levels, since some middle management supervisory tasks are now performed by computers.*

privacy rights.[17] Along the same lines, stress-related job disability claims have jumped dramatically for employees who sit hours on end staring into computer video monitors. **Ergonomics**, the science of designing machinery to better accommodate the human body, is getting greater attention from those who design computerized work stations. The hoped-for result is less physical and mental stress.

**ergonomics**   the science of designing machinery to better accommodate the human body

Another effect of computerization is the development of the *electronic cottage,* the home workplace that depends on computers linked to a central office. Recall the discussion of telecommuting in Chapter 7. Working at home has its pluses and minuses. For some, the flexibility of setting their own hours and working in the informal comfort of their home outweighs any disadvantages of such an arrangement, like the loss of the social life surrounding work. For others, though, such as the disabled or people in prison, the development of the electronic cottage can be an almost unqualified blessing. Such previously disadvantaged workers can now find employment in a much wider range of occupations.

# Supplement: Statistics in Business

A **statistic** is a number that is calculated to summarize data.[18] It describes certain characteristics of that group of numbers. The raw materials of statistics are thus numbers that represent counts and measurements of business activities and results.

# What Statistics Describe

Data, as mentioned earlier, does not become information until it is presented in a meaningful way. Statistics give us a vocabulary for describing numbers and turning data into information. For instance, when we list the hourly temperatures for each day in July, we have data. However, once we say that the temperature in July averaged 68 degrees or that this July was 3 degrees cooler than average, we have transformed the data into information that almost everyone can understand.

The numbers that a business is concerned with describing come from primary and secondary data collected and stored in its management information system (MIS). Businesses have such data as figures on costs, the time it takes to make each product, the hours it takes to perform specific processes, and the average time it takes to collect bills. Sometimes internal records do not contain sufficient data, so outside sources of data must be located. Research companies will often provide such data for a fee.

## *Samples*

Because collecting and storing many kinds of data are expensive, researchers often rely on a **sample**, a small group of representative units selected from a much larger group, to answer their questions.[19] Samples are also important in quality control. For many products, the only way to test them is to destroy them. The firm will therefore test only a certain number of items, to get an idea of the number of problems or failures it can expect in the entire production run.

Market research often relies on the use of samples, because it would be prohibitively expensive to ask, say, all persons between ages 18 and 25 living in the Detroit metropolitan area what they were looking for in a soft drink.

Many, but not all, surveys use a **random sample** in which any unit or person in a population has an equal chance of being chosen to appear in the sample.[20] Random samples are also known as *probability samples*. The results achieved with a sample should be representative of the results that would have been reached if the entire population had responded. Raw data for the sampling is obtained by either observations or surveys.

*Observations*   Observations are used to record overt behavior or physical characteristics. In many instances, a business's ordinary records supply this data. For example, a business should know how long it takes, on average, to collect its bills. The data to calculate the average would take into account the payment time on every bill that had been sent out. A restaurant might also use observation to determine how many customers ordered dinner every half hour, say, between 5 and 11 o'clock on weeknights. Such information could help managers determine the appropriate number of employees to schedule during those hours.

*Surveys*  When a company wants to know why people act as they do, surveys are important. Often it is not enough to know that 30 percent of the homeowners in a test market bought a company's new product. A company may decide to commission a survey of an entire population, called a **census**. Virtually all surveys done for businesses use only a sample of the population, however. The most common ways of carrying out a survey are by mail, personal interviews, and telephone interviews.

**census**  a survey of an entire population

Mail surveys are the lowest-cost option, but they present a number of drawbacks. This method takes time to implement and offers little flexibility, and the questionnaire must be short and fairly simple. Also, the number of people who will return a questionnaire is usually low, often less than 30 percent. In addition, people who answer mail surveys may not be representative of the whole population. After all, it is unusual for many to take the time to complete a survey.

Personal interviews consume the most time and cost the most money. They are, however, also the most flexible technique and offer the best opportunity to ask probing questions. Many companies conduct surveys in supermarkets or at malls or conduct panel interviews, called *focus groups,* to reduce the cost of personal interviews.

Telephone interviews, the most common survey method, are relatively inexpensive when compared to personal interviews, but they do not necessarily produce a representative sample. Many people have unlisted numbers or do not have a telephone at all. Eliminating these categories from the survey distorts the results. Dialing random numbers makes the surveys more representative, but many people refuse to answer survey questions over the phone. Even so, telephone surveys have a higher response rate than mail surveys and can be conducted quickly.

# Types of Statistics

Statistics are either descriptive or inferential. **Descriptive statistics** portray the characteristics of a larger set of data. A study of the payment patterns in a company's accounts receivable would produce descriptive statistics. **Inferential statistics** describe the behavior of a small group, from which the user may be able to predict the behavior of a larger group. Market research usually involves inferential statistics. Our main concern here is descriptive statistics.

Table 16.2 lists the number of onion-ring orders served in West Shore Community College's snack bar during a ten-day period. Firms commonly deal with data that contains hundreds or thousands of observations, but these ten days will serve our purposes here.

*6. Explain the role of statistics in a management information system.*

**descriptive statistics**  statistics which portray the characteristics of a larger set of data

**inferential statistics**  statistics which describe the behavior of a small group, from which the user may be able to predict the behavior of a larger group

## TABLE 16.2     Snack Bar Onion-Ring Sales

| Day of the Week | Number of Orders Sold |
|-----------------|:-----------------------:|
| Sunday | 15 |
| Monday | 30 |
| Tuesday | 18 |
| Wednesday | 35 |
| Thursday | 18 |
| Friday | 32 |
| Saturday | 37 |
| Sunday | 17 |
| Monday | 21 |
| Tuesday | 24 |
| Total | 247 |

**frequency distribution**
method of summarizing data by reducing the size of the listing or the number of items in the data set

A **frequency distribution** summarizes data by reducing the size of the listing or the number of items in the data set. With large quantities of data, this usually means grouping data into ranges. One first establishes reasonable ranges, then records the number of times actual observations occurred within each of them. Table 16.3 shows the onion-ring sales data transformed into ranges. Note that frequency distributions can be shown without grouping. For example, Table 16.2 shows that the snack bar twice served eighteen onion-ring orders but all other numbers just once.

## Measures of Size and Dispersion

**average** total number of observations divided by the number of occurrences of them

**arithmetic mean** technical name for average

*Arithmetic Mean*    The best-known statistical form is the **average,** technically referred to as the **arithmetic mean,** which is the total number of observation values divided by the number of occurrences of them. In our example, West Shore Community College's snack bar served a total of 247 orders over the ten-day period. The arithmetic mean or average daily sale is arrived at by dividing 247 by 10, for a figure of 24.7. Of course, the snack bar never sold 0.7 orders of onion rings. The closest we can get is to say that the snack bar sold approximately 25 orders each day.

**median** value that appears in the middle of the data when the observations are arranged in order from the lowest to the highest

*Median*    The figure called the **median** is the value that appears in the middle of the data when the observations are arranged in order from the lowest to the highest. This arrangement for the onion-ring sales in our sample is 15, 17, 18, 18, 21, 24, 30, 32, 35, 37. This particular series of numbers has no middle value. The two values closest to the middle are 21 and 24. Adding these two values and dividing by 2 produces 22.5 as the median value. An odd number of days would have a middle value that would become the median value, without any additional computation.

**mode** value in a collection of data that occurs most frequently

*Mode*    The **mode** of a collection of data is that value which occurs most frequently. In our example, 18 occurred twice. When no one value occurs more often than any other, there is no mode.

## TABLE 16.3   Onion-Ring Sales Frequency Distribution

| Number of Onion-Ring Orders | Frequency |
|:---:|:---:|
| 10–15 | 1 |
| 16–20 | 3 |
| 21–25 | 2 |
| 26–30 | 1 |
| 31–35 | 2 |
| 36–40 | 1 |

*Range*   Arithmetic means, medians, and modes are **measures of central tendency**, indicating how data will cluster about a central point. Frequently, however, a business will also want to look at what is called the **measure of dispersion**, an indication of how widely spread the data is. The principal measure of dispersion is the data's **range**, the difference between the highest and lowest observed values. In our example, we would calculate the range by subtracting the minimum value of 15 from the maximum value of 37, to get a range of 22.

> **measures of central tendency**   indications of how data will cluster about a central point
>
> **measure of dispersion**   indication of how widely spread the data is
>
> **range**   principal measure of the data's dispersion

*Variance and Standard Deviation*   Two sets of data may have the same arithmetic mean, yet have ranges that are vastly different. When the range of a set of data is small, the measures of central tendency will more accurately represent what actually occurred in each collection of observations. Of course, the arithmetic mean—a statistic—may or may not match an actual recorded event. The snack bar never sold 24.7 orders of onion rings in any day. The range is a rough notion of dispersion, but it is not usually relevant for analytical purposes.

Two more reliable indications of dispersion that describe the variability within data are its **variance** and **standard deviation**. Both measure the difference between each observed value and the arithmetic mean of the entire set of data. Computing variances and standard deviations is more complicated than calculating a range, and there is no need to explore such calculations here. The point to remember is that the greater the standard deviation or the variance, the greater the spread of the data. Measures of central tendency alone can deceive the user, so the astute manager will question the meaning of such statistics.

> **variance, standard deviation**   two indications of dispersion that measure the difference between each observed value and the arithmetic mean of the entire set of data

## Time Series Analysis

Managers will want explanations for any fluctuations in the recorded observations over time. **Time series analysis** or **trend analysis** is a statistical technique for examining the ways that observations of a variable move over time and then basing forecasts on the observations. Always keep in mind that trend analyses provide information that a manager must still test against his or her experience. Predicting the future is far from an exact science. Figure 16.6 represents in a line chart our snack bar's daily onion-ring sales

> **time series analysis (trend analysis)**   a statistical technique for examining the ways that observations of a variable move over time and then basing forecasts on the observations

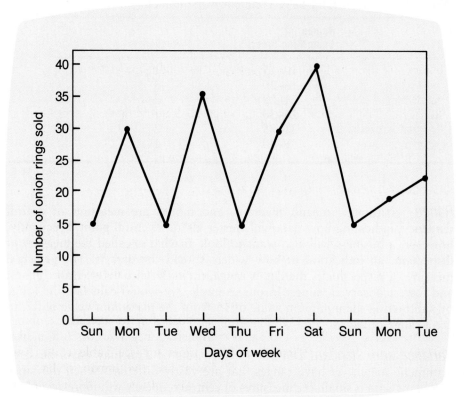

FIGURE 16.6   Line Chart

over a ten-day period. A chart like this one, if based on many more observations, could help a business compare demand on weekdays and weekends, for instance.

### Trend, Cyclical, and Seasonal Variations

**secular trend** fluctuation that consists of a smooth upward or downward movement over a long period

**cyclical fluctuations** business cycle movements over periods ranging from two to fifteen years

**seasonal trends** patterns that complete themselves within one year or less and then begin to repeat themselves

The first of the three recognized types of fluctuations, the **secular trend**, is a smooth upward or downward movement over a long period. For example, the number of home entertainment systems and the cost of housing would both reveal secular trends over the last twenty years. The second type, **cyclical fluctuations**, consists of business-cycle movements over periods ranging from two to fifteen years. No simple rationale can explain these movements. They result from widespread changes in economic activity, such as boom periods and recessions. The third type of fluctuation, **seasonal trends**, consists of patterns that complete themselves within one year or less and then begin to repeat themselves. Weather and such customs as the celebration of major holidays produce seasonal trends. Summer sees an upswing in ice-cream purchases, and Thanksgiving and Christmas mark the high points of the year for the turkey industry.

### Correlation Analysis

The arithmetic mean, median, and mode measure the central tendency and summarize the larger set of data into a single statistic. Trend analysis, coupled with a manager's judgment, permits certain predictions about the future.

**TABLE 16.4    Correlation Analysis**

| Variables | Correlation |
|---|:---:|
| Age of runner and time recorded in 40-yard dash | + |
| Community disposable income and $ value of food stamps issued | − |
| Population of college and number of basketball games won | 0 |
| Number of complimentary pizza coupons issued and number of pizzas ordered | + |
| Age of automobile and value of automobile | − |
| Number of Madonna albums displayed in store window and number of albums sold | 0 |

**Correlation analysis** is a statistical technique to measure the association between two or more variables. It helps managers identify the factors that can be used to predict fluctuations in one variable when changes in another are known. This ability can be especially valuable for industrial products that depend on derived demand (see Chapter 11), as, for example, prehung doors. Sales of such doors go up when housing starts go up and drop when housing starts drop. Sales of doors and housing starts therefore exhibit positive correlation. Other factors may demonstrate negative correlation, like the value of a car, which drops as its age goes up (see Table 16.4). And sometimes two factors show no correlation at all. The number of baseball bats sold in Oregon is unlikely to have any association with the amount of nail polish sold in Mississippi.

One caution is very important. Correlation analysis does *not* prove that changes in one variable cause changes in another. A drop in the sale of lobster may in fact positively correlate with a rise in the number of past-due car payments in a given community, but one cannot be said to have caused the other. Both changes probably resulted from an unfavorable change in the economy.

**correlation analysis** a statistical technique to measure the association between two or more variables

# Presenting Information

Proper presentation is the key to successfully conveying information. "A picture is worth a thousand words" is particularly true of statistical information in visual and tabular displays.

## *Visual Display*

A picture that portrays information items in a way that makes them easy to compare with one another or reflects trends among the items is a **visual display.** Some of the more popular forms include graphs, bar charts, and pie charts.

Graphs are particularly effective in showing how a situation changed over time. We saw this in Figure 16.6, the graph or line chart of onion-ring sales

**visual display** a picture that portrays information items in a way that makes them easy to compare with one another or reflects trends in items

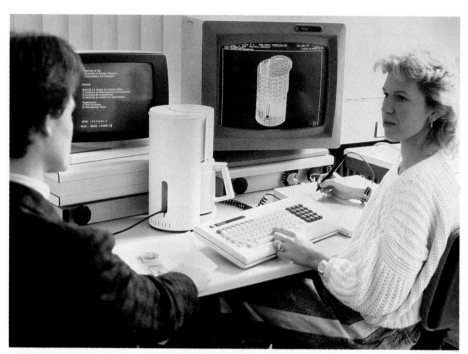

Viewing it on the screen *Computers can manipulate and present information in a number of ways. These engineers at Gillette work with a three-dimensional display of a coffee carafe to finetune its design before proceeding with manufacturing.*

**graph** visual display that indicates upward and downward movements of the values of a variable over a specified period

**bar chart** a comparison of several values at a stationary point in time, using either horizontal or vertical bars

**pie chart** a circle divided into pieces with each piece used to portray the kind and proportion of the data it represents

over a ten-day period. **Graphs** indicate upward and downward movements of the values of a variable over a specified period. They are constructed with a vertical Y axis (typically used to show the quantity or relative quantity of an item) and a horizontal X axis, which usually represents time or some other variable, such as cost.

A **bar chart** presents a comparison of several values at a stationary point in time. Either horizontal or vertical bars are used to show the quantity of an item, with the largest bar representing the greatest value. Figure 16.7 is a bar chart. Often symbols, called pictographs, are used instead of bars to convey information in a bar chart, as in Figure 16.8.

A **pie chart** is a circle that, like a pie, has been divided into pieces, with each piece used to portray the kind and proportion of the data it represents. Figure 16.9 is a pie chart. The whole pie equals 100 percent and each slice a relative percentage.

## Tabular Displays

**tabular display** an array or matrix of information in vertical columns and horizontal rows

An array or matrix of information in vertical columns and horizontal rows is a **tabular display.** Such a display shows the relationship between two or more variables and may contain either numeric or written data. Figure 16.10 is a two-column tabular display with numeric information about a single variable, the percent of sales. By contrast, Table 16.1, Information Needs by Functional Area, which we saw earlier, lists four variables—the four functional areas—and presents written information about each.

496

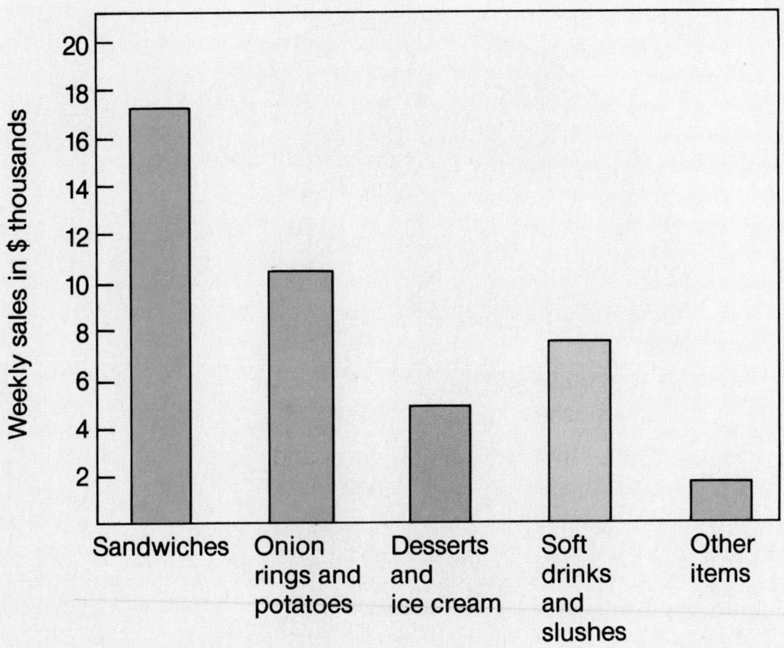

FIGURE 16.7
Bar Chart

Weekly sales in $ thousands

| | |
|---|---|
| 20 | |
| 18 | |
| 16 | |
| 14 | |
| 12 | |
| 10 | |
| 8 | |
| 6 | |
| 4 | |
| 2 | |

Sandwiches | Onion rings and potatoes | Desserts and ice cream | Soft drinks and slushes | Other items

FIGURE 16.8
Pictographs

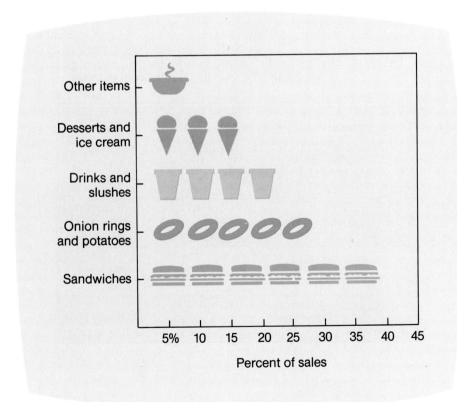

Other items

Desserts and ice cream

Drinks and slushes

Onion rings and potatoes

Sandwiches

5%  10  15  20  25  30  35  40  45

Percent of sales

FIGURE 16.9
Pie Chart

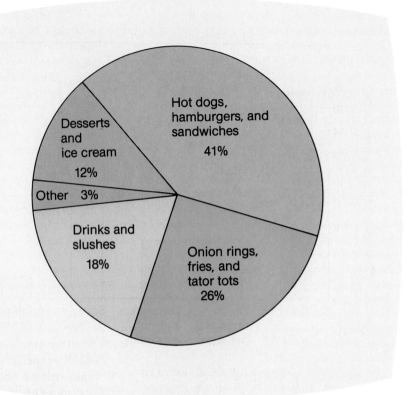

Desserts
and
ice cream
12%

Hot dogs,
hamburgers, and
sandwiches
41%

Other 3%

Drinks and
slushes
18%

Onion rings,
fries, and
tator tots
26%

FIGURE 16.10
Tabular Display

| Food group | Percent of sales |
|---|---|
| Burgers, hot dogs, sandwiches | 41% |
| Onion rings, fries, tator tots | 26% |
| Desserts, ice cream | 12% |
| Soft drinks, slushes | 18% |
| Other items | 3% |

Pie charts can be used to convey the same information as a tabular display. The more complex the visual display in terms of the number of its columns, however, the greater the need to put its information into the form of a pie chart. In general, tabular displays can convey more information in a smaller space, but they have less impact on their audience than do visual displays.

# CHAPTER HIGHLIGHTS

*1.* *Explain how data differs from information.*

*Data* consists of numbers, letters, facts, and figures that usually come from measurements or observations but have little or no meaning by themselves. Once data has been extracted or summarized so the result has meaning to the person who will use it, it becomes *information.*

*2.* *Describe the various components of a computer system.*

A *computer system* is a mechanical means of transforming data into information. It consists of hardware and software. *Hardware* refers to the electronic and mechanical components of a computer system. The three main types of hardware are the central processing unit (CPU), input devices, and output devices. *Software* is usually described in terms of programs, which are lists of instructions that tell the hardware how to behave.

*3.* *Classify the various types of computers used by business firms.*

We usually classify computers according to their cost, speed, size, and the number of users who can work on them at the same time. *Supercomputers,* used primarily for scientific, government, and military purposes, are the largest and most powerful computers made today. *Mainframe computers* represent the traditional workhorses of modern business. These computers have enormous memories and can support hundreds of terminals. *Minicomputers* are connected to networks of terminals to provide computing and word processing services for individual departments in large companies. *Personal computers* are suited for applications requiring moderate speed and memory capacity, like word processing and office management. Most are desktop models, but the power of personal computers has increased dramatically.

*4.* *Discuss the role of management information systems in a modern business.*

A *management information system (MIS)* is a collection of tools that provide information to a manager that facilitates that person's decision-making process. An MIS should help a manager make either a better decision or to make a decision more easily than he or she would without the system.

*5.* *List and describe the four functions of a management information system.*

A management information system must efficiently perform four functions: collect data; store data; update data; and process data. The value of an MIS lies in its ability to accumulate data so that it can be manipulated or processed into information.

*6.* *Explain the role of statistics in a management information system.*

Data does not become information until it is presented in a meaningful way. Statistics gives employees a vocabulary for describing numbers and turning numerical data into information. For example, market researchers often rely on a sample (a small group of representative units or persons selected from a much larger group) to answer questions about products or services. A random sample of all persons who own motorhomes, for example, can give us information about the total population of motorhome owners. This statistical technique can save large amounts of time and money and enable man-agement to make intelligent production, finance, and marketing decisions.

## KEY TERMS

Data
Information
Input
Data processing
Output
Computer system
Hardware
Peripherals
Central processing unit (CPU)
Main memory
Byte
Random access memory (RAM)
Control unit
Read-only memory (ROM)
Arithmetic-logic unit (ALU)
Auxiliary storage devices
Input device

Output device
CRT (cathode-ray tube)
Supercomputers
Mainframe computers
Terminals
Minicomputers
Personal computers (microcomputers)
Portable computers
Local area network (LAN)
Software
Program
Operating system
Programming
Menu
Booting
Utility program
Software applications package
Interactive mode

Cursor
Batch mode
Management information system (MIS)
Decision support system (DSS)
Executive information system
Sequential access
Random access
Manual updating
Batch system
Real-time updating
Ergonomics
Statistic
Sample
Random sample
Census
Descriptive statistics
Inferential statistics
Frequency distribution
Average

Arithmetic mean
Median
Mode
Measures of central tendency
Measure of dispersion
Range
Variance, standard deviation
Time series analysis (trend analysis)
Secular trend
Cyclical fluctuations
Seasonal trends
Correlation analysis
Visual display
Graph
Bar chart
Pie chart
Tabular display

## REVIEW QUESTIONS

1. What is the difference between data and information? Give examples of each.
2. In basic terms, what is a computer system?
3. What is the function of the central processing unit? What are the three main parts of the CPU?
4. What is the major difference between a supercomputer and a minicomputer?
5. What is the role of computer networks in the travel industry? How do travel agents benefit from this form of electronic data processing?
6. What is the role of software in modern computer systems? List and describe at least three software packages that are currently used to meet the data processing needs of business.
7. What is a management information system? What are the four functions of a management information system?
8. How do the information requirements of top management differ from first line management?
9. What is real-time updating? Give an example of an application of this procedure.
10. What is the difference between inferential and descriptive statistics? Describe how each might be used in a business setting.
11. How do managers use time series analysis?

# APPLICATION EXERCISES

1. In the near future you will open a bookstore near the campus of a large university. You have decided to develop a management information system. As the owner of a bookstore, what type of data would you collect? How might this data be classified? How long would you store the various types of data? Would you use manual or automatic (real-time) updating?

2. Assume the following monthly sales for your bookstore which opened in January:

| Month | Sales ($) |
|---|---|
| January | 42,000 |
| February | 40,000 |
| March | 43,000 |
| April | 45,000 |
| May | 48,000 |
| June | 48,500 |

| Month | Sales ($) |
|---|---|
| July | 50,000 |
| August | 52,000 |
| September | 54,000 |
| October | 56,000 |
| November | 60,000 |
| December | 66,000 |

What is the arithmetic mean for monthly sales figures? What is the median sales figure for the one-year period? What are the limitations of these two figures when assessing sales performance for the first year of the store's operation?

# CASES

## 16.1  Taking the High-Tech Road at Xerox

Xerox wanted more than just information from its [computer information] system. When he became president in 1986, Paul Allaire said, "We want to change the way we run our business." Chairman David Kearns brought Allaire back from Europe in 1983 to be chief of staff and asked him to figure out how to apply Xerox's technological experience to running the company better. The resulting "executive support system," probably the most far-reaching in any company, goes to the heart of management. Ken Soha, who oversees the system, relates that when the company's 20 strategic business unit chiefs used to gather for annual meetings with the top half-dozen executives at headquarters in Stamford, Connecticut, torrents of paper would rush back and forth in the preceding few days. Senior executives would get a fat black briefing book of documents, only partly read and little digested before the meeting, with no consistent format or terminology. Two similar units might have different definitions of a basic term like revenue. Much of a meeting would be spent trying to agree on facts.

As in many companies, devising the new computer system forced Xerox to rationalize and discipline reporting. Now when a business unit makes a presentation in Stamford, no papers fly to and fro. Instead, says Soha, each unit must submit its plan electronically five days in advance, compressed to a five-page format with standard definitions of terms. Each top executive should have read the plan on the screen of his Xerox 6085 workstation before the meeting, and business unit heads should not waste time going over basic facts. They can focus on issues.

As Allaire said in a Harvard business school case study, "Our management process is becoming inseparable from the technology which supports it."

## Questions

1. Is it reasonable to say that information management has become part of Xerox's formula for strategic success? Explain.
2. Why might some Xerox executives resist using the new "executive support system"?

Source: From Jeremy Main, "At Last, Software CEOs Can Use," *Fortune,* March 13, 1989, pp. 78, 80. Copyright 1989 *Fortune* Magazine. Reprinted by permission of the publisher.

## 16.2 Supervision or "Snoopervision" at Leprino Foods Company?

Vaughn Foster has U.S. 85 all to himself as he swings his truck onto the highway for his last trip of the day. To his right, the sun is disappearing behind the Rockies; ahead, the road stretches straight and empty for miles. With one eye on the speedometer, he eases into the right lane and starts creeping ahead at 50 miles an hour.

"I've been out all week," he says. "My wife's home, my kids are home, and I'd just as soon be there with them. There's no doubt about it: If that computer wasn't there I'd be running 60 easy."

Mr. Foster is talking about a black box the size of a dictionary that sits in a compartment above his right front tire. At the end of his trip, his boss at Leprino Foods Co. in Denver will pull a cartridge out of the box and pop it into a personal computer. In seconds the computer will print out a report showing all the times the truck was speeding. "It's like a watchdog," Mr. Foster grumbles. "You just can't get as far away from that supervisor as you used to. . . ."

At Leprino Foods, executives concede that their monitoring program has distasteful features. "There's no one in their right mind who'd want to have that computer watching them,"

admits Jerry Sheehan, the vice president of transportation for the closely held concern.

Like other trucking managers, Mr. Sheehan used to spend much of his time urging his drivers to observe the speed limit and take it easy on their engines. Truckers who drive too fast and strain their engines get too few miles per gallon and run up undue maintenance bills.

But urging wasn't accomplishing much. Leprino hired a vehicle-tailing service to follow a sampling of trucks and gauge their speeds. The service reported that most Leprino truckers were driving about 10 miles over the speed limit. That didn't surprise Mr. Sheehan, who has a theory about employee rules. "I'm a great one for believing that people really will do what's *in*spected and not what's *ex*pected," he says.

Three years ago, the nonunion company started outfitting its fleet with portable computers that hook up to sensors in a truck's engine and transmission. Now all 160 Leprino trucks have them. The devices gather detailed information about a truck's trip: what times it stopped and started, how fast the engine ran, how fast the truck was going throughout the trip.

The last statistic is especially potent at Leprino, which wields both carrot and stick to encourage its drivers to stay under 60 miles an hour (the extra five miles above the [old] national speed limit allows for speedometer errors and quick surges starting down a hill). A trucker gets a bonus of three cents a mile for every trip he makes without breaking 60.

But the first time a printout shows a driver sped at 65 miles an hour or faster, he gets an official reprimand. The second time, he is suspended without pay for a week. The third time, he is fired. Mr. Sheehan says Leprino has fired half a dozen truckers for speeding since the computers were installed.

Drivers at Leprino aren't enchanted with the system. "I started driving trucks because I'm kind of an independent sort of a guy that didn't like having the boss always looking over my shoulder," says E. K. Blaisdell, a former Leprino driver who recently became a dispatcher. "Then they managed to invent a machine that looks over my shoulder." Others gripe that they have become the butt of CB-radio jokes about states setting up extra-slow speed limits for Leprino drivers.

Mr. Sheehan, the vice president, sees another side. He says Leprino trucks now get 1.1 more miles per gallon—5.7 instead of 4.6—which is nearly a 25 percent improvement. A year after the first computers were installed, maintenance costs had dropped about one fifth and a declining accident rate had knocked $50,000 off the company's annual insurance premiums. Each $1,500 system paid for itself in about six months, Mr. Sheehan says, and in all, Leprino's $250,000 worth of computers have saved the company three times that much so far.

## Questions

1. On balance, do you think the computer monitoring of driver performance is a good or bad idea? Explain your reasoning.
2. Is this situation a sign of things to come? What sorts of actions and reactions are we likely to see in the area of computer monitoring of job performance?

Source: From Michael W. Miller, "Computers Keep Eye on Workers and See If They Perform Well," *Wall Street Journal*, June 3, 1985, pp. 1, 15. Reprinted by permission of *Wall Street Journal*, © Dow Jones & Company, Inc. 1985. All Rights Reserved Worldwide.

# Financial Management

PART SIX

*The once staid banking industry has taken on a new look in recent years. New services are being offered and traditional services such as checking accounts and loans have become more competitive. Since the deregulation of banking services, some of the changes have been quite dramatic. Citicorp, for example, chose to function as a national distribution company, with a full line of products and emphasis on new services and price tradeoffs. In Part VI we examine money, banking, and credit. Financial management, securities markets, and risk management are also covered in this section.*

# 17 Money, Banking, and Credit

## PRIME RATE
### BENCHMARK RATE USED IN SETTING BUSINESS AND SOME CONSUMER LOANS

9.00%
8.75
8.50
8.25
8.00

8  15  22  29  5  12
JANUARY        FEBRUARY

SOURCE: Riggs, Sovran, First American Bank

## MONEY MARKET MUTUAL FUNDS

■ 1ST VARIABLE RATE FUND
▨ DONOGHUE'S MONEY FUND AVERAGE
▨ GOVERNMENT INVESTOR TRUST

7.5%
7.0
6.5
6.0
5.5

28  4  11  18  25  1
DECEMBER  JANUARY      FEBRUARY

SOURCE: Donoghue's Money Fund Report

## MORTGAGE RATES
### LAST WEEK'S AVERAGES

30-YEAR FIXED         9.625%
15-YEAR FIXED         9.375%
3-YEAR A.R.M.         8.75%
1-YEAR A.R.M.      7.0%

4      6      8

SOURCE: The Peeke Report

Month...
Metrorail Riders...
Metrobus Riders...
Checks Cleared D.C...
Federal Payroll (millions)...
Federal Employes (excludes...
U.S. Consumer Price Index (CP...
Area Consumer Price Index[2]...
Area Food Store Price In...
Area Housing Cost I...
Avg. Daily Hotel...
Laventhol...
Area R...
Area...

To...

Foot...
Statistic...
Alexandr...

when we go get the earnin
will respond," he said.
Investors interested in Insi
alternate way

...was "upset with the perfor-
...pany last year" and has
..." to improve things.
...t to "cit"

69,200
23,900
3,395
...561                       $5,482,779
...485,277                   1,566,083,798
286,743,000                $90,775,744
                           1,015,002,000
$81,158,445                $61,274,389
115,878,497               168,222,497
...72                       213
191

|  | Qtr. Ended | Previous Qtr. | Year Ag |
|---|---|---|---|
| 31 | $92.75 | $91.07 | $87.1 |
| ar. 31 | $76.52 | $75.27 | $72.6 |
| Mar. 31 | $12.22 | $12.02 | $11. |

...revised   2. 1967 = 100  3. 2 Months Ago   4. SMSA-Standard Metropoli
...nery, Charles, Prince George's, Arlington, Fairfax, Prince William, Loudoun Counti
...assas.

## AREA RETAIL SALES
### IN BILLIONS OF DOLLARS

$2.8
2.6
2.4

## AREA DEPARTMENT STORE SALES
### IN MILLIONS OF DOLLARS

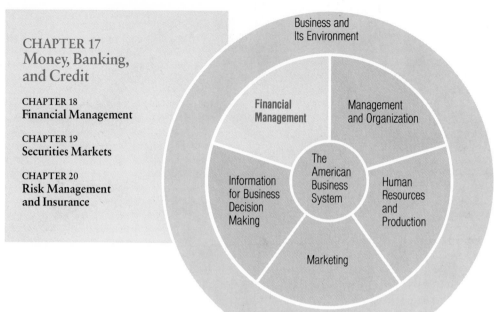

When Doug Pearson, president of NSS Corp., a Bedford, New Hampshire, company that sells computer hardware and software to banks, tried to increase the line of credit he had established at his bank, he was in for a surprise. In 1984, a year in which it had $500,000 in sales and earnings of $80,000, NSS had established a $30,000 line of credit. As more capital was needed, Pearson believed the bank would lend it to him. But when the account was given to a different lending officer, they "kind of reneged," recalls Pearson.

A source of credit is crucial to NSS's business for many reasons, not the least of which is that IBM requires NSS as a remarketer of IBM equipment to have a $1 million letter of credit. Pearson turned to his financial advisor, who steered him to Amoskeag Bank, a local bank, which lent him the money. By 1988, NSS had sales of $14 million, earnings of $300,000, and $1.9 million in operating lines of credit. Pearson makes a presentation to his loan officer every year to show him how NSS is performing against its business plan.

"The relationship is very important," says Pearson. "You have to show that you have a grip on reality. Over the years they have stayed with us and watched us grow."[1]

Doug Pearson knows firsthand about the importance of understanding money, banking, and credit. Without these three elements his business would be lost.

This chapter is about the nature of money. It also describes the function of credit, or how to get more money when it is needed, and surveys the major financial institutions.

# The Function of Money

Before money existed, the only way to acquire a good was to *barter*, to trade or exchange what one person owns for something another owns without using money. The problem with barter as a system of exchange is that every transaction is unique. If one shepherd trades three lambs and some wool for a new coat, this exchange offers little guidance to another shepherd who might want to make a similar transaction because the second shepherd's lambs, wool, and coat may be of a different quality.

Money solves the barter problem. **Money** is anything that is generally accepted in exchange for goods or in payment of debts, not necessarily valued for itself but because it can be used for the same purposes repeatedly.

*1.* Define money and list five of its characteristics.

**money** anything that is generally accepted in exchange for goods or in payment of debts

## The Purpose of Money

Money serves three essential purposes. It is

- A measure of value
- A medium of exchange
- A store of value

As a **measure of value**, money is a readily accepted means of relating or comparing the worth of different things. Money permits people to identify the relative value of two items—say, a blank videocassette at $4.99 and a videocassette of a recent movie for $39.95. Clearly, the price tag of the two videocassettes indicates that more value is placed on the movie videocassette.

Money is also a **medium of exchange**, anything that people are willing to accept in return for goods or services and that they in turn can exchange for

**measure of value** a readily accepted means of relating or comparing the worth of different things

**medium of exchange** anything that people are willing to exchange in return for goods and services

**Hot off the presses**
*These women are counting freshly printed yen notes, the currency used in Japan. Financial leaders in Japan are currently investigating ways of distributing yen more widely in world markets, to compete better with the U.S. dollar. Right now 70 percent of world trade is conducted in dollars.*

other goods or services. For example, when a consumer buys a new car stereo, the dealership may use the money it receives either to buy more inventory or to pay salaries.

In the United States, our money is no longer backed by a specific amount of gold. Thus, we use what is called *fiat money*—money that the government promises to be legally acceptable as a medium of exchange for products and services. The kind of fiat money most commonly used in exchanges is currency. Strictly speaking, **currency** refers only to coins and bills, but it may also refer to a nation's money. All countries that have a central government issuing money use some form of fiat money and currency.

**currency** coins and bills

Money is also a **store of value**, a means of holding and collecting wealth. A farmer could not amass wealth by keeping milk that his or her cows produce over the years. Instead, the farmer exchanges the milk, which would spoil in a few weeks, for money, which he or she can hold indefinitely without risk of spoilage.

**store of value** a means of holding and collecting wealth

## The Characteristics of Money

Money should have the following characteristics:

- Stability of value
- Divisibility
- Portability
- Durability
- Not easily counterfeited

*Stability of Value*   The value of money should not change significantly over the short run. An item valued at $100 today should be worth the same amount tomorrow or next month and approximately the same next year and the year after. Of course, inflation erodes the value of all currencies. The dollar has decreased in value over the last half century. For example, based on the **Consumer Price Index (CPI)**, the monthly governmental index of inflation, $1 today buys about what 37 cents bought in 1967. Countries like Brazil and Israel have even had inflation rates more than 200 times ours. Their people protect themselves against rapid declines in value by exchanging their currencies for something of predictable value, either goods or a stable currency. Often people will convert their savings to gold, land, or another "hard" asset when they fear that inflation will erode the value of their money. Table 17.1 shows the value of the U.S. dollar in various foreign currencies.

**Consumer Price Index (CPI)** the monthly governmental index that measures inflation

*Divisibility*   For a currency to work efficiently, its units of measure must permit precise valuation. The units should range from very small to extremely large and be divisible by the smallest unit. Goods and services in the United States can be precisely valued, and we can make exchanges in exactly the right amounts. It is no trick to buy a $1.29 bag of cheese popcorn with two $1 bills and get back 71 cents in coins. Similarly, it is not too difficult to figure out the divisibility of the British pound, which is equal to 20 shillings or 100 new pence.

**TABLE 17.1** World Value of the Dollar in Selected Countries on a Selected Date

| Country | Currency | Value on March 24, 1989 |
|---|---|---|
| Afghanistan | Afghani | 50.60 |
| Algeria | Dinar | 6.88 |
| Bahamas | Dollar | 1.00 |
| Botswana | Pula | 2.04 |
| Canada | Dollar | 1.18 |
| Chile | Peso | 252.74 |
| China | Renminbi Yuan | 3.72 |
| Cuba | Peso | 0.76 |
| Egypt | Pound | 0.70 |
| El Salvador | Colon | 5.00 |
| Finland | Markka | 4.21 |
| France | Franc | 6.31 |
| Germany, East | Ostmark | 1.86 |
| Germany, West | Mark | 1.86 |
| Greece | Drachma | 157.05 |
| Guatemala | Quetzal | 2.70 |
| Haiti | Gourde | 5.00 |
| Hong Kong | Dollar | 7.78 |
| India | Rupee | 15.53 |
| Israel | New Shekel | 1.81 |
| Italy | Lira | 1370.50 |
| Japan | Yen | 130.78 |
| Lebanon | Pound | 487.50 |
| Mozambique | Metical | 688.82 |
| Nicaragua | Cordoba | 5500.00 |
| Panama | Balboa | 1.00 |
| Philippines | Peso | 21.27 |
| Poland | Zloty | 571.48 |
| Saudi Arabia | Riyal | 3.75 |
| Somali Republic | Shilling | 238.00 |
| Spain | Peseta | 116.19 |
| United Kingdom | Pound sterling | 1.72 |
| Uruguay | Peso | 499.50 |
| USSR | Ruble | 0.62 |
| Yugoslavia | Dinar | 8247.11 |
| Zambia | Kwacha | 10.31 |

Source: From "World Value of the Dollar," *Wall Street Journal,* March 27, 1989, p. C3. Reprinted by permission of *Wall Street Journal,* © Dow Jones & Company, Inc. 1989. All Rights Reserved Worldwide.

But it's not always so easy. In the Yap Islands of the South Pacific, great stone wheels were still used as money at the beginning of the twentieth century. In East Africa, cows were money until very recently.[2] To arrive at an exchange that matched whole stones or cows required an infinitely more complicated process than our monetary exchanges. Today, virtually all currencies use a decimal system like ours.

*Portability*   The holders of a currency must be able to move it easily to wherever a transaction takes place. In facilitating exchanges, the advantage of a decimal currency over stone wheels and cows is obvious. In North America, people began using paper money in 1685.[3]

*Durability*   Any currency must be able to survive many transactions without wearing out. When it does need replacement, people must know that they can exchange it for new currency without its suffering any loss of value. The average $1 bill lasts one and a half years. It is equally a dollar for both its first and its last holder.

*Not Easily Counterfeited*   A currency's users must have confidence that what is in circulation is genuine. The federal government therefore goes to great lengths to make the design of bills difficult to counterfeit. The U.S. Bureau of Engraving and Printing uses paper containing silk threads as well as special inks and dyes to make paper money difficult to counterfeit.

## The Concept of Liquidity

The nature of money can be summed up by saying that it must be liquid. As we saw in Chapter 15, *liquidity* is the capacity of an asset to be turned into currency. Assets can be classified according to their liquidity. A *liquid asset* is one that can routinely be turned into cash at its market value within thirty days. Neither real estate nor an antique rocker, for instance, is a liquid asset, because liquidating either within thirty days would normally require the seller to take a lower-than-market price.

Bank accounts are certainly liquid assets, but their degree of liquidity depends on whether they are classified as demand deposits or time deposits. The most liquid assets other than currency are **demand deposits**, individual and business accounts from which depositors can withdraw funds at any time without prior notice to the bank. The *depositor,* a person or business in whose name funds have been put in a bank, can make withdrawals by check, automated bank teller (ATM), or some other means that allows him or her to access the account.

Until recently, most demand deposit accounts did not earn interest. Since Consumer Savings Bank of Worcester, Massachusetts, began offering the first **NOW (negotiable order of withdrawal) account** in June 1972, interest-bearing checking accounts began to be made available. NOW accounts were originally limited to savings banks in Massachusetts and New Hampshire, but they became available nationwide in 1980.[4] Credit unions also offer demand deposit accounts which are called **share draft accounts**.

A somewhat less liquid asset is a **time deposit**, funds deposited with a bank either in the form of a savings account or a certificate of deposit, under an agreement that the bank will pay interest on the funds and that the depositor will give notice to the bank a specified time before withdrawing funds. For instance, banks may require up to thirty days' notice before permitting a withdrawal (without penalty) from a savings account.

**demand deposits**   individual and business accounts from which depositors can withdraw funds at any time without prior notice to the bank

**NOW (negotiable order of withdrawal) account**   an interest-bearing checking account

**share draft accounts**   demand deposit accounts offered by a credit union

**time deposit**   funds deposited with a bank either in the form of a savings account or a certificate of deposit

# Financial Intermediaries

Just as marketing requires intermediaries to match producers and retailers, as we have seen, the financial system needs intermediaries to put together those who have funds with those who require funds. Financial intermediaries are institutions that take in funds, then loan them at a price (an interest charge) sufficient to reward the supplier adequately and make a profit for the intermediary.[5] Figure 17.1 illustrates the relationships among the suppliers and requirers of funds and financial intermediaries.

*2.* Explain what financial intermediaries are and distinguish their two major categories.

## Suppliers and Users of Funds

The cash flow of people and organizations rarely matches their cash needs. From time to time, individuals, businesses, and units of government supply excess cash to financial intermediaries and borrow from them.

*Individuals* Individuals invest money that they do not need immediately into life insurance, pension plans, and bank accounts. Many open Individual Retirement Accounts (IRAs) or, if they are self-employed, Keogh accounts, both of which can earn money on a tax-deferred basis. They use funds that financial intermediaries make available to them in the form of, say, home mortgage loans, bill consolidation loans, and student loans.

*Businesses* A combination of financially perilous times and increasingly sophisticated communications has made money management a key managerial function. Businesses can now shop worldwide for the best interest rates on short-term investments. Businesses supply their financial intermediaries with

FIGURE 17.1  How Financial Intermediaries Work

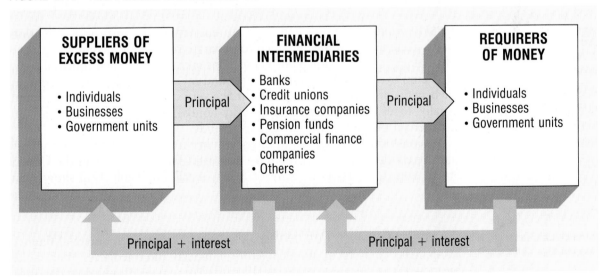

cash when, for example, they pay life insurance premiums on their employees and officers or make contributions to pension funds. Of course, businesses are also major requirers of funds, whether to solve a brief cash-flow problem or for a long-term transaction like a mortgage loan.

*Government Units*   Government units are also suppliers and users of funds. For instance, a town collects property taxes only once or twice a year, but it must meet payrolls every week. At times, towns must borrow for the short term in anticipation of receiving revenues. Towns borrow for the long term by issuing *bonds*, promises to pay interest and repay principal on a loan. Chapter 19 will look more closely at government bonds.

## Nondepository Institutions

There are two types of financial intermediaries: nondepository institutions and depository institutions. *Nondepository institutions* are, as the name suggests, financial intermediaries that do not accept deposits. The most common types are insurance companies, pension funds, commercial finance companies, consumer finance companies, and mutual funds (including stock, bond, and money market mutual funds). We will examine the first four of these in this section and the others in Chapter 19.

**premiums**   funds received by insurance companies from policyholders

*Insurance Companies*   An insurance company takes in funds, called **premiums**, from its policyholders. In return, the firm promises to pay the insured if a specific event occurs while its contract, the *policy*, is in force. For example, a life insurance company promises to pay if the person insured dies. Insurance companies make money by generating more premiums at higher rates than they must pay in claims and by earning interest on loans. They make short-term loans to policyholders and long-term loans to corporations, offer mortgages for real-estate developers, and purchase government bonds.

**pension funds**   accumulated funds intended to generate retirement income for participants

*Pension Funds*   The second type of nondepository institution, **pension funds**, accumulates funds intended to generate retirement income for people who belong to the pension plan. These plans take money, called contributions, from employees or employers (or both) and invest it so they can pay retirees the benefits promised. Pension funds make very conservative investments and usually focus on blue-chip stocks and bonds, high-quality mortgages on commercial property, and government bonds.

Pension funds have grown dramatically in recent years to the point where collectively they are one of the most powerful financial forces in the United States, with total assets in 1986 of $1.9674 trillion. Table 17.2 shows just how dramatic the growth in pension funds has been and where these funds have been invested.

**commercial finance companies**   intermediaries that make business loans

*Commercial Finance Companies*   The third category, **commercial finance companies**, consists of nondepository financial intermediaries that make business loans. Because commercial finance companies do not take deposits, they are not subject to the banking regulations discussed later in this chapter.

**TABLE 17.2** Growth of Pension Funds: Assets of Private and Public Pension Funds (in billions of dollars)

| Type of Pension Fund | 1980 | 1981 | 1982 | 1983 | 1984 | 1985 | 1986 |
|---|---|---|---|---|---|---|---|
| *Total, all types* | *913.9* | *987.8* | *1,152.4* | *1,358.3* | *1,477.2* | *1,738.3* | *1,967.4* |
| Private funds | 639.4 | 677.3 | 792.0 | 935.0 | 990.7 | 1,157.4 | 1,295.1 |
| Insured | 172.0 | 199.8 | 242.9 | 286.4 | 331.6 | 400.0 | 468.8 |
| Noninsured | 467.4 | 477.6 | 549.1 | 648.7 | 659.1 | 757.4 | 826.3 |
| Corporate equities | 231.3 | 210.0 | 258.1 | 311.3 | 297.2 | 383.0 | 436.6 |
| U.S. Government securities | 53.7 | 73.0 | 79.4 | 92.4 | 99.7 | 106.5 | 112.2 |
| Corporate bonds | 79.7 | 85.1 | 91.6 | 103.3 | 113.7 | 119.4 | 122.2 |
| Other | 102.7 | 109.5 | 120.0 | 141.7 | 148.5 | 148.5 | 155.2 |
| Public funds | 274.5 | 310.4 | 360.5 | 423.2 | 486.5 | 580.8 | 672.3 |
| State and local government | 198.1 | 224.2 | 262.5 | 311.2 | 356.6 | 432.1 | 502.7 |
| Corporate bonds | 94.5 | 103.8 | 107.3 | 106.6 | 118.1 | 123.3 | 131.4 |
| Corporate equities | 42.1 | 49.2 | 55.2 | 75.2 | 82.5 | 103.3 | 114.5 |
| U.S. Government securities | 40.0 | 51.8 | 71.2 | 88.2 | 111.2 | 128.7 | 149.7 |
| Other | 21.4 | 19.4 | 28.8 | 41.2 | 44.8 | 76.8 | 107.1 |
| U.S. Government | 76.4 | 86.2 | 97.9 | 112.0 | 130.0 | 148.8 | 169.6 |
| Civil service | 73.9 | 84.8 | 97.4 | 111.4 | 126.9 | 144.6 | 163.4 |
| Railroad retirement | 2.5 | 1.4 | .5 | .6 | 3.1 | 4.2 | 6.2 |

Source: *Statistical Abstract of the United States* (Washington, D.C.: Govt., 1988), p. 345, Table 569.

They fund their operations by borrowing large sums, then making loans to smaller businesses that cannot obtain bank financing. Such borrowers are not the best credit risks, so they must pay commercial finance institutions a higher rate of interest than they would a bank. Businesses pledge assets like equipment, inventory, real estate, or accounts receivable as collateral, in case they default on (are unable to repay) the loan.

*Consumer Finance Companies* The fourth type of institution, **consumer finance companies**, consists of nondepository financial intermediaries that lend to individuals. They operate much like commercial finance companies, making loans to individuals who cannot get bank loans and are thus willing to pay higher interest rates.

**consumer finance companies** financial intermediaries that lend to individuals

## Depository Institutions

A financial intermediary that accepts deposits is a depository institution. Lines once clearly divided the types of depository institutions, but the deregulation of financial services has largely erased the traditional boundaries, which existed until the 1970s.

*Commercial Banks* Originally, **commercial banks** served primarily business customers. They concentrated on attracting demand deposits, which paid no interest, and making loans to businesses. Commercial banks have broadened

**commercial banks** banks that attract demand deposits and make loans to individuals and businesses

Advertising for the banking market  *Great Western is a financial services corporation that owns commercial banks in several states. With this advertisement GW is hoping to reach the hefty consumer's market in Florida, the nation's fourth most heavily populated state.*

their services recently to penetrate the consumer-banking market. They now offer virtually all the different forms of customer products, including savings accounts and certificates of deposit, and services, including automated teller machines, credit cards, and brokerage services.

Some commercial banks are **national banks,** financial institutions organized with the approval of the U.S. Comptroller of the Currency, who issues them a charter. They are operated subject to federal banking regulations. National banks must be members of the Federal Reserve System. Other types of commercial banks, called **state banks,** are chartered by the state in which they operate. Many state banks also join the Federal Reserve System, but they do not have to. Sixty-six percent of all bank accounts are at state banks, whereas 60 percent of the total deposits at banks are at federal banks.

All members of the Federal Reserve System must insure their deposits against loss if the institution fails, through the **Federal Deposit Insurance Corporation (FDIC),** a corporation established by the Banking Act of 1933. Other financial institutions that meet the FDIC's requirements may also apply for insurance. The FDIC insures each account in a member bank for up to $100,000 per account. Today some people worry about this federal corporation's ability to handle the losses of large bank failures. In the case of a bank failure, the FDIC can borrow up to $3 billion from the U.S. Treasury. State insurance programs may or may not apply to accounts in institutions not covered by federal insurance. Unfortunately, some institutions have no insurance at all, and some state programs are not sufficient to protect depositors. Table 17.3 shows just how many FDIC-insured banks have closed because of financial difficulties from 1981 to 1986. Clearly, these closings are a growing concern.

**national banks**  commercial banks organized with the approval of the U.S. Comptroller of the Currency

**state banks**  commercial banks chartered by the state in which they operate

**Federal Deposit Insurance Corporation (FDIC)**  organization that insures each account in a member bank for up to $100,000 per account

## TABLE 17.3   FDIC-Insured Banks Closed, 1981 to 1986

|  | 1981 | 1982 | 1983 | 1984 | 1985 | 1986 |
|---|---|---|---|---|---|---|
| Total banks closed or assisted | 10 | 42 | 48 | 79 | 120 | 145 |
| Agricultural banks | 1 | 7 | 7 | 31 | 62 | 59 |
| Deposits, closed and assisted banks | 3,826 | 9,908 | 5,442 | 2,883 | 8,059 | 6,597 |
| Agricultural banks | 7 | 112 | 114 | 421 | 866 | 1,408 |
| Problem banks | 223 | 369 | 642 | 848 | 1,140 | 1,484 |

Source: *Statistical Abstract of the United States* (Washington, D.C., Govt., 1988): p. 474, Table 780.

The primary source of funds for commercial banks are demand and NOW accounts. Banks use a percentage of those funds to make loans to businesses and individuals. They are required by the federal government to keep a set percentage (3 to 17%) of their deposits available to meet depositors' needs.

*Thrift Institutions*   Originally, **thrift institutions**, such as savings banks and savings-and-loan associations, served individuals by providing safe, interest-bearing accounts for savings, mortgages, and other local, long-term loans. **Mortgages** are offered to individuals or businesses so they can purchase real estate. The real estate is used as collateral in case the buyer defaults on the loan.

With the entry of commercial banks into arenas previously restricted to the thrifts, any difference in the services offered by these two types of

**thrift institutions**
institutions that serve individuals by providing safe, interest-bearing accounts for savings

**mortgages**   payment arrangements offered to individuals or businesses so they can purchase real estate

**The Bailey Bros. Building & Loan**  *When tough times hit the town of Bedford Falls in the 1946 film* It's A Wonderful Life, *George Bailey manages to calm panicking depositors and keep the Bailey Bros. Building & Loan open through it all. Real-life S & Ls haven't met such a happy end: due to poor management and lack of government supervision 500 savings and loans had fallen bankrupt at the end of 1988.*

**savings-and-loan associations (S & L's)** thrift institutions that are usually owned by their depositors and offer a wide variety of financial services

depository institutions has almost disappeared. By the end of June 1987, in fact, savings and loans held only 32 percent of all residential mortgages, which amounted to $567 billion.

Nevertheless, the thrifts' organizational structure still distinguishes them from commercial banks. **Savings-and-loan associations (S & Ls)**, also known as building-and-loan associations, are thrift institutions that are usually owned by their depositors. They offer a wide variety of services, including checking accounts, and still invest, primarily in mortgages, within their communities. Perhaps the most memorable definition of a building-and-loan association came from George Bailey, a character played by Jimmy Stewart in the film *It's A Wonderful Life.* Pleading with Bedford Falls shareholders not to close their accounts at the Bailey Bros. Building & Loan Association, George says: "You're thinking of this place all wrong, as if I had the money back in a safe. The money's not here. Well, your money's in Joe's house; that's right next to yours. And in the Kennedy house and Mrs. Maitland's house—and a hundred others. You're lending them the money to build and then they're going to pay it back to you as best they can. Now what are you going to do, foreclose on them?"

*Mutual savings banks*, a class of thrift institutions found mainly in the Northeast, are also owned by their depositors. They have investment policies similar to those of the savings and loans. An increasing number of thrifts are turning themselves into shareholder-owned institutions in the same way that commercial banks have done.

The thrifts have a number of options when it comes to deposit insurance. They may participate in the FDIC or in the **Federal Savings and Loan Insurance Corporation (FSLIC)**, a corporation established by federal law to insure the deposits of thrift institutions. Like the FDIC, the FSLIC has a current maximum per account of $100,000. The FSLIC is funded by fees paid by member savings and loans. It can also borrow $750 million from the U.S. Treasury, raise its fees, and require its insured savings and loans to deposit up to 1 percent of their total savings should the FSLIC need to raise funds in the case of a bank failure. A variety of other state and private insurance programs exist. And like state-chartered commercial banks, thrifts also have the option of simply not insuring their accounts (see Business Issues).

*Credit Unions* A nonprofit savings-and-loan organization traditionally operated specifically for the benefit of its members (all of whom usually have some common link such as employment or ethnic background) is a **credit union**. For example, people of Lithuanian background may join the Taupa Lithuanian Federal Credit Union in South Boston, Massachusetts, and state employees in Ohio may join the Ohio State Employees' Credit Union. Credit unions primarily make automobile, student, and consumer loans. Because they operate as cooperatives, they channel their earnings back to their members in the form of higher interest rates while at the same time charging as much as 6 percent less than commercial rates to their members on loans and credit card purchases. Credit unions may insure their deposits, most commonly through the National Credit Union Administration, an agency of the federal government. The coverage is similar to that of the other federal deposit insurance programs. Table 17.4 shows how the total assets of credit unions relate to those of the other depository institutions we have discussed.

Credit unions have experienced tremendous growth in assets and members in recent years and have had half the number of failures as banks and savings

**Federal Savings and Loan Insurance Corporation (FSLIC)** a corporation established by federal law to insure the deposits of thrift institutions

**credit union** a nonprofit savings-and-loan organization operated specifically for the benefit of its members

TABLE 17.4   Total Number and Assets of Credit Unions Compared to Other Financial Institutions

| Institution | Total Number (1986) | Assets in Billions of Dollars |
|---|---|---|
| Credit Unions | 14,693 | 147.7 |
| FDIC-insured commercial banks | 14,198 | 2,940.9 |
| FSLIC-insured savings institutions | 3,227 | 1,165.3 |
| FDIC-insured savings banks | 472 | 237.0 |

Source: *Statistical Abstract of the United States* (Washington, D.C.: Govt., 1988), p. 470, Table 771.

# THE S & L CRISIS

The mid-1980s were a period of robust growth for the U.S. economy. Inflation, unemployment, and interest rates were all down. In the midst of this burgeoning economy, however, came a shocker—thrift institutions (of which savings and loan associations and savings banks are the most common type) were dropping like flies. The problem reached its pinnacle in 1988, when the Federal Home Loan Bank Board (FHLBB), which regulates the industry, sold off or liquidated 222 thrifts with combined assets of $100 billion, costing the government around $39 billion. Compare that to 1987, when 48 S & L liquidations or mergers and acquisitions at a cost of $3.8 billion was itself considered dire news.

At a time when the economy was thriving, how did the S & L industry find itself in such a fine mess? There is no simple answer. But part of the problem can be traced to the creation of money market mutual funds in the 1970s and the onslaught of deregulation in the 1980s.

In the old days, S & Ls followed a simple rule of charging borrowers 6 percent interest, paying depositors 3 percent interest on their savings, and using the 3 percent spread to keep operations running smoothly. That all worked fine until interest rates took off in the late 1970s and thrift deposits began to flow to the newly created money funds, which paid interest rates that kept pace with the double-digit inflation of the day.

Deregulation also took its toll. In 1980 interest restrictions were lifted on S & Ls, so they could offer tempting interest rates to lure back old depositors and attract new ones. The problem was that while they were paying out these high interest rates, they were not allowed to offer adjustable rate mortgages until a year later. Interest rates jumped to 13 percent in 1979 and more than 20 percent in 1980, and S & Ls tried to offer competitive rates while they were often only collecting 8 percent on their thirty-year mortgages. By 1981, 85 percent of all S & Ls were losing money.

To compound the problem, in 1982 S & Ls were granted permission to make loans not just for home mortgages but for all types of businesses, businesses that often were new territory for S & L management. Some began jumping into all kinds of businesses they didn't understand: casinos, airlines, and wind farms, to name a few. The result was often disastrous.

So in 1988 the FHLBB stepped in and sold off or liquidated more than 200 thrifts. Sixty-eight were sold in the month of December—twenty of these in the last two days of the month—because of a tax break that would end in 1988, making the thrifts much more attractive to buyers in 1988 than in 1989. The move resulted in a great deal of criticism of the FHLBB, and the press referred to the prices garnered as the "great S & L giveaway" or the "great S & L fire sale."

Even though the losses for the thrift industry for the third quarter of 1988 were down to $1.6 billion from the $3.9 billion posted in each of the two preceding quarters, the S & L crisis would not go away. President Bush stepped in with a plan designed to bail out the industry. His plan—which, among other things, calls for S & L owners to pay higher insurance premiums and increase their capital reserves from 3 percent to 6 percent of assets—could cost $200 billion over the next decade, with upwards of $60 billion of that to be footed by taxpayers.

Sources: Gisela Bolte, "Finally, the Bill Has Come Due," *Time,* February 20, 1989, pp. 68–73; Paul Duke, Jr., " 'Dual Banking' Faces a Possibly Crippling Blow in Bush's Plan to Curb State Powers Over S & Ls," *Wall Street Journal,* April 11, 1989, p. A24; Christine Gorman, "Cracks in the System," *Time,* August 29, 1988, pp. 54–55; "The Great S & L Giveaway," *Business Week,* January 16, 1989, p. 112.

and loans. Today, there are approximately 16,000 credit unions holding total assets of $193 billion.[6]

# The Federal Reserve System

From 1837 to 1907, panics marked by unstable currency and runs on banks punctuated American history. With the lesson of the Panic of 1907 fresh in their minds, Congress began to fashion a mechanism to stabilize the banking system. In 1913, President Woodrow Wilson signed the Federal Reserve Act, which created the **Federal Reserve System** as the United States' central bank. A *central bank* is the government agency responsible for acting as a government's bank, managing its monetary policy, serving as the primary bank of the banking system, and overseeing the nation's international financial relationships.

**Federal Reserve System** the United States' central bank

## *Its Structure*

As Figure 17.2 indicates, the Federal Reserve has a somewhat complex structure. Although we will examine the functions of each component in more detail later, an overview of the system here will be helpful.

*3. Describe the principal organizational elements in the Federal Reserve System.*

*The Board of Governors* The board of governors of the Federal Reserve System oversees the entire system. Its seven members are appointed by the president, and its chair serves as a principal government spokesperson on economic and monetary policy.

*The Federal Reserve Banks* The daily routine of ensuring the financial system's smooth operation falls to the twelve *Federal Reserve Banks*. Every day, these banks oversee the transfer of billions of dollars in currency and checks. Figure 17.3 shows the boundaries of each Federal Reserve District and of their branch territories, with the locations of their branches and other facilities. The twelve banks are located in Boston, New York, Philadelphia, Cleveland, Richmond, Atlanta, Chicago, St. Louis, Minneapolis, Kansas City (Missouri), Dallas, and San Francisco.

The twelve Federal Reserve Banks provide a number of services in addition to the ones discussed below. For instance, they issue **Federal Reserve Notes,** the nation's currency. They disburse funds and provide accounts for federal agencies. They also issue, service, and redeem U.S. savings bonds.

**Federal Reserve Notes** the nation's paper currency

The *members* or shareholders of the Federal Reserve System in each district own its Federal Reserve Bank. As noted earlier, all national banks must belong to the Federal Reserve System, and many state-chartered commercial banks also elect to join. As one condition of membership, a member bank must maintain a certain percentage of its deposits as a *reserve*, which is the liquid assets—usually currency—that are set aside in a bank's vault or on deposit with a regional Federal Reserve Bank.

Member banks are not the only institutions that use the Federal Reserve System's services. The Depository Institutions Deregulation and Monetary

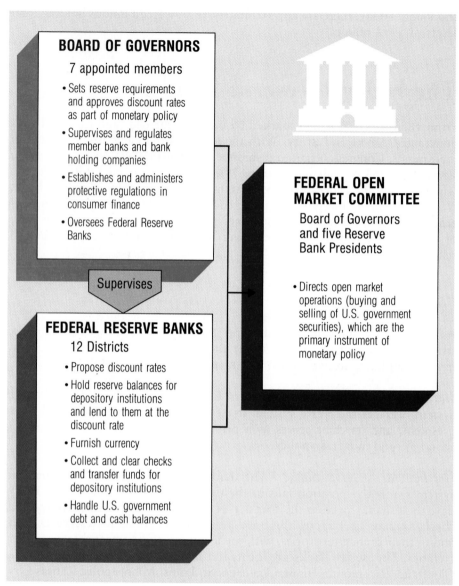

**BOARD OF GOVERNORS**

7 appointed members

- Sets reserve requirements and approves discount rates as part of monetary policy
- Supervises and regulates member banks and bank holding companies
- Establishes and administers protective regulations in consumer finance
- Oversees Federal Reserve Banks

Supervises

**FEDERAL RESERVE BANKS**

12 Districts

- Propose discount rates
- Hold reserve balances for depository institutions and lend to them at the discount rate
- Furnish currency
- Collect and clear checks and transfer funds for depository institutions
- Handle U.S. government debt and cash balances

**FEDERAL OPEN MARKET COMMITTEE**

Board of Governors and five Reserve Bank Presidents

- Directs open market operations (buying and selling of U.S. government securities), which are the primary instrument of monetary policy

FIGURE 17.2   Organization of the Federal Reserve System

Source: Board of Governors of the Federal Reserve System, *The Federal Reserve System: Purpose and Functions,* 7th ed. (Washington: 1984.)

Control Act of 1980 gave all depository financial institutions the right to use Federal Reserve services. Today member banks make up less than one-sixth of the more than 39,000 financial institutions subject to Federal Reserve System requirements. These approximately 6,000 member banks, however, hold about 70 percent of the deposits in commercial banks and 40 percent of all bank deposits.[7]

*Federal Open Market Committee*   The third major component of the Federal Reserve System is the Federal Open Market Committee. This twelve-

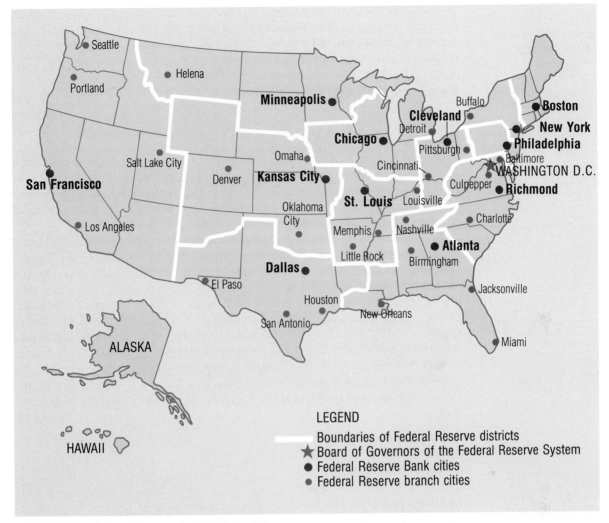

FIGURE 17.3   Federal Reserve District Boundaries

Source: From O. C. Ferrell and Geoffrey Hirt, *Business* (Boston: Houghton Mifflin, 1989), p. 535. Copyright 1989. Used by permission of the publisher.

member committee consists of the board of governors, the president of the New York Federal Reserve Bank, and the presidents of four other Federal Reserve Banks. The Open Market Committee's principal function is to carry out the Federal Reserve Board's monetary policy. This body directs the Federal Reserve System's buying and selling of U.S. government securities on the open market in order to increase or decrease the funds available for lending by member banks.

## Monetary Policy Responsibilities

The Federal Reserve's most publicized duties involve its control over the nation's **monetary policy**, the Federal Reserve System's management of

**monetary policy** the management of available credit and the money supply

available credit and the money supply. The level of credit and currency available strongly affects economic activity. By closely monitoring and regulating the supply of credit and money, the Federal Reserve works to stabilize fluctuations in the economy.

## Measuring the Money Supply

Every week, the Federal Reserve Board measures the money supply, the total amount of currency in circulation, deposits in checking and savings accounts, and other liquid assets. It uses four measures of the money supply.

The narrowest money measure, called $M_1$, primarily covers money held for the purpose of completing exchanges. This includes either currency or currency equivalents, like travelers' checks, and demand deposits. One major component, in the currency equivalents or "other checkable deposits" category, is the NOW accounts defined earlier.

The second classification in the money supply, $M_2$, expands $M_1$ by including all time deposits as well. Time deposits, or savings accounts, are deposit accounts that earn money at a specified interest rate. Although time deposits are supposed to remain in an account for their entire term, in practice they are quite liquid, subject to withdrawal with or without notice, although banks impose a penalty for early withdrawal. The measure called $M_3$ further expands $M_2$ by including large time deposits and investments in less liquid investment vehicles.[8] Major daily newspapers typically publish these figures weekly. See Figure 17.4 for a sample newspaper money supply table.

Once the Federal Reserve knows how much money is available in the system, it has three principal tools it can use to adjust the supply to meet its goals:

- Open-market operations
- The reserve requirement
- The discount rate

## Open-Market Operations

**open-market operations** the buying and selling of government securities on the open market

One Federal Reserve tool for carrying out its monetary policy is its **open-market operations**, the buying and selling of government securities on the open market, which are supervised by the Federal Open Market Committee discussed earlier. The securities are those issued by the U.S. Treasury and federal or federally sponsored agencies. When the Federal Reserve purchases securities, it issues a check on itself, which is deposited in the seller's bank. When the bank presents that check for payment, the Federal Reserve increases the amount in the bank's reserve account. Just the opposite happens when the Federal Reserve sells securities to member banks.

The Federal Reserve is interested in open-market operations because when financial intermediaries buy government securities, they have less money to loan to businesses and individuals. Conversely, when the Federal Reserve buys government securities, the financial intermediaries have more money to loan out. If conditions indicate that the economy needs a boost, the Federal Reserve will buy up government obligations, thus loosening credit. If inflation seems to be on the rise, however, the Open Market Committee will begin selling government obligations.

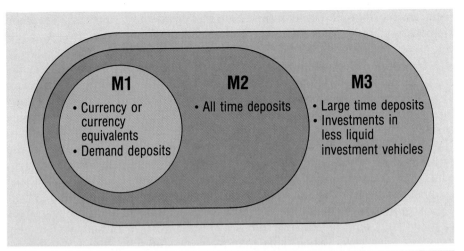

| Money supply | Total | Change from prior period |
|---|---|---|
| **M1** Week ended March 27 (in billions) | $787.1 | +$0.2 |
| **M2** Week ended March 27 (in billions) | $3,079.9 | −$5.4 |
| **M3** Week ended March 27 (in billions) | $3,962.8 | −$3.0 |

FIGURE 17.4  Money Supply Figures

Source: From *Wall Street Journal,* April 10, 1989, p. A16. Reprinted by permission of *Wall Street Journal,* © Dow Jones & Company, Inc. 1989. All Rights Reserved Worldwide.

*The Reserve Requirement*  As we have seen, the Federal Reserve's money supply measures include not just available currency but also bank deposits. Banks, of course, make loans against their deposits. They must also maintain some reserves, however, in order to meet customer demands. The Federal Reserve sets a **reserve requirement**, a specified percentage of deposits that a member bank must either deposit with the Federal Reserve or hold in its own vaults as cash and may not lend.

The reserve requirement in effect defines how much of a bank's deposits it may loan. If the reserve requirement happens to be 10 percent, a bank can lend as much as $1,000 for every $100 it has in deposits, as long as it maintains $100 in reserve. Thus, a financial intermediary in effect creates money through lending several times the amount of its deposits.

If the Federal Reserve increases the reserve requirement, it decreases the amount that depository institutions under its regulation can lend. The supply of credit available shrinks and the money supply therefore contracts. Lowering the reserve requirement has the opposite effect. Adjustments to the reserve

**reserve requirement** a specified percentage of deposits that a member bank must either deposit with the Federal Reserve or hold in its own vaults as cash and may not lend

requirement do take some time, though, before they ripple through the financial system and have any major effect on the economy.

### The Discount Rate

**discount rate** the amount the Federal Reserve charges on loans to all member depository institutions

A more sensitive and faster-acting economic lever is the **discount rate**, the amount the Federal Reserve charges on loans to all member depository institutions. In effect, the discount rate establishes a floor for interest rates charged by banks because banks tie the interest that they charge their customers to what the Federal Reserve is charging them. (Typically, as the discount rate is raised banks will raise their prime rate, the rate at which they offer to lend money to their best customers. Often, adjustable rate mortgages, home equity lines of credit, and revolving lines of credit such as credit cards are tied to fluctuations in the discount rate.) When the discount rate is lower than the rates charged banks by their other sources of funds, they tend to borrow from the Federal Reserve and use that money to make their own loans. This loan activity stimulates the economy by encouraging businesses and individuals to spend. When the Federal Reserve determines that too much money is available, it raises the discount rate and, at least theoretically, the process reverses itself. Figure 17.5 lists key U.S. and foreign interest rates including the discount and prime rate.

### Selective Credit Controls

**margin requirements** the minimum amount that a purchaser of securities must deposit with a broker in order to be able to buy securities on credit

The Federal Reserve has a number of other, more specifically targeted tools that it uses to fine-tune the monetary system. These techniques are lumped into the category of *selective credit controls*. The most important one is the Federal Reserve's ability to set **margin requirements**, the minimum amount that a purchaser of securities must deposit with a broker in order to be able to buy securities on credit. Like the reserve requirement, the margin requirement specifies how much securities dealers may lend to investors. (We will discuss margin requirements in detail in Chapter 19.)

## The Banking System's Bank

As the banks' bank, the Federal Reserve provides many of the same services to its members as banks provide their own customers. It makes loans, particularly when banks have liquidity problems, and it holds deposits.

### Check Clearing

The function of the Federal Reserve Banks that undoubtedly affects the most people and businesses every day is its check clearing. The Reserve Banks direct millions of transfers every day between districts and between banks. Figure 17.6 shows the clearing process for a check that goes through the Federal Reserve System.

### Other Means of Transferring Funds

Checks remain the most common means of transferring funds, but new means that are also regulated by the Federal Reserve are gaining rapid acceptance. For example, the *debit card*, a machine-readable plastic card, creates a receipt that authorizes a bank to transfer funds immediately from the debit-card holder's account to the business presenting the receipt. In effect, a debit card allows its holder to

## MONEY RATES

Tuesday, April 4

The key U.S. and foreign annual interest rates below are a guide to general levels but don't always represent actual transactions.

**PRIME RATE:** 11½%. The base rate on corporate loans at large U.S. money center commercial banks.

**FEDERAL FUNDS:** 9 15/16% high, 6% low, 6% near closing bid, 6½% offered. Reserves traded among commercial banks for overnight use in amounts of $1 million or more. Source: Fulton Prebon (U.S.A.) Inc.

**DISCOUNT RATE:** 7%. The charge on loans to depository institutions by the New York Federal Reserve Bank.

**CALL MONEY:** 10½% to 10⅞%. The charge on loans to brokers on stock exchange collateral.

**COMMERCIAL PAPER** placed directly by General Motors Acceptance Corp.: 9.80% 30 to 119 days; 9.70% 120 to 149 days; 9.65% 150 to 179 days; 9.50% 180 to 270 days.

**COMMERCIAL PAPER:** High-grade unsecured notes sold through dealers by major corporations in multiples of $1,000: 9.80% 30 days; 9.87% 60 days; 9.90% 90 days.

**CERTIFICATES OF DEPOSIT:** 9.20% one month; 9.30% two months; 9.45% three months; 9.72% six months; 9.95% one year. Average of top rates paid by major New York banks on primary new issues of negotiable C.D.s, usually on amounts of $1 million and more. The minimum unit is $100,000. Typical rates in the secondary market: 9.85% one month; 10% three months; 10.30% six months.

**BANKERS ACCEPTANCES:** 9.73% 30 days; 9.73% 60 days; 9.73% 90 days; 9.73% 120 days; 9.73% 150 days; 9.73% 180 days. Negotiable, bank-backed business credit instruments typically financing an import order.

FIGURE 17.5   Key U.S. and Foreign Annual Interest Rates

Source: From *Wall Street Journal*, April 5, 1989, p. C19. Reprinted by permission of *Wall Street Journal*, © Down Jones & Company, Inc. 1989. All Rights Reserved Worldwide.

buy now and pay now without using cash.

An *automated teller machine (ATM) card* is a form of debit card that allows the card holder to make certain bank transactions with a machine instead of having to interact with a teller. An ATM card is encoded with the customer's bank account number and can only be used when the customer's *personal identification number* (PIN), a series of letters or numbers that only the customer knows, is typed into the ATM keypad. At the end of 1973, 1,935 ATMs had been installed in the United States. The number mushroomed more than 3,000 percent by 1986, when 69,161 ATMs were installed.[9]

ATMs are often located in busy areas like supermarkets or shopping centers, far from the banks with which they are associated. According to the Bank Administration Institute, however, 79 percent of ATMs are located in bank branch offices and another 6 percent at main offices. The remaining 15 percent are in grocery and retail stores (4%), freestanding units (3.4%),

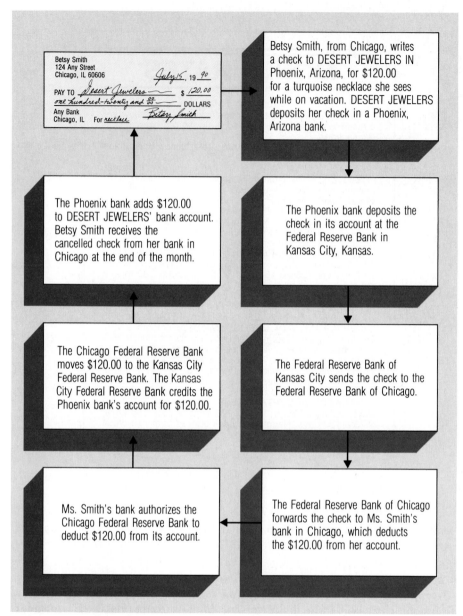

FIGURE 17.6 The Check-Clearing Process

Source: O. C. Ferrell and Geoffrey Hirt, *Business* (Boston: Houghton Mifflin, 1989), p. 540. Copyright 1989. Used by permission of the publisher.

shopping centers (2.1%), office complexes (2.1%), university campuses (1.4%), and hospitals (1.2%).[10]

*Point-of-sale terminals* also provide a direct link between a bank and computers at a place where consumers pay for goods or services. Using the customer's card, the machine will immediately transfer funds from the customer's account to the seller's. There is also a growing trend toward national networks of ATMs, where banks across the country allow other

Using ATMs to pay for college   *Automated teller machines or ATMs enable a customer to carry out a number of transactions without having to visit the bank during business hours. Students at the University of Iowa use ATMs to pay tuition bills by transferring funds from their accounts to the school's account.*

bank ATM cardholders to access their accounts. These networks include CIRRUS and PLUS. When a user does not have an account at a particular bank, he or she is typically charged an access fee through the network to use another bank's ATM.

Today many transfers between distant parties are accomplished directly by computer in a process called **electronic funds transfer (EFT)**. EFT includes *automated clearinghouses (ACHs)*, which allow for direct deposits to be made to and from a bank account by computer. ATMs and point-of-sale systems are both examples of electronic funds transfer systems. Consumers often authorize mortgage companies or insurance companies to make automatic withdrawals from their accounts for their regular monthly payments. The pay-by-phone services offered by some banks also fall into this category. Using EFT, employers deposit wages and the government deposits Social Security and pension payments directly to the recipients' accounts. EFT significantly reduces paperwork and the delays inherent in the check-clearing process. It also minimizes the risk of theft or loss as documents pass from hand to hand.

**electronic funds transfer (EFT)**   arrangement that allows for direct deposits to be made to and from a bank account by computer

## Deregulation and the New Financial Services Companies

Just as the computer was revolutionizing banking, the federal government began to dismantle the regulatory structure that had governed the industry since the 1930s. As noted earlier, the lines that used to exist between the types of financial intermediaries began to disappear. Deregulation opened banking to other businesses that began to invade the banks' territory. For instance, Sears, Roebuck and Company, the nation's largest retailer, entered the marketplace by offering financial counseling, insurance, and a general-purpose credit card it introduced in 1985 called the Discover Card. Such developments have placed the Federal Reserve System in a difficult position. Its authority to regulate these new financial intermediaries is not at all clear. Meanwhile, the intermediaries already subject to its regulations complain about the difficulties these regulations create for them in competing.

The course of banking and financial services regulation is difficult to predict. In the early 1980s, it seemed certain that banking regulation would die rather quickly. Record numbers of bank failures, however, including those of the Penn Square Bank and the first National Bank & Trust Company of Oklahoma City, and the near failure of Continental Illinois in Chicago, made further deregulation unlikely and even led to calls for reregulation (see Table 17.3).

# Credit

**credit** the ability of a business or a person to obtain money or property and to defer repayment

Let us examine the nature of **credit,** the ability of a business or a person to obtain money or property and to defer repayment or payment. This chain of events occurs because the lender makes a favorable appraisal of the debtor's ability to repay.

## The Five C's of Credit

*5. Define the five C's of credit and explain the function of credit bureaus.*

The five criteria most commonly applied by those evaluating credit applications can each be described by words beginning with the letter C. These criteria apply whether the borrower is applying for consumer or *commercial* (that is, business) *credit,* for *trade credit* (the sale of goods or services on the promise of payment in the future), or for *debit financing,* the lending of money at interest.

*Character* The reputation for honesty and integrity of the person or organization seeking credit is known as *character.* As with many of the C's of credit, character is difficult to evaluate, but it may be the most important of the five. Many lenders assess character by looking at a potential borrower's history of loan repayments. If the lender and the borrower are new to each other, the lender may do a credit check. The lender may also ask for a list of *references,* firms or banks with whom the borrower has done business in

**PERSONAL FINANCIAL STATEMENT**
**(CONFIDENTIAL)**

NAME _____     EMPLOYMENT _____
RESIDENCE
ADDRESS _____     POSITION _____
                                     BUSINESS
CITY, STATE, & ZIP _____     ADDRESS _____

OF _____

The following is submitted for the purpose of procuring, establishing and maintaining credit with you in behalf of the undersigned or persons, firms or corporations in whose behalf the undersigned may either severally or jointly with others execute a guaranty in your favor. The undersigned warrants that this financial statement is true and correct and that you may consider this statement as continuing to be true and correct until a written notice of a change is given to you by the undersigned.

Date: _____     Signed: _____

| ASSETS | | LIABILITIES & NET WORTH | |
|---|---|---|---|
| 1. Cash (on hand and in banks) (see schedule 1) | | 13. Notes Payable, Banks, Unsecured (see schedule 1) | |
| 2. U. S. Government and Agency Securities (see schedule 2) | | 14. Notes Payable, Banks, Secured (see schedule 1) | |
| 3. Marketable Securities (see schedule 2) | | 15. Notes Payable, Others (see schedule 7) | |
| 4. Non-Marketable Securities (see schedule 3) | | | |
| 5. Notes Receivable—Itemi… | | | |
| 6. Cash Value—Life Insuran… (do not deduct loan) (see… | | | |
| 7. Real Estate In Own Name (see schedule 5) | | | |
| 8. Partial Interests in Real Es… Values (see schedule 6) | | | |
| 9. Automobiles | | | |
| 10. Furniture and Personal Pro… | | | |
| 11. Other Assets—Itemize | | | |

**SUPPLEMENTARY SCHEDULES**

**SCHEDULE 1 — BANKING RELATIONSHIPS**

| Name of Bank | Location | Checking Balances | Savings Balances | Loan Balance | Terms or Maturity | Collateral | High Credit |
|---|---|---|---|---|---|---|---|
| | | | | | | | |
| | | | | | | | |

**SCHEDULE 2 — SECURITIES (GOV'T. AND MARKETABLE)**

| No. Shares or Face Value | DESCRIPTION | Cost | Market Value | Source of Valuation | Registered in Name of | Is Stock Pledged? |
|---|---|---|---|---|---|---|
| | | | | | | |

FIGURE 17.7   Sample Personal Financial Statement

Source: From Loren Gary, *Commercial Loan Forms Handbook* (Rolling Meadow, IL: Andover Parris Publishing Group/Bank Administration Institute, 1989), pp. 23–24. Copyright 1989 Andover Parris Publishing Group. Used by permission.

the past. Figure 17.7 shows a typical personal financial statement that is required when applying for a loan.

*Capacity*   The measure of a borrower's ability to live up to the terms of a credit agreement and to pay off an obligation as promised is known as *capacity*. Financial managers measure the capacity of individuals by evaluating their statements of assets and liabilities on the credit application. In the case of businesses, lenders review and analyze financial statements and historical trends and try to project historical performance.

*Collateral*   The security for a loan—usually an asset with enough value that it could be sold to satisfy the obligation—is called **collateral**. The collateral for a mortgage loan, for example, is the real estate on which the borrower gives the lender the mortgage. When collateral *secures* or assures the repayment of a loan, the borrower *assigns* or transfers ownership rights in the collateral

**collateral**   the security for a loan that could be sold to satisfy the obligation

unsecured loan   a loan for which the borrower does not provide collateral

to the lender in the event that the borrower defaults. An **unsecured loan**, one for which the borrower does not provide collateral, usually carries a higher interest rate than a secured loan. For example, unsecured credit extended on bank-issued credit cards routinely carries a much higher interest rate than secured loans granted by the same bank.

*Capital*   In the context of a credit application, *capital* means the financial resources that a borrower has available to assure the lender that the credit is secure. In this context, capital reflects the borrower's *net worth*, the amount by which assets exceed obligations. In making this calculation, a creditor looks at a business's financial statements or an individual's credit application.

*Conditions*   The fifth C, *conditions*, refers to the current economic environment. The ways in which outside factors might affect the borrower's ability to repay the obligation must be calculated as another element in a credit application.

## Consumer Credit

consumer credit   credit extended to individuals for nonbusiness personal, family, or household purposes

The credit extended to individuals for nonbusiness personal, family, or household purposes is **consumer credit**. Such transactions may be either secured or unsecured, long term or short term. A consumer may obtain credit from many sources, including banks, credit unions, stores, gasoline companies, or national credit card companies like Diners Club.

credit bureaus   businesses that keep records on the credit and payment practices of individuals and firms

Before extending credit, a financial institution will, as lender, carefully investigate the borrower and verify the information on the credit application. Lenders can check on consumer credit applicants by using **credit bureaus**, businesses that keep records on the credit and payment practices of individuals and firms. Credit bureaus also maintain data on consumers' employment and marital histories as well as other information that a lender might find relevant. Federal Reserve regulations restrict access to the information that credit bureaus maintain, to protect consumers from possible misuse of data. Persons on whom a credit bureau maintains information also have a right to see their files and to correct or add explanatory information to them.

## Credit Cards

credit card   a form of credit representing an agreement between the merchant and the card issuer, in which the merchant honors the card and the issuer pays the charge slips; and between the issuer and the card holder, in which the issuer extends a line of credit to the holder and the holder makes payments

A **credit card** is a card, usually made of plastic, which may represent two types of agreements. One agreement is between the card issuer and the merchant, to affirm that the merchant will honor the card and the issuer will pay the charge slips. The second is between the card issuer and the card holder, saying that the issuer will extend a certain amount of credit to the holder and that the holder will make payments in accordance with the contract. If a business, like Neiman Marcus, issues a credit card good only in its own stores, then the first element of the agreement in this definition would not of course apply.

Applicants for credit cards must fill out an application, on which the issuer then checks the information, as any lender would. Note that a business accepting a national credit card like Visa does not extend credit to the patron

**Credit cards are big business** *Credit cards enable approved card holders to postpone payment on purchases for the length of a predetermined grace period. Credit cards account for so many billions of dollars worth of purchases each year that relatively little currency is needed in our large economy.*

using the card. Rather, the business is extending credit to Visa, which has itself extended credit to the cardholder. The business's payment by Visa does not depend on the cardholder's paying Visa. Visa assumes the risk that its cardholders will not pay. Visa and the other national card issuers make money both by discounting each sale before paying the merchant and also by charging cardholders an annual fee as well as interest on bills not paid in full or on time.

Credit cards are big business today. More than 152 million Visa cards and 135 million MasterCards are in use, along with tens of millions of other cards.[11] These cards represent billions of dollars' worth of purchases each year and are a major reason why relatively little currency is needed in an economy the size of ours (see Experiencing Business).

## Commercial Credit

Businesses apply for credit in much the same way as consumers do. For a credit check, a lender can turn to a special credit investigative service or to a commercial rating firm like Dun & Bradstreet or TRW Information Services. Such firms provide relatively detailed reports on business borrowers. If sufficient information is available, they rate the potential borrower's financial strength and payment history. The services publish their ratings in reference volumes that they sell to credit managers.

In determining whether to extend trade credit to a new customer, a credit manager uses the rating firms and contacts the customer's trade and bank references to evaluate its creditworthiness. With this evaluation in hand, the

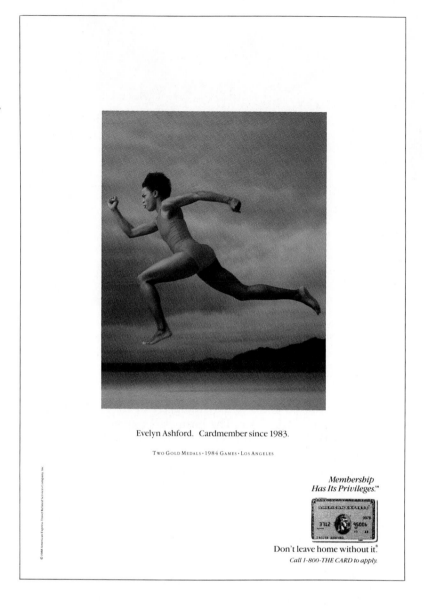

Evelyn Ashford.  Cardmember since 1983.

Two Gold Medals · 1984 Games · Los Angeles

*Membership Has Its Privileges.*℠

Don't leave home without it.®
*Call 1-800-THE CARD to apply.*

credit manager can decide whether to extend credit and, if so, how much. Generally, the amount of credit extended is small at the beginning of a relationship, often equaling just one or two orders. If the invoices covering this amount are paid promptly, the credit manager may increase the customer's line of credit. Over time, a credit manager evaluates the customer's payment practices and adjusts the borrower's credit limits as circumstances dictate. Quite often, credit managers share information with credit bureaus.

## The Collection Process

**6.** *Outline the collection process.*

Most firms and individuals pay their bills on time or at least meet the partial payment terms of their credit agreements. When payments are not made,

# TAKING CHARGE OF YOUR CREDIT

Like learning to ride a bicycle or drive a car or choosing the college to attend, getting a bank credit card is more and more becoming an American rite of passage. By 1986, 71 percent of American families owned a median of five cards per family. More than 250 million Visas and MasterCards were in circulation. And hundreds of billions of dollars were being charged annually.

Clearly, it pays to shop around for credit card rates and to have a clear understanding of just what you're getting into when you take hold of the plastic. Here are a few tips to remember.

If you plan on carrying over balances from one month to the next, you should try to find the lowest interest charge available. If you have a balance on a card charging you high interest, you can use a cash advance from the lower interest card to pay it down. But be sure to consider whether the savings will offset the cost of an annual card fee if you just paid one. For example, if you owe $1,000 and are paying monthly interest on it of $16.50 (at a rate of 19.8 percent a year), you'd save about $5.25 a month if you could get a card charging 13.5 percent interest. But you'd also have to pay that bank's annual card fee. If you just paid the 19.8 percent bank's card fee, it would take about three or four months to start saving money on the interest charges. The *Wall Street Journal* regularly publishes a list of bank credit card interest rates and card fees (see list).

If you're unable to get a credit card and really want one, collateral cards are available for almost anyone earning some income. You place a deposit in a bank issuing the card and that becomes your collateral account. Some banks will give you a credit line ranging from 50 to 75 percent of the collateral amount.

You also want to make sure that you understand how your billing works. If there's

## The Most Common Interest Rates Offered by the Ten Largest U.S. Issuers

| Bank | Interest Rate | Annual* Fee | Grace Days |
|------|------|------|------|
| Citibank | 19.80% | $20.00 | 30 |
| Chase Manhattan | 19.80 | 20.00 | 30 |
| Bank of America | 19.80 | 18.00 | 25 |
| First Chicago | 19.80 | 20.00 | 25 |
| Wells Fargo | 20.00 | 18.00 | 25 |
| Mfrs. Hanover | 17.80 | 20.00 | 25 |
| First Interstate | 21.00 | 20.00 | 25 |
| Maryland National | 18.90 | 18.00 | 25 |
| Bank of New York | 16.98 | 18.00 | 30 |
| Security Pacific | 20.40 | 15.00 | 25 |

*This fee applies to regular cards only, not premium cards.
Source: From "Bank Credit Card Interest Rates," *The Wall Street Journal*, April 10, 1989, p. C19. Reprinted by permission of *Wall Street Journal*, © Dow Jones & Company, Inc. 1989. All Rights Reserved Worldwide.

any confusion about what kind of grace period—the time period you have before the bank starts charging the interest—and whether it is erased if there are any carried-over balances, call your bank and ask. The wording on the backs of monthly bills varies from bank to bank and is often unintelligible. If you don't plan to carry over balances, but rather pay them off every month, it makes sense to get a card with a longer grace period so interest doesn't start accruing immediately on purchase.

In making a responsible selection of credit cards, remember as well that you have the power to shop around and choose the best deal for your personal situation.

Sources: "BRM Mortgage and Loan Rate Trends," *Bank Rate Monitor*, April 3, 1989, p. 2; tables 796 and 798; U.S. Bureau of the Census, *Statistical Abstract of the United States: 1988*, 108th ed. (Washington, D.C., 1987), pp. 481, 482; Jeffrey L. Seglin, "The Greatest Money Myths," *Boston*, August 1986, pp. 145, 148–150.

however, a credit manager or his or her staff initiates the process of collection, a system used to collect past-due accounts. Normally, the full process includes the following steps, in increasing urgency:

1. A series of computer-generated reminder letters
2. A strong personal letter
3. A telephone call or series of calls
4. Legal action

It is important to note that federal regulations limit how collection practices on consumer debts can be carried out. For example, a bill collector cannot call a consumer debtor after 9:00 P.M. or if the debtor has requested that no more phone calls be made.

# Credit: A Perspective

The restrictions mentioned on credit bureau reports and on collection activities became law as a result of one of the consumer movement's greatest triumphs. Four federal laws passed during one decade completely changed the face of consumer credit. The first of these laws, the *Truth in Lending Act*, was passed in 1969 and amended in 1980. In essence, this act requires lenders to present prospective borrowers with standard statements of all credit costs so that borrowers can compare prices. The act also limits consumer liability on a lost or stolen credit card to $50.

The next important consumer credit act was the *Fair Credit Reporting Act* of 1970, whose provisions relating to credit bureaus were discussed earlier. This act applies not only to consumer credit applications but also to credit reports supplied for decisions on hiring or retention in employment or for insurance applications.

In 1974, Congress enacted the *Equal Credit Opportunity Act,* which prohibited discrimination in evaluating and granting credit because of an applicant's race, color, sex, age, religion, marital status, or national origin. Last came the *Fair Debt Collection Practices Act* of 1978, which restricted abuses that had occurred in collection practices.

The irony of this new regulatory program lies in its timing. Just as deregulation was becoming the watchword in financial services, this new structured credit environment arrived. Yet in all the fervor for deregulation, no one seriously proposed abolishing the new credit practices acts.

# CHAPTER HIGHLIGHTS

*1.* Define money *and list five of its characteristics.*

*Money* is a measure of value, a medium of exchange, and a store of value. Five desirable characteristics of money are stability of value,

divisibility, portability, durability, and resistance to counterfeiting.

*2.* Explain what financial intermediaries are and distinguish their two major categories.

*Financial intermediaries* are middlemen that take in funds from various sources on a temporary basis and provide those funds to temporary users of funds at a price (the interest charge) that adequately rewards the suppliers and users of funds and also satisfies the intermediary's own earnings requirements. The major categories of financial intermediaries include insurance companies, pension funds, commercial and consumer finance companies, commercial banks, thrift institutions, and credit unions.

*3. Describe the principal organizational elements in the Federal Reserve System.*

The principal organizational elements in the Federal Reserve System are the board of governors, a seven-member board appointed by the President; twelve Federal Reserve Banks; and the Federal Open Market Committee, made up of the board of governors and five presidents of Federal Reserve Banks, one of whom must head the New York bank.

*4. Define* monetary policy *and explain the three principal ways the Federal Reserve has of implementing it.*

*Monetary policy* is the management of available credit and the money supply to regulate economic activity. The Federal Reserve uses three primary tools to implement its monetary policy: the reserve requirement, the discount rate, and open-market operations. All three tools affect the amount of money that is available for lending.

*5. Define the* five C's of credit *and explain the function of credit bureaus.*

The *five C's of credit* are character, the honesty and integrity of the loan applicant; capacity, the ability of the borrower to repay a loan; collateral, the security available for a loan; capital, the financial resources of the borrower; and conditions, the general economic environment. Credit bureaus keep records on the credit histories and payment practices of individuals and firms. The information they provide helps lenders evaluate an applicant's past payment history (character) and ability to repay (capacity).

*6. Outline the collection process.*

The collection process generally consists of four steps: (1) a series of computer-generated reminder letters, (2) a strong personal letter, (3) a telephone call or series of calls, and (4) legal action.

# KEY TERMS

Money
Measure of value
Medium of exchange
Currency
Store of value
Consumer Price Index (CPI)
Demand deposit
Negotiable order of withdrawal (NOW) account
Share draft account
Time deposit
Premium

Pension fund
Commercial finance company
Consumer finance company
Commercial bank
National banks
State banks
Federal Deposit Insurance Corporation (FDIC)
Thrift institution
Mortgage

Savings-and-loan association (S & L)
Federal Savings and Loan Insurance Corporation (FSLIC)
Credit union
Federal Reserve System
Federal Reserve Bank
Federal Reserve Note
Monetary policy
Open-market operations

Reserve requirement
Discount rate
Margin requirement
Electronic funds transfer (EFT)
Credit
Collateral
Unsecured loan
Consumer credit
Credit bureau
Credit card

# REVIEW QUESTIONS

1. What is the function of money? Before money existed, how did people acquire goods?
2. What are the five important characteristics of money?
3. Describe the concept of liquidity. Give some examples of liquid assets.
4. What is a financial intermediary? Describe the two types of financial intermediaries.
5. What is the difference between a thrift institution and a credit union?
6. What is the Federal Reserve System? In what ways does the Federal Reserve System stabilize the banking system?
7. Describe the open market operations of the Federal Reserve System.
8. What are the five C's of credit?
9. Describe consumer credit. How do lenders check on consumer credit applications?
10. What has been the impact of deregulation in the financial services industry?

# APPLICATION EXERCISES

1. At some time in the future you are very likely to seek credit for the purchase of an automobile, a home loan, educational needs, or the establishment of a small business. The lender will very probably apply the five C's in evaluating your credit application. How will you measure up? For each of the five C's of credit, circle one of the four ratings provided. On completion of this self-assessment, what do you think your chances are of obtaining a substantial loan?

|  | Poor | Fair | Good | Excellent |
|---|---|---|---|---|
| Character | 1 | 2 | 3 | 4 |
| Capacity | 1 | 2 | 3 | 4 |
| Collateral | 1 | 2 | 3 | 4 |
| Capital | 1 | 2 | 3 | 4 |
| Conditions | 1 | 2 | 3 | 4 |

2. Using the yellow pages of your local phone directory, prepare a list of nondepository and depository institutions that serve your community.

# CASES

## 17.1 Don't Bank on It

Once the great hope of electronic banking, the bloom seems to be off the rose of home banking. By the end of February 1989, after having invested tens of millions of dollars, Chemical Bank had canceled the accounts of its 25,000 individual and small business home-banking customers, signaling the defeat of a five-year effort it called "Pronto."

Overall, the reception of the home-banking movement has been lackluster at best. In early 1989, only 95,000 out of 3.3 million households having computers and modems were subscribers of the 41 home-banking services available.

Analysts cite several reasons why home banking has failed to catch on. First, the service fees banks charge range from $5 to $15 a month, and often with a phone-line surcharge of about $4.50 an hour. Second, the software that banks provide for using the system is the same as it was five years ago, so it is at times painfully slow, causing frustration and, if there's a phone-line surcharge, excess charges. Third, some customers who were using home banking simply to pay bills electronically found that $60 to $144 a year was a bit too steep a premium to pay for a more convenient checkbook register. Fourth, some of the systems only paid bills electronically to those companies that were equipped to accept electronic transfers. Some banks transferred this money but had to do so manually. Either way, someone ended up licking a stamp, putting a check in an envelope, and mailing it. Fifth, many of the banks froze payments for several days before transferring them from debtor to debtee, taking interest away from the user. Finally, users still had to trudge down to the bank to make deposits or get cash.

The verdict is still out on whether home-banking services will survive. Bank of America, Chase Manhattan, Citibank, Manufacturers Hanover, and others are still banking on it.

## Questions

1. What are some possible reasons why more of the 3.3 million computer and modem households did not sign up for home-banking services?
2. How might Chemical Bank have tailored its home-banking service to make it more appealing to customers?

For more information, see: Philip Elmer-DeWitt, "Back to the Velvet-Roped Lines," *Time*, January 9, 1989, p. 49; Jeffrey L. Seglin, *Bank Administration Manual* (Rolling Meadows, Ill.: Bank Administration Institute, 1988), pp. 199–200; and Laura Zinn, "Home Banking Is Here—If You Want It," *Business Week*, February 29, 1988, pp. 108–109.

## 17.2 Ethnic Loan Clubs

[Ethnic loan] clubs amount to informal small-scale banks organized primarily by immigrants to help one another. Though the loan clubs are not legally prohibited, they operate outside regular U.S. banking laws and safeguards. Even so, they have nurtured fledgling businesses from the barrio to Chinatown in cities as diverse as Houston, Los Angeles, Chicago and New York. With loans ranging from a few hundred dollars to $20,000 or more, Vietnamese *hui* (associations) in Texas played a crucial role in reviving the moribund shrimping industry in the Gulf of Mexico by financing the purchase of dozens of boats. An estimated $10 million in Korean *keh* (contracts) has financed the purchase of houses, restaurants and small grocery stores in the San Francisco Bay Area. . . .

Most of the clubs operate on the same basic principle: a group of people, often ten or 20, contribute the same amount of money each month to a kitty, which is immediately loaned to one of them. All club members including the borrower, continue to make the monthly payments until everyone has received the purse once. By that time, each participant has borrowed and repaid the entire loan.

In one type of West Indian *su-su* (among us) in Brooklyn, for example, ten people contribute $200 a month for ten months. Though many clubs assign the pool by drawing lots, each $2,000 collection in this kind of *su-su* goes to the person who everyone agrees needs it most urgently. After ten rounds, each member has contributed ten $200 installments and received one lump-sum payment of $2,000.

In many of the more elaborate loan clubs, participants bid for the privilege of taking the pool. Whoever offers the highest interest rate wins, although each member can take the pot only once. The entire interest payment is immediately deducted from the fund and paid out to the other members. . . .

No *hui, tanda* or *keh* can be successful without a great deal of trust. Individual members may not be acquainted with one another, but they must all know and believe in the organizer, called a *keh-ju* in Korean or a *chu-hui* in Vietnamese. She covers any defaults. As compensation, the first pool is traditionally hers: in a bidding club, she receives it interest-free. . . .

[H]ard-pressed immigrants will go on joining ethnic loan clubs. For many, the informal banks represent a leg up on the American dream. Someday the language and cultural barriers that hold back immigrants may start to crumble. Until then, the loan clubs will no doubt prosper.

## Questions

1. How do the *hui, keh, su-su, tandas,* and other ethnic loan clubs differ from banks and other lending institutions? Are there any similarities?
2. What dangers do members of these loan clubs run?

For more information, see: Christine Gorman, "Do-It-Yourself Financing," *Time*, July 25, 1988, p. 62. Copyright 1988 Time Inc. Reprinted by permission.

# 18 Financial Management

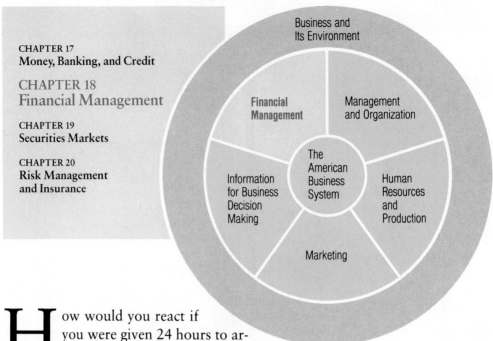

Business and
Its Environment

Financial
Management

Management
and Organization

Information
for Business
Decision
Making

The
American
Business
System

Human
Resources
and
Production

Marketing

How would you react if you were given 24 hours to arrange a $9.6 *billion* line of credit to enable your company to buy another company? Hans G. Storr, chief financial officer of Philip Morris Company, found himself in just such a position in late 1988. Within a single day of Philip Morris's hostile takeover announcement of Kraft, Inc., Storrs lined up the borrowing power for the $12.9 billion acquisition. In fact, Storrs actually piled up a $19 billion line of credit! Not only that, Storrs managed to fend off the threat of rising interest rates by locking in lower than average rates on half of the borrowed money. All this prompted an investment banker to tell *Business Week:* "By raising money quickly and keeping the cost of capital low, Hans did a terrific job."[1]

**financial management**
the process of obtaining money and using it effectively to achieve an organization's goals

This chapter is about **financial management**, the process of obtaining money and using it effectively to achieve an organization's goals. Financial management may serve goals ranging from Philip Morris's acquisition of Kraft, to a family-operated dry cleaner getting a bank loan to build an addition.

# The Nature of Financial Management

Every business has a person who manages its finances. The smallest firms, like a sandwich shop, may not have anyone who spends full time on financial management. In other words, the owner may wear all the hats. Or the firm may have someone like Mrs. J. Willard Marriott, Sr., who kept the Marriott Corporation's books on a yellow legal pad when it started in the 1920s.[2] Today, Mrs. Marriott's descendants oversee an $8 billion-a-year corporation requiring a platoon of highly trained financial managers.

## The Financial Managers

The best way to analyze the financial management function is in terms of how it operates in large corporations, because of the high degree of specialization in these firms. Figure 18.1 charts the typical finance activity within a large firm. At the top, the **vice president of finance** (or chief financial officer) is the officer in a corporation with overall responsibility for its financial functions. The **controller,** who reports to the vice president of finance, has responsibility for accounting, data processing, and taxes. Chapters 15 and 16 focused

**vice president of finance** the officer in a corporation with overall responsibility for the corporation's financial functions

**controller** the person responsible for accounting, data processing, and taxes within the corporation

FIGURE 18.1   Finance Activity Within a Firm

Source: Figure, p. 10 from *Principals of Managerial Finance,* 4th Edition, by Lawrence J. Gitman. Copyright © 1988 by the authors. Reprinted by permission of Harper & Row, Publishers, Inc.

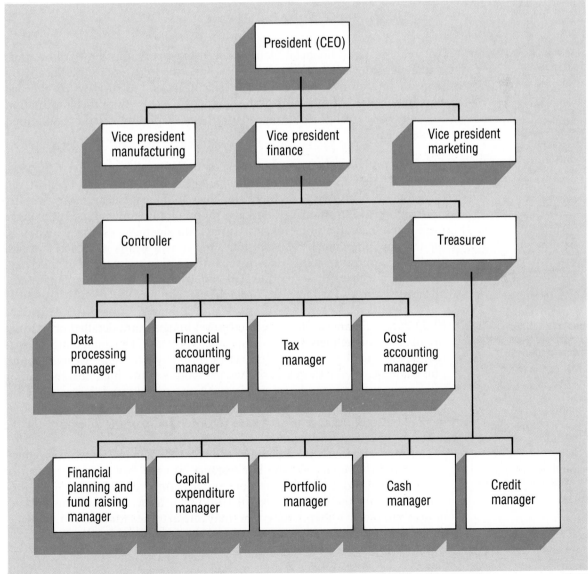

primarily on the controller's areas of responsibility. The **treasurer**, who also reports to the vice president of finance, has responsibility for overseeing and planning for the firm's expenditures and income.[3] In this section we will examine the treasurer's areas of responsibility. Clearly, the controller and the treasurer need to work together closely. In effect, the controller is the firm's scorekeeper, and the treasurer will need these up-to-the-minute reports before making important decisions.

We will refer to those making decisions in the treasurer's areas of responsibility as *financial managers* or *financial management*. Financial management performs three crucial functions:

1. Planning for a company's financial needs and reevaluating the plan after it is put into action.
2. Acquiring enough funds at the right times to keep the company moving.
3. Deciding how and when to spend the funds on hand.

## Developing a Financial Plan

To create a sound financial plan, financial managers must have a firm grasp of the company's aims for both the short and the long term. Once they know what these are, managers can draw up budgets and identify where the cash flow may exceed or fall short of the company's needs. With this information, managers can arrange in advance to invest any surplus or to acquire additional funds as needed.

*Establishing Objectives* Objectives of a financial plan must be precise enough so that managers can translate them into numbers. Then, if one objective conflicts with another, someone in management must establish priorities for these objectives. Suppose that a clothing manufacturer plans to introduce a new line of men's sportswear. Management, of course, wants to see the new line launched successfully, but it also wants its line of business clothes to continue to do well. In such a situation, management may have to decide which of these objectives is more important to the company and allocate the firm's resources accordingly.

*Budgeting* Financial plans for the future, **budgets**, are detailed projections of income and expenses over a specified period.[4] The budgeting process requires financial managers to predict a company's needs at various points. For example, a ski shop's cash budget would show high income during December and January but quite low income in July and August. Yet the pattern of the shop's cash needs may well be precisely the reverse of its income pattern, because it may have to order and pay for inventory for the next season during the summer.

The budget process can sometimes lead financial managers into involvement in matters of company policy. For instance, if **cash flow**, the movement of money into and out of a firm, is slow and accounts receivable are high, they may argue that the firm is extending too much trade credit (discussed later in this chapter). Other issues that may attract the attention of financial managers include the size of inventories, the amount of insurance coverage

Deep pockets   *To increase the capitalization of floundering, San Francisco–based Grocery Express, new owner Mary Garvey invested her own money. She also lowered prices on items sold through her delivery-only operation, in order to attract customers and increase revenue.*

that is desirable, the costs of marketing campaigns, the fate of older plants, the value of automation and computerization, as well as inflation and international currency fluctuations.

## Financing the Plan

From the financial manager's standpoint, implementing a plan consists primarily of financing it. The first option is **internal financing**, money generated from positive cash flow or **retained earnings**, profits plowed back into the business rather than paid out to stockholders in the form of dividends. This choice is often not available, for liquidity reasons or simply because the company has not yet begun to turn a profit. It might seem that a healthy business would not need the second option, **outside financing**, which is money generated by borrowing from or selling ownership interests to sources outside the business for its use. Most firms do require outside financing at one time or another, however.

*Short-term Needs*   Most firms discover that there is a gap between the time they must pay for inventory and the time when they can expect to receive income. To bridge this gap, a firm will usually obtain a loan. This type of loan is described as **short-term financing**, money that a firm will borrow for a year or less. Virtually every firm must resort to short-term financing at one point or another.

*3. Describe the two major sources of funds for a financial plan.*

**internal financing** money generated from cash flow

**retained earnings**   profits plowed back into the business rather than paid out to stockholders in the form of dividends

**outside financing**   money generated by borrowing from or selling ownership interests to sources outside the business for its use

**short-term financing** money that a firm will borrow for a year or less

The need for short-term financing is clear in Figure 18.2, which shows what happens when a computer store orders some disk drives. Even if sales of the drives are brisk, the store will probably have to pay its supplier before it can sell all the merchandise. If the store sells the drives on credit, it will have to wait thirty to sixty days for its money. In the meantime the firm must meet its overhead of rent, salaries, utility bills, and the like.

In seasonal industries, like Christmas tree farms, the time gap between expenses and income can prove especially troublesome. To prepare for the holiday season, such industries have to build up their inventories in advance and often pay for them before their season begins.

The need for short-term financing can also arise unexpectedly, as in emergencies. For instance, the roof on a warehouse may spring a major leak and require immediate replacement.

**long-term financing**
money that will not be repaid within one year

*Long-term Needs*   A business's stability depends on secure **long-term financing,** money that will not be repaid within one year. Generally, long-term financing is used for buying such assets as real estate, plants, and equipment. It may also be used to fund the purchase of another company. Because of a strong positive cash flow from its cigarette business, Philip Morris expected to pay off the long-term debt it needed to buy Kraft in just four years.[5]

As we will see later in this chapter, short-term and long-term financing meet very different needs. Nevertheless, the decision to use either should flow out of a detailed, systematic approach to financial management.

# The Uses of Funds

Once a business has raised money, in addition to using it to bridge an expense–income gap, its managers must put it to work.

FIGURE 18.2   The Time Gap Between Expenses and Income

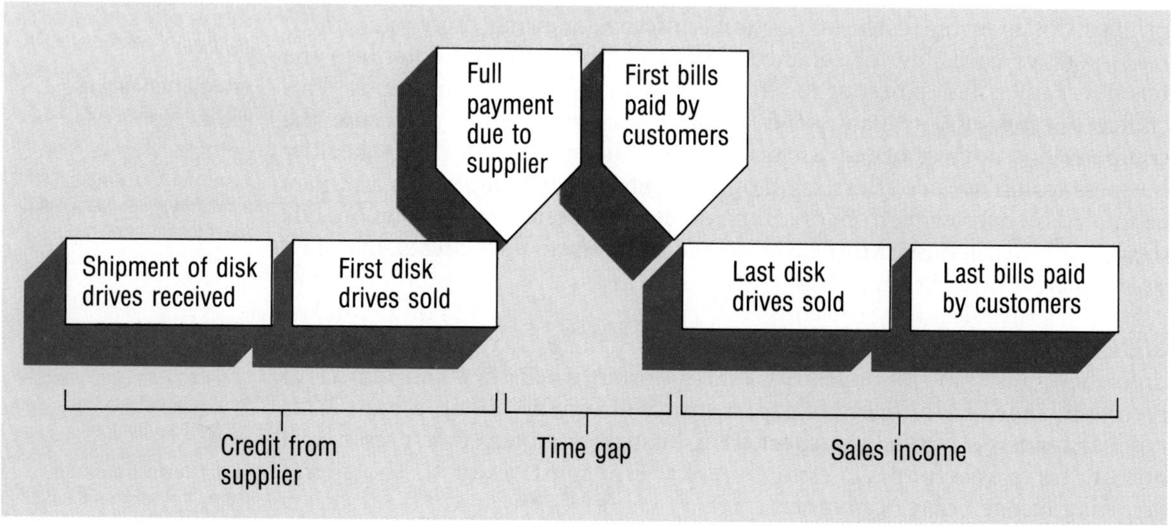

Investing for growth   *Walt Disney CEO Michael D. Eisner has committed $2 billion to a theme park in France. He does not expect it to show a profit before the year 2000.*

## The Nature of Investments

An **investment** is a financial tool for maintaining or increasing the expected value of today's funds. Gambling, in contrast, is a form of *entertainment* involving the use of current funds. Stepping up to a blackjack table in Atlantic City or Las Vegas or buying a state lottery ticket may be entertaining, but it certainly does not qualify as prudent investing. Every investment decision, whether business related or personal, requires weighing three key considerations: liquidity, risk, and return. The overriding goal is to make an **appropriate investment**, meaning one that fits a person's special combination of investment needs and risk tolerance.

*Liquidity*   Investment experts define **liquidity** as the "ability to convert an investment into cash quickly and without loss."[6] Shares of stock in a corporation listed on a major stock exchange are highly liquid because they can be converted to cash almost immediately through a stockbroker. Funds tied up in a piece of real estate, as discussed in Chapter 17, tend to have low liquidity because days, months, or even years must pass before a buyer can be found for the property. Cash, of course, is the most liquid asset a businessperson can own because it is ready for immediate expenditure or investment. On the down side, idle cash loses value from inflation. Extreme liquidity has its price.

Liquidity requirements vary depending on the needs of the investor. Cash or highly liquid investments can help a lumberyard owner meet weekly employee payrolls. Relatively less liquid investments, such as bank certificates

4. *Identify and discuss three key considerations that need to be weighed before making any investment.*

**investment**   a financial tool for maintaining or increasing the expected value of today's funds

**appropriate investment**   one that fits a person's special combination of investment needs and risk tolerance

**liquidity**   the ability to convert an investment into cash quickly and without loss

of deposit with penalties for early withdrawal, can be used to pay quarterly tax payments. As a general rule of thumb, the less liquid the investment, the more precise and longer term a financial manager's planning needs to be.

**risk**   the chance that an investor will be able to get his or her money back

*Risk*   To the investor, **risk** is a relative rather than absolute concept, involving the likelihood that an investor will be able to get his or her money back. In the words of a respected financial planner, "There is no such thing as *no risk*, only varying degrees of risk."[7] Three specific categories of risk are (1) business/financial risk, (2) market/interest rate risk, and (3) political/world events risk. Each category of risk needs to be weighed carefully prior to making an investment.

*Business/financial risk.* This type of risk, particularly relevant to those investing in corporate stocks and bonds or those extending trade credit to a buyer, is concerned with the financial health of the company. Some companies are an unreasonable financial risk because they have taken on too much debt. Others suffer from poor management. For example, as discussed in the last chapter many savings-and-loan institutions are being taken over by federal regulators because they have too many "nonperforming" loans made to bankrupt real estate speculators and oil and gas ventures. Company credit ratings from organizations such as Dun & Bradstreet help potential investors assess this aspect of business/financial risk. Business/financial risk is also tied to the earning potential of a company. In this regard, investors want to know how much in demand a company's goods/services are.

*Market/interest rate risk.* All markets are moving targets with their own dynamic relationships. This includes money markets, stock and bond markets, commodity markets, and markets for goods and services. Investors need to study historical patterns in a given market before investing. Real estate markets, for example, tend to suffer from exaggerated boom-and-bust cycles, whereas gold bullion markets react positively to bad news and stock markets react negatively to bad news. History, of course, is a helpful but not perfect predictor of future events. Interest rates, meanwhile, not only fluctuate in response to market variables such as investor confidence, they also are manipulated by the U.S. Federal Reserve as a way of stimulating or dampening the economy. A widely publicized benchmark for interest rates is the *prime rate* (discussed later).

*Political/world events risk.* In our increasingly globalized economy, financial markets are sensitive to worldly events. New tax legislation, revolutions, wars, and cartels take their economic toll. Far-flung people and situations can affect world markets in strange and complex ways. For example, when the supertanker *Exxon Valdez* ran aground in Alaska's Prince William Sound in March 1989 spilling 11 million gallons of crude oil (see Case 20.1), something unpredictable happened in the weeks that followed.[8] Exxon's price at the pump dropped while every other oil company's price went up! This turn of events can be explained in part by Exxon's desire to attract customers who might have been tempted to boycott its gas stations as well as by its competitors' desire to take advantage of a perceived shortage of crude oil. Wise investors stay abreast of world events to keep from being caught up in situations beyond their control.

**diversification**   the systematic attempt to balance varying types of risk through a range of different investments

A time-tested way of coping with the foregoing risks is diversification. **Diversification** is the systematic attempt to balance varying types of risk

548

through a range of different investments so as to increase overall return and reduce overall risk. For example, the risk of owning stock in a ski equipment company could be offset by owning stock in a tennis equipment firm. A winter with poor skiing conditions can spell financial disaster for the ski business, so a counterbalancing investment in a summer-oriented industry would be a good diversification strategy.

*Return*   Any profit that investors make from their investments is called their **return**. In effect, return is the reward for taking an investment risk. Two ever-present threats to investors' returns are inflation and taxes. Both erode value much like a stream slowly but steadily erodes its banks. Thus, it is important for investors to take inflation and applicable tax rates into effect when contemplating an investment. For example, a 10 percent interest rate does not look so good when 9 percent is subtracted for combined inflation and taxes.

**return**   any profit that investors make from their investments

## Risk and Return

One very important relationship needs to be mentioned at this point. That is the relationship between investment risk and return. Generally, the greater the risk, the greater the return. Figure 18.3 plots ten different investment options on a risk-return grid. Among other considerations, an appropriate investment depends on the investor's risk tolerance. Federally insured bank

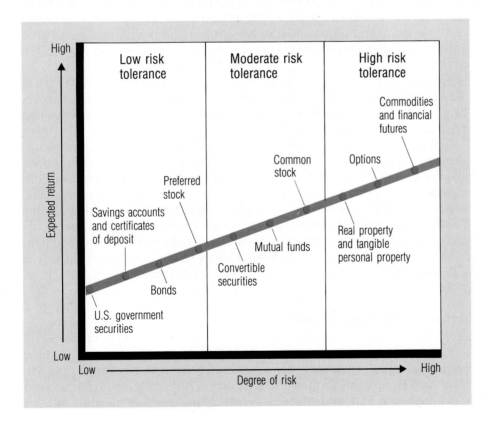

**FIGURE 18.3**
**The Risk-Return Relationship in Investing**

Source: Figure, p. 192 from FUNDAMENTALS OF INVESTING, 3/e by Lawrence J. Gitman and Michael D. Joehnk. Copyright © 1988 by the authors. Reprinted by permission of Harper & Row, Publishers, Inc.

savings accounts are for those with low risk tolerance, and real estate is more appropriate for investors with high risk tolerance. On the return side of the equation, real estate investors *expect* a greater return than they would receive by putting the same funds in a savings account.

## Acquiring Current Assets

Current assets are the most liquid form of assets, because they are to be used or converted into cash within one year. Cash is a current, potentially productive asset.

*Inventory*   The most obvious productive current asset is inventory. A business must have sufficient inventory to fill its orders, but not have so much that its cash is unnecessarily tied up. An automobile dealer's inventory of cars, for instance, usually consists of current assets because the dealer normally sells the cars within one year. Should sales slow down, though, the cars in stock will be much less useful to the dealer than cash would. By weighing the advantages of inventory against their business's need for liquidity, financial managers influence a firm's purchasing policy.

*Marketable Securities*   To maintain a desired level of liquidity, businesses often keep a certain amount of money in **marketable securities**, securities that can be easily converted into cash without being significantly discounted from market value. Besides the publicly traded stocks and bonds issued by corporations, businesses most commonly purchase commercial paper (discussed in the next section), treasury bills, and certificates of deposit. All three of these securities are **promissory notes**, written contracts involving a promise to pay money.

**Treasury bills (T-bills)** are short-term promissory notes issued weekly by the U.S. Treasury to finance the government's day-to-day cash requirements. Because the federal government's taxing power backs these obligations, they are a low-risk investment.

**Certificates of deposit (CDs)** are time deposits evidenced by promissory notes issued by a bank. These deposits may be in amounts as small as $500 and for periods from just days to years. Banks change their interest rates on CDs daily or weekly to reflect changes in the marketplace. Generally, banks pay higher rates for larger deposits and for those to be held for longer terms. Banks impose what is referred to as a penalty for cashing in a CD before the end of its term, but this penalty involves only a reduction in the interest paid. In some cases, holders of large-denomination CDs can sell them directly to a private investor and turn them into cash to avoid this penalty.

## Acquiring Fixed Assets

Assets that an organization will use for more than one year are called **fixed assets**. Accountants normally divide such assets into three classes: property, plant, and equipment. *Property*, in the context of fixed assets, refers to land, *plant* applies to buildings, and *equipment* means machinery and tools.

**marketable security** a security that can be easily converted into cash without being significantly discounted from market value

**promissory note** written contract involving a promise to pay money

**Treasury bill (T-bill)** a short-term promissory note issued by the U.S. Treasury

**certificate of deposit (CD)** a time deposit evidenced by a promissory note issued by a bank

**fixed asset** an asset that an organization will use for more than one year

The financial manager plays an especially critical role in acquiring fixed assets. Expenditures for doing so are sizable—a mainframe computer system can easily cost $1 million or more. To finance such assets can require a sophisticated approach. A commercial jet liner, for instance, costs over $20 million and is typically acquired through a commercial credit company like G.E. Credit. In evaluating such commitments, financial managers consider not only the effect such expenditures will have on cash flow and potential profitability but also the degree of risk involved.

# Sources of Short-term Financing

As we have seen, short-term financing refers to funds that a firm will use for a year or less. Short-term financing is normally unsecured, not backed by collateral.

*5.* *Identify the major sources of short-term financing.*

## Unsecured Short-term Financing

Some of the most common sources of unsecured short-term financing are trade credit, promissory notes to suppliers, bank loans, and commercial paper. These are discussed in this section.

*Trade Credit*   Many suppliers will grant buyers financing in the form of **trade credit**, an agreement whereby a supplier sells goods or services to a buyer but does not require immediate payment. In some cases, payment is not due for a specific period, such as thirty, sixty, or ninety days. In other arrangements, the buyer makes periodic installments. Trade credit is the most available form of credit. It is also the cheapest form, because the supplier usually spreads the cost of trade credit among its customers by building these costs into its own cost of goods sold.

**trade credit**   an agreement whereby a supplier sells goods or services to a buyer but does not require immediate payment

*Promissory Notes to Suppliers*   In some cases, a supplier may have reason enough not to grant trade credit to a customer. A poor credit rating, a history of slow payment, and a large order in relation to the customer's ability to repay are common reasons. In these situations, the supplier may insist that the customer sign a promissory note as a condition for extending credit.

One advantage of a promissory note is that it clearly specifies the customer's obligation, usually including the interest to be paid. Another advantage is that if the supplier needs cash before the note comes due, it may be able to sell the note to a bank. This process is called **discounting**, the sale of a promissory note to a bank for the amount of the note less a discount for the bank's services. The bank then assumes the responsibility for collecting from the customer when the note comes due.

**discounting**   the sale of a promissory note to a bank for the amount of the note less a discount for the bank's services

**compensation balance** an amount that the firm must keep on deposit with a financial institution during the term of a loan or the period covered by a line of credit

*Bank Loans*   Aside from suppliers, the most common sources of short-term financing are financial institutions. Companies with good credit ratings can often arrange unsecured short-term bank loans. In place of collateral, however, banks often require what is called a **compensation balance**, an amount that a firm must keep on deposit with a financial institution during the term of a loan or the period covered by a line of credit (discussed later). For example, a firm might have to maintain a $10,000 compensating balance in order to borrow $50,000.

The cost of borrowing from a bank is usually described in terms of the **prime rate** (or simply the "prime"), the interest rate large banks charge their largest and most reliable corporate customers. Other customers must pay from 2 to 4 percent above the prime, depending on the bank's evaluation of their creditworthiness. The prime fluctuates with the Federal Reserve Board's discount rate. Financial managers, therefore, need to monitor the economy regularly to try to time borrowings when the prime is relatively low.

Bank loans take three forms: promissory notes, lines of credit, and revolving credit agreements. A promissory note to a bank is the same as a promissory note to a supplier. A **line of credit** results from an agreement with a bank that over a specified period it will lend up to a certain amount at a set rate of interest, as the borrower needs the funds. The borrower pays interest only on what is actually borrowed. Note that the bank is not legally obligated to honor the line of credit. By contrast, a **revolving credit agreement** is a line of credit backed by a bank's legally enforceable guarantee that the money will be available whenever the borrower wants it. Banks will charge a **commitment fee** for such a guarantee and may also require a compensating balance.

*Commercial Paper*   Large corporations often acquire short-term financing by selling **commercial paper**, unsecured promissory notes issued by a corporation that mature in from 3 to 270 days. Such notes typically have a face value of $100,000 or more. This form of financing usually carries a lower rate of interest than a bank loan, and the issuer, the seller of the note, does not have to maintain a compensating balance. Commercial paper is normally sold at a discount from its face value. The difference between its actual price and its face value represents what the purchaser will earn on the loan. Typical buyers of commercial paper include banks, pension funds, and mutual funds.

## Secured Short-term Financing

Both commercial banks and commercial finance companies grant secured short-term loans. Small companies or new ones, companies with mediocre credit ratings, and firms that already owe a good deal of money are among the poorer candidates for unsecured financing. To minimize the lender's risk, such firms often have to put up collateral that may exceed the value of the loan by as much as 20 to 30 percent. Any relatively liquid asset will do, but lenders tend to look to inventory and accounts receivable to secure such loans. Often, lenders to such firms demand that the firm's owners cosign the note. The interest rates on such loans tend to be higher than on unsecured loans because of the borrower's lack of creditworthiness and the expenses of obtaining and liquidating collateral.

*Inventory as Collateral*   Companies that sell goods often have much of their capital tied up in inventory. Lenders prefer security in the form of

**prime rate**   the interest rate large banks charge their largest and most reliable corporate customers

**line of credit**   an agreement with a bank that over a specified period it will lend up to a certain amount at a set rate of interest as the borrower needs the funds

**revolving credit agreement**   a line of credit backed by a bank's legally enforceable guarantee that the money will be available whenever the borrower wants it

**commitment fee**   a bank charge for a loan guarantee

**commercial paper**   unsecured promissory notes issued by a corporation that mature in from 3 to 270 days

Seasoning   *Weather-dependent businesses may need short-term loans to carry them through predictably slow periods.*

finished, readily salable goods, but they will sometimes accept raw materials, parts, or components.

### Accounts Receivable as Collateral

Accounts receivable are usually created when trade credit is extended. Normally, these accounts are due in not more than sixty days. If a firm needs cash more quickly than it can collect these debts, however, it can pledge them as security for a loan. As it collects the accounts receivable, it repays the lender.

A related, but quite different practice, is called **factoring**, the selling of a firm's accounts receivable to another firm called a *factor*, which then owns and collects the debts. Customers are often told to pay the factor directly. Because a factor assumes all risk of bad debts, it pays considerably less than the face value of accounts receivable. A factor is thus an expensive source of short-term financing.

**factoring** the selling of a firm's accounts receivable to another firm that then owns and collects the debts

# Equity Financing

Long-term financing provides stability so that a company can expand, buy new equipment, develop products, acquire other companies, and make other capital expenditures. Long-term financing takes two forms. **Equity** represents the value of the owner's investments in a firm. A company can raise money by selling additional equity. **Debt**, discussed in the next section, represents borrowed money. Table 18.1 summarizes the growth of a hypothetical company and the ways it might meet its long-term financing needs.

**equity** the value of the owner's investment in a firm

**debt** borrowed money

TABLE 18.1    Financing Arrangements for a Hypothetical Company

Scenario: *Marcie and Jim meet and realize that Marcie has ideas for new types of software that Jim might be able to develop. They decide to go into business together as MJ Associates.*

**Year 1**

**Start-up Capital**

To begin, Marcie and Jim each contribute their savings to the business. Marcie has $2,000 and Jim has $142.12. This $2,142.12 is their initial equity financing.

**Trade Credit**

When they order company stationery, the printing company sends a thirty-day invoice. They plan to take advantage of this credit by waiting to pay until the full month expires.

**Promissory Note to Supplier**

When MJ Associates fails to pay for the stationery on time, the printer becomes impatient. Jim signs a note promising to pay within twenty additional days.

**Unsecured Bank Loan**

On the strength of the company's first large contract, a deal to adapt inventory-control software for a hotel chain, Marcie negotiates a small, short-term unsecured bank loan. With this, MJ Associates can cover its expenses until the contract begins to pay off.

**Year 2**

**Commercial Draft**

MJ purchases new computer equipment, signing a time draft that obligates the company to pay the supplier on a certain date.

**Secured Bank Loan**

Jim and Marcie convince the bank to supply additional funding, but this time the bank requires a written pledge of monies due from the hotel chain and other clients.

**Year 3**

**Stock Issue**

Incorporating their business, Marcie and Jim sell shares of the company—common stock—to relatives, friends, and other investors.

**Long-term Bank Loan**

With several employees and a multitude of contracts, MJ needs a bigger office. Jim and Marcie decide to buy a building that the company can grow into. A bank puts up a mortgage loan, which is secured by the building and land.

**Years 4–5**

**Retained Earnings**

Because the company's rapid growth demands plenty of cash, most of its earnings are retained rather than being distributed to the stockholders. But these are *after-tax* funds and the cost is high.

**Year 10**

**Commercial Paper, Bonds**

Now a major corporation, MJ can finance many of its short-term needs with commercial paper and its long-term needs with bonds. Because the firm's reputation is good because of strong earnings, these securities are very attractive to corporate investors.

## The Nature of Equity

All businesses start with some equity capital, the assets that owners invest to get their business off the ground. The monetary value of those assets stays in the business and forms the basis for the company's long-term financing. Owners of a small business may dig into their own pockets for these assets or seek partners to supply the cash. A business with seemingly great potential may attract a **venture capitalist**, an investor willing to put money into a business in exchange for a substantial block of stock.

Generally, when we speak of equity financing, we mean the issuing of additional stock by a corporation. **Stock** is a security in the form of an ownership interest in a corporation. In the next chapter, we will examine what a security is and what it means to have this designation. For now, the basic idea can be summed up in the following equation:

$$\text{Equity} = \text{Ownership} = \text{Stock}$$

By definition, shares of stock represent ownership interests in a corporation, but not all ownership rights are equal. Ownership brings with it a right to share in any distributions of profits, but again this right varies among the various classes and types of stock.

**6.** Describe the types of equity financing used by businesses.

**venture capitalist** an investor willing to put money into a business in exchange for a substantial block of stock

**stock** a security in the form of an ownership interest in the corporation

Other people's money
*Massachusetts-based Clean Harbors, an environmental protection company, was ready to expand. CEO Alan S. McKim arranged a successful stock offering to raise the needed money.*

## Common Stock

By law, every corporation must have common stock. A corporation may in fact have several classes of it, as General Motors and Wang Laboratories do, but one class of common stock must come with **voting rights**, the right to vote for directors and on extraordinary transactions, like a merger, that will affect the nature of the company. In other words, common shareholders (or one class of them) exercise the essential rights of ownership of the corporation.

*Share Valuation* A share of common stock, as depicted by the certificate in Figure 18.4, represents ownership of a portion of the net worth of a company. **Net worth** is determined by subtracting the value of a company's liabilities and preferred stock from the assets reflected on its balance sheet. Net worth is a relatively uncommon way to value shares, though.

The three most common ways to value shares are:

- Par value
- Book value
- Market value

The **par value** of a security is its stated or face value. Today, par value has virtually no meaning *as applied to common stocks*. Most states now permit corporations to issue **no-par shares**, or shares that are not assigned a dollar value.

**Book value** is the value of a company's net worth as represented by a common share. It can be calculated as follows:

$$\text{Book value} = \frac{\text{Assets} - (\text{Liabilities} + \text{Preferred stock})}{\text{Common shares outstanding}}$$

Book value gives a very conservative value to shares, because it does not reflect their potential for appreciation. It merely shows what the shares would bring if the company were to be liquidated.

One stock valuation method that does indicate a company's potential is called **market value**, the current price that a willing buyer will pay a willing seller. This price is the one published in newspapers if the stock is publicly traded and is the price one must pay in a private transaction (see Experiencing Business). The market price may be affected not only by a company's performance but also by its competitors' performance, the market's mood, the economy's general condition, and other factors having nothing to do with the company itself. A stock whose book value exceeds its market value is termed **undervalued**.

*Stock Splits* Individual investors today prefer to buy stocks in the $15 to $35 range because they can then afford to buy 100-share "round" lots and thus save on brokerage commissions. When a stock's market price is so high that many investors do not want to buy it, a company may decide to "split" its stock. When a **stock split** takes place, a company issues to shareholders one or more additional shares for each share currently held. A split increases the number of shares outstanding and reduces their market price proportionately, but it does not change the percentage that a shareholder owns.

voting rights the right to vote for directors and on extraordinary transactions that will affect the nature of the company

net worth determined by subtracting the value of a company's liabilities and preferred stock from the assets

par value a stated or face value of a security

no-par share a share that is not assigned a dollar value

book value the value of a company's net worth as represented by a common share

market value the current price of a stock that a willing buyer will pay a willing seller

undervalued a stock whose book value exceeds its market value

stock split takes place when a stock's market price is so high that many investors do not want to buy it and a company may decide to "split" its stock

556

FIGURE 18.4 A Stock Certificate

Source: Used with permission of Houghton Mifflin Company.

When the share price is too low to be attractive, the company's directors may implement a **reverse split**, reducing the number of shares outstanding and raising their market price.

*Preemptive Rights*    Under some states' laws, shareholders may have a **preemptive right**, the right to buy additional shares to preserve their ownership positions if the company issues additional shares to the public. Not all states recognize this right. Even where it is recognized, the articles of incorporation may deny it to shareholders.

*Dividends*    Ownership brings with it a right to share in **dividends**, that portion of a company's earnings that the board of directors votes to distribute to stockholders on a per-share basis in either cash or stock. The directors have no legal obligation to vote a dividend, or one of a certain amount.

Most growing companies do not declare cash dividends, preferring to retain any earnings in the business. Even some multibillion-dollar companies like the Tandy Corporation with its $2.8 billion in sales do not pay dividends. It might seem that retaining earnings is unfair to shareholders, but many shareholders are more concerned with appreciation in the value of their shares than they are with quarterly dividend checks. Still, some investors do look for a steady, high dividend. Table 18.2 lists some companies with extraordinary dividend records.

*Cash dividends* are dividends voted by the directors to be paid by the company to its shareholders. These dividends are expressed in terms of so many cents or dollars per share. Shareholders who owned their shares as of a specified date, the **record date**, receive dividends. Even if the shareholder

**reverse split**    a reduction of the number of shares outstanding, thus raising their market price

**preemptive right**    the right to buy additional shares to preserve ownership positions if the company issues additional shares to the public

**dividend**    that portion of a company's earnings that the board of directors votes to distribute to stockholders on a per-share basis in either cash or stock

**record date**    the specified date that shareholders who owned shares will receive dividends

TABLE 18.2   Companies Paying Annual Dividends
Since the 18th and 19th Centuries

| Began in | Stock | Began in | Stock |
|---|---|---|---|
| 1784 | Bank of New York Co., Inc. | 1882 | Affiliated Publications, Inc. |
| 1785 | Bank of Boston Corporation | 1882 | Bell Canada Enterprises Inc. |
| 1791 | Fleet Financial Group, Inc. | 1883 | Carter-Wallace, Inc. |
| 1804 | Norstar Bancorp Inc. | 1883 | Exxon Corporation |
| 1813 | Citicorp | 1885 | Consolidated Edison Co. |
| 1813 | First Fidelity Bancorporation | 1885 | Eli Lilly and Company |
| 1827 | Chemical New York Corp. | 1885 | UGI Corporation |
| 1840 | Morgan (J.P.) & Co. Inc. | 1886 | United Water Resources Inc. |
| 1841 | KeyCorp | 1889 | West Point-Pepperell, Inc. |
| 1848 | Chase Manhattan Corporation | 1890 | American Brands, Inc. |
| 1850 | Connecticut Energy Corp. | 1890 | Boston Edison Co. |
| 1851 | Connecticut Natural Gas Corp. | 1890 | Commonwealth Edison Co. |
| 1852 | Bay State Gas Co. | 1890 | Hydraulic Company |
| 1852 | Manufacturers Hanover Corp. | 1891 | Procter & Gamble Co. |
| 1852 | Washington Gas Light Co. | 1891 | Southern New England Telecommunications |
| 1853 | Cincinnati Gas & Electric Co. | 1892 | Times Mirror Company |
| 1853 | Continental Corporation | 1892 | Westvaco Corporation |
| 1863 | Pennwalt Corporation | 1893 | Coca-Cola Co. |
| 1863 | Singer Company | 1894 | Amoco Corp. |
| 1865 | Irving Bank Corp. | 1895 | Colgate-Palmolive Co. |
| 1865 | PNC Financial Corp. | 1895 | Mellon Bank Corp. |
| 1866 | First Wachovia Corp. | 1895 | Unisys Corp. |
| 1866 | Travelers Corporation | 1896 | BET Public Limited Co. |
| 1867 | CIGNA Corporation | 1898 | General Mills, Inc. |
| 1868 | American Express Co. | 1898 | "Shell" Transport & Trading Co., PLC |
| 1877 | Stanley Works | 1898 | Springs Industries, Inc. |
| 1879 | Cincinnati Bell Inc. | 1899 | Borden, Inc. |
| 1881 | American Tel. & Tel. Co. | 1899 | General Electric Co. |
| 1881 | Corning Glass Works | 1899 | PPG Industries, Inc. |
| 1881 | Security Pacific Corp. | 1899 | Washington Water Power Co. |

Source: From *Fact Book 1988* (New York: New York Stock Exchange, Inc., 1988), p. 37. Copyright 1988. Used by permission of the publisher.

**shareholder of record**
stockholder who owned shares when dividend is declared

**ex-dividend**   stock sold without the dividend

sells the shares between the record date and the payment date, payment will still be made to the **shareholder of record**. Sales of the shares after the record date are sold **ex-dividend**, that is, without the dividend.

Sometimes a company wishes to reward its shareholders but still conserve cash. In such a situation it may issue a *stock dividend*, a dividend in the form of shares in the corporation's stock. For example, a corporation might issue one new share for every ten already held, thus increasing the number of shares outstanding by 10 percent. The shareholders would then have the same percentage of ownership, but each share would be worth proportionately less.

## DEALING WITH A STOCKBROKER

If you do not own shares of corporate stock or have not dealt directly with a stockbroker, here is an opportunity to gain first-hand experience with the stock market.

1. Select the name and phone number of a stock brokerage firm from your local Yellow Pages.
2. Call and ask to talk to a broker. Give your name and where you are going to school and explain that you are working on a student project. You will find most stockbrokers to be friendly and helpful. However, if you run into one who is not, sim-

ply thank him or her for the time and call another broker. Tip: Make your call about 30 minutes after the New York Stock Exchange has closed for the day (4 p.m. Eastern), when brokers are under less pressure.

3. Select one or two local companies or one or two stocks from the list in Table 18.2 and ask the broker for their closing prices (price per share).
4. For future information, you might want to ask the broker how you would go about opening an account with his/her firm so you could buy and sell stock. Also ask what sort of commission they charge.

## Preferred Stock

In addition to raising money through common stock, some companies attract capital by issuing preferred stock. **Preferred stock** is a class of stock "that pays dividends at a specified rate and that has preference over common stock in the payment of dividends and the liquidation of assets."[9] Like a loan, preferred stock pays a specified dividend, stated either as a percentage of the par value or, more commonly, as a specific amount. The company must pay this preferred dividend before it can pay any dividend on its common stock. In addition, should the company be liquidated, the preferred shares are **redeemed** (paid at par) in full before anything is paid on the common stock. Frequently, a preferred stock's **indenture,** a formal legal agreement between the issuer and the holder, contains a **call feature**, a provision allowing the company itself to redeem it.

*Purposes* Companies usually issue preferred stock when they need funds and either cannot or do not wish to increase their debt levels (loans and bonds) or stockholder bases (common stock). The preferred's dividend, which is paid out of after-tax profits, has the advantage of being an identifiable expense that companies can plan for.

Sometimes a company issues preferred stock to pay for an acquisition when it wishes to limit the dilution of its existing shareholders' ownership while making the transaction attractive to the acquired company's share-

**preferred stock** a class of stock "that pays dividends at a specified rate and that has preference over common stock in the payment of dividends and the liquidation of assets"

**redeemed** the liquidation of shares before anything is paid to common stockholders

**indenture** a formal legal agreement between the issuer and the holder of a security

**call feature** a provision allowing the company itself to redeem a security

holders. In addition, if the acquiring company's financial planning is sound, the earnings of the acquired company will do three things:

■ Pay for the preferred dividends.
■ Generate a **sinking fund**, a fund set aside by the company, generally according to a formula based on profits or time, to redeem particular issues of preferred stock or debt.
■ Produce income or an improved marketplace opportunity for the acquiring company so that the common shareholders benefit further.

*Cumulative and Noncumulative Dividends* Preferred stock pays dividends rather than interest, and a company has no legal obligation to pay dividends. If dividends are to be paid, then, a company's preferred shareholders must receive theirs before the common shareholders do. The indenture, however, may specify that the dividends are **cumulative**, meaning that the company must pay all preferred dividends for past periods before paying any common stock dividends. A noncumulative issue's dividend will be higher than a cumulative one's on equivalent stock, to make up for the risk of its being skipped (see Table 18.3).

Suppose that a company **passed its dividend** (did not pay it) on its cumulative preferred in 1989. If the directors want to pay dividends on either preferred or common stock in 1990, they must first authorize payment of the 1989 preferred dividend. Then if they wish to pay a dividend on the common stock for 1990, they must pay the 1990 preferred dividend first.

TABLE 18.3    Types of Preferred Stock

| Type of Preferred | Description |
|---|---|
| Cumulative | If the corporation fails to make a dividend payment to preferred of this type, it must pay all accumulated unpaid dividends before it can pay any dividends on the common. |
| Noncumulative | If the corporation omits a dividend, the shareholders have no claim against the corporation for it; the opposite of cumulative. |
| Participating | In years when the corporation does well, shareholders receive a fixed dividend and, perhaps, after the common dividend is paid, a bonus. |
| Callable or redeemable | Stock that a corporation has a right to repurchase at its option; usually, the higher the dividend, the more rapidly it is called or redeemed. |
| Convertible | Stock that can be exchanged for common at a certain fixed ratio of preferred to common; this feature often allows a corporation to offer a lower dividend rate. |

The indenture will sometimes provide that if the dividends are passed for a certain period—often, three consecutive years—the preferred shareholders can then determine the composition of the board of directors and vote on the other decisions normally reserved for common shareholders.

*Participating and Nonparticipating Stock*   Stock called **participating preferred stock** is preferred stock that may, under circumstances specified in the indenture, participate in the dividend distributions on the common shares. Participating preferred stock is unusual. Most preferred stock is **nonparticipating**, meaning that it receives only the stated dividend.

*Convertibility*   Another way that companies limit their dividend and redemption obligations is by issuing **convertible preferred stock**, preferred stock whose indenture includes the right to convert a share into some number of common shares. Investors are motivated to exchange their convertible preferred stock for shares of common stock when the stock market is strong and the company's common stock is rising in value. Typically, investors forego a certain amount of interest as payment for convertibility. For a start-up company that expects to grow, offering investors convertible preferred stock provides the firm the advantage of a debt-like obligation in its early years and, after conversion, the advantage of capital appreciation.

> **participating preferred stock**   preferred stock that may, under circumstances specified in the indenture, participate in the dividend distributions on common shares
>
> **nonparticipating preferred stock**   stock that receives only the stated dividend
>
> **convertible preferred stock**   preferred stock whose indenture includes the right to convert a share into some number of common shares

# Debt Financing

Debt appeals to financial managers because it is a relatively predictable, stable source of long-term financing. A basic advantage that debt financing has over equity financing is that debt is not an indefinite or open-ended obligation. Shares last forever, but debt expires when it is paid off. Another key distinguishing factor between debt and equity involves tax deductibility. *All interest payments on debt are a tax-deductible business expense.* Dividends distributed to stockholders, in contrast, are paid in after-tax dollars.

Debt is associated with a predictable interest expense when a fixed rate of interest is involved. This is a desirable situation during inflationary times because today's debt is paid off with tomorrow's cheaper dollars. However, **floating interest rates**, those subject to change with the prevailing market rate, can hold some nasty surprises for management during an inflationary period. For example, in 1988 Marriott Corp. financed the repurchase of 25 million shares of its own stock with floating-rate loans. The Federal Reserve subsequently raised the discount rate, as an anti-inflationary move, and Marriott's average interest rate jumped from 7.2 percent to 9.6 percent. All this had the effect of driving Marriott's first-quarter interest expense from roughly $5 million in 1988 up to $31 million in 1989.[10] Of course, banks and other lenders prefer floating rate loans and adjustable rate mortgages (ARMS) as a hedge against inflation.

Debt takes two basic forms: loans and bonds. Again, though, as with equities, there are many variations on the forms.

> *7. List and describe the principal types of long-term debt financing.*
>
> **floating interest rates**   a rate subject to change with the prevailing market rate

## Loans

Long-term loans are often used to finance the purchase of new equipment or other major expenditures. Although repayment periods vary widely, they average between three and five years. The borrower signs a promissory note and makes payments on a regular schedule, just like an individual with an auto or a mortgage loan. The goods purchased with the proceeds of the loan usually secure the repayment of it, though the lender may demand other collateral, too. Common lenders include financial institutions, insurance companies, commercial credit companies, and pension funds. In some instances, manufacturers of heavy equipment will make the loans themselves, but on terms that resemble those of a bank loan rather than trade credit.

## Bonds

**corporate bond**  a long-term obligation to pay

**coupon rate**  a specified rate of interest

**maturity date**  the date on which the corporation will redeem the bond by paying its par value

You have probably heard the expression "his word is his bond." A bond in this context is an obligation to perform. A **corporate bond** is a long-term obligation to pay, usually represented by a certificate of indebtedness, as in Figure 18.5. By issuing such bonds a corporation promises to pay the investor a specified rate of interest (the **coupon rate**) on set dates until the bond's **maturity date**, the date on which the corporation will redeem the bond by paying its par value. The maturity date can be forty years in the future. Bonds are normally issued in par-value multiples of $1,000 and may reach $50,000 for a single bond. Public offerings of bonds work like those of stocks.

FIGURE 18.5   A Bond
Source: Used by permission of Consolidated Edison Co. of New York, Inc.

**Bond power** *San Francisco–based U.S. Windpower issued bonds to help finance development of alternative energy sources.*

Bonds do not bring with them an ownership interest in the **issuer**, an entity with the power to authorize the sale and distribution of securities on its behalf. Rather, the bondholder is entitled only to the payment of interest and principal in accordance with the terms of the bond's indenture. Should the issuer fail to make the payments on schedule, it can be forced into bankruptcy. The federal Trust Indenture Act of 1939 requires that each bond issue have an independent **trustee**, a person or (usually) a firm that protects the bondholders' interests by making sure that the issuer meets its obligations under the indenture.

**issuer** an entity with the power to authorize the sale and distribution of securities on its behalf

**trustee** a person or a firm that protects the bondholders' interests by making sure that the issuer meets its obligations under the indenture

*Secured and Unsecured Debt* Like all loans, bonds are either secured or unsecured, and the security can take various forms. Mortgage bonds, for instance, are secured by fixed assets like land and buildings, just as an individual's home mortgage loan is secured by the home itself. Collateral

**debenture** an unsecured bond

**bond rating** refers to the soundness of a specific bond offering

**junk bonds** low-quality, high-yield corporate bonds

**leveraged buyout (LBO)** when a current corporate management seizes control of its company by repurchasing all outstanding stock

trust bonds are secured by other securities that the issuer owns. Equipment bonds are secured by equipment and machinery used in the business, like railroad cars or an assembly line. In contrast, only the issuer's good faith and good reputation guarantee an unsecured bond, which is called a **debenture**.

*Bond Ratings* Investors have some help when choosing among thousands of corporate bonds. Each corporate bond offering is evaluated and rated by independent financial experts. Rating agencies such as Moody's and Standard & Poor's regularly publish their bond evaluations. Much like the grades given to students, bonds are given grades reflecting their investment quality. It is important to point out that a **bond rating** refers to the soundness of a specific bond offering, rather than being a rating of the offering company. As in the case of junk bonds, discussed next, some financially solid companies have in recent years issued some very speculative bonds. In the case of Moody's rating service, a simple A, B, C system devised by John Moody in 1909 is still in use today.[11] All told, including the various subcategories, there are nine different Moody's bond ratings (see Table 18.4). Standard & Poor's system is very similar, with ten different ratings. These bond ratings are closely watched by all parties because they influence bond interest rates and yields. Generally, the better the bond rating, the lower the yield.

A modern trend in the realm of corporate bonds that concerns many observers is the so-called "junk bond" (see Business Issues). On Moody's rating scale, junk bonds usually have a Ba rating or lower. Defined as low-quality, high-yield corporate bonds, **junk bonds** have become a popular tool for leveraged buyouts (LBOs) and mergers. In a **leveraged buyout**, current corporate management, generally with the help of an investment banker who underwrites junk bonds, seizes control of its company by repurchasing all outstanding stock. Among the more notable LBOs have been Safeway Stores, Seven-Up, and Reliance Electric. *Mergers* like that between Philip Morris and Kraft take place when one company buys another.

**TABLE 18.4    Moody's Bond Rating System**

| Rating Symbol | Explanation |
|---|---|
| Aaa | Best-quality bonds with smallest degree of investment risk; called "gilt edge bonds" |
| Aa | High-quality (high-grade) bonds |
| A | Upper-medium grade bonds |
| Baa | Medium grade bonds |
| Ba | Bonds with speculative elements |
| B | Speculative bond; long-term assurance of interest and principal payments is low |
| Caa | Bond in poor standing or in default |
| Ca | Highly speculative bonds typically in default (interest not being paid) |
| C | Lowest bond rating; no real investment standing |

Source: Adapted from *Moody's Bond Record,* March 1989, p. 1. Used with permission.

## JUNK BONDS: PRO AND CON

For earning the lordly sum of $550 million in 1987, financial wizard Michael R. Milken gained entry into the *Guinness Book of World Records*. The basis for Milken's extraordinary income was the sale of junk bonds, a business he pioneered. As might be expected of someone making so much money, Milken also earned considerable public attention. In 1989 Milken found himself first indicted (for insider trading), then wildly cheered by an adoring crowd as his lawyers led him from the courthouse to his waiting limousine. The accumulation of such a vast fortune in such a short time is perhaps the most bubbling ingredient in the American Dream. But, argue Milken's critics, his junk bonds and the leveraged buyouts they finance could cause the American economy to go flat.

In discussions about junk bonds, two questions usually rise to the surface: Are junk bonds good investments and is the use of junk bonds good for the American economy? The answer to the first question may depend on whether you take the short- or long-term view. Over the short term, junk-bond investors have done well. As high-risk investments, junk bonds have had to pay high yields. The total return—interest and appreciation—has been impressive. And overall, the default rate has been low, especially if you consider the higher profits that can be made. Take the long view, however, and you will see some disturbing signs. A 1988 study by Paul Asquith of Harvard University showed that as many as 34 percent of the junk bonds issued in the preceding decade had defaulted.

The $200-billion-a-year junk-bond business has exerted a dramatic effect on the U.S. economy. These bonds have generated the capital for corporate takeover artists, and they have forced reluctant corporations to protect themselves by taking measures not necessarily in their own interests. In either case, the result has been companies laboring under an increasing burden of debt. The taken-over companies must pay off the junk bonds with which they were purchased. The still-free companies may have maintained their independence by running up debts of their own—perhaps by buying back their own stock—to make them less appealing.

Junk-bond enthusiasts sing the praises of this debt. It creates a lean and hungry company, they maintain, and a lean and hungry company will find ways to succeed. Assets must be sold. Employees must be laid off. Duplicated functions must be eliminated. True, short-term profits will be down. But a streamlined operation means bigger profits in the long run.

It is about the long run, however, that junk-bond/leveraged-buyout critics worry. Even a lean and hungry company will suffer if the market for its products shrivels up, they say. Debt-laden companies are especially vulnerable to economic recession because interest payments must be made in both good times and bad.

Sources: Ellyn E. Spragins, *et al.,* "When Power Investors Call the Shots," *Business Week,* June 20, 1988, pp. 126–130; Mark Clayton, "Behind U.S. Merger Boom—Debt Bomb?" *The Christian Science Monitor,* October 28, 1988, pp. 1, 15; Brett Duval Fromson, "Life After Debt: How LBOs Do It," *Fortune,* March 13, 1989, pp. 91–98; and Gary Weiss, "Does Junk Have Lasting Value? Probably," *Business Week,* May 1, 1989, pp. 118–119.

*Redemption*    Bond issues can pose a major problem for an issuer that does not plan ahead. Normally, all the bonds in a particular issue mature on the same date. If a corporation sold, say, $400 million in one issue, it would

**serial bonds** bonds of one issue but that mature on different dates

have to repay the entire amount all at once. To avoid this problem, an issuer may choose to sell **serial bonds**, bonds of one issue but that mature on different dates. Another common method is to establish a sinking fund in which money is set aside each year for debt repayment. Often this fund is in the hands of an outside trustee, who is charged with ensuring that the company lives up to its obligations.

Quite commonly, the indenture will require the issuer to call bonds for redemption periodically. Before buying a bond, an investor should check to determine when and under what circumstances it is callable. Making a bond callable is a device designed to protect the issuer, not the holder. For example, in early 1985, Minstar, Inc., issued $300 million in $14\frac{7}{8}$ percent bonds to finance its acquisition of AMF, Inc. With interest rates running at about 9 percent, the bonds were trading at 112 percent of their par value, $1,000. Because of an obscure provision in the indenture, Minstar a year later began calling the bonds for redemption at par. Thus, the bondholders faced the prospect of losing the benefit of an excellent interest rate. But more important, those who paid a **premium**, more than par, for the bonds lost a portion of their original investment. From the company's point of view, however, for every $30 million it called Minstar saved $4.5 million annually in interest.[12]

**premium** an amount paid greater than par for bonds

*Convertibility* Some corporate bonds are convertible into shares of common stock. As with preferred stock, the indenture will specify a conversion rate, that is, the number of shares available for each $1,000 bond.

# Financial Management: A Perspective

As we have seen, financial management has responsibility for

- Performing financial analysis and planning
- Managing a firm's asset structure
- Managing a firm's financial structure

The balance sheet is financial management's report card. A firm's overall condition reflects the quality of the financial analysis and planning. The left side of the balance sheet reveals the firm's asset structure, and the right side shows its financial structure.

One way in which many people appraise financial management's report card has changed, as companies have come to use long-term debt instead of equity to finance expansion. An important financial ratio, **long-term debt to equity**, measures the relationship between bonds and shareholders' equity, as in this formula:

**long-term debt to equity** the ratio that measures the relationship between bonds and shareholders' equity

$$\frac{\text{Bonds}}{\text{Shareholders' equity}} = \text{Leverage ratio}$$

The resulting percentage represents the firm's **leverage**, its use of debt to improve the return on its shareholders' equity (see Figure 18.6).

Since the 1960s, managers have tended to operate with high degrees of leverage. They have done so because if they can use borrowed money to raise

**leverage** the use of debt to improve the return on shareholders' equity

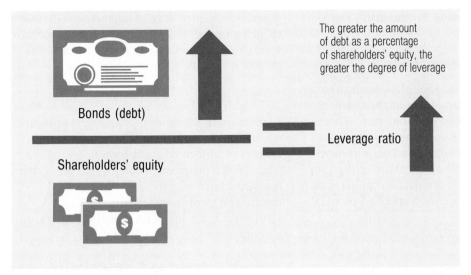

The greater the amount of debt as a percentage of shareholders' equity, the greater the degree of leverage

Bonds (debt)

Shareholders' equity

= Leverage ratio

FIGURE 18.6    Leverage

profits, the shareholders earn more for each dollar invested. Also, long-term debt eliminates the need to dilute the current shareholders' equity. Another major reason for borrowing, as mentioned earlier, is that the interest paid on either bonds or bank loans is tax deductible. Dividends paid to shareholders are not. Finally, when inflation dominates the economy, borrowing appears wise because the debt is repaid with cheaper dollars.

Traditionally, a 55 percent debt-equity ratio was regarded as the top percentage a financially sound firm could have and, from a potential lender's standpoint, the lower the better. Today, in the age of megamergers, LBOs, and junk bonds, a number of firms' debt-equity ratios exceed 70 percent. For instance, Minstar's debt equaled 77 percent of total equity in early 1986.[13] Highly leveraged balance sheets are now regarded with more skepticism. An old saying goes, "There's no such thing as a free lunch," and those who once bet that high inflation would last forever found that it at least paused in the mid-1980s. A declining inflation rate proved quite painful for those financial managers who had not recognized the risks of a potential change in the economic weather and taken cover under equity financing. Leverage can be a friend or a foe, depending on a company's condition and the state of the economy.

## CHAPTER HIGHLIGHTS

*1.* Describe the financial management function and distinguish it from the other finance-related activities within a business.

*Financial management* is the process of obtaining money and using it effectively to achieve an organization's goals. In a small business, the owner may manage the finances. In a large corporation, the finance manager is often given the title of vice president of finance. The controller reports to the vice president of finance and has responsibility for accounting, data processing, and taxes. The treasurer also reports to the vice president of finance and has responsibility for overseeing and planning for the firm's expenditures and income.

### 2. List the elements of a financial plan.

To create a sound financial plan, financial managers must have a firm grasp of the company's objectives for the short and long term. Once the company's objectives are identified, the managers can draw up budgets and identify where cash flow may exceed or fall short of the company's needs. Budgets are detailed projections of income and expenses over a specified period.

### 3. Describe the two major sources of funds for a financial plan.

From the financial manager's standpoint, implementing a financial plan consists primarily of financing it. The first option is internal financing, money generated from cash flow or retained earnings. The second option is outside financing, money generated by borrowing from or selling ownership interests to sources outside of the business.

### 4. Identify and discuss three key considerations that need to be weighed before making any investment.

Liquidity, risk, and return are three factors that both business and personal investors need to weigh carefully. Liquidity involves how quickly an investment can be converted to cash, without a significant loss. As a relative rather than absolute concept, risk involves the likelihood that an investor can get his/her money back. Business financial managers need to be concerned with three categories of risk: (1) business/financial risk; (2) market-interest rate risk; and (3) political/world events risk. Diversification is the generally accepted way of balancing risks and reducing overall risk. Regarding return, the investor's profit, greater risk typically means a greater return.

### 5. Identify the major sources of short-term financing.

In most cases, short-term financing is unsecured, not backed by collateral. The most common sources of unsecured short-term financing are: trade credit, promissory notes to suppliers, bank loans, commercial paper, and commercial drafts. The most common form of secured short-term financing is the use of inventory or accounts receivable as collateral.

### 6. Describe the types of equity financing used by businesses.

Most business firms start with some equity capital, such as the assets the owners invest to get the business off the ground. Generally, when we speak of equity financing, we mean the issuing of stock by a corporation. Stock is a security in the form of an ownership interest in the corporation. This ownership can take the form of common or preferred stock.

### 7. List and describe the principal types of long-term debt financing.

Debt is a relatively predictable, stable source of long-term financing. Long-term loans represent one form of debt financing. The repayment periods average between three and five years. Corporate bonds, a long-term obligation to pay usually represented by a certificate of indebtedness, are another form of debt financing. Bonds do not bring with them an ownership interest in the issuing company.

# KEY TERMS

| | | | |
|---|---|---|---|
| Financial management | Budgets | Short-term financing | Liquidity |
| Vice president of finance | Cash flow | Long-term financing | Risk |
| Controller | Internal financing | Investment | Diversification |
| Treasurer | Retained earnings | Appropriate investment | Return |
| | Outside financing | | Marketable security |

| | | | |
|---|---|---|---|
| Promissory note | Venture capitalist | Preferred stock | Maturity date |
| Treasury bill (T-bill) | Stock | Redeemed | Issuer |
| Certificate of deposit (CD) | Voting rights | Indenture | Trustee |
| Fixed asset | Net worth | Call feature | Debenture |
| Trade credit | Par value | Sinking fund | Bond rating |
| Discounting | No-par share | Cumulative | Junk bond |
| Compensation balance | Book value | Passed its dividend | Leveraged buyout (LBO) |
| Prime rate | Market value | Participating preferred stock | Serial bond |
| Line of credit | Undervalued | Non-participating preferred stock | Premium |
| Revolving credit agreement | Stock split | Convertible preferred stock | Long-term debt to equity |
| Commitment fee | Reverse split | Floating interest rates | Leverage |
| Commercial paper | Preemptive right | Corporate bond | |
| Factoring | Dividend | Coupon rate | |
| Equity | Record date | | |
| Debt | Shareholder of record | | |
| | Ex-dividend | | |

# REVIEW QUESTIONS

1. What is the major role of financial management in a modern business?
2. In what ways do the controller and the treasurer assist the vice president of finance in a corporate setting?
3. What is a budget? What is involved in the budgeting process?
4. What is the difference between internal and external financing?
5. What does the term *appropriate investment* mean?
6. What are current assets? Describe some common forms of current assets.
7. What are four sources of unsecured short-term financing?
8. What is equity financing? What are the advantages of financing through the sale of stock?
9. How does preferred stock differ from common stock? Why do companies issue preferred stock?
10. What is debt financing? What are the two basic forms of debt financing?

# APPLICATION EXERCISES

1. Obtain an annual report from a corporation. Study the report and list the following information: (a) the name and title of the officers involved in financial management; (b) the types of long-term financing used by the company.
2. You are planning to purchase a home for investment purposes. The home will be rented and rental income will be applied to monthly payments. Establish a budget showing your projected income and expenses for the first year.

# CASES

## 18.1 An ESOP Fable: Giving Workers a Piece of the Action

In theory, ESOP's [employee stock ownership plans] sound wonderful: companies sell stock to their workers to give them a financial stake in the companies. That, in turn, is supposed to heighten productivity. Since Congress passed the first ESOP bills in the 1970s, more than 10,000 companies with more than 10 million workers have signed on, according to estimates by the National Center for Employee Ownership (NCEO). The $4.3 billion worth of stock sales in the first three months of [1989] approaches the $6.5 billion figure for all of [1988]. Once a tool for small companies, ESOP's have gained favor in big corporations from J.C. Penney to Texaco. Procter & Gamble announced a $1 billion plan in January that would eventually put fully 20 percent of the company in workers' hands.

ESOP's look so good because of success stories like Avis—probably America's best-known employee-ownership plan, thanks to an aggressive advertising campaign. Its famous slogan, "We Try Harder," has been edited to read, "Owners Try Harder." Avis's program is not just any ESOP. It features an unusual degree of worker participation in day-to-day operations. ESOP's need that kind of cooperation to succeed, says Joseph Blasi, professor at California Polytechnic State University School of Business and author of "Employee Ownership: Revolution or Ripoff?" Says Blasi: "All of the evidence on employee ownership proves that it doesn't lead to improved product or performance, unless combined with employee involvement and problem-solving."

Not all ESOP's meet those criteria. Many do much more for bosses than for workers. Critics charge that management often uses tax-subsidized ESOP loans to restructure or dump poorly performing subsidiaries. ESOP's have also become a controversial takeover defense, since it puts large blocks of stock in relatively

friendly hands. Polaroid used one to thwart an attack by Shamrock Partners. Fairchild Industries expanded its ESOP while successfully resisting a takeover attempt—a move that the Department of Labor is now investigating.

### Questions

1. Why would nonemployee stockholders like or dislike an ESOP?
2. Why do you suppose employee participation in daily operations is apparently the key to ESOP success?
3. On balance, are you for or against ESOPs?

Source: Excerpted from John Schwartz, "Giving Workers a Piece of the Action," *Newsweek*, April 17, 1989, p. 45. From NEWSWEEK, April 17, 1989. © 1989, Newsweek, Inc. All rights reserved. Reprinted by permission.

## 18.2 New Venture Capital Funds Hope Doing Good Pays Off

There's a new source of capital for entrepreneurs—at least if they are socially responsible. The people who invented the "altruistic" mutual fund are branching into venture capital funds to finance new small businesses.

"We not only can do good but also make a decent return for our investors," says Wayne Silby of Calvert Social Venture Partners in Washington, D.C., one of the newly launched funds. Such funds will finance companies that appear particularly benevolent to employees, customers, communities and—their managers hope—investors. . . .

### Stimulating a New Breed

The venture funds don't plan to adopt an investment strategy any different from that of the altruistic mutual funds. They, too, will shun companies that do business in South Africa, make weapons systems or are involved in producing nuclear energy. But by providing capital to start-ups, they hope to stimulate the growth of a new breed of socially responsible ventures. These include companies with products or services for a clean environment and health care or others strongly committed to equal opportunity among employees.

Still, some institutional investors aren't sure funds with a narrow focus are the way to finance socially responsible ventures. . . .

In New York, Edward Tasch, a former partner of a venture fund specializing in health care deals, is launching Common Capital Partners, a $15 million fund. . . .

Common Capital's portfolio, according to Mr. Tasch, will range from retailers with explicitly stated social objectives to traditionally managed companies whose products or services address a major social need. He and the others are encouraged by the rapid growth and success of Ben & Jerry's Homemade Inc. and Body Shop International PLC, two small companies that have clear social goals as part of their overall business strategy.

At Ben & Jerry's, a Waterbury, Vt., ice cream retailer, the founders can't take a salary more than five times that of the lowest-paid employee. When it comes to supplies, for instance, Ben & Jerry's purchases its Brazil nuts from a producer that doesn't use slash-and-burn growing techniques. And it donates 7.5% of its pre-tax profits for distribution to not-for-profit organizations around the country.

Body Shop, a U.K.-based maker and seller of cosmetics with all natural ingredients, devotes space in each of its 370 stores to educate consumers on social and political issues like Amnesty International and Greenpeace. It also gives two hours a week to its employees to engage in community work.

## Questions

1. Is it a good idea to mix corporate finance and social responsibility?
2. Will socially responsible venture capital funds be a passing fad or a permanent feature on the corporate financial landscape? Explain your reasoning.

Source: From Udayan Gupta, "New Venture Capital Funds Hope Doing Good Pays Off," *The Wall Street Journal,* March 16, 1989, p. B2. Reprinted by permission of *Wall Street Journal,* © Dow Jones & Company, Inc. 1989. All Rights Reserved Worldwide.

# 19 Securities Markets

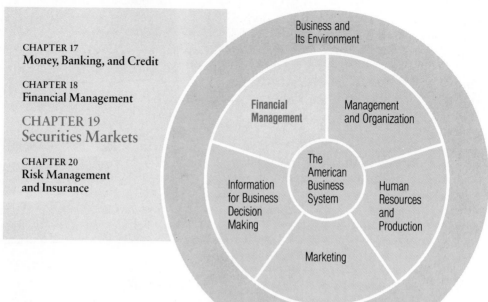

Business and
Its Environment

Financial
Management

Management
and Organization

Information
for Business
Decision
Making

The
American
Business
System

Human
Resources
and
Production

Marketing

A dams was a rabbit breeder. For $7,200, he sold a "rabbit kit" consisting of 12 female and 2 male rabbits to buyers who wanted to go into the rabbit-pelt business. Those 14 rabbits would produce an estimated 720 breeding females within a year. Adams promoted these rabbit kits by offering seminars on rabbit breeding across Florida. Part of his pitch—not included with the rabbit kit—was membership in a marketing association that he owned, which promised to find markets for the pelts. The state of Florida indicted him for selling an unregistered security, and a jury found him guilty.

When Adams appealed his conviction, the court had to decide whether or not a rabbit kit was a security. Most people think of securities as just stocks and bonds, so a rabbit kit seems a poor candidate for one. The term *securities*, however, takes in a host of investments—so many types, in fact, that no one has been able to develop a completely adequate definition of the term. For instance, the courts have held both a distributorship in a cosmetics firm and an ownership interest in an orange grove to be securities. State and federal securities laws, which require registration of securities in order to ensure that investors have sufficient information to evaluate investments, resort to listing dozens of examples of securities instead of attempting to define the word.

**security** an investment of money, a common enterprise, and an expectation of profit solely from the efforts of others

The U.S. Supreme Court eventually devised a solution to the problem. It created a three-part test, which the Florida District Court of Appeals applied in Adams's case. A **security** must show

- An investment of money
- A common enterprise
- An expectation of profit solely from the efforts of others

The rabbit kits did not satisfy the second test, because the buyers were not putting their money into a company or partnership—they were buying actual animals.[1] The rabbit kits failed the third test, too, so Adams's conviction was overturned. Once bought, the kits had to be turned into marketable pelts.

*1.* List the three attributes of a security.

Our focus here is on why and how people invest in the most common securities, stocks and bonds. In fact, we will focus even more narrowly on the stocks and bonds of the 10,000 or so corporations whose securities change hands on the national stock exchanges. This figure represents only .3 percent of all U.S. corporations, but transactions involving billions of dollars' worth of their securities occur every working day. Approximately 3 million corporations are **private** or "closely held" and their securities are not publicly traded. The securities of private companies can be traded only within limitations. Many professional corporations such as doctors' groups are closely held.

**private**  a corporation whose securities are not publicly traded

# How Securities Change Hands

A publicly traded stock can be transferred in three ways: in a private transaction between two parties, in a transaction on a primary market, or in a transaction on a secondary market (see Figure 19.1).

*2.* Describe the three basic processes by which securities change hands.

## Private Transactions

Suppose for a moment Adams's rabbit kits were in fact a security. The contract, for that is what a security is, would be between Adams and the

FIGURE 19.1   How Securities Change Hands

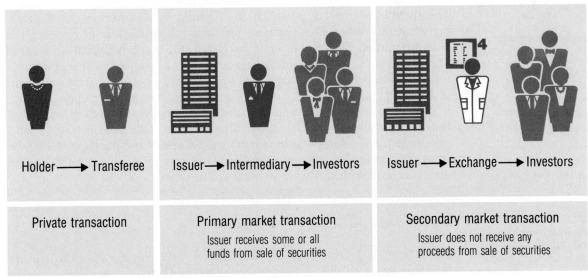

Holder ⟶ Transferee

Issuer ⟶ Intermediary ⟶ Investors

Issuer ⟶ Exchange ⟶ Investors

Private transaction

Primary market transaction
Issuer receives some or all funds from sale of securities

Secondary market transaction
Issuer does not receive any proceeds from sale of securities

buyer. No broker or other intermediary would have been involved. It is important to note that unless transfer of a security is somehow restricted, two persons can simply agree to the transfer. All that the holder must do to transfer the shares is to fill out the form on the back of the stock certificate and hand it to the **transferee**, the person to whom a security is transferred. Transactions of this sort occur every day of the year.

The publicly traded securities we are focusing on are also transferred by executing the transfer form on the back of the certificates. In such cases, however, the buyer and seller are brought together by intermediaries who make money by performing this service. The two contexts in which these transfers occur are called either primary markets or secondary markets.

**transferee** a person to whom a security is transferred

## *Primary Markets*

The company in which a stock represents ownership is the **issuer**. Those markets in which the issuer of a security receives some or all of the funds paid for the security are known as **primary markets**. Primary markets exist to market new issues of securities. In contrast, on the secondary market the issuer does not benefit from transactions, because they involve securities issued in the past, unless the issuer is selling its own stock.

One type of primary market transaction is **private placement**, the direct sale of stock by an issuer to investors. Securities and Exchange Commission regulations restrict the types of investors who may buy stock in private placements and limit how much money can be involved in any one issue.

More commonly, a primary market transaction is an indirect sale arranged through the efforts of an **underwriter**, an investment banker who agrees to buy a new issue and distribute it to the public. The process of initially selling a new issue of securities to the public is called a **public offering**. Generally, the issuer and the underwriter negotiate the amount that the issuer will receive and the price to be offered the public. The difference between the amount paid to the issuer and the amount paid by the public is the **spread**. The spread goes to the underwriter or group of underwriters, collectively known as a **syndicate**, as payment for their taking the risk in bringing the issue to market. The spread is comparable to the markup a retail store earns on merchandise. When an underwriter expects to be able to sell a stock with relatively little effort, as when a well-known strong company or government is the issuer, the spread is small. As the risk increases, the spread grows, too.

A public offering is a complicated procedure involving numerous steps and heavy expenses for the issuer. It also requires formal registration with governmental regulators, both federal (the Securities and Exchange Commission) and state, as, for example, the Ohio Department of Commerce's Division of Securities, for issuers who want to sell in Ohio.

**issuer** the company in which a stock represents ownership

**primary markets** those markets in which the issuer of a security receives some or all of the funds paid for the security

**private placement** the direct sale of stock by an issuer to investors

**underwriter** an investment banker who agrees to buy a new issue and distribute it to the public

**public offering** the process of initially selling a new issue of securities to the public

**spread** the difference between the amount paid to the issuer and the amount paid by the public

**syndicate** the underwriter or group of underwriters

## *Secondary Markets*

Those markets in which the sale of a security ordinarily does not involve any proceeds going to the issuer are **secondary markets**. When people refer to the stock market, they usually mean the various secondary markets for

**secondary markets** those markets in which the sale of a security ordinarily does not involve any proceeds going to the issuer

576

The heart of the trade   *The noisiest part of a securities transaction takes place on the floor of the stock exchange, where floor traders compete for the attention of harried specialists.*

securities. These markets include the national, regional, and international stock exchanges, the over-the-counter market (discussed later), and the bond exchanges. The **exchanges** are the actual markets where stocks and bonds are traded. They serve as continuous markets for the securities of the companies listed on them. On an average day, 300 million shares of common stock change hands on U.S. exchanges and $50 million worth of bonds are traded on the bond exchanges.

**exchanges**   the actual markets where stocks and bonds are traded

**3.** *Identify the principal secondary markets for securities and describe each.*

## Trading Securities on an Exchange

Let's take a look at how shares actually change hands on a secondary market.

*A Trade*   Suppose that an investor wants to buy 100 shares of Exxon Corporation common stock, which is traded on the New York Stock Exchange (NYSE). First, an investor who wishes to buy or sell stocks on an exchange must place an order with a stockbroker. This **broker**, sometimes called an account executive or a registered representative, works for a brokerage firm or a broker-dealer. Table 19.1 identifies several players who are important in the process of buying and selling stocks on an exchange. If the broker is not a member of the exchange on which the stock is traded, the broker must process the order through a member. (We will discuss membership on an exchange later.)

**broker**   person who buys and sells stocks after taking an order from a customer

An exchange processes each transaction in sequence, according to certain preestablished rules. Orders of up to 200 shares can now be executed by

## TABLE 19.1    The Key Players in Stock Transactions

| | |
|---|---|
| **Investor** | The individual seeking to buy or sell a security. |
| **Account executive** | Also known as a stockbroker or registered representative. Serves as the intermediary between the investor and market professionals. |
| **Floor broker** | The professional on the floor of an exchange who carries out an investor's order. |
| **Specialist** | A member of an exchange who, on the floor of the exchange, maintains a fair and orderly market by matching orders and by buying and selling as needed to balance the market. |

brokers automatically through an electronic system that matches, records, and reports trades automatically. Other orders are handled in the following time-tested manner. After taking the order, the broker immediately notifies the **floor broker**, a member of the firm who is on the floor of the exchange and whose job it is to execute customers' orders. The floor broker goes to the trading post on the floor of the exchange where Exxon is traded and tells the specialist there that he or she has a **market order**, an order at the market price, for 100 shares of Exxon. A **specialist** is a member of an exchange who is responsible for matching buy and sell orders or, if there is an imbalance of orders, for using his or her own portfolio to balance the buy and sell orders. The specialist may be holding many orders to sell shares of Exxon and will then match the market order to buy with the standing order to sell that has the lowest price. Thus a market order to buy will be matched with the lowest-priced order to sell, and a market order to sell will be matched with the highest-priced order to buy.

After the transaction at the trading post has been completed and the exchange has been properly recorded, the floor broker then notifies the broker about the execution of the transaction. At this point the broker notifies the investor, usually by phone, and follows up that notice with a written record detailing the transaction. The sale is manually recorded at the time of execution and is almost immediately displayed on the **ticker**, the electronic system that provides the public with notice of each transaction on the exchange. Investors can remain up to date by watching the ticker or by using a data terminal such as a Quotron in any brokerage office around the country.

*Other Types of Orders*    Instead of requesting a market order, our imaginary investor might have made the order more explicit. "Buy 100 shares of Exxon at 58" represents a **limit order**, an order specifying the maximum price acceptable to the investor. If 58 is lower than the market price, the transaction will not be executed until and unless the price reaches 58. The broker will hold the order until it can be completed or until the end of the day. An **open order** extends beyond the day's end and runs until it is canceled. A **stop order** is an explicitly priced sell order triggered when a stock price falls to or below a specified level. Stop orders and limit orders are rarely executed immediately and become open orders. Open orders are canceled at the end

---

**floor broker** a broker on the floor of the exchange whose job it is to execute customers' orders

**market order** an order at the market price

**specialist** a member of an exchange who is responsible for matching buy and sell orders or for using his or her own portfolio to balance the buy and sell orders

**ticker** the electronic system that provides the public with notice of each transaction on the exchange

**limit order** an order specifying the maximum price acceptable to the investor

**open order** an order that extends beyond the day's end and runs until it is canceled

**stop order** an explicitly priced sell order triggered when a stock price falls to or below a specified level

*PART VI / FINANCIAL MANAGEMENT*

of the trading day unless the investor gives instructions to maintain them in force overnight or keep them "good 'til canceled." An investor can also place a **discretionary order**, which puts the decision about whether to act or to wait into the broker's hands.

*Commissions*   Brokers make money by charging fees, called **commissions**, on the transactions they facilitate. Many brokerage firms have a minimum commission charge of $35 or $40 on any stock transaction. Commission rates, however, vary from one brokerage house to another and with the size of the order. For example, the commission on 100 shares of stock can vary all the way from a few dollars to over $100. In part, this variation occurs because brokerages offer different levels of service. **Full-service brokers** charge the highest commissions, because they provide advice, reports, research and analysis, portfolio management, and other services. **Discount brokers** charge the lowest commissions, because they merely execute their customers' instructions.

Generally, the commission per share drops as the number of shares in the transaction increases. An especially steep price break comes at the 100-share level. One hundred shares is a **round lot**; less than 100 shares is generally considered an **odd lot**. Odd-lot commissions are charged a premium because the transaction involves one extra step. Before an odd-lot order can be executed, one odd lot must be matched with another, either one ordered by another investor or one filled by a specialist. This extra effort explains why individual investors prefer to trade round lots and why companies split stock to keep prices low. In contrast, on very large orders the investor may negotiate an especially low commission.

*Margin*   A brokerage will extend credit to its individual customers to enable them to buy securities. These credit arrangements are called **margin accounts**. The Federal Reserve Board requires that the customer put up collateral, usually in the form of securities, to secure a brokerage's loan. The brokerage customer's margin is expressed as a percentage of the market value of the collateral plus the purchased securities, which remain in the brokerage's possession until the customer pays off the loan. The percentage has varied between 50 and 100 percent, depending on existing credit conditions.[2]

The customer's margin may go below the required percentage, if there is a decline in the market value of either the collateral or the purchased securities. In such a case, the brokerage issues a **margin call**, which demands additional collateral from the customer. If the customer fails to supply it, the brokerage will liquidate enough of the securities it holds for this customer to bring the margin up to the required level.

# The New York Stock Exchange

The New York Stock Exchange (NYSE) is the largest of the U.S. secondary markets. The first recorded exchange of stocks in New York dates to 1792. Today, the daily average trading volume exceeds 120 million shares, up from

**discretionary order** places the decision about whether to act or to wait into the broker's hands

**commission**   a fee charged on the transaction a broker facilitates

**full-service brokers** brokers who provide advice, reports, research and analysis, portfolio management, and other services

**discount brokers**   brokers who charge the lowest commissions, because they only execute their customers' instructions

**round lot**   100 shares of stock

**odd lot**   less than 100 shares of stock

**margin accounts**   credit arrangements by which a brokerage will extend credit to its individual customers to enable them to buy securities

**margin call**   a brokerage's demand for additional collateral from the customer

less than 50 million in 1981. Figure 19.2 is a New York Stock Exchange listing.

The New York Stock Exchange is a national exchange. The more than 2,230 issues of common and preferred stocks traded on it are those of over

FIGURE 19.2  New York Stock Exchange Listing

Source: *Wall Street Journal*, March 23, 1989. Reprinted by permission of *Wall Street Journal*, © Dow Jones & Company, Inc. 1989. All Rights Reserved Worldwide.

**High** Identifies the highest price paid for the stock in the last 52 weeks.

**Low** Identifies the lowest price paid for the stock in the last 52 weeks.

**Div** Indicates the value of dividends issued in the last 52 weeks. A **blank** (KeystnCon) indicates no dividends were paid. Note **j** signifies that although there has been a dividend paid this year, dividends were omitted or deferred at the last dividend meeting of the Board of Directors.

**Stock** Identifies the company and often includes special notes:

**s** (KoreaFd) signifies that there has been a stock split in the last 52 weeks.

**n** (Kroger) indicates a new issue in the last 52 weeks.

**pf** (KerrGlass) indicates that the issue is preferred stock.

↑ (KeyCorp)
New 52-week high

↓ New 52-week low

**Yld**
**%** The dividend paid as a percentage of stock price, an indication of investment return.

**P-E**
**Ratio** Stock price divided by earnings per share, an indication of investor assessment of risk and growth expectation.

**Vol**
**100s** The volume of shares sold the previous day, in hundreds of shares. A round lot, the normal transaction unit, is generally 100 shares.

**High** The highest price paid for the stock in the prior day's transactions

**Low** The lowest price paid for the stock in the prior day's transactions.

**Close** The last price paid for the stock in the prior day's transactions.

**Net**
**Chg.** The difference between the close in the prior day's trading of the stock and that of the previous day.

| | 52 Weeks High Low | Stock | Div. | Yld % | P-E Ratio | Vol 100s | High | Low | Close | Net Chg. |
|---|---|---|---|---|---|---|---|---|---|---|
| | 21   16½ | KerrGlass pf | 1.70 | 9.6 | .. | 4 | 17⅝ | 17⅝ | 17⅝ | ... |
| | 44½   32¾ | KerrMcGee | 1.10 | 2.6 | 18 | 1416 | 41⅞ | 41 | 41¾ | +¾ |
| ↑ | 23⅜   19½ | KeyCorp | 1.20 | 5.2 | 8 | 351 | 23½ | 23⅛ | 23⅛ | −⅛ |
| | 18   8¾ | KeystnCon | | ... | ... | 16 | 13½ | 13¼ | 13¼ | +¼ |
| | 24   17⅛ | Keystnint | .56 | 2.9 | 16 | 227 | 19½ | 19⅜ | 19½ | −¼ |
| | 65¾   51⅛ | KimbClark | 2.60 | 4.3 | 13 | 2246 | 60⅜ | 59¾ | 60 | −¼ |
| | 27⅜   15⅞ | KingWorld | | ... | 9 | 879 | 24¾ | 24¼ | 24¾ | +¼ |
| | 12½   8¾ | KleinBenAus | 1.77e | 19.1 | ... | 233 | 9⅜ | 9¼ | 9¼ | ... |
| | 48⅝   37 | KnghtRidder | 1.22 | 2.8 | 16 | 452 | 44⅛ | 43¾ | 44 | −⅛ |
| | 19¾   17½ | KyUtil | 1.40 | 7.6 | 10 | 332 | 18½ | 18⅜ | 18½ | +⅛ |
| | 12¼   8 | KerrGlass | .44 | 4.6 | ... | 8 | 9½ | 9½ | 9½ | −⅛ |
| | 25⅞   12 | Kollmrgn | .32 | 1.3 | 19 | 374 | 25 | 24½ | 25 | +½ |
| s | 36½   18⅜ | KoreaFd | .94e | 2.7 | ... | 1312 | 35 | 34½ | 34½ | −½ |
| n | 11   7¼ | Kroger | | ... | 42 | 1875 | 10¼ | 10⅛ | 10⅛ | −⅛ |

Financial capital *The monumental architecture of Wall Street suggests power and unshakable reliability: while the massive columns support the building, the activity inside supports the economy.*

1,675 national and international companies. Only the stocks of companies that can meet certain specific criteria for size and breadth of ownership can qualify for listing on the NYSE.

Membership in the New York Stock Exchange is limited to individuals, although the brokerage house for which a member works often pays for the membership and advertises itself as a Member of the New York Stock Exchange. The 1,336 regular members are said to have seats on the exchange, which are bought and sold. Their price has ranged from a low price of $4,000 in 1876 to $625,000 in 1929. As late as 1986 a seat sold for as little as $550,000, but in 1987 a seat on the New York Stock Exchange sold for $1,100,000.

## Other Stock Exchanges

Virtually all stock exchanges function like the New York Stock Exchange, and their rules and regulations governing their members' conduct also resemble the NYSE's.

*American Stock Exchange (Amex)* The American Stock Exchange, also located in New York, is the second of the national exchanges. Because different issues trade on the New York Stock Exchange and the Amex, most brokerage houses also employ Amex members. Only about 930 issues trade on the Amex. It is regarded, somewhat inaccurately, as the appropriate exchange for newer, smaller, and more speculative companies.

*Regional Exchanges*   The several regional exchanges are similar in structure to the major exchanges but are much smaller in size and scope. They primarily serve the demand for stocks of regional companies, but the stocks of national companies trade on them, too. For example, the Boston Edison Company, an electric utility, is listed on both the New York Stock Exchange and the Boston exchange.

In recent years, the number and importance of the regional exchanges has declined. In 1930 there were more than thirty regionals; today there are five. The Midwest, Pacific, and Philadelphia regional exchanges are significantly larger than the others. The Cincinnati exchange functions quite differently from the others. Since 1978 it has operated a computerized exchange—without a trading floor. Brokers transmit orders to a central computer, which receives, stores, displays, matches, and executes the orders. It functions on a first-come, first-served basis. Whether this new method of handling orders will succeed over the long run remains to be seen.

Today, foreign stock exchanges are gaining in importance to the American investor. More foreign investors are buying U.S. stocks and U.S. investors are buying more foreign securities. Consequently, foreign companies such as Sony Corp. and Hitachi can be purchased on U.S. exchanges, and the stock of many U.S. companies can be purchased on the London, Tokyo, Toronto, and Hong Kong stock exchanges. In addition, new exchanges are opening around the world. Even Shanghai and Moscow now have exchanges where securities are publicly traded.

*The Over-the-Counter Market (OTC)*   The telecommunications network linking broker-dealers for transactions in securities not listed on exchanges is called the **over-the-counter market (OTC)**. Some 4,700 stocks trade over the counter. These are primarily stocks issued by smaller and newer companies, although the stocks of large corporations such as Apple Computer and MCI Communication trade in the over-the-counter market (see Figure 19.3). Some trade frequently, others only occasionally. The annual OTC transaction volume is about the same as the NYSE's, however.

The OTC is not an exchange like the NYSE or the Amex. It functions through the members of the **National Association of Securities Dealers (NASD)**. This organization has set up **NASDAQ (National Association of Securities Dealers Automatic Quotations)**, a computerized system enabling dealers to determine instantly the current market price for the more popular OTC shares and see who is making a market in them. The NASDAQ system reports the best available prices to buy or sell a stock based on the prices quoted by all participating market makers in that stock. A transaction occurs when a dealer acting as a market maker agrees to buy or sell at a price acceptable to the investor. In essence, the investor using NASDAQ negotiates the transaction through the broker.[3] For issues not included in NASDAQ, brokers must call dealers to find a participant willing to complete the transaction.

**over-the-counter market (OTC)** the telecommunications network linking broker-dealers for transactions in securities not listed on exchanges

**National Association of Securities Dealers (NASD)** organization through which the over-the-counter market functions

**National Association of Securities Dealers Automatic Quotations (NASDAQ)** a computerized system enabling dealers to determine instantly the current market price for the more popular OTC shares and see who is making a market in them

**High** Identifies the highest price paid for the stock in the last 365 days.

**Low** Identifies the lowest price paid for the stock in the last 365 days.

**Stock** Identifies the company and often includes special notes:

**s**(DEP) signifies that there has been a stock split since January.

**.12e**(DairyMrtA) dividend paid in the last twelve months, but no regular dividend rate

↓ (DaisySys) New 52-week low

↑ New 52-week high

**Vol 100s** The volume of shares sold the previous day in hundreds of shares.

| | 52 Weeks High | Low | Stock | Div. | Yld % | PE | Vol 100s | High | Low | Close | Net Chg. |
|---|---|---|---|---|---|---|---|---|---|---|---|
| | 15 | 7¼ | D&N Fncl | .60 | 4.6 | 4 | 87 | 13⅛ | 12¾ | 13 | ... |
| | 27¼ | 14½ | DBA Sys | | ... | 10 | 257 | 15½ | 15 | 15 | ... |
| | 3⅝ | 2½ | DDI Pharm | | ... | 9 | 14 | 2¾ | 2¾ | ¾ | −⅛ |
| s | 11½ | 7⅝ | DEP | | ... | 12 | 160 | 9 | 8¾ | 8⅞ | −⅛ |
| | 14 | 10⅛ | DF Southeast | | ... | ... | 133 | 13¼ | 13 | 13 | ... |
| | 9⅛ | 4½ | DH Tech | | ... | 12 | 71 | 8⅛ | 7⅞ | 8 | −⅛ |
| | 5⅝ | 3¼ | DNA PitTch | | ... | ... | 51 | 3⅝ | 3½ | 3½ | −⅛ |
| | 31¼ | 19¼ | DS Bcp | .72 | 3.2 | 16 | 84 | 23 | 22¼ | 22¼ | −¼ |
| | 9⅝ | 6⅛ | DSC Comm | | ... | 33 | 1185 | 9¼ | 9 | 9⅛ | ... |
| | 18½ | 11¼ | DST Sys | .16 | 1.3 | 20 | 22 | 12¼ | 11¾ | 12¼ | +½ |
| | 13½ | 7½ | DahlbgElec | | ... | 28 | 10 | 8¼ | 8¼ | 8¼ | −⅜ |
| | 15½ | 12½ | DlyJrnl | | ... | ... | 2 | 15¼ | 13¾ | 15¼ | ... |
| | 10¾ | 8 | DairyMrtB | .12e | 1.3 | 9 | 1 | 9½ | 9½ | 9½ | +⅜ |
| | 10¾ | 7¾ | DairyMrtA | .12e | 1.4 | 8 | 10 | 8⅝ | 8⅝ | 8⅝ | ... |
| ↓ | 11½ | 4¼ | DaisySys | | ... | ... | 607 | 4½ | 4⅛ | 4⅛ | −¼ |

**High** The highest price paid for the stock in the prior day's transactions.

**Low** The lowest price paid for the stock in the prior day's transactions.

**Close** The last price paid for the stock in the prior day's transactions.

**Net Chg.** The difference between the close in the prior day's trading of the stock and that of the previous day.

FIGURE 19.3 Over-the-Counter Listing

Source: *Wall Street Journal,* March 23, 1989. Reprinted by permission of *Wall Street Journal,* © Dow Jones & Company, Inc. 1989. All Rights Reserved Worldwide.

## The Bond Markets

In Chapter 18, we discussed corporate bonds as certificates of indebtedness offered to the public. It is important to note that anyone—individuals, partnerships, or governments—can issue such certificates. We are concerned here, however, only with those issued by larger corporations and the different units of local, state, federal, and foreign governments, because they trade on secondary markets. The bond markets are separate from the stock markets. Corporations whose stock trades on the NYSE may thus list their bonds on the Amex, and OTC markets exist for government bonds (see Figure 19.4).

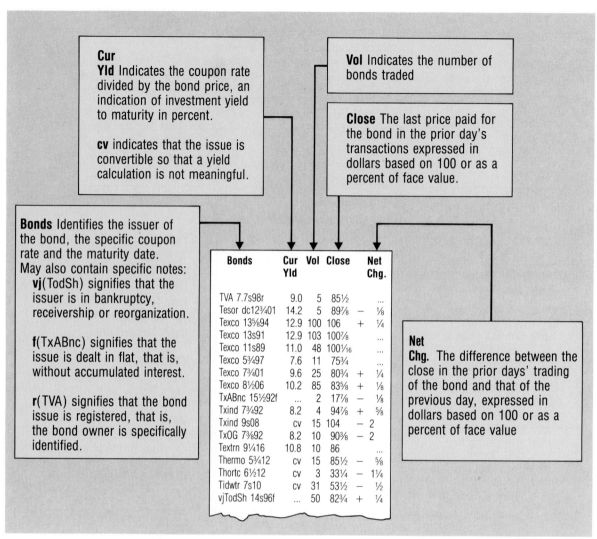

**Cur Yld** Indicates the coupon rate divided by the bond price, an indication of investment yield to maturity in percent.

**cv** indicates that the issue is convertible so that a yield calculation is not meaningful.

**Vol** Indicates the number of bonds traded

**Close** The last price paid for the bond in the prior day's transactions expressed in dollars based on 100 or as a percent of face value.

**Bonds** Identifies the issuer of the bond, the specific coupon rate and the maturity date. May also contain specific notes:

- **vj**(TodSh) signifies that the issuer is in bankruptcy, receivership or reorganization.
- **f**(TxABnc) signifies that the issue is dealt in flat, that is, without accumulated interest.
- **r**(TVA) signifies that the bond issue is registered, that is, the bond owner is specifically identified.

**Net Chg.** The difference between the close in the prior days' trading of the bond and that of the previous day, expressed in dollars based on 100 or as a percent of face value

| Bonds | Cur Yld | Vol | Close | Net Chg. |
|---|---|---|---|---|
| TVA 7.7s98r | 9.0 | 5 | 85½ | ... |
| Tesor dc12¾01 | 14.2 | 5 | 89⅞ | − ⅛ |
| Texco 13⅝94 | 12.9 | 100 | 106 | + ¼ |
| Texco 13s91 | 12.9 | 103 | 100⅞ | ... |
| Texco 11s89 | 11.0 | 48 | 100 1/16 | ... |
| Texco 5¾97 | 7.6 | 11 | 75¾ | ... |
| Texco 7¾01 | 9.6 | 25 | 80¾ | + ¼ |
| Texco 8½06 | 10.2 | 85 | 83⅝ | + ⅛ |
| TxABnc 15½92f | ... | 2 | 17⅞ | − ⅛ |
| Txind 7¾92 | 8.2 | 4 | 94⅞ | + ⅝ |
| Txind 9s08 | cv | 15 | 104 | − 2 |
| TxOG 7⅜92 | 8.2 | 10 | 90⅜ | − 2 |
| Textrn 9¼16 | 10.8 | 10 | 86 | ... |
| Thermo 5¾12 | cv | 15 | 85½ | − ⅝ |
| Thortc 6½12 | cv | 3 | 33¼ | − 1¼ |
| Tidwtr 7s10 | cv | 31 | 53½ | − ½ |
| vjTodSh 14s96f | ... | 50 | 82¾ | + ¼ |

FIGURE 19.4 Bond Listing

Source: *Wall Street Journal,* March 23, 1989. Reprinted by permission of *Wall Street Journal,* © Dow Jones & Company, Inc. 1989. All Rights Reserved Worldwide.

**government bonds** the debt certificates issued by federal, state, and local governments and their agencies

**U.S. government issues** all bonds issued by any unit of the federal government or issued as municipal bonds

*Government Bonds* The debt certificates issued by federal, state, and local governments and their agencies are called **government bonds.** Government bonds are classified as **U.S. government issues,** which includes all bonds issued by any unit of the federal government or issued as municipal bonds.

Bonds issued by the U.S. Treasury are considered the safest investment available in the United States and perhaps in the world. Because the taxing power of the U.S. government backs them, they carry the lowest net interest rate of any bond. (Recall our discussion in Chapter 18 of the relationship between risk and return). Treasury issues provide operating funds for the federal government. Also, as we saw in Chapter 17, the Federal Reserve buys

and sells U.S. bonds as part of its monetary policy.

Other federal bonds are generally considered somewhat more risky, even though neither the federal government nor any federal agency has defaulted on an obligation in this century. The most active markets are for the bonds of the Federal National Mortgage Association (FNMA, "Fannie Mae") and the Government National Mortgage Association (GNMA, "Ginnie Mae"). The FNMA purchases and sells residential mortgages as part of its effort to stabilize the availability of mortgages and promote residential construction. The GNMA, a part of the Department of Housing and Urban Development, guarantees mortgages and buys and sells mortgages in the same way the FNMA does.[4]

**Municipal bonds** are debt obligations of state and local governments and their agencies. In other words, a government bond that is not issued by the federal government, a federal agency, or a foreign government is a municipal bond. The interest these bonds pay is not taxed by either the federal government or the state that benefits from their being issued. What this means is that the interest on a bond issued by the city of Buffalo, for example, is not subject to the New York state income tax. An Ohio resident, however, would have to pay Ohio state income taxes on this bond's interest.

**municipal bonds** debt obligations of state and local governments and their agencies

Once the tax benefits are factored back in, it becomes clear that municipal bonds carry a higher interest rate than federal bonds. The reason is simply that municipals are riskier. In 1983, for instance, the Washington Public Power Supply System defaulted on over $2 billion in bonds. In the mid-1970s, New York City nearly defaulted on its bonds.

## Mutual Funds

Mutual funds are not secondary markets themselves. Rather, they are major participants in the secondary markets. **Mutual funds** are poolings of various people's investments that are managed for a fee by professional investment managers toward a particular goal or according to a particular philosophy. Individual investors may thus invest a modest sum and participate in a portfolio that they could not otherwise afford to create by themselves. The mutual-fund investor spreads the risk of loss across a whole portfolio and can take advantage of professional management.

**mutual funds** poolings of various people's investments that are managed for a fee by professional investment managers toward a particular goal or according to a particular philosophy

*Investment Objectives* Mutual funds are not all alike. Each has a different philosophy and set of principles that guide its investments. Even within a particular type of mutual fund, philosophies and performance may vary widely.

Mutual funds may choose to invest in common stocks, corporate bonds, government bonds, or combinations of these securities. They may invest principally in just certain types of investments, such as energy stocks, aerospace stocks, high-technology stocks, or other specialized categories. Mutuals may characterize themselves as **growth funds** (offering limited dividends and investing in more speculative stocks), as **income funds** (concentrating on a high-yield portfolio with limited growth and risk), or as **balanced funds** (seeking to provide modest income and growth from a generally conservative portfolio).

**growth funds** funds that offer limited dividends and invest in more speculative stocks

**income funds** funds that concentrate on a high-yield portfolio with limited growth and risk

**balanced funds** funds that seek to provide modest income and growth from a generally conservative portfolio

**Loads, No-Loads, and Management Fees**  A sales charge, usually ranging from 2.5 to 8.5 percent, assessed on the purchase of a share in a mutual fund is a **load**. A fund salesperson or, more commonly, a stockbroker markets load funds, and the load goes principally to them. In other words, for a fund to break even in its first year on an 8.5 percent load, the fund must have a total return (dividends plus price appreciation) of more than 8.5 percent to the investor. Having made up for the load, the investor can then finally start to earn something on the investment.

A **no-load mutual fund** has no sales charge, so all of the purchaser's money is invested. Investors buy no-load fund shares directly from the fund itself. Studies conducted so far have been inconclusive on whether load or no-load funds perform better.

In recent years, **low-load** and **reverse-load mutual funds** have been introduced. A fund is considered to be low load if the sales charge is less than 5 percent. A reverse-load fund does not have a sales charge at the time of purchase but charges a fee for selling the shares. Frequently the reverse load will be 5 or 6 percent if fund shares are sold the first year, and the percent is reduced each year until it disappears. On funds of this type, a continuing sales charge is applied that may be as high as 1.25 percent per year. The proliferation of approaches to charging for sales has caused some confusion for investors. The Securities and Exchange Commission continually evaluates new developments in an effort to assure that the investor can make informed investment decisions.

All funds charge a management fee to compensate the funds' managers and pay administrative costs. Generally, the fee is based on a percentage of the assets and is often on a sliding scale. Management fees vary widely from less than .5 percent to 2.5 percent of the assets under management. All fees charged by a fund must be reported in the fund's prospectus or official offering circular.

# Sources of Financial Information

*4. List the principal sources of financial information and give an example of each.*

In years past, investors had to seek out the business and financial news on their own. Today, television and radio include stock summaries in their daily newscasts. Special programs also deal exclusively with business and financial news. There is even a cable television service, Financial News Network, that covers business news exclusively throughout the day. Even with all this electronic coverage, though, the major sources of business and financial news remain the magazines and newspapers.

## Magazines

Many weekly magazines cover different aspects of business. Among the most popular are *Business Week, Industry Week,* and *Fortune. Barron's* is a weekly securities-oriented tabloid owned by Dow Jones, the publisher of the *Wall Street Journal.* And *Forbes,* a biweekly, offers an assortment of stories about

---

**load**  a sales charge ranging from 2.5 to 8.5 percent, assessed on the purchase of a share in a mutual fund

**no-load mutual fund**  a fund with no sales charge; all of the purchaser's money is invested

**low-load mutual fund**  a mutual fund with sales charge of less than 5 percent

**reverse-load mutual fund**  a fund that does not have a sales charge at the time of purchase but charges a fee for selling the shares

**Read all about it** *Specialized magazines supply investors with basic information and commentary. Here* Business Week *advises its readers to be wary of a popular investment, the "Penny Stock Scam" (see Case 22.2).*

business and investing but does not try to cover current events. Hundreds of other publications each cover a specific market or subject, like *Aviation Week, Sheep & Goat Ranchers Magazine,* and *Publishers Weekly.*

## Newspaper Coverage

Some industries have their own newspapers. The women's apparel industry, for one, now has *W,* formerly called *Women's Wear Daily.* In the past, only the *Wall Street Journal* covered the securities markets extensively. Today, *Investors' Daily* and *USA Today* provide millions of investors with information on a daily basis. Also, many papers devote a whole section or part of one to business news several times a week. Most newspapers carry complete NYSE and Amex listings and selected listings from other markets. Recall, for instance, Figure 19.2, an excerpt from a NYSE listing; Figure 19.3, from an over-the-counter listing; and Figure 19.4, from a bond marketing listing.

The source of the data in these listings is the computerized record of the daily transactions in each market. It is this same record that produces the ticker data described earlier. At the end of each trading day, this information is transmitted electronically to newspapers and any others who order it. It is also available to subscribers, like brokerages, who have the proper micro-computer equipment. Some individual investors use these computerized listings to manage their own portfolios (see Experiencing Business).

## Other Sources

An investor seeking specific information on a firm can go directly to a particular company's shareholder or investor-information department. Public companies will provide annual reports, SEC Form 10-K reports, and many other reports.

The key investor protection offered by the securities regulations discussed in the next section is their requirement that the issuer fully and fairly disclose the nature of the investment to all prospective buyers. This disclosure comes in the form of two documents. All issuers must file a **registration statement** with the Securities and Exchange Commission and state securities regulators that fully describes the investment and the issuer. The second document, the **prospectus**, summarizes the information contained in the registration statement. Full-service brokerages or the companies themselves are the best sources for these documents.

Full-service brokerages also provide detailed reports on investments, prepared by their own in-house analysts. Often, brokerages' larger branches have libraries with financial information services like *Value Line, Moody's Industrial Directories, Moody's Million Dollar Directory,* and *Standard & Poor's Reports.* Public libraries, which often have substantial collections in business and finance, usually also subscribe to some of these services.

**registration statement** document filed with the Securities and Exchange Commission and state securities regulators that fully describes an investment and the issuer

**prospectus** a summary of information contained in the registration statement

## Stock Averages

Several statistical averages measure the activity of the New York Stock Exchange and the stock market in general. These include

- The Dow Jones Averages (NYSE)
    - 30 Industrials
    - 20 Transportation stocks
    - 15 Utilities
    - The Composite (the 65 stocks of the other three averages)
- The Standard & Poor's 500 stock average (NYSE)
- The NYSE average price of all issues traded
- The Amex average price of all issues traded
- The NASDAQ index

These closely watched averages are computed constantly during the trading day. Over time, they should reflect trends in the markets. The charts shown in Figure 19.5 depict the movement over six months of the three most

## WATCHING YOUR STOCK

Suppose you own stock in a retail chain called Pay-Less Stores. Pay-Less is a fast-growing discount retailer with over 1,300 stores in twenty-five states. The company plans to open 150 new stores this year. Pay-Less is one of the largest retailers in the United States—behind only K mart, Wal-Mart, and Sears. Pay-Less sells clothes, shoes, small appliances, cosmetics, and a variety of other goods usually found in a discount retail store.

Which of the following hypothetical news items would cause the price of your Pay-Less stock to rise? To fall? Explain. Check your responses against those in the back of the book.

1. Sears decides to become a discount retailer and offer its merchandise at prices competitive with Pay-Less.
2. The index of leading economic indicators suggests that the economy will be strong in the forseeable future and that personal incomes are likely to rise.
3. The CEO of Pay-Less, along with the Chairman of the Board and three top vice presidents die in airplane crash.
4. K mart announces a spring sale on lawn mowers.
5. A large Japanese conglomerate announces that it has purchased 10 percent of the stock of Pay-Less and is considering a takeover.
6. A major European retail company announces that it will open four large stores in the United States to sell designer clothes and other exclusive merchandise.
7. Pay-Less is sued by several employees for age discrimination.
8. Pay-Less opens ten new stores in France and announces that it plans to open fifty more in Europe in the next three years.

important Dow Jones averages. Also shown are the stocks included in the computations, which change from time to time, because of mergers, bankruptcies, and other factors.

The Standard & Poor's Corporation prepares a broader set of averages similar to the Dow Jones averages. The NYSE, Amex, and NASDAQ averages are broader still, since they include all the stocks traded each day.

# Regulation of Securities Trading

Before World War I, most securities trading involved a few knowledgeable investors and some highly sophisticated speculators. Then, during the postwar boom of the 1920s, ordinary people increasingly became involved in the market. At the same time, many investors and speculators overextended themselves, bidding the market up to record levels. When the bubble burst, on "Black Tuesday," October 29, 1929, the stock market crashed. At its lowest point, on July 1, 1932, the values of the stocks on the New York Stock Exchange had declined more than 82.5 percent from their pre-crash

**FIGURE 19.5** Dow Jones Averages

highs.[5] The time line shown in Figure 19.6 identifies the major securities legislation that followed the election of Franklin D. Roosevelt in 1932.

The success of this sequence of regulations appeared to be beyond question until 1987. Up to that time, the United States had not suffered a crash that even slightly resembled that of 1929–32. But on October 19, 1987, now referred to as "Black Monday," the stock market took an unprecedented 508-point plunge (see Business Issues). The 1987 crash prompted calls for new regulation. Various investigations and studies pointed to a need for

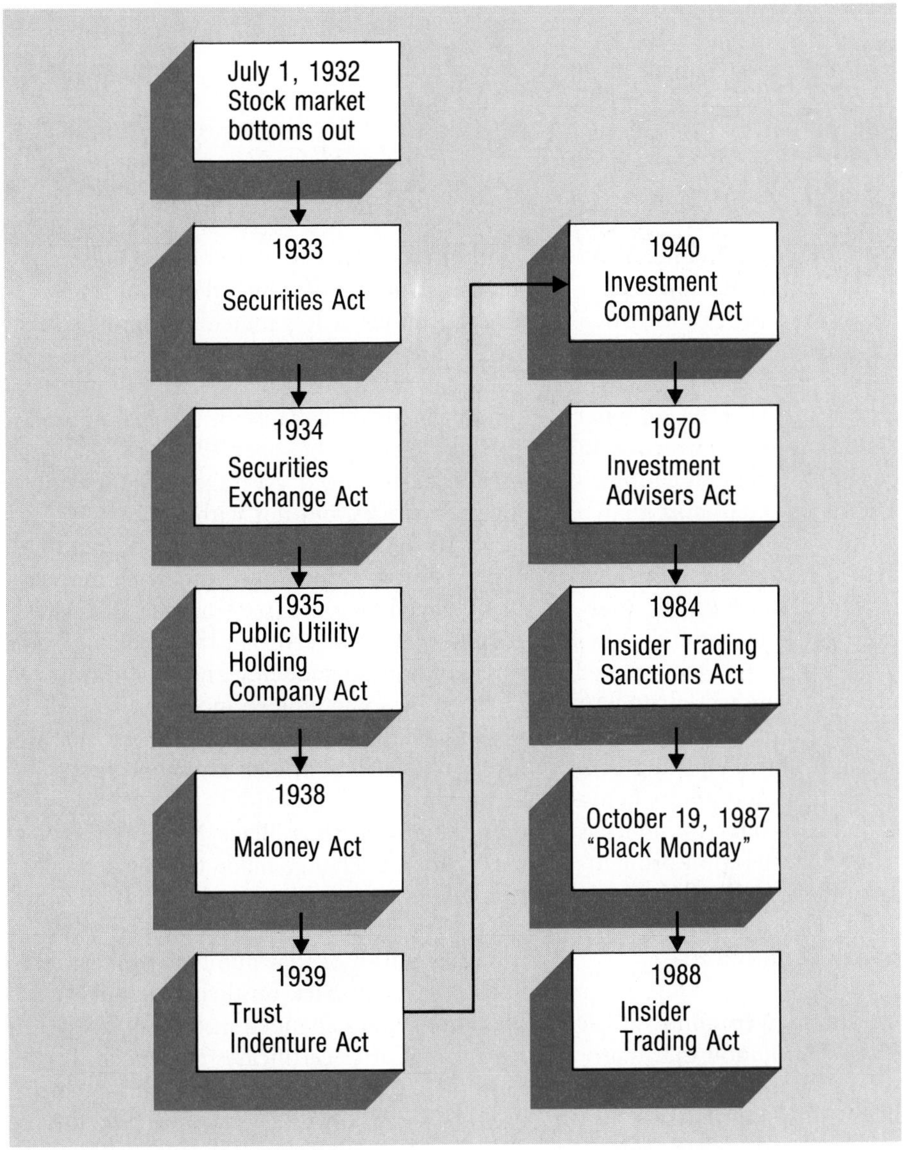

FIGURE 19.6
Securities Regulation
Time Line

| | |
|---|---|
| July 1, 1932 Stock market bottoms out | |
| 1933 Securities Act | 1940 Investment Company Act |
| 1934 Securities Exchange Act | 1970 Investment Advisers Act |
| 1935 Public Utility Holding Company Act | 1984 Insider Trading Sanctions Act |
| 1938 Maloney Act | October 19, 1987 "Black Monday" |
| 1939 Trust Indenture Act | 1988 Insider Trading Act |

changes in trading rules but not new major regulation. Some procedural rules have been changed to assure fair access to markets for small and large investors alike, even in volatile markets.

## Federal Securities Legislation

*The Securities Act of 1933* The first major piece of legislation on our timeline, the **Securities Act of 1933**, is a disclosure act requiring that the issuer of a public offering file a registration statement providing specific information about the issuer, its financial condition, management, properties,

**Securities Act of 1933** a disclosure act requiring that the issuer of a public offering file a registration statement providing specific information about the issuer, its financial condition, management, properties, and general operation

# A LOOK BACK AT THE MARKET CRASH OF 1987

In August 1987, the Dow Jones Industrial Average (DJIA) reached 2722.42, having risen from less than 2000 at the start of the year. Many analysts were warning of imminent danger, but some of those had been "crying wolf" for months, or years. Then began what many considered a normal price correction in August as prices began to decline in choppy trading. That decline represented more than a 17 percent drop by the close of trading on October 16. Markets in Europe were open before those in the United States on Monday morning, October 19, and they were all down 7 to 10 percent by the time the NYSE opened. European investors were trying to sell stocks for which they could find no buyers, so New York had heavy selling from the opening bell. The DJIA dipped more than 200 points before buyers came in and pulled it back to minus 100 around noon. But the afternoon brought further selling and the market closed down 508 points at 1738.74. That day set a record for the greatest one day decline ever— 22.6 percent.

By mid-afternoon rumors were rampant on Wall Street. There was speculation that many brokerage firms were in financial difficulty. The exchanges remained open and active to provide markets for buyers and sellers, but not without confusion and fear. The potential existed for a complete collapse of the financial institutions in the United States in the next day's trading. However, the Federal Reserve Board notified banks and brokerage companies that monies would be available in the system to provide liquidity to the financial markets. Also, many corporations, which were quite profitable at the time, began to enter the markets to buy the stock of their own companies. These and other actions helped to stabilize the securities markets at that point.

Could it happen again? The history of our kind of economy is cratered by periodic crashes, from all of which the economy has emerged more or less intact. We may be relatively sure, however, that if present trends continue, we will not witness exactly the same kind of financial collapse in the near future.

In the wake of October 19, 1987, the stock market has changed. Average investors still invest in stocks, but not with the same speculative fervor and not to the same degree. Big-time investors turned from the stock market to leveraged buyouts (see Chapter 18). And corporations, alarmed that their financial picture could be so suddenly and so radically changed by something so incomprehensible, began to buy back their stock. Fewer shares are available to be traded now, and fewer shares are traded.

In the aftermath of Black Monday the New York Stock Exchange made technical changes that would permit it to handle a billion shares a day. The average daily volume rarely approaches a fifth of that number. Brokerage houses have cut back on their stock-market operations and expanded into other fields. (Most now offer certificates of deposit, for example.) Whatever other kinds of financial dangers we may face, chances are that the stock-market palpitations of 1987 will be remembered more as a soap-opera episode than as an American tragedy.

---

Sources: "Six Months Later: The Crash," *Business Week,* Apr. 18, 1988, pp. 55–65. F. Norris, "Crash Course: What Happened on October 19 and What It Means," *Barrons,* 68:12–13, Jan. 4, 1988. K. Labart, "Anatomy of a Panic," *Financial World,* 156:18–19, Dec. 1, 1987. J. Edgerton, "Crash of '87: How the Small Investor Got the Shaft," *Money,* 17:13–14, Jan. 1988. D. A. McIntyre, "The Crash Revisited," *Financial World,* 157, Nov. 1, 1988, p. 124(1). "What Caused the Meltdown," *The Economist,* Dec. 19, 1987, p. 65+. J. Egan, "A Crashing Anniversary," *U.S. News & World Report,* Oct. 17, 1988, pp. 56–58. K. Pennar, "Did the Crash Make a Dent?" *Business Week,* Oct. 17, 1988, pp. 88–90.

and general operation. This act also prohibits false and misleading statements in registration statements or in connection with public offerings.

*The Securities Exchange Act of 1934*  The Securities and Exchange Commission was established by the **Securities Exchange Act of 1934**. This act requires periodic disclosures in the form of reports to the SEC by companies whose securities are publicly held. It also greatly strengthens the government's hand in regulating the ways in which securities change hands in public transactions. Later amendments to the act provided for the registration of brokers and dealers and established periodic reporting requirements for the issuers of listed securities.

The key point to remember about the 1933 and 1934 acts is that they mandate disclosure of relevant financial information to the public so that investors can make up their own minds about the merits of an investment. It must be emphasized that these acts do not try to keep people from making bad investments.

**Securities Exchange Act of 1934** act requiring periodic disclosures in the form of reports to the SEC by companies whose securities are publicly held

*The Public Utility Holding Company Act of 1935*  The SEC is empowered by the **Public Utility Holding Company Act of 1935** to regulate the companies that control public utilities, notably the electric utilities, natural-gas pipeline companies, and their subsidiaries. Because utility companies usually have legal monopolies, utility holding companies exercise enormous power over their customers and markets.

**Public Utility Holding Company Act of 1935** regulates the companies that control public utilities

*The Maloney Act of 1938*  The present self-regulation of the OTC market was authorized by the **Maloney Act of 1938**. It led to the creation of the National Association of Securities Dealers, which now regulates the market.

**Maloney Act of 1938** act that authorized the self-regulation of the OTC market

*The Trust Indenture Act of 1939*  The next important regulatory act, the **Trust Indenture Act of 1939**, requires that any corporate debt offered to the public be registered with the SEC and conform to certain requirements relating to maturity, interest, and financial backing. This act also requires the appointment of an independent trustee for each issue of long-term debt.

**Trust Indenture Act of 1939** act that requires that any corporate debt offered to the public be registered with the SEC and conform to certain requirements relating to maturity, interest, and financial backing

*The Investment Company Act of 1940*  The **Investment Company Act of 1940** made mutual funds subject to SEC registration and reporting requirements.

**Investment Company Act of 1940** act that made mutual funds subject to SEC registration and reporting requirements

*The Investment Advisers Act of 1940*  Those who advise investors, whether or not they actually handle investor funds, must register with the SEC, as required by the **Investment Advisers Act of 1940**. This act provides penalties for improper actions, fraud, and conflict of interest.

**Investment Advisers Act of 1940** act that requires those who advise investors, whether or not they handle investor funds, to register with the SEC

*The Securities Act of 1964*  Companies whose securities trade over the counter were brought under SEC jurisdiction by the **Securities Act of 1964**, if the company and its stockholders met certain criteria. This act broadened the SEC's jurisdiction to include companies that had avoided regulation by staying off the exchanges. After the passage of this act, many of the larger OTC companies applied to the national exchanges for listing.

**Securities Act of 1964** act that broadened the SEC's jurisdiction to include companies that had avoided regulation by staying off the exchanges

5. Identify the principal federal securities statutes.

Securities Investors
Protection Act of 1970
act that created the Securities
Investors Protection Corporation (SIPC)

Securities Investors
Protection Corporation
(SIPC)   a regulatory agency
that oversees the liquidation of
failed broker-dealers and
insures investors when the
assets of a failed firm are
insufficient to cover its
obligations to its customers

*The Securities Investors Protection Act of 1970*   Until 1970, such legislation of the Roosevelt era as that just described provided most of the regulatory structure in the securities marketplace. Market activity grew rapidly in the late 1960s, however, and a number of brokerage houses that could not cope with those changes failed, bringing great losses to their customers.

The **Securities Investors Protection Act of 1970** created the **Securities Investors Protection Corporation (SIPC)**, which oversees the liquidation of failed broker-dealers and insures investors when the assets of a failed firm are insufficient to cover its obligations to its customers. The SIPC insures investor accounts held by the brokerage houses for up to $500,000 in total and $100,000 in cash deposits. Like the FDIC and FSLIC in the banking industry, members of the securities exchanges, who are required to join, and other brokers, dealers, and fund managers, who may elect to join, fund the SIPC.

*The Insider Trading Sanctions Act of 1984*   One of the results of deregulation was a dramatic change in the enforcement of the antitrust laws. Under the Reagan administration, and in the face of foreign competition, the antitrust laws were applied in a less restrictive manner than ever before. The 1980s became the era of the megamerger, as giant oil companies merged, conglomerates like Beatrice Foods merged with other conglomerates and then went private, and diversified giants like R. J. Reynolds swallowed related companies like Nabisco and then were themselves devoured by others. Information about merger plans became valuable to stock-market speculators, whose activities brought into serious question the fairness of the market. Trading on **insider information**, information available only to persons who owe a fiduciary duty (a trust relationship) to a corporation's shareholders, had long been illegal under the 1934 SEC act, but many believed the penalties to be inadequate. The **Insider Trading Act of 1984** subjected those guilty of insider trading to forfeiture of up to three times their gain on the illegal trades and expanded the SEC's powers to investigate such trading.

insider information
information available only to
persons who owe a fiduciary
duty to a corporation's
shareholders

Insider Trading Act of
1984   act that subjected
those guilty of insider trading
to forfeiture of up to three
times their gain on the illegal
trades and expanded the SEC's
powers to investigate such
trading

Insider Trading Act of
1988   act that increased the
criminal penalties for insider
trading and extended the reach
of the law

*The Insider Trading Act of 1988*   In the late 1980s, investigators continued to uncover insider trading abuses. Some violations were the result of activity of brokers and even managers of brokerage firms. The **Insider Trading Act of 1988** increased the criminal penalties for insider trading and extended the reach of the law. The act made brokerage firms and their managers legally responsible for identifying and reporting trades that represent insider trading. Managers, for instance, could be subject to fines of up to $1 million. Neither of the two insider trading acts specifically defined insider trading. That omission has caused controversy in the investment and legal communities.

# Options

option   a security contract
that gives the option buyer the
right to buy or sell 100 shares
of stock at a specified price for
a specific period of time

An **option** is a security contract that gives the option buyer the right to buy or sell 100 shares of stock at a specified price for a specific period of time. For example, an investor may believe that the price of IBM is going to rise

**Ivan Boesky goes inside** *Great profits can be made through illegal, insider trading, but only at great risk. Trading on illegally obtained information about various companies, Ivan Boesky made a fortune, got caught, and went to jail.*

over the next month from its price of $125 per share. He or she might purchase an option to buy IBM for $125 at any time during the next two months. The investor would pay the seller of the option a small amount, perhaps $3 per share for the right. If IBM were to rise to $135 per share before the option expires, the option buyer could **exercise** the option, buying the stock at $125 for a profit. On the other hand, if IBM goes down to $120, the option buyer would let the option **expire** worthless and have a small loss of only $300. The option buyer can control large amounts of stock with small amounts of money and limited risk.

**exercise** acting upon a purchased option

**expire** letting the specified time period for an option run out, making the option worthless

The obvious question is, why would someone sell an option? The owner of IBM stock may be very happy to sell IBM for $125 per share and also receive $3 per share over the next two months. After all, the option price represents 14 percent return on an annualized basis. In addition, if the price of IBM remains the same, or goes down, the option seller pockets $300 and keeps the stock.

Options have become important investment vehicles for both individuals and institutions since the options contracts became standardized and trading started on major exchanges in the mid-1970s. Options trade actively on the American, Midwest, Philadelphia, and Pacific exchanges. People who buy options are usually speculators who wish to benefit from large price moves while risking small amounts of money. Sellers of options are conservative investors who usually are trying to increase the return on their investments while reducing the risk of owning stock.

# Commodities

**commodities** basic resources and agricultural products, such as gold, silver, wheat, cotton, pork bellies, and orange juice

**commodities contracts** commitments to buy a quantity of a commodity at a particular time

**6.** Describe the process by which commodities contracts are traded.

Gold, silver, wheat, cotton, pork bellies, and orange juice—in other words, our basic resources and agricultural products—are **commodities. Commodities contracts**—commitments to buy a quantity of a commodity at a particular time—are bought and sold on secondary markets. Investors may purchase a contract up to eighteen months before it is due to expire. Most investors do not actually want the commodity itself. They expect to sell the contract before it matures and hope to make money by doing so.

Most investors purchase on margin, which the industry margin requirement of 5 percent encourages. They speculate that the price of a contract will rise so that the contract can be sold at a profit before it expires. Buyers bet that by putting a small amount down they will make a very high return on their investment and not have to take title to the goods. The risk of loss is at least as great as the chance for gain, though.

For example, say that a contract is for 112,000 pounds of sugar. Its price is, perhaps, 20.88 cents per pound. On margin, a speculator is able to buy a sugar contract for only $1,169.28 plus the commission. An increase in the sugar's market price of only 1 cent per pound would result in a profit of $1,120.00, or 95.8 percent, less commission. A drop of 1 cent would result in a loss of the same $1,120.00, however. Because an investor needs only to put down 5 percent, very small price movements have large impacts. A failure to sell before maturity will result in the delivery of 112,000 pounds of sugar and a demand by the seller for $22,216.32. Furthermore, speculators usually magnify these consequences by buying or selling several contracts at once.

Let us be clear that the commodities market is not only for speculation. Often, businesses that expect to require certain quantities of the commodities contract for delivery through the exchanges, assuring themselves of a supply when needed and at a predictable cost.

# Speculating and Investing: A Perspective

When we discussed commodities, we used the term *speculate*. This word, often associated with both commodities and stocks, implies the kind of gambling that knowledgeable football bettors engage in. It is true that early information about crop reports, long-range weather forecasts, and political changes could make a knowledgeable investor's fortune, but the speculative nature of commodities trading is easily exaggerated.

Commodities market regulators have taken a tolerant view of insider trading. In fact, unlike securities issuers, the issuers of commodities contracts are not subject to reporting requirements. Ever since the Securities Act of 1933, though, the watchword for all issuers has been *disclosure*. In recent years, insider-trading scandals have rocked Wall Street. These cases mainly involved people who had access to confidential information about coming takeover attempts or mergers. Some cases, however, simply involved passing

**Commodities gone bad**  *In the excitement of trading, commodities speculators may easily forget that there are real products behind their transactions. Oversupply means that the price of contracts declines. It could also mean that the product goes to waste.*

on information that would affect a stock's price. For example, a Deputy Secretary of Defense in the Reagan administration went to jail for four years for obstructing an SEC investigation into tips he had given friends.[6]

Why is a certain type of conduct with respect to securities a crime when the same conduct with respect to commodities is simply sound trading? More and more people are asking this question. The philosophy behind the securities laws is that securities are investments and all investors should have equal access to relevant information. Is this really possible, since markets always operate on an information advantage?

The regulatory philosophy seems to be that an investment somehow has positive qualities that a speculation does not. It is difficult to feel sorry for those convicted of insider trading. Almost without exception, they knew that what they were doing was wrong. Still, it is worth considering whether the law as it stands makes sense and whether people who buy and sell commodities or stocks are in fact engaged in the same types of transactions and should thus be treated the same way.

# CHAPTER HIGHLIGHTS

**1.** *List the three attributes of a security.*

A security must show (1) an investment of money; (2) a common enterprise; and (3) an expectation of profit solely from the efforts of others.

**2.** *Describe the three basic processes by which securities change hands.*

Transfer of a publicly traded stock can occur in three ways: (1) In a private transaction between two parties. Unless transfer of a security is somehow restricted, two persons can simply agree to the transfer. (2) In a transaction on a primary market. *Primary markets* are those in which the issuer of a security receives some or all of the funds paid for the security. Primary markets are markets for new issues of securities. (3) In a transaction on a secondary market. When people refer to the "stock market," they usually mean the secondary markets for securities. *Secondary markets* are those markets in which the sale of a security ordinarily does not involve any proceeds going to the issuer.

**3.** *Identify the principal secondary markets for securities and describe each.*

Secondary markets for securities include the national, regional, and international stock exchanges, the over-the-counter market and the bond exchanges. The New York Stock Exchange is the oldest and largest of the U.S. secondary markets. The NYSE is a national exchange. The American Stock Exchange, also located in New York, is the second of the national exchanges. Regional exchanges are similar in structure to the major exchanges but are much smaller in size and scope. The over-the-counter market refers to a telecommunications network linking broker-dealers for transactions in securities not listed on exchanges. The bond markets are separate from the stock markets. Government bonds and municipal bonds are common bond listings.

**4.** *List the principal sources of financial information and give an example of each.*

The major sources of business and financial news remains magazines and newspapers. Several magazines, *Business Week, Industry Week,* and *Fortune* feature financial information. Newspaper coverage of financial information is provided in the *Wall Street Journal* and the financial section of many daily papers. Full service brokerages also provide detailed reports on investments prepared by in-house analysts. Some investors go directly to the company's shareholder or investor information department.

**5.** *Identify the principal federal securities statutes.*

The regulation of securities trading was triggered by the stock market crash of 1929. The Securities Act of 1933 is a disclosure act requiring that the issuer of a public offering file a registration statement providing specific information about the issuer. The Securities Exchange Act of 1934 established the SEC. This act requires periodic disclosures in the form of reports to the SEC by companies whose securities are publicly held. It also greatly strengthened the government's hand in regulating the ways in which securities changed hands in public transactions.

**6.** *Describe the process by which commodities contracts are traded.*

*Commodities* are basic resources and agricultural products such as gold, silver, wheat, cotton, pork bellies, and orange juice. A *commodity contract* is a commitment to buy at a particular time a quantity of a commodity that is bought and sold on secondary markets. Investors purchase the contract up to eighteen months before it is due to expire. In most cases, investors do not want the commodity. They expect the price of the contract will rise and that the contract may be sold at a profit before expiration.

# KEY TERMS

Security
Private
Transferee
Issuer
Primary markets
Private placement
Underwriter
Public offering
Spread
Syndicate
Secondary markets
Exchanges
Broker
Floor broker
Market order
Specialist
Ticker
Limit order
Open order
Stop order
Discretionary order
Commission

Full-service brokers
Discount brokers
Round lot
Odd lot
Margin accounts
Margin call
Over-the-counter
market (OTC)
National Association
of Securities Dealers
(NASD)
National Association
of Securities Dealers
Automatic Quota-
tions (NASDAQ)
Government bonds
U.S. government issues
Municipal bonds
Mutual funds
Growth funds
Income funds

Balanced funds
Load
No-load mutual fund
Low-load mutual fund
Reverse-load mutual
fund
Registration statement
Prospectus
Securities Act of 1933
Securities Exchange
Act of 1934
Public Utility Holding
Company Act of
1935
Maloney Act of 1938
Trust Indenture Act of
1939
Investment Company
Act of 1940

Investment Advisers
Act of 1940
Securities Act of 1964
Securities Investors
Protection Act of
1970
Securities Investors
Protection Corpora-
tion (SIPC)
Insider information
Insider Trading Act of
1984
Insider Trading Act of
1988
Option
Exercise
Expire
Commodities
Commodities contracts

# REVIEW QUESTIONS

1. Describe the major ways a publicly traded stock transfer can occur.
2. What is the function of a secondary market?
3. Describe how shares change hands on a secondary market.
4. How does the New York Stock Exchange operate? How does this exchange differ from the over-the-counter market?
5. What is a government bond? How do U.S. government bonds differ from municipal bonds?
6. If you want to begin investing in stocks or bonds, what sources of financial information are available to you?
7. Describe the role of the Securities and Exchange Commission. Why was it established?
8. By law, the issuer of stock must provide investors with two disclosure documents. List and describe each one.
9. Why is insider trading a problem? What has the U.S. government done to curb it?
10. What is an option?

# APPLICATION EXERCISES

1. Select two companies listed on the New York Stock Exchange. Chart the closing price and price changes for a two-week period from newspaper stock quotations. Also list the annual dividend and earnings for each stock. At the end of the two-week period, decide which stock is most attractive in terms of an investment plan that stresses growth. Explain your reasoning.

2. Select one company listed on the New York Stock Exchange. Find the Standard and Poor's report on the company at the library or a nearby brokerage firm. Identify and summarize the factors that would cause you to buy or not to buy stock in this company and explain your reasoning.

# CASES

## 19.1  Management's Job

Many corporate buyouts in the 1980s were leveraged buyouts (LBOs) in which a small group of managers or investors bought all publicly held shares from the shareholders ("took the company private") using borrowed money for most of the purchase. The borrowed money was a debt obligation of the corporation, not of the individuals buying the company. Often the purchase price was substantially higher than the previous market price of the shares. The shareholders benefited from the price increase and the new owners assumed the risk of full ownership. Banks and brokerage firms often made large profits in a short period of time by providing financing and arranging the deal.

In theory, at least, leveraged buyouts worked because owners could and would run the companies more efficiently than hired managers. If management did a good job, it could make a handsome profit. Increasing the corporate debt, however, also lowered the quality of existing debt and increased the risk of loss. In many cases, the debt was partially repaid by selling off divisions of the corporation to other companies.

In 1988 eight top managers of RJR Nabisco, Inc., a major consumer products conglomerate, made a $17.6 billion offer to buy the stock of their own company and take it private. The group was led by Ross Johnson, the chief executive officer of RJR Nabisco, who was responsible to the board of directors for running the company on behalf of the investors. Part of the management plan was to cut back operations in some areas and sell divisions that included a number of valuable consumer brands. In the process Johnson and his seven colleagues, who put up $200 million of their own money, would reap profits estimated to be as high as $2.6 billion. The bid prompted other offers from investor groups and eventually resulted in the 1989 sale of RJR Nabisco for $25 billion to Kohlberg Kravis Roberts & Co. (KKR), a company specializing in leveraged buyouts. That was slightly less than the final offer of $25.4 billion bid by the management group, but the board of directors did not want to show favoritism in the deal and they felt that KKR had a plan that would not require the sale of major assets.

### Questions

1. Is it ethical for the managers who are hired to run a company on behalf of stockholders to buy the company with the potential of making huge profits for themselves?
2. What effect would borrowing huge amounts of money have on the price of existing RJR Nabisco bonds?

For more information, see *Time*, December 12, 1988, p. 56; *Time*, December 5, 1988, p. 66; "RJR Sued by Noteholders," *Wall Street Journal*, December 7, 1988, p. A5; J. A.

White, "ITT Sues RJR, Saying Buy-out Devalues Bonds," *Wall Street Journal,* November 17, 1988, p. C1; A. C. Wallace, "A Growing Backlash Against Greed: Even Republican Leaders Are Disturbed by Debt-Financed Takeovers," *New York Times,* November 13, 1988, p. F1; B. J. Stein, "A New Low? The RJR LBO Makes a Travesty of Fiduciary Responsibility," *Barron's,* November 14, 1988, p. 16; J. H. Dobrzynski, "Was RJR's Ross Johnson Too Greedy for His Own Good?" *Business Week,* November 21, 1988, p. 95.

## 19.2   Insider Information

Individuals and investment firms, trying to cash in on the rash of corporate takeovers in the 1980s, used money and accurate information that a takeover attempt was in the works to buy the stock of target firms before the company attempting the takeover bid up the stock's price.

The SEC prohibits using insider information before it is made public. At least a few players have been unable to resist the temptation to profit from what they know.

One was Dennis Levine, a young investment banker. The SEC charged him with using inside knowledge of potential takeover attempts. Levine supposedly profited (allegedly $12.6 million worth) by secretly buying stocks of fifty-four target firms through a Bahamian subsidiary of a Swiss bank.

He pled guilty to four felony counts, for which he could receive twenty years in prison and fines up to $610,000. Levine agreed to help the SEC investigation of insider fraud. He

was sentenced to two years in jail and fined $362,000. He was also barred from the securities business for life.

Levine's cooperation helped the government to prosecute and convict Ivan Boesky of insider trading in December, 1987. Boesky was a key player in a massive web of insider trading. In return for information and evidence that led to numerous indictments of Wall Street figures, Boesky was given less than the maximum five-year jail sentence—three years and a $50 million fine, plus the return of $50 million in illegal profits. That evidence also led to a guilty plea and $650 million fine for insider trading by the Drexel Burnham Lambert brokerage. Drexel had been involved in many takeovers on behalf of its corporate clients by selling low-quality "junk" bonds and arranging bank loans to finance the deals.

### Questions

1. How can insider trading affect securities markets?
2. How could Drexel Burnham Lambert's admission of insider trading affect firms attempting takeovers?

For more information, see *Time,* June 23, 1986, p. 61; *Fortune,* June 9, 1986, p. 101; *New York Times,* June 6, 1986, p. A1; *Newsweek,* December 21, 1987, p. 51; *U.S. News & World Report,* December 28, 1987, p. 13; *Wall Street Journal,* December 22, 1988, p. A1.

# 20 Risk Management and Insurance

After you have completed this chapter, you will be able to do the following:

*1.* Define the types of risk and describe the four main ways of handling risk.

*2.* Define insurance and explain how insurance reduces risk.

*3.* Outline the four principles of insurance.

*4.* List the major forms of public insurance and private insurance coverage.

*5.* Describe the applications of insurance to business risks.

*6.* Compare term life insurance with cash value life insurance.

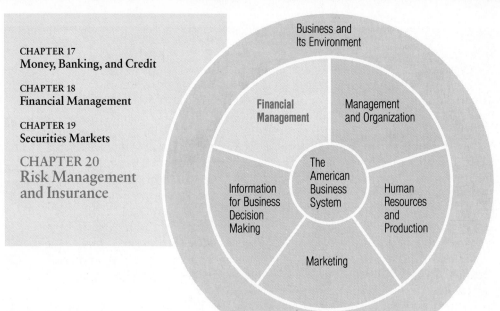

In 1975, the Gillette Company opened a plant in Manaus, Brazil, to manufacture razor blades and pens for the Brazilian and other markets. As time passed, the plant became increasingly important to the company's success; so much so that management began to worry about the potential for huge losses should a fire break out. By 1986, the company stood to lose $30 million in business interruption costs and $15 million in direct building and contents losses if a fire destroyed the plant. The potential business interruption losses were especially high because destruction of the plant would require importing and paying heavy import duty on products to meet Brazilian demand. These possibilities called for careful risk management. The company's risk managers planned for the construction of a sophisticated sprinkler system in addition to purchasing $100,000 of fire insurance. The sprinkler system was not completed without serious obstacles for the planners, however: the steep cost of the project needed to be approved by company management, and qualified technical Brazilians who could work on the project proved hard to find. Eventually, after a few years of work and planning, the Manaus sprinkler system was completed. The money to fund the project was approved, and a team of Brazilian contractors and New York engineers were found to build the system. Gillette management sleeps easier these days, knowing that the Manaus facility is well protected.[1]

> Insurance is not the only—or necessarily the best—way to cope with risk. Risk managers at Gillette opted for a combination of fire insurance and a specialized sprinkler system to reduce the risk of fire damage at their Manaus, Brazil, plant. At one extreme, a firm might simply take its chances and hope that an undesirable event will not occur. At the other, the company might avoid an activity because of its potential risk. Between those two extremes lie the options that this chapter examines.

# The Nature of Risk

The uncertainty about whether an event will or will not occur is **risk**. Note that risk is not the same as the odds that an event will occur.

An event that has a 95 percent chance of occurring is highly certain and is therefore of low risk. Facing such a likely occurrence, a business will either avoid activities that might lead to the event or plan how to deal with it when it happens. For example, Federal Express knows that accidents involving its thousands of delivery vans are inevitable. Its strategy for dealing with this risk is both to put a premium on accident-free records for its drivers and also to maintain stores of replacement parts and vehicles. Federal Express is in a high-certainty, low-risk situation. The contrary is also true, however: a "one in a billion" event is also a low risk, because there is a high degree of certainty that it will not happen. Normally, businesses assume the risk of such events. The greatest risk occurs when the odds are neither extremely high nor extremely low or are unknown. These risks are the ones a business must focus on.

**risk** the uncertainty about whether an event will or will not occur

*1.* Define the types of risk and describe the four main ways of handling risk.

**Liability** *Unocal Corporation carries insurance to protect itself against the financial loss a petroleum-refinery fire would cause. It also tries to minimize such loss by training its refinery workers in fire-fighting procedures.*

There are two categories of risk. **Speculative risk** offers the potential for gain as well as loss. Starting a new business or buying securities involves speculative risk. **Pure risk**, the second type, offers only the potential for loss. Fires, automobile accidents, and illnesses exemplify pure risk. Firms can buy insurance to protect against pure risk, but not against speculative risk. Figure 20.1 outlines the classifications of risk.

## Risk Management

In a business, **risk management** is the process of identifying exposures to risk, choosing the best method for handling each exposure, and implementing it.

The managing of speculative risks is a general responsibility of the overall management team. Managing pure risks, though, is in many firms the job of a **risk manager**, a person whose job it is to preserve company assets and a business's earning power against pure risks. Over 4,000 risk managers attended the 1988 annual meeting of the Risk and Insurance Management Society.

Among the risk manager's most common concerns are **property risks**, the potential direct loss of the firm's property due to fire or similar causes.

FIGURE 20.1   A Classification of Risk

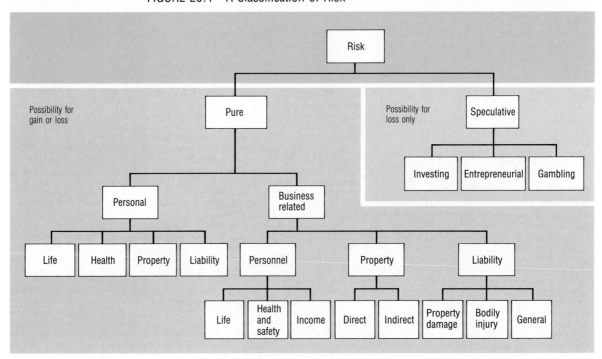

Indirectly, property losses can cause revenue losses if, say, fire destroyed an automobile dealership's paint shop. A risk manager's other major area of concern is **liability risks**, those risks that involve the potential that a firm might be held legally responsible for losses suffered by a person or another firm. Personal injury liability for automobile accidents is the most common type. For manufacturers, another critically important type of risk management is product liability insurance.

At a major corporation, the risk manager is likely to have a high rank and control a large, important budget line with a relatively small staff. One example is *Business Insurance* magazine's "Risk Manager of the Year" for 1988, William L. Mather of the Gillette Company. Gillette is a major consumer products company (razors, razor blades, toiletries, and pens) with operations in over 50 countries. Mather and his staff of four full-time and two half-time professionals were responsible for about $21 million in risk management expenditures in 1988. Mr. Mather is responsible for protecting the company from losses ranging from those arising out of its operation of almost 4,000 vehicles to the complexities of using hydrocarbons in aerosol spray cans.[2]

## The Techniques of Risk Management

When deciding how to handle a risk, the risk manager has four basic methods from which to choose (see Figure 20.2):

- Risk avoidance
- Risk assumption
- Risk transfer
- Risk reduction

**Risk avoidance** requires a firm not to engage in an activity or to own property that might lead to an exposure to risk. For example, in the mid-1980s many companies decided not to extend their operations to the Union of South Africa in order to avoid the risks of the political instability there.

By contrast, **risk assumption** requires that a firm consciously recognize a particular risk and accept it as an integral part of its activities. As mentioned, risk assumption may be in order when the odds are strongly against an event's happening or when the potential loss is low. In some instances, **insurers**, any organizations that provide insurance coverage, force their policyholders into risk assumption so that they can keep coverage affordable. They may issue a policy with a **deductible**, an amount the policyholder must pay before the insurer's obligation to pay becomes effective. Most automobile policies require at least a $250 deductible. The other principal method that insurers have of forcing risk assumption is coinsurance, which we will discuss later.

**Risk transfer** shifts risk to another party. Insurance can be a prime example of risk transfer. When an insurance company agrees to pay the losses of an insured, the risk faced by the insured is transferred. But insurance does more; it also reduces risk.

**liability risks** risks that involve the potential that a firm might be held legally responsible for losses suffered by a person or another firm

**risk avoidance** way of handling risk which requires that a firm not engage in an activity or own property that might lead to an exposure of risk

**risk assumption** way of handling risk which requires that a firm consciously recognize a particular risk and accept it as an integral part of its activities

**insurers** any organizations that provide insurance coverage

**deductible** an amount the policyholder must pay before the insurer's obligation to pay becomes effective

**risk transfer** the shift of risk to another party

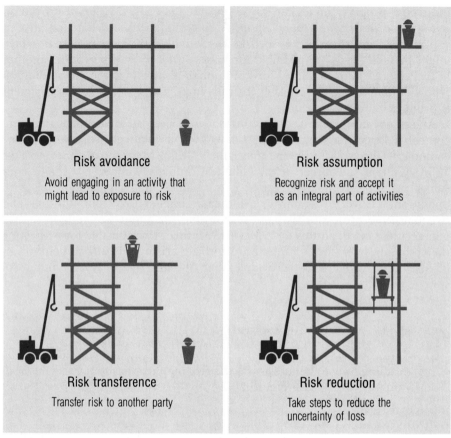

**Risk avoidance**
Avoid engaging in an activity that
might lead to exposure to risk

**Risk assumption**
Recognize risk and accept it
as an integral part of activities

**Risk transference**
Transfer risk to another party

**Risk reduction**
Take steps to reduce the
uncertainty of loss

FIGURE 20.2   Four Risk Management Strategies

**risk reduction**   the lessening of the uncertainty of financial loss in a risky situation

**Risk reduction** is the lessening of the uncertainty of financial loss in a risky situation. Many companies go to great lengths to promote worker safety so as to avoid not only the financial costs of injury but the down time and disruption of work that would accompany it. Risk reduction can be achieved in several ways. *Hazard reduction* involves reducing the odds that a loss will occur, as in providing training programs for operators of heavy construction equipment. *Loss reduction* involves reducing the severity of the loss, as in installing a sprinkler system in a high-rise office building. The major way to reduce risk, however, is to buy insurance.

*2. Define insurance and explain how insurance reduces risk.*

**insurance**   a contract that reduces risk of loss and requires one party to pay a specified sum to another if a previously identified event occurs

**insured**   a person or firm that buys insurance

# The Nature of Insurance

A contract that reduces risk of loss and requires one party to pay a specified sum to another if a previously identified event occurs is called **insurance**.

By means of an insurance contract, the **insured**, a person or firm that buys insurance, exchanges an uncertain situation for the certainty of paying an

**insurance premium**. The contract between the insurer and the insured, the **insurance policy**, contains the terms of the insurance.

Insurance can be divided into life insurance and *all* other types. The two groups share several important characteristics, but fundamental differences distinguish them, as we will see. Insurance generally works on four principles:

- The law of large numbers
- Indemnification
- The concept of insurable risk
- The concept of insurable interest

**insurance premium** a fee paid to the person or firm providing insurance

**insurance policy** the contract between the insurer and the insured which contains the terms of the insurance

*3. Outline the four principles of insurance.*

## The Law of Large Numbers

As the number of units in a group increases, predictions about the group become more accurate and therefore more certain, according to the **law of large numbers**. Insurance reduces the risk for an entire class of insured entities because the number and degree of losses are mathematically certain. Insurance giants like Allstate or State Farm, which have had tens of millions of policyholders over the years, can make extremely accurate predictions, based on their extensive research and experience.

**law of large numbers** law which states that as the number of units in a group increases, predictions about the group become more accurate and therefore more certain

*Self-insurance*  The law of large numbers also works to the advantage of firms with experience running many stores, outlets, or plants. They may choose **self-insurance**, a mechanism by which a business establishes a fund to cover losses caused by particular types of events. Usually, firms assign each unit its share of the losses that are likely to occur to all the units in a given period. Suppose that a retail firm has 500 stores, each valued at $500,000. If the firm projects one fire loss per year, it could assess each store $1,000 for the year rather than buying fire insurance. If no fires occur, the fund earns interest until it is needed. If more than one fire occurs in the first year, however, the firm could find itself strapped for cash. Plainly, self-insurance is only for large firms like Safeway Stores, Inc., and the K mart Corporation. Small firms whose facilities are concentrated in only a few places should avoid self-insurance.

**self-insurance** a mechanism by which a business establishes a fund to cover losses caused by particular types of events

Another method employed by large corporations to control insurance costs is to form or buy a "captive" insurance company that will write the insurance plans needed by the parent company. Nissan Motor Corporation has formed such a company to provide worker's compensation and property/casualty protection for its U.S. dealers.[3]

## Indemnification

The principle of **indemnification**, which does not apply to life insurance, requires an insurer to pay no more than the financial loss actually suffered. Otherwise, the insured might be tempted to try to gain from a loss. For a standard property insurance policy, for example, an insurer will pay only a loss's **actual cash value**, the purchase price of an item of personal property

**indemnification** the principle which requires an insurer to pay no more than the financial loss actually suffered

**actual cash value** the purchase price of an item of personal property less its depreciation

## CATASTROPHIC EVENTS CAN CAUSE CATASTROPHIC LOSSES

On July 6, 1988, an offshore oil and natural gas platform in the North Sea off Scotland exploded, killing 164 workers. In addition to the tragic human loss and suffering, this accident represented the largest insured manmade disaster to that date. Loss estimates ranged from a low of $1 billion to over $1.4 billion. Initial loss estimates included $795 million for the platform itself, $175 million for the removal of the wreckage, $225 million for business interruption costs, $100 million in seepage and pollution costs, and $100 million in employer liability losses. This estimate did not include the cost of the temporary shutdown of six oil fields in the North Sea as a result of

the explosion. A consortium of four oil companies owned the platform. One of the owners, Occidental Petroleum, had deductibles of $3 and $10 million on two of its insurance policies. Well over ten different insurers and reinsurers, in addition to virtually every syndicate and company in the London market, participated in providing various types of protection for the platform.

Sources: Stacey Shapiro, "$1 Billion Loss," *Business Insurance*, July 11, 1988, pp. 1, 33, 34; Stacey Shapiro and Carolyn Aldred, "Brokers Review Coverage for Devastated Oil Platform," *Business Insurance*, July 18, 1988, pp. 69, 70; William E. Smith, "Screaming Like a Banshee," *Time*, July 18, 1988, p. 36.

less its depreciation, rather than its replacement value. After a fire, a firm without replacement-value coverage may have to go out of business because the insurance proceeds will not replace lost equipment. At that point, the extra cost of replacement-value coverage will look like a missed bargain.

In life insurance the principle of indemnification is difficult to apply because the dollar loss from a death is so difficult to determine in advance. Therefore, a life insurance policy will specify a predetermined face amount to be paid at the death of the insured. A policy application with an unrealistically high face amount will be rejected.

### *Insurable Risk*

**insurable risks**  the risks for which an insurance policy can be purchased

The risks for which an insurance policy can be purchased are **insurable risks**. Emotional or sentimental values are irrelevant in respect to insurability. For all types of insurance other than life insurance, insurable risks must be financial, measurable, and predictable. A sufficiently large number of similar situations must have occurred before an insurance company can generate accurate estimates of risk. When a pianist "insures" his or her hands, what actually occurs is a transference of risk. Remember that insurance is a reduction of risk through the working of the law of large numbers. That is why insurance policies generally exclude losses from catastrophes like wars, earthquakes, or floods. Catastrophes like these are neither predictable nor isolated. Insurers base their premiums on the average of isolated losses. It is nevertheless still possible to obtain policies covering some catastrophic risks. (See Business Issues).

In general, an insurable risk is a loss that is not intentionally caused by the insured. Again, life insurance policies are an exception. Insurers will pay on a suicide's policy if it has been in effect for more than a specified period, usually two years. They will never pay the murderer of an insured, though.

Insurers also have the right to set standards for the risks they accept. They can, for instance, refuse to insure drivers who have had numerous accidents. And in terms of setting standards for financial liability, an insurable risk may be neither too big nor too small. Increasingly, insurers have avoided taking on large individual risks, unilaterally, particularly in the areas of medical malpractice and product liability, where a single claim can run into the millions. Instead, portions of the coverage are sold off to other companies through a process called **reinsurance**. In contrast, insurers will not cover losses so small that the cost of processing a claim would make the premium prohibitively high. Deductibles exist specifically to bridge this gap between the costs of claim processing and premiums.

**reinsurance** the portions of the coverage that are sold off to other insurance companies

## Insurable Interest

A person applying to purchase insurance must have an **insurable interest,** which means that he or she must stand to suffer a measurable dollar loss if the insured-against event were to occur. This principle keeps insurance from

**insurable interest** having a measurable dollar loss if an insured-against event were to occur

Insurable interest   *Those who just sold the property in question could not collect on damage caused by this flooding. If the new owners do not have their insurance in place, they are out of luck.*

becoming a means of gambling on another's death or misfortune. The insurable-interest principle applies in different ways to property insurance and life insurance.

With property insurance, an insurable interest must exist at the time of the loss. For instance, a person who might continue to pay the premiums on a fire insurance policy on a house he had sold could not collect if it burned down. However, a firm can obtain insurance on goods that it expects to receive, although the policy will not take effect until the risk of loss shifts over to the insured.

With life insurance, an insurable interest can arise from either family or business relationships. The insurable interest must exist at the time the policy was issued. If, for example, a wife takes out a life insurance policy on her husband and they then divorce, she can still keep it in force and collect when he dies.

## Insurance Companies

Over 6,000 companies write insurance. With assets exceeding $1.47 trillion, the insurance industry is one of the major investors in real estate, government securities, and corporate securities. Over 2 million people work in the insurance industry.

The two major types of insurance companies are stock insurance companies and mutual insurance companies. **Stock insurance companies**, owned by stockholders, provide insurance protection for a profit. Like other for-profit corporations, stock insurance companies distribute profits to shareholders in the form of dividends. One major stock insurance company is Aetna Life & Casualty Co.

**Mutual insurance companies** are owned by their policyholders. Any profits they earn go to the policyholders in the form of insurance dividends. Mutual of New York (MONY) is one such leading mutual insurance company.

**stock insurance companies** insurance companies owned by stockholders which provide insurance protection for a profit

**mutual insurance companies** insurance companies owned by their policyholders, in which any profits earned go to the policyholders in the form of insurance dividends

## The Types of Coverage

Most people are familiar with the five major categories of insurance: property, liability, health, life, and income. It is not until one considers that even a medium-sized firm may require as many as three dozen types of insurance that the breadth of these categories becomes apparent, however. For the remainder of this chapter, we will examine the types and sources of coverage, as given in Figure 20.3.

# Public Insurance

*4. List the major forms of public insurance and private insurance coverage.*

The federal government is an important source of insurance. In fact, over one-third of national government expenditures go for programs that provide insurance benefits of one kind or another.

FIGURE 20.3 Types
of Insurance Coverage

| Property | Losses due to destruction of or damage to property or possessions |
|---|---|
| Liability | Losses when the insured is legally liable for another's losses |
| Health | Losses arising out of illness or injury |
| Life | Losses which result from the insured's death, but payment is not based on indemnification |
| Income | Loss of income attributable to property loss or to health or disability; often a feature of property or health policies |

## Unemployment Insurance

Federal law and the laws of all fifty states make employers financially responsible when they lay off employees, and in some cases when they fire them. **Unemployment insurance** provides partial, temporary replacement income for eligible unemployed workers. A state payroll tax on employers funds the insurance program. The level of this tax varies. Employers with high rates of claims among their employees pay more than those with low rates. The state administers the program, but during periods of high unemployment the federal government offers supplemental benefits.

**unemployment insurance** insurance that provides partial, temporary replacement income for eligible unemployed workers

## Worker's Compensation

The state-administered insurance program that provides employees with protection from losses caused by injury or illness resulting from employment is called **worker's compensation.** In effect, worker's compensation is a form of **no-fault insurance,** an insurance program that compensates losses regardless of who, if anyone, is responsible for their occurrence. In the early part of this century, state legislatures devised worker's compensation systems as a means of avoiding suits against employers and as a way to see that employees received enough to live on. The program covers medical care, lost income, rehabilitation, and survivors' benefits. Worker's compensation usually covers not more than 75 percent of the worker's lost wages, but these benefits are tax free. The benefits cease when the employee returns to work.

**worker's compensation** a state-administered insurance program that provides employees with protection from losses caused by injury or illness resulting from employment

**no-fault insurance** an insurance program that compensates losses regardless of who, if anyone, is responsible for their occurrence

Whether an employer must buy worker's compensation insurance from the government or from a private insurer varies from state to state. Some states allow self-insurance. Premiums vary according to the safety of the industry in question and the employer's record of claims.

## Social Security

**Social Security Act of 1935** act that established the federal Old-Age Survivors, Disability, and Health Insurance (OASDHI) program that provides retirement, survivors', disability, and health insurance

Under the **Social Security Act of 1935,** the federal *Old-Age, Survivors, Disability, and Health Insurance (OASDHI)* program provides retirement, survivors', disability, and health insurance. The federal government spends more than $350 billion each year on the four major Social Security programs. The program is funded primarily through a payroll tax. In 1989, employers and employees each paid in 7.51 percent of the employee's first $48,000 in wages. In 1990, the rate increased to 7.65 percent. Self-employed workers pay both the employee and employer tax. The maximum dollar amount to which the rate applies is adjusted for inflation each year.[4] Figure 20.4 shows some changes in Social Security.

*Retirement Benefits* Retirement benefits are based on the covered worker's income during his or her years of employment. In 1989, the maximum

FIGURE 20.4  Changes in Social Security
Source: *Social Security Bulletin* 51, 11 (November 1988), p. 37.

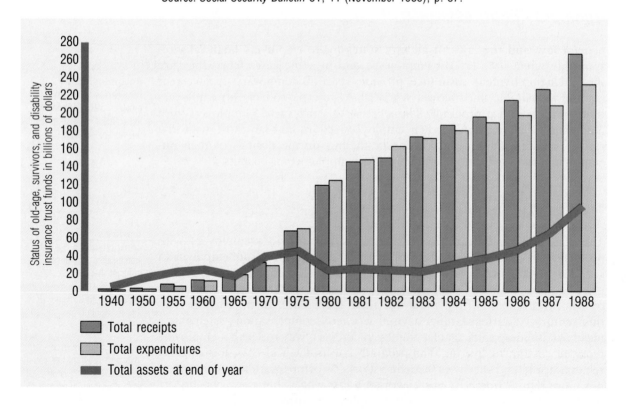

benefits were $899 per month. The benefits schedule is annually adjusted for inflation. Eligible retirees can begin receiving benefits at age 62, but they are permanently reduced a certain amount for each month before age 65 that the retiree elects to receive them. Late retirement—that is, after age 65— adds 3 percent per year to benefits. Starting in the year 2000, the full-benefit retirement age will gradually increase to 67.

*Survivors' Benefits*   Survivors of workers who paid Social Security taxes can collect these benefits if the worker dies before retirement. These benefits are a form of life insurance payable to the worker's spouse, dependent children, or dependent parents. Survivors' benefits can potentially reach $16,000 per year and last for fifteen years or more.

*Disability Benefits*   Totally disabled workers who have paid Social Security taxes, and their immediate families, can collect benefits if the disability is expected to last more than twelve months or until death. Like survivors' benefits, these benefits vary according to the worker's wages, the length of time worked, and the number of dependents.

*Medicare*   The federal health insurance program known as Medicare is for persons 65 or older, people of any age with permanent kidney failure, and certain disabled people. It provides both hospital and medical coverage.

## Other Types of Public Insurance

Federal and state governments offer many other insurance programs, such as the sampling that follows.

*Deposit Insurance*   As discussed in Chapter 17, federal and state agencies insure deposits in banks, thrift institutions, and credit unions.

*Mortgage Insurance*   Mortgage lenders always run the risk that their borrowers will default. To protect themselves, they often require borrowers to obtain mortgage insurance. Normally, borrowers buy a policy issued by an insurance company, but the federal government also issues insurance for eligible borrowers, through the Veterans Administration (VA) and the Federal Housing Administration (FHA).

*Flood Insurance*   Because floods are catastrophes, insurance companies have not offered insurance against losses caused by them. To fill this need, the National Flood Insurance Act of 1968 authorized the federal government to provide such insurance at subsidized rates.

*Crime Insurance*   Because of the high probability of losses, insurance companies do not like to write insurance against crime covering people and businesses located in high-crime areas. The federal government will step in to fill the gap if no private insurer will take the risk.

**More than it could chew** *We pay insurers money to assume risks for us. Insurers try to avoid taking on more risk than they feel they can afford. In drought-plagued 1988, Chubb received applications for $350 million in rain insurance—70 times the amount for which they wrote policies the preceding year.*

*Crop Insurance*   The Federal Crop Insurance Corporation sells crop insurance through the licensed agents of private insurers.

*Pension Insurance*   Until 1974, employees often lost their pension benefits if their employer filed for bankruptcy, went out of business, or simply terminated its pension plan. In that year, Congress enacted the **Employee Retirement Income Security Act (ERISA)**, which created the Pension Benefit Guaranty Corporation to guarantee pension plans.

**Employee Retirement Income Security Act (ERISA)**   act which created the Pension Benefit Guaranty Corporation to guarantee pension plans

# Private Insurance

The total spent on private insurance in the United States exceeds $286 billion each year, or more than $1,200 per person. Very little economic activity takes place without insurance to cover it. When NBC bought the rights to televise the Moscow Olympics in 1980, for instance, the network took out insurance coverage in case the United States did not field a team, which it decided not to do, in fact.

## Property and Liability Insurance

Property owners always run the risk that their property may be damaged or destroyed. A good-sized hurricane, for example, can easily cause $500 million in property damage. Property owners also run the risk that someone will hold them liable for injuries that occurred on or were caused by their property. In New Jersey, for instance, a bar can be liable if a patron drinks too much and causes an auto accident in which a third person is injured. Risks like these are covered by property and liability insurance. These two forms of insurance are distinctly different types, but insurers typically sell them together. See the various types of liability insurance in Table 20.1.

*Fire and Homeowner's Insurance*   Fires cause more than $7 billion in damage each year. *Fire insurance* protects the insured from losses to the covered property, considered usually to be both a building and its contents, that are caused by fire and, often, other perils such as hail and windstorms. The premiums on fire insurance vary according to the property's value, the type of building it is, the use the property is put to, the value of its contents, and other factors. Fire insurance policies often require extensive risk-reduction efforts, such as the installation of sprinkler systems and smoke alarms.

The maximum insurance claim paid is generally the actual cash value of the loss up to the policy limits. Many fire policies contain a **coinsurance**

**coinsurance**   a clause that requires the policyholder to pay a portion of any loss to an insured building if the policy maximum is less than a specified percentage of the building's value at the time of the loss

TABLE 20.1   Types of Liability Insurance

| Types | Coverage |
| --- | --- |
| *General liability* | Basic liability coverage for a firm; other types added to it. |
| *Owners', landlords', and tenants' (OLT)* | Losses suffered by individuals other than employees as a result of the firm's use of the premises it occupies. |
| *Manufacturers' and contractors' (M & C)* | Premises coverage plus coverage for off-premises activities. |
| *Comprehensive general liability* | Umbrella liability protection, including general liability, OLT, and G & C coverage. |
| *Product liability* | Losses suffered as a result of products sold by manufacturers, wholesalers, and retailers. |
| *Professional liability (malpractice)* | Losses arising out of the rendering of services by certain professionals. |

clause, however, which requires the policyholder to pay a portion of any loss to the insured building if the policy maximum is less than a specified percentage (usually 80 percent) of the building's value at the time of the loss. For example, suppose that J & J Construction owns a garage valued at $200,000. The policy covering it has a maximum of $120,000, with $1,000 deductible and an 80 percent coinsurance clause. Assume that a fire does $101,000 damage to the garage. To determine the insurer's liability to J & J, the formula is as follows:

$$\frac{\text{Policy maximum}}{(\text{Coverage \% required}) \times (\text{Property value})} \times (\text{Loss} - \text{Deductible}) = \text{Liability}$$

The insurer's liability to J & J would therefore be

$$\frac{\$120,000}{(.80) \times (\$200,000)} \times (\$101,000 - 1,000) = \text{Liability}$$

$$\frac{\$120,000}{\$160,000} \times \$100,000 = \$75,000$$

Thus, J & J will have to absorb a $26,000 loss ($101,000 − $75,000).

Many fire insurance policies feature **business interruption insurance**, a form of income insurance that protects a firm against lost earnings as the result of a fire or similar peril. It covers expenses like taxes and payrolls, which continue even though the business may be closed. Fire policies for the home are covered under **homeowner's insurance**, which often covers apartments as well as houses. These package policies include both property and liability protection.

*Automobile Insurance*  Insurance from property and liability losses arising from the ownership or operation of motor vehicles is *automobile insurance*. This type of insurance is usually a package containing four distinct forms of coverage. Table 20.2 outlines the coverage common to personal and family automobile policies. Normally, personal auto policies have a single maximum amount that would be paid for all liability arising from any one accident. Family policies, in contrast, usually contain separate limits, often expressed as "15/40/10," or the like. In this example, in one accident any person's injuries will be covered up to $15,000, all personal injuries will be covered up to $40,000, and all property damage will be covered up to $10,000.

Business auto policies are somewhat different. For one thing, liability coverage for bodily injury covers only nonemployees, because worker's compensation already covers employees. Also, a business auto policy usually has one overall limit on liability.

A major criticism of auto insurance over the years has been the need to determine who was at fault for an accident. Such determinations can result in expensive and time-consuming lawsuits. About one-half of the states have adopted some form of **no-fault automobile insurance**, which has two essential elements: direct payments regardless of fault from one's own insurance company under the medical payments/personal injury protection part of the policy and limitations on the right to sue. The most effective no-fault laws combine generous benefits under medical payments/personal injury protection

**business interruption insurance** a form of income insurance that protects a firm against lost earnings as the result of a fire or similar peril

**homeowner's insurance** a form of insurance that covers apartments as well as houses for both property and liability protection

**no-fault automobile insurance** insurance that permits direct payments regardless of fault from one's own insurance company under the medical payments/personal injury protection part of the policy and limitations on the right to sue

**TABLE 20.2    Family and Personal Automobile Policies**

| Policy Part | Type of Coverage | Person Covered | Property Covered |
|---|---|---|---|
| 1. | Liability insurance | Pays when the driver of the insured car is at fault and that person is the owner of the car or is driving with the permission of the owner. The insurance company may require that some drivers be excluded, however. | — |
| | Bodily injury liability | Passengers of other cars and pedestrians injured as a result of the accident. Passengers of the at-fault driver will be covered only if their losses exceed that covered in Part 2 (below). | — |
| | Property damage liability | — | Automobiles and other property damaged through the fault of the covered driver. |
| 2. | Medical payments insurance | The covered at-fault driver and his/her passengers. | — |
| 3. | Property damage insurance | — | The insured automobile. |
| | Collision | — | The insured automobile when damaged as a result of a collision or rollover caused by a covered driver. |
| | Comprehensive | — | The insured automobile and its contents when damaged as a result of fire, theft, windstorm, and other perils. |
| 4. | Uninsured/ underinsured motorists | Driver and passengers of insured car when bodily injuries are caused by an uninsured or underinsured motorist. | The insured automobile when losses are caused by an uninsured or underinsured motorist. |

with strong limitations on lawsuits. The least effective also allow generous benefits but place minimal limitations on lawsuits. This allows injured parties to collect from their own company and file a lawsuit against the other driver as well. This raises the cost of auto insurance for all.

Figure 20.5 compares fault and no-fault auto insurance.

*5. Describe the applications of insurance to business risks.*

*Business Liability Insurance*    As a result of new laws and court decisions, businesses are now legally responsible for a far greater scope of losses than they were even ten years ago. As we have seen, **liability insurance** is coverage against legal responsibility for another's losses. Table 20.1 listed the most

**liability insurance**
coverage against legal responsibility for another's losses

FIGURE 20.5 No-Fault versus Fault Insurance

Source: Adapted from Lawrence S. Clark & Peter D. Kinder, *Law and Business* (New York: McGraw-Hill, 1986), p. 617, Copyright 1986. Used by permission of the publisher.

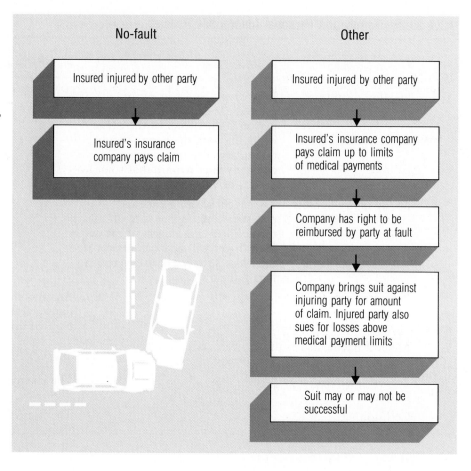

common general types. Virtually all liability policies also obligate the insurance company to provide a legal defense for the insured, up to the policy limits. If a lawsuit seeks more than the policy limits, the insured must pay for lawyers to defend against the excess liability.

*Malpractice* or **professional liability insurance** covers responsibility for losses arising out of professional services rendered by doctors, lawyers, accountants, and certain other professionals. A doctor who operates on a patient's left ear instead of the right or a lawyer who loses a client's money or an accountant who carelessly certifies a false financial statement would all be liable for their acts, and their insurers would have to pay. An explosion of litigation in this area has resulted in malpractice insurance's becoming extremely expensive.

**Product liability insurance** covers a manufacturer's or seller's responsibility for losses caused by goods placed in commerce. Makers of everything from football helmets to polio vaccines need to protect themselves against liability for injuries their products may cause. Chapter 22 explores product liability in more detail.

*Transportation (Marine) Insurance* That form of property insurance designed to protect goods as they are moved from place to place is called

**professional liability insurance** insurance that covers responsibility for losses arising out of professional services rendered by doctors, lawyers, accountants, and certain other professionals

**product liability insurance** insurance that covers a manufacturer's or seller's responsibility for losses caused by goods placed in commerce

*transportation insurance* or *marine insurance*. The insurance industry commonly refers to it as marine insurance, revealing its ancient function of insuring cargo shipped by sea. The first form of marine insurance appeared originally in Babylon over 2,000 years ago. Today, it comes in two types. *Inland marine insurance* covers cargo carried by every form of transportation not involving water. An inland marine policy would cover cargo carried on a space shuttle, for instance. *Ocean marine insurance* covers cargo carried on any body of water.

*Theft Insurance and Fidelity Bonds*    The general term for insurance covering losses resulting from the unlawful taking of property belonging to another is *theft insurance.* In a business context, theft insurance applies only to theft by nonemployees. Usually, but not always, theft insurance covers *robbery,*

Risk control    *Many companies are exceptionally susceptible to risk because of the nature of their business. Because Chiquita ships its bananas all over the world, exchange rates can effect profits. By taking advantage of Chicago Mercantile Exchange's currency features and options, the risks are greatly reduced.*

theft involving the threat or actual use of force, and *burglary*, theft from a building involving forcible entry into it. Theft insurance is often part of a property insurance package. A business can purchase robbery or burglary insurance separately or purchase an umbrella theft insurance policy that covers both kinds of loss.

Businesses that wish to insure themselves against theft by employees purchase **fidelity bonds**. For example, banks obtain fidelity bonds to cover their tellers so that the banks are protected against embezzlement.

*Surety Bonds*   On major construction projects, particularly those under government contracts, contractors must supply **surety bonds**, insurance policies that provide for compensation to the beneficiary should a contract not be completed on time.

*Title Insurance*   The purchaser of real property to which the seller did not have a clear or marketable title is insured against losses by **title insurance**. It protects the purchaser against the risk that he or she might not actually have legal ownership of the property. Banks usually require title insurance as a condition of a mortgage loan.

*Credit Insurance*   Insurance paid for by a borrower that compensates a lender for any losses if the borrower defaults is *credit insurance*. In theory, such insurance makes lenders willing to loan to less creditworthy borrowers or lend at lower rates. In practice, creditors often encourage or require borrowers to buy it because they receive a commission on the sale of it.

## Health Insurance

As Chapter 8 noted, *health insurance*, which reimburses expenses arising from illness or accident, costs employers more than $90 billion each year. Employees consider health insurance a vital benefit, given that national health-care expenses exceed $2,000 per person per year.[5] The health insurance that employers provide is sold to employees collectively, so it is called *group health insurance*. Premiums for group insurance policies are lower than for individual policies, because the risk is spread across a wider, often healthier group. The principal types of health insurance coverage can be bought separately, but they are most commonly sold together in what is called a comprehensive health insurance plan.

*Hospitalization*   The central element in virtually all health insurance policies is *hospitalization coverage*, insurance covering all expenses of being in a hospital except doctors' charges. The covered expenses usually include charges for the room, routine laboratory tests, basic drugs, and the like. Many policies set a maximum amount covered per day for a certain number of days, with any excess paid by the insured. This type of coverage is called *first-dollar coverage* because it pays, for example, the first $150 per day.

*Surgical Coverage*   Surgeons' and anesthesiologists' fees, surgical nurses' charges, operating room charges, and similar expenses are paid through

**High risks**  *Some workers routinely risk serious personal injury or even death. The right kind of insurance will cover medical expenses and even home mortgage payments during a period of recuperation.*

*surgical coverage.* Many insurers pay whatever is charged for surgery as long as it is "usual, customary, and reasonable." Other companies may set a maximum they will pay for particular procedures, like $1,200 for an appendectomy. In either case, it is first-dollar coverage.

*Medical Expenses*   Medical and doctor expenses other than those related to surgery are paid by *medical expense coverage.* These expenses may include office visits, X-rays, drugs, and the like. Medical expense coverage may be first-dollar with annual maximums, but more commonly it specifies an annual deductible or coinsurance percentage and annual per-item maximums.

*Major Medical Expense*   When a major illness or accident strikes, the types of health coverage we have just discussed often run out quickly. *Major medical expense coverage* reimburses a broad range of losses associated with major or catastrophic illnesses or injuries. The policy limits on this coverage can reach $100,000, and the deductible may be as high as $5,000. Coinsurance provisions are the standard 80/20, with the insured paying 20 percent, though there is usually a cap that establishes a maximum out-of-pocket payment by the insured.

*Dental and Vision*   Some health policies include dental and vision care. Coinsurance and deductible provisions are commonly part of such coverage.

*Disability Income Insurance*   Income lost as a result of an illness or injury can be replaced by *disability income insurance.* This coverage is sometimes included in health policies but is routinely sold separately. Disability benefits usually begin after a waiting period of from three to thirty days. The benefits replace between 50 and 70 percent of an employee's income, but they are not taxable.

## Health Maintenance Organizations

Until twenty years ago, private doctors and hospitals had no real competition for patient and insurance company dollars. Also, by that time advances in medical technology had led to the introduction of extraordinarily expensive treatments like coronary bypass surgery and million-dollar diagnostic tools like the CAT scanner. These increases brought about government cost-containment programs, which largely failed, and resulted in private efforts to cut medical costs. They also led to competition in the medical marketplace.

The most important competitor to develop was the **health maintenance organization (HMO)**, a prepaid health-care provider that operates clinics and, in some cases, hospitals. HMOs provide health care, not insurance. Their members pay a monthly fee (HMOs offer both individual and group plans) and receive almost unlimited care. If the HMO cannot provide the treatment a member needs, the member is referred to an outside provider, whom the HMO pays. HMOs tend to emphasize "wellness" and attention to good health practices as a way to reduce health-care expenses. The California-based Kaiser-Permanente program is the largest HMO in the country. To control health insurance expenditures, many employers have begun limiting health-care-related fringe benefit options to HMOs only.

# Life Insurance

There are five forms of life insurance. They differ on the period of their coverage and how, if any, the cash value builds. The forms of life insurance are term, whole life, limited life, endowment, and universal life. The latter four forms are referred to collectively as cash value life insurance.

Upon the death of an insured, *life insurance* pays a set amount to the policy's beneficiary. A **beneficiary** is the person or organization named to receive the proceeds from a life insurance policy. The key characteristic distinguishing life insurance from the other types of insurance is that the principle of indemnification is applied in a different way to the payment of benefits under life policies. As mentioned earlier, the amount to be paid is set at the inception of the policy rather than at the time of the loss. Insurance companies base their life insurance premiums on the experience represented by mortality tables. Thus, the price of the same amount of life insurance increases with the age of the insured. All other things being equal, a 40-year-old will pay more for fifty thousand dollars in life insurance than a 30-year-old. Other factors that enter into the calculation of premiums include the insured's health and whether he or she smokes.

## Term Life Insurance

The type of life insurance that pays the policy amount to the beneficiary only if the insured dies within the period covered by the last premium is known as **term life insurance**. It works much like automobile or health insurance in that regard. If the insured wishes to renew the policy, he or she must typically make a new contract with the insurer. Policies with a guaranteed renewability option are generally available and recommended, however.

6.Compare term life insurance with cash value life insurance.

## Cash Value Life Insurance

Cash value life insurance, sometimes referred to as whole life insurance, is a class of life insurance policies that requires premium payments on the insured's behalf until death or until the insured reaches a certain age. Upon the insured's death, no matter how long the policy has been in force, the insurer pays the value of the policy. Cash value life insurance has two characteristics that distinguish it from term insurance. First, it has a savings aspect. The insurer uses a portion of each premium for term insurance while investing the balance. The accumulation of funds and interest it earns is the policy's cash value or surrender value. Even if a policy lapses, or ends because the premiums are not paid, the insured is entitled to its cash value. Second, a cash value life policy is permanent. Once the policy is issued, it never has to be renewed and the premiums need never change, unlike those for term insurance, which change with each new contract. Its cash value and permanence features, however, make whole life much more expensive than term.

**cash value life insurance (whole life insurance)** a class of life insurance policies that requires premium payments on the insured's behalf until death or until the insured reaches a certain age

**cash value (surrender value)** the accumulation of funds and interest a policy earns

*Straight Life Insurance*    There is a form of cash value insurance, **straight life insurance**, that has the lowest relative premium per $1000 of permanent life insurance. The premium payments take place over the lifetime of the insured. Consequently, the cash surrender value is the lowest of the cash value policies. The face value of the policy is payable to the beneficiary upon the insured's death.

**straight life insurance** a form of cash value insurance that has the lowest relative premium per $1000 of permanent life insurance

*Limited-Pay Life Insurance*    One type of cash value insurance, **limited-pay life insurance**, allows premium payments to stop at some time before death. Two common types are "twenty pay life," which requires premiums for only twenty years, and "paid at sixty-five," which requires premiums until the age of 65. Cash values build rapidly to allow for the years when no premiums will be paid.

**limited-pay life insurance** a form of cash value insurance that allows premium payments to stop at some time before death

*Universal Life Insurance*    In recent years, many candidates for insurance have regarded term life as a better buy than cash value, because the rate of return on the cash value was less than they could obtain by investing the money themselves. Some insurers therefore began offering **universal life insurance**, a form of cash value insurance that combines term insurance with an investment plan guaranteeing higher rates than are usually available on cash value policies. When these policies were first introduced, the advertised returns often were considerably higher than the actual returns proved to be after commissions and other fees were deducted.

**universal life insurance** a form of cash value insurance that combines term insurance with an investment plan guaranteeing higher rates than are usually available on cash value policies

**endowment life insurance** form of insurance which provides for payment of the face amount either at the insured's death or at some specified time before the insured's death, whichever comes first

*Endowment Life Insurance*    Another form of cash value insurance, **endowment life insurance**, provides for payment of the face amount either at the insured's death or at some specified time before the insured's death, whichever comes first. The idea is to build up cash value so that if the insured does not die, the cash value will pay for, say, children's education or parents' retirement. Endowment policies are the most expensive policies.

## Business Uses of Life Insurance

**key person insurance**
a form of term life insurance designed to protect a business against the loss of vital employees

Businesses often purchase life insurance. In many cases, they buy group life insurance as a benefit for their employees. The employees, in this case, designate their beneficiaries. In other cases, businesses buy a form of term life insurance called **key person insurance** designed to protect themselves against the loss of vital employees, particularly those in upper management or ones who have crucial scientific or engineering expertise. Sometimes the coverage can be as high as $1 million.

Many partnerships and closely held corporations also buy life insurance. As Chapter 3 discussed, when a partner or shareholder in a closely held corporation dies, his or her heirs often do not want the business. What they want is the value of the decedent's interest. In anticipating this situation the partners or shareholders may agree to purchase specified amounts of life insurance on themselves so that their heirs can receive their money and the remaining partners and shareholders get the business. Such buy-sell agreements, which must appear in either the partnership agreement or the corporate articles or bylaws, should provide for regular appraisals of the business and adjustments in the amount of insurance so that the heirs do not feel cheated by what they receive (See Experiencing Business).

# The Debate over Insurance: A Perspective

National news magazines, the television networks, and every other information medium has regularly carried major stories about the crisis in liability insurance and the legislative proposals intended to cure it. The issues can be presented in a clear-cut manner. Greedy plaintiffs with trumped-up claims, abetted by unscrupulous lawyers, have squeezed the insurance system to a point where companies and municipalities with clean records cannot afford insurance. That is one point of view. Another is that, in an effort to capture greater market shares, the insurance companies lowered their insurability standards during the late 1970s and early 1980s so that they are now facing mounting claims on the bad risks they took on.

Because they oversimplify the situation, such arguments conceal an extremely important and highly complex problem. Let's take a brief look at one aspect of the insurance crisis.

As we saw in Chapter 2, until the early twentieth century the principles of laissez faire put the risk of buying defective goods primarily on the user or consumer. Today, much of the burden has shifted to sellers and manufacturers. For example, Jeanne Leichtamer Samples received a $2.2 million judgment against American Motors (AMC) for injuries she suffered when the jeep in which she was a passenger flipped over. Negligence by the driver caused the accident, but a defective roll bar, and this jeep model's tendency

# DEVELOPING A RISK MANAGEMENT PLAN FOR YOUR COMPANY

You have been the assistant to the Director of Manufacturing for a medium-sized firm that makes molded plastic household items, including plates, drinking glasses, eating utensils, and the like. Your company has grown to the point that it has become advantageous to set up a separate corporation to operate a warehouse facility for the parent firm. You have been selected to be the operations manager for the new firm. Initial plans call for a staff of three truck drivers to transport goods from the manufacturing plant in your firm's three trucks; six warehouse workers, including two forklift drivers; and an office staff of three individuals, including your assistant. You have been asked to develop a risk management plan for the new firm. What pure risks will the new firm face? What hazard reduction, loss reduction, and risk reduction efforts might you employ to address those risks? What other insurance needs might you have?

to roll over, probably increased the severity of Ms. Samples' injuries.[6]

Given the driver's negligence, should AMC have had any responsibility to Ms. Samples? Even thirty years ago, Ms. Samples could not have collected from AMC. Also, until the 1970s the insurance laws of most states would not have allowed her, as a guest in the vehicle, to recover from the driver either, unless she could prove extreme recklessness. These factors have caused courts and juries faced with people like Ms. Samples, who at twenty-one is permanently paralyzed from the waist down, to look to manufacturers and their insurers. The logic ran that large companies could spread the costs of injuries like hers across millions of customers. At one point, AMC faced claims exceeding $1.6 billion arising out of over five hundred similar lawsuits.

How many times and how much should a manufacturer have to pay for a defective design, assuming that the design was in fact faulty and did lead to injuries and deaths? One could argue that liability should be limited only by what the courts will award. What did the potential liability mean, though, for the jobs of those working at AMC, a company that after years of losing money had just crept into the black and was eventually bought out by Chrysler Corporation?

At the moment, society offers no alternatives to those who are injured except to file lawsuits against the manufacturers. Aside from the very rich, no one has the financial resources to cope with such seious injuries as spinal cord damage. Without an insurance system to pay for catastrophic nonfatal injuries, victims have a choice only between accepting impoverishment or hoping to win a lawsuit. If insurance paid for all victims' injuries, however, what mechanism would remain to force manufacturers to maintain high safety standards?

The debates raging about malpractice, automobile, and property insurance are every bit as complex as those about product liability insurance. As we have seen with product liability insurance, these debates are really about where responsibility belongs: to society, businesses, or individuals.

# CHAPTER HIGHLIGHTS

**1.** *Define the types of risk and describe the four main ways of handling risk.*

*Speculative risk* offers the potential for gain as well as loss. *Pure risk,* on the other hand, offers the potential for loss only. A business can handle risk through risk avoidance, risk assumption, risk reduction, and risk transfer.

**2.** *Define insurance and explain how insurance reduces risk.*

Insurance is a contract that reduces risk of loss and requires one party to pay a specified sum to another if a previously identified event occurs. Insurance reduces risk because the insured party exchanges an uncertain situation for the certainty of paying an insurance premium. Risk is also reduced for society as a whole because the insurance company applies the law of large numbers, which provides high accuracy in the predictions about losses caused by the insured-against event.

**3.** *Outline the four principles of insurance.*

The *law of large numbers* holds that as the number of units in a group increases, one can make more accurate and more certain predictions about the group. The *principle of indemnification* requires that an insurer pay an insured no more than the financial loss actually suffered. *Insurable risks,* those for which an insurance policy can be purchased, must be financial, measurable, and predictable. An *insurable interest* is one the person making the claim must have in the property or life insured. It keeps insurance from becoming a means of gambling on someone else's misfortune.

**4.** *List the major forms of public insurance and private insurance coverage.*

The major forms of public insurance are unemployment insurance, worker's compensation, and Social Security (Old-Age, Survivors, Disability, and Health Insurance). The primary categories of private insurance coverage are property and liability insurance, health insurance,

and life insurance. Property and liability insurance includes fire and homeowner's insurance, automobile insurance, business liability insurance, malpractice or professional insurance, and product liability insurance. It also includes transportation or marine insurance, theft insurance, and fidelity and surety bonds, as well as title and credit insurance. Health insurance generally consists of hospitalization, surgical, medical expenses, and major medical expenses coverage. It may also include dental and vision care coverage and disability income insurance. Life insurance may be term, cash value, limited-pay life, or universal life policies.

**5.** *Describe the applications of insurance to business risks.*

Businesses purchase property and liability insurance to protect themselves from the loss of their assets and from the loss of income produced by those assets. Liability insurance protects a business from claims against it. Public insurance offers important protection to the firm's employees. Health and life insurance, which are frequently offered as part of the employee benefits package, may be an important factor in attracting and retaining qualified workers. A business may also purchase key person insurance to protect itself from loss should a partner or a key manager die.

**6.** *Compare term life insurance with cash value life insurance.*

*Term life insurance* will pay the beneficiary a stated sum should the insured die during the term of the policy. At the end of the term, a new policy would then have to be taken out at a new premium rate. *Cash value life insurance,* on the other hand, lasts for the insured's entire life, unless the policy is canceled. Premiums continue until death or until a prespecified time and need not change over the life of the policy. In addition, cash value life policies build up a cash value and thus have a savings dimension to them.

# KEY TERMS

Risk
Speculative risk
Pure risk
Risk management
Risk manager
Property risks
Liability risks
Risk avoidance
Risk assumption
Insurers
Deductible
Risk transfer
Risk reduction
Insurance
Insured
Insurance policy
Law of large
  numbers

Self-insurance
Indemnification
Actual cash value
Insurable risks
Reinsurance
Insurable interest
Stock insurance
  companies
Mutual insurance
  companies
Unemployment
  insurance
Worker's
  compensation
No-fault insurance
Social Security Act of
  1935

Employee Retirement
  Income Security Act
  (ERISA)
Coinsurance
Business interruption
  insurance
Homeowner's insurance
No-fault automobile
  insurance
Liability insurance
Professional liability
  insurance
Product liability
  insurance
Fidelity bonds
Surety bonds
Title insurance

Health maintenance
  organization (HMO)
Beneficiary
Term life insurance
Cash value life
  insurance (whole life
  insurance)
Cash value (surrender
  value)
Straight life insurance
Limited-pay life
  insurance
Universal life insurance
Endowment life
  insurance
Key person insurance

# REVIEW QUESTIONS

1. What is risk and how is it different from odds or probability? How does speculative risk differ from pure risk?
2. What is risk management? Describe the four methods for handling risk that are available to the risk manager.
3. Define insurance and distinguish between its risk transfer and risk reduction characteristics.
4. Describe one risky situation that is insurable and one that is uninsurable. Why is the uninsurable risk uninsurable?
5. What is required for a firm to be able to engage in self-insurance?
6. Distinguish stock insurance companies from mutual insurance companies.
7. Describe the four major benefits provided under Social Security.
8. Discuss the liability risks faced by business firms and the insurance coverage programs available to reduce these risks.
9. What types of insurance should a business firm consider when seeking to reduce its risks from dishonest acts?
10. How does major medical insurance fit into an overall health insurance plan?
11. How is term life insurance different from cash value life insurance? What common points do they share?
12. Why should a business consider purchasing life insurance on its key employees? What special problems might life insurance solve for a small business that is not a sole proprietorship?

# APPLICATION EXERCISES

1. You are the general manager of a plant that does metal plating for other plants in your area that supply automobile manufacturers with small bolts, tubing, clips, and the like.

The plating processes you use rely on various hazardous chemicals and on heavy metals such as mercury, cadmium, and lead. Your state legislature is considering a bill that would require extensive disclosure of information to your employees of the health hazards resulting from working with these chemicals and metals. Given this information, respond to the following questions. What are some of the positives and negatives of this type of legislation? If enacted, how might this bill affect your worker's compensation plan, especially in terms of claims made and premiums charged? What risk reduction techniques might you use to soften the impact from this type of legislation?

2. Three small trucking companies with about 100 employees and 60 trucks each have recently merged. You have been hired as their first risk manager. During your first few weeks on the job, you realize that none of the three firms has ever really taken an adequate risk management approach to the risks they face. Thus, you see the need to develop a risk management plan for presentation to the board of directors, which consists of the previous three owners. What three risks would you present as most critical to the company? What risk management methods would you emphasize in your presentation? How might you include self-insurance in your analysis?

# CASES

## 20.1 The *Exxon Valdez* Disaster

On March 24, 1989, the oil supertanker *Exxon Valdez* collided with a reef near the south coast of Alaska, spilling 10.1 million gallons of oil into Prince William Sound. Within days, a flurry of debate erupted among Exxon, its insurers, environmentalists, local fishermen, the state of Alaska, and the U.S. government. The debate centered around attempts to assess the magnitude of the loss and responsibility (or depending on point of view, the blame) for the damage and the clean-up.

Fueling the debate were a number of factors that combined to make the spill an example of risk management at its worst, in the eyes of some observers. First, the ship was being piloted by the uncertified third mate. Second, the captain failed an alcohol breathalyzer test after the accident and had a history of driving a car under the influence of alcohol. Third, the ship and its cargo were virtually uninsured because of Exxon's policy deductibles. Fourth, the cost of the clean-up will not be known for years, if ever, because of the necessarily long-range impact on the environment and the Alaska fishing industry. Fifth, the clean-up effort appeared to

be slowly organized and implemented because of misunderstandings and miscommunications among those responsible for its implementation. Sixth, Exxon faces deductibles in the hundreds of millions of dollars for liability coverage (much of it provided by an Exxon captive insurer) related to the clean-up.

### Questions

1. What methods of risk management might have been applied by Exxon before the accident to minimize its losses?
2. What methods of risk management might have been applied by Exxon after the accident to minimize its losses?
3. On what grounds might Exxon's insurer attempt to deny coverage for this event?
4. What role should government play when events occur that exhaust the customary liability and insurance mechanisms?

For more information, see *Time*, April 17, 1989, pp. 56–66; *Business Insurance*, April 3, 1989, pp. 1, 45, 46; *Business Week*, April 17, 1989, p. 18; *Newsweek*, April 10, 1989, pp. 54–57.

## 20.2 Americans Face Rising Health Insurance Costs

By 1988, health-care expenditures in the United States topped $500 billion per year, representing over 11 percent of the gross national product. Corresponding figures for 1965 were $42 billion and 5.9 percent. The percentage of GNP is expected to rise to 13 percent by 1992. Per capita expenditures were over $2,000 in 1988. The cost of providing treatment to AIDS victims and the inevitable growth in the population of those over age 65 will add considerably to these figures through the end of the century.

As arresting as these figures are, they only begin to take on meaning when viewed in terms of who pays the bills. The single most important bill payer is the government, at 39.6 percent. Next is private insurance, with 31.4 percent, followed by direct patient payments, at 27.8 percent. Over 35 million Americans have no public or private health insurance coverage, however. And many others find, usually after an illness, that their coverage is woefully inadequate.

A major impact of these changes has been in the way employers have designed their group health-care fringe benefit plans. In 1984, 96 percent of these plans fit into the hospital/surgical/medical expense/major medical insurance format outlined in the chapter. By 1988, only 28 percent fit such a format. The basic coverages remained the same but were reformulated under the euphemism of "managed care." In other words, a worker is still insured for the same losses but his usage of health care is managed. Controls include requiring prior approval for hospital stays (implying that disapproval is possible), forced membership in an HMO, increased deductibles and coinsurance requirements, and strong incentives (through possible higher patient payments) to use preferred providers who give discounts to the employer and have agreed to the employers overseeing the type of care provided to patients. Of course, an employee does not need to agree to any of these restrictions if he or she wishes to pay for his or her own health care. Gone are the days when employers bought health insurance plans for their employees, allowing workers and their families access to virtually unlimited free health-care subject only to their own desires and that of their freely chosen physician.

### Questions

1. Are employers and the managers of the group health insurance plans they offer justified in their move toward managed health care? Explain.

2. What actions might patients take in the effort to bring the health-care expenditure explosion under control? How might higher deductibles and coinsurance requirements encourage such actions?

3. Government programs and employer-paid health insurance plans provide over 50 percent of the health-care financing in this country. What impact does this have on taxpayers and consumers?

For more information, see *Newsweek,* January 30, 1989, pp. 44–51; *Fortune,* September 26, 1988, pp. 145–150; *Business Insurance,* July 18, 1988, pp. 1, 61, 62; *Business Week,* September 26, 1988, pp. 66, 67.

# Business and Its Environment

*Approximately 600,000 Americans are lawyers, and many of them are working for business firms. Many of the laws that influence business operations are complex, and require legal interpretation. Firms that are involved in international trade must be familiar with the laws of the countries where they do business. Lawyers are also busy helping business firms cope with many government regulations. Business law is a major topic in Part VII. We will also describe government and business, and international business in this section.*

**PART SEVEN**

# 21 Business Law

LEARNING

OBJECTIVES

After you have completed this chapter, you will be able to do the following:

1. Identify each of the sources of U.S. law.

2. Describe the various ways we classify laws in the United States.

3. Describe the dispute-resolution system and the two principal alternatives to it.

4. Define tort and identify the classifications of torts.

5. Describe the forms a contract may take and list the elements of a contract.

6. Classify the types of property.

7. Describe the Uniform Commercial Code.

8. Classify the major types of bankruptcy proceedings and describe each.

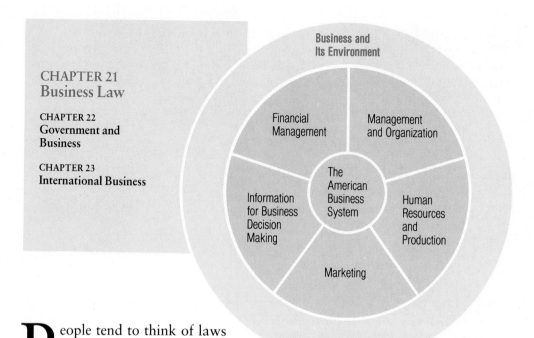

**CHAPTER 21**
Business Law

**CHAPTER 22**
Government and Business

**CHAPTER 23**
International Business

Business and Its Environment

Financial Management

Management and Organization

Information for Business Decision Making

The American Business System

Human Resources and Production

Marketing

P eople tend to think of laws as being permanent. They are by no means unchanging, however, and modifications in them have profound effects on individuals, businesses, and society. Consider the case of Lorena Weeks. In 1966 she had worked for the Southern Bell Telephone & Telegraph Company for nineteen years. Under her union's contract with the company, unionized employees had the right to bid on any job that came open. The job was to be awarded to the bidder with the most seniority who also met the job's qualifications. When a switchman's job opened, Ms. Weeks and a man with less seniority than she had both bid on it. According to the job description, a switchman had to maintain, test, and operate equipment in the telephone company's central office. Southern Bell rejected her bid solely because it had decided not to assign women to switchmen's jobs.

Ms. Weeks filed a complaint with the U.S. Civil Rights Commission. Three years, almost to the day, after she had bid on the job, a federal appeals court held that the company had unlawfully discriminated against her. The court based its decision on Title VII of the Civil Rights Act of 1964. That federal law, discussed in detail in Chapter 8, makes it unlawful for an employer to discriminate against an individual because of that person's sex.[1]

**preventive law** structuring operations to achieve goals and avoid legal problems by knowing what the law requires

Businesspeople need to know how the law affects their operations. Ideally, once they know what the law requires, they can structure their operations to achieve their goals and avoid legal problems. Business-law courses stress this perspective, which is called **preventive law**. For example, human resources personnel must be careful during hiring interviews to avoid questions about a woman's marital status and childbearing plans. Under most circumstances, such questions violate Title VII.

Businesspeople rightly understand that what they need to know about law is its practical aspects. Yet in order to make sense of what the law requires and to apply it to their affairs, they also need a working knowledge of how laws are made and how they have developed historically.

# The Sources of American Law

American law originates not only in each branch of government—legislative, executive, and judicial—but also at each level of government—federal, state, and local. Ultimately, of course, all laws must meet the test of the United States Constitution.

*1. Identify each of the sources of U.S. law.*

## The U.S. Constitution

It would be easy, but incorrect, to think of Title VII as being just another business regulation. Title VII also represents Congress's interpretation of its duties under the Fifth and Fourteenth Amendments to the Constitution.[2] The U.S. Constitution, dating from 1789, states in rather specific terms how the federal government is to be organized and what its legal relationships to the states and the people are to be. It lists in general terms the fundamental principles on which our society is based.

Ms. Weeks's case was one of the first decided under the Civil Rights Act of 1964. Today, cases like hers rarely come up. Society has largely accepted and incorporated the Civil Rights Act's goals into everyday life. Before the law changed in 1964, however, the courts would have rejected Ms. Weeks's claim of discrimination. Until that time, businesses and government agencies routinely barred women and minorities from certain types of jobs. Title VII of the Civil Rights Act forced all employers—at no little cost—to change their hiring practices. Against that cost, though, must be balanced the benefits to society of opening up jobs to new pools of talented individuals. More important, the Civil Rights Act brought the nation closer to the ideal of equal protection under the law for all citizens. These considerations are typical of those that Congress, state legislatures, county commissioners, and city councils must routinely weigh before making new laws within the context of already existing principles.

Our system works because our Constitution and the system of government it defines facilitate the interaction between our deeply held principles and the constantly changing circumstances of American life. In this chapter and the next, we will survey the major areas of American law that affect business.

## Statutes and the Common Law

The specific obligations imposed by government on the way business operates take the form of *statutes*, laws passed by Congress or state legislatures and signed by, respectively, the president or a state governor. Businesses routinely

Statutory law *Malcolm-Jamal Warner, known on* The Cosby Show *as Theo Huxtable, is more than just a real person. He is also a legal entity. For business purposes, he has incorporated. Malcolm's lawyers refer to him as Mal-Jam, Inc.*

**statutory**  the federal and state laws specifying obligations imposed by government on the way business operates

**administrative regulations**  the binding requirements designed by a government agency to accomplish the purposes of a specific statute

**common law**  the body of legal principles developed over centuries by judges in deciding cases

deal with statutes. The federal and state laws governing securities discussed in Chapter 17 are **statutory**. All tax laws are statutory, as are the laws permitting incorporation and those regulating environmental hazards. Statutes also authorize government agencies to issue **administrative regulations**, legally binding requirements designed by a government agency to accomplish the purposes of a specific statute. For example, Congress authorized the Occupational Safety & Health Administration (OSHA) to issue regulations covering workplace hazards. In the next chapter, we will take a close look at administrative regulations.

Another familiar form of the law is **common law**, a body of legal principles developed over centuries by judges in deciding cases. Where there is no statute by which to resolve a dispute, judges have to apply general principles to the specific facts of the particular case. Though the principles are not written down, the decisions are. These decisions, contained in reports and digests, become binding precedents.

Common law evolved in England from the thirteenth century onward and came to this continent with British colonists. Common law exists only at the state level, because the U.S. Constitution effectively limits federal laws to statutes and administrative regulations (see Figure 21.1). Every state has its own body of common law, which consists primarily of the law relating to contracts, torts, and property. (Louisiana is the sole exception, because of its legal roots in the French tradition.) It is important to note that constitutional amendments and statutes supersede common-law principles. As you will see, the Uniform Commercial Code, a statute, has replaced much of the common law of contracts as it applies to businesses.

## The Classification of Laws

There are several ways to classify laws, but the divisions that follow are the most common.

*Public Law and Private Law*  Duties imposed by governments to protect the rights of individuals or preserve social order are termed **public law**. In this country, public law is found in constitutions, statutes, and administrative regulations. It is never found in common law. By contrast, **private law** is law that defines the relationships between and among individuals and other nongovernmental entities like corporations (see Business Issues). Private law comes mainly in the form of statutes and common law.

*Criminal Law and Civil Law*  Statutes that specify the duties owed to society and that prescribe penalties like fines, imprisonment, or loss of life for violating them are called the **criminal law**. Of these laws, those involving

*2. Describe the various ways we classify laws in the United States.*

**public law**   the duties imposed by governments to protect the rights of individuals or preserve social order

**private law**   the law that defines the relationships between and among individuals and nongovernmental entities

**criminal law**   statutes that specify the duties owed to society and that prescribe penalties

FIGURE 21.1   Classification of Law

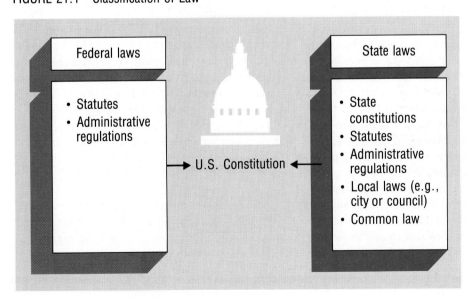

# VIDEO COMBAT

By most accounts the video-game business is no place for sweet, good-natured fun. If you are out to make some money, however, and if you like a good fight, this might be just the place for you. Nintendo, the superpower of the industry, with its hugely successful series of games of adventure and strategy such as "Adventures of Zelda" and "Mike Tyson's Punchout" controlled three-quarters of the $2.3 billion in U.S. video-game sales in 1988. Sales for 1989 were predicted to rise 50 percent, with Nintendo showing no signs of loosening its hold on the market. Frustrated competitors, notably Atari Games and a subsidiary, Tengen Inc., struggled to match Nintendo in the toy stores and also took the market leader to court.

The charge? Monopoly. Atari/Tengen claimed that Nintendo was practicing unfair restraint of trade.

The huge market share enjoyed by Nintendo would make it a monopoly in the eyes of the court. Most antitrust judgments, however, hinge not just on the size of a company's market share, but also on the methods by which a company maintains that market share. Atari/Tengen was not concerned with the utter dominance of the leader's hardware. What it wanted, and claimed it was not getting, was an unrestricted opportunity to create and sell compatible software.

Nintendo hardware incorporated a "lockout" chip, which prevented it from playing any but Nintendo software. That software was manufactured by Nintendo itself and by 39 software companies in the United States and Japan, licensed by Nintendo. Nintendo restricted both the number of games and the number of copies of each game that its licensees could market. The source of Nintendo's problems with Tengen, a licensee, lay in Tengen's impatience with its limited access to a booming market. Tengen circumvented Nintendo's rules and began marketing unauthorized software. It also went to court, screaming violation of antitrust laws.

In its defense, Nintendo argued that it was only doing what it had to do if it were to operate successfully. Lack of quality and market control, Nintendo claimed, were the reasons why the video-game business, which had achieved $3 billion in sales in the early 1980s, had collapsed to $100 million before Nintendo came along. The lockout chip and the short leash for its licensees were not monopolistic practices; they were simply good business.

Nintendo countered the Atari/Tengen suits with legal action of its own. It sued Tengen for breach of contract and patent and trademark infringement. It hinted darkly that, once the slings and arrows of its tiny competitors had been fought off, it would file infringement charges against retailers who carried Nintendo-compatible Tengen products.

The resolution of these and other suits against Nintendo is likely to take years. By then, some industry analysts suggest, the video-game craze may have faded. The gladiators may find that, while they fought, the fans left the coliseum. Hardly a suitable ending for a video contest.

---

Sources: Maria Shao, "There's a Rumble in the Video Arcade," *Business Week,* February 20, 1989, p. 37; Jerry Adler et al., "The Nintendo Kid," *Newsweek,* March 6, 1989, pp. 64–68; "Nintendo Prohibited from Suing Retailers," *Wall Street Journal,* March 7, 1989, p. A12; and Douglas A. McGill, "A Nintendo Labyrinth Filled with Lawyers, Not Dragons," *New York Times,* March 9, 1989, pp. A1, D23.

white-collar crime, like embezzlement or theft by computer, affect business the most. Still, criminal law has relatively little impact on business when compared to **civil law**, which simply is all law that is not classified as criminal law.

*Substantive Law and Procedural Law*   All laws are either substantive or procedural. **Substantive law** describes rights or duties. A seller's obligation to deliver goods that conform to his or her contract with a buyer is a matter of substantive law.

By contrast, **procedural laws** are the provisions in constitutions or statutes that describe how something is to be done by, or in relation to, government. If, for instance, a seller fails to deliver conforming goods, procedural laws define how—not on what grounds—the buyer might take the seller to court. As another example, when you apply for a driver's license, procedural laws list the steps that you and the Department of Motor Vehicles must each follow in filing and acting on the application. And when the legislature adopts a state budget, it must follow procedural laws. These three examples hint at the importance of procedural laws. In short, the "mere technicalities" that unsuccessful **litigants**—persons involved in lawsuits—often complain about are the procedural laws. Without these laws, we would have chaos, not a legal or a social system.

Procedural laws are virtually always written, so the law presumes that people have been given adequate notice of the requirements in them. Ignorance of the law is, in fact, no excuse. When it comes to getting a dog license or a title transferred on a car, an ordinary person can deal quite effectively with procedural requirements. For more complicated matters, coping with the procedural laws probably requires a lawyer's help.

# The Dispute-Resolution System

No society could function without a peaceful means for resolving disputes. The formal system must be regarded as a last resort, however. Preventive law principles dictate that everything that can be done to avoid disputes should be done. If a dispute arises, the **parties**—the people involved—should first do everything they can to resolve it themselves. Failing that, the parties may enter the **dispute-resolution system**, the structure that society has established for resolving differences. The idea of disputes immediately brings to mind the courts as a means of resolving them. The costs associated with litigation, or lawsuits, have soared over the last thirty years, however, and much effort has gone into devising alternatives to lengthy court actions.

## The State and Federal Court Systems

The federal government and each of the states have court systems. Figure 21.2 is a much-simplified diagram of the federal and state court systems. Each system is divided into trial courts and appellate courts.

**civil law**   all law that is not classified as criminal law

**substantive law**   law that describes rights or duties

**procedural laws**   the provisions in constitutions or statutes that describe how something is to be done by, or in relation to, government

**litigants**   the persons involved in lawsuits

**parties**   the people involved in a dispute

**dispute-resolution system**   the structure that society has established for resolving differences

*3. Describe the dispute-resolution system and the two principal alternatives to it.*

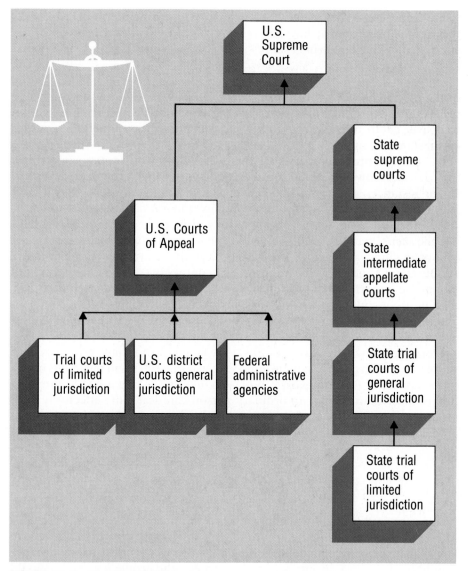

FIGURE 21.2   The Court System

Source: Illustration from *Business Law,* Fourth Edition, by Rate A. Powell, John R. Allison, and Robert A. Prentice. Copyright © 1989 by The Dryden Press, a division of Holt, Rinehart and Winston, Inc., reproduced by permission of the publisher.

*Trial Courts*   Litigation that does not begin in administrative agencies or commissions starts in the *trial courts.* Like our economic system, our system of dispute resolution rests on competition. If the two sides are allowed the chance to present their own version of the facts aggressively in a neutral forum, we believe that the truth will emerge. Because of this characteristic, our dispute-resolution institutions are called an *adversary system.*

At a trial both sides are permitted to present evidence. This may take the form of either (1) *testimonial* or (2) *real* or *demonstrative* evidence. For

**The dispute-resolution system** *Tiny Blue Mountain Arts, a Colorado-based greeting-card company, felt giant Hallmark was appropriating its ideas. Owners Susan Polis Schutz and Stephen Schutz took Hallmark to court, sued for a hefty sum, and won. Hallmark also had to buy back remaining cards from its outlets.*

example, in a dispute over whether the terms of an employment contract have been breached by the employer, witnesses may be called to testify that the employee failed to perform the duties for which he or she was hired. This is testimonial evidence. In addition to witnesses who will testify that he or she did in fact perform his or her duties, the employee will offer into evidence his or her own testimony because it speaks for itself.

Usually, both a judge and a jury hear the case. After all the evidence has been presented and the attorneys for each side have made closing arguments in which they try to persuade the jury that the facts favor their side, the judge instructs the jury on what the law is. The jury then decides what the facts really are, applies the law to the facts, and returns a verdict for one side or the other. If a judge alone hears a case, he or she makes both the findings of fact and the conclusions of law.

There are two types of trial courts. **Trial courts of general jurisdiction** can hear any matters that a trial court in its system has authority or **jurisdiction** to hear. In the federal system, such courts are called U.S. District Courts. In state systems, they have many names, including *superior courts, courts of common pleas, circuit courts,* and *district courts.* Both state and federal systems also have **trial courts of limited jurisdiction,** courts with authority to hear only particular types of cases or cases involving less than a certain dollar amount. In the state systems, the courts of this type that have the most impact on business are the small-claims courts—like Judge Wapner's *People's Court*—and the courts with names like *county court, municipal*

**trial courts of general jurisdiction** courts that can hear any matters that a trial court in its system has authority to hear

**jurisdiction** the authority that a court has to hear a particular matter

**trial courts of limited jurisdiction** courts with authority to hear only particular types of cases or cases involving less than a certain dollar amount

court, or *district court,* which hear only cases involving less than $10,000. In the federal system, these include the tax court and the bankruptcy courts.

In an important sense, all federal trial courts have limited jurisdiction. They are allowed to hear only the cases involving substantial questions of federal law or cases in which the parties on the two sides live in different states and the amount at issue exceeds $10,000. By contrast, state courts have the power to resolve any dispute, including those that a federal court might decide, unless the U.S. Constitution or a federal statute assigns jurisdiction exclusively to the federal courts. State courts regularly decide questions of federal statutory and constitutional law and disputes involving more than $10,000 between residents of different states. The Constitution assigns all cases involving treaties to the federal courts, however.

### Intermediate Appellate Courts

**appeal** the right to ask a higher court to review the record of the case for errors

**appellant** a person who appeals an adverse judgment by a court

**intermediate appellate courts** courts that hear appeals of trial-court decisions but are not the supreme court of their particular jurisdiction

**briefs** the written arguments relative to an issue

**affirm** the appellate court's approval of a trial court's judgment

**reverse** the appellate court's overturning of the trial court's judgment

In virtually all cases, the losing party in a trial-court case has a right to **appeal**, to ask a higher court to review the record of the case for errors in the trial court's interpretation and application of law. Which court an **appellant**, a person who appeals an adverse judgment by a court, may choose to appeal to depends on the court system. Some less populated states, like Nebraska, have only one appellate court, the supreme court. The federal court system and more than thirty states have **intermediate appellate courts**, courts that hear appeals of trial-court decisions but that are not the supreme court of their particular jurisdiction.

Appellate courts never listen to witnesses or accept new evidence. Rather, they look at what happened in the trial court, read the written arguments, called **briefs**, and listen to lawyers' oral presentations. Possibly weeks or months later, the judges will issue a written decision. Unless the trial court made an error of law that could have materially affected the case's outcome, the appellate court will normally approve or **affirm** the trial court's judgment. If the trial court made an error of law that might have materially affected the case's outcome, however, the appellate court will **reverse** or overturn the trial court's judgment. Only in the most extreme circumstances will an appellate court reverse a trial court's decision because of errors in its findings of fact. When an appellate court reverses a trial court's judgment, it returns the case to the trial court with instructions about what to do with the case. The trial court will often have to hold a new trial on some or all of the issues in the original trial.

### Supreme Courts

**supreme court** the highest appellate court in the court system

Every court system has a **supreme court**, the highest appellate court in an American court system. A state's supreme court is the ultimate authority on the state's law and constitution. As long as a state supreme court's decision does not touch on matters of federal law or the U.S. Constitution, the U.S. Supreme Court lacks jurisdiction to review the state decision. Where the case involves the interpretation of a federal statute or a provision of the federal constitution, however, the case may be appealed directly from the highest state court to the U.S. Supreme Court. In every system with intermediate appellate courts, the supreme court chooses the cases it will review. In the others, the supreme court hears all the cases appealed to it. The U.S. Supreme Court reviews only about 180 of the more than 3,000 cases appealed to it annually. In effect, in cases that a supreme court declines to review, the judgments are affirmed.

## The Importance of Judicial Review

The courts have the last word on the interpretation of a constitutional provision or a statute. When faced with a question of law, courts seek guidance in **precedents**, earlier decisions on similar or identical questions of law. Precedents are of two types. A persuasive precedent is a case decided by a court in any other judicial system except the U.S. Supreme Court. It is important to note that a court does not have to follow a persuasive precedent. By contrast, a binding precedent is a case decided by a higher court in the same system. Under the rule of **stare decisis**, a Latin term meaning literally "to stand by decisions," a court must follow a decision by a higher court in its own system or by the U.S. Supreme Court. *Stare decisis* is among the most important stabilizing factors in our legal system.

**precedents** earlier decisions on similar or identical questions of law

**stare decisis** a Latin term that means a court must literally follow a decision by a higher court in its own system or by the U.S. Supreme Court

## Alternative Dispute-Resolution Mechanisms

Perhaps the most common alternative to litigation is *arbitration*, a procedure in which the parties agree to submit a dispute to a third party and to be bound by that party's decision. Normally, a contract provision will require the submission of disputes involving it to the arbitration process. Construction contracts for complicated projects often have arbitration clauses, for example. And the sports pages regularly report the arbitration of salary disputes between professional athletes and their teams. Note that even if a contract does not require arbitration, the parties can agree to it.

Another alternative in dispute resolution is *mediation*, in which the parties agree to submit a dispute to a third party, the **mediator**, but are not bound by his or her recommendations. A mediator tries to bring the parties together.

**mediator** one who tries to bring parties together in a dispute

Finally, entrepreneurs are entering the dispute resolution business, competing in price with the judicial system. The wheel of retailing, discussed in Chapter 13, seems to work here, too! Some firms offer services in which they supply a retired judge to hear and decide a dispute that the parties have agreed to submit. Similarly, some corporations have staged private minitrials in front of their executives to resolve disputes.

# The Law of Torts

A **tort** is a legal wrong as defined by the common law. A legal wrong is one that causes an injury for which society has determined that the injured party deserves compensation from the party responsible for the injury. Suppose that Jane invites Ben for dinner at 7:00 P.M. sharp. He shows up at 8:00 P.M. and the dinner is ruined. Ben has indeed wronged Jane, but the law does not consider mere bad manners to be a legal wrong.

**tort** a legal wrong as defined by the common law

*4. Define* tort *and identify the classifications of torts.*

Over the last eight centuries or so, the common law has come to define the rights of people with which others may not interfere without being responsible, or **liable**, in **damages**, money paid to an injured party to compensate for the injury. The law of torts grew out of the need to prevent violence between parties and to compensate the injured party.

**liable** being held responsible because of interference with others' rights

**damages** monies paid to an injured party to compensate for the injury

# Intentional Torts

**intentional torts** acts for which the person who starts a lawsuit does not have to prove monetary loss in order to collect damages

**plaintiff** the person who starts a lawsuit

**defendant** the party against whom a lawsuit is brought

**intent** refers to a voluntary act or omission that is reasonably likely to bring about a particular consequence

The clearest indication of these ancient purposes comes in the class of torts called **intentional torts,** acts for which the **plaintiff,** the person who starts a lawsuit, does not have to prove a monetary loss in order to collect damages. These acts are ones the law regards as so serious that once the plaintiff proves that the act did in fact occur, the **defendant,** the party against whom the lawsuit is brought, is presumed to have intended its consequences. **Intent** here simply refers to a voluntary act or omission that is reasonably likely to bring about a particular consequence.

Retailers who arrest suspected shoplifters sometimes find themselves subjected to large damage awards for *false arrest,* the wrongful confinement or restraint of freedom of movement of someone. By contrast, a business could sue an employee who wrongfully took for personal use office supplies for *conversion,* the use of a person's property inconsistent with that person's ownership rights. Another common intentional tort is *fraud,* the intentional misrepresentation of the truth to convince someone to give up something of value. One of the largest jury verdicts in history came in a recent suit based on the intentional tort of *inducing breach of contract,* the act of convincing a person to violate an existing contractual duty. A Houston jury awarded Pennzoil over $11 billion because it decided that Texaco had convinced Getty Oil to abandon its agreement to sell to Pennzoil and to sell to Texaco instead.

# Negligence

There is a broad range of torts known as *negligence torts,* which do not require the plaintiff to prove that the defendant intended to commit them. Instead, the plaintiff must prove that the defendant had a duty to act with a certain degree of care but failed to do so. Suppose that a customer in a grocery store drops a jar of pickles that breaks. An employee cleans up the mess and mops the floor. Before the floor can dry, the plaintiff comes along, starts across the wet floor, slips, and falls. For the plaintiff to recover damages, he or she must prove that the store had a duty to keep patrons off the wet floor and that the store employee's conduct fell below the requirements of that duty. The plaintiff must also prove that actual harm occurred that can be calculated in terms of a dollar amount of damages.

*Strict Liability* Certain types of activity, such as the use of explosives or the keeping of wild animals, are so inherently dangerous that the law imposes *strict liability* for any injury that occurs, even if reasonable care was taken to prevent it. Thus, for example, no matter what precautions are taken, if someone is hurt at a construction site when dynamite is used the construction company or some agent involved in the activity will be held liable for the injury.

*Product Liability* The law takes a similar view, though for rather different reasons, of *product liability.* When products were few in number and simple in design, the consumer could be expected to discover any defect that might cause injury. As products have become specialized and complex, the responsibility for ensuring their safety has shifted to the manufacturer and retailer. Under the principles of product liability, the buyer may bring suit for any injury caused by a defect in the product.

# The Law of Contracts

The word *contract* may bring to mind the familiar multipage, single-spaced documents that no ordinary person seems able to read. There are, of course, contracts like that, but the contracts that fuel our economy are the ones we make every day in buying groceries, clothes, or a fast-food chain's hamburger. A **contract** is simply a promise or promises that the courts will enforce. Fortunately, the courts have to enforce only a minuscule percentage of the huge number of contracts made each year in the United States. Nonetheless, the principles of preventive law dictate that businesspeople should put all important contracts into a form that courts will readily enforce.

**contract** a promise or promises that the courts will enforce

## The Form of Contracts

In theory, all contracts are oral, and oral contracts are usually enforceable. A written contract just lists what the parties to the oral contract have promised. The promises and not the writing form the contract.

Oral contracts are enforceable, but written contracts are preferable. They reduce the possibility of disagreement and the courts give them great weight

*5. Describe the forms a contract may take and list the elements of a contract.*

Contracts *Pepsico, Inc., reaps handsome profits from its ownership of Pizza Hut, Kentucky Fried Chicken, and Taco Bell. The soft-drink manufacturer also sells a lot of Pepsi through these outlets. As provided in their contracts, the fast-food chains sell no other brand of cola.*

in a lawsuit. A written contract can consist of a sales slip, a notation on a check, or any other writing that evidences the promises that the parties made.

## The Elements of a Contract

The elements of a contract are the signs that a court looks for in deciding whether a contract is enforceable (see Experiencing Business). The five elements are:

1. Mutual assent
2. Consideration
3. Contractual capacity
4. Legal purposes
5. In writing, if required by law

*Mutual Assent*   All contracts must satisfy this equation:

$$\text{Offer} + \text{Acceptance} = \text{Mutual assent}$$

**offer** a proposal of what one party will or will not do in exchange for another party's act or promise

**offeror** the party making an offer

**offeree** the party receiving an offer

**acceptance** the offeree's agreement to the terms of an offer

**mutual assent** the parties' agreement on a contract's terms as expressed in the offer and acceptance

**consideration** something of legal value that each party agrees to exchange

**contractual capacity** the ability to understand the nature of a contract

An **offer** is a proposal of what one party will or will not do in exchange for the other party's act or promise. The party making the offer is the **offeror**, the party receiving the offer, the **offeree**. An **acceptance** is the offeree's agreement to the terms of the offer. **Mutual assent** is the parties' agreement on the contract's terms as expressed in the offer and acceptance. Normally, mutual assent consists of an exchange of promises. The offer may be, "I'll give you five dollars for your calculator." The acceptance may be simply, "Okay." Mutual assent is present; therefore, the contract is valid if the other elements of a contract are present too.

*Consideration*   In our example, note that each party's promise involved **consideration**, something of legal value that each party agrees to exchange. For a contract to be enforceable, one party's consideration need not be even approximately equal in value to the other's. If the considerations are grossly or absurdly unequal, however, a court may question whether mutual assent was really present.

*Contractual Capacity*   A party has **contractual capacity** if he or she has the ability to understand the nature of a contract. The mentally retarded and the infirm are among those presumed to lack this capacity. Some persons under eighteen lack contractual capacity in certain circumstances, but it is wrong to assume that they lack it in all situations.

*Legal Purposes*   Just as the law will not enforce a contract in which one of the parties lacks contractual capacity, the law will not enforce a contract that has an illegal purpose. For example, contracts for the sale of illegal drugs or agreements to pay gambling debts (even in Nevada) are not enforceable.

## HELPING RACHEL WILLIAMS WITH HER MODELING CONTRACT

Successful fashion models make very good money. The top models in the world, models like Paulina Porizkova and Christie Brinkley, make several million dollars a year. The agencies that represent these models, managing their bookings, coaching them, and even housing the younger ones, also make very good money. By charging clients such as *Vogue* 20 percent of the model's fee as a service charge and by retaining as a commission 15 to 20 percent of the model's fee, a big agency like Elite, whose models include Porizkova, Carol Alt, and Cindy Crawford, can earn over $40 million a year. Nevertheless a single star model represents a substantial amount of an agency's business, and when a rising star under contract to one agency switches to another, a substantial lawsuit can develop.

Rachel Williams, a six-foot-one, athletic blond, began modeling with the Click agency when she was seventeen. "I think I look like any tall blond girl," she says, "but apparently not. Everybody thinks I'm strong looking." Her "strong" look is special enough and Click's management sharp enough that within three years Williams was earning as much as $5,000 a day. She became a star; and her ad for Absolut-vodka, in which she appears clad in a shimmery minidress with the Absolut logo emblazoned on it, became a classic of recent advertising. When Williams notified Click that she had switched to the Ford agency, Click responded with an $11 million breach-of-contract suit against her and Ford.

Williams's contract with Click was a one-page agreement with only basic provisions about consent and commissions. One of the terms stated that the contract was for one year but would be automatically renewed without a signature if written notice were not given 90 days before the anniversary. The second anniversary passed without any exchange written or spoken between Williams and Click about the contract. Two weeks later Williams went to Ford.

Although a lot of money is involved, models and model agencies continue to use short, standard agreements of the type that is at issue in the Williams/Click lawsuit. What inadequacies do you see in this type of contract? Think about the legal elements of a contract—(1) assent; (2) consideration; (3) capacity; (4) legal purposes; (5) writing if necessary. If you were Rachel Williams, just starting out, what specifics would you want in your contract? If you were running the Click agency, what provisions would you add to make sure you could hold on to your next rising star?

Sources: Stephen O'Shea, "Role Models," *Elle*, June 1989, pp. 138–143; Michael Gross, "Those Lips, Those Eyebrows," *New York*, February 13, 1989, pp. 24–25; Dinah Prince, "Girl Crazy," *New York*, January 25, 1988, pp. 32–41; Armen Keteyian, "Follow That Girl," *New York*, March 6, 1989, pp. 38–41.

## *Relation to the Law of Agency*

The law of agency, discussed in Chapter 3, is an outgrowth of contract law. An **agent**, you may recall, is an individual who represents another. The other, the **principal**, can be another individual, a partnership, or a corporation.

**agent** an individual who represents another

**principal** an individual, partnership, or corporation represented by an agent

Agency relationships—and therefore an agent's authority—are always defined by contract. The law of partnerships, also discussed in Chapter 3, developed from the concept of agency. The relations between partners are thus also a matter of contract. By contrast, corporations are created under statutes. There is no such thing as a common-law corporation. A corporate charter or certificate of incorporation is a contract between the corporation and the state issuing it. A corporation's relationships with employees, vendors, and customers, however, are matters of contract negotiated by its agents.

# The Law of Property

**real property** land and everything attached to it

*6. Classify the types of property.*

**personal property** all property that is not either a fixture or real property

When parties make a contract, the subject is usually property. Property takes two forms. **Real property** is land and everything attached to it. A tree is part of real property; a condominium is real property; a garage or a barn is real property; built-in bookshelves are real property. Technically, the bookshelves are *fixtures,* personal property that is permanently attached to real property.

**Personal property** is all property that is not either a fixture or real property. Personal property is also of two types. *Tangible personal property* is property that one can touch, like a baseball, a book, furniture, jewelry, or a blouse. *Intangible personal property* is property that one cannot touch, like a share of stock or a bank account. In both these cases, the owner has something—a certificate or a bankbook—that represents the property but is not the property itself. Trademarks (discussed in Chapter 12), patents, and copyrights are other forms of intangible personal property. A *patent* is a seventeen-year monopoly granted by the federal government to exploit new processes, machines, or manufactured goods, or significant improvements to existing processes. A *copyright* is a monopoly granted by the federal government on the exploitation of literary or artistic works. The creator of the works holds the monopoly for his or her lifetime plus fifty years.

# The Uniform Commercial Code

**Uniform Commercial Code (UCC)** a body of statutes that replaces several areas of business law formerly covered individually by each state's common law of contracts

*7. Describe the Uniform Commercial Code.*

Any list of the great developments in American law would have near its top the adoption of the **Uniform Commercial Code (UCC)**, a body of statutes that replaces several areas of business law formerly covered individually by each state's common law of contracts. Every state except Louisiana has adopted most or all of the UCC. Doing business across state lines has thus now become quite stabilized. Table 21.1 lists the subject areas covered in the UCC, a few of the many topics the UCC covers.

## Sales

**goods** personal property that is both tangible and movable

Despite its name, the law of sales contained in UCC Article 2 covers only the sale of **goods,** personal property that is both tangible and movable. It

does not affect the sale of real property or of services, which are covered by common law or other statutes. Article 2 does not fundamentally alter the common-law contract concepts, but it does bring the details associated with those concepts into line with modern commercial practice.

*Warranties*    In one area, the UCC significantly changes the common law. Under this provision, a seller of goods makes certain **warranties**, guarantees or assurances. These warranties relate to the seller's title to the goods and to the satisfactory performance of the goods. Before the introduction of warranties, a buyer's only remedy for defective goods, if the seller would not voluntarily offer to make good, was a lawsuit for breach of contract. In such a suit, the buyer would have to prove precisely what representations the seller had made about the goods and establish that he or she had relied on these representations. Under the UCC, however, it is often the seller who must prove that he or she did not make the warranty in question.

**warranties**    guarantees or assurances

As its name implies, a *warranty of title* guarantees that the seller has the right to transfer to the buyer the title to the goods. When you buy a stereo,

TABLE 21.1    Topics Covered in the Uniform Commercial Code (UCC)

| | |
|---|---|
| Article 2 | Sales |
| Article 3 | Commercial Paper |
| Article 4 | Bank Deposits and Collections |
| Article 5 | Letters of Credit |
| Article 6 | Bulk Transfers |
| Article 7 | Warehouse Receipts, Bills of Lading, and Other Documents of Title |
| Article 8 | Investment Securities |
| Article 9 | Secured Transactions; Sales of Accounts and Chattel Paper |

*The statutes in the Uniform Commercial Code are divided topically into eleven articles. Three deal with definitional and procedural matters. The titles of the other eight articles are listed here.*

the store *warrants* its right to sell it. As for this warranty alone, courts virtually never allow a seller to protect itself against liability by means of a *disclaimer*, a refusal to make a warranty. A seller can disclaim almost all other warranties, though.

*Warranties of performance* guarantee that the goods will conform to certain standards. These warranties are of two sorts. An *express warranty* is an oral or written promise that the seller makes to the buyer. If a seller represents a certain car as being a 1985 Mustang, that is an express warranty. Suppose that instead the buyer plainly says, "This is a 1985 Mustang, isn't it?" If the seller does not contradict the statement, the buyer can accept the seller's silence as being an express warranty.

The second type of warranties of performance is *implied warranties*, or warranties imposed by Article 2 of the UCC rather than those created by a seller's representations. Implied warranties themselves fall into two classes. *Warranties of merchantability* are warranties, made only by merchants, that a product is fit for the ordinary purposes for which it is sold. A merchant who sells microwave ovens warrants them to be fit for use in cooking. It does not warrant that the oven is safe for drying pottery or clay statues.

The second class of implied warranties relates to *warranties of fitness for a particular purpose,* warranties made when a seller knows that a buyer is purchasing goods to be used in a certain way. Suppose that the sole proprietor of a small business describes the business's bookkeeping and word-processing needs to a salesperson. Then the proprietor buys the hardware and software that the salesperson recommends. If the goods are not sufficient for the business's needs, the computer store has breached its warranty of fitness for a particular purpose.

A federal fly in the ointment   *There are federal laws forbidding selling something for what it is not. There are also federal laws forbidding selling something for what it is. For some reason Avon's Skin So Soft products repel insects. Prohibited from saying so directly, Avon makes the point indirectly, through its advertising.*

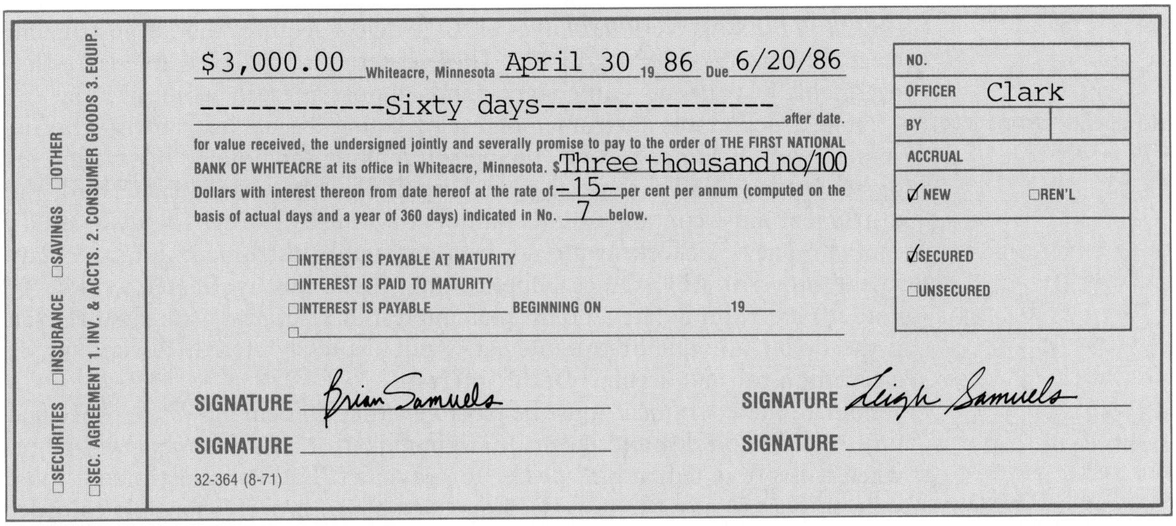
□SECURITIES □INSURANCE □SAVINGS □OTHER
□SEC. AGREEMENT 1. INV. & ACCTS. 2. CONSUMER GOODS 3. EQUIP.

$3,000.00 Whiteacre, Minnesota April 30 19 86 Due 6/20/86

------------Sixty days--------------- after date.

for value received, the undersigned jointly and severally promise to pay to the order of THE FIRST NATIONAL BANK OF WHITEACRE at its office in Whiteacre, Minnesota. $ Three thousand no/100 Dollars with interest thereon from date hereof at the rate of -15- per cent per annum (computed on the basis of actual days and a year of 360 days) indicated in No. 7 below.

□INTEREST IS PAYABLE AT MATURITY
□INTEREST IS PAID TO MATURITY
□INTEREST IS PAYABLE ______ BEGINNING ON ______ 19___
□

NO.
OFFICER Clark
BY
ACCRUAL
✓NEW □REN'L
✓SECURED
□UNSECURED

SIGNATURE Brian Samuels SIGNATURE Leigh Samuels
SIGNATURE SIGNATURE
32-364 (8-71)

FIGURE 21.3 A Note

Source: Reprinted by permission from *West's Business Law: Text and Cases,* Fourth Edition, by Kenneth W. Clarkson, et al., copyright © 1989 by West Publishing Company. All rights reserved.

## The Law of Negotiable Instruments

The UCC Article 2 law of sales probably has the greatest day-to-day impact on a business. Article 3 is in second place. Article 3 covers the law of **negotiable instruments**, written contracts containing a promise to pay money to one person who may then assign this right to another. Negotiable instruments function in effect as another form of currency. For this reason, the Federal Reserve includes them in its counting of the money supply, as we saw in Chapter 17.

**negotiable instruments** written contracts containing a promise to pay money to one person who may then assign this right to another

*Types of Negotiable Instruments* Negotiable instruments include promissory notes (Figure 21.3), checks (Figure 21.4), and certain types of warehouse receipts and bills of lading. The most important of these are notes and checks.

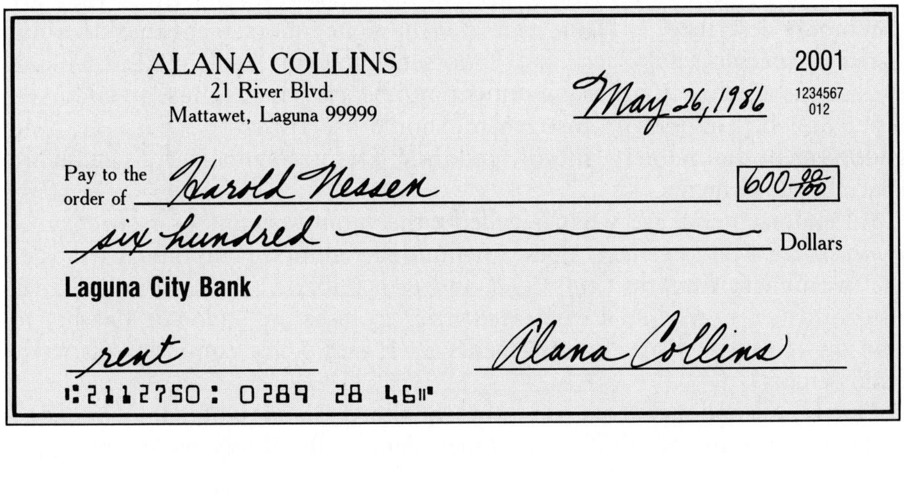
ALANA COLLINS
21 River Blvd.
Mattawet, Laguna 99999

2001
May 26, 1986
1234567
012

Pay to the order of Harold Nessen 600-00/100

six hundred —————— Dollars

Laguna City Bank

rent Alana Collins

⑆2112750⑆ 0289 28 461⑈

FIGURE 21.4 A Check

## Requirements for Negotiability

UCC Article 3 requires that an instrument meet six criteria to be negotiable. These criteria are designed to ensure that negotiable instruments can change hands almost as freely as money.

First, a negotiable instrument must of course be an **instrument**, that is, something in writing. Second, the person making the note or instructing his or her bank to pay the check must himself sign the instrument. Third, the instrument must contain an unconditional promise or order to pay a certain sum in money. A check would not be a negotiable instrument if it said, "Pay to the order of ABC Office Supplies only if the postage meter works." A note for a certain dollar amount plus interest at a set rate is negotiable even if the dollar amount of the interest is not expressly stated. A very simple calculation can put a value on the interest.

Fourth, the instrument must be payable either on demand or at a specified time. **Payable on demand** means that the maker of an instrument will pay it when it is presented to him or her for payment. Fifth, the instrument must state that it is "payable to order" or "payable to bearer." **Payable to order** on an instrument signifies that it can be transferred by means of an endorsement, discussed in the next section. An **endorsee**, the person to whom an instrument is endorsed, may demand payment. **Payable to bearer** means that anyone who has possession of the instrument may demand payment. Sixth, the front of the instrument must plainly show that it satisfies the five previous criteria.

An instrument that does not satisfy these criteria is not negotiable, but that does not mean it is worthless. Rather, it means that the rights that UCC Article 3 grants to persons to whom the instrument may be transferred do not apply. The instrument still remains a contract and may be enforced under either the common law or the law of sales.

## Endorsements

Whatever appears on the reverse side of an instrument has no effect on its negotiability. The front establishes that. What is on the reverse side, however, does affect how an instrument can be transferred. All instruments, except those payable to bearer, called *bearer instruments,* are transferred by **endorsement**, a notation, usually on the back of an instrument. Bearer instruments can be transferred simply by changing who is in possession of them.[3]

All endorsements are made either "in blank" or "specially," as they are commonly described. A *blank endorsement* is an endorsement that does not name a specific endorsee. Like endorsement 1 in Table 21.2, a blank endorsement turns an order instrument into bearer paper. Thus, an **endorser**, a person who endorses an instrument, should use a *special endorsement*, an endorsement that names a specific endorsee. Endorsements 2, 3, 5, and 6 are special endorsements.

All endorsements are what is called either nonrestrictive or restrictive. A *nonrestrictive endorsement* does not limit the endorsee's ability to transfer the instrument. Endorsements 1, 2, and 6 in Table 21.2 are nonrestrictive. In contrast, a *restrictive endorsement* tries to limit the endorsee's ability to transfer the instrument. Endorsements 3, 4, and 5 are common restrictive endorsements.

Finally, all endorsements are either qualified or unqualified. A *qualified endorsement* indicates that the endorser denies all liability under the rights

---

**instrument** something in writing

**payable on demand** means that the maker of an instrument will pay it when presented for payment

**payable to order** means that it can be transferred by means of an endorsement

**endorsee** the person to whom an instrument is endorsed

**payable to bearer** means that anyone who has possession of the instrument may demand payment

**endorsement** a notation required to permit the transfer of an instrument

**endorser** a person who endorses an instrument

TABLE 21.2    A Classification of Endorsements

| Endorsement | In Blank | Special | Restrictive | Nonrestrictive | Qualified | Unqualified |
|---|---|---|---|---|---|---|
| \|s\| Michael Manson | X | | | X | | X |
| Pay Susan Gray<br>\|s\| Michael Manson | | X | | X | | X |
| Pay Susan Gray only<br>\|s\| Michael Manson | | X | X | | | X |
| For deposit only<br>\|s\| Michael Manson | X | | X | | | X |
| Pay Susan Gray for<br>account of Robert Gray<br>\|s\| Michael Manson | | X | X | | | X |
| To Susan Gray,<br>without recourse<br>\|s\| Michael Manson | | X | | X | X | |

*Note:* The symbol |s| means "signed."
Source: From Lawrence S. Clark and Peter D. Kinder, *Law and Business* (New York: McGraw-Hill, 1986), p. 652. Copyright 1986. Used by permission of the publisher.

of subsequent holders of the instrument in the event that the instrument is not accepted or paid. Endorsement 6 in Table 21.2 is a qualified endorsement.

# The Law of Bankruptcy

Bankruptcy, whether your own or someone else's, is an ordinary risk of doing business. UCC Article 9, covering secured transactions, provides a first line of defense for creditors. A second line of defense commonly used by creditors of small businesses is to require the owners to cosign notes with their businesses. In the event of bankruptcy, the creditor therefore has a claim on the individual cosigner's personal assets as well as the business's.

The cosigner strategy is perfectly legal, but it defeats one of the goals of a bankruptcy proceeding: to give the **bankrupt**, the person or business in a bankruptcy proceeding, a clean slate to start over with. The other principal purpose is to give the creditors as much of what is owed them as possible.

**bankrupt** the person or business in a bankruptcy proceeding

## The Bankruptcy Code

Bankruptcy is a matter of federal law. The most recent revisions of the Bankruptcy Code, the Bankruptcy Reform Act of 1978 and the Bankruptcy Amendments of 1984, almost totally rewrote the law. Special federal bankruptcy courts hear such cases.

Proceedings under the bankruptcy statutes are commonly referred to by their chapter numbers in the Bankruptcy Code. The three most common types of proceedings are

*8. Classify the major types of bankruptcy proceedings and describe each.*

- Chapter 7: Straight bankruptcy or liquidation
- Chapter 11: Reorganization (mainly used for businesses)
- Chapter 13: Regular income plans (individuals only)

**discharged** when a business's debts are terminated

In Chapter 7 proceedings, the most common type, businesses are dissolved, their assets liquidated, and their debts **discharged** or terminated. Individuals emerge from Chapter 7 with a minimal amount of assets. Everything else is liquidated and paid to their creditors. Proceedings in Chapter 11 and Chapter 13 shield businesses and individuals from their creditors while they work out payment arrangements. The famous bankruptcy cases of the 1980s—the Manville Corporation, Continental Air Lines, and the A. H. Robins Manufacturing Company—were Chapter 11 proceedings (see Table 21.3).

## Bankruptcy Proceedings

Bankruptcy proceedings are either voluntary or involuntary. The bankrupt initiates voluntary proceedings, and creditors initiate involuntary proceedings. Normally, Chapter 13 proceedings are voluntary.

**creditors' committee** all of the bankrupt's creditors called together by the court to review the bankrupt's documentation of debts and assets and to elect a permanent trustee in bankruptcy

Once bankruptcy papers are filed, all bankruptcy proceedings follow essentially the same pattern (see Figure 21.5). The court will grant the bankrupt relief from the creditors' collection efforts, appoint an interim trustee to protect the bankrupt's assets, and order the creditors' committee to meet. The **creditors' committee** is simply all of the bankrupt's creditors called together by the court to review the bankrupt's documentation of his or her debts and assets and to elect a permanent trustee in bankruptcy. The permanent trustee's job is to protect the existing assets, sort out the liabilities, and rule on the validity of claims. If the bankrupt is an individual, the trustee segregates the assets that he or she may keep. Depending on the bankrupt's state of residence, for example, he or she may keep a vehicle worth up to $1,200, plus household goods, furnishings, and clothing totaling up to $4,000. What remains is distributed to creditors in the order of their priority

TABLE 21.3   Bankruptcy Filings, by Type of Business and Chapter: 1980–1986

|  | 1980 | 1981 | 1982 | 1983 | 1984 | 1985 | 1986 |
|---|---|---|---|---|---|---|---|
| **Total** | 277,880 | 360,329 | 367,866 | 374,734 | 344,275 | 364,536 | 477,856 |
| **Type** | | | | | | | |
| Business | 36,449 | 47,415 | 56,423 | 69,818 | 62,170 | 66,651 | 76,281 |
| Non-business | 241,431 | 312,914 | 311,443 | 304,916 | 282,105 | 297,885 | 401,575 |
| Voluntary | 276,691 | 358,997 | 366,331 | 373,064 | 342,828 | 362,939 | 476,214 |
| Involuntary | 1,189 | 1,332 | 1,535 | 1,670 | 1,447 | 1,597 | 1,642 |
| **Chapter** | | | | | | | |
| Chapter 7 | 214,357 | 265,721 | 255,098 | 251,322 | 232,994 | 244,650 | 332,679 |
| Chapter 11 | 5,302 | 7,828 | 14,059 | 21,207 | 19,913 | 21,425 | 24,443 |
| Chapter 13 | 58,216 | 86,778 | 98,705 | 102,201 | 91,358 | 98,452 | 120,726 |

Source: *Statistical Abstract of the United States* (Washington, D.C. Govt., 1988), p. 501, table 838.

*PART VII / BUSINESS AND ITS ENVIRONMENT*

FIGURE 21.5
Resolving a Bankruptcy

```
┌─────────────────────────┐              ┌─────────────────────────┐
│        Voluntary         │              │       Involuntary        │
│                          │              │                          │
│  Debtor may petition     │              │  Creditors bring legal   │
│  bankruptcy court        │              │  action against debtor   │
│  for bankrupt status     │              │                          │
│                          │              │  Debtor must answer      │
│                          │              │  creditors' charges      │
└─────────────────────────┘              └─────────────────────────┘
                    │                         │
                    ▼                         ▼
            ┌───────────────────────────────┐
            │  Creditors elect trustee(s)    │
            └───────────────────────────────┘
                           │
                           ▼
            ┌───────────────────────────────┐
            │  Trustee converts all          │
            │  assets to cash                │
            └───────────────────────────────┘
                           │
                           ▼
            ┌───────────────────────────────┐
            │  Resulting cash is used to pay │
            │  necessary expenditures and    │
            │  priority claims               │
            └───────────────────────────────┘
                           │
                           ▼
            ┌───────────────────────────────┐
            │  Remaining cash is distributed │
            │  to unsecured creditors        │
            └───────────────────────────────┘
```

as established by the Bankruptcy Code. Once the distributions are completed, the court discharges the debtor.

The court's discharge order ends the proceeding and the bankrupt's liability on all debts covered in it. The bankrupt's financial slate may still be far from clean, though. Some debts are **nondischargeable**, meaning not releasable in a bankruptcy proceeding. These debts include those that may be owed to the government in the form of taxes, fines, penalties, or—in most circumstances—educational loans. Judgments in tort actions based on a claim other than negligence are not dischargeable, either, nor are alimony, separate maintenance, and child-support payments.

**nondischargeable** when a debt is not releasable in a bankruptcy proceeding

# Business Law: A Perspective

It is often said that ours is a government of laws, not people. This saying accurately reflects the respect we share for the principles that govern us. Those principles and the laws that express them, however, apply to people

Liquidating assets   *A borrower went broke and so did his bank. In this way a half-century-old, motorless ferryboat fell into the hands of the Federal Deposit Insurance Corporation. Charged with settling the bank's debts and selling off its assets, the FDIC must pay upkeep on such items, while it searches for buyers.*

and are applied by people. Therefore, our political laws cannot be as inflexible as the physical laws, like $E = MC^2$. For the businessperson, preventive law is one more planning tool. The law makes predicting or structuring the outcome of transactions significantly easier. Still, the prudent businessperson will keep in mind the famous saying of our most practical philosopher, Benjamin Franklin: "In this world nothing is certain but death and taxes."

# *CHAPTER HIGHLIGHTS*

*1.* *Identify each of the sources of U.S. law.*

U.S. law originates in each branch of government—legislative, executive, and judicial—and at each level of government—federal, state, and local.

*2.* *Describe the various ways we classify laws in the United States.*

The three major divisions include public law and private law, criminal law and civil law, and substantive law and procedural law.

*3.* *Describe the dispute-resolution system and the two principal alternatives to it.*

The structure that society has established for resolving differences is called the *dispute-*

*resolution system.* This system includes trial courts, intermediate appellate courts, and supreme courts. The two major alternative dispute-resolution mechanisms include *arbitration* and *mediation.*

**4.** *Define* tort *and identify the classifications of torts.*

A *tort* is a legal wrong defined by the common law. A legal wrong is one that causes an injury for which society has determined the injured party deserves compensation from the party responsible for the injury. Torts are classified as *intentional torts, negligence, strict liability,* and *product liability.*

**5.** *Describe the forms a contract may take and list the elements of a contract.*

In simple terms, a *contract* is a promise or promises that the courts will enforce. Contracts may be in written or oral form. While oral contracts are enforceable, written contracts are often preferable because they reduce the possibility of disagreement. In case of lawsuit, the courts give a written contract greater weight in most instances. The elements of a contract are mutual assent, consideration, contractual capacity, legal purposes, and writing, if required by law.

**6.** *Classify the types of property.*

Property takes two forms. *Real property* is land and everything attached to it. A home, and the trees surrounding the house, are examples of real property. *Personal property* is all property that is not a fixture or real property. The suit you wear to work, the boat you take to the lake on weekends, and your bank account represent types of personal property.

**7.** *Describe the Uniform Commercial Code.*

The *Uniform Commercial Code* is a body of statutes that replaces several areas of business law formerly covered by each state's common law of contracts. It has been adopted by nearly every state, so doing business across state lines is now quite predictable.

**8.** *Classify the major types of bankruptcy proceedings and describe each.*

Proceedings under the bankruptcy statutes are commonly referred to by their chapter numbers in the Bankruptcy Code. Three of them are:
Chapter 7: Straight bankruptcy or liquidation
Chapter 11: Reorganization (mainly businesses)
Chapter 13: Regular income plans (individuals only)

# KEY TERMS

| | | | |
|---|---|---|---|
| Preventive law | Jurisdiction | Intentional torts | Uniform Commercial |
| Statutory | Trial courts of | Plaintiff | Code (UCC) |
| Administrative | limited jurisdiction | Defendant | Goods |
| regulations | Appeal | Intent | Warranties |
| Common law | Appellant | Contract | Negotiable instruments |
| Public law | Intermediate appel- | Offer | Instrument |
| Private law | late court | Offeror | Payable on demand |
| Criminal law | Briefs | Offeree | Payable to order |
| Civil law | Affirm | Acceptance | Endorsee |
| Substantive law | Reverse | Mutual assent | Payable to bearer |
| Procedural laws | Supreme court | Consideration | Endorsement |
| Litigants | Precedents | Contractual capacity | Endorser |
| Parties | *Stare decisis* | Agent | Bankrupt |
| Dispute-resolution | Mediator | Principal | Discharged |
| system | Tort | Real property | Creditors' committee |
| Trial courts of general | Liable | Personal property | Nondischargeable |
| jurisdiction | Damages | | |

# REVIEW QUESTIONS

1. What is preventive law?
2. Identify the sources of U.S. law. How do we classify U.S. law?
3. Describe the dispute-resolution system.
4. What is a tort? An intentional tort?
5. What is the Uniform Commercial Code? What are some of the topics it covers?
6. Describe the law of property.
7. Describe the law of negotiable instruments. What are the six requirements for their negotiability?
8. What is the best way to endorse checks made out to you?
9. What are the goals of a bankruptcy proceeding? List and describe three common chapter numbers in the Bankruptcy Code.
10. Why is it a mistake to consider personal bankruptcy an easy way out of excessive indebtedness?

# APPLICATION EXERCISES

1. As the owner of a small auto agency, you have decided to expand the service department. The new construction will cost approximately $75,000, according to a local building contractor who happens to be a close friend. Your lawyer has suggested that the details of the construction project be outlined in a contract. Should you follow the lawyer's advice? If a contract is to be prepared, what information will be required for a valid contract?

2. Prepare a list of four current court cases that involve business firms. What appear to be the major issues in each case? What steps could each business have taken, if any, to avoid legal action?

# CASES

## 21.1  Where There's Smoke, There's Fire

"I remember they used to be so glamorous," said Rose Cipollone about the women celebrities who graced the advertisements for L&M, her brand of cigarettes for years. "They always used to wear evening gowns." When these dreams clashed sharply with her own fatal bout with lung cancer, Mrs. Cipollone waged a battle with the tobacco industry which severely wounded some of America's most smoothly running and most profitable corporations.

Rose Cipollone filed suit against the Liggett Group Inc., Philip Morris Inc., and Lorillard, Inc., makers of the cigarettes she smoked. Her husband carried on the legal action after her death in 1984. The tobacco industry sent three dozen lawyers, backed by $75 million, into the battle. The Cipollone's lawyers, from relatively small firms with relatively small war chests, spent about $2 million. In 1988, a jury awarded Mr. Cipollone $400,000. Do these figures add up to a victory? Both sides say they do.

According to Marc Edell, the lead lawyer for the Cipollones, the case shattered the tobacco industry's image of invincibility. Before Cipollone, the manufacturers had never lost a health-related liability suit. As to the issue of profitability, Edell admits that the Cipollone case was a bust. He states that future successful suits are more likely to earn money for the lawyers who file them, however. Prying over 100,000 secret internal documents out of the tobacco companies was one of Edell's major expenses. These documents are now available at minimal expense.

And yet the tobacco companies continue to smile the whitest of smiles. Judgment was rendered against only one of the three firms, Liggett, and that on the narrow grounds that L&M filters were promoted as "Just What the Doctor Ordered." The award was made to Mr. Cipollone, rather than to the estate of Mrs. Cipollone, because she was deemed at least 50 percent responsible. The amount of the award was small change to a mega-million-dollar firm. And federal appeals courts have ruled that the health caution printed on every pack of cigarettes since 1966 frees the manufacturers from liability.

A related suit may support this projected confidence. In a Seattle case, an alcoholic couple sued Jim Beam Brands Co., makers of the bourbon they favored, for drinking-induced birth defects in their child. The jury decided in favor of the distiller.

## Questions

1. Tobacco and liquor companies argue against the inclusion of mandatory health cautions on their packages. Is this a wise strategy? Why or why not?
2. Does the Cipollone verdict pose a long-tem threat to the tobacco industry? Why or why not?

For more information see *Business Week,* June 27, 1988, pp. 32–33; *Newsweek,* June 27, 1988, p. 48; *Time,* June 27, 1988, pp. 48–50; *New York Times,* April 21, 1989, p. A12; and *Wall Street Journal,* May 18, 1989, p. C9.

## 21.2   A Bankruptcy in Health Care

The story of Maxicare is a story about an organization that bit off more than it could chew. Back in the days when it was the largest publicly traded health-maintenance organization in the United States, Maxicare negotiated a deal in an expansive move which proved to be too big for it to digest. In 1986 the stock of then robust Maxicare was selling for $28 a share. By the fall of 1988 the price had plummeted to 93 cents.

A fairy tale? A parable about the dangers of not looking before you leap? Analysts attribute the decline of Maxicare to its acquisition of HealthAmerica, another health-maintenance organization. The deal doubled Maxicare's size but plunged it into a $460 million debt, from which it seemed unable to emerge. Some experts maintain that Maxicare might have weathered the crisis if health-care costs had not surged and if the company had hired sufficient middle- and upper-level management to handle the larger operation. Others argue that HealthAmerica was not a healthful acquisition—that it represented assets with little or no real value.

Whatever the cause, Maxicare found itself unable to pay its debts. Creditors forced the company to sell off components to raise money. Maxicare still could not improve its financial picture. In March of 1989 it sought protection under Chapter 11 of federal bankruptcy law. At the time it filed, Maxicare had assets of $498.8 million and liabilities of $535.4 million. Most of its assets, however, were "goodwill." They reflected the prices Maxicare had paid for its acquisitions, but not the prices those acquisitions might bring if sold. The stock had dropped to below 19 cents a share.

Guarded from its past creditors, Maxicare set out to rebuild its reputation and its business. All new debts, the company promised, would be promptly paid. Its over 900,000 remaining subscribers would continue to be covered.

## Questions

1. The doctors expected to provide future health care to Maxicare subscribers were also creditors well back on the list of those to be paid under the Chapter 11 rules. Might this affect their willingness to work for Maxicare?
2. To satisfy its creditors before filing for Chapter 11, Maxicare had to sell off many of its more appealing assets. How would this affect the company's ability to recuperate? Should Maxicare have considered filing for Chapter 11 earlier? Why?

Sources: For more information see *U.S. News & World Report,* August 22, 1988, p. 45; *Wall Street Journal,* March 17, 1989, p. B12; *New York Times,* March 17, 1989, pp. D1–D2; *Wall Street Journal,* April 6, 1989, p. A20.

# 22 Government and Business

## LEARNING

## OBJECTIVES

After you have completed this chapter, you will be able to do the following:

**1.** Describe the three principal areas of government's relations with business.

**2.** Explain the origins and purposes of the antitrust laws.

**3.** Identify the two major prohibitions included in the Sherman Act.

**4.** Define the three restraints on trade forbidden by the Clayton Act.

**5.** List and describe the three forms of mergers.

**6.** Outline the Federal Trade Commission's role in policing the marketplace.

**7.** Describe the theory underlying environmental, health, and safety regulations.

**8.** Explain the various meanings of the term deregulation.

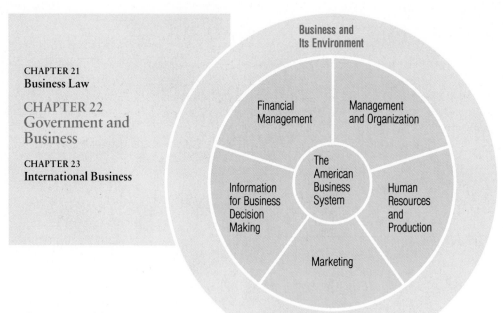

Business and
Its Environment

Financial
Management

Management
and Organization

The
American
Business
System

Information
for Business
Decision
Making

Human
Resources
and
Production

Marketing

The great humorist Will Rogers once noted, "The business of government is to keep the government out of business—that is, unless business needs government aid."[1] This saying no doubt has a familiar ring to persons associated with the American textile industry. In the early 1970s, the federal government aggressively implemented occupational health standards, which had a serious economic impact on many textile mills. One of these health standards limited the concentration of cotton dust allowable in the air because this contaminant had been associated with lung disease among textile workers.[2] To reduce the concentration of cotton dust in the air required remodeling plants and installing expensive equipment. Needless to say, this government involvement in business was not welcomed.

In the early 1980s, the American textile industry was struggling to compete with low-cost imports from many foreign countries. Some companies were able to reduce the size of their labor forces, but others had to close plants. Many textile executives voiced the need for government action to save the industry. They recommended, among other things, a series of tariffs on imported textiles. These tariffs would raise the price of imports, thus making them less attractive to consumers, the argument ran.

# Government's Roles

*1. Describe the three principal areas of government's relations with business.*

Government's relations with business can be described in terms of the three S's: subsidy, support, and supervision (Figure 22.1). As we look at each of these activities, keep in mind that they occur at all three levels of government: local, state, and federal.

## Subsidy

Imagine what our country would be like if private companies owned the highways and bridges. Suppose that each 5-mile segment belonged to a different company, which would make money by charging tolls on vehicles using its road segment or bridge. This system may sound ridiculous, but it existed in France until the 1880s and in parts of New England even until the 1920s. In this country, the question of whether government should fund the railroads, canals, and highways dominated the political agenda between 1789 and about 1850. Only the coming of railroads resolved the question in favor of government subsidy. In fact, government money and other assistance led to the construction of virtually all the railroads built west of the Appalachian Mountains.

Today, relatively few highways still have tolls, and government agencies oversee the maintenance of these roads. State and local governments assist business with financing and by giving tax breaks for new plants, like General Motors' Saturn auto plant in Tennessee. The federal government also subsidizes commercial space ventures by using NASA rockets and space shuttles. In addition, electric and gas companies receive special privileges to enable them to bring their services to homes and businesses. The list of subsidies seems endless.

## Support

Government at all levels offers tangible support to business. One important way in which government supports business is in its purchasing of private-sector goods and services. The government produces only a tiny proportion of the goods it uses, so it buys tons of paper, for example, from private suppliers. And in order to keep public payrolls lean, government units contract with businesses for a whole array of services ranging from computer maintenance to prison management.

FIGURE 22.1  Government's Role in Business

| Subsidy | Support | Supervision |
|---|---|---|
| 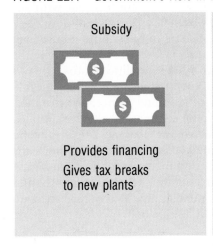 | 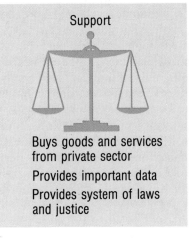 | 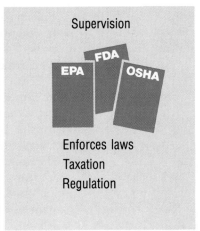 |
| Provides financing<br>Gives tax breaks to new plants | Buys goods and services from private sector<br>Provides important data<br>Provides system of laws and justice | Enforces laws<br>Taxation<br>Regulation |

**Government support** *When the government wanted a new airport in Ruidoso, New Mexico, it hired private businesses to do the work. Elf Aquitaine Applied Asphalt of St. Louis, Missouri, received the contract to lay the runways.*

Many of government's support services to business are less obvious than the financial subsidies. For instance, no major business does any long-term planning or market research that is not in some way influenced by data from the U.S. Department of Commerce and the U.S. Department of Labor. Likewise, in the mineral-producing states, federal and state agencies supply invaluable information about promising geological formations. And businesses that develop goods for the government can often apply the same technology to other, private-sector, products. Commercial jet aviation began with the Boeing 707, a modified version of a cargo plane that Boeing had developed for the Air Force. Farmers, the commercial fishing industry, and amusement parks, among many others, rely on weather forecasts supplied by the Department of Commerce that are based on NASA satellite photos.

Perhaps the most important support that government provides business—and, indeed, all citizens—is a stable system of laws and justice. For instance, the value to business of the predictability in the commercial climate supplied by the Uniform Commercial Code (discussed in Chapter 21) is beyond calculation. Commerce as we know it simply could not exist without the laws and constitutional amendments permitting incorporation (discussed in Chapter 3). And a system of courts and regulations (discussed in Chapter 21) protects American businesses from unfair competition by foreign companies.

## Supervision

It is far easier to complain about the burdens that government imposes in the form of regulation and taxation than it is to acknowledge the benefits that government provides. Like any other member of society, business finds its freedom of action limited by laws and regulations. Unlike the average citizen, however, businesses, and large ones in particular, have the ability to make their complaints heard. For the past fifteen years, business has complained about the heavy hand of government regulation. What is government regulation, and does it really harm business? These questions do not have simple answers.

The government regulation of business takes three forms (see Figure 22.2). First, business must observe the same laws that all other members of society must obey. The criminal laws apply to businesses and individuals alike. Corporations obviously cannot serve jail terms or suffer the death penalty, but their managers can. Prosecutors have become increasingly aggressive in their efforts to convict errant executives and managers. In one highly publicized recent case, a jury found certain executives of the Film Recovery Systems Corporation guilty of manslaughter in the death of a worker from cyanide poisoning on the job.[3]

The second form of government regulation is designed to encourage competition and keep the marketplace free of abusive practices. These laws

FIGURE 22.2   Government Regulation of Business

1890
Sherman Act
- Prohibits anything which restrains trade such as price fixing, and monopolies

1969
National Environmental Policy Act
- Expressed environmental concerns; forerunner to Environmental Protection Agency in 1970 which enforces air and water pollution legislation

1890   1900   1910   1920   1930   1940   1950   1960   1970

1914
Clayton Act
- Prevents restraints on trade by prohibiting tying arrangements, reciprocal-dealing arrangements, and exclusive-dealing arrangements
- Regulates mergers
- Prohibits interlocking directorates

1914
Federal Trade Commission Act
- Gives Federal Trade Commission power to enforce antitrust laws, and prevent any unfair trade practices not covered by earlier acts

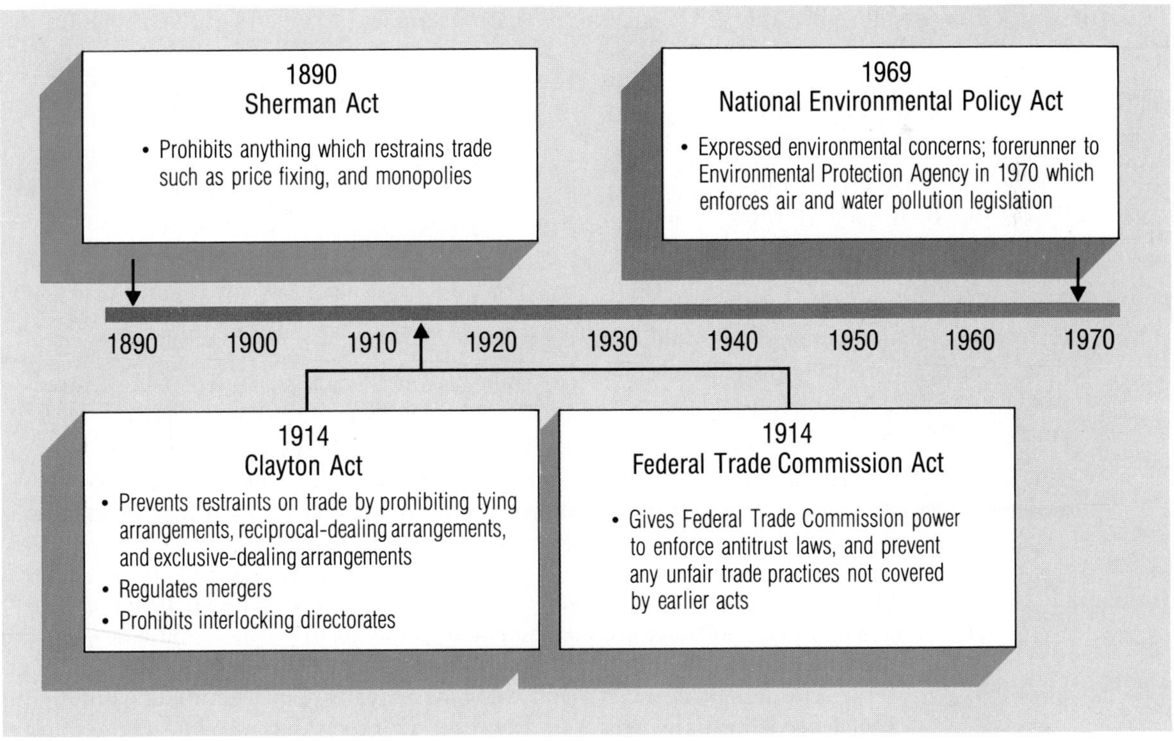

# HOW TO SELL GUNS

Politicians and media spokespeople pondering the rightness or wrongness of a product might do well to also consider the effects of their decisions on supply and demand. If they don't, they may find that their actions have unexpected consequences.

How else explain the smile that filled the face of Mark Pace, owner of Bama Gun and Pawn Shop? It was March of 1989. President Bush had just announced that he would ban the import of semiautomatic rifles. And Pace's sales of such guns was faster than ever. "I had them in corners and all over the place until the national press created the demand. What they have done is put one in everybody's home." Many buyers felt the need to justify their purchases, but they were making them nonetheless. Said a purchaser in line at a Georgia gun shop: "You have a lot of people like me out here who aren't fascists but are just afraid they won't have another chance to get these guns." Prices were up as much as 300 percent over a month earlier.

The basis for the President's decision seemed clear enough at the time. Because of the prevalence of semiautomatic weapons among drug dealers and other criminals, hospitals were now treating wounds virtually unknown except in wartime. Not long before his announcement, a man armed with a semiautomatic had gone on a well-publicized killing rampage. Foreign importers, who had brought just 4,000 of the weapons into the country in 1986, were requesting to bring in over 113,000 in just the first three months of 1989. Polls showed that close to three-quarters of the U.S. population favored banning semiautomatics. Politically, it seemed, the President, a long-time member of the National Rifle Association, had made a smart move.

Practically, at least in the short term, one might have questioned the President's declaration. It, together with an announcement by Colt Industries that the company would stop making the AR-15, civilian cousin to the famed military M-16, created the illusion of a coming shortage. In fact, a temporary ban on importing semiautomatics was not likely, in itself, to have had a significant immediate impact on supply. Retail outlets were well stocked. Only a third of all semiautomatics sold in the United States were imported. Domestic manufacturers, this having been a time of relative peace, could presumably have filled any gap in demand. And Colt Industries, while still at the heart of the legend of the semiautomatic, had diversified away from gun manufacture. By March of 1989 it controlled no more than 5 percent of the domestic semiautomatic market.

Sources: Kirk Johnson, "Past Associations Tied to Colt's Abandonment of Semiautomatics," *The New York Times*, March 17, 1989, p. A18; Ronald Smothers, "Assault Rifles Selling Like Hot Stocks, Stores Say," *The New York Times*, March 17, 1989, p. A1; Jacob V. Lamar, "Gunning for Assault Rifles," *Time*, March 27, 1989, p. 39; and "Lock and Load for the Gunfight of '89," *U.S. News & World Report*, March 27, 1989, p. 9.

fall into the two broad categories of antitrust and consumer protection.

The third form includes all the government regulations designed to achieve the results that an unfettered free market will not produce. Under free enterprise, the market mechanism works wonderfully in meeting consumer and social needs in many areas. In areas like worker safety, however, the market mechanism does not provide enough encouragement to guarantee that there will be at least minimally safe conditions in all workplaces. Virtually all occupational health and safety, equal employment, labor, environmental, and public-health regulations fall into this category. The first three of these areas were covered in Parts 2 and 3. We will discuss environmental and public-health regulations later in this chapter (see Business Issues).

# The Antitrust Laws: Regulations Promoting Competition

One of the most important governmental regulatory functions is the encouragement of fair and open competition. The marketplace would seem not to need this help, but, as the free market's great apostle Adam Smith noted, "People of the same trade seldom meet together, even for merriment and diversion, but the conversation ends in a conspiracy against the public, or in some contrivance to raise prices."[4] What Smith observed in England in 1776 proved prophetic of late nineteenth- and early twentieth-century America. Society's response took the form of what are now called the antitrust laws.

## The Nature of the Antitrust Laws

The antitrust laws are misnamed—they should be called the procompetition laws. Most states have their own antitrust laws, but they are of limited scope and for the most part, they duplicate the federal laws. We will therefore discuss only the federal statutes.

*Antitrust* means literally "against trust." In the context of the late nineteenth century, a trust was a legal device designed to get around certain restrictions on the ownership of corporations. These restrictions disappeared in the 1880s and 1890s, but the name *trust* remained as a term to describe giant industrial and natural-resource consortiums that attempted to absorb or destroy all other companies in their markets. Once a trust controlled a market, it was free to charge what it wanted for its goods, as John D. Rockefeller's Standard Oil Company did. What was worse, it could use its economic power to make or break businesses that relied on its commodity. Sometimes one trust even had enough power to break another.

*2. Explain the origins and purposes of the antitrust laws.*

## The Sherman Act

The first federal legislation aimed at controlling trusts was the **Sherman Act** of 1890, named for its sponsor Senator John Sherman. The Sherman Act contains two broad prohibitions. Section 1 declares illegal "every contract, combination in the form of trust or otherwise, or conspiracy in restraint of trade or commerce. . . ." Section 2 prohibits the wrongful acquiring of a monopoly, attempting to monopolize, and conspiring to monopolize.

**Sherman Act** the first federal legislation aimed at controlling trusts

*3. Identify the two major prohibitions included in the Sherman Act.*

## Restraints of Trade

The restraints of trade and commerce targeted by the Sherman Act include price fixing, allocation of markets among competitors, boycotts, and certain types of monopolies.

**price fixing** an agreement between two or more parties on the prices to be charged for goods

**Price fixing** is an agreement between two or more parties on the prices to be charged for goods. Such agreements, whether explicit or implicit, can have no other purpose but to limit competition. The government has only to prove that the forbidden conduct actually occurred; there is no defense for the conduct. Such antitrust violations are called **per se violations**. Agreements to fix prices may be between competitors or between a buyer and a seller. If a seller requires a buyer to agree to charge not less than a certain amount for a product when it is resold, the seller has violated the Sherman Act.

**per se violation** when the government has only to prove that forbidden antitrust conduct has actually occurred

**market allocations** agreements to divide markets among potential competitors

**Market allocations** are agreements to divide markets among potential competitors. **Horizontal market allocation** is the division of a market among independent competitors. It is a per se violation of the Sherman Act. Suppose, for example, that the Widget Corporation, International Widgets, and Widgets, Ltd., agree to divide the California market for industrial widgets. Their agreement would limit the number of sellers from which buyers could choose, leaving buyers with only a "take it or leave it" option.

**horizonal market allocation** the division of a market among independent competitors

**vertical market allocation** the division of a market among related entities

By contrast, **vertical market allocation** is the division of a market among related entities, like franchisees or subsidiaries. Such allocations may or may not be violations of the Sherman Act. The courts apply to these allocations what is called a **rule-of-reason standard**, meaning that the defendant in an antitrust case is given the opportunity to prove that the conduct does not unreasonably restrict trade. For example, if our widget companies were all franchisees of Worldwide Widgets, which had divided California among them, a court would probably not find a violation. There would be no horizontal market allocation because the franchisees would still have to compete against other businesses selling widgets.

**rule-of-reason standard** the defendant in an antitrust case is given the opportunity to prove that the conduct does not unreasonably restrict trade

**boycott** an agreement among competitors not to sell to or buy from a particular entity

A **boycott** is an agreement among competitors not to sell to or buy from a particular entity. It is a per se violation of the Sherman Act.

## Monopolies

**monopoly** the power to control prices and exclude competition

"A **monopoly** is the power to control prices and exclude competition."[5] Monopoly violations are particularly hard to prove. They are rule-of-reason offenses, which require highly sophisticated economic and demographic analyses. One type of monopoly violation is relatively easy to prove, though. **Predatory pricing** is an abuse of monopoly power involving the pricing of products in such a way as to eliminate competition. Suppose that B. C. Bowling Balls has been the only source of balls for miniature bowling until A. D. Bowling Balls decides to enter the market. When B. C. hears the news, it drops its prices to below its costs to prevent A. D. from successfully entering the market. A company that has a legal monopoly violates the Sherman Act if it tries to keep its monopoly by preventing another company from entering the market.

**predatory pricing** an abuse of monopoly power involving the pricing of products in such a way as to eliminate competition

Some monopolies are completely legal and even socially desirable. Suppose that B. C. Bowling Balls had acquired its monopoly as a result of simply staying in the field after its competitors had dropped out, for one reason or another. B. C. would then have acquired a **natural monopoly**, a monopoly acquired as a result of market forces, without violating the antitrust laws. In some instances, statutes and even the U.S. Constitution allow the granting

**natural monopoly** a monopoly acquired as a result of market forces

of monopolies. As noted in Chapter 3, public utilities have monopolies in their service areas because having, say, natural-gas companies compete for residential service would be inefficient. Another example of allowed monopolies, copyrights and patents, which are authorized by the U.S. Constitution, give their holders monopolies on the benefits derived from creative works or inventions. Without such monopolies, people would have little incentive to create or innovate.

## The Clayton Act

The **Clayton Act** (1914) broadened the scope of the Sherman Act by trying to prevent anticompetitive behavior rather than by dealing with its consequences.

*Preventing Restraints on Trade*    The Clayton Act focuses on three devices—tying arrangements, reciprocal-dealing arrangements, and exclusive-dealing arrangements—that can lessen competition or lead to the gaining of monopoly power.

A **tying arrangement** results when the seller agrees to sell a product that the buyer wants (the *tying* product) only if the buyer also purchases another product that the buyer does not want (the *tied* product). Suppose that the Nadir Corporation is the sole source for left-handed sky hooks. Nadir decides to sell sky hooks only to buyers who also agree to buy certain quantities of widgets. Nadir has thus committed a per se violation of the Clayton Act. Note that a tying arrangement violates the Clayton Act only if the seller has so much power in the market that the buyer will buy the tying product without regard for what else it must buy to get what it wants. If the buyer has the choice of an adequate substitute elsewhere, the seller's conduct does not violate the Clayton Act.

A **reciprocal-dealing arrangement** occurs when a buyer can force a seller to buy something from it as a condition of the buyer's making the purchase. A reciprocal-dealing arrangement is, of course, the opposite of a tying arrangement. Now it is the buyer's market power that forces a seller to buy what it does not want.

An **exclusive-dealing arrangement** is an agreement by one party to sell all its output of a certain product to the other party, or to buy all it requires of a product from that party, in exchange for that party's promise not to engage in similar transactions with anyone else. These cases are enormously technical and complicated, and there are many exceptions to the general rule against exclusive-dealing arrangements.

*Regulating Mergers*    Section 7 of the Clayton Act prohibits mergers that "substantially lessen competition." A **merger** is one company's acquisition and absorption of another.

Mergers take one of three forms (see Figure 22.3). A **vertical merger** is a merger of two companies in the same chain of supply. For instance, if Coca-Cola acquires an independently owned Coca-Cola bottler, a vertical merger

**Clayton Act** broadened the scope of the Sherman Act by trying to prevent anti-competitive behavior rather than by dealing with its consequences

*4. Define the three restraints on trade forbidden by the Clayton Act.*

**tying arrangement** results when the seller agrees to sell a product that the buyer wants only if the buyer also purchases another product that the buyer does not want

**reciprocal-dealing arrangement** occurs when a buyer can force a seller to buy something from it as a condition of the buyer's making the purchase

**exclusive-dealing arrangement** an agreement by one party to sell all its output of a certain product to the other party, or to buy all it requires of a product from that party, in exchange for that party's promise not to engage in similar transactions with anyone else

**merger** one company's acquisition and absorption of another

**vertical merger** a merger of two companies in the same chain of supply

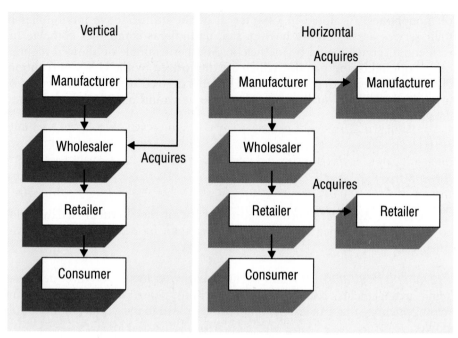

FIGURE 22.3   Forms of Mergers

**horizontal merger**
the merging of two competitors

**conglomerate mergers**
the acquisition of companies in different markets

*5. List and describe the three forms of mergers.*

**interlocking directorates**
the presence of the same individual on the boards of two companies that are in similar product markets if the combined total capital of the two companies exceeds $1 million

has occurred. A **horizontal merger** occurs when two competitors merge. Horizontal mergers are of special concern to regulators. **Conglomerate mergers**, by contrast, are of little concern to government regulators because they involve the acquisition of companies in different markets. For example, the nation's leading seller of bathroom fixtures, American Standard, once owned American Bank Stationery and Mosler Safe, two businesses unrelated to its main business.

The government regulates mergers because they may remove competitors, or at least potential competitors, from the marketplace. In recent years, the government has taken a very relaxed attitude toward mergers. Because lawsuits can often take a decade or more to resolve, the Clayton Act authorizes the government to issue merger guidelines specifying the permissible boundaries. Since 1976, when Congress passed the Hart-Scott-Radino Antitrust Improvements Act, acquiring firms with assets exceeding $100 million have had to submit proposed mergers for government clearance before they can take place.

*Interlocking Directorates*   The Clayton Act also prohibits **interlocking directorates**, the presence of the same individual on the boards of two companies that are in similar product markets if the combined total capital of the two companies exceeds $1 million (see Figure 22.4). A person sitting on the boards of two competing companies could easily give information about one to the other, with serious anticompetitive results.

## The Robinson-Patman Act

The Robinson-Patman Act bans **price discrimination**, the sale of goods at different prices by a commercial seller to two or more nonretail buyers. The law's goal is to prevent large buyers from obtaining price advantages over small ones. Thus, a shaving-cream manufacturer must sell its product to both a giant chain and a corner drugstore at the same price. If volume discounts are available they must be offered to all buyers. The Robinson-Patman Act does not apply to retail sales, so it still permits the corner drugstore to sell the same product at different prices to two customers. (Other laws may affect the drugstore's pricing, of course.) The workings of this act are extremely complicated and go beyond our scope here.

## The Federal Trade Commission Act

The **Federal Trade Commission Act** of 1914 created the **Federal Trade Commission (FTC)** and gave it extremely broad authority to police the marketplace. Its authority includes not only jurisdiction over some antitrust cases but also the power to act against unfair trade practices, as we will see in the next section. The act gives the Federal Trade Commission the power to regulate any "unfair methods of competition," which includes any anti-competitive behavior that falls short of being a violation of the other acts discussed earlier.

## Enforcing the Antitrust Laws

The federal and state governments have the duty to enforce the antitrust laws. Private entities, however, whether individuals or businesses, also have

FIGURE 22.4   Interlocking Directorates

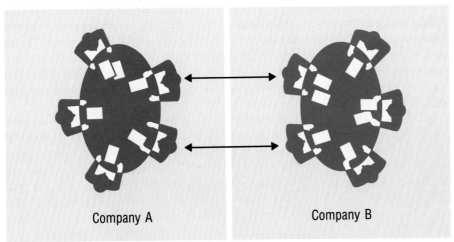

Company A        Company B

the right to enforce any antitrust laws except the Federal Trade Commission Act by means of lawsuits if they are injured by anticompetitive behavior. The law provides a strong incentive for private antitrust actions: triple damages for a successful plaintiff. Big business has mounted a serious attack on the triple damages remedy, claiming that it has created a "bounty hunter" mentality among greedy lawyers. Thus far, smaller businesses and lawyers have had the better of the argument. They have noted that the extreme length and complexity of antitrust cases makes successful claims expensive, as well as the fact that many victims of anticompetitive practices are bankrupted, so they could not sustain the costs of a suit if all that they were to recover was what they had originally lost.

# Policing the Marketplace

As noted earlier, the antitrust laws are really procompetition laws designed to ensure that the heart of our capitalist system, competition, flourishes in the marketplace. Market competition is not like war. Laws and regulations define what society regards as fair, and competitors must observe them.

In Chapter 19, we encountered the Securities and Exchange Commission (SEC), which has the responsibility for maintaining a fair market for securities. Various other federal and state agencies are responsible for policing other markets. The beneficiaries of these regulations are businesses and consumers alike.

## The Federal Trade Commission

*6. Outline the Federal Trade Commission's role in policing the marketplace.*

The Federal Trade Commission's enabling act charges it to prevent "unfair or deceptive acts or practices in commerce." We have already seen the effect of that provision in the antitrust area, but this provision also gives the FTC powers over the marketplace that go well beyond antitrust's narrow limits. In general, unfair or deceptive practices include any that tend to fool the consumer. For example, a sign over a tape deck in Looney Louie's Stereo Store may advertise that the price is "$250 off!" If the sign means "$250 off the manufacturer's list price," it probably is deceptive, since almost no stereo retailers sell at that deep a discount. In order to avoid being deceptive, Louie must either indicate on the sign what the discount really means or else sell the tape deck at $250 below his normal prices.

Sellers can also make deceptive presentations about the quality of their goods. If Louie claims that the tape deck has four recording heads when it has only two, his representation is deceptive. A celebrity who endorses a product must actually use the product, unless he or she obviously would not be expected to use it. The classic example of the exception to this rule was All-Pro quarterback Joe Namath's endorsement of a certain brand of pantyhose. Another important area of marketplace regulation concerns consumer credit. If a credit card issuer advertises a specific rate, for example, it is obligated to charge that rate.

**More than just a pretty face** *Elizabeth Taylor is well paid for lending her image to Elizabeth Taylor's Passion, one of the ten best-selling perfumes in the United States. The FTC insists that she wear the scent as a condition of their permitting her to promote it.*

The Federal Trade Commission's rules do not inhibit tough competition, like advertisements comparing competing products. They do, however, enforce minimum fairness standards.

## State Regulations

Almost all states have consumer-protection laws similar to the provisions of the Federal Trade Commission Act. Virtually any case involving deceptive practices can be brought by a state as well as the FTC.

States enforce many other laws that ensure honest dealings. For instance, all cities and counties have laws regulating the weights and measures used in trade. Inspectors check scales in supermarkets, pumps in gas stations, and the like to make sure that customers receive what they are charged for. The states also set and enforce standards for the practice of the professions: doctors, lawyers, accountants, engineers, and others.

# Environmental, Health, and Safety Regulations

*7. Describe the theory underlying environmental, health, and safety regulations.*

Our country's experience has convinced most Americans of the superiority of a market-based economy and social system. The market mechanism is not perfect, however. It cannot achieve some goals that we as a society need and want. These social aims are expressed primarily in environmental, health, and safety regulations.

## When Market Incentives Do Not Work

Theoretically, the invisible hand working through the marketplace described by Adam Smith should guide businesses toward producing the greatest good for the greatest number. Unfortunately, though, doing the right thing sometimes lessens a firm's ability to compete. In these cases, the government must supply incentives for a business to take action. Here's an example.

When firms discharge pollutants into the air or water, they may create a serious danger to human health. No firm has a direct incentive to stop, however—particularly when stopping costs money. Success in a competitive marketplace requires companies to keep costs to a minimum and maintain a healthy profit margin. Suppose that three competing manufacturing firms each discharge pollutants into the same river from identical plants, and that it will cost each one $2 million to install pollution-control systems to eliminate the problem. It might also cost $1 million per year to operate each system. Clearly, if one of the three firms refuses to install such a system, that company will have a continuing cost advantage over its two competitors. In this case, open competition provides an incentive *not* to solve the environmental problem. Thus, society must step in, acting through government. At the very least, it must remove the disincentive to meet the public's needs.

## Air, Water, and Conservation Regulations

The most recent measures designed to meet societal needs are the environmental regulations. Although some American water-pollution regulations date from the early 1900s, comprehensive regulation dates only from the mid-1960s. Air-pollution regulation began about the same time. The National Environmental Policy Act of 1969 provided a framework for the expression of environmental concerns and for the inclusion of such considerations in national decision making. In 1970, the Environmental Protection Agency came into existence to take charge of most air and water regulations. The 1970s saw water and air legislation begin to assume an important place on the national agenda.

Government regulations and our government *EG&G, Inc., a contractor for the Department of Energy, specializes in conducting simulated spills of such fluids as ammonia and liquefied natural gas in order to monitor the effects of these spills on the environment. Companies trying to conform to government regulations might ask the Department of Energy to have EG&G provide them with information about spill effects.*

Perhaps the most remarkable aspect of these regulatory programs was the national consensus that developed around them. When the Reagan administration set out to abolish the environmental programs created in the 1970s, the public offered no support for its efforts. The administration did weaken or eliminate enforcement to a degree, but it abandoned its push to eliminate the programs.

Other programs affecting natural resources and conservation were adopted in the 1970s. For instance, the first comprehensive federal regulation of surface mining began in 1977. Regulation of the offshore exploration for oil and gas was revised, for the first time in twenty-five years. The federal Coastal Zone Management Act encouraged the first comprehensive examination of our coasts as national and state resources.

## Regulation of Food and Drugs

Every state has a department of agriculture and a department of health, which share responsibility for policing the quality of the food produced and consumed within the state. On the federal level, the United States Department of Agriculture and the Food and Drug Administration (FDA) share these duties in regard to goods in interstate commerce. The FDA is responsible for enforcing the Pure Food and Drug Act, one of the earliest efforts to regulate the marketplace. Under this act the FDA evaluates new drugs coming onto the American market, for instance, and develops standards for food additives.

## Regulation of the Workplace

As we saw in Parts 1 and 3, government regulation of the workplace has a long history. These regulations, on the federal, state, and local levels, have not always kept pace with modern technology. Ironically, the consensus that developed around the environmental legislation of the 1970s never formed for the Occupational Safety and Health Act enacted by Congress during the same era. The Reagan administration had a significantly easier time not enforcing these laws than the environmental laws.

## Contemporary Regulatory Issues

Several major regulatory issues have dominated the news for much of this decade and seem likely to continue to do so well into the next. These issues include the questions of what to do about hazardous wastes and acid rain and how to anticipate what has come to be called the greenhouse effect. All three problems are phenomenally complicated, the first two no less for having been with us for so long (see Experiencing Business).

*Hazardous Waste*   Even seemingly clean industries like semiconductor manufacturing produce *hazardous wastes*. Older disposal methods once thought safe, like burial and injection into deep wells, have proven inadequate—or worse. Ignoring for a moment the companies that did not act responsibly, we must still ask if it is fair to pursue, years later, the companies that acted in good faith from the beginning in disposing of their wastes. Congress has answered this question in part by creating the so-called Superfund to finance the cleanup of old dumps, like California's Stringfellow acid pits and New York's Love Canal. Cleanup costs, however, have exceeded even the highest early estimates. Worse still, we have no assurances yet that current technologies will ultimately work any better than the older ones did.

*Acid Rain*   *Acid rain* is gradually destroying biological life in lakes and botanical life in forests from New York to Maine and in southeastern Canada. Most experts believe the major culprits to be sulfur particles that are released when coal is burned in midwestern power plants. This sulfur combines with water in the atmosphere to form low concentrations of deadly sulfuric acid, which returns to earth in the form of acid rain, often hundreds of miles away.

Fitting all power plants with pollution-control devices to minimize sulfur emissions would cost billions. And if the plants chose instead to burn low-sulfur western coal, the eastern coal industry would collapse. Neither alternative

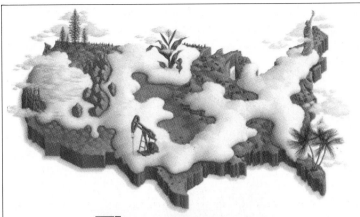

Suppressing hazardous waste    *Companies such as 3M are getting involved in the contemporary regulatory issues concerning our environment. The company has developed a vapor suppressing foam to fight hazardous vapors, dust, and odors produced by industrial operations.*

appeals to the public utilities that own the plants or to the residents of the states that would have to pay higher electric bills, lose mining jobs, or both. A contributing problem is that in the 1960s a number of Midwestern utilities constructed major coal-fired stations employing "high stack" technology. These huge smokestacks were designed to reduce air pollution near the plants by sending the smoke into the upper atmosphere and dispersing it over a wide area. It is generally believed that this early solution to air pollution led to a great acceleration in the acidification of rainfall.

*The Greenhouse Effect*    Perhaps no threat to the environment has ever rivaled the consequences that some scientists believe will follow from the gradual warming of the earth's atmosphere, a condition that has been dubbed the **greenhouse effect**. With the gradual depletion of the thin layer of ozone

**greenhouse effect** the gradual warming of the earth's atmosphere

## MANAGING THE BIG COST OF TOXIC WASTE

Imagine that you are the chief financial officer of your company, a relatively small manufacturer of semiconductors for the computer industry. Your company is in a highly competitive field and that means watching costs at every turn. The responsibility to earn a profit is often equivalent to the responsibility of staying in business for your company, at least that is the way your board of directors sees it. Naturally the way the board sees it is the way you tend to see it.

Now assume that you want to address the problem of hazardous waste costs for your company. In the United States roughly 300 million tons of hazardous waste are produced each year. All manufacturers of semiconductors use toxic chemicals and create their share of this waste. Because of EPA environmental regulations the costs of toxic waste disposal have reached $2500 per ton within the United States and are climbing. This is a cost your company has to face squarely.

Suppose you discover some companies in West Africa, where environmental regulations are minimal, that will dispose of your waste for only $3 per ton. At that price even the cost of transportation would keep your costs far below the going U.S. disposal price of $2500 per ton. The numbers are simple: if you were to export your company's hazardous waste to a third-world country, you could boost your company's profits. Furthermore, you learn that be-cause of their large foreign debts poor countries facing a choice between poverty and poison willingly accept the risks of hazardous waste. And so the legal aspects are relatively simple too. Exporting is just as legal as meeting all EPA and federal regulations, only cheaper.

You have to decide whether to accept the high costs of U.S. hazardous waste disposal or to take advantage of the lost costs of exporting waste. As you think this over, you can't help wondering about ethics. Is exporting hazardous waste, even legally, taking unfair advantage of someone else's desperation? Yet how can it be unethical to export hazardous waste if you do it legally and the importer accepts it willingly? You have to consider that by taking on higher costs you may be risking the survival of your company. Is it ethical to risk the survival of your company and the hundreds of jobs it provides? Considering everything—the finances, the laws, and different ethical points of view, what would you do? And what reasons would you give to your board of directors when they asked you to back up your choice?

Sources: Betsey Carpenter, "Superfund, Superflop," *U.S. News & World Report,* February 6, 1989, pp. 47–49; Joshua Hammer with Elizabeth Bradburn, "The Big Haul in Toxic Waste," *Newsweek,* October 3, 1988, pp. 38–39; Paul Ruffins, " 'Toxic Terrorism' Invades Third World Nations," *Black Enterprise,* November 1988, p. 31.

that shields the earth and its inhabitants from the full force of the heat and harmful rays given off by the sun, temperatures will increase and the polar caps will begin to melt. At the same time the ozone layer has begun to tear away, enormous areas of tropical vegetation, especially in the Amazon rain forests, have been systematically destroyed, depriving the earth of one of its principal natural means by which carbon dioxide is drawn out of the atmosphere. The combined effect of these two phenomena is a gradual warming of the earth's surface, one which, according to some predictions, will result in drastic climactic changes. The effort to inhibit the greenhouse effect has already led some countries to change their policies toward economic development. The future, to say the least, is uncertain. But it is reasonable to assume that increased government regulation will be one of the consequences of widening awareness of the greenhouse effect.

*The Dilemma*   The great progress made in just the last twenty years to clean up the environment seems easy compared to solving the problems that remain. As open sewers have been capped and industrial discharges ended, salmon have returned to rivers like the Connecticut, in which only carp swam twenty years ago. Smokestacks pouring out soot and ash have largely disappeared. The remaining tasks are the relatively more difficult ones that involve attacking largely invisible hazards at costs that are staggering.

Much the same problem exists in the field of health and safety regulation. Cars have become much safer since the publication of Ralph Nader's indictment of automobile quality, *Unsafe at Any Speed* in 1965. How to assess the social cost of safety still focuses on whether the number of lives saved and injuries prevented warrants the extra expense to society of more and more costly safety devices.

# Deregulation

As discussed in Chapter 1, the pace of business regulation began to accelerate in the 1930s and reached its high point in the early 1970s. At that time, a reaction set in and deregulation became the watchword. The impact of deregulation on financial services was discussed in Chapter 17.

## The Two Types of Deregulation

**Deregulation** has two meanings. This term originally referred to the stripping away of regulations restricting competition in entire industries, particularly in regard to railroads, airlines, and trucking. The second meaning has the sense of nonregulation, the elimination or avoidance of regulation, particularly in the environmental, health, and safety areas where it cannot be readily justified on a strict cost-benefit basis.

*Industry Deregulation*   The process of industry deregulation, begun under the Carter administration, has proven an enormous success.

Beginning in the nineteenth century, the transportation sector in particular came under close government regulation. The railroads were the first to trigger regulation by abusing their hold over national transportation. The Depression then saw a surge of regulation. The Roosevelt administration felt that it not only had to protect the public interest against industry abuses but

**deregulation**   refers to the stripping away of regulations restricting competition in entire industries or the elimination or avoidance of regulation

*8. Explain the various meanings of the term deregulation.*

**featherbedding** requiring more workers than needed to do a job

also had to protect jobs. These often conflicting goals led to **featherbedding**, the requiring of more workers than needed to do a job and transportation rules and routes that make little sense now. Perhaps the greatest achievement of the Carter administration was its dismantling of these regulatory structures. Changes in technology, the economy, and the nation's shifting population patterns dictated the end of these regulations. For instance, at the start of the 1970s, the railroads were known for their bankruptcies and aged equipment. Today, the rail industry carries 35 percent more tonnage than it did in the 1940s, but it is using less than 25 percent of its 1940s work force.[6]

*Nonregulation*  Deregulation also became synonymous with not regulating, particularly in the areas of the environment, health, and safety. After failing to convince Congress to repeal much of the legislation in this area, administrators in the Reagan era simply stopped enforcing the parts of laws with which they disagreed. This approach led to scandals in the Environmental Protection Agency and Department of the Interior—the two principal environmental agencies—and the Department of Labor. Nonregulation remains highly controversial and lacks the broad support that true deregulation has. Still, nonregulation has succeeded in drastically reducing what its advocates regard as an unjustifiable intrusion into the marketplace by the government.

# Taxation

"The power to tax involves the power to destroy," wrote U.S. Chief Justice John Marshall in 1819.[7] The argument about how much deregulation is appropriate centers on whether tax dollars are being used to destroy businesses. There can be little doubt that President Reagan aimed his aggressive domestic budget cutting at preventing such an abuse of power.

Taxes today are of course a far more complicated matter than they were in Chief Justice Marshall's day. Now they are instruments of social and economic policy, which is why federal and state tax legislation has dominated the news since 1980. The power to tax involves the power to foster and protect as well as to destroy.

## Federal Taxation

The tax that first comes to mind is of course the federal income tax. This tax applies to both corporations and individuals and is the government's principal source of revenue. A special tax funds the Old Age, Survivors, Disability, and Health Insurance (OASDHI) program, better known as Social Security. **Excise taxes** have the effect of raising prices of liquor, jewelry, and cigarettes. Liquor and cigarette taxes are often called "sin taxes." Some justify them as a way to discourage consumption, even though there is no evidence that these taxes have done anything but increase government revenues. A **sales tax** on gasoline supports the so-called highway trust fund, which collects money for highway and mass-transit improvements. The

**excise tax** designed to discourage use and exact a premium for use

**sales tax** a tax based on the value of a transaction

*"Yes, we have a profit-sharing plan. It goes to the government."*

federal government also taxes any deceased persons' estates that have a value exceeding $500,000.

**Tariffs**, which we will discuss in the next chapter, are taxes on goods imported into the United States. Tariffs can be selectively raised on particular goods so that imported goods become more expensive than the same type of goods made in the United States.

Another type of government charge is **user fees**, charges to the public designed to compensate the government for services it performs. Fees for the use of national parks and campgrounds, for power-boat inspections, and the issuing of water-fowl hunting stamps are among the thousands of charges that are not called taxes but still feed the public treasury.

**tariffs** taxes on goods imported into the United States

**user fees** charges to the public designed to compensate the government for services it performs

## State and Local Taxes

State governments impose many of the same types of taxes as the federal government. The U.S. Constitution, however, forbids states to impose tariffs either on foreign goods or on goods made in another state.

The two principal sources of state revenues directly affect business. The first is the **property tax**, a tax imposed by a state or local government on

**property tax** a tax imposed by a state or local government on real property

Taxation  *Under the 1986 federal tax-reform bill, children under 14 must pay taxes—and suffer the penalties for not paying taxes—as adults. Children with over $500 in unearned income now must pay at least some of their tax at their parents' rate, which is probably higher than theirs.*

real property. Real property includes land, buildings, and fixtures, discussed in detail in Chapter 21. Normally, businesses and individuals pay different rates on their property taxes, with the higher rates being charged to businesses. The second major source of government income is sales and gross receipts taxes. Both taxes are collected by business for government. Figure 22.5 presents a breakdown of state tax receipts.

Many states have income taxes, and all have estate taxes. States also impose "sin" taxes and other excise taxes. And their repertoire of user fees probably exceeds the federal government's. For instance, any business constructing a new plant must pay a sewer-connection fee. Building-inspection departments often charge significant fees.

# Government and Business: A Perspective

Regulation and taxation are issues that generate great emotion among businesspeople. Not a few have questioned whether they are getting their money's worth from government. Of course, given the many considerations we have examined in this chapter, it is impossible to answer this question in any concrete way.

For all the negative factors surrounding government control, consider how much a government employee like Jerome Kelley could accomplish. In 1982, Kelley became the director of development for the Vermont Department of Agriculture. His goal was to recreate the farm economy that Vermont had had fifty years before, when 23,000 farms had covered the tiny state. With only a $100,000 budget, Kelley embarked on a campaign to persuade

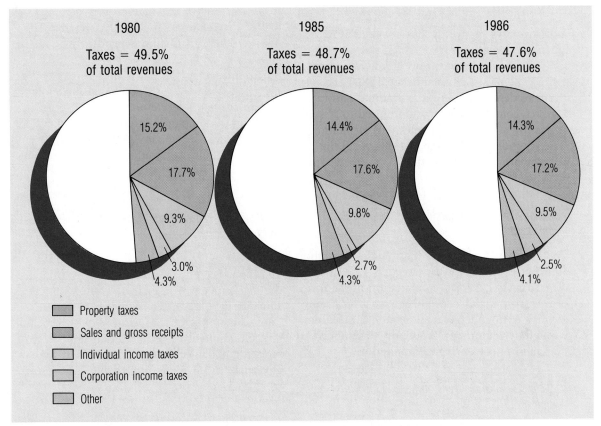

| 1980 | 1985 | 1986 |
|---|---|---|
| Taxes = 49.5% of total revenues | Taxes = 48.7% of total revenues | Taxes = 47.6% of total revenues |

1980: 15.2%, 17.7%, 9.3%, 3.0%, 4.3%

1985: 14.4%, 17.6%, 9.8%, 2.7%, 4.3%

1986: 14.3%, 17.2%, 9.5%, 2.5%, 4.1%

Legend:
- Property taxes
- Sales and gross receipts
- Individual income taxes
- Corporation income taxes
- Other

FIGURE 22.5   State and Local Tax Receipts

Source: *Statistical Abstract of the United States*, Washington, D.C.: 1988, Table 431.

Vermont food producers to take advantage of their state's image. He encouraged them to use the word *Vermont* on their labels and package their goods to capitalize on the state's "down home" image. For instance, maple syrup that used to be packaged in nondescript tins now comes in reusable Mason jars. Today, Vermont has a vibrant specialty food industry that knows how to market itself.[8]

# CHAPTER HIGHLIGHTS

*1.* Describe the three principal areas of government's relations with business.

The government's relations with business can be described in terms of the three S's: (1) *subsidy,* the use of government money and other assistance to build highways, subsidize commercial space ventures, and help develop other projects deemed beneficial for the general public; (2) *support* in the form of purchases of private sector goods, weather forecasts supplied by the Department of Commerce, and other forms of assistance; (3) *supervision,* in the form of various government regulations that enforce criminal law, ensure fair trade, and ensure safety in the work place.

*2. Explain the origins and purposes of the antitrust laws.*

Antitrust laws support a series of regulatory functions that encourage fair and open competition. Antitrust means literally "against trust." The term was used in the 1880s and 1890s to describe giant industrial and natural resource combinations that attempted to absorb or destroy all other companies in their markets. When Standard Oil Company controlled the petroleum market, it was free to charge what it wanted.

*3. Identify the two major prohibitions included in the Sherman Act.*

The Sherman Act was the first federal legislation aimed at controlling trusts. Section 1 declares illegal "every contract, combination in the form of trust or otherwise, or conspiracy in restraint of trade or commerce. . . ." Section 2 prohibits wrongfully acquiring a monopoly; attempting to monopolize; conspiring to monopolize.

*4. Define the three restraints on trade forbidden by the Clayton Act.*

The Clayton Act broadened the effect of the Sherman Act. It was designed to prevent anti-competitive behavior rather than deal with its consequences. The act focused on three devices that restrain trade: (1) tying arrangements which result when the seller only agrees to sell a product the buyer wants (the tying product) if the buyer also purchases another product the buyer does not want (the tied product); (2) a reciprocal dealing arrangement occurs when a buyer can force a seller to buy something from it as a condition of the buyer's original purchase. It is the opposite of a tying arrangement; (3) exclusive dealing arrangements arise out of an agreement by one party to sell all of its output of a product to, or to buy all it requires of a product from, the other party in exchange for the party's promise not to engage in similar transactions with anyone else. Each of these three arrangements can lessen competition.

*5. List and describe the three forms of mergers.*

A *vertical merger* is a merger of two companies in the same chain of supply. If American Airlines purchases a small independently owned regional airline, a vertical merger has occurred. A *horizontal merger* occurs when two competitors merge as when U.S. Air purchased Piedmont Airlines. *Conglomerate mergers* involve the acquisition of companies in different markets. If Miller Brewing Company purchases B.E.L.-Tronics Limited, a manufacturer of radar detection equipment, then a conglomerate merger has taken place.

*6. Outline the Federal Trade Commission's role in policing the marketplace.*

The Federal Trade Commission, created in 1914, has been given broad authority to police the marketplace. The Federal Trade Commission Act gave the FTC the power to pursue "unfair methods of competition" which include any anticompetitive behavior that falls short of violation of the other acts. Federal and state governments have the duty to enforce the antitrust laws.

*7. Describe the theory underlying environmental, health, and safety regulations.*

Theoretically, the marketplace should guide businesses toward producing the greatest good for the greatest number. But sometimes doing the right thing (such as spending large sums of money to improve safety in a coal mine) lessens a firm's ability to compete. In these cases, the government must supply the incentives for a firm to take action. A firm is less likely to discharge pollutants into a nearby body of water if such an action may result in a large fine.

*8. Explain the various meanings of the term* deregulation.

Deregulation has two meanings. In the past it referred to the stripping away of regulations that restricted competition in entire industries such as railroads, airlines, and trucking. The second meaning is nonregulation, the elimination or avoidance of regulations particularly in the environmental, health, and safety areas that cannot be justified on a strict cost-benefit basis.

# KEY TERMS

Sherman Act
Price fixing
Per se violation
Market allocations
Horizontal market
allocation
Vertical market
allocation
Rule-of-reason standard
Boycott

Monopoly
Predatory pricing
Natural monopoly
Clayton Act
Tying arrangement
Reciprocal-dealing
arrangement
Exclusive-dealing
arrangement
Merger

Vertical merger
Horizontal merger
Conglomerate mergers
Interlocking
directorates
Price discrimination
Federal Trade
Commission Act
Federal Trade
Commission (FTC)

Greenhouse effect
Deregulation
Featherbedding
Excise tax
Sales tax
Tariffs
User fees
Property tax

# REVIEW QUESTIONS

1. Describe the three principal areas of government's relations with business.
2. Government regulation of business takes three forms. Discuss how these regulations apply to the production and distribution of agricultural products.
3. What are the major purposes of the antitrust laws?
4. Name and describe the first federal legislation aimed at controlling trusts.
5. Why is it difficult to prove monopoly violations?
6. What are the three major restraints of trade forbidden by the Clayton Act?

7. What is a merger? What are the three major forms of mergers?
8. Describe the Robinson-Patman Act.
9. Describe the Federal Trade Commission's role in policing the marketplace.
10. Explain why it is necessary for government agencies to establish environmental, health, and safety regulations.
11. What are two of the most important contemporary regulatory issues?
12. What are the major types of taxation?

# APPLICATION EXERCISES

1. The deregulation of the airlines has created major changes in this industry. How have consumers benefited from deregulation? What problems have consumers faced since this industry was deregulated? What has been the impact of deregulation on commercial airlines?
2. In recent years, you have, let's say, operated a small women's apparel store in a county that enforces a blue law. This law prohibits the operation of certain types of business firms on Sundays. With only a few exceptions—service stations, food stores, drugstores, and the like—most stores cannot open for business on Sundays. The Chamber of Commerce decides to seek repeal of the blue law and wants every business owner to sign a petition requesting that the law be put before the voters at the next election. Would you sign the petition? What are some of the common arguments in favor of this form of government regulation? What are some of the major arguments against blue laws?

# CASES

## 22.1 The Case of the Evaporating Border

Trade negotiators are used to cutting through knotty problems, but perhaps none as knotty as the problem raised by Canadian lumber interests in 1987. It seems the knots in American lumber are larger than the knots in Canadian lumber. This, claim the Canadians, means the U.S. boards are inferior to Canadian boards. Therefore, the argument runs, the U.S. product should not go up against the Canadian on an equal board footing.

Until recently, this was not a problem. Canadian woodchoppers were protected by lofty tariffs that left their neighbors to the south uncompetitive. With the U.S.-Canadian Free Trade Agreement, however, a free reign at home no longer seemed so certain. The agreement was intended to trigger legislation that would eventually abolish all trade barriers between the two countries. Before that could happen, it triggered anxieties within Canadian citizens and some Canadian businesses chilled by the shadow cast by the massive U.S. society and economy.

The issue was absorption. If the agreement were fully realized, would there still be a Canada? As of the signing of the agreement, a near majority of Canadians fear there will not. They foresee a Canada beset by the U.S. social afflictions of crime, unemployment, and homelessness. They have visions of American companies gobbling up their Canadian counterparts. Protected Canadian businesses, like the lumber industry, share the latter concern. In Ontario, for example, people fear that the automobile and auto parts industries—largely American owned—will close down if GM and Ford could import their products without penalty. Protected U.S. businesses have expressed similar concerns. There is some doubt whether the U.S. uranium and zinc-alloy industries can hold their own against the Canadians.

On the whole, however, government and business on both sides of the border have applauded the signing of the agreement. Experts predict that before the year 2000 the Canadian economy will expand by 5 percent and the U.S. by 1 percent. That would mean 750,000 jobs and $45 billion for the U.S. economy. To be sure, proponents admit, some jobs will be lost and some industries will suffer in the short run. In the long run, however, the united economy of English-speaking North America is expected to prosper.

### Questions

1. Would U.S. wine makers, with no significant competition in Canada, be differently affected by free trade than the lumber industry? How?
2. Free traders say a world without tariffs is their objective. Might a free-trade block in North America and another in Western Europe support or threaten such a possibility? Why?

For more information see *U.S. News & World Report,* June 27, 1988, pp. 38–39; *Time,* June 6, 1988, pp. 39–40; *Inc.,* July, 1988, pp. 37–38; and *Business Week,* January 9, 1989, pp. 54–55.

## 22.2 Now You See It, Now You Don't

If science has its science fiction, should business have its business fiction? Its larger than life characters? Its improbable scenarios? Exasperated securities investigators and defrauded, naive investors say such a fiction already exists—not, unfortunately, on the pages of cheap paperbacks, but in the "boiler rooms" of penny-stock firms, where an overheated telephone sales force markets illusions of profit to the hopeful but inexperienced.

Penny stocks are securities that sell for $3 or less. They are not offered through any exchange, and you may not find them listed in any newspaper. Their function is to capitalize developing businesses. Knowledgeable investors may put their money into penny stocks, hoping to cash in on the next Polaroid or Xerox. But knowledgeable investors investigate before they take out their checkbooks. They are willing to assume a high risk for a potential high rate of return. They are not willing to invest their money in phantoms.

Knowledgeable investors are not, in other words, willing to invest in a firm that has supposedly mastered the technique for extracting gold from Costa Rican beach sand. They would not seek their fortunes in a "blind pool," a company with no other function than to invest people's money in firms about which the investors remain uninformed. Nor would they write out a check for stock in a company that was owned, under a fake name, by the brother-in-law of the head of the brokerage firm and that turned out no real product.

Yet, through intensive telephone sales techniques, disreputable brokers are able to unload such questionable issues, mainly to the timid and the trusting. Through a series of clever manipulations, the brokers then work up the price of the stock dramatically and sell their own holdings. Investors eager to cash in on their good fortune find it difficult. Brokers may refuse to accept their sell orders or insist they reinvest their earnings in another, equally questionable stock. All the while there is hype, perhaps through a newsletter that acknowledges no connection to the firm. Eventually, the balloon will burst: People will realize that the company has no significant product or perhaps no product at all and the price of its stock will shrivel. The gullible investor's money is gone.

So, quite possibly, is the broker. Such firms may operate out of sturdy office buildings and paint conservative logos on their doors. But they may also set up shop illegally in cheap motels, from which they can sneak away in the middle of the night—only to head for another cheap motel, perhaps in another state, where they will continue their operation.

All brokers charge a percentage on transactions. This is how they earn their living. For more visible brokers dealing in listed stocks, this may amount to 5 percent. The more imaginary the stock, however, the more imaginative the fee. Mobile penny-stock dealers may appropriate 50 percent of what they collect as a commission. In some cases, even if you wish to—and are able to—resell the stock to the broker immediately after buying it, you will only get half your money back.

Owners of these firms are not necessarily pillars of the financial community. Many have been reprimanded and even fined. Some are no longer permitted to operate as brokers—although that doesn't stop them. Most seem to enjoy living on the frontier of financial responsibility, ever ready to hop onto their horses and ride off to new, and perhaps even more lawless, territory. One of the practitioners who most infuriates enforcement authorities wears snakeskin boots to work. The sales force of a now defunct Oklahoma office referred to itself as The-Hole-in-the-Wall Gang, after Butch Cassidy and the Sundance Kid.

## Questions

1. Are penny stocks necessarily questionable investments? Explain.
2. Might it help reduce fraud if penny stocks were listed in the newspapers, like New York Stock Exchange stocks? Why?
3. Does the government have the duty to protect people from foolish investment decisions? Explain.

For more information see *Business Week*, January 23, 1989, pp. 74–82; *Business Week*, February 20, 1989, p. 132; *Business Week*, March 13, 1989, p. 128; and *Newsweek*, April 10, 1989, p. 52.

# 23 International Business

After you have completed this chapter, you will be able to do the following:

**1.** Describe the importance of foreign trade in our global economy.

**2.** Identify two major types of trade advantages.

**3.** Explain how a nation's balance of trade and balance of payments influence economic stability.

**4.** Identify four common types of protectionism and summarize the arguments pro and con.

**5.** Describe those factors that have created a global marketplace.

**6.** Explain the problem of ethnocentrism and what can be done to curb it.

**7.** Explain the different ways a purely domestic business can become an international operation.

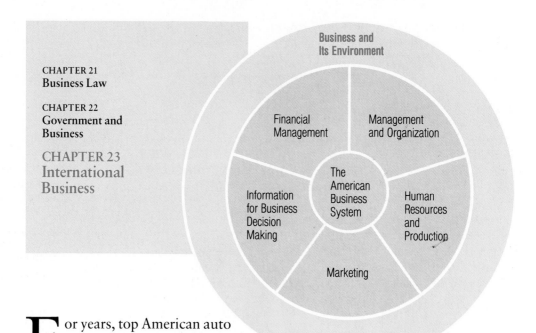

**Business and
Its Environment**

Financial
Management

Management
and Organization

Information
for Business
Decision
Making

The
American
Business
System

Human
Resources
and
Production

Marketing

F or years, top American auto executives railed against their Japanese competitors at every turn of the wheel. Chrysler chairman Lee Iacocca launched some of his best barbs to protest what he considered unfair Japanese tactics. Lately, the big guns have been remarkably silent. But then again, who would criticize his business partner? The old antagonists have suddenly started working together on the same assembly lines.

Customers may not realize it, but the world auto industry is fast becoming one great partnership. Consider this: Mazda designed and built Ford's sporty new Probe. The classic Japanese Toyota Corolla now rolls out of an American plant half owned by General Motors. The peppy "American" Pontiac LeMans was engineered by Opel (GM's West German subsidiary) and is built by Daewoo in South Korea. The Corvette, often described as the epitome of the American-made sports car, comes with a high-performance transmission built by ZF, a West German company.[1]

*1. Describe the importance of foreign trade in our global economy.*

Like it or not, and prepared or not, American business managers and consumers have been thrust into a vigorous global economy. It is commonplace for Americans to wake to the sound of a Japanese alarm clock, catch the morning news on an Asian-assembled TV, have a breakfast including orange juice from Brazil, slip on Italian shoes, gas up the Japanese-made family car with 45-percent imported fuel, and rush off to work at a major U.S. company owned by stockholders from every point of the compass. In fact, an estimated 26 cents of every dollar Americans now spend on consumer goods goes for imports.[2] This sort of global interdependence has powerful and lasting implications for job security, the health of the national economy, national defense, international relations, and a host of other considerations. Consequently, in this final chapter we explore some basic principles of doing business across national boundaries.

# The Elements of Trade

The word *business* in this chapter will have a broader meaning than the more usual sense of just commercial transactions between individuals or business entities. *Business* can also mean **trade**, the buying or selling of goods or services among companies, states, or countries. **International trade** is trade that involves the crossing of national boundaries.

Trade develops when two entities, called **trading partners**, recognize that there are mutual benefits in a transaction or series of transactions and decide to undertake them. **Foreign trade** is thus trade between partners of different nationalities. A nation can gain by specializing in those goods or services that it can produce with relative efficiency and trade for what it cannot produce efficiently. For example, Brazil has a large, unskilled labor force. This factor, along with its climate and soil, makes Brazil an ideal producer of oranges and coffee. In contrast, West Germany has a large, highly skilled, well-educated work force that allows it to produce goods requiring intensive capital investment. These conditions make West Germany an ideal producer of technologically sophisticated equipment, appliances, and chemicals.

**trade** the buying or selling of goods or services among companies, states, or countries

**international trade** trade that involves the crossing of national boundaries

**trading partners** trade between two entities

**foreign trade** trade between partners of different nationalities

## *Specialization*

Two countries with different work forces and levels of capital investment will have different production costs if they both produce the same product. This fact argues for **specialization**, the concentration of economic activity in those areas in which the country, the individual, or the business has either natural or acquired advantages.[3]

*2. Identify two major types of trade advantages.*

**specialization** the concentration of economic activity in those areas in which the country, the individual, or the business has either a natural or acquired advantage

### *Absolute Advantages*
In general, economic theory recognizes two main types of advantages: absolute and comparative. An **absolute advantage** exists when one country can produce a product more efficiently than any other country. South Africa has an absolute advantage in the production of diamonds, for example. No other country has such extensive deposits of these gems; therefore, no other country can produce them as cheaply. Absolute advantages are rare.

**absolute advantage** exists when one country can produce a product more efficiently than any other country

### *Comparative Advantages*
More commonly, a country will have a **comparative advantage**, which is the ability to produce a product at a lower cost than a competitor can. Suppose that the United States can produce a ton of aluminum for $100, whereas Brazil's costs are $200. In this instance, the United States has a comparative advantage in aluminum and should specialize in producing it. Let's assume also that Brazil can produce a ton of orange concentrate for juice at $100 per ton when a ton of concentrate costs $200 to produce in the United States. In this case, Brazil is the country with the

**comparative advantage** the ability to produce a product at a lower cost than the competitor can

comparative advantage and should specialize in orange concentrate. According to the principle of comparative advantage, such specialization by these two countries should result in more efficient use of both countries' resources.

In today's fast-paced world, comparative advantages can disappear rather quickly. Asian countries such as Taiwan, South Korea, Singapore, and Hong Kong, for example, prospered during the 1970s and 1980s because of comparative advantages involving plentiful labor and low wages. But consider Tandy Corp.'s recent experience: in 1972, when the cost of Korean labor was low, the company built an electronics manufacturing facility in that country. In March 1989, however, Tandy was forced to shut down its factory because of anti-American labor demonstrations. This unrest coupled with the rapid increase in Korean labor costs no longer made it advantageous for Tandy to assemble computer components there.[4]

Indeed, Japan, once the leading "low-wage country," has become one of the world's high-cost producers. This is true because of dramatically higher wage rates, heavy dependence on costly imported natural resources, and astronomical real estate and transportation costs.

## Exporting and Importing

**exports** goods produced in one country but sold in another

**imports** goods that are sold in one country but produced in another country

Economic theory holds that, as a consequence of specialization, countries will produce more of the products in which they have a comparative advantage than they need for their own consumption. The excess quantities thus become available for foreign trade. There are two sides to foreign trade. **Exports** are goods produced in one country but sold in another. Reversing the order of things, **imports** are goods sold and consumed in one country but produced in another. For example, PepsiCo manufactures cola concentrate for Pepsi-Cola in the United States. When it sells the concentrate to the Soviet Union, the concentrate becomes an American export. Conversely, when PepsiCo buys Stolichnaya vodka from the Soviet Union and resells it here, this liquor becomes an import.[5]

**balance of trade** the relationship between the value of goods and services imported and goods and services exported during a particular period

3. Explain how a nation's balance of trade and balance of payments influence economic stability.

**balance of payments** measures the relationship between payments coming into and going out of a country during a particular period

*Balance of Trade*   Nations watch very closely their **balance of trade**, the relationship between the value of goods and services imported and goods and services exported during a particular period. A favorable balance of trade exists when the value of exports exceeds that of imports. When imports exceed exports, as in the case of the United States today, there is an unfavorable balance of trade (see Figure 23.1).

*Balance of Payments*   A country's balance of trade is only one element in a much more important economic index, its balance of payments. The **balance of payments** measures the relationship between payments coming into and going out of a country during a particular period. In this context, *payments* includes all transfers of assets across the nation's boundaries. For example, a calculation of payments leaving the United States would include foreign aid, military assistance, private overseas investment, and tourist spending abroad (see Figure 23.2). It is possible for a nation to have a favorable balance of payments but an unfavorable balance of trade, or vice versa.

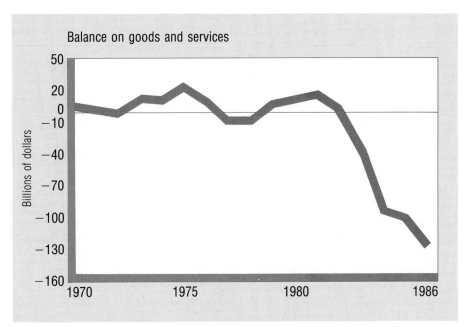

FIGURE 23.1    The Dramatic Growth of America's Trade Imbalance

Source: U.S. Department of Commerce, *Statistical Abstract of the United States 1988,* figure 29.2, p. 754.

## *The Valuation of Currency*

The condition of a nation's balance of payments directly affects the value of its currency. Currency can be a synonym for money, which is how we will use the term in this chapter. Currency includes not only coins and bills but everything commonly accepted in place of cash. As we saw in Chapter 17, a nation's currency serves three purposes. It is a measure of value, a store of value, and a medium of exchange.

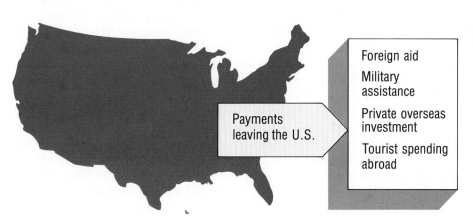

FIGURE 23.2    Balance of Payments

**exchange rate** the value of a currency expressed in terms of another currency

## Exchange Rates

In international trade, a currency's value is its **exchange rate,** the value of a currency expressed in terms of another currency. For example, on a particular day the price of a U.S. dollar might be 12 Indian rupees, 1,500 Italian lira, or .8 Argentine australs. In most of the free world, the law of supply and demand establishes the prevailing exchange rates, at least to some degree. Good financial managers, such as Philip Morris's Hans G. Storr (introduced in Chapter 18), know how to take advantage of fluctuating exchange rates. Anticipating in late 1984 that the dollar would be pulled under by the massive U.S. trade deficit, he converted $2 billion into foreign currencies for a profit to Philip Morris of $400 million in the next three years.[6]

If a country has a balance of payments deficit like that the United States has been experiencing, it is sending out more currency than it is taking in. The supply of its currency among its trading partners will rise as a result, and its value against other currencies should decline. In short, its exchange rate will drop. That is precisely what happened to the value of the U.S. dollar in relation to Japanese yen, starting in the mid-1970s. Americans overwhelmingly came to prefer Japanese electronics at the same time that a large segment of the U.S. population began buying Japanese cars. The Japanese did import more goods from America than from any of their other trading partners at this time, but their balance of payments with the United States still showed a huge surplus.

## The Problem of Imbalance

This persistent imbalance caused the dollar to decline in value in terms of the yen. There are two standard remedies to this problem. The artificial solution is to institute either devaluation or revaluation. **Devaluation** is an arbitrary downward adjustment of one country's currency in terms of another country's. The converse of devaluation is **revaluation,** an arbitrary upward adjustment of one country's currency in terms of another country's. In essence, a country sets a fixed rate of exchange for its currency, which it hopes will then accomplish the desired result in terms of the balance of payments. The government enforces the new fixed exchange rate by imposing civil and criminal penalties on people and businesses that exchange currency at other rates.

**devaluation** an arbitrary downward adjustment of one country's currency in terms of another country's

**revaluation** an arbitrary upward adjustment of one country's currency in terms of another country's

Until 1971, most of the free world operated on a fixed rate of exchange. In that year, most of the major industrial countries abandoned fixed rates of exchange because they no longer reflected economic realities. Today, only the less developed nations and the communist countries rely on them. For example, in 1989 the official exchange rate for the Russian ruble was $1.63. Meanwhile, on the illegal black market, where natural forces of supply and demand were operating, a ruble fetched only 7 cents.[7]

The free market solution for an imbalance in payments is to increase exports to the nation enjoying the favorable balance of payments. In other words, the United States should sell Japan more of the goods and services in which it enjoys a comparative advantage, to reduce its trade deficit with that country. The solution to payment imbalances may thus be seen to lie in specialization and in the removal of artificial barriers to free trade between nations, as Adam Smith urged in 1776 in *The Wealth of Nations.*

The trading room  *These specialists buy and sell government securities on the open market as directed by the Federal Reserve Bank. By prescribing buying or selling the Fed controls the money supply, and thus works to stabilize the dollar and the balance of U.S. international payments.*

## Protectionism

Although Adam Smith's free-trade argument has been around for over 200 years, the debate it stirred is hotter than ever. At the heart of this debate is the concept of **protectionism**, creating artificial barriers to free trade to protect domestic industries and jobs. Among the major protectionist barriers to trade are tariffs, import quotas, embargoes, and bureaucratic red tape. Before examining each of these forms of protectionism, however, let us briefly review both sides of the argument.

**protectionism**  the creation of artificial barriers to free trade to protect domestic industries and jobs

*Arguments Pro and Con*  Lining up squarely behind the concept of protectionism are labor unions and managers of domestic industries facing competition from abroad. American steel and textile companies have pushed hard for trade barriers to stem the tide of foreign competition. They promote their cause with the slogan "Buy American." Unions fear foreign competition and imports because they are perceived to be a serious threat to job security.

**"Jobs for Americans"** *The Wal-Mart chain of retail outlets may not have the power to erect trade barriers. Still, the firm tries to protect American jobs. "Buy American" is, in the words of Wal-Mart's promotional literature, the company's "focused program committed to exhausting every comparable domestic opportunity prior to placing off-shore orders." The company claims to have made or saved over 19,000 U.S. jobs.*

During the 1980s, hundreds of thousands of jobs did in fact disappear in the U.S. automobile and steel industries. This was partly because of intense foreign competition and partly because of short-sighted management, among a complex combination of other factors.

*4. Identify four common types of protectionism and summarize the arguments pro and con.*

Antiprotectionist arguments are offered by industries heavily dependent on exports and "free traders" in political and academic circles who are philosophically opposed to tampering with the natural forces of free markets. Ronald Reagan repeatedly vetoed protectionist legislation in the belief that the economy's long-run interests would best be served by an unfettered marketplace. Researchers say American consumers are forced to foot the bill for protectionism, to the tune of an estimated $65 to $75 billion a year.[8] In fact, according to one study, it costs consumers (in the form of artificially higher prices) about $42,000 to save one job in the U.S. textile industry and $105,000 to prevent a single automobile industry job from going overseas.[9] Critics of protectionism believe this sort of subsidy is far too costly.

Of course, some want it both ways. Some American farmers and loggers, for example, want to be protected by trade barriers around U.S. markets but not be hampered by them when exporting to other countries. Still others, like the managers at Harley-Davidson Motorcycle who benefited from such an arrangement, call for *temporary* trade protection while a struggling company or industry gets back on its feet (refer back to the opening example in Chapter 10). Given the highly political nature of the protectionist debate, the net result is a worldwide patchwork of inconsistent signals to importers and exporters.

*Tariffs*   Historically, nations have protected themselves against imports by using **tariffs** or *duties,* taxes imposed by a country on imported goods. These taxes take two forms. **Revenue tariffs** are imposed solely to generate income for a government. For example, the United States imposes a duty on Scotch whisky solely for revenue purposes. Those who favor free trade have less trouble with revenue tariffs than they do with the other form of import duty, the **protective tariff,** a tariff imposed to protect a domestic industry from competition by keeping the price of competing imports level with or higher than the price of domestic products. The French and Japanese agricultural sectors would both shrink drastically if their nations abolished the protective tariffs that keep the price of imported farm products high.

*Import Quotas*   A limit on the quantity of a particular good that can be brought into a country is an **import quota.** The most important quota imposed by the United States in recent years was one on Japanese cars in response to Japanese dominance in the economy car market. Japanese auto makers responded to the import quota in classic free-market style simply by exporting more expensive cars. Such cars provided them with greater per-car profit margins, thus making up for the lost volume.

*Embargoes*   A law or government order forbidding either the importing or exporting of certain specified goods is an **embargo.** More often than not, countries impose embargoes not to protect a domestic industry but to punish another country. In 1961, the United States placed an embargo on Cuban goods that is still in force. In 1973, a number of Arab oil-exporting countries imposed an embargo on the United States and certain Western European countries that supported Israel. More recently, South Africa's racist apartheid policies triggered trade embargoes by the United States and other Western nations.

*Bureaucratic Red Tape*   This last form of protectionism is more subtle than the forms discussed so far. Yet bureaucratic red tape can be the most frustrating trade barrier of all. It can cause unexplained delays and generate great confusion. Motorola's recent experience in Japan is a prime example. When Motorola introduced the world's smallest portable telephone to the Japanese market in early 1989, it was given permission by the Japanese government to sell the new phones only in the western half of the country. Unfortunately, the majority of Japan's $720 million cellular phone market, including Tokyo, was in the eastern half of the country. According to *Business Week*: "When Motorola protested, Japan compromised. Motorola could attach adapters to its phones so they could be used in Tokyo. But the adapters only work on car phones, while 90 percent of the customers use portable phones on the train."[10] Frustrated by all this bureaucratic red tape, Motorola turned to U.S. government trade negotiators for help in forcing open the lucrative Japanese cellular phone market.

**tariffs**   taxes imposed by a country on imported goods

**revenue tariffs**   taxes imposed solely to generate income of the government

**protective tariff**   tax imposed to protect a domestic industry from competition

**import quota**   a limit on the quantity of a particular good that can be brought into a country

**embargo**   a law or government order forbidding either the importing or exporting of certain specified goods

## Trade Agreements

**trade agreement**   a negotiated relationship between nations that regulates the commerce between them

A negotiated relationship between nations that regulates the commerce between them is called a **trade agreement**. Since 1947, the United States has relied far more heavily on trade agreements than on protective tariffs. By that time, many historians and economists had concluded that the Smoot-Hawley Tariff Act of 1930 had greatly increased the severity of the Depression by setting off a tariff war with our trading partners and ourselves. The effect on our exports was disastrous.

**General Agreement on Tariffs and Trade (GATT)**   a treaty which established an international mechanism for mutual adjustments of trade barriers and regulations

**reciprocity**   the belief that one country's markets can be only as free as its trading partners'

*GATT*   In 1947, the United States and twenty-two other nations signed the **General Agreement on Tariffs and Trade (GATT)**, which established an international mechanism for mutual adjustments of trade barriers and regulations. GATT expresses the principal concept on which the United States has based its trade policy ever since. This concept is called **reciprocity**, the belief that one country's markets can be only as free as its trading partners'.[11] Each year the GATT nations meet to review recommendations, settle disputes, and devise ways to reduce trade barriers between countries.

The United States has not relied solely on GATT to implement its free trade philosophy. Representatives from the United States and its six major trading partners hold an annual economic summit to resolve trade problems.

*New Regional Trade Agreements*   One of the most significant trade agreements in recent years is the U.S.-Canadian Free Trade Agreement that went into effect on January 1, 1989. Already the world's two biggest trading partners, the United States and Canada have agreed to dismantle all trade barriers over a period of years. The ultimate result will be a truly unified North American marketplace.[12] Next on the horizon is a unified European regional market by 1992 (see Business Issues).

# Trade in a Shrinking World

International trade existed even before there really were nations. From records and the wreckage of ancient ships, we know that trade crossed certain geographic boundaries at least five thousand years ago. In some ways, particularly in transportation, little changed for thousands of years. For instance, in the 1830s it still took as long for a message to go from London to Rome as it had eighteen hundred years earlier.[13] In only another forty years, however, trains had replaced horse-drawn coaches, and steamships had outmoded sailing vessels. The transatlantic telegraph cable ultimately linked the United States and Europe with instantaneous communications.

## A Global Marketplace

*5. Describe those factors that have created a global marketplace.*

The pace at which the world grew smaller in the nineteenth century accelerated in the twentieth. Automobiles, jet planes, and satellites that could handle

# THE UNITED STATES IN A UNITED EUROPE

"The United States is a European nation," said President Bush early in his administration. The President had not forgotten his primary school geography. Rather, he was expressing the hope that U.S. business would be able to prosper in an economically united European Economic Community.

The EEC, also known as the Common Market, consists of the United Kingdom, Ireland, Denmark, Belgium, the Netherlands, Luxembourg, West Germany, France, Spain, Portugal, Italy, and Greece: 12 proud countries, each with its distinctive history and particular economic strengths and weaknesses.

At the time of the President's declaration, Europeans, who had for some time agreed in principle that a united Europe would be a stronger and more prosperous Europe and that 1992 would be a good year for this united Europe to show its face, were still strenuously arguing over just how far they should go. On one side of the debate, the United Kingdom's Margaret Thatcher insisted that the union meant no more than the creation of a free-trade bloc. To many EEC officials in the organization's Brussels headquarters, the union meant much more. If vast social and economic dislocations were not to occur, all 12 countries would have to agree to changes. Denmark did not wish to be penalized for the added cost to its products attributable to its strong environmental-protection laws. Nor did that Scandinavian country wish to be forced by economic pressure to repeal those laws. To accommodate Denmark, would the rest of Europe become more environmentally conscious? West German labor, with its high wages, strict regulations, and strong say in management, felt it could only lose if forced to go head to head with the work force of Spain, where wages were lower and work rules more lax. Should EEC-wide work rules be passed, equalizing wages, benefits, and influence throughout the community?

As of early 1989, when the President was declaring the United States to be European, the exact form of the economic union was not certain. What American businesses were relatively sure of, however, was that the union would be mighty and that, proclamations about the glories of unrestricted free trade not withstanding, it would be to some degree exclusive. Firms not based within the EEC and firms based in strongly protectionist nations would be at a competitive disadvantage. With this in mind, some American companies began to establish a European presence. Some did this through mergers. Others began to expand and consolidate their existing European operations. For Walt Disney, it was off to work we go on a $2 billion theme park in France. AT&T opened a $200 million microchip plant in Spain. Federal Express began to gobble up delivery services throughout Europe. All these firms had visions of sharing, without penalty, in a market 320 million people strong, which in 1987, had a combined gross domestic product of $4.3 trillion.

Sources: Richard I. Kirkland, "Outsider's Guide to Europe in 1992," *Fortune*, October 24, 1988, pp. 121–122, 126–127; Scott Sullivan, "Who's Afraid of 1992?" *Newsweek*, October 31, 1988, pp. 321–334; and Frank J. Comes and Jonathan Kapstein, "Reshaping Europe: 1992 and Beyond," *Business Week*, December 12, 1988, pp. 48–51.

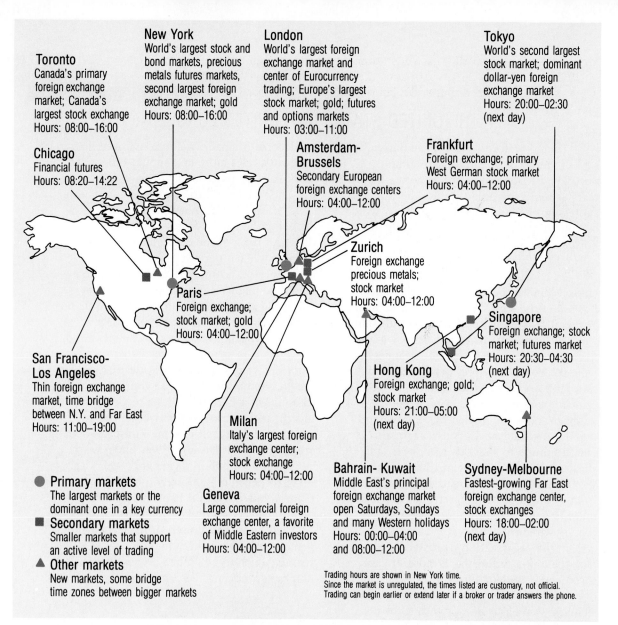

**Toronto**
Canada's primary foreign exchange market; Canada's largest stock exchange
Hours: 08:00–16:00

**Chicago**
Financial futures
Hours: 08:20–14:22

**New York**
World's largest stock and bond markets, precious metals futures markets, second largest foreign exchange market; gold
Hours: 08:00–16:00

**London**
World's largest foreign exchange market and center of Eurocurrency trading; Europe's largest stock market; gold; futures and options markets
Hours: 03:00–11:00

**Tokyo**
World's second largest stock market; dominant dollar-yen foreign exchange market
Hours: 20:00–02:30 (next day)

**Amsterdam-Brussels**
Secondary European foreign exchange centers
Hours: 04:00–12:00

**Frankfurt**
Foreign exchange; primary West German stock market
Hours: 04:00–12:00

**Zurich**
Foreign exchange precious metals; stock market
Hours: 04:00–12:00

**Paris**
Foreign exchange; stock market; gold
Hours: 04:00–12:00

**Singapore**
Foreign exchange; stock market; futures market
Hours: 20:30–04:30 (next day)

**San Francisco-Los Angeles**
Thin foreign exchange market, time bridge between N.Y. and Far East
Hours: 11:00–19:00

**Hong Kong**
Foreign exchange; gold; stock market
Hours: 21:00–05:00 (next day)

**Milan**
Italy's largest foreign exchange center; stock exchange
Hours: 04:00–12:00

**Bahrain- Kuwait**
Middle East's principal foreign exchange market open Saturdays, Sundays and many Western holidays
Hours: 00:00–04:00 and 08:00–12:00

**Sydney-Melbourne**
Fastest-growing Far East foreign exchange center, stock exchanges
Hours: 18:00–02:00 (next day)

● **Primary markets**
The largest markets or the dominant one in a key currency

■ **Secondary markets**
Smaller markets that support an active level of trading

▲ **Other markets**
New markets, some bridge time zones between bigger markets

**Geneva**
Large commercial foreign exchange center, a favorite of Middle Eastern investors
Hours: 04:00–12:00

Trading hours are shown in New York time.
Since the market is unregulated, the times listed are customary, not official.
Trading can begin earlier or extend later if a broker or trader answers the phone.

**FIGURE 23.3  World Financial Centers**

Source: From *The New York Times,* Sunday, May 4, 1986. Copyright © 1986 by the New York Times Company. Reprinted by permission.

routine telephone calls completely revitalized transportation and communications. Most recently, the computer and the microchip have again revolutionized communications and information processing.

Since the dawn of this phenomenal era, optimists have persisted in predicting the disappearance of national boundaries and identifications in the face of the accelerating speed of transportation and the homogenizing effect of mass communications. We find ourselves instead living in a "global village" with quite distinct neighborhoods whose residents trade in a global marketplace. Even as recently as fifty years ago, the world's principal financial centers were New York and London. Today the centers are spread across the globe (see Figure 23.3).

## America's Position in the Global Marketplace

Contrary to the impression created by dramatic and pessimistic media coverage of the trade deficit, the United States still is the dominant player in the global economy. But, as indicated in Figure 23.4, America's slice of the pie is shrinking and Japan is coming on fast. This rearrangement has fostered new ways of looking at things. For example, the dollar is no longer the automatic choice for the world's business currency. Moreover, newly industrialized

FIGURE 23.4   America's Large But Shrinking Share of the World Economy

Source: Data from the Econoclast Advisory Service. Chart adapted from Horn and Rapaport in *The Christian Science Monitor* © 1989 TCSPS.

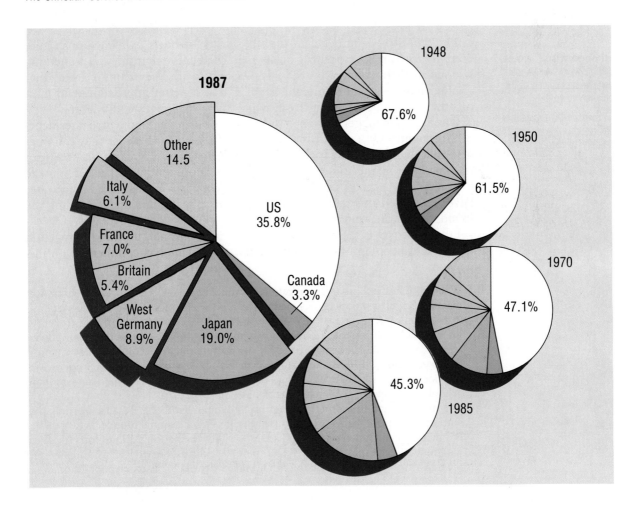

countries (NICs) such as Taiwan and South Korea are demanding and getting greater respect at the trade negotiating table.

There is a vital hidden lesson here: neither the United States nor any other country can deal with its economic problems in isolation. Whether we like it or not, we are all in the same marketplace.

## Thinking Internationally

Americans have rightly been criticized for knowing, and caring, too little about the rest of the world. The tiny number of people born in this country who can speak more than one language fluently testifies to the truth of this criticism. (Europeans, among others, routinely master at least two languages besides their own.) It is ironic that Americans, who have done so much to make the world smaller, are quite ill prepared to deal with those from different cultures. It is also ironic that a nation like ours, which is based on immigrants, should fall into having narrow attitudes about the way foreigners live. These preconceptions are attitudes that we as a nation of businesspeople simply cannot afford.

**ethnocentrism** a belief that the way something is done in their country is the only way to do it

**6.** Explain the problem of ethnocentrism and what can be done to curb it.

*Ethnocentrism* The belief in the superiority of one's own race or culture is **ethnocentrism**. Ethnocentric businesspeople believe that the way something is done in their country is the only way to do it. They cannot admit that another nation or culture might have devised a better approach, or at least one that works better for it, from which they themselves could learn.

Often, U.S. managers assigned to foreign countries will not entrust residents of that country with significant decision-making power because they can't believe that foreigners are capable of making decisions. As a result, an American or someone from the home office will make decisions that would be better made by someone who knows the culture and the country. Sophisticated companies have recognized this reality for years and have made this understanding the foundation of their international successes.

Ethnocentrism is, as we have suggested, an irrational, unthinking reaction to different peoples and cultures. *Fortune* magazine has commented on this phenomenon:

> When it comes to Hispanic marketing, a little knowledge is a dangerous thing. Remember Braniff's blooper? The airline's ads told Hispanics to fly *en cuero*—or "naked." Tropicana advertised *jugo de china* in Miami. *China* means orange to Puerto Ricans, but Miami's Cubans thought it was juice from the Orient. Jack in the Box goofed with a commercial featuring a band of Mexican mariachis accompanying a Spanish flamenco dancer. "That's like having Willie Nelson sing while Michael Jackson does the moonwalk," says Bert Valencia, a marketing professor at the American Graduate School of International Management in Glendale, Arizona.
>
> Why do companies sometimes end up looking like *idiotas*? Because learning this market takes more than a few lessons at Berlitz. An occasional blunder is forgivable. But many companies are designing advertising for the nation's 19 million Hispanics without understanding the differences among Mexicans, Puerto Ricans, Cubans, and the rich array of other nationalities that make up the U.S. Hispanic population.[14]

Entering the global marketplace   *While some U.S. companies ponder the difficulties of penetrating foreign markets, others quietly work their way in. Mead Johnson has been marketing Isocal, a complete nutritional product for patients, to Japanese hospitals since 1987.*

It is not necessarily true, however, that a company with a policy or technique that does not fit a local culture is ethnocentric. In fact, such a firm may be smart. For example, in Japan the concept of a commitment to equal job opportunities for women is not as generally accepted as it is in the United States. IBM is committed to this concept worldwide, however. As a result, women students in Japan rank IBM as their most desirable employer.[15] Thus, IBM gets its pick of the brightest women graduates.

*Avoiding the Trap*   A successful international manager must acknowledge that deep differences separate cultures but that each culture has undeniable merits, and for those belonging to it (see Experiencing Business). Only those who have lived in a culture for a considerable time can understand it sufficiently to function effectively in it. Managers taking this view will strongly favor hiring local personnel to run foreign operations and give them considerable discretion in decision making. Such managers will also favor intensive training for their American employees going to overseas jobs.

## DEVELOPING INTERCULTURAL AWARENESS AND SENSITIVITY

*Instructions:* Please read the following incident and jot down some notes to explain what happened before looking up the interpretation at the end of the text.

Yoko was one of the best employees Katherine had ever supervised. Precise and hard working, Yoko was a joy to be with and was well liked by her office coworkers.

Katherine, however, began to notice that Yoko, although very skilled, was reluctant to carry out duties without being specifically told to

do so. This reluctance to take initiative was frustrating for Katherine, and Yoko's coworkers began to feel that an unfair portion of the workload was falling on their shoulders.

What was happening? Why would an otherwise good, responsible employee hesitate to take initiative on duties that were obviously familiar to her?

Source: Excerpted from Sondra Thiederman, "Breaking Through to Foreign-Born Employees," *Management World,* May/June 1988, pp. 22–23.

---

**Foreign Corrupt Practices Act** forbids the bribing of foreign officials by U.S. companies or their employees to obtain favorable treatment

In a few important ways, employees of an American corporation cannot and should not adapt their practices to fit local customs. The most important of these differences is bribery. The federal **Foreign Corrupt Practices Act** forbids the bribing of foreign officials by U.S. companies or their employees to obtain favorable treatment. Does this put American businesspeople at a competitive disadvantage in countries where bribery is common practice? According to a recent study of business dealings in the Middle East, the answer is, "Apparently not."[16]

# Entering the International Marketplace

*7. Explain the different ways a purely domestic business can become an international operation.*

When a firm decides to expand from being a purely domestic business to an international operation, it can choose to become one of several types of venture. Among these are the following alternatives:

- Exporting
- Licensing
- Joint ventures
- Direct foreign investment

## *Exporting*

As we have seen, exporting occurs when goods are produced in one country for consumption in another. For example, Komatsu Ltd., a Japanese heavy-equipment maker, exports its construction equipment worldwide, as does

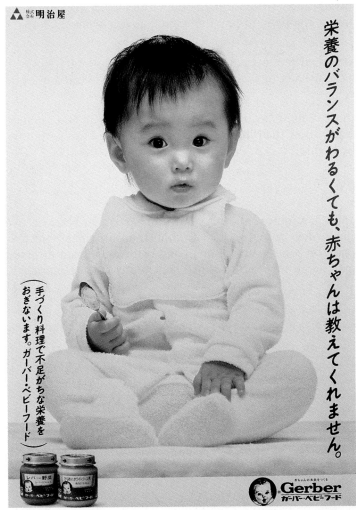

株式会社 明治屋

栄養のバランスがわるくても、赤ちゃんは教えてくれません。

手づくり料理で不足がちな栄養を
おぎないます。ガーバー・ベビーフード

レバー野菜
チキン＆ホワイトソース

ガーバー・ベビーフード

赤ちゃんの未来をつくる
Gerber
ガーバー・ベビーフード

**Licensing** *Gerber baby foods are sold in Japan through a Japanese licensee—the Meidi-Ya Company. Meidi-Ya promotes its products almost like vitamins—supplements to the traditional infant diet. To successfully market products in other cultures, local customs may have to be understood and respected.*

the Caterpillar Company of Illinois. The Swedish firms Begus Inter and Faluhus export prefabricated modular homes to the United States.[17]

## Licensing

In international business, a **license** is a privilege to manufacture or sell a product in all or part of a country or to extract a natural resource from a particular location. Coca-Cola, for example, has had to obtain licenses to produce and sell its soft drinks in the over 155 countries in which it does business.[18]

**license** a privilege to manufacture or sell a product in all or part of a country or to extract a natural resource from a particular location

A license is a contract, and its provisions are therefore subject to negotiation. A license can require a company to pay the issuing government

- A one-time fee
- A percentage of annual receipts
- A **royalty** or share, usually of the gross output, from the extraction of a natural resource

**royalty** the share of payment to the issuing government for the extraction of a natural resource

Licenses often have a limited duration. Some licenses grant monopolies, whereas others simply allow their holders to compete for business within the country issuing the license.

## Joint Ventures

**joint venture** an agreement between two businesses to combine their resources to accomplish a particular objective

As we saw in Chapter 3, a **joint venture** is simply an agreement between two businesses to combine their resources to accomplish a particular objective. Here we are focusing on joint ventures involving companies from different countries. They may agree to produce a product jointly or just market it,

Adaptability   *Even transporting cases of cola from bottler to warehouses is a different proposition in Thailand than it is in the United States. Pepsi manages the complexities of its international operations with the aid of sophisticated computer systems.*

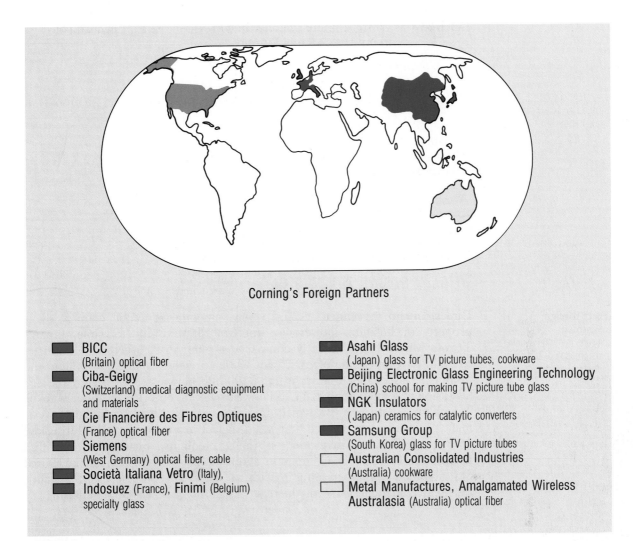

Corning's Foreign Partners

BICC
(Britain) optical fiber
Ciba-Geigy
(Switzerland) medical diagnostic equipment
and materials
Cie Financière des Fibres Optiques
(France) optical fiber
Siemens
(West Germany) optical fiber, cable
Società Italiana Vetro (Italy),
Indosuez (France), Finimi (Belgium)
specialty glass

Asahi Glass
(Japan) glass for TV picture tubes, cookware
Beijing Electronic Glass Engineering Technology
(China) school for making TV picture tube glass
NGK Insulators
(Japan) ceramics for catalytic converters
Samsung Group
(South Korea) glass for TV picture tubes
Australian Consolidated Industries
(Australia) cookware
Metal Manufactures, Amalgamated Wireless
Australasia (Australia) optical fiber

FIGURE 23.5   Corning's Global Tie-Ups

Source: Based on materials that originally appeared in Louis Kraar, "Your Rivals Can Be Your Allies," *Fortune,* March 27, 1989, p. 68. Copyright 1989 *Fortune* Magazine. Reprinted by permission of the publisher.

store it, or transport it. Financial arrangements between **coventurers,** the parties in a joint venture, can vary as much as in a partnership. For small firms, joint ventures can provide entry into international business that they could not otherwise afford. In other instances, companies form joint ventures with foreign corporations to crack a foreign market. Since 1980, AT&T, for example, has formed joint ventures with Dutch, Italian, Spanish, South Korean, Taiwanese, and Japanese coventurers.[19] Regarding the scope of this trend, *Fortune* magazine has reported that in the 1980s U.S. corporations formed over 2,000 alliances with European companies alone.[20] Corning Glass Works, with over fifteen foreign partners, has been a leader in extending its global reach through joint ventures (see Figure 23.5).

**coventurers**   the parties in a joint venture

TABLE 23.1   Which Country Has the Greatest Direct Foreign Investment
in the U.S.? Some Surprises . . .

| Country | Total at end of 1987 (billions of U.S. dollars) | 1987 ranking |
|---|---|---|
| Britain | $102 | 1 |
| Japan | $53 | 2 |
| Netherlands | $49 | 3 |
| Canada | $27 | 4 |
| West Germany | $24 | 5 |

Source: Data from "Total Foreign Investment in the U.S.," *Fortune*, July 31, 1989, p. 81.

## Direct Foreign Investment

**direct foreign investment** occurs when someone from one country owns property or business interests in another country

**Direct foreign investment** occurs when someone from one country owns property or business interests in another country. For example, Japan's Toyota Motor Corp. recently completed a plant in Georgetown, Kentucky to build its Camry line of cars.[21] By 1988, foreigners had $250 billion tied up in U.S. assets and Americans had $300 billion invested in foreign assets.[22] Sensationalist news reports in recent years about how Japan appears to be buying up America have alarmed many Americans. Although Japan's investment position in the United States did in fact grow significantly during the 1980s, total Japanese investment in America remains a distant second behind Britain (see Table 23.1). Complaints about Japanese investments in the United States (called "Japan bashing"), with no apparent concern about Britain's far greater financial grip on America, has raised concerns about racism.

# The Multinational Corporation

**multinational corporation** a large firm with a home base in one country operating wholly or partially owned subsidiaries in other countries

A large firm with a home base in one country operating wholly or partially owned subsidiaries in other countries is a **multinational corporation.**[23] The point at which a company engaged in international business becomes a true multinational is a subject of debate. Most people would agree that a company with subsidiaries in several countries is a multinational. A firm, however, need not operate in all—or even most—industrial countries to be considered a multinational.

## The Scale of Multinationalism

Multinationals come in many types. Exxon, McDonald's, Philip Morris, General Electric, and American Express are some of the better known U.S.-based multinationals. Phillips NAV, Mitsubishi Heavy Industries, British

A Big Mac's a Big Mac *McDonald's has made its international fortune by offering a standardized product worldwide. A Big Mac and fries in Montreal do not differ appreciably in taste from a Big Mac and fries in Rio de Janiero.*

Petroleum, and Nestlé are some well-known foreign multinationals. As these examples illustrate, multinationals typically control vast assets (see Table 23.2). They generally tend to be conglomerates, though many, like the Royal Dutch/Shell Group, are not.

As with domestic companies, profit—not national boundaries—determines the business strategies that these corporate giants develop. In a fully developed

TABLE 23.2   The Ten Largest U.S. Multinational Corporations

| 1987 rank | Company | Total revenue (mil) | Foreign revenue as percent of total | Foreign assets as percent of total |
|---|---|---|---|---|
| 1 | Exxon | $ 76,416 | 75.1 | 51.0 |
| 2 | Mobil | 52,256 | 60.5 | 48.9 |
| 3 | IBM | 54,217 | 54.0 | 54.1 |
| 4 | General Motors | 101,782 | 23.7 | 23.4 |
| 5 | Ford Motor | 73,145 | 32.8 | 39.4 |
| 6 | Texaco | 34,372 | 49.8 | 31.1 |
| 7 | Citicorp | 27,519 | 48.4 | 45.1 |
| 8 | E. I. du Pont de Nemours | 30,468 | 38.2 | 27.5 |
| 9 | Dow Chemical | 13,377 | 55.6 | 49.0 |
| 10 | Chevron | 26,015 | 22.7 | 20.2 |

Source: Excerpted from "The 100 Largest U.S. Multinationals," Excerpted by permission of *Forbes*, July 25, 1988. © Forbes Inc., 1988. p. 248.

multinational corporation, capital, technology, personnel, information, goods, and services flow freely from one country and one subsidiary to another.

## Global Influence

Many critics claim that the intense concentrations of power that multinationals can bring to bear corrupt the political processes of the countries in which they operate. These complaints have centered most often on mineral extraction and oil companies, though ITT also was a major focal point for critics in the 1970s because of allegations of illicit meddling in U.S. and Chilean politics.

It is a mistake, however, to view multinationals as a passing phenomenon or only in negative terms. Instead, they are visible and lasting proof of our

**Multinational corporation**   *The international delivery service, UPS, is a successful multinational corporation. Its home base in the United States operates branches all over the world.*

shrinking world and globalized economy. Without question, the managers of multinational corporations are constantly confronted by decisions that have large political and economic consequences. They know that they are in a global marketplace and that their actions have global implications. They face the never-ending challenge of being good world citizens.

# CHAPTER HIGHLIGHTS

*1. Describe the importance of foreign trade in our global economy.*

Foreign trade is one of the most important factors that contributes to the economic development of a nation. When Korea began exporting the Hyundai automobile to the United States, the production of this car created many new jobs. The currency received from the sale of these autos could be used by Korea to purchase goods and services from the United States and other nations. The end result should be an increase in the standard of living for the citizens of Korea.

*2. Identify two major types of trade advantages.*

Economic theory recognizes two major types of advantages. An absolute advantage exists when a country can produce a product more efficiently than any other country. This type of advantage is quite rare. A comparative advantage exists when a country can produce a product at a lower cost than a competitor can.

*3. Explain how a nation's balance of trade and balance of payments influence economic stability.*

Balance of trade is the relationship between the value of goods and services imported and the value of goods and services exported during a particular period. A favorable balance of trade exists when the value of exports exceeds that of imports. The balance of payments measures the relationship between payments coming into and payments going out of a country during a given period. Payments include all transfers of assets across the nation's boundaries. When American tourists spend money in England, they are transferring assets (cash) overseas.

*4. Identify four common types of protectionism and summarize the arguments pro and con.*

Nations often attempt to protect their domestic industries by means of *trade barriers*. Tariffs represent one method of placing imports at a disadvantage in their competition with domestic goods. A tariff is a tax imposed by a country on imported goods. A second barrier to imports is the *import quota*, a limit on the quantity of a particular good that may be brought into a country. An *embargo* is a law or government order forbidding either the importing or the exporting of specified goods. *Bureaucratic red tape* is a subtle but very frustrating form of protectionism. Those in favor of protectionist trade barriers, primarily labor unions and domestic industries hurt by imports, fear the loss of jobs and markets. Opponents of protectionism say the end consumer has to subsidize it through artificially higher prices.

*5. Describe those factors that have created a global marketplace.*

In many ways the world has grown smaller in the twentieth century. Jet planes permit faster business travel between nations, satellites now permit us to make international phone calls with ease, and ships are now bigger and faster. Most important, Americans and people from many other nations are beginning to think internationally.

*6. Explain the problem of ethnocentrism and what can be done to curb it.*

*Ethnocentrism* is the belief that one's own race or culture is superior to others. Such attitudes constitute a major barrier to intercultural business dealings. Intercultural awareness and sensitivity along with knowledge of foreign languages can help curb ethnocentrism.

*7. Explain the different ways a purely domestic business can become an international operation.*

When an American business decides to move from a purely domestic business to an international operation, it can choose from several types of ventures. One option is *exporting*. Exporting occurs when goods are produced in one country for consumption in another. A second option is *licensing*. A license is a privilege to manufacture or sell a product in all or part of a country or to extract a natural resource from a particular location. The third option is the *joint venture,* an agreement between two businesses to combine their resources to accomplish a particular objective. *Direct foreign investment,* a fourth option, describes a situation in which a company purchases assets or forms a subsidiary in another country for the purpose of producing a product and marketing it in that country or elsewhere.

## KEY TERMS

| | | | |
|---|---|---|---|
| Trade | Balance of trade | Embargo | Royalty |
| International trade | Balance of payments | Trade agreement | Joint venture |
| Trading partners | Exchange rate | General Agreement on | Coventurers |
| Foreign trade | Devaluation | Tariffs and Trade | Direct foreign |
| Specialization | Revaluation | (GATT) | investment |
| Absolute advantage | Protectionism | Reciprocity | Multinational |
| Comparative | Tariffs | Ethnocentrism | corporation |
| advantage | Revenue tariffs | Foreign Corrupt | |
| Exports | Protective tariff | Practices Act | |
| Imports | Import quota | License | |

## REVIEW QUESTIONS

1. Provide a definition of foreign trade. What are some of the common reasons countries engage in foreign trade?
2. Distinguish between absolute advantages in foreign trade and comparative advantages.
3. Why do nations seek to achieve a favorable balance of trade?
4. A nation can have a favorable balance of payments and an unfavorable balance of trade, or vice versa. Why?
5. What is meant by the term *exchange rate*?
6. In recent years, Japan's balance of payments with the United States has showed a huge surplus. What is the free market solution to this imbalance in payments?
7. List and describe four of the most common trade barriers used by nations wishing to establish barriers to imports.
8. How does a trade barrier differ from a trade agreement?
9. What factors have contributed to the creation of a global marketplace?
10. What is ethnocentrism? How does ethnocentrism serve as a barrier to cooperation between nations?

# APPLICATION EXERCISES

1. In recent years America has used import quotas to reduce the number of automobiles imported from Japan. Prepare a list of the arguments for and against this practice using concepts taken from this chapter. Then indicate what your position would be regarding future import quotas for Japan, Korea, or any other country that is providing strong competition for the American auto industry.

2. Assume the position of vice president of marketing for a small manufacturing company. This company manufactures a series of high-quality tools used by cabinetmakers. Research indicates that a market for these tools exists in several European countries including Germany, France, and Italy. You are considering the direct export of these tools which will require setting up a sales and marketing network in these countries. Another option under consideration is a joint venture with a manufacturing firm in Europe that also makes woodworking tools. What are the advantages and disadvantages of each option?

# CASES

## 23.1  Mobil's Big Pullout

For some 20 years Mobil Corp. resisted pressure from antiapartheid groups to withdraw from South Africa. Instead, the oil giant, which was the largest U.S. company still operating in the country, pushed for social change from within. Last week it gave up that tough struggle. Mobil announced plans to sell its $400 million refinery and service stations to a South African concern, General Mining Union Corp., for a bargain price of about $150 million.

The sale had little to do with Mobil's view of apartheid and everything to do with the bottom line. Congress last year eliminated credits for taxes paid in South Africa, costing the company $5 million. It said the change meant a 72 percent tax rate.

Mobil's decision could add new fuel to the stalled disinvestment movement. Over 190 U.S. companies have quit South Africa since 1986, but only a handful left last year. With Mobil gone, the remaining U.S. companies will find it harder to maintain that it's better to fight apartheid than quit.

### Questions

1. Thinking back to the definition of corporate social responsibility in Chapter 2, do you believe Mobil was a socially responsible multinational corporation when it pulled out of South Africa?

2. Will South Africa's black population be better off because of the withdrawal of U.S. companies?

Source: "Mobil's Big Pullout," *Newsweek,* May 8, 1989, p. 42. From NEWSWEEK, May 8, 1989. © 1989, Newsweek, Inc. All rights reserved. Reprinted by permission.

## 23.2  Those Strange Americans

A group of Arab oil workers sent to Texas for training found American teaching methods impersonal. Several Japanese workers at a U.S. manufacturing plant had to learn how to put courtesy aside and interrupt conversations when there was trouble. Executives of a Swiss-based multinational couldn't understand why its American managers demanded more autonomy than their European counterparts.

To all these people, America is a foreign country with a strange corporate culture. Just as Americans doing business abroad must grapple with unfamiliar social and commercial practices, so too must the European, Asian and Latin American managers of U.S. subsidiaries, a growing number of whom are coming to work here.

The U.S. Department of Immigration and Naturalization says that last fiscal year 65,349 intercompany transferees, up from 21,495 in 1978, were brought here to work in an administrative or managerial capacity or to use some specialized knowledge. . . .

To lessen the culture shock, many companies are relying on consultants to provide books, movies and special programs that educate foreign employees about corporate life in the U.S. Some have taken the language instruction, tax advice and orientation techniques used when Americans are sent abroad and modified them to accommodate foreigners transferred here. Others are trying a sort of buddy system, pairing foreign newcomers with American managers.

**"Culturally Determined"** "Most people think that culture is manners, food, dress, arts and crafts," says Clifford Clarke, president of IRI International, a Redwood City, Calif., consulting company. "They don't realize that how you motivate a guy is culturally determined. Every managerial task is culturally determined."

Occasionally, transferees find that behavior suitable at home may irritate coworkers here. *Living in the U.S.A.*, a recent training film, portrays a Japanese employee angering an American colleague by repeatedly apologizing for a late report; the American expects explanations and solutions. "In America, if you talk around things people get frustrated with you," says Lennie Copeland, who helped produce the film.

Jose Carlos Villates, a business manager for animal health products at American Cyanamid Co., also had a problem with office protocol. Back in Puerto Rico and the Dominican Republic, where he was raised, business people would begin meetings with relaxed chitchat. At the company's headquarters in Wayne, N.J., though, he says he picks up "signals or body language" that Americans find such sociability time wasting. But even after 15 months in the U.S., Mr. Villates feels uncomfortable plunging abruptly into business. "It strikes us as cold-blooded," he says.

Europeans, on the other hand, can be flummoxed by "a deceiving appearance of informality," says French-born Andre Rude. "They don't realize the urgency of the request and find themselves in trouble" when work isn't done on time. Mr. Rude counsels international transferees at Hewlett-Packard Co. in Palo Alto, Calif.

**Classroom Difficulties** Many foreigners also have a hard time with American-style classroom training. Mr. Clarke of IRI says his firm teaches Japanese to be more outspoken in such situations and recommends that American teachers "count to 10" while waiting for a reply. He adds that Arab oil workers, for their part, learned more quickly when classroom time was supplemented with individual sessions and even home visits by teachers.

## Questions

1. What factors would make it particularly difficult for someone from another culture to live and work in the United States?
2. Have you ever experienced "culture shock"? Explain.
3. Why is a "buddy system" for visiting foreign employees probably a good idea?

Source: Excerpted from Amanda Bennett, "American Culture Is Often a Puzzle for Foreign Managers in the U.S.," *Wall Street Journal*, February 12, 1986, p. 29. Reprinted by permission of *Wall Street Journal*, © Dow Jones & Company, Inc. 1989. All Rights Reserved Worldwide.

# Answers to Experiencing Business

Chapter 1

1. Deregulation 2. NeXT 3. McDonald's 4. True; Theory X, the management theory developed by Douglas McGregor, assumes that managers must closely supervise workers 5. Post-its; 3M 6. c. Fab detergent 7. Sam Walton [founder and head of the Wal-Mart department store chain] 8. GNP (gross national product) 9. the United States and Canada 10. Ford's Taurus

Chapter 2

Here are the average responses for samples of 124 American managers, 72 French managers, and 70 German managers. (The French and German managers were given specially translated versions of the questionnaire.)

| Situation 1 | | Situation 2 | |
|---|---|---|---|
| American | 4.0 | American | 3.3 |
| French | 6.9 | French | 5.7 |
| German | 5.8 | German | 5.2 |

As this exercise shows, ethical judgments are rarely a matter of black and white. There is a lot of room for personal and cultural interpretations. Generally speaking, the lower your score, the stricter your moral interpretation.

Chapter 5

If you have seven or more ["Yes"] answers, your EQ (executive quotient) is high enough to qualify for advancement. But go back and review your "no" answers, as well as the ones where you wavered. These are the areas that should be addressed in the future.

Richard Sbarbaro, president of the Chicago firm, analyzes each question in the following way:

1. Companies are looking for "idea people," not just caretakers. The long haul is considered to be more important than the immediate benefits. . . .
2. Consider that many times business can be conducted in a leisuretime mode, and, in fact, many of the most successful deals have been closed in a nonbusiness atmosphere. . . .

Candidates who have an active social and cultural life are considered to be more aware of and knowledgeable about the world around them. Employers are not looking for people with tunnel vision.
3. Even the best plan must first be sold to management. The candidate that can communicate effectively is heads above those that can't put a plan down on paper. Also, in order for a plan to be effective it must be communicated to those people who are charged with its implementation.
4. Those who can't enjoy life are in big trouble. Humor can often relieve the tension in a stressful environment.
5. The specialists (engineers, scientists, computer experts, etc.) who have moved into senior management are those who have taken an interest in the entire company and have become team players.

The most successful managers are willing to get their fingers dirty on occasion. Also, they never forget that bottom line results are the only results that count.
6. Sometimes a gut reaction is the best one. Don't, however, operate that way on a regular basis.
7. Fast track executives normally are more interested in

salary and bonus than in pension and profit-sharing plans.

8. Know your allies within the company. Use your mentor when needed. Just because the plan is good, don't expect it to roll right through. Jealousy is a reality among peers.

9. It's easier to determine who is promotable if you follow a hands-off policy. Don't create drones. Remember, though, that you are responsible for those you supervise.

10. Have fun, but play to win. That's a good idea whether it's golf or business . . . or both.

Source: "For Your Information," *Personnel Journal,* September 1984, p. 10.

## Chapter 7

How employees ranked the importance of morale-building factors in their work:

1. Interesting work
2. Full appreciation of work done
3. Feeling of being in on things
4. Job security
5. Good wages
6. Promotion and growth in the organization
7. Good working conditions
8. Personal loyalty to employees
9. Tactful discipline
10. Sympathetic help with personal problems

How managers thought their employees would rate these factors:

1. Good wages
2. Job security
3. Promotion and growth in the organization
4. Good working conditions
5. Interesting work
6. Personal loyalty to employees
7. Sympathetic help with personal problems
8. Full appreciation of work done
9. Tactful discipline
10. Feeling of being in on things

Source: Data from Kenneth A. Kovach, "What Motivates Employees? Workers and Supervisors Give Different Answers," *Business Horizons* 30 (September-October 1987: 58–65.

## Chapter 8

1. b (Refer to discussion in this chapter.)
2. a (See Figure 8.1.)
3. a (In 1987, American women working full time earned on the average 69 percent of what men earned, up 8 percent from 1978. The gender gap in pay is narrowing but is still large.[22])

4. c (Refer to discussion in this chapter.)
5. d (See Figure 8.5.)
6. b (Refer to discussion in this chapter.)
7. b ("there's considerable documentation that older workers are . . . extremely productive.")[23]
8. b (According to the U.S. Department of Labor, the five occupations with the largest job growth between now and 1995 will be cashiers; registered nurses; janitors, cleaners, maids; truck drivers, and waiters and waitresses.)[24]
9. d (Refer to discussion in this chapter.)
10. c (Refer to discussion in this chapter.)

## Chapter 12

The ten most powerful brand names in America are:

1. Coca-Cola
2. Campbell's
3. Pepsi-Cola
4. AT&T
5. McDonald's
6. American Express
7. Kellogg's
8. IBM
9. Levi's
10. Sears

Source: Edward C. Baig, "Name That Brand," *Fortune,* July 4, 1988, p. 11–12.

## Chapter 15

1. Net profit margin: 3.2%
2. Return on equity: 17.3%
3. Earnings per share: $6.11
4. Working capital: $1,099.4 million
5. Current ratio: 1.45
6. Acid-test ratio: 0.74
7. Inventory turnover: 5.07
8. Debt-to-assets ratio: 0.69
9. Debt-to-equity ratio: 1.21

## Chapter 16

On close inspection, each of these ten items turns out to be an excuse, not a *valid reason,* for not using a computer.

1. A stated desire to not want to use a computer often is an emotional response motivated by fear of failure.
2. Computers don't make mistakes, people do. Because billing mistakes and other administrative problems are often blamed on computers, people have come to mistrust them. Computers do what they are instructed to do. If they are given faulty instructions,

they will produce faulty results. "Garbage in—garbage out!"

3. True, computers generally are associated with the young. But that is no reason for older people to shy away from them. James A. Michener, the widely read novelist, did not launch his writing career until he was forty. Age is a state of mind, not a number.

4. A trip to the nearest computer store for some browsing will open up a whole new world of possibilities for using a computer for work and/or play.

5. Technically, computers are complicated. But user friendly hardware and software are making them accessible for the average individual.

6. Computer users do indeed often engage in terminology overkill. Again, as computer hardware and software become more user friendly, the technical jargon will be pushed aside. Think of the modern telephone. It is a highly complex piece of telecommunications equipment. But it is so user friendly that you do not need a technical vocabulary to make a phone call. All it takes is pushing a few bottons.

7. This item involves two mistaken notions. First, although computers often are used for complex mathematical problems, you do not need to be a math whiz to operate the typical business program. Second, you do not have to be a computer programmer to be able to do work on a computer. All the programming has already been performed for you when you buy an application program for word processing, spreadsheets, and so on. Analogously, you do not have to know how to build and repair an automobile in order to drive one.

8. Though it helps to be a fast touch typist when entering data on a keyboard, many computer users do very nicely with their own version of hunt-and-peck. Moreover, other input devices such as a point-and-push "mouse" eliminate the keyboard altogether.

9. True, computer technology changes rapidly. But the key to buying a computer is finding one that adequately performs the jobs you need to accomplish, for a reasonable price. Even when new computers come on the market, you will still have one that "gets the job done."

10. Personal computers have been around long enough to permit the growth of a used computer market. Used personal computers, still in good working order, can be purchased for surprisingly little today.

## Chapter 19

1. The stock would fall. Sears is a formidable competitor; this decision would hurt Pay-Less's sales.

2. The stock would rise. If the economy is strong, retail sales should be up and the company should benefit.

3. The stock would fall. When the visionary leaders of a fast growing company leave the company for any reason, it is likely to hurt the company—particularly if they die. Charter Companies experienced a loss of its leadership due to an airplane crash in the 1980s. Many stockholders sold on the news and the confusion in the company that followed resulted in the company being forced into bankruptcy.

4. There would be no effect on the stock. A routine sales promotion by a competitor should have no particular effect on the stock of the company.

5. The stock would rise. When a well financed company announces interest in buying another company, the stock of the target company almost invariably rises.

6. There would be no effect. The European company is not establishing many stores and they are selling merchandise to a different market than Pay-Less.

7. Stock price would fall. When there is a major judgment against a company, the profits may be adversely affected, hurting the stock price. Even before any judgement, the negative publicity may hurt employee morale and cause customers to go to the competition.

8. Effect cannot be determined. Opening new stores overseas may be a great move in the long term; however, it is too early to tell whether U.S. marketing methods will work in France. In addition, there are major costs involved in establishing new operations in foreign countries.

## Chapter 20

1. The risks the new firm will face can be classified as property and liability risks. Among the property risks are those related to destruction of your building and its contents because of fire or some other event, business interruption risk, damage to your trucks from collisions, and theft by employees or others. The primary liability risks arise out of the operation of your trucks and injuries to your employees on the job.

2. Hazard reduction efforts might include training programs for your employees so that they will not cause accidents. Loss reduction might include installing a sprinkler system and fire alarms to reduce the potential loss should a fire occur. These would be especially important since plastics are highly flammable. Risk reduction would involve the purchase of insurance. Fire, business interruption, worker's compensation, automobile (property and liability), theft, general liability, marine, and key person (life) insurance are among the types of insurance you would need to purchase.

3. You would probably be interested in group life, health, dental, and disability income insurance as fringe benefits for your employees.

The answer in this case rested in cultural differences. These differences are the result of variations in training and values. Hesitance to take independent intiative on tasks is just one of the challenges faced by managers of multi-cultural workforces.

Some foreign-born employees also resist admitting that instructions have not been understood. This problem relates to language and accent barriers within the office.

Keep in mind that any statement regarding a given group is, of necessity, a generality. Generalities about cultures must be applied cautiously. Each individual and each case must be considered separately. The information supplied in articles such as this are only guidelines. They are starting points for your exploration into the world of cultural diversity. They are not final absolute statements of fact that can be applied in any situation or to any individual.

## Strong Respect

The tendency to resist taking initiative on duties exists among a wide variety of immigrant groups, but it is most common among Asian or Hispanic populations. The reluctance to take independent action grows out of two culturally rooted attitudes that differ radically from those held in the United States.

The first of these perspectives is a strong respect for authority. This dictates that actions should be undertaken only after the boss has ordered or approved them. For many foreign-born employees, beginning a task without specific instructions shows disrespect and defiance to their superiors. This action is disruptive to the careful hierarchy of power found in many countries.

A second, related attitude is the fear of loss of face. To lose face—or *kibun*, as Koreans refer to it—is to suffer embarrassment in front of others. Similarly, Tagalog-speaking Filipinos speak of suffering from *hiya*, or shame. An employee who undertakes a task on his or her own, especially an unfamiliar task, is risking failure and humiliation. This view stands in sharp contrast to the traditional American perspective: "Nothing ventured, nothing gained."

The solution to this problem lies in awareness and education. Newly hired foreign-born employees must be told that in the United States, taking a well-considered move on one's own, even if a mistake is made, is better than always waiting to be told what to do. A manager should emphasize that acting independently does not show disrespect for authority, and that initiative is considered a sign of dedication and loyalty.

Mistakes inevitably will be made when these employees take initiative. These mistakes present the greatest challenge to the cross-cultural manager, who must correct the error while preserving the pride of the employee. If pride and face are lost through such an error, the chances of that employee ever taking initiative again is greatly diminished.

Although the manager obviously must correct the error, he or she should also praise the employee for having taken the initiative. Only this way can the employee's confidence be raised and independent action encouraged.

A manager should also clearly state which tasks can be undertaken independently and which require further direction. The foreign-born employee, unlike a native-born employee will probably not make this distinction on his or her own. Being specific can avoid confusion, minimize errors and go far toward relieving this often frustrating problem.

## Face Saver

Loss of face can also be a partial reason why foreign-born employees are reluctant to admit that instructions have not been understood. This employee is not only concerned with losing face for him- or herself, but is also worried about causing embarrassment for the person giving the instruction. The foreign-born employee believes that the instructor may lose face because of the implication that if the material is not understood, it must not have been explained properly. This is an important point. The employee is concerned not only with being embarrassed, but with causing embarrassment as well.

The solution to this problem is straightforward and within the grasp of any manager with good observation skills and who knows the significance of nonverbal communication.

A manager probably needs to go over information again if the foreign-born employee gives the following responses:

- repetitive nodding and smiling;
- repetition of "Yes, I understand";
- distracted facial expression; and
- failure to ask any questions.

When a manager observes signs of poor understanding, he or she can encourage the asking of questions by essentially speaking the employee's "cultural language."

The manager should explain to the employee that management, too, will lose face if tasks are not completed correctly by employees. By discussing "saving face," a concept that the employee can understand and relate to, the manager is using a successful motivation strategy as well as showing the employee the kind of respect that will generate future cooperation and productivity.

# Notes

## Chapter 1

1. Walter Guzzardi Jr., "The U.S. Business Hall of Fame," *Fortune*, March 14, 1988, pp. 144–145.
2. Data from Jeremy Main, "Breaking Out of the Company," *Fortune*, May 25, 1987, pp. 82–88.
3. See Robert A. Peterson, George Kozmetsky, and Nancy M. Ridgway, "Perceived Causes of Small Business Failures: A Research Note," *American Journal of Small Business*, July–September 1983, pp. 15–19.
4. Complete details may be found in Ron Zemke, "The Honeywell Studies: How Managers Learn to Manage," *Training*, August 1985, pp. 46–51.
5. Richard I. Kirkland, Jr., "The Death of Socialism," *Fortune*, January 4, 1988, p. 65.
6. Karl Marx, *Critique of the Gotha Programme* (1875), as reprinted in *Karl Marx and Frederick Engels, Selected Works*, vol. 2 (London: Lawrence & Wishart, Ltd., 1962), pp. 1, 24.
7. Kirkland, "Death of Socialism," pp. 66, 71.
8. See Adam Smith, *The Wealth of Nations* (New York: Modern Library, 1937).
9. Data from Edward J. Toth, "The International Outlook for U.S. Business," *Government Finance Review*, February 1988, pp. 19–23.
10. Lawrence M. Friedman, *A History of American Law* (New York: Simon & Schuster, 1972), p. 166.
11. Milton Moskowitz, et al., eds., *Everybody's Business* (New York: Harper & Row, 1980), pp. 152, 153–154.
12. Samuel Eliot Morison, *The Oxford History of the American People* (New York: Oxford Univ. Press, 1964), pp. 666–669.
13. Christopher Power and Aaron Bernstein, "The Fren-zied Skies," *Business Week*, December 19, 1988, p. 72.
14. See Catherine Yang and Howard Gleckman, "The S&L Mess—and How to Fix It," *Business Week*, October 31, 1988, pp. 130–136.
15. Data from Peter Nulty, "The Economy of the 1990s: How Managers Will Manage," *Fortune*, February 2, 1987, pp. 47–50.
16. William B. Johnston and Arnold H. Packer, *Workforce 2000: Work and Workers for the Twenty-first Century* (Indianapolis: Hudson Institute, 1987), pp. 105–106.

## Chapter 2

1. See "Adopting' an Entire Class," *Business Week*, January 12, 1987, p. 130; Roger Thompson, "A Father of Innovation," *Nation's Business*, April 1987, pp. 61–62; and Elizabeth Ehrlich, "Business Is Becoming a Substitute Teacher," *Business Week*, September 19, 1988, pp. 134–135.
2. Adapted from Thomas M. Jones, "Corporate Social Responsibility Revisited, Redefined," *California Management Review*, Spring 1980, pp. 59–60.
3. Milton Friedman, "A Friedman Doctrine—The Social Responsibility of Business is to Increase its Profits," *New York Times Magazine*, September 13, 1970, p. 126.
4. Amy Borrus, "Japan Digs Deep to Win the Hearts and Minds of America," *Business Week*, July 11, 1988, p. 73.
5. David Vogel, foreword to Thornton Bradshaw & David Vogel, *Corporations and Their Critics* (New York: McGraw-Hill, 1982), viii-ix.

6. Stuart Jackson and Harris Collingwood, "Business Week/Harris Poll: Is an Antibusiness Backlash Building?" *Business Week,* July 20, 1987, p. 71.
7. See Ron Powers, "Businessmen Wear Black Hats," *Business Month,* December 1987, pp. 70–74.
8. Eric Jay Dolin, "Industry Is Going on a Waste-Watcher's Diet," *Business Week,* August 22, 1988, p. 94.
9. Louis W. Fry, Gerald D. Keim, and Roger E. Meiners, "Corporate Contributions: Altruistic or For-Profit," *Academy of Management Journal,* March 1982, p. 105.
10. For example, see Joseph Nolan and David Nolan, "The Path to Social Responsibility," *Across the Board,* May 1986, pp. 54–58.
11. William L. Prosser, *The Law of Torts,* 4th ed. (St. Paul, Minn.: West, 1971), pp. 641–643. The example is based on MacPhearson *v.* Buick Motor Co., 217 N.Y. 382, 111 N.E. 1050 (1916).
12. Irving Howe, *World of Our Fathers* (New York: Harcourt Brace Jovanovich, 1976), pp. 304–305.
13. W. A. Haas, Jr., "Corporate Social Responsibility: A New Term for an Old Concept with New Significance," in Bradshaw and Vogel, eds. *Corporations and Their Critics,* p. 135.
14. Amy L. Domini and Peter D. Kinder, *Ethical Investing* (Reading, Mass.: Addison-Wesley, 1984), p. 71.
15. Milton R. Moskowitz, "Company Performance Roundup," *Business and Society Review,* Summer 1988, p. 68.
16. See *1985 Annual Report* (Downers Grove, Ill.: ServiceMaster Industries, Inc., 1986); Jay McCormick, "Amazing Grace," *Forbes,* June 17, 1985, p. 83.
17. Robert T. Gray, "Making Ethics Come Alive," *Nation's Business,* June 1988, p. 65.
18. Data from Jackson and Collingwood, "Business Week/Harris Poll."
19. See Joe Queenan, "Juice Men," *Barron's,* June 20, 1988, pp. 37–38.
20. Thomas R. Horton, "The Ethics Crisis Continues: What to Do?" *Management Review,* November 1986, p. 3.
21. Karen L. Koman, "General Dynamics People Get Lessons In Ethics," *St. Louis Post-Dispatch,* March 30, 1986, pp. 1A, 8A.
22. "Business' Big Morality Play," *Dun's Review,* August 1980, p. 56.
23. See, for example, Janet P. Near, "Whistle-Blowing: Encourage It!" *Business Horizons,* January–February 1989, pp. 2–6.
24. Data from William H. Wagel, "A New Focus on Business Ethics at General Dynamics," *Personnel,* August 1987, pp. 4–8.

### Chapter 3

1. Todd Mason, "Big John Connally Falls to Earth near Austin," *Business Week,* December 15, 1986; Peter Nulty, "John Connally's Time of Trouble," *Fortune,* June 23, 1986, p. 101; Harlan S. Byrne, "Trials and Tribulations: More on John Connally's Business Ventures," *Barron's,* July 14, 1986.
2. Uniform Partnership Act, §6 (1).
3. Model Business Corporation Act, §54 (a), (c)–(f), (h)–(j).
4. Ibid., §55.
5. *The Coca-Cola Company Annual Report 1985* (1986), p. 41.
6. *General Electric Co. Annual Report 1984* (1985), p. 30.
7. Laura Landro and Carolyn Phillips, "Pulitzer Family Feud Widens Over Bid," *The Wall Street Journal,* April 11, 1986, p. 6; Alex S. Jones, "And Now the Pulitzers Go to War," *The New York Times,* April 13, 1986, p. F4.
8. "The Fortune 500," *Fortune,* April 24, 1989, pp. 346–401.
9. Model Business Corporation Act, §50.
10. "Corporate Odd Couples," *Business Week,* July 21, 1986, pp. 100–105.

### Chapter 4

1. Dawn Bethe Frankfort, "Milkman with the Midas Touch," *USAir,* October 1986, p. 65.
2. Ibid., p. 65.
3. Nicholas C. Siropolis, *Small Business Management,* 3rd ed. (Boston: Houghton Mifflin, 1986), p. 37.
4. Quoted by Office of Economic Research, The New York Stock Exchange, *Economic Choices for the 1980s* (January 1980), p. 9, as quoted in Siropolis, *Small Business Management,* p. 37.
5. W. L. Gore, letter to the editor, *Inc.,* December 1985, p. 7.
6. "The *Savvy* 60," *Savvy,* April 1985, pp. 50, 51–52.
7. M. Beauchamp, "Son Knows Best, for Now," *Forbes,* December 16, 1985, pp. 62, 66.
8. Calvin A. Kent, Donald L. Sexton, and Karl H. Vesper, *Encyclopedia of Entrepreneurship,* 1982, p. 29.
9. "The 1988 Inc. 500," *Inc.,* December 1988, p. 88.
10. Carol J. Loomis, "IBM's Big Blues: A Legend Tries to Remake Itself," *Fortune,* January 19, 1987, p. 34.
11. Siropolis, *Small Business Management,* p. 7.
12. "The 1988 Inc. 500," *Inc.,* December 1988, p. 88.
13. David L. Birch, *Job Creation in America* (New York: The Free Press, 1987), pp. 7–24.
14. "Nine Who Dare," *Forbes,* November 21, 1983, p. 123; John A. Conway, "Follow-Through," *Forbes,* January 13, 1986, p. 10.
15. Sheila Lukins and Julee Rosso (New York: Workman, 1981), xi-xiii.

16. David Gray, "Prematurely Gray," *Inc.*, November 1988, p. 23.
17. Bro Uttal, "Inside the Deal that Made Bill Gates $350,000,000," *Fortune,* July 21, 1986, pp. 23–33.
18. J. Bettner and C. Donahue, "Now They're Not Laughing," *Forbes,* November 21, 1983, pp. 116, 117–118.
19. "Home Business," U.S. Small Business Administration Bibliography, (Washington, D.C.: U.S. Government Printing Office), no. 2 1985, p. 2.
20. "New Economic Realities: The Rise of Women Entrepreneurs," *A Report of the Committee on Small Business,* House of Representatives, June 28, 1988 (Washington, D.C.: U. S. Government Printing Office, 1988), iii.
21. Tom Richman, "The New American Start-Up," *Inc.,* September 1988, p. 54.
22. SBA figures as quoted in R. Greene, "Do You Really Want to Be Your Own Boss?" *Forbes,* October 21, 1985, p. 86.
23. Calvin Trillin, "Competitors," *The New Yorker,* July 8, 1985, p. 31.
24. W. Baldwin, "Too Much of a Good Thing?" *Forbes,* December 16, 1985, pp. 102–103.
25. Mark Leepson, "Building a Business: A Matter of Course," *Nation's Business,* April 1988, p. 42.
26. Clay Chandler, "Hatching Business," *Roanoke Times and World News,* October 9, 1988, p. F-1.
27. U.S. Department of Commerce, Bureau of Industrial Economics and the Minority Business Development Agency, *The Franchise Opportunities Handbook* (Washington, D.C.: U.S. Government Printing Office, 1983), p. 24.
28. A. Spector, "5 Franchisors Discuss Growth," *Independent Restaurants,* October, 1985, pp. 42, 45.
29. See the Automobile Dealer's Day in Court Act of 1956 and the Petroleum Marketers Practices Act of 1979.

### Chapter 5

1. Kenneth Labich, "The Seven Keys to Business Leadership," *Fortune,* October 24, 1988, p. 59.
2. Data from Andrea L. Woolard, "The Rebuilding of a Nonprofit," *Association Management,* February 1986, pp. 86–90. Also see V. V. Murray, "Why Can't Voluntary Organizations Be More Business-like?" *Canadian Business Review,* Spring 1987, pp. 19–21.
3. Adapted from discussion in Robert L. Katz, "Skills of an Effective Administrator," *Harvard Business Review,* Sept.–Oct. 1974, pp. 90–102.
4. Adapted from Henry Mintzberg, "The Manager's Job: Folklore and Fact," *Harvard Business Review,* July–Aug. 1975, pp. 49–61.
5. Kenneth Labich, "At Corning, A Vision of Quality," *Fortune,* October 24, 1988, p. 64.
6. Ibid.

7. Gary Hector, "Yes, You *Can* Manage Long Term," *Fortune,* November 21, 1988, p. 68.
8. See Carol Davenport, "America's Most Admired Corporations," *Fortune,* January 30, 1989, pp. 68–75.
9. Adapted from Robert J. House, "A Path Goal Theory of Leader Effectiveness," *Administrative Science Quarterly,* September 1971, pp. 321–338.
10. See Thomas Moore, "Make-or-Break Time for General Motors," *Fortune,* February 15, 1988, pp. 32–42 and David Pauly, "GM Gets Back in High Gear," *Newsweek,* February 20, 1989, p. 39.
11. Terrence E. Deal and Allan A. Kennedy, *Corporate Cultures* (Reading, MA: Addison-Wesley Publishing Co., 1982), p. 15.
12. Anne B. Fisher, "Glamour: Getting It—or Getting It Back," *Fortune,* May 12, 1986, pp. 18–22.

### Chapter 6

1. Alex Taylor III, "The Tasks Facing General Motors," *Fortune,* March 13, 1989, p. 52.
2. Data from Ron Zemke, "Putting the Squeeze on Middle Managers," *Training,* December 1988, pp. 41–46.
3. See James W. Walker, "Managing Human Resources in Flat, Lean, and Flexible Organizations: Trends for the 1990's," *Human Resource Planning,* no. 2, 1988, pp. 125–132.
4. John A. Byrne, "Caught in the Middle," *Business Week,* September 12, 1988, p. 88.
5. Adam Smith, *The Wealth of Nations* (Harmondsworth, Eng.: Penguin, 1982), pp. 109ff.
6. Taylor, "Tasks Facing General Motors," p. 53.
7. See Patrick Houston, "Why Honeywell Bull Is on a Turnaround Track," *Business Week,* February 22, 1988, pp. 152, 154.
8. Based on Maria Shao, "Apple Turns from Revolution to Evolution," *Business Week,* January 23, 1989, pp. 90, 92.
9. Adapted from John R. P. French and Bertram Raven, "The Bases of Social Power," in *Studies in Social Power,* ed. Dorwin Cartwright (Ann Arbor: University of Michigan Press, 1959), pp. 150–167.
10. See Philip M. Podsakoff and Chester A. Schriesheim, "Field Studies of French and Raven's Bases of Power: Critique, Reanalysis, and Suggestions for Future Research," *Psychological Bulletin,* May 1985, pp. 387–411.
11. Richard E. Krafve, *Boston Sunday Globe,* May 22, 1960; as quoted in Robert W. Kent, ed., *Money Talks* (New York: Facts on File, 1985), p. 214.
12. Adapted from Jerry M. Rosenberg, *Dictionary of Business and Management,* p. 296. Copyright © 1983 by John Wiley & Sons. Reprinted by permission of John Wiley & Sons, Inc., New York.
13. Harvey F. Kolodny, "Managing in a Matrix," *Business Horizons,* March–April 1981, pp. 17–24. Also

see Erik W. Larson and David H. Gobeli, "Matrix Management: Contradictions and Insights," *California Management Review*, Summer 1987, pp. 126–138.

14. Data from Roy Rowan, "Where Did *That* Rumor Come From?" *Fortune*, August 13, 1979, pp. 130–137.

15. "Executives Favor Plucking the Fruits from Employee Grapevine," *Association Management*, April 1984, p. 105. Also see Alan Zaremba, "Working with the Organizational Grapevine," *Personnel Journal*, July 1988, pp. 38–41.

16. Carol Davenport, "America's Most Admired Corporations," *Fortune*, January 30, 1989, p. 71.

## Chapter 7

1. Robert Levering, *A Great Place to Work* (New York: Random House 1988), pp. 33–39.
2. Ibid., p. 33.
3. Barry L. Reece and Rhonda Brandt, *Effective Human Relations in Organizations* (Boston: Houghton Mifflin, 1987), p. 4.
4. Keith Davis, *Human Behavior at Work* (New York: McGraw-Hill, 1981), p. 12. Donna Fenn, "The Kids Are All Right," *Inc.*, January 1985, pp. 48–54.
5. Robert Levering, Milton Moskowitz, and Michael Katz, *The 100 Best Companies to Work for in America* (New York: New American Library, 1985), pp. 110–115.
6. Ibid., p. 251.
7. "America's Fitness Binge," *U.S. News & World Report*, May 3, 1982, p. 60.
8. Terri Minsky, "Stride-Rite Dampers Down Smoking," *Boston Globe*, May 14, 1985, p. 45, 47.
9. Adapted from Ricky W. Griffin and Gregory Moorhead, *Organizational Behavior* (Boston: Houghton Mifflin, 1986), p. 140, and Richard M. Steers and Lyman W. Porter, *Motivation and Work Behavior*, 3rd ed. (New York: McGraw-Hill, 1983).
10. As quoted in "Thoughts on the Business of Life," *Forbes*, October 7, 1985, p. 192.
11. Ricky W. Griffin, *Management* (Boston: Houghton Mifflin, 1984), p. 571.
12. David R. Hampton, *Contemporary Management*, 2nd ed. (New York: McGraw-Hill, 1981), pp. 15–19.
13. Robert Kreitner, *Management*, 4th ed. (Boston: Houghton Mifflin, 1989), p. 67.
14. Abraham H. Maslow, *Motivation and Personality* (New York: Harper & Row, 1954).
15. Levering, *Great Place to Work*, pp. 63, 64.
16. Levering et al., *100 Best Companies to Work for*, pp. 199–202.
17. "How Bosses Get People to Work Harder," *U.S. News & World Report*, January 29, 1979, p. 63.
18. Hampton, *Contemporary Management*, p. 52.
19. Douglas McGregor, *The Human Side of Enterprise* (New York: McGraw-Hill, 1960).
20. Levering et al., *100 Best Companies to Work for*, pp. 225–228.
21. Kenneth Blanchard and Spencer Johnson, *The One Minute Manager* (New York: William Morrow & Co., 1982), p. 40.
22. Keith Davis, *Human Behavior at Work* (New York: McGraw-Hill, 1977), p. 61.
23. "Idea Man," *The Wall Street Journal*, July 26, 1976, p. 1.
24. Saul Rubinstein, "QWL [Quality of Work Life], the Union, the Specialist, and Employment Security," *Training and Development Journal*, March 1984, p. 82.
25. *A Conference on Quality of Work Life: Issues Affecting the State-of-the Art* (Washington, D.C.: U.S. Dept. of Labor, 1984), p. 1.
26. Tom St. George, "Quality of Work Life: Why Things Get Tougher as You Go," *Training/HRO*, January 1984, p. 70.
27. Paul D. Bush, "The Argument for Employee Participation," *Boston Globe*, November 12, 1985, p. 30.
28. William G. Ouchi, *Theory Z* (Reading, Mass.: Addison-Wesley, 1981).
29. Bush, *Boston Globe*, p. 30.
30. Philip I. Morgan and H. Kent Baker, "Taking a Look at Flexitime," *Supervisory Management*, February 1984, p. 38.
31. Ellen Wojohn, "Bringing Up Baby," *Inc.*, November 1988, pp. 64, 65.
32. Levering et al., *100 Best Companies to work for*, p. 104.
33. Glenn Collins, "Many in Work Force Care for Elderly Kin," *The New York Times*, January 6, 1986, p. B5.
34. Telecommuting: An Idea Whose Time Has Almost Come," *Management Technology*, January 1984, p. 29.
35. Karl Albrecht and Ron Zemke, *Service America* (Homewood, Ill.: Dow Jones-Irwin, 1985).
36. Julia H. Martin and Donna J. Tolson, "Changing Job Skills in Virginia: The Employer's View," in University of Virginia Institute of Government *Newsletter*, 62: 6 (January 1986), p. 34.
37. Robert W. Kent, ed., *Money Talks* (New York: Facts on File, 1985), p. 219.

## Chapter 8

1. Karen Berney, "Child Care by Consortium," *Nation's Business*, May 1988, p. 24.
2. Data from "Caring for the Children," *Nation's Business*, May 1988, pp. 18–25; Robert T. Jones, "The Year 2000 Worker," *Association Management*, June 1988, pp. 14, 16; and Anthony Ramirez, "Making Better Use of Older Workers," *Fortune*, January 30, 1989, pp. 179–180, 184, 186–187.

3. Pat Choate, vice president of public policy at TRW, as quoted in Louis S. Richman, "Tomorrow's Jobs: Plentiful, But . . .," *Fortune*, April 11, 1988, p. 48.
4. Jeffrey J. Hallett, "America at Work: The U.S. Workforce 1988–2015," *Electric Perspectives*, Summer 1988, p. 35.
5. See Alan Farnham, "Holding Firm on Affirmative Action," *Fortune*, March 13, 1989, pp. 87–88.
6. For more, see Richard Koenig, "Toyota Takes Pains, and Time, Filling Jobs at Its Kentucky Plant," *The Wall Street Journal*, December 1, 1987, pp. 1, 27.
7. Ibid.
8. Lee Bowes, *No One Need Apply: Getting and Keeping the Best Workers*, quoted in Brian Dumaine, "The New Art of Hiring Smart," *Fortune*, August 17, 1987, p. 78.
9. Karen M. Evans and Randall Brown, "Reducing Recruitment Risk Through Preemployment Testing," *Personnel*, September 1988, pp. 55–56.
10. Dumaine, "New Art of Hiring Smart," p. 80.
11. See James G. Frierson, "New Polygraph Test Limits," *Personnel Journal*, December 1988, pp. 84–92.
12. Data from Eric Rolfe Greenberg, "Workplace Testing: Results of a New AMA Survey," *Personnel*, April 1988, pp. 36–44.
13. Paul L. Blocklyn, "Making Magic: The Disney Approach to People Management," *Personnel*, December 1988, p. 32.
14. Data from Barry C. Campbell and Cynthia L. Barron, "How Extensively Are HRM Practices Being Utilized by the Practitioners?" *Personnel Administrator*, May 1982, pp. 67–71. Also see William L. Hunter, "Relieving the Pain of Performance Appraisals," *Management World*, June 1988, pp. 7–9.
15. Data from Dale A. Masi and Seymour J. Friedland, "EAP Actions & Options," *Personnel Journal*, June 1988, pp. 61–67.
16. See Theodore H. Rosen, "Identification of Substance Abusers in The Workplace," *Public Personnel Management*, Fall 1987, pp. 197–207.
17. Data from John Brecher, "Taking Drugs on the Job," *Newsweek*, August 22, 1983, pp. 52–60.
18. Data from Chris Lee, "Where the Training Dollars Go," *Training*, October 1987, pp. 51–65.
19. See Patricia A. Galagan, "IBM Gets Its Arms Around Education," *Training & Development Journal*, January 1989, pp. 35–41.
20. For practical advice on terminations, see Steven A. Jesseph, "Employee Termination, 2: Some Dos and Don'ts," *Personnel*, February 1989, pp. 36–38.
21. Data from Morton E. Grossman and Margaret Magnus, "The Boom in Benefits," *Personnel Journal*, November 1988, pp. 50–55.
22. Data from Gene Koretz, "A Shifting Labor Market Cuts Male-Female Wage Gap," *Business Week*, August 10, 1987, p. 18.
23. Ramirez, "Making Better Use of Older Workers," p. 186.
24. Data from Hallett, "America at Work: The U.S. Workforce 1988–2015," p. 32.

### Chapter 9

1. "Mr. Smith Goes Global," *Business Week*, February 13, 1989, p. 66–72.
2. Page Smith, *The Nation Comes of Age* (New York: McGraw-Hill, 1981), pp. 795–796.
3. Paul A. Samuelson and William D. Nordhaus, *Economics*, 12th ed. (New York: McGraw-Hill, 1985), p. 635.
4. Harold C. Livesay, *Samuel Gompers and Organized Labor in America* (Little Brown, Boston), 1978.
5. The Clayton Act, §6.
6. Handbook of Labor Statistics, Wages, and Industrial Relations. 1978.
7. Data from Bureau of Labor Statistics, Wages, and Industrial Relations, Washington, D.C.; Laurent Belsie, "Industrial Unions on the Rebound," *The Christian Science Monitor*, January 23, 1989, p. 7.
8. L. Bernstein, "Unions Revert to 1930s-style Organizing Tactics."
9. "The Killing Cost Stalking Business," *Fortune*, February 27, 1989, pp. 58–68.
10. Livesay, *Samuel Gompers*.
11. W. Serrin, "Historians See Lessons for Present in Fate of Dead Anthracite Coal Towns," *New York Times*, December 29, 1985, p. 30.
12. "A Work Revolution in U.S. Industry," *Business Week*, May 16, 1983, p. 100.

### Chapter 10

1. Shirley Cayer, "Harley's New Manager-Owners Put Purchasing Out Front," *Purchasing*, October 13, 1988, p. 50.
2. See James R. Evans et al., *Applied Production and Operations Management* (St. Paul, Minn.: West, 1984), pp. 341–344.
3. Data from Alex Taylor III, "The Tasks Facing General Motors," *Fortune*, March 13, 1989, pp. 52–59.
4. See Michael L. Rothberg, "IBM PC: No Accident," *Computer Decisions*, July 1988, p. 16.
5. See, for example, Roger Rowand, "GM Defends Its Outsourcing," *Automotive News*, July 18, 1988, pp. E32–E33.
6. "The Hollow Corporation," *Business Week*, March 3, 1986, p. 56.
7. For more, see Lucien Rhodes, "High on the Hog," *Inc.*, March 1987, pp. 77–84, and Charles R. Day Jr., "What a Dumb Idea," *Industry Week*, January 2, 1989, pp. 27–28.
8. Evans et al., *Applied Production and Operations Management*, p. 618.

9. Rux Martin, "Gourmet Foods from the Green Mountains," *Vermont Life,* Winter 1985, p. 23.
10. See Michael Rogers, "Coors Comes Bubbling Back," *Fortune,* March 17, 1986, pp. 51, 53.
11. See Jeffrey Rothfeder, "These Maps Can Find Oil—Or Sell Burgers," *Business Week,* March 13, 1989, p. 134.
12. Louis Kraar, "Japan's Gung-Ho U.S. Car Plants," *Fortune,* January 30, 1989, p. 98.
13. John A. Byrne, "Is Your Company Too Big?" *Business Week,* March 27, 1989, p. 92.
14. Gene Bylinsky, "A Breakthrough in Automating the Assembly Line," *Fortune,* May 26, 1986, pp. 64–66.
15. Bill Saporito, "IBM's No-Hands Assembly Line," *Fortune,* September 15, 1986, p. 105.
16. R. H. Anthony and J. S. Reese, *Management Accounting* (Homewood, Ill.: Richard D. Irwin, Inc., 1975).
17. Adapted from Jerry M. Rosenberg, *Dictionary of Business and Management,* 2nd ed. Copyright © 1983 by John Wiley & Sons. Reprinted by permission of John Wiley & Sons, Inc., pp. 266–267.
18. A good background source is Sumer C. Aggarwal, "MRP, JIT, OPT, FMS?" *Harvard Business Review,* September-October 1985, pp. 8–10, 12, 16.
19. Based on John A. Byrne, "Culture Shock at Xerox," *Business Week,* June 22, 1987, pp. 106–110.
20. Data for (3) from Patricia Sellers, "Getting Customers to Love You," *Fortune,* March 13, 1989, pp. 38–49.
21. Jack Meredith and Thomas E. Gibbs, *The Management of Operations,* 2nd ed. (New York: John Wiley and Sons, 1984), p. 539.
22. Brian Dumaine, "How Managers Can Succeed Through Speed," *Fortune,* February 13, 1989, p. 54.

Chapter 11

1. Bill Saporito, "The Fly in Campbell's Soup," *Fortune,* May 9, 1988, pp. 67–70.
2. "Marketing's New Look," *Business Week,* January 26, 1987, pp. 64–69.
3. "AMA Board Approves New Marketing Definition," *Marketing News,* March 1, 1985, p. 1.
4. Greg Edwards, "Dairymen Told Milk Campaign Boosted Consumption 10%," *Roanoke Times and World News,* January 29, 1987, p. D4.
5. William M. Pride and O. C. Ferrell, *Marketing,* 4th ed. (Boston: Houghton Mifflin, 1985), p. 6.
6. John Downes and Jordan E. Goodman, *Dictionary of Finance and Investment Terms* (Woodbury, N.Y.: Barron's 1985), p. 439.
7. American Marketing Association, *Marketing Definitions* (Chicago: American Marketing Association, 1960), p. 13.
8. Ibid., p. 22.

9. General Electric Company, *Annual Report: 1952* (New York: General Electric Co., 1953), p. 21.
10. Gerald L. Manning and Barry L. Reece, *Selling Today* (Boston: Allyn & Bacon, 1987), p. 5.
11. Nancy L. Croft, "Casting Stoves Upon the Waters," *Nation's Business,* February 1986, pp. 44R–45R.
12. Shawn Tully, "Nestlé Shows How to Gobble Markets," *Fortune,* January 16, 1989, pp. 74–78.
13. Lynn G. Reiling, "Wrangler Womenswear Outfits Sales Staff with Portable Computers," *Marketing News,* March 1, 1985, p. 31.

Chapter 12

1. Richard W. Stevenson, "Brand-Name Vegetables on the Way," *Roanoke Times & World News,* November 26, 1986, p. 10.
2. Bryan Salvage, "Branded Produce: Sign of the Times," *Grocery Marketing,* March 1988, p. 40.
3. William M. Pride and O. C. Ferrell, *Marketing,* 4th ed. (Boston: Houghton Mifflin, 1985), p. 11.
4. "Record New Product Intros in 1987," *Food Institute Report,* January 16, 1988, p. 3.
5. Philip Kotler, "New Products Management for 1980" (New York: Booz, Allen & Hamilton, 1982), pp. 339–340.
6. Brian Dumaine, "How Managers can Succeed Through Speed," *Fortune* February 13, 1989, p. 54.
7. New? Improved? *Business Week,* October 21, 1985, pp. 108, 109.
8. Bill Saporito, "Ganging Up on Black & Decker," *Fortune,* December 23, 1985, pp. 63–72.
9. Alex Taylor III, "Why the Bounce at Rubbermaid?" *Fortune,* April 13, 1987, pp. 77–78.
10. Carol Davenport, "America's Most Admired Corporations," *Fortune,* January 30, 1989, p. 70.
11. William E. Sheeline, "Making Them Rich Down Home," *Fortune,* August 15, 1988, pp. 51–55.
12. John Huey, "The New Power in Black and Decker," *Fortune,* January 2, 1989, pp. 89–94.
13. Saporito, "Ganging Up on Black and Decker," pp. 63–72.

Chapter 13

1. John Huey, "Wal-Mart—Will It Take over the World?" *Fortune,* January 30, 1989, p. 53.
2. Huey, "Wal-Mart," pp. 52–61.
3. Michael Oneal, "Can Sears Get Sexier But Keep the Common Touch?" *Business Week,* July 6, 1987, p. 93.
4. American Marketing Association, *Marketing Definitions* (Chicago: American Marketing Association, 1960), p. 9.
5. "Why Rivals Are Quaking as Nordstrom Heads East," *Business Week,* June 15, 1987, pp. 99–100.

6. Susan Buschbaum, "A Nation of Shopkeepers," *Inc.*, November 1985, p. 72.
7. "Risks and Hard Work Pay Off for the Limited," *Roanoke Times & World News*, January 1, 1989, p. E-6.
8. "The Final Word in No-Frills Shopping," *Fortune*, March 13, 1989, p. 30.
9. "Carrefour Hypermarket Sees Its First U.S. Test," *Supermarket News*, February 8, 1988, p. 1 and 8.
10. "At Home," *Changing Times*, January 1986, p. 18.
11. Mary Rowland, "How the Busy Go Shopping," *Working Women*, January 1989, pp. 47–53.
12. Francine Schwadel, "Attention K-Mart Shoppers: Style Coming to the Store," *Wall Street Journal*, August 9, 1988, p. 6.
13. Cadillac's Bill for Airmailing Allantes May Be $20 Million," *AutoWeek*, December 30, 1985, p. 4.
14. Huey, "Wal-Mart," pp. 52–61.
15. Adapted from Robert A. Sigafoos, *Absolutely Positively Overnight!* (New York: Mentor Books, 1984).

## Chapter 14

1. Larry Edsall, "Weather or Not," *Autoweek*, July 18, 1988, p. 60.
2. Leo Kiley, Vice President, Marketing, Frito-Lay, Inc., Dallas, Texas.
3. American Marketing Association, *Marketing Definitions* (Chicago: American Marketing Association, 1963), p. 9.
4. William M. Pride and O. C. Ferrell, *Marketing*, 4th ed. (Boston: Houghton Mifflin, 1985), p. 352.
5. Mark Lewyn, "Coke, IBM Put Their Brands on the World," *USA Today*, November 15, 1988, p. B-1.
6. Stephen Koepp, "All Wrapped up in Company Logos," *Time*, December 2, 1985, p. 70.
7. Pat Sloan, "Made in America Greets Shoppers," *Advertising Age*, December 19, 1985.
8. Edward C. Baig, "Trying to Make Beef Appetizing Again," *Fortune*, November 25, 1985, p. 64.
9. Richard L. Lynch, Herbert L. Ross, and Ralph D. Wray, *Introduction to Marketing* (New York: McGraw-Hill Book Co., 1984), p. 403.
10. John O'Toole, "Stay Tuned, America, It Could Be Fun," *U.S. News & World Report*, January 13, 1986, p. 53.
11. "This TV Season Is Prime Time for Advertisers," *Business Week*, June 13, 1988, p. 35.
12. Gerald L. Manning and Barry L. Reece, *Selling Today*, 3rd ed. (Boston: Allyn & Bacon, 1987), p. 11.
13. "Computerized Assisted Car Sales," *Personal Selling Power*, January/February 1985, p. 28.
14. Manning and Reece, *Selling Today*, p. 57.
15. George A. Kestler, "Strategic Motivation and Incentives for Professional Telemarketing," *Telemarketing*, April 1984, p. 36.
16. Adapted from Ernan Roman, "Telemarketing Rings in New Business Era," *Advertising Age*, January 27, 1986.
17. American Marketing Association, *Marketing Definitions*, (Chicago: American Marketing Association, 1963), p. 20.
18. Lynch, Ross, and Wray, *Introduction to Marketing*, p. 40.
19. Felix Kessler, "The Costly Coupon Craze," *Fortune*, June 9, 1986, p. 84.
20. "Coupon Eater Has Trouble Digesting Coupon Problems," *Grocery Marketing*, September, 1988, p. 32.
21. Pride and Ferrell, *Marketing*, p. 375.
22. "Iacocca Gets Good Marks for Odometer Case Actions," *Roanoke Times and World News*, July 3, 1987, p. D9.
23. Kevin McManus, "If You Can Find Another Iacocca, Publish Him!" *Insight*, March 31, 1986, pp. 52–54.

## Chapter 15

1. William Nack, "Thrown for Heavy Losses," *Sports Illustrated*, March 24, 1986, pp. 40–47.
2. Adapted from Ralph Estes, *Dictionary of Accounting*, 2nd Ed. (Cambridge, Mass.: MIT Press, 1984), p. 2. Copyright © The Massachusetts Institute of Technology Press. Used by permission.
3. Ibid., pp. 34, 38.
4. B. Needles, Jr., Henry R. Anderson, and James C. Caldwell, *Principles of Accounting*, 2nd ed. (Boston: Houghton Mifflin, 1984), p. 105.
5. Adapted from John Downes and Jordan E. Goodman, *Dictionary of Finance and Investment Terms* (Woodbury, N.Y.: Barron's, 1985), p. 184.

## Chapter 16

1. Jeremy Main, "The Winning Organization," *Fortune*, September 26, 1988, pp. 50–51.
2. For some helpful computer buying tips from now until 1993, see Cary Lu, "Coping with Chaos," *Inc.*, September 1988, pp. 129–130, 132.
3. Paul B. Finney, "The Invisible Machines that Keep Disney Humming," *Management Technology*, June 1985, p. 28.
4. Data from Stuart Gannes, "Tremors from the Computer Quake," *Fortune*, August 1, 1988, pp. 42–60 and Joel Dreyfuss, "Catching the Computer Wave," *Fortune*, September 26, 1988, pp. 78–82.
5. See, for example, Carrie Gottlieb, "Intel's Plan for Staying on Top," *Fortune*, March 27, 1989, pp. 98–100.
6. Data from Gannes, "Tremors from the Computer Quake."
7. David R. Sullivan et al., *Using Computers Today* (Boston: Houghton Mifflin, 1986), pp. 15–16, 33.
8. Ibid., p. 33.

9. See Lynda M. Applegate, James I. Cash, Jr., and D. Quinn Mills, "Information Technology and Tomorrow's Manager," *Harvard Business Review*, November-December 1988, pp. 128–136; Jeremiah J. Sullivan and Gretchen O. Shively, "Expert System Software in Small Business Decision Making," *Journal of Small Business Management*, January 1989, pp. 17–26; and Brian O'Reilly, "Computers that Think Like People," *Fortune*, February 27, 1989, pp. 90–93.

10. Paul B. Finney, "The Invisible Machines that Keep Disney Humming," p. 32.

11. Jeffrey Rothfeder, "Dow Jones Makes A Young Dog Do New Tricks," *Business Week*, January 16, 1989, pp. 89–92.

12. Stephanie K. Walter, "A CEO's Recipe for Mixing Management and Machines," *Management Technology*, July 1984, p. 43.

13. "How Personal Computers Can Trip Up Executives," *Business Week*, September 24, 1984, p. 94.

14. Data from Dreyfuss, "Catching the Computer Wave."

15. See Jeremy Main, "At Last, Software CEOs Can Use," *Fortune*, March 13, 1989, pp. 77–83.

16. Kenneth Labich, "The Arrival of the Baby-Boomer Boss," *Fortune*, August 15, 1988, p. 60.

17. See John Hoerr, "Privacy," *Business Week*, March 28, 1988, pp. 61–65, 68.

18. David W. Pearce, ed., *The Dictionary of Modern Economics*, rev. ed. (Cambridge, Mass.: MIT Press, 1983), p. 417.

19. William M. Pride and O. C. Ferrell, *Marketing*, 4th ed. (Boston: Houghton Mifflin, 1985), p. 120.

20. Ibid.

## Chapter 17

1. Jeffrey L. Seglin, "Court a Banker Now, Borrow Money Later," *Venture*, August 1988, pp. 65–68.

2. Adam Smith, *The Money Game* (New York: Random House, 1967), p. 54; Arthur Fromm, *The History of Money* (New York: Archer House, 1957), p. 31.

3. Mark Goodman, "Designing the Dollar," *Money*, November 1986, pp. 112–118.

4. Jeffrey L. Seglin, *Bank Administration Manual*, 3rd ed. (Rolling Meadows, Ill.: Bank Administration Institute, 1988), p. 270.

5. Lawrence Gitman, *Principles of Managerial Finance*, 3rd ed. (New York: Harper & Row, 1982), p. 59.

6. Nathaniel C. Nash, "Clouds on Credit Union Horizon," *New York Times*, Friday, March 31, 1989, pp. D1, D18.

7. Board of Governors of the Federal Reserve System, *The Federal Reserve System: Purposes and Functions*, 7th ed. (Washington, D.C.: Board of Governors of the Federal Reserve System, 1984), pp. 9–10.

8. Board of Governors of the Federal Reserve System, *The Federal Reserve System: Purposes and Functions*, 7th ed. (Washington, D.C.: Board of Governors of the Federal Reserve System, 1984), pp. 22–23; John Downes and Jordan Elliot Goodman, *Dictionary of Finance and Investment Terms* (Woodbury, N.Y.: Barron's, 1985), pp. 117, 235–236, 336–337.

9. Seglin, *Bank Administration Manual*, pp. 34–35.

10. Ibid., p. 35.

11. Jeffrey Kutler, "MasterCard, Visa Hit American Express Co. with Both Barrels," *American Banker*, September 24, 1987), pp. 14, 15.

## Chapter 18

1. Leah J. Nathans, "The Money Magician at Philip Morris," *Business Week*, April 10, 1989, p. 78.

2. A CEO's Recipe for Mixing Management and Machines," *Management Technology*, July 1984, p. 43.

3. Lawrence J. Gitman, *Principles of Managerial Finance*, 3rd ed. (New York: Harper & Row, 1982), pp. 8–10.

4. Research on devious budget games that managers tend to play is presented in Frank Collins, Paul Munter, and Don W. Finn, "The Budgeting Games People Play," *The Accounting Review*, January 1987, pp. 29–49.

5. Data from Nathans, "The Money Magician at Philip Morris."

6. Lawrence J. Gitman and Michael D. Joehnk, *Fundamentals of Investing*, 3rd ed. (New York: Harper & Row, 1988), p. 131.

7. Personal interview with Bernie Kestler, CFP, President, Kestler Associates, Inc., Phoenix, Arizona, April 24, 1989.

8. For details, see Sharon Begley, "Smoothing the Waters," *Newsweek*, April 10, 1989, pp. 54–57; and Andrea Rothman, "Who's That Screaming at Exxon? Not the Environmentalists," *Business Week*, May 1, 1989, p. 31.

9. John Downes and Jordan Elliot Goodman, *Dictionary of Finance and Investment Terms* (Woodbury, N.Y.: Barron's Educational Series, Inc., 1985), pp. 299–300.

10. See Tim Smart, "A Buyback Backfires," *Business Week*, May 1, 1989, p. 29.

11. Drawn from *Moody's Bond Record*, March 1989, preface.

12. Peter Nulty, "Irwin Jacobs Stirs a Junk Bond Brawl," *Fortune*, June 9, 1986, p. 104.

13. Ibid.

## Chapter 19

1. *Adams v. State*, 443 So. 2d 1003 (Fla. Dist. Ct. App. 1983).

2. John Downes and Jordan Elliot Goodman, *Dictionary of Finance and Investment Terms* (Woodbury, N.Y.: Barron's Educational Series, Inc., 1985), p. 220.

3. Frank K. Reilly, *Investments,* 2nd ed. (New York: CBS College Publishing, The Dryden Press, 1986), p. 84.
4. David M. Darst, *The Handbook of the Bond and Money Markets* (New York: McGraw-Hill Book Company, Inc., 1981), pp. 208, 235.
5. Frank J. Fabozzi and Frank G. Zarb, eds., *Handbook of Financial Markets: Securities, Options, Futures* (Homewood, Ill.: Dow Jones-Irwin, 1981), p. 63.
6. Tamar Lewin, "The Dilemma of Insider Trading," *The New York Times,* July 21, 1986, p. D1.

## Chapter 20

1. Kathryn J. McIntyre, "Bringing Risk Management to the Jungle," *Business Insurance,* April 18, 1988, p. 152.
2. *Business Insurance,* April 18, 1988, pp. 148–162.
3. Douglas McCleod, "Nissan Establishes Captive to Reinsure Dealers' Risk," *Business Insurance,* January 23, 1989, pp. 1, 38.
4. *Social Security Bulletin,* 52, 1 (January 1989): 2.
5. "Can You Afford to Get Sick?" *Newsweek,* March, 1989.

## Chapter 21

1. *Weeks v. Southern Bell Telephone & Telegraph Co.,* 408 F. 2d 228 (5th Cir. 1969).
2. John E. Nowak et al., *Constitutional Law,* 2nd ed. (St. Paul, Minn.: West, 1983), pp. 718–30, 1077–78.
3. Lawrence S. Clark and Peter D. Kinder, *Law and Business* (New York: McGraw-Hill, 1986), pp. 649–52.

## Chapter 22

1. Robert W. Kent, ed., *Money Talks* (New York: Facts on File Publications, 1985), p. 94.
2. Ricky W. Griffin, *Management* (Boston: Houghton Mifflin, 1984), p. 638.
3. David R. Spiegel, "Enforcing Safety Laws Locally," *The New York Times,* March 1986, p. 11.
4. Adam Smith, *The Wealth of Nations* (Harmondsworth, Eng.: Penguin Books, 1982), p. 232.
5. Lawrence S. Clark and Peter D. Kinder, *Law and Business* (New York: McGraw-Hill, 1986), p. 782.
6. Jerry Flint, "Here Come the Truckbusters," *Forbes,* June 30, 1986, p. 87.
7. As quoted in Kent, *Money Talks,* p. 89.
8. Rux Martin, "Gourmet Foods from the Green Mountains," *Vermont Life,* Winter 1985, pp. 22–24.

## Chapter 23

1. Frank Washington and David Pauly, "Driving To-ward a World Car?" *Newsweek,* May 1, 1989, p. 48.
2. Data from James C. Cooper, "Rising Interest Rates Will Keep Demand on a Short Leash," *Business Week,* May 30, 1988, p. 23.
3. David W. Pearce, ed., *The Dictionary of Modern Economics,* rev. ed. (Cambridge, Mass.: MIT Press, 1983), p. 411.
4. Dori Jones Yang and Laxmi Nakarmi, "Is the Era of Cheap Asian Labor Over?" *Business Week,* May 15, 1989, p. 45.
5. Milton Moskowitz et al., eds., *Everybody's Business* (New York: Harper & Row, 1980), pp. 64–65.
6. Leah J. Nathans, "The Money Magician at Philip Morris," *Business Week,* April 10, 1989, p. 78.
7. Data from Peter Galuszka, " 'I'll Take It. What Is It?' The Shopping Spree in Russia," *Business Week,* May 1, 1989, p. 41.
8. See Howard Banks, "Managing 'Free' Trade," *Forbes,* October 31, 1988, p. 29.
9. Data from Karen Pennar, "Protectionism: Making It Pay For Itself," *Business Week,* April 7, 1986, p. 24. Also see Karen Pennar, "The Gospel of Free Trade Is Losing Apostles," *Business Week,* February 27, 1989, p. 89.
10. Neil Gross, "Motorola Is Pounding on Japan's 'Open Door,' " *Business Week,* May 8, 1989, p. 58.
11. "The History of Protectionism Proves the Value of Free Trade," *Insight,* June 30, 1986, p. 14.
12. For more, see Chuck Hawkins and William J. Holstein, "The North American Shakeout Arrives Ahead of Schedule," *Business Week,* April 17, 1989, pp. 34–35.
13. Colin Thubron, *The Ancient Mariners* (Alexandria, Virginia: Time-Life Books, 1981).
14. Julia Lieblich, "If You Want a Big, New Market . . .," *Fortune,* November 21, 1988, p. 181.
15. See Kenneth Labich, "America's International Winners," *Fortune,* April 14, 1986, pp. 34–35.
16. Details may be found in Kate Gillespie, "Middle East Response to the U.S. Foreign Corrupt Practices Act," *California Management Review,* Summer 1987, pp. 9–30.
17. Anthony J. Yudis, "Swedish-Made Homes Rising on N.E. Lots," *Boston Globe,* July 26, 1986, p. 37.
18. The Coca Cola Company, *1985 Annual Report* (Atlanta, 1986), p. 15.
19. "Corporate Odd Couples," *Business Week,* July 21, 1986, p. 100.
20. Data from Louis Kraar, "Your Rivals Can Be Your Allies," *Fortune,* March 27, 1989, p. 66.
21. See Richard Koenig, "Toyota Takes Pains, and Time, Filling Jobs at Its Kentucky Plant," *Wall Street Journal,* December 1, 1987, pp. 1, 27.
22. Data from Gene Koretz, "The Buying of America: Should We Be Worried?" *Business Week,* May 9, 1988, p. 36.
23. Pearce, *Dictionary of Economics,* p. 299.

# Glossary

## A

**absolute advantage** exists when one country can produce a product more efficiently than another country (Ch 23)

**acceptance** the offeree's agreement to the terms of the offer (Ch 21)

**accommodation strategy** when a company assumes more social responsibility because of pressure from an interest group or the government (Ch 2)

**accounting** the process of recording financial information, interpreting it, and then communicating it (Ch 15)

**accounting cycle** the five-step process that takes a transaction from being mere raw data to its being summarized in financial statements (Ch 15)

**accounting equation** the formula that sets liabilities and owner's equity together as claims against assets (Ch 15)

**accounting period** any regular period of one year or less for which a business decides to have financial statements prepared (Ch 15)

**accounts payable** debts owed to suppliers of goods and services that are due during the next accounting period (Ch 15)

**accounts receivable** any amounts owed to an organization by its customers (Ch 15)

**accrued expenses** various kinds of obligations that were incurred during the accounting period but are not yet actually due or owing (Ch 15)

**acquisition** the purchase of other companies (Ch 3)

**actual cash value** the purchase price of an item of personal property less its depreciation (Ch 20)

**administered vertical-marketing system** system in which one channel member dominates all the others in its channel or channels (Ch 13)

**administrative expenses (general expenses)** the overall costs of operating a firm, excluding selling expenses and cost of goods sold (Ch 15)

**administrative regulations** the binding requirements designed by a government agency to accomplish the purposes of a specific statute (Ch 21)

**advertising** nonpersonal promotion of ideas, goods, or services paid for by an identified sponsor (Ch 14)

**advertising media** the means of communication used by major advertisers, including magazines, newspapers, direct mail, radio, television, and outdoor advertising (Ch 14)

**affirm** the appellate court's approval of a trial court's judgment (Ch 21)

**affirmative action programs** programs that consist of written plans to hire, train, and promote minority workers and women (Ch 8)

**agency shop** one in which employees may choose not to join the union (Ch 9)

**agent (broker)** an intermediary who receives a commission for bringing together buyers and sellers for the purpose of negotiating an exchange but never takes title to property (Ch 13 and 21)

**alien corporation** American corporation that does business in a foreign country (Ch 3)

**altruism** an unselfish concern for others' well-being (Ch 2)

**American Federation of Labor (AFL)** an umbrella organization for craft unions (Ch 9)

**antidiscrimination laws** laws that forbid treating people differently on the basis of their religion, color, sex, race, age, or national origin (Ch 8)

**appeal** the right to ask a higher court to review the record of the case for errors (Ch 21)

**appellant** a person who appeals an adverse judgment by a court (Ch 21)

**approprite investment** one that fits a person's special combination of investment needs and risk tolerance (Ch 18)

**arbitration** the submission of a dispute to a neutral third party (Ch 9)

**arbitrator** the neutral third party who makes a decision binding on the parties who submit a dispute (Ch 9)

**arithmetic-logic unit (ALU)** part of the CPU that handles arithmetic computations (Ch 16)

**arithmetic mean** technical name for average (Ch 16)

**assets** everything of value that an organization owns, its economic resources (Ch 15)

**association** a voluntary organization of people with a common interest (Ch 3)

**atmospherics** the variables considered in designing retail stores (Ch 13)

**attrition** the normal loss of employees from retirement, job changes, death, and the like (Ch 8)

**audit** a formal examination of a firm's financial records (Ch 15)

**authority** the designated right to control the use of specified organizational resources (Ch 6)

**authorization card** form signed by employees that either authorizes the union to represent them or to request a representation election or both (Ch 9)

**automation** the substitution of mechanical for human labor and sensory applications (Ch 10)

**auxiliary storage devices** units on a computer system such as the floppy or hard disk drive that supplement the main memory storage (Ch 16)

**average** total number of observations divided by the number of occurrences of them (Ch 16)

## B

**balance of payments** measures the relationship between payments coming into and going out of a country during a particular period (Ch 23)

**balance of trade** the relationship between the value of goods and services imported and goods and services exported during a particular period (Ch 23)

**balance sheet (statement of financial position)** summary of an organization's financial status at the end of an accounting period (Ch 15)

**balanced funds** funds that seek to provide modest income and growth from a generally conservative portfolio (Ch 19)

**bankrupt** the person or business in a bankruptcy proceeding (Ch 21)

**bar chart** a comparison of several values at a stationary point in time, using either horizontal or vertical bars (Ch 16)

**bargaining unit** a group of employees who share common interests in wages and working conditions and have common skills (Ch 9)

**barter** trading goods for goods or services rather than for money (Ch 1)

**base pay** the basic wages or salaries that workers receive (Ch 8)

**base wage rate** the minimum paid per hour to any worker in the bargaining unit (Ch 9)

**batch mode** mode in which software runs directly from the operating system like a utility program (Ch 16)

**batch system** manual-updating system in which data is first collected, then stored in a batch until time to process it (Ch 16)

**beneficiary** the person or organization named to receive the proceeds from a life insurance policy (Ch 20)

**benefit variable** segmentation variable which considers economy, convenience, and prestige (Ch 11)

**benefits** services that employees receive that are paid for by the employer, like health insurance, pensions, and vacations (Ch 8)

**board of directors** group of individuals elected by the shareholders to oversee business operations (Ch 3)

**bond rating** refers to the soundness of a specific bond offering (Ch 18)

**bonus** a payment beyond the employees' base pay or commissions (Ch 8)

**book value** the value of a company's net worth as represented by a common share (Ch 18)

**bookkeeper** a clerical employee who records day-to-day business transactions (Ch 15)

**booting** to "pull the operating system up by its boot-straps," or start it (Ch 16)

**boycott** an agreement among competitors not to sell to or to buy from a particular entity (Ch 22)

**brand** a name, term, symbol, design, or any combination of these elements used to identify a specific product and distinguish it from its competition (Ch 12)

**brand name** that part of a brand that can be spoken (Ch 12)

**brand symbol** a graphic portrayal of an element that identifies a product or firm (Ch 12)

**breakeven analysis** a method used to determine the demand or sales volume required at a given price for the firm to break even (Ch 12)

**briefs** the written arguments relative to an issue (Ch 21)

**broker** person who buys and sells stocks after taking an order from a customer (Ch 19)

**budget** an organization's financial plan for the future in which it describes how it will use its resources to meet its goals (Ch 15 and 18)

**business** the profit-motivated buying, producing, and selling of goods and/or services (Ch 1)

**business ethics** the study of the moral problems that confront members of business organizations and others who engage in business transactions (Ch 2)

**business incubator programs** programs that nurse fragile new enterprises in an artificially supportive environment until they are strong enough to make it on their own (Ch 4)

**business interruption insurance** a form of income insurance that protects a firm against lost earnings as the result of a fire or similar peril (Ch 20)

**business representative (business agent)** person employed by a union to represent it in matters with management (Ch 9)

**business unionism** the philosophy which emphasizes that American unions exist primarily for the economic improvement of their workers (Ch 9)

**bylaws** rules adopted for the corporation's internal operations (Ch 3)

**byte** eight binary digits or bits (Ch 16)

## C

**cafeteria-style benefit programs** programs that permit employees to choose from an array of benefit programs, up to a preset limit (Ch 8)

**call feature** a provision allowing the company itself to redeem a security (Ch 18)

**capacity** the rate at which an operation can produce output over a given period (Ch 10)

**capital** assets that are exchanged for an ownership interest in a business (Ch 4)

**capital contribution** a partner's investment—whether in cash or property—in the business (Ch 3)

**capitalism** an economic system based on the belief that private citizens should be free to produce and sell goods and services for profit, without government interference (Ch 1)

**captioned photograph** a photo of a new product, a corporate officer, or something else of interest, accompanied by a brief description (Ch 14)

**carrier** a firm which offers transportation services (Ch 13)

**carrying costs** expenses incurred because an item is held in inventory (Ch 10)

**cash flow** the movement of money into and out of a firm (Ch 18)

**cash value (surrender value)** the accumulation and interest a policy earns (Ch 20)

**cash value life insurance (whole life insurance)** a class of life insurance policies that requires premium payments on the insurer's behalf until death or until the insured reaches a certain age (Ch 20)

**catalog showroom** type of discount store in which only one unit of each product the store carries is on display (Ch 13)

**caveat emptor** a Latin terms meaning "let the buyer beware" (Ch 2)

**census** a survey of an entire population (Ch 16)

**central processing unit (CPU)** the computer system's brain, where the data processing actually occurs (Ch 16)

**centralization** an organizational arrangement in which all decisions are passed along to top management before being implemented (Ch 6)

**certificate of deposit (CD)** a time deposit evidenced by a promissory note issued by a bank (Ch 18)

**certified management accountant** management accountant who has passed the National Association of Accountants' test and has satisfied its educational and professional criteria (Ch 15)

**certified public accountant (CPA)** an accountant who has passed an examination prepared by the American Institute of Certified Public Accountants (AICPA) and satisfied a state's educational and experience requirements (Ch 15)

**chain of command** the vertical reporting and authority relationships in an organization chart (Ch 6)

**chain stores** a retail outlet under common (usually corporate) ownership and management (Ch 13)

**channel of distribution (marketing channel, distribution channel)** a group of intermediaries or middlemen that direct products to customers (Ch 11 and 13)

**chief steward** an elected union official for the employee's department or plant who represents the members in grievances and oversees the execution of the collective bargaining agreement (Ch 9)

**civil law** all law that is not classified as criminal law (Ch 21)

**Civil Rights Act of 1964 (Title VII)** law that declares it illegal to discriminate in employment against any individual in respect to his or her compensation as well as the terms of employment because of that individual's race, color, religion, sex, or national origin (Ch 8)

**Clayton Act** broadened the scope of the Sherman Act by trying to prevent anticompetitive behavior rather than by dealing with its consequences (Ch 22)

**closed shop** one that requires workers to belong to the union before they can be hired (Ch 9)

**closely held corporation** firm with fifty or fewer shareholders (Ch 3)

**clutter** broadcast messages that are not part of a t.v. program (Ch 14)

**co-owner** a joint owner, as in a partnership (Ch 3)

**coercive power** power achieved by threatening people with punishment or actually punishing them (Ch 6)

**coinsurance** a clause that requires the policyholder to pay a portion of any loss to an insured building if the policy maximum is less than a specified percentage of the building's value at the time of the loss (Ch 20)

**collateral** the property securing a loan; the security of a loan that could be sold to satisfy the obligation (Ch 4 and 17)

**collective bargaining** negotiation of the terms and conditions of employment between management and an organization representing employees (Ch 9)

**commercial banks** banks which attract demand deposits and make loans to individuals and businesses (Ch 17)

**commercial finance companies** intermediaries that make business loans (Ch 17)

**commercial paper** unsecured promissory notes issued by a corporation that mature in from 3 to 270 days (Ch 18)

**commission** a fee charged on the transaction a broker facilitates (Ch 19)

**commission basis** an incentive system in which sales employees receive either a fixed amount or a percentage of the value of the sales they make (Ch 8)

**commitment fee** a bank charge for a loan guarantee that may also require a compensating balance (Ch 18)

**commodities** basic resources and agricultural products, such as gold, silver, wheat, cotton, pork bellies, and orange juice (Ch 19)

**commodities contracts** commitments to buy a quantity of a commodity at a particular time (Ch 19)

**common carrier** a firm that offers transportation services to the public (Ch 13)

**common law** the body of legal principles developed over centuries by judges in deciding cases (Ch 21)

**communism** an economic system in which there are no social classes, and no privately owned property (Ch 1)

**comparitive advantage** the ability to produce a product at a lower cost than the competitor can (Ch 23)

**compensation** the money or benefits or both for which an employee exchanges work (Ch 8)

**compensation balance** an amount that the firm must keep on deposit with a financial institution during the term of a loan or a period covered by a line of credit (Ch 18)

**competition** when two or more businesses offering similar goods or services go after the same customers (Ch 1)

**competition-based pricing** pricing based on competitive price levels (Ch 12)

**compressed work week** a scheduling system that permits workers to vary the number of days they work from the traditional five without changing the total number of hours worked (Ch 7)

**computer-integrated manufacturing (CIM)** a computerized operations-management system that manages data flow while at the same time directing the movement and processing of material (Ch 10)

**computer system** a mechanical means of transforming data into information (Ch 16)

**concentrated strategy** aiming a single strategy at one specific market segment (Ch 11)

**conceptual skills** the ability to understand all the organization's activities, how its various parts fit together, and how the organization relates to others (Ch 5)

**conglomerate** a corporation that owns several other corporations that are in different industries (Ch 3)

**conglomerate mergers** the acquisition of companies in different markets (Ch 22)

**Congress of Industrial Organizations (CIO)** an umbrella organization for industrial unions (Ch 9)

**consent election** a representation election agreed on by union and management (Ch 9)

**consideration** something of legal value that each party agrees to exchange (Ch 21)

**consultative selling** a sales approach used today in which salespeople serve as consultants to customers, diagnosing problems, identifying needs, and offering sound recommendations on products (Ch 14)

**consumer credit** credit extended to individuals for non-business, personal, family, or household purposes (Ch 17)

**consumer-oriented layout** an operational layout designed to facilitate the customer's interactions with the firm's services (Ch 10)

**Consumer Price Index (CPI)** the monthly governmental index that measures inflation (Ch 9 and 17)

**consumer product** goods and services purchased in the consumer market (Ch 11 and 13)

**continuous-flow system (continuous process system)** the production-to-stock process that produces large quantities of a single standardized product (Ch 10)

**contract** an agreement between two or more parties that the law will enforce (Ch 2 and 21)

**contract carrier** a carrier which provides service to one shipper or a limited number of shippers (Ch 13)

**contractual capacity** the ability to understand the nature of the contract (Ch 21)

**control** the process of measuring an organization's performance against its plans to make certain that the actual operations conform with the plans (Ch 10)

**control unit** the main part of the CPU that tells the computer what to do and where to find or put data (Ch 16)

**controller** the person responsible for accounting, data processing, and taxes within the corporation (Ch 18)

**controlling** the process of measuring an organization's performance against its plans (Ch 5)

**convenience goods** products that consumers purchase frequently, generally at low prices, and for which they are willing to spend only a minimum of effort in completing the exchange (Ch 11)

**convenience store** a small store which offers a limited range of items at prices considerably higher than super-market prices, but stays open from 18 to 24 hours a day (Ch 13)

**convertible preferred stock** preferred stock whose indenture includes the right to convert a share into some number of common shares (Ch 18)

**cooperative** corporation or association formed to perform services so its owners or members can make a profit but without making any profit itself (Ch 3)

**corporate bond** a long-term obligation to pay (Ch 18)

**corporate culture** a system of informal rules that spells out how people are to behave most of the time (Ch 5)

**corporate officers** a president, one or more vice presidents as specified in the bylaws, a secretary, and a treasurer, elected by the board (Ch 3)

**corporate social responsibility** encompasses obligations to society above and beyond making a profit for stockholders, obeying laws, or honoring contracts (Ch 2)

**corporate vertical-marketing system** system in which the firm performs all the channel functions (Ch 13)

**corporation** the form of business organization authorized by state law that comes into existence when that state's secretary of state issues a *certificate of incorporation* (Ch 3)

**correlation analysis** a statistical technique to measure the association between two or more variables (Ch 16)

**cosmetic change** an alteration in a product that has little or no effect on its basic function (Ch 12)

**cost-based pricing** a pricing strategy derived from the cost of producing or purchasing a good (Ch 12)

**cost of goods sold** the amount that an organization spent to buy or produce the goods it sold during an accounting period (Ch 15)

**cost-of-living adjustments (COLAs)** changes to the base wage rate to reflect increases in the inflation rate for the preceding quarter or year (Ch 9)

**council bargaining** form of negotiation in which several local unions join to negotiate together (Ch 9)

**coupon rate** a specified rate of interest (Ch 18)

**coventurers** the parties in a joint venture (Ch 23)

**credit** an entry on the right side of the account (Ch 15); the ability of a business or a person to obtain money or property and to defer payment (Ch 17)

**credit bureaus** businesses that keep records on the credit and payment practices of individuals and firms (Ch 17)

**credit card** form of credit representing an agreement between the merchant and the card issuer, in which the merchant honors the card and the issuer pays the charge slips; and between the issuer and the card holder, in which the issuer extends a line of credit to the holder and the holder makes payments (Ch 17)

**credit union** a nonprofit savings-and-loan organization operated specifically for the benefit of its members (Ch 17)

**creditors' committee** all of the bankrupt's creditors called together by the court to review the bankrupt's documentation of debts and assets and to elect a permanent trustee in bankruptcy (Ch 21)

**criminal law** statutes that specify the duties owed to society and prescribe penalties (Ch 21)

**critical path** the path with the longest total time for completion of a series of sequential events in the production process (Ch 10)

**CRT (cathode-ray tube)** device in the monitor that allows images to appear on the screen (Ch 16)

**cumulative** kind of dividend that requires the company to pay all preferred dividends for past periods before paying any common stock dividends (Ch 18)

**currency** coins and bills (Ch 17)

**current assets** cash and any other assets that are likely to be used up or converted into cash, usually within a year (Ch 15)

**current liabilities** debts that will fall due within the next twelve months (Ch 15)

**cursor** a movable blinking symbol (Ch 16)

**customer orientation** basing marketing decisions on customers' wants (Ch 11)

**customer satisfaction** a positive reaction of customers toward the goods and services they buy (Ch 11)

**cyclical fluctuations** business cycle movements over periods ranging from two to fifteen years (Ch 16)

## D

**damages** monies paid to an injured party to compensate for the injury (Ch 21)

**data** numbers, letters, facts, and figures that usually come from measurements or observations (Ch 16)

**data processing** functions that a computer performs on the data (Ch 16)

**debenture** an unsecured bond (Ch 18)

**debit** an entry on the left side of an account (Ch 15)

**debt** borrowed money (Ch 18)

**decentralization** an arrangement in which decisions are pushed down the organization to the level where the functional expertise lies (Ch 6)

**decision** a choice of actions by means of which a manager seeks to achieve the organization's goals (Ch 5)

**decision support system (DSS)** a computer system that permits managers to call up whatever specific information they need whenever they need it (Ch 16)

**decisional roles** roles that center on solving problems and making choices (Ch 5)

**decline stage** the stage which begins when sales begin to decrease and normally ends with the firm abandoning the product (Ch 12)

**deductible** an amount the policyholder must pay before the insurer's obligation to pay becomes effective (Ch 20)

**defendant** the party against whom a lawsuit is brought (Ch 21)

**defense strategy** involves the use of public relations, legal maneuvering, and whatever other means are necessary to avoid assuming additional obligations (Ch 2)

**delegation** involves the assignment of varying degrees of decision-making authority to subordinates (Ch 6)

**demand** the willingness of purchasers to buy specific quantities of a good or service at a particular price and particular time (Ch 1 and 12)

**demand-based pricing** a pricing strategy which assigns price according to how much will need to be sold in order for the firm to break even (Ch 12)

**demand curve** the line reflecting the relationship between each price and the quantities demanded (Ch 1)

**demand deposits** individual and business accounts from which depositors can withdraw funds at any time without prior notice to the bank (Ch 17)

**demographic variable** segmentation variable which considers age, sex, family size, income, occupation, education, religion, race, nationality, and social class (Ch 11)

**department store** a retail outlet that carries a diverse assortment of merchandise grouped into departments (Ch 13)

**departmentalization** the arranging of divided tasks into meaningful groups (Ch 6)

**depreciation** the process of distributing the original value of a long-term value asset over the years of its useful life (Ch 15)

**deregulation** refers to the stripping away of regulations restricting competition in entire industries or the elimination or avoidance of regulation (Ch 22)

**derived demand** products for which the demand is caused by the demand for other products (Ch 11)

**descriptive statistics** statistics which portray the characteristics of a larger set of data (Ch 16)

**detail (missionary) salespeople** salespeople who develop good will and stimulate demand for the manufacturer's products in target markets (Ch 14)

**devaluation** an arbitrary downward adjustment of one country's currency in terms of another country's (Ch 23)

**differentiated strategy** aiming individualized appeals at particular market segments (Ch 11)

**direct foreign investment** occurs when someone from one country owns property or business interests in another country (Ch 23)

**direct inventory** in manufacturing this includes raw materials, work in process, and finished products; in retail and service operations it includes all goods bought for resale (Ch 10)

**direct-mail advertising** any advertising sent through the mail directly to a target market (Ch 14)

**discharge** a permanent separation initiated by the employer, usually for cause, such as absenteeism or poor job performance (Ch 8)

**discharged** when a business's debts are terminated (Ch 21)

**discount brokers** brokers who charge the lowest commissions because they only execute their customers' instructions (Ch 19)

**discount rate** the amount the Federal Reserve charges on loans to all member depository institutions (Ch 17)

**discount store** a retail outlet that competes primarily on the basis of price (Ch 13)

**discounting** the sale of a promissory note to a bank for the amount of the note less a discount for the bank's services (Ch 18)

**discretionary income** more income than is required to obtain the necessities of life (Ch 1 and 11)

**discretionary order** places the decision about whether to act or to wait into the broker's hands (Ch 9)

**display advertising** product exhibits in places like airports, railroad stations, billboards, and civic centers (Ch 14)

**dispute-resolution system** the structure that society has established for resolving differences (Ch 21)

**dissolution** an act that indicates that a partner has ended the business relationship (Ch 3)

**diversification** the systematic attempt to balance varying types of risks through a range of different investments (Ch 18)

**dividend** that portion of a company's earnings that the board of directors votes to distribute to stockholders on a per-share basis in either cash or stock (Ch 18)

**domestic corporation** what a corporation is called in the state in which it receives articles of incorporation (Ch 3)

**double-entry bookkeeping** a system of recording business transactions in which each transaction is recorded in at least two separate accounts (Ch 15)

**E**

**economic strike** a strike called because of failure to reach agreement on wages and benefits (Ch 9)

**economic system** the way in which a society produces and distributes goods and services (Ch 1)

**economics** the study of how individuals and society choose to employ limited resources and distribute the resulting goods and services (Ch 1)

**effective organization** an organization that satisfies multiple effectiveness criteria ranging from profitability to social responsibilities (Ch 6)

**electronic funds transfer (EFT)** arrangement that allows for direct deposits to be made to and from a bank account by computer (Ch 17)

**embargo** a law or government order forbidding either the importing or exporting of certain specified goods (Ch 23)

**emotional buying motive** a buying motive which includes the wish for social approval, a desire to be different, and a need to be free of fear (Ch 11)

**employee assistance program** program that offers constructive help and counseling for employees with personal problems (Ch 8)

**Employment Retirement Income Security Act (ERISA)** act that created the Pension Benefit Guaranty Corporation to guarantee pension plans (Ch 20)

**employment test** a standardized screening device intended to predict the applicant's potential for successful job performance (Ch 8)

**endorsee** the person to whom an instrument is endorsed (Ch 21)

**endorsement** a notation required to permit the transfer of an instrument (Ch 21)

**endorser** a person who endorses an instrument (Ch 21)

**endowment life insurance** a form of insurance which provides for payment of the face amount either at the insured's death or at some specified time before the insured's death, whichever comes first (Ch 20)

**enlightened self-interest** involves the belief that a business ultimately helps itself when it helps to solve society's problems (Ch 2)

**entrepreneur** a person who organizes, operates, and assumes the risk of a business venture in the hope of making a profit (Ch 1 and 4)

**entrepreneurship** the capacity for innovations, investment, and expansion in new markets, products, and techniques (Ch 4)

**environmental analysis** a study of conditions that might affect an organization (Ch 5)

**Equal Employment Opportunity Act** act that created the Equal Employment Opportunity Commission (EEOC) (Ch 8)

**Equal Employment Opportunity Commission (EEOC)** agency that enforces the employment-related aspects of the antidiscrimination laws (Ch 8)

**equilibrium** the location at which supply and demand are in balance (Ch 1 and 12)

**equity** ownership interest, either in a home or accumulated value in a life-insurance policy or in a savings account (Ch 4); the value of the owner's investment in a firm (Ch 18)

**ergonomics**   the science of designing machinery to better accommodate the human body (Ch 16)

**esteem**   how a person is regarded by others and by himself or herself (Ch 7)

**ethics**   the study of moral, as contrasted with legal, obligations (Ch 2)

**ethnocentrism**   a belief that the way something is done in their country is the only way to do it (Ch 23)

**ex-dividend**   stock sold without the dividend (Ch 18)

**exchange process**   the transfer of money or its equivalent for goods (Ch 11)

**exchange rate**   the value of a currency expressed in terms of another currency (Ch 23)

**exchanges**   the actual markets where stocks and bonds are traded (Ch 19)

**excise tax**   designed to discourage use and exact a premium for use (Ch 22)

**exclusive-dealing arrangement**   an agreement by one party to sell all its output of a certain product to the other party, or to buy all it requires of a product from that party, in exchange for that party's promise not to engage in similiar transactions with anyone else (Ch 22)

**exclusive distribution strategy**   strategy which relies on a single retail outlet or a very few outlets in a market area (Ch 13)

**executive information system**   an easy-to-use computerized information system designed specifically for executives who might not be familiar with computers but who need to call up information quickly (Ch 16)

**exercise**   acting upon a purchased option (Ch 19)

**expert power**   power achieved by sharing knowledge or expertise with others (Ch 6)

**expire**   letting the specified time period for an option run out, making the option worthless (Ch 19)

**exports**   goods produced in one country but sold in another (Ch 23)

## F

**factfinding**   the process by which an outside factfinder narrows the issues that are before the negotiating parties (Ch 9)

**factoring**   the selling of a firm's accounts receivable to another firm that then owns and collects the debts (Ch 18)

**factors of production**   land, labor, and capital: the three ways in which people make money from their property (Ch 1)

**Fair Labor Standards Act**   law that requires time and a half for overtime work (Ch 9)

**family brand (blanket brand)**   an approach based on the use of one brand name for all of a firm's products (Ch 12)

**featherbedding**   requiring more workers than needed to do a job (Ch 22)

**feature article**   manuscript longer than a news release, which the firm usually has prepared for a specific publication (Ch 14)

**Federal Deposit Insurance Corporation (FDIC)**   organization which insures each account in a member bank for up to $100,000 per account (Ch 17)

**Federal Reserve Notes**   the nation's paper currency (Ch 7)

**Federal Reserve System**   the U.S. central bank (Ch 17)

**Federal Savings and Loan Insurance Corporation (FSLIC)**   a corporation established by federal law to insure the deposits of thrift institutions (Ch 17)

**Federal Trade Commission (FTC)**   regulates any "unfair method of competition," which includes any anticompetitive behavior that falls short of being a violation of the other acts (Ch 22)

**Federal Trade Commission Act**   created the Federal Trade Commission (FTC) (Ch 22)

**fidelity bonds**   insurance for businesses that wish to insure themselves against theft by employees (Ch 20)

**financial management**   the process of obtaining money and using it effectively to achieve an organization's goals (Ch 18)

**financial ratios**   certain mathematical relationships between numbers to the components of the financial statements (Ch 15)

**financial statements**   an organization's reports of its financial condition (Ch 15)

**First In, First Out (FIFO)**   the system which assumes that the first items brought into inventory are also the first sold (Ch 15)

**fixed assets (plant and equipment assets)**   those assets that a firm expects to use for more than a year (Ch 15 and 18)

**fixed costs**   costs that do not vary with the level of output or production (Ch 12)

**fixed-position layout**   an operational arrangement in which workers and equipment come to the product, instead of the usual arrangement (Ch 10)

**flexitime**   a plan in which traditionally fixed work hours are replaced with a more flexible time schedule within a company's guidelines (Ch 7)

**floating interest rates** a rate subject to change with the prevailing market rate (Ch 18)

**floor broker** a broker on the floor of the exchange whose job it is to execute customers' orders (Ch 19)

**for-profit corporation** organization created to make profits for its owners (Ch 3)

**foreign corporation** what a corporation is called in any state other than the one in which it was incorporated (Ch 3)

**Foreign Corrupt Practices Act** forbids the bribing of foreign officials by U.S. companies or their employees to obtain favorable treatment (Ch 23)

**foreign trade** trade between partners of different nationalities (Ch 23)

**Four P's** the marketer's major tools, consisting of the product strategy, price strategy, place (distribution) strategy, and promotion strategy (Ch 11)

**franchise** a license to sell another's products or to use another's name in business, or both (Ch 4)

**franchise tax** a fee for the privilege of doing business as a corporation (Ch 3)

**franchisee** person who buys a franchise (Ch 4)

**franchiser** company that sells a franchise (Ch 4)

**free-enterprise system** an economy based on the principle of voluntary association and exchange (Ch 1)

**freight forwarder** a common carrier that will often lease space from other carriers and combine small individual shipments into economical lot sizes (Ch 13)

**frequency distribution** method of summarizing data by reducing the size of the listing or the number of items in the data set (Ch 16)

**full-service brokers** brokers who provide advice, reports, research and analysis, portfolio management, and other services (Ch 19)

**full-service wholesaler** wholesaler who offers the widest variety of services to its customers (Ch 13)

**functional organization** a system in which the various functions involved in supervising a worker are divided into separate tasks performed by specialists (Ch 6)

## G

**General Agreement on Tariffs and Trade (GATT)** a treaty which established an international mechanism for mutual adjustments of trade barriers and regulations (Ch 23)

**general partnership** the usual form of partnership (Ch 3)

**generic term** a trademark which has passed into common, everyday language (Ch 12)

**geographic variable** a segmentation variable which considers regions, counties, cities, and climate areas (Ch 11)

**givebacks** a union's foregoing of wages or benefits or working conditions won in earlier collective bargaining (Ch 9)

**goods** personal property that is both tangible and movable (Ch 21)

**goodwill** a firm's extra earning power compared to other firms in the same industry (Ch 15)

**government bonds** the debt certificates issued by federal, state, and local governments and their agencies (Ch 19)

**grading** the assignment of "predetermined standards of quality classifications to individual units or lots of a commodity" (Ch 11)

**grapevine** the informal, unofficial communication network within an organization (Ch 6)

**graph** visual display which indicates upward and downward movements of the values of a variable over a specified period (Ch 16)

**greenhouse effect** the gradual warming of the earth's atmosphere (Ch 22)

**grievance** an employee complaint about wages, hours, working conditions, or disciplinary action (Ch 9)

**grievance committee** a union committee that meets with management to resolve matters relating to the contract that the stewards are unable to resolve (Ch 9)

**gross profit (gross margin)** the difference between cost of goods sold and net sales (Ch 15)

**gross sales** the total value of all goods or services sold during the accounting period (Ch 15)

**growth funds** funds that offer limited dividends and invest in more speculative stocks (Ch 19)

**growth stage** the stage which begins when sales start to increase and ends when sales begin to level off (Ch 12)

## H

**hardware** the electronic and mechanical components of a computer system (Ch 16)

**Hawthorne studies** experiments conducted in the 1920s to determine relationships between changes in physical working conditions and employee productivity (Ch 7)

**health maintenance organization (HMO)** a prepaid health-care provider that operates clinics and, in some cases, hospitals (Ch 20)

**hierarchy** classification of an organization according to the rank or authority of the positions within it (Ch 5)

**hierarchy of needs** the order in which people tend to satisfy their basic human needs (Ch 7)

**high technology** new and innovative types of businesses that depend heavily on advanced scientific and engineering knowledge (Ch 4)

**hollow corporations** American firms that import components or products from low-wage countries, place their own names on them, and sell them in America (Ch 10)

**homeowner's insurance** a form of insurance that covers apartments as well as houses for both property and liability protection (Ch 20)

**horizontal market allocation** the division of a market among independent competitors (Ch 22)

**horizontal merger** when two competitors merge (Ch 22)

**human relations** refers to all the types of interaction among people: conflicts, cooperative efforts, and group relationships (Ch 7)

**human resource management** the process of acquiring, deploying, and developing people for organizational success (Ch 8)

**human resource planning** the systematic process of forecasting the future demand for employees and estimating the supply available to meet that demand (Ch 8)

**human skills** the ability to work with and for people, to communicate with others, and to understand others' needs (Ch 5)

## I

**idea** a concept, a philosophy, an image, or an issue (Ch 12)

**import quota** a limit on the quantity of a particular good that can be brought into a country (Ch 23)

**imports** goods that are sold in one country but produced in another country (Ch 23)

**in-home retailer** someone who sells directly to customers in their homes (Ch 13)

**incentive rate formulas** pay increments awarded for increased productivity (Ch 9)

**incentives** bonuses and other plans designed to encourage employees to produce work beyond the minimum acceptable levels (Ch 8)

**income funds** funds that concentrate on a high-yield portfolio with limited growth and risk (Ch 19)

**income statement** a summary of what an organization has earned and spent over a given period (Ch 15)

**incorporator** person who signs and files two copies of the proposed articles of incorporation with the secretary of state of that state (Ch 3)

**indemnifications** the principle that requires an insurer to pay no more than the financial loss actually suffered (Ch 20)

**indenture** a formal legal agreement between the issuer and the holder of a security (Ch 18)

**independent bargaining** form of negotiation in which a local negotiates for itself, without any help from the national or any other local unions (Ch 9)

**independent retailer** retail stores which operate independently, and are most often proprietorships or partnerships (Ch 13)

**indirect inventories** the supplies a business uses that are not purchased with the intention of reselling them (Ch 10)

**individual brand strategy** an approach that calls for a different brand name for each product (Ch 12)

**industrial product** a product used in the production of another good or service (Ch 11)

**industrial union** a union whose membership includes all the workers in an industry, regardless of the tasks they perform (Ch 9)

**inferential statistics** statistics which describe the behavior of a small group, from which the user may be able to predict the behavior of a larger group (Ch 16)

**informal organization** a behind-the-scenes network based on voluntary personal relationships rather than on formal authority (Ch 6)

**information** data that has been extracted or summarized so that it has meaning to the person who will use it (Ch 16)

**informational roles** roles that require a manager to gather and communicate information within the hierarchy and to the outside world (Ch 5)

**informative advertising** a form of advertising which provides the consumer with product information (Ch 14)

**infringement** violation of brand names or symbols (Ch 12)

**injunction** a court order forbidding certain actions (Ch 9)

**input** data put into a computer (Ch 16)

**input device** that part of a computer system that converts data from an outside source to signals which the CPU can use (Ch 16)

**inside salespeople** salespeople who rely almost totally on telephone orders and usually follow a regular customer-contact schedule (Ch 14)

**insider information** information available only to persons who owe a fiduciary duty to a corporation's shareholders (Ch 19)

**Insider Trading Act of 1984** act that subjected those guilty of insider trading to forfeiture of up to three times their gain on the illegal trades and expanded the SEC's powers to investigate such trading (Ch 19)

**Insider Trading Act of 1988** act that increased the criminal penalties for insider trading and extended the reach of the law (Ch 19)

**inspection** the determination of whether an input or output conforms to the organization's standards of quality (Ch 10)

**institutional advertising** advertising used to generate good will or enhance a firm's image rather than for selling a specific product (Ch 14)

**instrument** something in writing (Ch 21)

**insurable interest** having a measurable dollar loss if an insured-against event were to occur (Ch 20)

**insurable risks** the risks for which an insurance policy can be purchased (Ch 20)

**insurance** a contract that reduces risk of loss and requires one party to pay a specific sum to another if a previously identified event occurs (Ch 20)

**insurance premium** the cost of the insurance (Ch 20)

**insurance policy** the contract between the insurer and the insured which contains the terms of the insurance (Ch 20)

**insured** a person or firm that buys insurance (Ch 20)

**insurers** any organizations that provide insurance coverage (Ch 20)

**intangible assets** long-term assets that have no physical substance but have a value based on rights or privileges that belong to the owner (Ch 15)

**integrated marketing** viewing marketing as the job of everyone in the company because each employee can influence the firm's ability to gain and retain customers (Ch 11)

**intensive distribution strategy** strategy which takes advantage of all available retail outlets (Ch 13)

**intent** refers to a voluntary act or omission that is reasonably likely to bring about a particular consequence (Ch 21)

**intentional torts** acts for which the person who starts a lawsuit does not have to prove monetary loss in order to collect damages (Ch 21)

**interactive mode** the display of prompts by the software to the user (Ch 16)

**interlocking directorates** the presence of the same individual on the boards of two companies that are in similar product markets if the combined total capital of the two companies exceeds $1 million (Ch 22)

**intermediary (middleman)** a firm beween the manufacturer and the ultimate user in the channel that takes title or directly assists others to take title to goods (Ch 11)

**intermediate appellate courts** courts that hear appeals of trial-court decisions but are not the supreme court of their particular jurisdiction (Ch 21)

**internal financing** money generated from cash flow (Ch 18)

**international trade** trade that involves the crossing of national boundaries (Ch 23)

**interpersonal roles** roles that primarily require a manager to deal with people (Ch 5)

**interview** a private meeting of corporate officials or employees with the news media (Ch 14)

**introduction stage** the stage in the life cycle in which the product is first brought to market (Ch 12)

**inventory** certain classes of goods that are assets to a business (Ch 10 and 15)

**inventory control** a system which develops and maintains levels and assortments of products appropriate for a firm's target markets (Ch 13)

**investment** a financial tool for maintaining or increasing the expected value of today's funds (Ch 18)

**Investment Advisers Act of 1940** act that requires those who advise investors, whether or not they handle investor funds, to register with the SEC (Ch 19)

**Investment Company Act of 1940** act that made mutual funds subject to SEC registration and reporting requirements (Ch 19)

**involvement** the element of the QWL process that brings employees, unions, and management closer together for their mutual benefit (Ch 7)

**issuer** an entity with the power to authorize the sale and distribution of securities on its behalf (Ch 18); the company in which a stock represents ownership (Ch 19)

## J

**job analysis** a systematic study of each employee's duties, tasks, and work environment (Ch 8)

**job description** a written summary of the duties, tasks, and responsibilities associated with a job (Ch 8)

**job enlargement** adding similar duties from the same job level to a worker's basic responsibilities (Ch 7)

**job enrichment programs** programs whose major goal is to make routine jobs more challenging and interesting by giving employees more independence and responsibility (Ch 7)

**job rotation** a system in which workers switch for a time from one job to another (Ch 7)

**job sharing** a program in which two people share one job (Ch 7)

**job specification** a listing of the key qualifications a person needs to perform a job successfully (Ch 8)

**joint venture** an association of individuals for a limited, specific, for-profit business purpose (Ch 3 and 23)

**journal (book of original entry)** a chronological list of transactions each assigned to a particular account (Ch 15)

**junk bonds** low-quality, high-yield corporate bonds (Ch 18)

**jurisdiction** the authority that a court has to hear a particular matter (Ch 21)

**just-in-time inventory system** a program designed to ensure a continuous flow of manufacturing input from suppliers while at the same time minimizing the amount of goods held in inventory (Ch 10 and 13)

## K

**key person insurance** a form of term life insurance designed to protect a business against the loss of vital employees (Ch 20)

**Knights of Labor** an organization formed in 1869 whose goal it was to organize all workers, regardless of their skills or industry, into one organization (Ch 9)

## L

**label** that part of the package or product that contains information (Ch 12)

**labeling** the presentation of information on a package or product (Ch 12)

**Landrum-Griffin Act** provides a bill of rights for members, guaranteeing them the right to vote in union elections, speak at union meetings, receive union financial reports, and be treated like other members (Ch 9)

**Last In, First Out (LIFO)** the system which assumes that the last items taken into inventory are the first sold (Ch 15)

**law of large numbers** law that states that as the number of units in a group increases, predictions about the group become more accurate and therefore more certain (Ch 20)

**layoff** a separation caused by the employer's lack of work (Ch 8)

**layout** the physical arrangement of a production facility (Ch 10)

**lead time** the period that elapses between the time of placing an order and its receipt (Ch 10)

**leading/motivating** involves influencing, persuading, and directing people to accomplish an organization's objectives (Ch 5)

**ledger** a book or computer file in which each account appears separately (Ch 15)

**legitimate power** power achieved because of formal authority (Ch 6)

**leverage** the use of debt to improve the return on shareholders' equity (Ch 18)

**leveraged buyouts** when a current corporate management seizes control of its company by repurchasing all outstanding stock (Ch 18)

**liabilities** amounts that a firm owes to others (Ch 15)

**liability insurance** coverage against legal responsibility for another's losses (Ch 20)

**liability risks** risks that involve the potential that a firm might be held legally responsible for losses suffered by a person or another firm (Ch 20)

**liable** being legally responsible for any and all debts of the partnership (Ch 3); being held responsible because of interference with others' rights (Ch 21)

**license** a privilege to manufacture or sell a product in all or part of a country or to extract a natural resource from a particular location (Ch 23)

**limit order** an order specifying the maximum price acceptable to the investor (Ch 19)

**limited partner** investor in a partnership whose liability is restricted to the amount invested (Ch 3)

**limited partnership** form of business in which the general partners have the same rights and liabilities as partners in a general partnership while the limited partners have virtually no management rights (Ch 3)

**limited-pay life insurance** a form of cash value insurance that allows premium payments to stop at some time before death (Ch 20)

**limited-service wholesaler** wholesaler who offers a narrower range of services to customers (Ch 13)

**line of credit** an agreement with a bank that over a specified period it will lend up to a certain amount at a set rate of interest as the borrower needs the funds (Ch 4 and 18)

**line organization** organizational structure in which top management has total, direct control and each subordinate reports to a single supervisor (Ch 6)

**liquidity** the ease with which asset accounts can be turned into cash (Ch 15 and 18)

**litigants** the persons involved in lawsuits (Ch 21)

**load** a sales charge ranging from 2.5 to 8.5 percent, assessed on the purchase of a share in the mutual fund (Ch 19)

**local area network (LAN)** a network linking computers in a small geographical area or a particular building (Ch 16)

**lockout** management technique in which doors are closed to unionized workers (Ch 9)

**long-term debt to equity** the ratio that measures the relationship between bonds and shareholders' equity (Ch 18)

**long-term financing** money that will not be repaid within one year (Ch 18)

**long-term liabilities** debts that will fall due more than a year after the date of the balance sheet (Ch 15)

**low-load mutual fund** a mutual fund with sales charge of less than 5 percent (Ch 19)


## M

**mail-order retailer** a retailer who issues a catalog from which consumers can choose items and place their orders by mail or telephone (Ch 13)

**main memory** part of the CPU that holds data and programs while the computer is manipulating them (Ch 16)

**mainframe computers** large systems with high processing speeds and considerable storage capacity (Ch 16)

**maintenance (hygiene) factors** the elements that form the work environment (Ch 7)

**maintenance shop** one in which an employee who has joined a union must remain in it only so long as he or she works in that bargaining unit (Ch 9)

**Maloney Act of 1938** act that authorized the self-regulation of the OTC market (Ch 19)

**management** the process of coordinating human, informational, physical, and financial resources to accomplish organizational goals (Ch 5)

**management by objectives (MBO)** employee performance-appraisal technique based on objectives established jointly by the employee and his or her supervisor (Ch 8)

**management information system (MIS)** a collection of tools that provides information to a manager to facilitate that person's decision-making processes (Ch 16)

**manager** a person who coordinates an organization's resources (Ch 5)

**manual updating** an alteration of the existing data by a person (Ch 16)

**manufacturing** the management of the resources necessary to convert raw material into finished goods (Ch 19)

**margin accounts** credit arrangements by which a brokerage will extend credit to its individual customers to enable them to buy securities (Ch 19)

**margin call** a brokerage's demand for additional collateral from the customer (Ch 19)

**margin requirements** the minimum amount that a purchaser of securities must deposit with a broker in order to be able to buy securities on credit (Ch 17)

**market** a group of people or firms who currently demand or might potentially require a product or service and who have the ability, willingness, and authority to buy it (Ch 11)

**market allocations** agreements to divide markets among potential competitors (Ch 22)

**market coverage** producer's choice of the number and types of outlets it wants for its products (Ch 13)

**market niche** the area in which a firm specializes or holds a unique position (Ch 4)

**market order** an order at the market price (Ch 19)

**market price** the point of equilibrium between supply and demand (Ch 1 and 12)

**market research** the systematic gathering and analyzing of data on a particular marketing problem (Ch 11)

**market segmentation** the process of dividing all potential customers into distinctive groups that might merit a specific type of marketing effort (Ch 11)

**market value** the current price of a stock that a willing buyer will pay a willing seller (Ch 18)

**marketable security** a security that can be easily converted into cash without being significantly discounted from market value (Ch 15 and 18)

**marketer** a person who works in marketing (Ch 11)

**marketing** the process of planning and executing the conception, pricing, promotion, and distribution of ideas, goods, and services to create exchanges that satisfy individual and organizational objectives (Ch 11)

**marketing concept** the "belief that the firm should dedicate all of its policies, planning, and operations to the satisfaction of the customer" (Ch 11)

**marketing information system** a combination of people, equipment, and procedures organized to gather, process, and disperse information needed for making marketing decisions (Ch 11)

**marketing intermediary (middleman)** a firm between the manufacturer and the ultimate user or consumer that take title to the goods (Ch 13)

**marketing mix** the combination of the Four P's in any strategy (Ch 11)

**marketplace** the forum where individuals and businesses exchange money for goods and services (Ch 1)

**markup** a predetermined percentage of the cost which is then added to the cost in computing the price (Ch 12)

**mass production** the production-to-stock process that produces large quantities of identical or nearly identical products (Ch 10)

**master budget** an overall financial plan for the entire firm (Ch 15)

**materials handling** the physical handling of items during transportation and warehousing (Ch 13)

**materials requirements planning (MRP)** the computerized technique used to plan and control manufacturing inventories (Ch 10)

**matrix organizational structure** one that combines horizontal and vertical lines of authority and also functional and product departments (Ch 6)

**maturity date** the date on which the corporation will redeem the bond by paying its par value (Ch 18)

**maturity stage** the stage which begins when sales start to level off and ends when sales eventually begin to decline (Ch 12)

**measure of dispersion** indication of how widely spread the data is (Ch 16)

**measure of value** a readily accepted means of relating or comparing the worth of different things (Ch 17)

**measures of central tendency** indications of how data will cluster about a central point (Ch 16)

**median** value that appears in the middle of the data when the observations are arranged in order from the lowest to the highest (Ch 16)

**mediation** the process in which an impartial third party helps the parties settle their unresolved issues (Ch 9)

**mediator** the impartial third party who helps negotiating teams settle their unresolved issues (Ch 9 and 21)

**medium of exchange** anything that people are willing to exchange in return for goods and services (Ch 17)

**menu** a display of available programs to help the computer user carry out tasks (Ch 16)

**merchant** an intermediary who takes title to goods and resells them (Ch 13)

**merger** one company's acquisition and absorption of another (Ch 22)

**minicomputers** intermediate sized computers originally designed to be connected directly to scientific and medical instruments to control their operation and analyze data produced (Ch 16)

**minutes** secretary of the board's record of the votes in a board meeting (Ch 3)

**mode** value in a collection of data that occurs most frequently (Ch 16)

**modified capitalism** the American brand of capitalism, in which a relatively free marketplace is constrained by governmental rules and regulations (Ch 1)

**monetary policy** the management of available credit and the money supply (Ch 17)

**money** anything that is generally accepted in exchange for goods or in payment of debts (Ch 17)

**monopolistic competition** occurs when a relatively large number of sellers market similar but not identical products (Ch 1)

**monopoly** occurs when one company alone offers a good or service and therefore controls the market and price for it (Ch 1 and 22)

**morale** a state of psychological well-being based on such factors as a sense of organizational purpose and confidence in the future (Ch 7)

**mortgage** a security interest in real property (Ch 4); payment arrangements offered to individuals or businesses so they can purchase real estate (Ch 17)

**Motivation-Maintenance Model** Herzberg's model for human behavior at work, in which people require certain motivational and maintenance factors (Ch 7)

**motivation** the factors that cause people to behave in a certain way (Ch 7)

**motivational factors** work experiences that tend to motivate employees to achieve higher production levels and feel more committed to their jobs (Ch 7)

**multiple-unit pricing** the practice of providing discounts for purchases of two or more units (Ch 12)

**multinational corporation** a large firm with a home base in one country operating wholly or partially owned subsidiaries in other countries (Ch 23)

**municipal bonds** debt obligations of state and local governments and their agencies (Ch 19)

**mutual agency** the authority of each partner to act on behalf of the other partners and the partnership as a whole (Ch 3)

**mutual assent** the parties' agreement on the contract's terms as expressed in the offer and acceptance (Ch 21)

**mutual funds** poolings of various people's investments that are managed for a fee by professional investment managers toward a particular goal or according to a particular philosophy (Ch 19)

**mutual insurance companies** insurance companies owned by their policyholders in which any profits they earn go to the policyholders in the form of insurance dividends (Ch 20)

## N

**National Association of Securities Dealers (NASD)** organization through which the over-the-counter market functions (Ch 19)

**National Association of Securities Dealers Automatic Quotations (NASDAQ)** a computerized system enabling dealers to determine instantly the current market price for the more popular OTC shares and see who is making a market in them (Ch 19)

**national banks**   commercial banks organized with the approval of the U.S. Comptroller of the Currency (Ch 17)

**national brand (manufacturer's brand)**   a manufacturer-owned brand (Ch 12)

**National Labor Relations Act (NLRA)**   also known as the Wagner Act; act that made labor-management relations a federal matter and established the National Labor Relations Board to regulate them (Ch 9)

**National Labor Relations Board (NLRB)**   a five-member board appointed by the president to carry out the federal labor laws (Ch 9)

**national negotiation**   form of negotiation in which national union negotiates wages and benefits on an industry- or companywide basis and the local unions negotiate working conditions (Ch 9)

**natural monopoly**   a monopoly acquired as a result of market forces (Ch 22)

**need**   something that disturbs our satisfied physical or psychological state (Ch 7)

**negotiable instruments**   written contracts containing a promise to pay money to one person who may then assign this right to another (Ch 21)

**net income**   the difference between the total operating expenses and the gross profit (Ch 15)

**net sales**   the amount the firm added to its assets by selling goods during the accounting period (Ch 15)

**net worth**   determined by subtracting the value of a company's liabilities and preferred stock from the assets (Ch 18)

**new-product development process**   the six-step procedure for testing, developing, and selling a product (Ch 12)

**news release**   printed copy, usually in the form of brief newspaper stories, circulated generally to the news media (Ch 14)

**no-fault automobile insurance**   insurance that permits direct payments regardless of fault from one's own insurance company under the medical payments/personal injury protection part of the policy and limitations on the right to sue (Ch 20)

**no-fault insurance**   an insurance program that compensates losses regardless of who, if anyone, is responsible for their occurrence (Ch 20)

**no-load fund**   a fund with no sales charge; all of the purchaser's money is invested (Ch 19)

**no-par share**   share that is not assigned a dollar value (Ch 18)

**non-participating preferred stock**   stock that receives only the stated dividend (Ch 18)

**nondischargable**   when a debt is not releasable in a bankruptcy proceeding (Ch 21)

**nonprofit corporation (not-for-profit corporation)**   an organization set up for charitable, educational, or fraternal purposes (Ch 3)

**nonstore retailer**   a retailer which does not operate in conventional store facilities (Ch 13)

**notes payable**   notes that will fall due during the next twelve months (Ch 15)

**NOW (negotiable order of withdrawal) account**   an interest-bearing checking account (Ch 17)

## O

**objective**   what is to be accomplished; the goal (Ch 5)

**odd/even pricing**   strategies in which prices ending in odd numbers are meant to suggest a low price and in which even-numbered prices suggest prestige (Ch 12)

**odd lot**   less than 100 shares of stock (Ch 19)

**offer**   a proposal of what one party will or will not do in exchange for the other party's act or promise (Ch 21)

**offeree**   the party receiving the offer (Ch 21)

**offeror**   the party making the offer (Ch 21)

**oligopoly**   a market dominated by a few large sellers, usually in industries that require huge initial investments in plant and equipment (Ch 1)

**open-market operations**   the buying and selling of government securities on the open market (Ch 17)

**open order**   an order that extends beyond the day's end and runs until it is cancelled (Ch 19)

**open shop**   one in which union membership is not a condition of employment (Ch 9)

**operating expenses**   all costs of running the business except the cost of goods sold (Ch 15)

**operating system**   a program that does the detailed work of running the computer's hardware (Ch 16)

**operational planning**   the scheduling of an organization's day-to-day needs and the designing of how to meet them (Ch 5 and 10)

**operations management**   the process of planning and coordinating the production of goods and services (Ch 10)

**option**   a security contract that gives the option buyer the right to buy or sell 100 shares of stock at a specified price for a specific period of time (Ch 19)

**order processing**   the receiving and filling of customers' orders (Ch 13)

**ordering costs** expenses incurred whenever a business places an order for inventory goods with a vendor (Ch 10)

**organization** exists when two or more people coordinate their efforts, on an ongoing basis, to strive for a common purpose (Ch 6)

**organization chart** a diagram of the positions and reporting relationships within an organization (Ch 6)

**organizational goals** a firm's long-range goals (Ch 11)

**organizational structure** a pattern of task groupings reporting relationships, and authority within an organization (Ch 6)

**organized labor** workers represented by unions (Ch 9)

**organizing** assigning to the appropriate position the tasks required to achieve the organization's objectives, along with the authority and responsibility for accomplishing those tasks (Ch 5)

**organizing drive** taking the steps toward unionization (Ch 9)

**orientation** the systematic introduction of new employees to their new organization, job, and coworkers (Ch 8)

**outdoor advertising** advertising consisting of posters, billboards, and signs (Ch 14)

**outplacement program** a program that teaches laid-off employees job-hunting skills and helps them find suitable employment (Ch 8)

**output device** that part of a computer system that transmits processed data from the computer and presents it to the user (Ch 16)

**output** information that comes out of the computer system after processing (Ch 16)

**outside (field) salespeople** salespeople who work on the road, calling on potential buyers (Ch 14)

**outside financing** money generated by borrowing from or selling ownership interests to sources outside the business for its use (Ch 18)

**outsourcing** the practice of buying parts from outside vendors (Ch 10)

**over-the-counter (OTC) market** the telecommunications network linking broker-dealers for transactions of securities not listed on exchanges (Ch 19)

**owners' equity** the amount the owners would have left if they used the firm's assets to pay all its liabilities (Ch 15)

*P*

**packaging** the development of a container and a graphic design for a product (Ch 12)

**par value** a stated or face value of a security (Ch 18)

**participating preferred stock** preferred stock that may under circumstances specified in the indenture, participate in the dividend distributions on common shares (Ch 18)

**parties** the people involved in a dispute (Ch 21)

**partnership** an association of two or more persons to carry on as co-owners of a business for profit (Ch 3)

**partnership agreement** a contract between two persons stating the terms on which they agree to be partners (Ch 3)

**passes its dividend** when a company has not paid a dividend (Ch 18)

**pattern bargaining** form of negotiation in which local unions in a single company or industry negotiate on their own under the supervision of the national union (Ch 9)

**pay structure** the relationship among the rates of pay for various jobs within the company (Ch 8)

**payable on demand** means that the maker of an instrument will pay it when presented for payment (Ch 21)

**payable to bearer** means that anyone who has possession of the instrument may demand payment (Ch 21)

**payable to order** means that it can be transferred by means of an endorsement (Ch 21)

**penetration pricing strategy** pricing which calls for introducing a new product at a low price to attain a strong grip on a sizable market share (Ch 12)

**pension funds** accumulated funds intended to generate retirement income for participants (Ch 17)

**per se violations** when the government has only to prove that forbidden conduct has actually occurred (Ch 22)

**performance appraisal** a formal assessment of how well employees are doing their jobs (Ch 8)

**periodic inventory method** method that calculates the effect of sales on inventory only at the end of an accounting period (Ch 15)

**peripherals** all hardware devices other than the CPU (Ch 16)

**perpetual inventory system** system that records every change in inventory as soon as it happens (Ch 15)

**personal computers (microcomputers)** smaller computers which sit on the desktop, have limited storage capacity, and usually include a monitor and a keyboard (Ch 16)

**personal property** all property that is not either a fixture or real property (Ch 21)

**persuasive advertising** advertising which firms use to influence the target market's beliefs, attitudes, or behavior (Ch 14)

**physical distribution** the process of transporting goods, including materials handling, order processing, and inventory control (Ch 13)

**physiological needs** food, clothing, sleep, and shelter; the "survival" needs (Ch 7)

**picketing** the patrolling of entrances to an employer's facilities by members of a labor union often carrying signs to inform other employees and the public that a strike is in progress (Ch 9)

**pie chart** a circle divided into pieces with each piece used to portray the kind and proportion of the data it represents (Ch 16)

**piece-rate system** an incentive system that compensates a worker according to the number of units of a product he or she produces (Ch 8)

**piece-work rates** rates that pay employees according to what they produce, not by the time they work (Ch 9)

**plaintiff** the person who starts a lawsuit (Ch 21)

**planning** the process of formulating objectives and determining how to achieve those objectives with available resources (Ch 5)

**point-of-purchase display** a special rack, sign, or display set up to increase consumer product awareness (Ch 14)

**police powers** state and local governments' powers to protect the health, safety, and welfare of their citizens (Ch 2)

**portable computers** range of machines from hand-held programmable calculators to laptop computers that can perform most functions that large heavier PCs can (Ch 16)

**positive reinforcement** actions following particular behavior that are designed to increase the likelihood of that behavior being repeated (Ch 7)

**posting** the process of transferring information from the journal to the ledger (Ch 15)

**power** the ability to control the actions of others (Ch 6)

**preapproach** planning that takes place before meeting with the customer (Ch 14)

**precedents** earlier decisions on similar or identical questions of law (Ch 21)

**predatory pricing** an abuse of monopoly power involving the pricing of products in such a way as to eliminate competition (Ch 22)

**preemptive rights** the right to buy additional shares to preserve ownership positions if the company issues additional shares to the public (Ch 18)

**preferred position** advertising in specific sections of newspapers which are are more likely to be read by the target market (Ch 14)

**preferred stock** a class of stock "that pays dividends at a specified rate and that has preference over common stock in the payment of dividends and the liquidation of assets" (Ch 18)

**premium** anything of value that customer receives in addition to the purchased item or service (Ch 14); an amount paid greater than par for bonds (Ch 18)

**premium placement** a newspaper's placement of an ad on a specific page (Ch 14)

**premiums** funds received by insurance companies from policyholders (Ch 17)

**prepaid expenses** the services and supplies an organization has paid for but has not yet used (Ch 15)

**press conference** a public meeting of corporate officials with the news media at which written and photographic materials are often supplied (Ch 14)

**prestige pricing** setting a very high price on an item to give an impression of high quality (Ch 12)

**preventive law** structuring operations to achieve goals and avoid legal problems by knowing what the law requires (Ch 21)

**price discrimination** the sale of goods at different prices by a commercial seller to two or more nonretail buyers (Ch 22)

**price fixing** an agreement between two or more parties on the prices to be charged for goods (Ch 22)

**price lining** pricing strategy in which the firm selects a limited number of key prices for certain classes of products (Ch 12)

**price points** key prices chosen for certain classes of products in the price lining process (Ch 12)

**price-quality relationship** where price is directly related to quality, so that high price means high quality (Ch 12)

**primary boycott** an action by a union to try to persuade others not to deal with an employer against whom it has a dispute (Ch 9)

**primary-brand (generic) advertising** type of advertising which does not distinguish between brands (Ch 14)

**primary markets** those markets in which the issuer of a security receives some or all of the funds paid for by the security (Ch 19)

**prime rate** the interest rate large banks charge their largest and most reliable corporate customers (Ch 18)

**principal** an individual, a partnership, or a corporation represented by an agent (Ch 21)

**private** a corporation whose securities are not publicly traded (Ch 19)

**private accountant (management accountant)** an accountant who is an employee of a company or government agency (Ch 15)

**private carrier** a carrier owned and operated by a shipper (Ch 13)

**private corporation** corporation organized by private individuals or companies for some purpose other than for providing utility service (Ch 3)

**private label brand** one owned by a retailer (Ch 12)

**private law** the law that defines the relationships between and among individuals and nongovernmental agencies (Ch 21)

**private placement** the direct sale of stock by an issuer to investors (Ch 19)

**private warehouse** a warehouse owned by a firm that has sole access to it (Ch 13)

**privatization** the selling of government-controlled companies and industries to private investors (Ch 1)

**proaction strategy** voluntary, constructive social action (Ch 2)

**problem** the difference between actual and desired (Ch 5)

**procedural laws** the provisions in constitutions or statutes that describe how something is to be done by, or in relation to, government (Ch 21)

**process layout** a layout model which groups machinery or activities according to their purposes (Ch 10)

**product** any good or service that may be the subject of an exchange for money (Ch 1 and 10)

**product differentiation strategy** a program designed to give a product distinctive characteristics that can serve as competitive advantages over similar products (Ch 12)

**product layout** a layout model in which the equipment arrangement relates to the sequence of operations performed in manufacturing a product (Ch 10)

**product liability insurance** insurance that covers a manufacturer's or seller's responsibility for losses caused by goods placed in commerce (Ch 20)

**product life cycle** the four identifiable stages in a product's life: introduction, growth, maturity, and decline (Ch 12)

**production planning and control** the management function which involves the scheduling and monitoring of operations relating to the production of goods or services (Ch 10)

**production-to-order system** system that produces only what customers or clients demand (Ch 10)

**production-to-stock system** system that produces goods to be held in inventory (Ch 10)

**professional corporation** newest form of corporation, in which shareholders offer such professional services as medical, legal, and engineering work (Ch 3)

**professional liability insurance** insurance that covers responsibility for losses arising out of professional services rendered by doctors, lawyers, accountants, and certain other professionals (Ch 20)

**profit** the excess of revenues over expenses (Ch 1 and 15)

**profit-sharing program** program that distributes a set portion of a company's profits to its employees, according to a standard formula (Ch 8)

**program** a set of instructions for the computer to follow (Ch 16)

**Program Evaluation and Review Technique (PERT)** a scheduling technique for production control (Ch 10)

**programming** the designing and writing of computer programs (Ch 16)

**promissory note** written contract involving a promise to pay money (Ch 18)

**promotion** an advancement granted to an employee to a higher position, greater responsibility, or more prestige (Ch 8); the communications that an organization uses to inform, persuade, or remind a target market about its products, its services, or itself (Ch 14)

**promotional mix** the way a firm combines advertising, personal selling, sales promotion, and publicity and public relations in its promotion strategy (Ch 14)

**property risks** the potential direct loss of the firm's property due to fire or similar causes (Ch 20)

**property tax** a tax imposed by a state or local government on real property (Ch 22)

**prospecting** developing a list of potential customers (Ch 14)

**prospects** firms or individuals who qualify as potential customers because they have the authority and financial ability to buy the product (Ch 14)

**prospectus** a summary of information contained in the registration statement (Ch 19)

**protectionism** the creation of artificial barriers to free trade to protect domestic industries and jobs (Ch 23)

**protective tariff** tax imposed to protect a domestic industry from competition (Ch 23)

**psychographic variable** segmentation variable which considers personality characteristics, lifestyle, and buying motives (Ch 11)

**psychological (secondary) needs** the needs of the mind (Ch 7)

**public accountant** an independent professional whom individuals or companies may hire to perform specific accounting services (Ch 15)

**public corporation** corporation set up by Congress or a state legislature for a specific public purpose (Ch 3)

**public law** the duties imposed by governments to protect the rights of individuals or preserve social order (Ch 21)

**public offering** the process of initially selling a new issue of securities to the public (Ch 19)

**public relations** the activities designed to create and maintain favorable relations between an organization and its various publics (Ch 14)

**Public Utility Holding Company Act of 1935** regulates the companies that control public utilities (Ch 19)

**public warehouse** a storage building that can be used by the general public to store goods for a fee (Ch 13)

**publicity** communication in news-story form about a company or its products transmitted by a mass medium at no charge (Ch 14)

**publicly traded** when shares are bought and sold on stock exchanges (Ch 3)

**pull strategy** strategy which promotes a product or service directly to the consumer (Ch 14)

**purchases** the value of what a firm bought for inventory during the accounting period (Ch 15)

**purchasing** the operations function by which a business obtains the goods and services it requires (Ch 10)

**pure competition** occurs when no single seller can control the price of a good or service (Ch 1)

**pure risk** offers only the potential for loss (Ch 20)

**push strategy** promotion strategy which involves selling goods or services directly to the next intermediary in the channel of distribution (Ch 14)

## Q

**quality circles** groups of workers that volunteer to meet regularly to discuss ways to improve work procedures, eliminate defects, and perform their work more efficiently (Ch 7)

**quality control** the operations management function meant to ensure that output meets product design specifications (Ch 10)

**Quality of Work Life movement (QWL)** the drive to achieve a better workplace environment for employees while increasing profitability for the employer (Ch 7)

**quasi-public corporation (public utility)** corporation granted a monopoly by a government unit to provide certain kinds of services to the public (Ch 3)

## R

**random access** a computer's ability to retrieve any piece of data from the source in the same amount of time as any other piece (Ch 16)

**random access memory (RAM)** memory cells used to store changeable data or instructions (Ch 16)

**random sample** sample in which any unit or person in a population has an equal chance of being chosen to appear in the sample (Ch 16)

**range** principal measure of the data's dispersion (Ch 16)

**rational buying motive** a buying motive which includes the desire for dependability, durability, efficiency, financial gain, and economy (Ch 11)

**reaction strategy** when business denies responsibility for something while at the same time developing an argument for continuing the status quo (Ch 2)

**read-only memory (ROM)** memory cells that hold permanently stored programs (Ch 16)

**real property** land and everything attached to it (Ch 21)

**real-time updating** interaction of computer hardware and software to automatically make changes to the database as new data becomes available (Ch 16)

**reciprocal-dealing arrangement** occurs when a buyer can force a seller to buy something from it as a condition of the buyer's making the purchase (Ch 22)

**reciprocity** the belief that one country's markets can be only as free as its trading partners' (Ch 23)

**record date** the specified date that shareholders who own shares will receive dividends (Ch 18)

**recruitment** the process of attracting qualified people to apply for jobs (Ch 8)

**redeemed** the liquidation of shares before anything is paid to common stockholders (Ch 18)

**referent power** power achieved through being liked or in response to your charisma (Ch 6)

**refund** the return of a portion of an item's purchase price (Ch 14)

**registration statement** document filed with the Securities and Exchange Commission and state securities regulators that fully describe an investment and the issuer (Ch 19)

**reinsurance** the portions of the coverage that are sold off to other insurance companies (Ch 20)

**reliable employment test** test that consistently measures what it is supposed to measure (Ch 8)

**reminder (reinforcement) advertising** advertising which seeks to remind the target market about something (Ch 14)

**representation election** an election to determine whether a union will represent a particular group of workers (Ch 9)

**reserve requirement** a specified percentage of deposits that a member bank must either deposit with the Federal Reserve or hold in its own vaults as cash and may not lend (Ch 17)

**retailer** a businessperson who acquires goods from manufacturers, producers, or wholesalers, and then sells them to consumers (Ch 4 and 13)

**retained earnings** profits kept in the business after any dividends are paid (Ch 15 and 18)

**return** any profit that investors make from their investments (Ch 18)

**revaluation** an arbitrary upward adjustment of one country's currency in terms of another country's (Ch 23)

**revenue** the cash and accounts receivable a firm generates from its operations (Ch 15)

**revenue tariffs** taxes imposed solely to generate income for the government (Ch 23)

**reverse-load mutual fund** a fund that does not have a sales charge at the time of purchase but charges a fee for selling the shares (Ch 19)

**reverse** the appellate court's overturning of the trial court's judgment (Ch 21)

**reverse split** a reduction of the number of shares outstanding and raising their market price (Ch 18)

**revolving credit agreement** a line of credit backed by a bank's legally enforceable guarantee that the money will be available whenever the borrower wants it (Ch 18)

**reward power** power achieved by promising or granting rewards (Ch 6)

**right to employment** the methods by which promotions, transfers, and layoffs are determined within a bargaining unit (Ch 9)

**right-to-work law** a law that outlaws union shops (Ch 9)

**risk** the chance that an investor will be able to get his or her money back (Ch 18); the uncertainty about whether an event will or will not occur (Ch 20)

**risk assumption** way of handling risk that requires that a firm consciously recognize a particular risk and accept it as an integral part of its activities (Ch 20)

**risk avoidance** a way of handling risk that requires that a firm not engage in an activity or own property that might lead to an exposure of risk (Ch 20)

**risk management** the process of identifying exposures to risk, choosing the best method for handling each exposure, and implementing it (Ch 20)

**risk manager** a person whose job it is to preserve company assets and a business's earning power against pure risks (Ch 20)

**risk reduction** the lessening of the uncertainty of financial loss in a risky situation (Ch 20)

**risk transfer** the shift of risk to another party (Ch 20)

**robot** a reprogrammable machine capable of performing a variety of tasks requiring programmed manipulations of tools and materials (Ch 10)

**round lot** 100 shares of stock (Ch 19)

**royalty** the share of payment to the issuing government for the extraction of a natural resource (Ch 23)

**rule-of-reason standard** the defendant in an antitrust case is given the opportunity to prove that the conduct does not unreasonably restrict trade (Ch 22)

## S

**salary** compensation calculated usually on a weekly, monthly, or yearly basis and not normally related to the number of hours actually worked (Ch 8)

**sales engineers** salespeople who have precise, detailed knowledge of their products and are able to discuss technical matters (Ch 14)

**sales promotion** marketing activities other than personal selling, advertising, and publicity that stimulate consumer purchasing and dealer effectiveness (Ch 14)

**sales tax** a tax based on the value of a transaction (Ch 22)

**sample** a free package or container of a product (Ch 14); a small group of representative units selected from a much larger group to answer researchers' questions (Ch 16)

**savings and loan associations (S & Ls)** thrift institutions that are usually owned by their depositors and offer a wide variety of financial services (Ch 17)

**scheduling** the function of production control that sets the time for and duration of tasks (Ch 10)

**seasonal trends** patterns that complete themselves within one year or less and then begin to repeat themselves (Ch 16)

**secondary boycott** a refusal to work for, purchase from, or handle the products of another company with which the union has no dispute in order to force that company to stop doing business with the company with which the union does have a dispute (Ch 9)

**secondary markets** those markets in which the sale of a security ordinarily does not involve any proceeds going to the issuer (Ch 19)

**secular trend** fluctuation that consists of a smooth upward or downward movement over a long period (Ch 16)

**Securities Act of 1933** a disclosure act requiring that the issuer of a public offering file a registration statement providing specific information about the issuer, its financial condition, management, properties, and general operation (Ch 19)

**Securities Exchange Act of 1934** act requiring periodic disclosure in the form of reports to the SEC by companies whose securities are publicly held (Ch 19)

**Securities Act of 1964** act that broadened the SEC's jurisdiction to include companies that had avoided regulation by staying off the exchanges (Ch 19)

**Securities Investors Protection Act of 1970** act that created the Securities Investors Protection Corporation (SIPC) (Ch 19)

**Securities Investors Protection Corporation (SIPC)** a regulatory agency that oversees the liquidation of failed broker-dealers and insures investors when the assets of a failed firm are insufficient to cover its obligations to its customers (Ch 19)

**security** an investment of money, a common enterprise, and an expectation of profit solely from the efforts of others (Ch 19)

**security interest** a financial interest in personal property or fixtures that secures the payment of a debt or obligation (Ch 4)

**selection** the identification of appropriate candidates (Ch 8)

**selective (brand) advertising** promotion designed to encourage a consumer to buy a certain brand of product and thereby build customer patronage (Ch 14)

**selective distribution strategy** an approach that centers on a moderate proportion of the retailers likely to carry a particular product in a given market area (Ch 13)

**self-actualization** self-fulfillment or the tapping of one's potential to one's own satisfaction (Ch 7)

**self-insurance** a mechanism by which a business establishes a fund to cover losses caused by particular types of events (Ch 20)

**selling expenses** all costs directly associated with selling products or services to customers (Ch 15)

**seniority** a system in which the order of hiring determines the order of promotions, layoffs, rehirings, and the exercise of all other employment rights (Ch 8 and 9)

**seniority differential** an incremental pay increase determined by the length of the worker's service with the employer (Ch 9)

**separation** the ending of the employment relationship (Ch 8)

**sequential access** the process the computer undergoes of reading all the entries preceding a user's file before it can access the file (Ch 16)

**serial bonds** bonds of one issue but that mature on different dates (Ch 18)

**Service Corps of Retired Executives (SCORE) and Active Corps of Executives (ACE)** volunteer agencies funded by the SBA to provide advice for small firms (Ch 4)

**service** work that is done for others that does not involve the production of goods (Ch 4 and 12)

**service sector** consists of businesses that perform work for others that does not involve producing goods (Ch 1)

**setups** modifications of a process or a machine to meet the specifications for a new order (Ch 10)

**share** unit into which ownership of a corporation is divided (Ch 3)

**share draft accounts** demand deposit account offered by a credit union (Ch 17)

**shareholder** person who owns shares in a corporation (Ch 3)

**shareholder of records** stockholder who owned shares when dividend is declared (Ch 18)

**Sherman Act** the first federal legislation aimed at controlling trusts (Ch 22)

**Sherman Antitrust Act** legislation originally designed to curb large companies' abuses of the market system (Ch 9)

**shift differential** an incremental pay increase for working nonstandard time periods (Ch 9)

**shop steward** a union member elected to represent the other members employed in a particular work unit in their day-to-day dealings with the employer (Ch 9)

**shoppers' guides** advertising circulars featuring both display and classified ads that are delivered door to door (Ch 14)

**shopping goods** goods which are purchased infrequently, have a relatively high unit price, and bought only after comparison with other product alternatives (Ch 11)

**short-term financing** money that a firm will borrow for a year or less (Ch 18)

**sinking fund** a fund set aside by the company itself to redeem particular issues of preferred stock or debt (Ch 18)

**skills inventory** a data bank containing each employee's history, skills, interests, and performance record (Ch 8)

**skimming price strategy** pricing which involves charging a high price when the product is first introduced (Ch 12)

**small business** any business that is independently owned and operated, is not dominant in its field, and does not employ more than 500 persons (Ch 4)

**Small Business Administration (SBA)** an agency of the federal government that offers both managerial and financial assistance to small businesses (Ch 4)

**small business development center (SBDC)** a business clinic usually located on a college campus that is set up to provide counseling at no charge and training at only a nominal charge (Ch 4)

**Small Business Institute (SBI)** program in which business students assist small business owners with their problems, under the supervision of faculty members (Ch 4)

**social audit** an annual assessment of a company's effects on society and the environment (Ch 2)

**Social Security Act of 1935** act that established the federal Old-Age, Survivors, Disability, and Health Insurance (OASDHI) program that provides retirement, survivors' disability, and health insurance (Ch 20)

**socialism** an economic system in which the state owns the principal means of production, though private property of some sort still exists (Ch 1)

**software** a set of intangible commands that instruct a computer to read data into its memory from a peripheral device and perform various functions with it (Ch 16)

**software applications package** the program a user employs to tell the CPU what to do with the data entered (Ch 16)

**sole proprietorship** form of business in which one individual (sole proprietor) owns all the assets of the business and is alone responsible for its debts (Ch 3)

**span of management** determined by the number of people who report directly to a manager (Ch 6)

**specialist** a member of an exchange who is responsible for matching buy and sell orders or for using his or her own portfolio to balance the buy and sell orders (Ch 19)

**specialization** the concentration of economic activity in those areas in which the country, the individual, or the business has either a natural or acquired advantage (Ch 23)

**specialty advertising** producing small, inexpensive items bearing the advertiser's name, address, and occasional brief messages for free distribution (Ch 14)

**specialty goods** products for which consumers develop a strong preference and loyalty (Ch 11)

**specialty store** a store carrying a limited line of merchandise (Ch 13)

**speculative risk** offers the potential for gain as well as loss (Ch 20)

**spread** the difference between the amount paid to the issuer and the amount paid by the public (Ch 19)

**staff** employees and managers not directly involved in producing or distributing the goods and services an organization sells (Ch 6)

**staffing** the process of locating, selecting, and assigning people to the tasks designed to achieve an organization's objectives (Ch 5)

**standardization** establishing a set of uniform specifications against which particular manufactured goods are measured, or a set of classes in which agricultural and mined products are sorted or assigned (Ch 11)

**stare decisis** a Latin term that means a court must literally follow a decision by a higher court in its own system or by the U.S. Supreme Court (Ch 21)

**state banks** commercial banks chartered by the state in which they operate (Ch 17)

**statement of changes in financial position** summary of changes in the firm's generation and use of cash that have taken place during the accounting period being analyzed (Ch 15)

**statistic** number that is calculated to summarize data (Ch 16)

**statutory** the federal and state laws specifying obligations imposed by government on the way business operates (Ch 21)

**stock** a security in the form of an ownership interest in the corporation (Ch 18)

**stock insurance companies** insurance companies owned by stockholders which provide insurance protection for a profit (Ch 20)

**stock split** takes place when a stock's market price is so high that many investors do not want to buy it and a company may decide to "split" its stock (Ch 18)

**stop order** an explicitly priced sell order triggered when a stock price falls to or below a specified level (Ch 19)

**store of value** a means of holding and collecting wealth (Ch 17)

**straight life insurance** a form of cash value insurance that has the lowest relative premium per $1000 of permanent life insurance (Ch 20)

**strategic planning** involves determining what business the company is in and generally how it intends to remain in business (Ch 5)

**stress interview** interview in which the interviewer deliberately annoys, embarrasses, or frustrates the applicant to determine his or her action (Ch 8)

**strike** practice in which a union, in an effort to put economic pressure on management, calls on its members not to work (Ch 9)

**strikebreaker (scab)** a person hired to replace striking employees (Ch 9)

**structured interview** interview in which the interviewer asks a series of prepared questions based on the job specifications (Ch 8)

**Subchapter S (S corporation)** corporation with thirty-five or fewer shareholders that elects under Subchapter

S of the Internal Revenue Code to be treated for federal tax purposes essentially as a partnership (Ch 3)

**substantive law** law that describes rights or duties (Ch 21)

**supercomputers** the largest, most powerful computers made today (Ch 16)

**supermarket** a large, predominantly self-serve food store which offers relatively low prices and carries nationally recognized brands (Ch 13)

**superstore, hypermarket** a large store carrying a broad selection of food, specialty food, and nonfood items (Ch 13)

**supply** the willingness of sellers or producers to provide goods or services at a particular price and particular time (Ch 1 and 12)

**supply curve** the line reflecting the relationship between the price and the quantity supplied (Ch 1)

**supreme court** the highest appellate court in the court system (Ch 21)

**surety bonds** insurance policies that provide for compensation to the beneficiary should a contract not be completed on time (Ch 20)

**syndicate** temporary association that forms to carry out a specific, usually short-term investment (Ch 3); the underwriter or group of underwriters (Ch 19)

*T*

**tabular display** an array or matrix of information in vertical columns and horizontal rows (Ch 16)

**tactical planning** involves allocating available resources to specific purposes (Ch 5)

**Taft-Hartley Act** act that reflected the public's wish to blunt union drives for more wages, benefits, and—most importantly—power (Ch 9)

**target marketing** choosing specific markets on which to focus marketing activities (Ch 11)

**targeted television advertising** television advertising aimed at specific audiences (Ch 14)

**tariffs** taxes imposed by a country on imported goods (Ch 22 and 23)

**technical skills** the ability to use the tools, equipment, procedures, and techniques of a specialized field (Ch 5)

**telecommuters** persons who work at home or in a satellite office and electronically transfer the information needed to do their job between home/satellite and headquarters (Ch 7)

**telemarketing** the art and science of marketing goods and services through telephone contact (Ch 14)

**term life insurance** the type of life insurance that pays the policy amount to the beneficiary only if the insured dies within the period covered by the last premium (Ch 20)

**terminals** input devices consisting of a keyboard and a CRT linked to the central computer (Ch 16)

**termination** recognition of the fact that the winding up is complete and the partnership has therefore ended (Ch 3)

**test market** sample market areas, the sales from which are used to predict the behavior of the entire market (Ch 12)

**Theory X** McGregor's theory that people really do not want to work and will avoid it if possible (Ch 7)

**Theory Y** McGregor's theory that work is as natural to people as recreation and rest (Ch 7)

**Theory Z** William Ouchi's 1981 book that outlined how American business could meet the challenges Japan poses (Ch 7)

**thrift institutions** institutions which serve individuals by providing safe, interest-bearing accounts for savings (Ch 17)

**ticker** the electronic system that provides the public with notice of each transaction in the exchange (Ch 19)

**time deposit** funds deposited with a bank either in the form of a savings account or a certificate of deposit (Ch 17)

**time series analysis (trend analysis)** a statistical technique for examining the ways that observations of a variable move over time and then basing forecasts on the observations (Ch 16)

**title** the right to own property that usually comes with physical possession of tangible personal property or real property (Ch 13)

**title insurance** insurance of losses to the purchaser of real property to which the seller did not have a clear or marketable title (Ch 20)

**tort** a legal wrong as defined by the common law (Ch 21)

**total costs** the sum of the fixed and variable costs (Ch 12)

**trade** the buying or selling of goods or services among companies, states, or countries (Ch 23)

**trade (craft) union** a union made up of skilled workers of the same or related vocations (Ch 9)

**trade agreement** a negotiated relationship between nations that regulates the commerce between them (Ch 23)

**trade credit** a commercial buyer's open account arrangements with suppliers of goods or services (Ch 4, 11, 13, 18)

**trade show** a large exhibit of products that are usually common to one industry (Ch 14)

**trademark** a brand name or symbol registered with the U.S. Patent and Trademark Office (Ch 12)

**trading partners** trade between two entities (Ch 23)

**training and development** the process of changing employee attitudes and/or behavior through some type of structured experience (Ch 8)

**transferee** a person to whom a security is transferred (Ch 19)

**transformation** the conversion of input (resources) into output (goods or services) (Ch 10)

**transportation** the process of actually moving goods from one location to another (Ch 13)

**treasurer** the person responsible for overseeing and planning the firm's expenditures and income (Ch 18)

**Treasury bill (T-bill)** short-term promissory note issued by the U.S. Treasury (Ch 18)

**trial balance** a step taken before preparing financial statements to make sure that a credit offsets every debit and that the arithmetic was done correctly (Ch 15)

**trial courts of general jurisdiction** courts that can hear any matters that a trial court in its system has authority to hear (Ch 21)

**trial courts of limited jurisdiction** courts with authority to hear only particular types of cases or cases involving less than a certain dollar amount (Ch 21)

**Trust Indenture Act of 1939** act that requires that any corporate debit offered to the public be registered with the SEC and conform to certain requirements relating to maturity, interest, and financial backing (Ch 19)

**trustee** a person or a firm that protects the bondholders' interests by making sure that the issuer meets its obligations under the indenture (Ch 18)

**tying arrangement** results when the seller agrees to sell a product that the buyer wants only if the buyer also purchases another product that the buyer does not want (Ch 22)

## U

**U.S. government issues** all bonds issued by any unit of the federal government or issued as municipal bonds (Ch 19)

**undercapitalization** the lack of sufficient funds to operate a business normally (Ch 4)

**undervalued** a stock whose book value exceeds its market value (Ch 18)

**underwriter** an investment banker who agrees to buy a new issue and distribute it to the public (Ch 19)

**unemployment compensation** payments from a pool created by employer contributions and required by state law to be made for a certain perod to laid-off workers (Ch 9)

**unemployment insurance** insurance that provides partial, temporary replacement income for eligible unemployed workers (Ch 20)

**unfair labor practice** a violation of the laws that the NLRB enforces (Ch 9)

**Uniform Commercial Code (UCC)** a body of statutes that replaces several areas of business law formerly covered individually by each state's common law of contracts (Ch 21)

**union** an organization through which employees combine their strength to advance their common interests (Ch 9)

**union shop** one in which workers do not have to be union members when hired but must later join (Ch 9)

**universal life insurance** a form of cash value insurance that combines term insurance with an investment plan guaranteeing higher rates than are usually available on cash value policies (Ch 20)

**unsecured loan** a loan for which the borrower does not provide collateral (Ch 17)

**unstructured interview** interview in which the interviewer does not have a firmly set structure for the interview and the interviewee does most of the talking (Ch 8)

**user fees** charges to the public designed to compensate the government for services it performs (Ch 22)

**utility** the satisfaction that goods and services yield to their buyers (Ch 11)

**utility program** a program provided by the manufacturer of the operating system that does routine file maintenance (Ch 16)

## V

**valid employment test** test that measures what it is supposed to measure (Ch 8)

**variable costs** costs that depend on the number of units produced (Ch 12)

**variance, standard deviation** two indications of dispersion that measure the difference between each observed value and the arithmetic mean of the entire set of data (Ch 16)

**variety store** a relatively small store that offers a wide range of small, inexpensive items (Ch 13)

**vending machine** an electromechanical device which dispenses items when a customer inserts money, a credit card, or a code (Ch 13)

**venture capitalist** an investor willing to put money into a business in exchange for a substantial block of stock (Ch 18)

**vertical-channel integration** the combination of two or more entities within the channel stretching from the producer to the consumer or end user (Ch 13)

**vertical market allocation** the division of a market among related entities (Ch 22)

**vertical merger** a merger of two companies in the same chain of supply (Ch 22)

**vice president of finance** the officer in a corporation with overall responsibility (Ch 18)

**visual display** a picture that portrays information items in a way that makes them easy to compare with one another or reflects trends in items (Ch 16)

**voting rights** the right to vote for directors and on extraordinary transactions that will affect the nature of the company (Ch 18)

## W

**wage/salary survey** a review of pay rates at companies within comparable industries in a particular region (Ch 8)

**wages** compensation usually calculated according to the number of hours an employee actually worked (Ch 8)

**warehouse club** usually a large store, which charges a membership fee and offers high-quality merchandise at very low prices (Ch 13)

**warehouse receipt** the record that a public warehouseman gives a person who is storing goods (Ch 13)

**warehouse store** a discount or off-price food store that offers approximately the same merchandise as supermarkets but has virtually no ambience (Ch 13)

**warehousing** the set of activities designed to ensure that goods are available when they are needed (Ch 13)

**warranties** guarantees or assurances (Ch 21)

**wheel of retailing** a method of describing the evolution of retailing and retailers over time, as new competitors continue to enter the market (Ch 13)

**whistle blowers** employees who report unethical or illegal conduct to their superiors or a government agency (Ch 2)

**wholesaler** a business or individual who buys and resells products to other merchants, but not to consumers (Ch 13)

**winding up** liquidation of the partnership's assets, payment of its debts, repayment of the partners' capital contributions, and division of the remaining funds (Ch 3)

**worker's compensation** a state-administered insurance program that provides employees with protection from losses caused by injury or illness resulting from employment (Ch 20)

**working capital** the money necessary to fund the business's regular operations (Ch 4)

**working conditions** a catch-all term to describe all aspects of the relationship between employer and employee that are not related to the area of compensation (Ch 9)

# Credits

**Chapter 1** p. 8 Ann States/Picture Group; p. 10 Richard Wood; p. 13 © Joyce Ravid; p. 16 Chris Niedenthal/Time Magazine; p. 19 Enrico Ferorelli; p. 25 UPI/Bettmann Newsphotos; p. 28 Damon Corporation; p. 26 AT&T

**Chapter 2** p. 40 Peter Freed; p. 45 Southwestern Bell Corporation; p. 49 Andy Freeberg; p. 52 Robert Holmgren; p. 53 Steve Smith; p. 55 Rick Friedman; p. 57 Rob Kinmonth

**Chapter 3** p. 71 Robert Frerck/Odyssey Productions; p. 73 Koala Blue, Inc.; p. 79 Will McIntyre; p. 82 Arthur Meyerson Photography; p. 84 © 1989 Roger Ressmeyer/Starlight; p. 89 Blue Diamond Growers; p. 86 Courtesy of Kinder-Care Learning Centers, Inc. Hutcheson Schutz Advertising

**Chapter 4** p. 98 © Nancy Rica Schiff 1988; p. 101 Edmund Nagele/FPG International; p. 104 Reprinted with permission of NYNEX Corporation, Bill Varie, copyright 1987; p. 110 Rex Rystedt Photography; p. 113 Andy Goodwin; p. 118 Nancy J. Pierce

**Chapter 5** p. 131 Michael Melford; p. 134 © Jim Henson Productions, Henson Associates, Inc.; p. 137 SuperStock International; p. 139 John Still; p. 146 Robert Holmgren

**Chapter 6** p. 159 Kathy Schenker Associates; p. 158 Reprinted with permission American International Group, Inc.; p. 164 © Lou Jones; p. 170 Jonathan Levine/ONYX; p. 176 Stacy Pick/Stock, Boston; p. 177 Louie Psihoyos/Matrix International

**Chapter 7** p. 189 Lee Balterman; p. 192 Michael Melford; p. 198a,b,c James Schnepf; p. 203 Courtesy, Stone Container Corporation

**Chapter 8** p. 221 John Chiasson/Ganima-Liaison; p. 224 Fredrich Cantor; p. 227 Alan D. Levenson; p. 238 John S. Abbott; p. 242 Armen Kachaturian; p. 243 Liane Enkelis/Stock, Boston

**Chapter 9** p. 252 Culver Pictures; p. 261 © Camille Vickers; p. 262 Bill Campbell/Picture Group; p. 265 Quaker State Corporation; p. 271 George Glod/SuperStock International; p. 273 Richard Mackson/FPG International

**Chapter 10** p. 287 Mark Seliger; p. 288 Doug Menuez/Time Magazine; p. 293 Ovak Arslanian; p. 296 Arthur Meyerson Photography; p. 299 Steve Dunwell; p. 301 Mead Corporation

**Chapter 11** p. 315 Rob Kinmonth; p. 321 Diana Walker/Time Magazine; p. 323 Andy Snow/Picture Group; p. 326 David R. Frazier; p. 327 Levi Strauss & Co.; p. 331 Air Products and Chemicals, Inc., Allentown, PA

**Chapter 12** p. 344 Philip Saltonstall/Onyx Enterprises, Inc.; p. 343 Courtesy Thomas J. Lipton, Inc., Englewood Cliffs, N.J.; p. 347 Zeva Oelbaum; p. 351 Courtesy of Dean Foods; p. 353 Warner-Lambert Company; p. 360 Andy Freeberg

**Chapter 13** p. 372 Barry Bomzer; p. 375 Arthur Meyerson Photography; p. 382 Jay Dickman/Matrix International; p. 383 Reprinted Courtesy Lands' End Catalogue © Lands' End, Inc.; p. 389 Courtesy of Household International; p. 390 John S. Abbott

**Chapter 14** p. 402 Walter Bibikow; p. 405 Courtesy Philips, Consumer Electronics Company; p. 408 America's Dairy Farmers. National Dairy Board.; p. 414 Photograph courtesy of Fuji Photo Film U.S.A., Inc.; p. 417 Louis Bencze; p. 421 Bob Kramer; p. 422 Courtesy of The Reebok Foundation

**Chapter 15** p. 434 Courtesy of Deluxe Corporation; p. 437 Sepp Seitz/Woodfin Camp; p. 446 Tom & Michele Grimm/After Image; p. 452 Photo courtesy of Walgreen Co.; p. 457 Photo by William Thompson, Chief Photographer-Communications, for Gulfstream Aerospace, a Chrysler company

Chapter 15 p. 434 Courtesy of Deluxe Corporation; p. 437 Sepp Seitz/Woodfin Camp; p. 446 Tom & Michele Grimm/ After Image; p. 452 Photo courtesy of Walgreen Co.; p. 457 Photo by William Thompson, Chief Photographer-Communications, for Gulfstream Aerospace, a Chrysler company

Chapter 16 p. 477 Gianni Giansanti/Sygma; p. 478 Reprinted with permission, International Business Machines Corporation; p. 483 Louie Psihoyos/Matrix International; p. 485 Ovak Arslanian; p. 489 Mark Joseph Photography; p. 496 Courtesy: The Gillette Company

Chapter 17 p. 509 Ethan Hoffman; p. 516 Courtesy of Great Western Financial Corporation; p. 518 The Museum of Modern Art/Film Stills Archive; p. 529 Jim Heemstra/Picture Group; p. 533 Steve Starr/Picture Group; p. 534 Courtesy American Express Travel Related Co., Inc.

Chapter 18 p. 545 Cindy Charles; p. 547 David Strick/Onyx Enterprises, Inc.; p. 553 Geoffrey Clifford/Wheeler Pictures; p. 555 © 1988 Edward Slaman; p. 563 Ed Linton/U.S. Windpower

Chapter 19 p. 577 Paul Solomon/Wheeler Pictures; p. 581 Steve Benbow/Woodfin Camp; p. 587 Bob Fingerman; p. 595 Stephen Ferry/Gamma-Liason; p. 597 Peter Menzel/Stock, Boston

Chapter 20 p. 605 Bob Thomason; p. 611 Dan Miller/Woodfin Camp; p. 616 Michael L. Abramson; p. 621 Chicago Mercantile Exchange; p. 623 Bob Kramer

Chapter 21 p. 638 Oscar Abolafia/Time Magazine; p. 643 Rocky Thies; p. 647 "Reproduced with Permission, © PepsiCo, Inc. 1989"; p. 651 Sandy Roessler/The Stock Market; p. 652 Kip Brundage/Wheeler Pictures; p. 658 Rob Kinmonth

Chapter 22 p. 666 Photo by Carlos Mercacto, courtesy of Elf Asphalt, Inc.; p. 675 © Peter C. Borsari; p. 677 Photo courtesy of EG & G, Inc. Wellesley, MA; p. 679 Courtesy of 3M; p. 684 A. Gallant/The Image Bank

Chapter 23 p. 697 Andy Freeberg; p. 698 Wal-Mart Stores, Inc.; p. 705 Bristol-Myers Company; p. 707 Photo courtesy of Gerber Products Company-International Division; p. 708 Courtesy of Compaq Computer Corporation, Black Star Photography; p. 711 Robert Frerck/Odyssey Productions; p. 712 Courtesy of United Parcel Service of America, Inc.

## Cartoons

Chapter 2 p. 56 Reprinted from *Harvard Business Review*, March/April 1988, by permission of Donald Reilly; Chapter 7 p. 200 Reprinted from *Harvard Business Review*, January/ February 1988, by permission of James Stevenson; Chapter 8 p. 240 © 1989 John Bush *Corporate Report Minnesota*; Chapter 14 p. 412 Drawing by Stevenson; © 1980 The New Yorker Magazine, Inc.; Chapter 15 p. 451 Reprinted from *Harvard Business Review*, January/February 1988, by permission of James Stevenson; Chapter 17 p. 517 Reprinted with permission of The Times-Picayune. Chapter 22 p. 683 From *Wall Street Journal*— Permission, Cartoon Features Syndicate.

Ivory Soap, 345–346
Izod, 350

Jack in the Box, 704
Jackson, Mary Ann, 106
J.C. Penney Co., Inc., 206
Johnson & Johnson Products, Inc.,
    41, 179, 191, 348, 352–353
John Wannamaker's, 378
Jones, Janice, 105
Jones & Laughlin Steel, 268

Kaiser-Permanente, 624
Kanaga, William S., 56–57
Keebler Co., Inc., 343
Kelley, Jerome, 684–685
Kellogg's, 351, 412
Kennedy, Allan A., 146–148
King's Collar, 378
K mart Corporation, 378, 385, 411,
    609
Kodak, 87, 157, 350
Komatsu Ltd., 706
Kraft, Inc., 542, 546, 564
Kroc, Ray, 102
Kroger Company, 315, 381
Kwik-Kopy, 116

Land o' Lakes, 87
Land's End, 383
Lane Bryant, 379
Lang, Eugene, 38
Lauren, Ralph, 350
Lean Cuisine dinners, 341
Lemmon, Jack, 193
Leonard, Stew, 96
Lerner stores, 379
Lerner Woman, 379
Lever Brothers Company, 350
Levi Strauss, 24, 50
Lewis, John L., 254, 256
Limited, The, 379, 468
Limited Express, 379
Limited Stores, 379
L.L. Bean, Inc., 107, 303, 411
Longs Drug Stores, Inc., 170
Los Angeles Raiders, 436
Los Angeles Rams, 319
Lotus 1-2-3, 482
Lowe's Companies, Inc., 322
Lukins, Sheila, 102

*McCall's* magazine, 403
McCormick, Cyrus, 24

McDade & Company, Inc., 380
McDonald's Corporation, 98, 102,
    116, 145, 223, 258, 313, 406–
    407, 710
McGregor, Douglas, 195
Macy's, 378
Manville Corporation, 80, 656
Marriott, J.W., Jr., 484
Marriott, Mrs. J. Willard, Sr., 542
Marriott Corporation, 325, 351,
    542, 561
Marshall, John, 78, 682
Maruchan, 312
Marx, Karl, 14–15
Mary Kay Cosmetics, Inc., 192, 382
Maslow, Abraham H., 190, 191,
    193, 198
MasterCard, 533
Mather, William L., 607
Mayo, Elton, 188–190
Maytag, 197
Mazda, 692
MCI Communications, 582
Meany, George, 256
Melitta, Inc., 423
Mercedes-Benz automobiles, 361
Merle Norman Cosmetics, Inc., 371
Meyer, Jerome J., 162
Microsoft, 103
Midas Muffler, 116
Miller's saddlery, 347
Minolta copiers, 424
Minstar, Inc., 566, 567
Missouri Pacific Railroad, 251
Mitsubishi Heavy Industries, 711
Mobil Oil Company, 52–53, 350,
    409
Monaghan, Tom, 19
Monsanto, 175
Moody, John, 564
*Moody's Indusrial Directories*, 588
*Moody's Million Dollar Directory*,
    588
Moog, Bill, 196–197
Moog, Inc., 196
Moscow Olympics, 617
Mosler Safe, 672
Mother Myrick's, 290
Motorola, 197, 303, 699
*Motorweek* magazine, 6
Mutual of New York, 612
MV series, 473
My Own Meals Inc., 106

Nabisco Brands, Inc., 343, 594
Nader, Ralph, 51, 681
Namath, Joe, 674
National Bank & Trust Company
    of Oklahoma City, 530
National Broadcasting Company,
    616–617
National Cash Register Company,
    199
National Coal Association, 52
National Dairy Research and Pro-
    motion Board, 313
National Decorating Products
    Show, 421
National Ocean Industries
    Association, 52
National Video Stores, 100
NBA Players Association, 254
NBC, 616–617
NCR, 199
Nemeth, Lane, 101–102
Nestlé Food Corporation, 205, 319,
    711
New Pig Corp., 289–290
New York State Department of
    Law, 205
New York Telephone Company,
    206
Nieman Marcus, 532
Nike, 349
Nissan Motor Corporation, 294,
    609
Nissan Motor Manufacturing Corp.
    USA, 40
Nissin Foods, 312, 319
Nordstrom department stores, 375–
    376
Northland Industrial Trucks, 372
Northwestern Mutual Life Insur-
    ance Company, 186, 197
Norton, Peter, 100
NSS Corp., 508
Nucor Corporation, 107

Occidental Life Insurance Company,
    205
Ocean Spray, 87
Ohio State Employees Credit Union,
    519
Olivetti, 87
Opel, 692
Open Pantry Food Marts, Inc., 381

Obsorne Computer Corporation, 345–346
Ouchi, William G., 201

Pace Membership Warehouse, 381
Parker Hannifin Corp., 297
Patterson, John H., 199
Pearson, Doug, 508
Pella Windows & Doors, 403
Pellon, 348
Penn Square Bank, 530
Pennzoil, 646
Pepperidge Farm cookies, 350
PepsiCo, 694
Perkins Geddis Eastman, 205
Perot, Ross, 4
Peter Norton Computing Inc., 99, 100
Peters, Thomas J., 148–149
Peugeot, 400
Philip Morris Company, 542, 546, 564, 696, 710
Phillips NAV, 711
Pic n Save Corporation, 381
Pikes Peak Auto Hill Climb, 400
Pioneer Electronics, 347
Planters peanuts, 350
PLUS, 529
Pontiac LeMans, 692
Porsche automobiles, 361, 406
PPG Industries, 283
Price Club, 381
Pritchard, Beth, 126
Procter, Harley, 346
Procter & Gamble Company, 149, 342–343, 345–346, 403, 409
Progresso, 312
Prudential Insurance Company, 60
*Publishers Weekly*, 587
Publix Super Markets, Inc., 186, 319
Pulitzer Publishing Company, 80
Purolator Courier Corporation, 388

Quaker Oats Company, 236

Ralphs Grocery Company, 371
Reagan, Ronald, 28, 51, 682, 698
Reliance Electric, 564
Remington, Eli, 25
Rent-a-Wreck, 115–116
Residence Inns, 325
Reuther, Walter, 200, 256
Revlon, 83

Reynolds, Russell, Jr., 229
R.H. Macy Company, Inc., 378
R.J. Reynolds Tobacco Company, 409, 594
Rockefeller, John D., 25
Rogers, Will, 664
Rolex watches, 361
Roosevelt, Franklin D., 25, 50
Rosso, Julee, 102
Royal Dutch/Shell Group, 711
Rubbermaid, 141, 344
Runyon, Marvin T., 40
Ryan Transfer, 244

Safeway Stores, Inc., 315, 381, 564, 609
Samples, Jeanne Leichtener, 626–627
Sarah Coventry, Inc., 382
Schloemer, Paul G., 297
S.C. Johnson Wax, 126
Scott's Turf Builder, 324
Sears, Roebuck and Company, 351, 368, 372–373, 383, 411, 530
ServiceMaster Industries, 55
Service Merchandise Company, Inc., 380
Seven-Eleven Convenience Food Stores, 381
Seven-Up, 64
*Sheep & Goat Ranchers Magazine*, 587
Silver Palate, The, 102
Simmons, John, 201
Simmons Construction Company, 201
Simon, Neil, 188
Singer, 315
Skippy peanut butter, 350
Smith, Adam, 16 161, 669, 696, 697
Smith, Frederick W., 186, 250, 393
Smith, Roger B., 145, 156
Smokey Mountain Log Cabins, Inc., 116
Sony Corp., 406, 582
Source, 475
Southern Bell Telephone & Telegraph Company, 636
*Southern Living* magazine, 403
*South Florida Home & Garden* magazine, 327
Southland Stores, 381

Sprague Electric, 201
*Standard & Poor's Reports*, 588
Standard Oil Company, 370, 669
State Farm, 609
Steinway, 289
Stew Leonard's Dairy, 96
Stolichnaya vodka, 694
Stonyfield Farm Yogurt, 353
Stop & Shop Companies, Inc., 349
Stop n Go, 381
Storr, Hans G., 542, 696
Strawberry's, 324
Stride-Rite Corporation, 188
Student Loan Marketing Association, 81
Sunbeam, 361
Sun Refining & Marketing Company, 372
*Supermarket News*, 420
Super X, 411

Tandy Corporation, 556, 694
Target discount chain, 378
Taupa Lithuanian Federal Credit Union, 519
Taylor, Frederick, 173
Technical Equities Corporation, 436
Tennessee Valley Authority, 81
Texas Instruments, 175
Texas Instruments 9914A, 360
Texas Oil Company, 372, 646
Thomas J. Lipton, 312, 319
Thorne, Jack, 114
3M Corporation, 43–44, 346
Tidewater, Inc., 111
Tiger International, Inc., 250, 388
*Time* magazine, 409
Toyota Motor Company, 221, 225, 294, 332, 692, 710
Travelers Insurance Company, 205
Triangle Shirtwaist Company, 49
Tropicana, 704
TRW, 174
Tubby's Sub Shops, 117
Tupperware, 382
Tylenol, 327, 352–353
Tysons Corner Play and Learn Children's Center, 216

United Parcel Service, 388
U.S. Postal Service, 387
U.S. Steel Corporation, 355–356
University City Science Center, 114

UNIX, 473
*Unsafe at Any Speed*, 681
*USA Today*, 587

Valencia, Bert, 704
*Value Line*, 588
VAX series, 473
Venture Stores, Inc., 371
Vermont Castings, 319
Victoria's Secret, 379
Visa, 532–533

Waggoner, Robert, 104
Wal-Mart Stores, Inc., 319, 368,
    371, 373, 378, 390–391

*Wall Street Journal, The*, 483, 586
Walt Disney Productions, 473, 481
Walt Disney World, 232
Wang Laboratories, 46, 556
Warehouse Foods, 381
Washington Public Power Supply
    System, 585
Waterman, Robert H., Jr., 148–149
Weeks, Lorena, 636
Wendy's International, Inc., 116, 370
Weyerhaeuser, Frederick, 24–25
Whitney, Eli, 24
Whitney National Bank, 111
Wilkinson, Wallace, 294
Williams, Jerry O., 220

Williams-Sonoma, 383
Wilson, Woodrow, 521
W.L. Gore & Associates, 169
*W* magazine, 587
*Women's Wear Daily*, 587
Woolworth Company, 380
World Book, Inc., 382
Wrangler Womenswear, 328–329

Xerox Corporation, 45, 61, 147,
    300, 350

Yankelovich, Daniel, 186
Yugo automobiles, 355

ZF, 692

# Subject Index

Absolute advantages, international trade and, 693

Academic references, employee selection and, 231–232

Acceptance, contracts and, 648

Accommodation strategy, 51(fig.), 53

Accountability, business ethics and, 59

Accountants, public and private, 436

Accounting, 430–460
balance sheet and, 442(fig.), 444–447
budgeting and, 456–460
definition of, 432
double-entry bookkeeping and, 438–439, 439(fig.)
income statement and, 447–452
interpreting financial statements and, 452–456
relationship to bookkeeping, 435, 435(fig.)
statement of changes in financial position and, 452
users of accounting information and, 433(fig.), 433–435

Accounting cycle, 439–443
calculating trial balance and, 442–443
entering transactions in journal and, 440, 441(fig.)

examining source documents and, 439–440
posting transactions in ledger and, 441–442, 442(fig.)
preparing financial statements and, 443

Accounting equation, 438–439, 439(fig.)

Accounting firms, the nation's largest 436, 436(table)

Accounting information
sources of, 483, 586–588
users of, 433(fig.), 433–435

Accounting period, 443

Accounts payable, 440–443, 447

Accounts receivable, 445
as collateral, 553

Accrued expenses, 447

ACE, see Active Corps of Executives

Achievement-oriented leadership, 143–144

ACHs, see Automated clearinghouses

Acid rain, regulation and, 678–679

Acid-test ratio, 455

Acquisitions, 87, 89–90

Action plans, planning and, 141

Action statement, planning and, 139

Active Corps of Executives (ACE), 114

Activity ratios, 454(table), 456

Actual cash value, 609–610

Adjusting entries, 443

Administered vertical-marketing system, 372–373

Administrative expenses, 451

Administrative regulations, 637–638

Advantages
absolute, 693
comparative, 693–694

Adversary system, 642

Advertising, 403–415
brand, 405–408
direct-mail, 410–411
display, 414
franchises and, 116
generic, 408–409
informative, 404
institutional, 409
objectives of, 404–405
outdoor, 413
persuasive, 404
primary demand, 408–409
reminder or reinforcement, 404
selective, 405–408
specialty, 414
television, targeted, 415
types of, 405–409

Advertising media, 409–415, 410(table)

Affirmation, of trial court's judgment, 644

Affirmative action programs, 220

AFL, *see* American Federation of Labor

Age, of American work force, 217

Age Discrimination in Employment Act of 1967, 219(table)

Agency law, relation to law of contracts, 648–649

Agency shop, 256

Agent, 369, 648
  budinrdd, of union, 267

AICPA, *see* American Institute of Certified Public Accountants

Air, transportation by, 388

Airline industry deregulation, 28

Alcohol abuse, employee assistance programs and, 234–235

Alien corporation, 84

Allowances, 448

Alternative work patterns, 203–206, 204(fig.)

Altruism, social responsibility and, 43

ALU, *see* Arithmetic-logic unit

Amalgamated Clothing & Textile Workers, 254, 259, 261

Amalgamated Transit Union, 263

American Arbitration Association, 267

American Federation of Labor (AFL), 252–253

American Institute of Certified Public Accountants (AICPA), 436

American Stock Exchange (Amex), 581–582, 595

American Stock Exchange (Amex) average, 589

Amortization, 446

Antidiscrimination laws, 218–220, 219(table)

Antitrust laws, 669–674
  enforcing, 673–674
  nature of, 669

Appeal, 644

Appellant, 644

Appellate courts, intermediate, 644

Appropriate investment, 547

Arbitration
  as alternative to litigation, 645
  collective bargaining and, 272–273
  grievance procedures and, 267

Arbitrator, 267

Arithmetic-logic unit (ALU), 472

Arithmetic mean, 492

Arrest, false, 646

Articles of incorporation, 74–75

Artificial intelligence, 478–479

Assembly-line production, 285

Assembly language, 476

Assets, 438, 445–446
  current, 445, 550
  fixed (plant and equipment), 445–446, 550–551
  intangible, 446
  liquid, 512
  ratio of debt to, 456

Association, partnership as, 71

ATM, *see* Automated teller machine

Atmospherics, 376

Attrition, 222

Audit, 436
  social, *see* Social audit

Authority, 166(fig.), 166–167
  delegation of, 171–172, 172(fig.)

Authorization cards, 261

Automated clearringhouses (ACHs), 529

Automated teller machine (ATM), 527–528
  national networks of, 528–529

Automation, 297

Automobile insurance, 618–619, 619(table)
  no-fault, 618–619, 620(table)

Auxiliary storage devices, 472, 487

Average, 492

Awards, motivation and, 199–200

Background investigations, employee selection and, 230–232

Balanced funds, 585

Balance
  compensation, 551–552
  of payments, 694
  of trade, 694
  trial, computing, 442–443

Balance sheet, 442(fig.), 444–447, 566
  assets on, 445–446
  liabilities on, 446–447
  owner's equity on, 447

Bank(s)
  central, 521
  commercial, 515–517
  deregulation of, 530

FDIC-insured, 516, 517(table)
Federal Reserve, 521–522, 523(fig.)
  national, 516
  savings, 517, 518–519
  state, 516

Bank accounts
  liquidity of, 512
  in\money supply, 524

Bank loans, *see* Loan(s)

Bankruptcy Amendments of 1984, 655

Bankruptcy law, 655–657
  Bankruptcy Code and, 655–656
  proceedings and, 656–657

Bankruptcy Reform Act of 1978, 655

Bar chart, 496, 497(fig.)

Bargaining unit, 262

Barter, 23

Base pay, 240

Base wage rate, 264

Batch mode, 477

Batch processing, 285

Batch systems, 488

Bearer instruments, 654

Beginning inventory, 450

Beneficiary, 624

Benefits, 240–242, 264–265
  collective bargaining and, 264–265
  of marketing, 332–333

Benefit variables, market segmentation and, 326

binary digit, 472

binary notation, 472

Bit, 472

"Black Monday," 590–591

"Black Tuesday," 589–590

Blank endorsement, 654

Blanket brand strategy, 350

Board of directors, 83
  in corporate management, 85–86
  interlocking directorates and, 672

Board of Governors, of Federal Reserve System, 521

Bond(s), 514
  bond ratings and, 564
  callable, 566
  collateral trust, 563–564
  convertibility of, 566

convertible into common stock, 566
corporate, 562
equipment, 564
fidelity, 622
financing by, 562(fig.), 562–566
government, 584–585
junk, 564
listing for, 584(fig.)
mortgage, 563
municipal, 585
premium on, 566
redemption of, 565–566
secured and unsecured debt and, 563–564
serial, 566
surety, 622
Bond markets, 583–585
Bond ratings, 564
Bonus, 243
Bookkeeper, 435
Bookkeeping
double-entry, 438–439, 439(fig.)
relationship of accounting to, 435, 435(fig.)
Book of original entry, 440
Book value, 556
Booting, 476
Boston exchange, 582
Boycotts
primary and secondary, 274
Sherman Act and, 670
Brand(s), 349
blanket, 350
family, 350
individual, 350
manufacturer's, 349
national, 349
private label, 349
Brand advertising, 405–408
Branding, 349–351
brand strategies and, 350–351
names and symbols and, 349–350
Brand name, 349
Brand strategies, 350–351
Brand symbol, 349
Breech of contract, inducing, 646
Breakeven analysis, 358(fig.), 358–359
Briefs, 644
Brokers, 369
discount, 579
floor, 578

full-service, 579
trading securities and, 577
Budget, 456–457
capital, 457
cash, 457
master, 457
operating, 457
Budgeting, 456–460
control and, 460
financial plan and, 544–545
responsibility for, 459
types of budgets and, 457, 459
zero-based, 459
Building-and-loan associations, 517, 518
Bureaucratic red tape, protectionism and, 699
Burglary, insurance against, 622
Business(es). See also Corporation(s); Organizations(s)
challenges for, 29
cooperatives as, 87
economic foundations of, 11–23
finance activity within, 543, 543(fig.)
government subsidies and, 665
government supervision of, 667–669. See also Regulation
government support of, 665–666
international, see International trade
joint ventures as, 74–75, 87, 708–709
learning about, 9–10
nature of, strategic operations planning and, 289
partnership form of, 71–77, 626
reasons to study, 5–8
small, see Small business
social responsibility and, see Social responsibility
software applications packages for, 477–478
sole proprietorship form of, 69–71
as suppliers and users of funds, 513–514
syndicates as, 87
topical model for study of, 30, 31(fig.)
Business agent, of union, 267
Business analysis, in new-product development process, 342

Business ethics, 56–62
encouraging, 60–61
improving, 61–62
reasons for, 59–60
scope of, 57–59
Business/financial risk, 548
Business incubator programs, 114
Business interruption insurance, 618
Business law, 634–658
bankruptcy and, 655–657
classification of, 639, 639(table), 641
contracts and, 647–650
dispute-resolution system and, 641–645
property and, 650
statutes and common law and, 637–639
torts and, 645–647
U.S. Constitution and, 637
Uniform Commercial Code and, 650–655, 651(table)
Business liability insurance, 619–620
Business plan, failure to develop, 108–109
Business representative, of union, 267
Business unionism, 253
Buying. See also Purchase(s); Purchasing
emotional motives for, 328
marketing and, 316
rational motives for, 328
wholesalers and, 377
Bylaws, corporate, 86
Byte, 472

CAD, see Computer-aided design
CAD/CAM, seeComputer-aided manufacturing systems
Cafeteria-style benefit programs, 241(fig.), 241–242
Callable bonds, 566
Call feature, 559
CAM, see Computer-aided manufacturing systems
Canada, trade agreement with United States, 700
Capacity
contractual, 648
credit and, 531
facility layout and, 296–297

Court(s), 641–644, 642(fig.)
   appellate, intermediate, 644
   circuit, 643
   of common pleas, 643
   county, 643
   district, 643
   municipal, 643
   superior, 643
   supreme, 644
   trial, 642–644
Coventurers, 709
CPA, *see* Certified public accountant
CPI, *see* Consumer Price Index
CPU, *see* Central processing unit
Craft unions, 252–253
Credit, 440–443, 530–536
   collection process and, 534, 536
   commercial, 530, 533–534
   consumer, 530, 532, 536
   credit cards and, 532–533
   five C's of, 530–532
   line of, 112, 552
   revolving, 552
   trade, 112, 314, 377, 530, 551
   wholesalers and, 376
Credit cards, 532–533
   lost or stolen, 536
Credit controls, selective, 526
Credit insurance, 622
Creditors' committee, 656
Credit unions, 512, 519, 519(table), 521
Crime insurance, 615
Criminal law, 639, 641
Critical path, 291
Crop insurance, 616
CRT, *see* Cathode ray tube
Culture
   corporate, 146–148
   international trade and, 705–706
Cumulative dividends, 560–561
Currency, 510
   devaluation of, 696
   in money supply, 524
   revaluation of, 696
Currency equivalents, in money supply, 524
Currency valuation, 695–696
   exchange rates and, 696
   imbalance and, 696
Current assets, 445
   acquiring, 550

Current liabilities, 447
Current ratio, 455
Cursor, 477
Customer departments, 163–164
Customer orientation, marketing and, 318
Customer satisfaction, marketing and, 319, 323–324
Cyclical fluctuations, 494

Damages, under tort law, 645
Data
   collection of, management information systems and, 487
   information versus, 469–470
   market, 328–330
   sources of, 482–484
   storage of, management information systems and, 487
   turning into information, 490
   updating, management information systems and, 487–488
Data processing, 470
Debit, 440–443
Debit card, 526–527
Debt, 553. *See also* Leverage
   secured and unsecured, 563–564
Debt financing, 561–566
   bonds and, 562(fig.), 562–566
   loans and, 562
Debt-to-assets ratio, 456
Debt-to-equity ratio, 456
Decentralization, 169, 169(fig.), 170
Decision(s), 135
   high-tech versus low-tech, 289–290
   make-or-buy, 288–289
   strategic, in operations planning, 287–288
Decisional roles, of managers, 134–135
Decision making, 135(fig.), 135–137
   employee involvement in, 200–203
   evaluating alternatives and, 136
   follow-up and, 137
   identifying alternatives and, 136
   implementation and, 136–137
   problem definition in, 135–136
Decision support systems (DSS), 484–485

executive information systems and, 485
   human error and, 484–485
Decline stage of product life cycle, 347
Deductibles, 607
   insurance and, 611
Defendant, 646
Defense strategy, 51(fig.), 52–53
Delegation, 171–172, 172(fig.)
Demand, 19–20, 356, 356(fig.)
   derived, 332
   for workers, forecasting, 221–222
Demand accounts, 517
Demand-based pricing, 358–359
Demand curve, 20, 20(fig.)
Demand deposits, 512
Democratic socialism, 15
Demographic variables, market segmentation and, 325–326
Demonstrative (real) evidence, 642
Dental insurance, 623
Departmentalization, 162–166, 163(fig.)
   by customer, 163–164
   functional, 162
   by location, 164
   multiple, 165(fig.), 165–166
   by product/service, 162–163
Department stores, 378, 379(fig.)
Deposit insurance, 615
Depositor, 512
Depository institutions, 515–521
   commercial banks as, 515–517
   credit unions as, 519, 519(table), 521
   thrift institutions as, 519–521
Depository Institutions Deregulation and Monetary Control Act of 1980, 521–522
Depreciation, 445–446
Deregulation, 28, 681–682
   of airline industry, 28
   of banking industry, 530
   industry, 681–682
   nonregulation as, 682
Derived demand, for industrial products, 332
Descriptive statistics, 491
Detail salespeople, 419
Devaluation, 696
Differentials, seniority and shift, 264

Differentiated strategy, target marketing and, 327
Direct foreign investment, 710
Direct inventory, 298
Directive leadership, 143, 144
Direct loans, from Small Business Administration, 112
Direct-mail advertising, 410–411
Disability insurance, 623
  Social Security, 615
Discharge
  of debts, bankruptcy and, 656, 657
  of employees, 239
Disclaimer, warranties and, 652
Disclosure, securities and, 596–597
Discount(s)
  cash, 448
  promissory notes and, 551
Discount brokers, 579
Discount rate, 526, 527(fig.)
Discount stores, 378
Discretionary income, 27, 317
Discretionary order, 579
Disk drives, 472
Dispersion, measure of, 493
Display advertising, 414
Dispute-resolution system, 641–645
  alternatives to courts and, 645
  judicial review and, 645
  state and federal court systems and, 641–644, 642(fig.)
Disseminator, manager as, 133
Dissolution, of partnership, 76
Distress sales, 356
Distribution, physical, see Physical distribution
Distribution channels, see Channels of distribution
Distribution strategy, 322, 366–393
  channels of distribution and, 369–373
  exclusive, 374
  intensive, 374
  market coverage and, 374–376
  in marketing mix, 322
  physical distribution and, 386–391
  retailers and, 378–386
  selective, 374
  wholesalers and, 376–377
District courts, 643
Disturbance handler, manager as, 134

Diversification, of investments, 548–549
Dividend(s)
  passing, 560–561
  stock, 558
  cash, 557–558
  on common stock, 557–558
  cumulative and noncumulative, 560–561
Division of Labor, 161–162, 162(table)
  transformation and, 283
Dollar, exchange rate and, 696
Domestic corporation, 84
Double-entry bookkeeping, 438–439, 439(fig.)
Dow Jones averages, 589, 590(fig.)
Drug(s), regulation of, 678
Drug abuse, employee assistance programs and, 234–235
Drug testing, employee selection and, 229–230
DSS, see Decision support systems
Dual reporting problem, in matrix-structured organization, 174–175
Dun & Bradstreet
  commercial credit and, 533
  financial ratios and, 456

EAPs, see Employee assistance programs
Earnings per share, 453
Economic conditions, credit and, 532
Economics
  competition and markets and, 21–23, 22(fig.)
  definition of, 12–13
  demand, supply, and equilibrium and, 19–21
  fundamental questions of, 13
Economic strike, 275
Economic systems, 13, 14(fig.), 14–17
  American, development of, 23–29
Economic theory-based pricing, 356(fig.), 356–357
Economy, planned, 15
Education, of American work force, 217
EEOC, see Equal Employment Opportunity Commission

Effective organizations, 177–179
  corporations ranked as, 178(table), 179
  criteria for, 178–179
EFT, see Electronic funds transfer
Election
  consent, 262
  representation, 261–263
Electronic cottage, 489
Electronic funds transfer (EFT), 529
Electronic news services, 484
Embargo, 699
Employee(s). See also Human resource management; Union(s)
  attracting, 239
  availability of, facilities location and, 292
  estimating supply of, 222–223
  exempt and nonexempt, 242
  forecasting demand for, 221–222
  involving in decision making, 200–203
  motivating, see Motivation
  orientation of, 225, 233
  promotion, transfer, and discharge of, 238–239
  recruiting, 225–226
  retaining, 240
  selection of, 225, 226–233
  social responsibility and, 46–47
  sources of, 226, 226(table)
Employee assistance programs (EAPs), 234–236
Employee Polygraph Protection Act of 1988, 229
Employee Retirement Income Security Act of 1974 (ERISA), 219(table), 616
Employment, right to, 266
Employment application, 227–229, 228(fig.)
Employment process, 225(fig.), 225–233
  orientation in, 233
  recruiting in, 225–226
  selection in, 227–233
Employment references, employee selection and, 231
Employment tests, 229–230, 230(table)
  reliable, 229
  valid, 229
Endorsee, 654

Endorsements, 654–655, 655(table)
  bland, 654
  nonrestrictive, 654
  qualified, 654–655
  restrictive, 654
  special, 654
Endorser, 654
Endowment life insurance, 625–626
Energy, availability of, facilities location and, 293
Enlightened self-interest, social responsibility and, 43–47, 46(fig.)
Entrepreneur(s), 19, 96, 105
  characteristics of, 97–98, 99(table)
  manager as, 134
  training programs for, 113–114
  women as, 105–106, 106(fig.)
Entrepreneurship, 96–98. *See also* Small business
  risks of, 106–107
Environment, legal, of human resource management, 218–220, 219(table)
Environmental analysis, planning and, 140
Environmental Protection Agency, 676
Environmental regulation, 676–677
Equal Credit Opportunity Act of 1974, 536
Equal Employment Opportunity Act of 1972, 220
Equal Employment Opportunity Commission (EEOC), 220
  employee selection and, 227, 229
  Sexual Harassment Guidelines of, 219(table)
Equal Pay Act of 1963, 219(table)
Equilibrium, 20–21, 21(fig.), 356(fig.), 357
Equipment, 550
Equipment bonds, 564
Equity, 553, 555
  ratio of debt to, 456, 566
  return on, 453
  in small businesses, 111
Equity financing, 553–561, 554(table)
  common stock and, 556–558
  nature of equity and, 555
  preferred stock and, 559–561
Ergonomics, 489

ERISA, *see* Employee Retirement Income Security Act of 1974
Error, decision support systems and, 484–485
Estate taxes, 683, 684
Esteem, need for, 192–193
Ethics, 57. *See also* Business ethics
Ethnocentrism, 704–705
Event, in Program Evaluation and Review Technique, 290
Evidence
  real (demonstrative), 642
  testimonial, 642–643
Excellence, in management, 148(table), 148–149
Exchange(s), 577. *See also* Stock exchanges
  marketing and, 313
  money as medium of, 509–510
Exchange rates, 696
Excise taxes, 682, 684
Exclusive-dealing arrangement, 671
Exclusive distribution strategy, 374
Ex-dividend stock, 558
Executive information systems, 485
Executive Order 11246, 219(table)
Executive Order 11375, 219(table)
Exempts, 242
Exercise, of option, 595
Expenses
  accrued, 447
  administrative, 451
  general, 451
  operating, 451
  prepaid, 451
  selling, 451
Expert power, 167
Expert systems, 479
Expiration, of option, 595
Export(s), 694
Exporting, 706–707
  balance of payments and, 694
  balance of trade and, 694
Express warranty, 652
External motivators, 198–200

Facility, 445, 550
  location of, 291–294
Facility layout, 294–297
  capacity and, 296–297
  computerized automation and, 297
  consumer-oriented, 296

design considerations and, 294, 295(fig.), 296–297
  fixed-position, 294
  for manufacturing, 294, 295(fig.)
  for nonmanufacturing operations, 294, 296
  process, 294
  product, 294
  robots and computer-integrated manufacturing and, 297
Factfinding, collective bargaining and, 273
Factoring, 553
Factors of production, 18, 18(fig.)
Failure, of small businesses, 107–109
Fair Credit Reporting Act of 1970, 536
Fair Debt Collection Practices Act of 1978, 536
Fair Labor Standards Act of 1938, 219(table), 242, 263
False arrest, 646
Family brand, 350
"Fannie Mae," 585
FDA, *see* Food and Drug Administration
FDIC, *see* Federal Deposit Insurance Corporation
Featherbedding, 682
Feature articles, for publicity, 423
Federal courts, supreme, 644
Federal Deposit Insurance Corporation (FDIC), 516
  banks insured by, 516, 517(table)
Federal Mediation and Conciliation Service, 267, 272
Federal National Mortgage Association (FNMA, "Fannie Mae"), 585
Federal Open Market Committee, 522–523
Federal Reserve Act, 521
Federal Reserve Banks, 521–522, 523(fig.)
Federal Reserve Board
  margin accounts and, 579
  prime rate and, 552
Federal Reserve Notes, 521
Federal Reserve System, 521–530, 552, 579
  as banking system's bank, 526–529

deregulation and, 530
members of, 516, 521
monetary policy and, 523–526
new financial intermediaries and, 530
structure of, 521–523, 522(fig.)
Federal Savings and Loan Insurance Corporation (FSLIC), 519
Federal Trade Commission (FTC), 673, 674–675
franchisee protections of, 117
infringement and, 350
Federal Trade Commission Act of 1914, 673, 674
Federal trial courts, 643, 644
Fiat money, 510
Fidelity bonds, 622
Field salespeople, 419
FIFO, *see* First In, First Out
Figurehead, manager as, 133
Finance, information requirements for, 482
Finance companies
commercial, 514–515
consumer, 515
Financial assistance, wholesalers and, 377
Financial incentives, 240
motivation and, 200
Financial information, sources of, 483, 586–588
Financial institutions. *See also* Bank(s)
small business financing and, 111–112
Financial intermediaries, 513(fig.), 513–521
depository institutions as, 515–521
new, 530
nondepository institutions as, 514–515
suppliers and users of funds and, 513–514
Financial management, 540–567, 543(fig.)
debt financing and, 561–566
definition of, 542
developing financial plans and, 544–545
equity financing and, 553–561, 554(table)
financial managers and, 543–544

financial plans and, 544–546
sources of short-term financing and, 551–553
uses of funds and, 546–551
Financial plan, 544–546
budgeting and, 544–545
establishing objectives and, 544
financing, 545–546
Financial ratios, 452, 453(table), 454–456
applying, 456
short-term, 453, 454(table), 455
Financial references, employee selection and, 231
Financial risk, 548
Financial statements, 434–435
certification of, 436
interpreting, 452–456
preparing, 443
Financing
outside, 545
debt, 561–566
equity, 553–561, 554(table)
of franchises, 117
internal, 545
long-term, 546
marketing and, 313–314
short-term, 545–546, 551–553
of small businesses, 110–112
Fire insurance, 617–618
First-dollar coverage, 622, 623
First In, First Out (FIFO), 450
Fixed-position layout, 294
Fixed assets, 445
acquiring, 550–551
Fixtures, 650
Flexibility, of small businesses, 107
Flexible-benefit programs, 241(fig.), 241–242
Flexitime, 203–205
Floating interest rates, 561
Flood insurance, 615
Floor broker, 578
Floppy disk, 472, 487
FNMA, *see* Federal National Mortgage Association
Focus, of small businesses, 107
Focus groups, 491
"Follow the leader" pricing, 355–356
Food(s), regulation of, 677–678
Food and Drug Administration (FDA), 678

Foreign corporation, 84
Foreign Corrupt Practices Act, 706
Foreign investment, direct, 710
Foreign stock exchanges, 582
Foreign trade, 693. *See also* International trade
Form utility, 323–324
For-profit corporation, 82
Four P's, 321–322
Franchise, 115
Franchisee, 115
Franchiser, 115
Franchise tax, 79
Franchising, 115–117
advantages and disadvantages of, 116–117
franchising relationship and, 115–116, 116(table)
Fraud, 646
Freedom, in free-enterprise system, 18
Free-enterprise system, 17–19
freedom and individualism and, 18
free markets and, 17, 17(fig.)
private property and profit in, 18–19
Free markets, 17, 17(fig.)
Freight forwarder, 387
Frequency distribution, 492
Friendship groups, 175
FSLIC, *see* Federal Savings and Loan Insurance Corporation
Full-service brokers, 579
Functional departments, 162
Functional organization, 173
Fundamental economic questions, 13
Funds transfer, 526–529

Gambling, 547
Garment labels, 354
General Agreement on Tariffs and Trade (GATT), 700
General expenses, 451
General partnership, 74
Generic advertising, 408–409
Generic name, 350
Geographic variables, market segmentation and, 325
Geosystems, 292
Gigabyte, 472
"Ginnie Mae," 585

Givebacks, collective bargaining and, 267–269
global marketplace, 700, 720–704
America's position in, 703(fig.), 703–704
GNMA, *see* Government National Mortgage Association
Going rate, of compensation, 239
Good(s), 340
convenience, 330
sale of, 650–652
shopping, 331
specialty, 332
Goodwill, 446
Government, 662–685. *See also* Business law; Law(s); Regulation; Tax(es)
Federal Trade Commission and, 117, 350, 673, 674–675
insurance provided by, *see* Public insurance
subsidies and, 665
as supplier and user of funds, 514
support provided by, 665–666
Government bonds, 584–585
Government inducements, facilities location and, 293–294
Government National Mortgage Association (GNMA, "Ginnie Mae"), 585
Government securities, open-market operations and, 524
Grading, marketing and, 314
Grapevine, 176
Graphs, 495–496, 497(fig.), 498(fig.)
Great Depression, 25
regulation and, 50
Greenhouse effect, regulation and, 679–681
Grievance, 266
process of, collective bargaining and, 266–267, 267(fig.)
Grievance committee, 267
Gross profit, 450
Gross sales, 448
Group health insurance, 622
Growth funds, 585
Growth stage of product life cycle, 346
Guaranteed loans, from Small Business Administration, 112

Hard disk, 472, 487
Hardware, 470–473, 471(fig.)
choosing, 479
Hart-Scott-Rodino Antitrust Improvements Act, 672
Hawthorne studies, 188–190
Hazardous wastes, regulation and, 678
Hazard reduction, 608
Health care, costs of, 240–241, 264–265
Health insurance, 264–265, 622–623
dental, 623
disability income, 623
group, 622
for hospitalization, 622
major medical expenses under, 623
medical expenses under, 623
surgical coverage under, 622–623
vision, 623
Health maintenance organization (HMO), 624
Hierarchy
management, 128–129, 129(fig.)
of needs, 190, 191(fig.), 193
"High stack" technology, 679
High technology, small businesses in, 102–104
HMO, *see* Health maintenance organization
Hollow corporations, 289
Home-based businesses, 105
Homeowner's insurance, 618
Hong Kong exchange, 582
Horizontal market allocation, 670
Horizontal merger, 89, 671–672
Hospitalization insurance, 622
Hours, collective bargaining and, 265
Human error, decision support systems and, 484–485
Human relations, 184–207
alternative work patterns and, 203–206, 204(fig.)
employee involvement in decision making and, 200–203
morale and, 187–188
motivation and, 188–190, 197–200
Motivation-Maintenance Model and, 194, 195(fig.)

needs and, 190–193, 191(fig.)
Theory X and Theory Y and, 194–197
Human resource management, 214–244
compensation and benefits and, 239–244
employment process and, 225(fig.), 225–233
evaluating and developing job performance and, 232–239
evolution of, 217–221
information requirements for, 481
planning in, 221–224
responsibility for, 220–221
Human resource planning, 221–224
estimating supply of workers and, 222–223
forecasting demand and, 221–222
job analysis and, 223–224
Human skills, for management, 129–131
Hygiene factors, 194
Hypermarkets, 381

Idea(s), 341
generation of, for new products, 341–342
Implied warranties, 652
Import(s), 694
Importing
balance of payments and, 694
balance of trade and, 694
Import quota, 699
Incentive(s), financial, 200, 240
Incentive rate formulas, 264
Incentive systems, 242–243
Income
discretionary, 27, 317
net, 451–452
Income funds, 585
Income statement, 447–452
cost of goods sold in, 448–451
net income in, 451–452
operating expenses in, 451
revenues in, 447–448, 449(fig.)
Income tax, 682, 684
Incorporation
articles of, 74–75
certificate of, 78
Incorporator, 78
Indemnification, 609–610
Indenture, 559

Independent bargaining, 270
Independent retailers, 378
Indirect inventory, 298
Individual brand strategy, 350–351
Individualism, in free-enterprise
    system, 18
Individual Retirement Accounts
    (IRAs), 513
Industrial products, 332
    distribution channels for, 371–
        372
    overlap with consumer products,
        332
    unqique market features and, 332
Industrial Revolution
    specialization and, 161
    unions and, 251
    U.S. economic system and, 23–26
Industrial unions, 254
Industry. *See also* Manufacturing
    U.S. economic system and, 24
Industry deregulation, 681–682
Inferential statistics, 491
Inflation
    cost-of-living adjustments and,
        264
    returns and, 549
    value of money and, 510
Informal organization, 175–176
    friendship groups in, 175
    grapevine and, 176
Information
    accounting, *See also* Accounting
        information
    data versus, 469–470
    financial, sources of, 483, 586–
        588
    insider, 594
    market, 313, 376, 377
    tabular display of, 496, 498(fig.),
        499
    turning data into, 490
    visual display of, 495–496,
        497(fig.), 498(fig.)
Informational roles, of managers,
    133
Information processing system, 470,
    470(fig.)
Information requirements
    by functional area, 481(table),
        481–482
    by management level, 482
Information sector, rise of, 28

Informative advertising, 404
Infringement, 349–350
In-home retailers, 382
Initial interview, employee selection
    and, 232
Injunction, 253
Inland marine insurance, 621
Input, 470
Input devices, 472
Insider information, 594
Insider Trading Act of 1984, 594
Insider Trading Act of 1988, 594
Inside salespeople, 419
Inspection, 302
Institutional advertising, 409
In-store retailers, 378–381
Instrument
    definition of, 654
    negotiable, *see* Negotiable instru-
        ments
Insurable interest, 611–612
Insurable risk, 610–611
Insurance, 608–627
    automobile, 618–619, 619(table)
    business interruption, 618
    business liability, 619–620
    credit, 622
    crime, 615
    crop, 616
    debate over, 626–627
    definition of, 608
    dental, 623
    deposit, 615
    disability income, 623
    fidelity bonds and, 622
    fire, 617–618
    flood, 615
    health, 264–265
    health maintenance organizations
        and, 624
    homeowner's, 618
    hospitalization, 622
    indemnification and, 609–610
    insurable interest and, 611–612
    insurable risk and, 610–611
    insurance companies and, 612
    key person, 626
    law of large numbers and, 609
    life, cash value, 625–626
    life, term, 624–625
    for major medical expense, 623
    malpractice, 620
    for medical expenses, 623

mortgage, 615
    no-fault, 613
    pension, 616
    product liability, 620
    professional liability, 620
    self-insurance and, 609, 614
    Social Security, 614–615
    surety bonds and, 622
    surgical, 622–623
    theft, 621–622
    title, 622
    transportation (marine), 620–621
    type of, 612, 613(fig.)
    unemployment, 613
    vision, 623
    worker's compensation, 613–614
Insurance companies, 514, 612
    "captive," 609
    mutual, 612
    stock 612
Insurance policy, 514, 609
Insurance premium, 514, 608–609,
    614
Insured, 608
Insurers, 607
Intangible assets, 446
Intangible personal property, 650
Integrated marketing, 318–319
Intelligence, artificial, 478–479
Intensive distribution strategy, 374
Intent, torts and, 646
Interactive mode, 477
Interest, on checking accounts, 512,
    517, 524
Interest rate(s)
    floating, 561
    municipal bonds and, 585
    prime, 548, 522
Interest rate risk, 548
Interlocking directorates, 672
Intermediaries, *see* Financial inter-
    mediaries; Marketing interme-
    diaries
Intermediate appellate courts, 644
Intermittent processing, 285
Internal financing, 545
Internal motivators, 197–198
Internal Revenue Service
    depreciation calculations and,
        445–446
    as user of accounting
        information, 435

International trade, 690–713
  absolute advantages and, 693
  balance of payments and, 694
  balance of trade and, 694
  bureaucratic red tape and, 699
  comparative advantages and, 693–694
  currency valuation and, 695–696
  direct foreign investment and, 710
  embargoes and, 699
  entering, 706–710
  ethnocentrism and, 704–705
  exporting and, 694, 706–707
  global marketplace and, 700, 702–703
  importing and, 694
  import quotas and, 699
  intercultural awareness and, 705–706
  joint ventures and, 708–709
  licensing and, 707–708
  multinational corporations and, 710–713
  protectionism and, 697–699
  specialization and, 693–694
  tarriffs and, 699
  trade agreements and, 700
  U.S. role in, 703(fig.), 703–704
International Workers of the World ("Wobblies"), 252
Interpersonal roles, of managers, 133
Interstate Commerce Commission, 25
Interviews
  employee selection and, 232–233
  personal, 491
  for publicity, 423
  stress, 232–233
  structured and unstructed, 232
  telephone, 491
Introduction stage of product life cycle, 346
Inventory, 445
  acquiring, 550
  beginning, 450
  as collateral, 552–553
  direct, 293
  First In, First Out, 450
  indirect, 298
  just-in-time system for, 299–300, 392

Last In, First Out, 450–451
  periodic inventory system for, 448, 450
  perpetual iventory system for, 448–450
  of skills, 223
  wholesalers and, 376, 377
Inventory control, 298–300, 390–391
  costs of inventory and, 298–299
  just-in-time inventory and, 299–300
Investment(s), 547–549
  appropriate, 547
  foreign, direct, 710
  liquidity and, 547–548
  return and, 549
  risk and, 548–549
Investment Advisers Act of 1940, 593
Investment Company Act of 1940, 593
Involement, Quality of Work Life movement and, 201
IRAs, see Individual Retirement Accounts
Issuer
  of bonds, 563
  of stock, 576

Japan
  comparative advantage and, 694
  import quotas and, 699
Japanese yen, exchange rate and, 696
Job analysis, 223–224
Job creation, computer and, 488
Job description, 224
Job enlargement, 197
Job enrichment programs, 197
Job loss, computers and, 488
Job-order processing, 285–286
Job performance
  employee assistance programs and, 234–236
  performance appraisal and, 234
  promotion, transfer, and discharge and, 238–239
  training and development programs and, 236–238
Job rotation, 198
Job security, collective bargaining and, 266

Job sharing, 205
Job-shop processing, 285–286
Job specification, 224
Joint ventures, 87
  international business and, 708–709
  partnerships as, 74–75
Journal, 440
  entering transactions in, 440, 441(fig.)
Judicial review, 645
Junk bonds, 564
Jurisdiction, 643
Just-in-time inventory systems, 299–300, 392

Keough accounts, 513
Key person insurance, 626
Kilobytes, 472
Knights of Labor, 251–252

Labeling, 353–354
Labor
  division of, 161–162, 162(table), 283
  organized, 250. See also Union(s)
Labor-management relations, 248–275
  changing role of unions in, 257–258
  collective bargaining process and, 269–275, 270(fig.)
  early union movement and, 251–253
  regulation of, 253–257
  subjects of collective bargaining and, 263–269
  unionization process and, 259, 261–263
Labor theory of value, 15
Laissez faire, 25
  caveat emptor and, 48
LAN, see Local area network
Landrum-Griffin Act of 1959, 255(table), 256
Last In, First Out (LIFO), 450–451
Law(s). See also Business Law
  antidiscrimination, 218–220, 219(table)
  antitrust, 699–674
  civil, 641
  common, 638–639
  corporations and, 650

criminal, 639, 641
dispute-resolution system and, 641–645
governing securities trading, 591(fig.), 591, 593
human resource management and, 218–220, 219(table)
labor, 254–256, 255(table)
of large numbers, 609
of partnerships, 650
preventive, 636
private, 639
procedural, 641
public, 639
right-to-work, 256
statutory, 637–638
substantive, 641
U.S. Constitution and, 637
Layoffs, 239
collective bargaining and, 266
unemployment compensation and, 266
Layout, *see* Facility layout
LBOs, *see* Leveraged buyouts
Leader, manager as, 133
Leadership
effective, keys to, 144, 144(table)
as management function, 142–144
situation theory of, 143–144
Leadership style, 142–144, 143(fig.)
achievement-oriented, 143–144
directive, 143, 144
participative, 143
supportive, 143
Lead time, purchasing and, 301
Ledger, posting transactions in, 441–442, 442(fig.)
Legal purposes, contracts and, 648
Legislation, *see* Law(s)
Legitimate power, 167
Leverage, 566–567, 567(fig.) *See also* Debt
Leveraged buyouts (LBOs), 564
Liability(ies), 438, 446–447
current, 447
definition of, 74
long-term, 447
of partners, 74, 75
product, 646–647
of shareholders, 80–81
strict, 646
under tort law, 645

Liability insurance, 619–629
product, 620
professional, 620
types of, 617(table)
Liability risks, 607
Liaison, manager as, 133
Licensing, international business and, 707–708
Lie detector tests, employee selection and, 229
Life, unlimited, of corporations, 79
Life insurance, 624–626
business uses of, 626
cash value, 625–626
endowment, 625–626
indemnification and, 610
insurable interest and, 612
insurable risks and, 611
key person, 626
limited-pay, 625
straight, 625
term, 624–625
universal, 625
whole life, 625–626
LIFO, *see* Last In, First Out
Limited partners, 76
Limited partnerships, 76
certificate of, 77(fig.)
Limited-pay life insurance, 625
Limit order, 578
Line-and-staff organization, 173
Line of credit, 112, 552
Line organization, 173
Liquid asset, 512
Liquidity, 445, 512
investment and, 547–548
short-term financial ratios and, 453, 455
of stock, 80
Litigants, 641
Load, 586
Loan(s)
bank, 551–552
collateral and, 531–532
direct, 112
financing by, 562
floating rate, 561
guaranteed, 112
participation, 112
from Small Business Administration, 112
unsecured, 532
Local area network (LAN), 475

Local taxes, 683–684
Location departments, 164
Lockouts, 274
London exchange, 582
Long-term-debt ratios, 454(table), 456
Long-term debt to equity ratio, 566
Long-term financing, 546
Long-term liabilities, 447
Loss reduction, 608
Low-load mutual funds, 586

$M_1$, 524
$M_2$, 524
$M_3$, 524
Machine language, 476
Magazines
advertising in, 409
as sources of financial information, 586–587
Magnetic tape, 487
Mail-order retailers, 382–383, 384(fig.)
Mail surveys, 491
Mainframe computers, 473, 475
Main memory, of computer, 471–472, 487
Maintenance factors, 194
Maintenance shop, 256
Major medical expenses insurance, 623
Make-or-buy decision, 288–289
Maloney Act of 1938, 593
Malpractice insurance, 620
Management, 124–149. See *also*(table) Labor-management relations
controlling function of, 144–145
corporate, 85–86
corporate cultures and, 146–148
decision-making process for, 135(fig.), 135–137
excellence in, 148(table), 148–149
expectations of, motivation and, 199
financial, *see* Financial management
hierarchy of, 128–129, 129(fig.)
of human resources, *see* Human resource management
information needs of, 480–484
leading/motivating function of, 142–144

Measures of central tendency, 492, 493
Median, 492
Mediation
  as alternative to litigation, 645
  collective bargaining and, 272
Mediator, 272, 645
Medical expenses insurance, 623
Medicare, 615
Medium of exchange, money as, 509–510
Megabyte, 472
Memory
  main, of computer, 471–472, 487
  random access, 472
Merchant, 369
Merchantability, warranties of, 652
Mergers, 89, 564
  conglomerate, 672
  horizontal, 89, 671–672
  insider trading and, 594
  regulation of, 671–672
  vertical, 89, 671
Merit pay, 200
MESBIC, see Minority Enterprise Small Business Investment Companies
Microcomputers, 473–475
Middlemen, see Marketing intermediaries
Midwest exchange, 582, 595
Minicomputers, 473
Minimum wage law, see Fair Labor Standards Act
Minorities, in work force, 258
Minority Enterprise Small Business Investment Companies (MESBICs), 112
Minutes, of board of directors, 86
MIS, see Management information system
Missionary sales people, 419
Mission statement, planning and, 141
Mode, 492
Modem, 475
Modified capitalism, 16–17
Monetary policy, 523–526
  discount rate and, 526, 527(fig.)
  measuring money supply and, 524, 525(fig.)
  open-market operations and, 524
  reserve requirement and, 525–526

selective credit controls and, 526
Money, 509–512. See also Currency
  characteristics of, 510–512
  counterfeiting of, 512
  divisibility of, 510–511
  durability of, 512
  fiat, 510
  liquidity and, 512
  as measure of value, 509
  as medium of exchange, 509–510
  portability of, 512
  stability of value of, 510
  as store of value, 510
Monitor
  computer, 472
  manager as, 133
Monopolistic competition, 22–23
Monopoly, 22
  natural, 670–671
  Sherman Act and, 670–671
Moody's bond ratings, 564
Morale, 187–188
Mortgage(s), 112, 517
  adjustable rate, 561
  title insurance and, 622
Mortgage bonds, 563
  federal, 585
Mortgage insurance, 615
Moscow exchange, 582
Motivation, 188–190
  employee involvement in decision making and, 200–203
  external motivators and, 198–200
  Hawthorne studies of, 188–190
  internal motivators and, 197–200
  as management function, 142–144
  Motivation-Maintenance Model and, 194, 195(fig.)
  needs and, 190–193, 191(fig.)
  Theory X and Theory Y and, 194–197
Motivational factors, 194
Motivation-Maintenance Model, 194, 195(fig.)
Motives, rational and emotional, for buying, 328
MRP, see Materials-requirement planning systems
Multinational corporations, 710–713
  competition among, 319
  global influence and, 712–713

scale of multinationalism and, 710–712
Multiple departmentalization, 165(fig.), 165–166
Multiple-unit pricing, 361
Municipal bonds, 585
Municipal court, 643
Mutual agency, partnerships and, 71
Mutual assent, contracts and, 648
Mutual funds, 585–586
  investment objectives and, 585
  loads, no-loads, and management fees of, 586
Mutual insurance companies, 612
Mutual savings banks, 518–519

NASD, see National Association of Securities Dealers
NASDAQ, see National Association of Securities Dealers Automatic Quotations
National Association of Accountants, 436
National Association of Securities Dealers (NASD), 582, 593
National Association of Securities Dealers Automatic Quotations (NASDAQ), 582
National Association of Securities Dealers Automatic Quotations (NASDAQ) averages, 589
National banks, 516
National Credit Union Administration, 519
National Education Association, 256
National Environmental Policy Act of 1969, 676
National Labor Relations Act of 1935 (NLRA), 254–255, 255(table)
National Labor Relations Board (NLRB), 25, 254–255
  representation elections and, 261–263
National negotiation, 270
Natural monopoly, 670–671
NBA Players Association, 254
Need(s), 190–193
  hierarchy of, 190, 191(fig.), 193
  physiological, 190–191

Organizational structure, 158–159

Organization chart, 159–161, 160(table)

Organized labor, 250. *See also* Union(s)

Organizing, as management function, 142

Organizing drive, 259, 261

Orientation, of workers, 225, 233

OSHA, *see* Occupational Safety & Health Administration

OTC, *see* Over-the-counter market

Outdoor advertising, 413

Outplacement programs, 239

Output, 470
voice, 473

Output devices, 472–473

Outside financing, 545

Outside salespeople, 419

Outsourcing, 289

Over-the-counter (OTC) market, 582
listing for, 583(fig.)
self-regulation of, 593

Owner's equity, 438, 447

Ownership
of corporations, 79–84, 83(fig.)
forms of, 66–90
possession utility and, 324
of small businesses, 104–109

Ozone layer, regulation and, 679–681

Pacific exchange, 582, 595

Packaging, 351–353

"Paid at sixty-five" life insurance, 625

Participating preferred stock, 561

Participation loans, from Small Business Administration, 112

Participative leadership, 143

Parties, to legal disputes, 641

Partnership(s), 71–77
advantages and disadvantages of, 75–76, 76(table)
ending, 76–77
general, 74
joint ventures as, 74–75
law of, 650
life insurance purchased by, 626
limited, 76, 77(fig.)
partnership contributions and, 73

partnership shares and, 72–73
partners' liability and, 74
profit-making nature of, 74–75
types of partners and, 75(table)
voluntary nature of, 71–72

Partnership agreement, 72, 72(fig.)
dissolution and, 77

Partnership shares, 72–73

"Party sales," 382

Par value, 556

Passed its dividend, 560–561

PATCO, *see* Professional Air Traffic Controllers Organization

Patent, 650

Pattern bargaining, 270

Pay, *see* Compensation; Wage(s)

Payable on demand, 654

Payable to bearer, 654

Payable to order, 654

Pay-by-phone services, 529

Payments, 694
balance of, 694

Pay scale, 239

Pay structure, 240

Penetration pricing strategy, 360

Pension Benefit Guaranty Corporation, 616

Pension funds, 264, 514, 515(table)

Pension insurance, 616

Percentage of net sales, 453, 455(fig.)

Perfect competition, 22

Performance. *See also* Job performance
warranties of, 652

Performance appraisal, 234

Performance checklists, 234, 235(fig.)

Performance measurement, management control and, 145

Performance standards, management control and, 144–145

Periodic inventory system, 448, 450

Peripherals, 471

Perpetual inventory system, 448–450

Per se violations, antitrust, 670

Personal computers, 473–475

Personal identification number (PIN), 527

Personal injury liability, 607

Personal interviews, 491

Personal problems, employee assistance programs and, 234–236

Personal property, 650
tangible and intangible, 650

Personal references, employee selection and, 231

Personal selling, 416–420
for manufacturers, 419
for retailers, 418
selling process and, 416–418
of services, 419
telemarketing and, 419–420
for wholesalers, 419

Personnel, *see* Employee(s)

Personnel managers, 217

Persuasive advertising, 404

PERT, *see* Program Evaluation and Review Technique

Philadelphia exchange, 582, 595

Photographs, for publicity, 423

Physical distribution, 386–391
inventory control and, 390–391
materials handling and, 389
order processing and, 390
transportation and, 387–388
warehousing and, 388–389

Physical examinations, employee selection and, 232

Physiological needs, 190–191

Picketing, 274

Pictographs, 496, 497(fig.)

Piece-work rates, 243, 264

Pie chart, 496, 498(fig.), 499

Piggyback service, 388

PIN, *see* Personal identification number

Pipelines, 388

Place strategy, in marketing mix, 322

Place utility, 324

Plaintiff, 646

Plan
business, failure to develop, 108–109
components of, 138–139
marketing, 321

Planned economies, 15

Planning
financial, 544–546
for human resources, *see* Human resource planning
as management function, 138–142

Planning (*Cont.*)
  operational, 140, 298
  operations, *see* Strategic operations planning
  process of, 140–142, 141(fig.)
  production, 290–291
  of products, 290
  strategic, 139–140
  tactical, 140
Plant, 550. *See also* Facility; Facility layout
Plant and equipment assets, 445
Point-of-purchase displays, sales promotion and, 421
Point-of-sale terminals, 528–529
Police powers, 49
Policies and procedures, 167–168
Policy
  insurance, 514, 609
  monetary, *see* Monetary policy
Political/world events risk, 548
Polygraphs, employee selection and, 229
Portable computers, 475
Positive reinforcement, motivation and, 198–199
Possession utility, 324
Posting, 441–442, 442(fig.)
Power, 166(fig.), 166–167
  coercive, 167
  expert, 167
  legitimate, 167
  referent, 167
  reward, 167
Preapproach, 416
Precedents, persuasive and binding, 645
Predatory pricing, 670
Preferred position, advertising and, 410
Preferred stock, 559–561
  convertibility of, 561
  cumulative and noncumulative, 560–561
  participating and nonparticipating, 561
  purposes of, 559–560
  types of, 560(table), 560–561
Pregnancy Discrimination Act of 1978, 219(table)
Premium(s)
  on bonds, 566
  insurance, 514, 608–609, 614

motivation and, 199–200
  sales promotion and, 420
Premium placement, advertising and, 410
Prepaid expenses, 445
Press conferences, for publicity, 423
Prestige pricing, 361
Preventive law, 636
Price(s), market, 21, 357
Price fixing, Sherman Act and, 670
Price lining, 361
Price points, 361
Price-quality relationship, 361
Price strategy, in marketing mix, 322
Pricing, 354–356
  competition-based, 359
  cost-based, 357
  demand-based, 358–359
  economic theory-based, 356(fig.), 356–357
  market share as objective of, 355
  predatory, 670
  profit maximization as objective of, 355
  resource allocation and, 354–355
  status quo as objective of, 355–356
  survival as objective of, 356
  target return on investment as objective of, 355
Pricing strategies, 322, 359–361
  mutiple-unit, 361
  for new products, 359–360
  odd/even, 361
  penetration, 360
  prestige, 361
  psychological, 361
  skimming, 359–360
Primary-demand advertising, 408–409
Primary boycott, 274
Primary markets, securities and, 576
Prime rate, 548, 552
Principal, agency law and, 648
Printers, 472
Private accountants, 436
Private carrier, 387
Private corporation, 82, 575
Private insurance, 616–624
  automobile, 618–619, 619(table)
  business liability, 619–620
  credit, 622

fidelity bonds and, 622
  fire, 617–618
  homeowner's, 618
  malpractice, 620
  product liability, 620
  professional liability, 620
  surety bonds and, 622
  theft, 621–622
  title, 622
  transportation (marine), 620–621
Private label brand, 349
Private law, 639
Private placement, 576
Private property, in free-enterprise system, 18
Private warehouse, 389
Privatization, 15
Proaction strategy, 51(fig.), 53
Probability samples, 490
Problem, 135
  defining, 135–136
Procedural law, 641
Process layout, 294
Producers, *see* Manufacturers
Product(s), 18, 283, 340–341. *See also* New-product development process
  branding and, 349–351
  consistency of, franchises and, 117
  consumer, 330–332, 369–371
  cosmetic changes in, 348
  industrial, 332, 371–372
  labeling and, 353–354
  more frequent use of, 348
  new users for, 348
  new uses for, 348
  operations management and, 283
  packaging and, 351–353
  planning, 290
  pricing and, 354–356
  promotion of, 333
  responsibility for, 48
Product departments, 162–163
Product differentiation strategy, 346, 347
Production, factors of, 18, 18(fig.)
Production era, 24–25
  marketing and, 317
Production facility, *see* Facility; Facility layout
Production planning and control, 290–291

Production processes
  assembly-line, 285
  batch processing and, 285
  classification of, 284–286,
    286(fig.)
  continuous-flow, 284
  job-shop processing and, 285–
    286
  mass production and, 285
  production-to-order, 284
  production-to-stock, 284
  project processing and, 286
Production-to-order system, 284
Production-to-stock system, 284
Productivity, as basis of
  compensation, 242–244
Product layout, 294
Product liability, 646–647
Product liability insurance, 607, 620
Product life cycle, 344–348,
    345(fig.)
  decline stage of, 347
  extending product life and, 348
  growth stage of, 346
  introduction stage of, 346
  maturity stage of, 346–347
Product strategy, 322, 340–344
  in marketing mix, 322
  new-product development process
    and, 341(fig.), 341–343
Professional Air Traffic Controllers
  Organization (PATCO), 274–
  275
Professional corporation, 83
Professional liability insurance, 620
Profit
  in free-enterprise system, 19
  gross, 450
  maximization of, as pricing
    objective, 355
  net, 453
  partnerships and, 74–75
Profitability ratios, 453, 454(table)
Profit-sharing program, 243–244
Program(s), 475. See also Software
  spreadsheet, 482
  utility, 476
Program Evaluation and Review
  Technique (PERT), 290–291,
  291(fig.), 481
Programming, 476
Project management, 174–175
Project processing, 286

Promissory notes, 550, 653,
    653(fig.)
  to bank, 552
  as source of short-term financing,
    551
Promotion(s), 238–239, 333
  collective bargaining and, 266
  franchises and, 116
  objectives of, 400–401
  sales, 420–421
  wholesalers and, 376, 377
Promotion mix, 403, 404(fig.)
Promotion strategy, 322, 398–424,
    401(fig.)
  advertising and, 403–415
  in marketing mix, 322
  personal selling and, 416–420
  publicity and public relations and,
    422–423
  pull, 401(fig.), 403, 420
  push, 401(fig.), 402–403
  sales promotion and, 420–421
Prompts, 477
Property, 550
  law of, 650
  personal, 650
  private, 18
  real, 547, 650
Property insurance, 617–619,
    619(table)
  insurance interest and, 612
Property risks, 606–607
Property tax, 683–684
Prospect(s), 416
Prospecting, 416
Prospectus, 588
Protectionism, 697–699
  arguments pro and con, 697–699
  bureaucratic red tape and, 699
  embargoes and, 699
  import quotas and, 699
  tariffs and, 699
Protective tariffs, 699
Psychographic variables, market
  segmentation and, 326
Psychological needs, 191–193
Psychological pricing strategies, 361
Public accountants, 436
Publications, 10, 12(table)
  as sources of financial
    information, 483, 586–588
Public corporation, 81–82
Public insurance, 612–616

  crime, 615
  crop, 616
  deposit, 615
  flood, 615
  mortgage, 615
  pension, 616
  Social Security, 614–615
  unemployment, 613
  worker's compensation, 613–614
Publicity, 422–423
  social responsibility and, 46
Public law, 639
Publicly traded corporation, 80, 82–
  83
Public offering, 576
Public opinion, business ethics and,
  59, 60(fig.)
Public relations, 423
Public utility, 82
Public Utility Holding Company Act
  of 1935, 593
Public warehouse, 389
Pull strategy, 401(fig.), 403
  for promotion, 420
Purchase(s), 450. See also Buying;
  Purchasing
  on margin, 596
  net, 450
Purchasing, 300–301. See also Buy-
  ing; Purchasing
  franchises and, 117
Pure competition, 22
Pure risk, 606
Push strategy, 401(fig.), 402–403

Qualified endorsement, 654–655
Quality circles, 202–203
Quality control, 301–302,
  303(table)
Quality of Work Life (QWL)
  movement, 201
Quasi-public corporation, 82
Quick ratio, 455
Quitting, 239
QWL, see Quality of Work Life
  movement

Radio, advertising on, 411–412
Railroads, transportation by, 387
Railway Labor Act of 1926,
  255(table)
RAM, see Random access memory
Random access, 487

Random access memory (RAM), 472
Random sample, 490
Range, 493
Rank-order appraisals, of job performance, 234
Rational buying motives, 328
Raw materials, proximity to, 292
Reaction strategy, 51(fig.), 52
Read-only memory (ROM), 472
Real (demonstrative) evidence, 642
Real property, 650
  liquidity of, 547
Real-time updating, 488
Rebates, sales promotion and, 420
Reciprocal-dealing arrangement, 671
Reciprocity, trade agreements and, 700
Record date, 557
Recruitment, 225–226
  social responsibility and, 46
Redeemed stock, 559
Redemption, of bonds, 565–566
References
  credit and, 530–531
  employee selection and, 231–232
Referent power, 167
Reform, of U.S. economic system, 25–26
Refunds, sales promotion and, 420
Registration statement, 588
Regulation(s)
  administrative, 637–638
  during 1970s, 50–51
  of air, water, and conservation, 676–677
  antitrust laws and, see Antitrust laws
  beginnings of, 49–50
  contemporary issues in, 678–681
  deregulation and, 681–682
  of food and drugs, 677–678
  forms of, 667(fig.), 667–669
  of labor relations, 253–257
  of mergers, 671–672
  of monopolies, 670–671
  nonregulation and, 682
  reaction to, 51
  of securities trading, 589–594
  social responsibility and, 49–51
  state, 675–676
  of trade restraints, 670, 671

U.S. economic system and, 25–26
  of workplace, 678
Reinforcement, positive, 198–199
Reinforcement advertising, 404
Reinsurance, 611
Reliable employment test, 229
Reminder advertising, 404
Replacement-value coverage, 610
Reports, management information systems and, 484
Representation election, 261–263
Reputation
  of small business, 107
  social responsibility and, 44–45
Reserve, 521
Reserve requirement, 525–526
Resource allocation
  pricing and, 354–355
  as manager's role, 134
Restrictive endorsement, 654
Retailers, 371, 378–386
  in-home, 382
  in-store, 378–381
  independent, 378
  mail-order, 382–383, 384(fig.)
  nonstore, 381–384
  selling for, 418
  vending machines as, 383–384
  wheel of retailing and, 384–386, 385(fig.)
  wholesalers' services to, 376–377
Retailing, small businesses in, 102
Retail strategy, choosing, 375–376
Retained earnings, 447, 545
Retirement, 239
  Social Security benefits and, 614–615
Return, risk and, 549(fig.), 549–550
Return on equity ratio, 453
Return on investment, 549
  as pricing objective, 355
Return on sales ratio, 453
Reevaluation, 696
Revenue, 447–448, 449(fig.)
Revenue tariffs, 699
Reversal, of trial court's judgment, 644
Reverse-load mutual funds, 586
Reverse split, 557
Revolving credit agreement, 552
Reward power, 167
Rights
  of unions and management, 263

voting, of common stock, 556
Right to employment, 266
Right-to-work laws, 256
Risk, 605–608
  business/financial, 548
  classification of, 606(fig.)
  diversification and, 548–549
  entrepreneurship and, 19
  insurable, 610–611
  investment and, 548–549
  liability, 607
  marketing and, 316
  market/interest rate, 548
  municipal bonds and, 585
  political/world events, 548
  property, 606–607
  pure, 606
  return and, 549(fig.), 549–550
  of small business ownership, 106–107
  speculative, 606
  stock issue and, 576
Risk assumption, 607
Risk avoidance, 607
Risk management, 606–608
  technique of, 607–608, 608(fig.)
Risk manager, 606
Risk reduction, 608
Risk transfer, 607
Robbery, insurance against, 621–622
Robinson-Patman Act, 673
Robots, 297
ROM, see Read-only memory
Round lot, 579
Royalty, international business and, 708
Rule-of-reason standard, 670
Russia, economy of, 15
Russian ruble, exchange rate and, 696

S&Ls, see Savings-and-loan associations
Safety, need for, 191
Salary, 242. See also Compensation; Wage(s)
Sale(s). See also Selling
  closing, 418
  distress, 356
  gross, 448
  net, 448
  return on, 453

servicing, 418
Uniform Commercial Code and, 650–652
warranties and, 651–652
wholesalers and, 376
Sales and marketing era, 26–27, 317
Sales demonstration, 417
Sales engineers, 419
Salespeople
detail or missionary, 419
inside, outside, and field, 419
Sales presentation, 417
preparing for, 416
Sales promotion, 420–421
sales resistance, negotiating, 418
Sales returns, 448
Sales tax, 682, 684
Samples, 490–491
observations and, 490–491
probability, 490
random, 490
sales promotion and, 420
surveys and, 491
Savings accounts, in money supply, 524
Savings-and-loan associations (S&Ls), 517, 518
Savings and loan industry, deregulation of, 28
Savings banks, 519
mutual, 518–519
SBA, see Small Business Administration
SBDCs, see Small Business Development Centers
SBI, see Small Business Institute
Scabs, 274–275
Scheduling, in production planning and control, 290–291
SCORE, see Service Corps of Retired Executives
S corporation, 84
Screening, in new-product development process, 342
Seasonal trends, 494
Secondary boycott, 274
Secondary markets, 576–577
Secondary needs, 191
Secular trend, 494
Securities, 572–597
definition of, 574–575
government, open-market operations and, 524

marketable, 445, 550
primary markets and, 576
private transactions and, 575–576
regulation of trading of, 589–594
secondary markets and, 576–577
trading on an exchange, 577–579
Securities Act of 1933, 591, 593
Securities Act of 1964, 593
Securities and Exchange Commission (SEC), 25, 674
empowerment of, 593
establishment of, 593
mutual funds and, 586
private placement and, 576
public offerings and, 576
registration with, 588, 593
statement of changes in financial position and, 452
Securities Exchange Act of 1934, 593
Securities Investors Protection Act of 1970, 594
Securities Investors Protection Corporation (SIPC), 594
Security, need for, 191
Security interest, 112
Segmentation variables, 325–326
Selection, 225, 227–233
background investigations and, 230–232
employment application and, 227–229, 228(fig.)
employment tests and, 229–230, 230(table)
interviews and, 232–233
physical examinations and, 232
selection decision and, 233
Selective advertising, 405–408
Selective credit controls, 526
Selective distribution strategy, 374
Self-actualization, need for, 193
Self-insurance, 609, 614
Selling. See also sale(s)
consultative, 416
as marketing function, 313
Selling expenses, 451
Seniority, promotions, transfers, layoffs and rehiring and, 239, 266
Seniority differential, 264
Separation, of employees, 239
Sequential access, 487
Serial bonds, 566

Service(s), selling, 419
Service Corps of Retired Executives (SCORE), 114
Service departments, 162–163
Service sector
rise of, 27–28
small businesses in, 102
work force and, 257–258, 258(fig.)
Setups, 290
Shanghai exchange, 582
Share(s)
earnings per, 453
no-par, 556
partnership, 72–73
of stock, 80, 556, 557(fig.)
Share draft accounts, 512
Shareholder(s), 80
in corporate management, 85
limited liability of, 80–81
of record, 558
Sheet Metal Workers, 263
Sherman Antitrust Act of 1890, 253, 669–671
monopolies and, 670–671
restraints of trade and, 670
Shift differential, 264
Shop, 256
Shoppers' guides, 415
Shopping goods, 331
Shop steward, 266
Short-term financial ratios, 453, 454(table), 455
Short-term financing, 545–546, 551–553
secured, 552–553
unsecured, 551–552
"Single sourcing," 300
Sinking fund, 560, 566
SIPC, see Securities Investors Protection Corporation
Situational theory of leadership, 143–144
Skills, for management, 129–131, 130(fig.)
Skills inventory, 223
Skimming price strategy, 359–360
Small business, 99–144. See also Entrepreneur(s)
economic importance of, 100–102, 101(table)
failure of, 107–109
fields attracting, 102–104

Small business (*Cont.*)
  financing, 110–112
  home-based, 105
  keys to success of, 107
  rewards of owning, 105, 105(table)
  risks of owning, 106–107
  sources of help for, 113–114
  women as owners of, 105–106, 106(fig.)
  working definition of, 100
Small Business Administration (SBA), 100
  financing provided by, 112
  management assistance provided by, 114
Small Business Development Centers (SBDCs), 114
Small Business Institute (SBI), 114
Smart machines, 297
Smoot-Hawley Tariff Act of 1930, 700
Social audit, 54–56
  developing, 54(fig.), 54–55
  future of, 56
  objections to, 55
Socialism, 14–15
  democratic, 15
Social needs, 192
Social responsibility, 39(table), 39–56
  accommodation strategy for, 51(fig.), 53
  arguments for and against, 41(table)
  caveat emptor and contracts and, 48–49
  defense strategy for, 51(fig.), 52–53
  definition and background of, 39–47, 41(table)
  increasing, 42
  motivation for, 43–47, 46(fig.)
  proaction strategy for, 51(fig.), 53
  reaction strategy for, 51(fig.), 52
  regulation and, 49–51
  social audit and, 54–56
  voluntary actions and, 40–41, 42(fig.)
Social Security, 614–615
  changes in, 614(fig.)
  disability benefits under, 615
  Medicare under, 615

retirement benefits under, 614–615
  survivors' benefits udner, 615
  taxes for, 682
Social Security Act of 1935, 614
Software, 470–471, 475–476
  choosing, 479
  languages and, 476
  operating systems and, 476
  stored programs and, 476
Software applications packages, 476–478
  artificial intelligence and, 478–479
  business applications and, 477–478
  modes and, 476–477
Sole proprietorships, 69–71
  advantages and disadvantages of, 70, 70(table)
Source documents, for accounting, 439–440
South Korea
  comparative advantage and, 694
  in global marketplace, 703
Span of management, 168
Special endorsement, 654
Specialist, securities exchange and, 578
Specialization, 161–162, 162(table)
  international trade and, 693–694
  transformation and, 283
Specialty advertising, 414
Specialty goods, 332
Specialty stores, 378–379
Speculative risk, 606
Speed, as competitive advantage, 303
Spokesperson, manager as, 133
Spread, 576
Spreadsheet programs, 482
Staff, 173. *See also* Employee(s)
Staffing, as management function, 142
Standard & Poor's average, 589
Standard & Poor's bond ratings, 564
Standard deviation, 493
Standardization, marketing and, 314
Stare decisis, 645
State banks, 516
State courts, 643

Statement of changes in financial position, 452
Statement of financial position, *see* Balance sheet
State regulation, 675–676
State taxes, 683–684, 685(fig.)
Statistics, 490–495
  descriptive, 491
  inferential, 491
  samples and, 490–491
  size and dispersion measures and, 492–493
  time series analysis and, 493–495
Status quo, as pricing objective, 355–356
Statutory law, 637–638
Steelworkers, 257
Stock, 555. *See also* Common stock
  ex-dividend, 558
  liquidity of, 547
  preferred, 559–561
  share of, 80, 556, 557(fig.)
  valuation of, 556
Stock averages, 588–589
Stock dividend, 558
Stock exchanges, 577–582
  commissions and, 579
  foreign, 582
  margin and, 579
  regional, 582
Stock insurance companies, 612
Stock market crash, of 1929, 589–590
  of 1987, 590–591
Stock split, 556–557
  reverse, 557
Stop order, 578
Storage
  computer, 471–472, 487
  marketing and, 315
Storage devices, auxiliary, 472
Store(s)
  chain, 378
  convenience, 381
  department, 378, 379(fig.)
  discount, 378
  specialty, 378–379
  variety, 380–381
  warehouse, 381
Stored-program computers, 476
Store of value, money as, 510
Straight life insurance, 625

Strategic decision, in operations planning, 287–288
Strategic operations planning, 287–294
  facilities location and, 291–294
  high-tech versus low-tech decisions and, 289–290
  make-or-buy decision and, 288–289
  nature of the business and, 289
  production planning and control and, 290–291
  strategic decision and, 287–288
Strategic planning, 139–140
Strategy
  brand, 350–351
  concentrated, 327
  differentiated, 327
  distribution, *see* Distribution strategy
  price, 322
  pricing, *see* Pricing strategy
  product, *see* Product strategy
  product differentiation, 346, 347
  promotion, *see* Promotion strategy
  retail, 375–376
  for social responsibility, 51(fig.), 52–53
  target marketing and, 326–327
Stress, computers and, 489
Stress interview, employee selection and, 232–233
Strict liability, 646
Strike(s), 274
  economic, 275
Strikebreakers, 274–275
Structured interview, employee selection and, 232
Subchapter S corporation, 84
Subsidies, 665
Substantive law, 641
Supercomputers, 473, 474(fig.)
Superior courts, 643
Supermarkets, 381, 385
Superstores, 381
Supervision
  government, *see* Regulation
  in matrix-structured organization, 174–175
Supply, 20, 356(fig.), 356–357
Supply curve, 20, 20(fig.)
Supportive leadership, 143

Supreme courts, 644
Surety bonds, 622
Surgical insurance, 622–623
Surrender value, of life insurance, 625
Surveys, 491
Survival, as pricing objective, 356
Survivors' benefits, Social Security, 615
Syndicates, 87
  stock issue and, 576

Tabular display, 495–496, 497(fig.), 498(fig.)
Tactical planning, 140
Taft-Hartley Act of 1947, 255(table), 256, 263, 267, 269
Taiwan, in global marketplace, 703
Tangible personal property, 650
Targeted television advertising, 415
Target market(s)
  direct-mail advertising and, 411
  retail strategy and, 375–376
Target marketing, 326–327
  concentrated strategy and, 327
  differentiated strategy and, 327
Tariffs, 683, 699
  protective, 699
  revenue, 699
Tax(es), 682–684
  accounting information and, 435
  corporate, 80
  on estates, 683, 684
  excise, 682, 684
  federal, 682–683
  franchise, 79
  income, 682, 684
  property, 683–684
  returns and, 549
  sales, 682, 684
  Social Security, 682
  state and local, 683–684, 685(fig.)
  tariffs as, 683
  user fees as, 683, 684
T-bills (Treasury bills), 550
Teamsters Union, 256
Technical skills, for management, 129–131
Technology. *See also* High technology
  "high stack," 679
Telecommuters, 206

Telemarketing, 419–420
Telephone interviews, 491
Television advertising, 412–413, 413(fig.)
  targeted, 415
Terminals, 473
  point-of-sale, 528–529
Termination
  of employees, 239
  of partnership, 77
Term life insurance, 624–625
Testimonial evidence, 642–643
Test market(s), 342
  in new-product development process, 342–343
Theft insurance, 621–622
Theory X, 195
Theory Y, 195–197
Theory Z, 201–202, 202(fig.)
Thrift institutions, 519–521
Ticker, 578
Time, as basis of compensation, 242, 243–244
Time deposits, 512
  in money supply, 524
Time series analysis, 493–495
  correlation analysis and, 494–495, 495(table)
  trend, cyclical, and seasonal variations and, 494
Time utility, 324
Title
  merchants and, 369
  warranty of, 651–652
Title insurance, 622
Title VII, *see* Civil Rights Act of 1964
Tokyo exchange, 582
Toronto exchange, 582
Torts, 645
  intentional, 646
  law of, 645–647
  negligence, 646–647
Trade, 693
  balance of, 694
  foreign, 693
  international, *see* International trade
Trade agreements, 700
Trade credit, 112, 314, 530, 551
  wholesalers and, 377
Trade journals, as source of data, 483

Trademarks, 349–350, 650
Trade restraints
    Clayton Act and, 671
    Sherman Act and, 670
Trade show, 421
Trade unions, 252–253
Trading partners, 693
Training and development, 236–
    238. *See also* Management
    training
    for entrepreneurs, 113–114
    franchises and, 116–117
Transfer(s), 239
    collective bargaining and, 266
Transferee, 576
Transformation, 283–286, 284(fig.)
    classification of production proc-
        esses and, 284–286, 286(fig.)
    division of labor and specializa-
        tion and, 283
Transportation, 387–388
    by air, 388
    marketing and, 315
    pipelines and, 388
    railroads and, 387
    trucks and, 388
    types of carriers and, 387,
        387(table)
    by water, 388
Transportation costs, facilities loca-
    tion and, 292
Transportation facilities, 292
Transportation (marine) insurance,
    620–621
Treasurer, 544
Treasury bills (T-bills), 550
Treasury bonds, 584
Trend analysis, *see* Time series anal-
    ysis
Trial balance, calculating, 442–443
Trial courts, 642–644
    of general jurisdiction, 643
    of limited jurisdiction, 643
Trucks, transportation by, 388
Trustee, bond issue and, 563
Trust Indenture Act of 1939, 563,
    593
Truth in Lending Act of 1969, 536
TRW Information Services, com-
    mercial credit and, 533
"Twenty pay life" insurance, 625
2/10 net 30, 448
Tying arrangement, 671

UCC, *see* Uniform Commercial
    Code
Undercapitalization of small
    businesses, 109
Undervalued stock, 556
Underwriter, 576
Unemployment compensation
    insurance, 266, 613
Unfair labor practices, 254
Uniform Commercial Code (UCC),
    639, 650–655, 651(table)
    law of negotiable instruments
        and, 653–655
    sales and, 650–652
Uniform Guidelines on Employee
    Selection Procedures of 1978,
    219(table)
Union(s), 250–253, 257–275
    boycotts and, 274
    business agent of, 267
    business representative of, 267
    collective bargaining and, 263–
        275
    craft, 252–253
    emerging service sector and, 257–
        258
    first efforts to organize, 251
    givebacks and, 267–269
    grievance process and, 266–267,
        267(fig.)
    growing number of women and
        minorities in, 258, 259(fig.)
    hours and, 265
    industrial, 254
    job security and, 266
    legal restraints and, 274
    lockouts and, 274
    mediation, arbitration, and fact-
        finding and, 272–273
    membership of, 256, 257,
        257(fig.)
    negotiating teams and, 270–271
    organizing drive and, 259, 261
    preparations for bargaining and,
        269
    representation election and, 261–
        263
    respective rights of management
        and, 263
    strikebreakers and, 274–275
    strikes and, 274
    strong, emergence of, 251–253
    trade, 252–253

wages and benefits and, 264–265
working conditions and, 265–266
Union shop, 256
United Auto Workers, 254, 257,
    270, 275
United Farm Workers, 274
United Mine Workers, 254, 256,
    265
United Rubber Workers, 254
United States
    development of economic system
        in, 23–29
    position in global marketplace,
        703(fig.), 703–704
U.S. Bureau of Engraving and
    Printing, 512
U.S.-Canadian Free Trade
    Agreement, 700
U.S. Comptroller of the Currency,
    516
U.S. Constitution, 637
U.S. Department of Agriculture,
    677–678
U.S. District Courts, 643
U.S. dollar, exchange rate and, 696
U.S. government issues, 584
U.S. Supreme Court, 644
U.S. Treasury bills, 550
U.S. Treasury bonds, 584
Universal life insurance, 625
Unlimited life, of corporations, 79
Unsecured loan, 532
Unstructured interview, employee
    selection and, 232
User fees, 683, 684
Utility, 323–324
    form, 323–324
    place, 324
    possession, 324
    time, 324
Utility program, 476
Utility Workers, 254

Valid employment test, 229
Value
    book, 556
    labor theory of, 15
    market, 556
    of money, stability of, 510
    money as measure of, 509
    money as store of, 510
    par, 556
Variance, 493

Variety store, 380–381
Vending machines, 383–384
Venture capitalist, 555
Vertical-channel integration, 372–373, 373(table)
Vertical market allocation, 670
Vertical-marketing systems, administered, 372–373, orate, 372
Vertical merger, 89, 671
Vice president of finance, 543
Vietnam War, regulation and, 50–51
Vision insurance, 623
Visual display, 495–496, 497(fig.), 498(fig.)
Vocational Rehabilitation Act of 1973–1974, 219(table)
Voice output, computers and, 473
Voluntary actions, social responsibility and, 40–41, 42(fig.)
Voting rights, 556

Wage(s), 242, 264. *See also* Compensation
  base pay and, 240
  base rate for, 264
  collective bargaining and, 264
  cost-of-living adjustments and, 264
  differentials and, 264

incentive rates and, 264
  motivation and, 194, 200
Wage/salary survey, 239
Wages and hours law, *see* Fair Labor Standards Act
Wagner Act, *see* National Labor Relations Act of 1935
Warehouse(s), public and private, 389
Warehouse club, 381
Warehouse receipt, 388
Warehouse store, 381
Warehousing, 388–389
Warranties, 651–652
  disclaimer and, 652
  express, 652
  of fitness for a particular purpose, 652
  implied, 652
  of merchantability, 652
  of performance, 652
  of title, 651–652
Water, transportation by, 388
Wheel of retailing, 384–386, 385(fig.)
Whistle blowers, 61
Whole life insurance, 625–626
Wholesaler, 371
Wholesalers, 376–377
  full-service, 376
  limited-service, 376

selling for, 419
  services to procedures, 376, 377(fig.)
  services to retailers, 376–377
Winding up, partnerships and, 76–77
"Wobblies," 252
Women
  as entrepreneurs, 105–106, 106(fig.)
  in work force, 217, 258, 259(fig.)
Workers, *see* Employee(s)
Worker safety, responsibility for, 48–49
Worker's compensation insurance, 613–614
Work force, changing, 217, 257–258, 258(fig.)
Working capital, 110–111, 455
Working conditions, collective bargaining and, 265
Workplace, regulation of, 678
Workshops, for entrepreneurs, 114
World events risk, 548
World War II
  regulation and, 50
  U.S. economic system and, 26


Zero-based budgeting, 459
Zoning, facilities location and, 293